1927	Congress passes first legislation specifically dealing with "broadcasting"
1928	Columbia Broadcasting System (CBS) founded
1930	NBC establishes nightly network radio newscasts
1933	President Franklin Roosevelt begins broadcasting "fireside chats"; Armstrong patents FM radio technology
1934	Congress passes Communications Act; Mutual Broadcasting System created
1938	Orson Welles panics nation with Halloween broadcast on CBS
1939	Edward Murrow begins broadcasting reports of London being bombed; David Sarnoff demonstrates RCA's television system at World's Fair
1941	U.S. enters World War II; all manufacturing resources devoted to war effort; FCC adopts technical standards for black-and-white television
1945	NBC sells Blue Network, creating American Broadcasting Company (ABC)
1948	FCC places freeze on new TV station licenses until 1952
1953	FCC adopts technical standards for color television
1956	Ampex Corporation introduces videotape recorder
1961	FCC adopts standards for stereo FM broadcasting
1962	Congress requires all TV sets to have UHF and VHF tuners
1963	Syncom launched (first geosynchronous communications satellite)
1975	Home videotape recorders come on the market; HBO begins satellite distribution of programming
1986	Fox established the fourth television broadcast network
1996	FCC mandates conversion to digital TV broadcasting
2004	Janet Jackson's "wardrobe malfunction," leading to stiffer indecency enforcement
2009	Conversion from analog to digital television broadcasting

Why You Need This New Edition

To be brief, the reason you need this new edition of *Broadcasting in America* is because the previous edition is hopelessly outdated. If you tried using the previous edition of this text in your current introduction to electronic media class you would undoubtedly find yourself profoundly confused.

Consider just a few of the changes in electronic media that have occurred in the nearly 10 years since the publication of the Ninth Edition:

▶ The transition of television broadcasting from analog to digital transmission
▶ The maturation of satellite-delivered television and radio services as competitors to cable systems and broadcasters
▶ The emergence of telephone companies as providers of multichannel video and Internet services
▶ The widespread consolidation of media ownership
▶ The increased power of consumers to decide when and where to access programming
▶ The diversity, ease of use, and ubiquity of the Internet

And this is truly a very short list.

Because of these significant changes in the media landscape, almost every section of this text has been rewritten. History, operations, programming, and regulation chapters have been substantially updated, the technology chapters have been completely overhauled, and coverage of audience measurement includes new information on measuring the impact of new technologies. Additionally, the former chapter on media effects now focuses on both media theories and effects while the chapter on international media, recognizing the importance of emerging media globally, is much less Eurocentric than previous editions. Finally, the Tenth Edition offers a vibrant full-color presentation and visual program and is now accompanied by video, audio, and online resources through MyCommunicationKit.

You need this new edition because the electronic media have seen dramatic change in the past decade. This text documents those changes and provides informed insights in the exciting, and mostly unpredictable, changes yet to come.

Head's Broadcasting in America

A Survey of Electronic Media

tenth edition

Michael A. McGregor
Indiana University

Paul D. Driscoll
University of Miami

Walter McDowell
University of Miami

Allyn & Bacon

Boston New York San Francisco
Mexico City Montreal Toronto London Madrid Munich Paris
Hong Kong Singapore Tokyo Cape Town Sydney

Acquisitions Editor: *Jeanne Zalesky*
Development Editor: *Deb Hanlon*
Editorial Assistant: *Megan Lentz*
Marketing Manager: *Wendy Gordon*
Production Supervisor: *Patty Bergin*
Production Management and Composition: *Progressive Publishing Alternatives*
Manufacturing Buyer: *JoAnne Sweeney*
Cover Administrator: *Kristina Mose-Libon*
Photo Researcher: *Sue McDermott Barlow*
Interior Design: *Ellen Pettengell*

Chapter Opener photo credit: © *Colin Anderson/Blend Images/Corbis*

Library of Congress Cataloging-in-Publication Data

Head's broadcasting in America : a survey of electronic media. — 10th ed. /
  Michael Mcgregor, Paul Driscoll, Walter Mcdowell.
    p. cm.
  Rev. ed. of: Broadcasting in America / Sydney W. Head. 9th ed. 2001.
  ISBN-13: 978-0-205-60813-3
  ISBN-10: 0-205-60813-2
1. Broadcasting—United States. I. Head, Sydney W. Broadcasting
in America. II. Title: Broadcasting in America.
  HE8689.8.H43 2009
  384.540973—dc22

2008048224

10 9 8 7 6 5 4 3 2 1 CIN 13 12 11 10 09

Allyn & Bacon
is an imprint of

www.pearsonhighered.com

ISBN10: 0-205-60813-2
ISBN 13: 978-0-205-60813-3

Brief Contents

Contents

chapter 3
Cable and Newer Media 41

List of Exhibits

Preface

The First Edition of *Broadcasting in America* appeared in 1956. Founding author Sydney Head (1913–1991) launched a text that introduced thousands to the study of broadcasting by viewing electronic media in a broad, academic perspective and treating media in context, both as products of contemporary social forces and as social forces in their own right. Later co-authors Christopher Sterling, Lemuel Schofield, and Tom Spann carried on this vision, and we hope that vision continues in this Tenth Edition. Although their names do not appear on this edition, we gratefully acknowledge that much of what is good about this text is directly attributable to Chris, Lem, and Tom, and we thank them.

Electronic media have experienced tremendous change in the nearly 10 years since the Ninth Edition was published. This has required major revisions to every chapter in this book, including those on history, which must now acknowledge and assess the importance of the digital revolution and the power media consumers now wield.

Changes in the Tenth Edition

The Tenth Edition marks the beginning of a new era for *Broadcasting in America*. We have a new publisher, Pearson Education, which has given the text new life. Two new members of the authorship team, Paul Driscoll and Walt McDowell, both of the same university where Sydney Head's legacy originated, the University of Miami, add new perspectives, energy, and a fresh approach throughout the text. A new four-color design and visual program further the contemporary appeal of this text and bring the content to life.

In the Tenth Edition, we have heavily updated each chapter to include new information on the vast changes that have taken place in the field of broadcasting since the last edition was published. We have streamlined historical discussions and fine-tuned our presentation of topics to eliminate any repetitiveness. We also consolidated Chapters 8 and 9 on programming in response to both formal and informal comments from professors. By consolidating these two chapters, we have created a more coherent discussion of the creation and distribution of program content in a complicated media environment.

Developments in the Tenth Edition include:

► The transition in broadcasting from analog to digital transmission
► Discussion of the changing business models of electronic media
► The continued development of the Internet as both a complement and competitor to traditional media
► The increasingly perplexing problems of audience measurement in a world of untold viewing and listening options
► A confusing regulatory environment that is both deregulatory and re-regulatory, depending on the topic of regulation
► Globalization and its effects on media industries and consumers

Chapter-by-Chapter Updates and Summaries

► Chapter 1 (*Introducing Electronic Media*) introduces students to the exciting changes taking place in electronic media as we enter the second decade of the new century. This updated chapter examines the accelerating convergence of various electronic media forms and the increasing ability of consumers to control the time and place of their media consumption, while also introducing new concepts and vocabulary explored in more detail in later chapters.
► Chapter 2 (*From Radio to Television*) reviews the history of television and radio, including new exhibits featuring President Roosevelt's fireside chats and the fast fading effect of television as a unifying social agent during times of crisis.
► Chapter 3 (*Cable and Newer Media*) covers the history of cable and other newer media technologies. There are several new sections in the Tenth Edition: a section detailing advanced cable services such as digital cable, broadband, and telephone over cable; a section on satellite services; a section on telephone companies and their move into the multichannel television business; and a separate section on the history of the Internet. New graphics illustrate the changing nature of the multichannel program distribution market,

with cable losing share to satellite and telephone delivery systems. Another new graphic highlights the growth of Internet use in terms of people using the Internet and broadband penetration.

▶ Chapter 4 (*How Electronic Media Work*) retains the text's traditional overview of conventional electronic media technology but also provides an expanded discussion of how digital media work, with a special emphasis on DTV transmission and reception.

▶ Chapter 5 (*Distribution by Wired Relays, Wireless Relays, and over the Internet*) concludes with a revised and expanded introduction to the Internet. This chapter explores the promise, but also the problems, associated with these new technologies.

▶ Chapter 6 (*Commercial Operations*) takes a closer look at the underlying economic models influencing electronic media companies today. To that end, it unravels some of the business complexities surrounding the trend toward media convergence in which companies must blend "old" and "new" media to sustain a profitable business venture.

▶ Chapter 7 (*Noncommercial Services*) provides updated information on noncommercial services, most notably public broadcasting in the United States. In addition, the chapter focuses on two intertwined and often controversial issues of (first) defining exactly what noncommercial program content should be in the digital era, and (second) what is the best means for funding this service.

▶ Chapter 8 (*Programs and Programming Basics*) consolidates what used to be Chapters 8 and 9 in prior editions in an effort to provide a more coherent understanding of the creation and distribution of program content in a complicated media environment. As with other chapters in this edition, the goal is to present not only factual knowledge about this arena but also the underlying principles and theories that guide decision-making.

▶ Chapter 9 (*Audience Measurement*) updates the reader on the latest audience measurement techniques for conventional media, such as radio, television, and cable, and also addresses the flurry of new attempts to track Internet traffic by on-line audiences.

▶ Chapter 10 (*Media Theory and Effects*) better reflects the contemporary multimedia environment and not only explains different approaches to the study of media effects, but also enables the reader to become a more critical consumer of media research.

▶ Chapter 11 (*The Communications Act, Licensing, and Structural Regulation*) outlines the legal system in the United States and focuses on FCC licensing and structural regulation. Changes in regulation covered in this edition include new broadcast licensing procedures involving filing windows and auctions,

new cable franchising regulations designed to speed up the franchising process for new entrants (e.g., the telephone companies), and revised ownership regulations including the partial rescission of the broadcast/newspaper cross-ownership ban.

▶ Chapter 12 (*Constitutional Issues and Content Regulation*) updates the government's continuing efforts to regulate content in the media, with significant revisions in the sections on indecency and profanity in broadcasting. We have also expanded the coverage of copyright issues in a digital age for this edition.

▶ Chapter 13 (*A Global View*) presents a substantially revised presentation on the ways different countries approach the development and supervision of both public and private media enterprises. This encompasses not only the inner workings of a nation's media system but also external operations intended to reach the outside world. The chapter also looks at the dynamics of business globalization and how media technologies are shaping a new international media environment.

Ancillary Support

Instructor's Manual and Test Bank. The Instructor's Manual and Test Bank includes chapter outlines, lecture topics, learning objectives, and discussion questions. Also included are over 500 questions in multiple choice, true/false, and essay question format.

MyTest Computerized Test Bank. The printed test questions are also available electronically through our new, web-based, computerized testing system, MyTest. The user-friendly interface enables instructors to view, edit, and add questions, transfer questions to tests, and print tests from any computer with internet access! Available at www.pearsonmytest.com (access code required).

PowerPoint Presentation Package. The PowerPoint slides provide main ideas and key examples from each chapter of the text. Select figures from the text can also be found in this presentation, which is available to adopters through Pearson Education's Instructor's Resource Center, www.pearsonhighered.com/irc (access code required).

MyCommunicationKit for Broadcasting. MyCommunicationKit is an electronic supplement that offers book-specific learning objectives, chapter summaries, flashcards, and practice tests as well as video clips and activities to aid student learning and comprehension. Also included in MyCommunicationKit are Research Navigator and Weblinks that give you access to powerful and reliable research material. Available at www.MyCommunicationKit.com (access code required).

Acknowledgments

Many people deserve our thanks and appreciation. Professors Walter Gantz, Rob Potter, Ron Osgood, and Jim Krause, all colleagues of Mike McGregor at Indiana University, provided information, encouragement, and support for this project. Thanks also to Reed Nelson, Tamera Theodore, and Corey Harrison for finding time in their busy schedules to help Mike with tedious but crucial technical support.

Among their colleagues at the University of Miami, Professors Walter McDowell and Paul Driscoll wish to thank professors Michel Dupagne, Ed Pfister and Sallie Hughes plus Steve Yavner of UMTV and PhD graduate student Paola Prado. Recognition of assistance from academics at other universities include Max Grubb at Kent State University and Steven Dick at the University of Louisiana at Lafayette.

From the business world, a special thanks to Alan Batten, media brand consultant; Anne Elliot, Vice President of Communication for Nielsen Media Research; Erwin Krasnow, media attorney; Chuck Bortnick, Executive Vice President of Jack FM; the executive management team at WFOR-TV, Miami; and finally, our undergraduate and graduate students who keep us in touch with today and curious about the future.

Our editorial team at Allyn & Bacon deserves special mention. Many thanks to Karon Bowers and Jeanne Zalesky for resurrecting *Broadcasting in America* and assigning so many valuable resources to the Tenth Edition. One of those valuable resources, development editor Deb Hanlon, was instrumental in the completion of this text. She was part cheerleader, head coach, and mentor, all wrapped in one. She provided excellent suggestions for additions and deletions, and kicked us in the pants (gently but persuasively) when we invariably let our timetable slide.

Finally, we would like to thank the following reviewers for their comments and suggestions:

Stephen Adams, Cameron University
George Bagley, University of Central Florida
Marvin R. Bensman, University of Memphis
Craig Breit, Cerritos College
Constance Book, Elon University
Timothy F. Brown, University of Central Florida
Butler Cain, University of Alabama
John Chapin, Pennsylvania State University
Donald G. Godfrey, Arizona State University
Wayne Hepler, Hartford Community College
Robert Jordan, San Diego City College
Tommy Morahan, San Francisco State University
Peter B. Seel, Colorado State University
Donald R. Simon, Columbia College Chicago
Jennifer Smith, University of Georgia
Christine M. Stover, Oakland University
Mary Vavrus, University of Minnesota
James A. Wall, Southern Illinois University at Colorado
Marjorie L. Yambor, Western Kentucky University

Mike McGregor
Paul Driscoll
Walter McDowell

Introducing Electronic Media

You already knew a great deal about American electronic mass media even before you picked up this book. You probably grew up using radio, television, cable, video cassette recorders, and computers. More recently many of you have used satellite TV and radio, picture phones, and wireless laptop computers. You routinely "share" MP3 files and store them on your computer, and then download them into a portable player such as the Rio or iPod. Increasingly, you watch video programs on those same devices or your smart phone. You send text messages, have scores of friends on MySpace or Facebook, and spend hours each week surfing the Internet.

So why, then, read a textbook about something you use daily, something that's an integral part of your normal lifestyle? What can you possibly learn that you don't already know?

Well, test yourself with the following questions:

► What did the terrorist attacks of September 11, 2001, and the destruction of Hurricane Katrina teach us about our media systems in the United States? What media policy changes did those events trigger?

► How can a stand-up comic on Comedy Central make racist or sexually explicit references in every other sentence and get away with it, but your favorite radio DJ got fired for using such language only once?

► What limitations are there on the government's ability to protect children against pornography and chat room predators on the Internet?

► Shows you and all your friends like always seem to get canceled. How accurate are those TV ratings we hear about?

► Why do so many radio stations across the country sound so similar?

► What is the origin of the Internet?

► Why don't advertisers like DVRs?

► What is digital TV? Is it the same as high-definition TV?

► Do people in some countries really have to pay an annual tax on each radio and TV set they own? Why would they?

► What's the difference between a broadcast station and a cable network?

Studying electronic media has been exciting since the invention of the telegraph because the ability to communicate instantly over great distances has changed the world dramatically. But studying electronic media in the new century is especially exciting because the changes happening are increasingly rapid. Staying on top of what many regard as a media revolution, with all of its twists and turns, its subtleties and implications, is a challenge for any serious student of communication.

One thing that makes studying media challenging is the large number of new terms and concepts one must learn. Media professionals and scholars often simplify discussion by replacing longer terms with abbreviations and acronyms. The discussion that follows introduces many of these frequently used shortcuts. Although we have taken care to explain an acronym or abbreviation when it is introduced, it's easy to become confused later when one pops up again. The inside rear cover of this text provides a list of the acronyms and abbreviations introduced in this book and you may find it helpful as you make your way through the alphabet soup that follows.

1.1 What It Means

No book, including this one, can be completely up to date. We envy historians who write almost exclusively about the past. While new information about the American Revolution may be discovered, the outcome of the conflict is not in doubt. We have no such insight about what may happen next year, or even next week, regarding developments in electronic media. That's why it is important that you, as students of electronic media, remain alert to changes taking place constantly, changes that may make some of the material we present in the following pages inaccurate or, we hope more often, simply incomplete.

In spite of the media's mind-numbing rate of change, there are a few trends worth noting before we get too far along in our explorations.

Convergence

Media scholars most often think of convergence as a technological phenomenon, and that is certainly a major component of the trend. With respect to communication, technological convergence means the coming together of, and blurring of lines between, what previously had been essentially separate ways of distributing information, for example, broadcasting, cable, telephony, computers, and mail. But convergence is not only about technologies, "hardware," and the means of transmission and delivery—convergence also relates to the content transmitted and delivered.

An example of content convergence is provided by cable. The typical cable subscriber is unaware of the significant differences between a broadcast station carried on the system and a cable network. The programs from each source are often identical, they enter the home on the same wire, and both are seen on the same display device (a TV set). It is little wonder that consumers tend to think of them as being the same thing—television. Many people also access the Internet, with its vast array of text, data, graphics, still images, sound and video—what many people call **multimedia**—through the same wire that brings TV programs from broadcast stations and cable networks into their home. In many places, cable also provides telephone service over that same technological link, and telephone companies increasingly offer video programming.

Most people still split these various converged services by using separate, purpose-specific technologies such as the TV receiver, the conventional telephone handset, and the home computer. Some futurists, however, believe that the interface for using these services will converge into a single device. The computer's ability to display video, text, and graphics, as well as reproduce sound, makes it the most likely device to serve this role. Indeed, today's computers can be configured to perform the functions of a TV and radio receiver, a fax machine, a telephone, and a host of other duties formerly performed by separate devices.

Another important characteristic, or perhaps consequence, of convergence is **interactivity.** Traditional electronic media such as radio and television broadcasting are essentially **unidirectional** (one-way) technologies. Convergence technologies tend to make **bidirectional** (two-way) transmissions possible, blurring the distinction between creators of content and consumers of content. Recognizing the attraction of interactivity, especially among younger audiences, traditionally one-way media, such as broadcasting and newspapers, are struggling to find ways audience members can engage interactively with the content being provided.

Many observers argue that another consequence of technological and content convergence is the effect they are having on patterns of media ownership. Although some may argue that convergence is more accurately described as an excuse for, rather than a cause of, the dramatic changes in media ownership in the last two decades, it must be acknowledged that convergence is at least a factor. In a world of converging technologies and content, some say consolidation, diversification, vertical integration, and synergy are necessary if media companies are to prosper, or even survive.

Consolidation (combining two similar organizations into one) can theoretically result in a stronger entity than either organization standing alone. While it may not be true that "two can live as cheaply as one," there are potential cost savings. Two small-market radio stations in adjacent towns may be unable to survive independently but, if allowed to consolidate and share resources (office space, sales staff, and engineers), they may both prosper.

Diversification (providing more than one product or service) can also theoretically make a company stronger. A company that can sell advertising for distribution through both its broadcast stations and its newspapers is probably in a stronger position than one that can sell only newspaper advertising. Similarly, a company that can **bundle** video, Internet access, and telephone services may be a more effective competitor than the company that can only offer one of these services.

As typically applied to media industries, **vertical integration** refers to the control of the production and distribution of content by one company. A media company, such as the Walt Disney Company, benefits financially from the fact that it can both produce programs (through its Disney studios) and also distribute the programs it produces (through its ABC television network). A company that can only produce programs or only distribute them is in a theoretically weaker competitive position.

𝒳 **Synergy** refers to the idea that the action of two or more companies working together may produce a benefit greater than the combined effect of the same companies operating separately. Synergy is often presented as an argument to support consolidation. For example, the owners of the small-market radio stations mentioned before might argue that not only will consolidation save the two stations, the consolidated entity will have enough resources to improve the programming broadcast by both. Likewise, the company that can provide multiple services will be able to use its increased revenues to upgrade its technical facilities.

Volatile Markets

In the second half of the twentieth century Americans had filled their homes, their cars, and even their pockets with electronic devices. By the turn of the century more than 98 percent of American homes had a television set, and many homes had three or more sets. About 58 percent of those homes were connected to cable and another 20 percent subscribed to satellite TV services. Cell phones were so commonplace they were already considered hazards to public safety, if not sanity, in some towns and cities. Many young people had cars filled with electronic entertainment hardware worth more than the car itself.

Perhaps most dramatically, use of the Internet in the second half of the 1990s had mushroomed. The **National Telecommunications and Information Administration (NTIA)** reported in 1999 that the number of homes with computers connected to the Internet had increased rapidly. Harris Interactive surveys suggested more than 50 percent of U.S. adults were using computers at home, and almost half of them were accessing the Internet. The U.S. Education Department's **National Center for Educational Statistics (NCES)** estimated that more than 95 percent of the nation's public schools had Internet access, ensuring that future consumers would grow up considering Internet access a basic right of citizenship.

American entrepreneurs, seeing an opportunity to make huge profits through telecommunications technologies, formed start-up companies promising to capitalize on the "information economy." The stock price of an Internet-based company would often double, triple, or quadruple on the day of its **initial public offering (IPO).** It seemed to many people that any company with a name ending in "dot-com" (.com) was destined for success. Some observers argued that **electronic commerce (e-commerce)** was a new paradigm representing a radical break with the rules governing traditional brick-and-mortar businesses. Cautionary words from seasoned investors were ignored. Warnings, coming as early as 1996 from then-Federal Reserve Chairman Alan Greenspan about the "irrational exuberance" of investors, had little effect.

A measure of that "irrational exuberance" is the **National Association of Securities Dealers Automatic Quotation System (NASDAQ)** index that tracks the price of stocks sold "over-the-counter," as most dot-com companies are. During a period of only a few months in late 1999 and early 2000, the NASDAQ soared past 3,000 and then 4,000, and finally, in mid-March 2000, the index screamed past 5,000.

The decline was even more rapid. Less than a year after hitting 5,000 the NASDAQ index was barely hanging on to 2,000. "New economy" companies such as Furniture.com, Pets.com, Mortgage.com, Quepasa.com, MotherNature.com, and Garden.com were history.

Perhaps the demise of such small start-up companies should come as no surprise, since under-capitalized new companies often fail. But the carnage was not limited to fledgling entrepreneurs. In January 2000 one of the "new media" giants, **America Online (AOL),** announced plans to acquire Time Warner, an "old media" company in a merger that would give AOL controlling interest in the new firm. Time Warner owned magazines such as *Fortune, Time,* and *Sports Illustrated,* plus popular cable networks *HBO, CNN, TCM,* and others. It also owned a major movie studio, cable companies serving many cities, and other media-related properties. The idea that any "new media" company formed in the mid-1980s could take over such a huge mass media conglomerate with a history dating to the 1920s was staggering to many observers. But, at the time, AOL was the nation's largest online company, with more than 20 million Internet subscribers and, of even more importance, a market value of more than $160 billion, dwarfing that of Time Warner by billions of dollars.

AOL co-founder, Steve Case, made it clear that the merger was largely about convergence:

"We're at the cusp of what we think will be a new era as the television and the PC and the telephone start blurring together and the promise of the Internet. . . . . Consumers love the fact they have new ways to get information, new ways to communicate, new ways to buy products, new ways to learn things, new ways to be entertained. And they want to figure out how to take what's happening on the PC, what's happening on the television, what's happening on the telephone and have it a little more integrated so it's more convenient." (*The NewsHour with Jim Lehrer*, January 12, 2000)

Three years and one day after that interview, Steve Case announced he would step down as chairman of AOL Time Warner Inc. Although AOL had added another 15 million subscribers and was generating billions in subscription fees, advertising revenues had plummeted and the company formed by the merger had not been as successful as expected. AOL Time Warner stock had fallen from about $72 at the time of the merger to less than $15. During the last year of Case's tenure as chairman, the company posted losses of almost $100 billion, the largest in corporate history. That same year, the company dropped AOL from its corporate name.

On the other hand, the beginning of the new century has seen some market success stories; perhaps the most spectacular involves Google. Begun as a two-person research project in 1996, the company incorporated in 1999 with a series of individuals investing a total of nearly one million dollars. When the company went public in 2005, stock was initially offered at $85 per share; the initial offering raised $1.67 billion. By the end of 2007, Google stock had reached more than $800 per share. To increase its presence in the market, Google acquired other suddenly successful Internet companies such as YouTube in 2006 for $1.65 billion and DoubleClick in 2007 for $3.1 billion.

Power to the People: The Democratization of Media

"The old cliché that content is king has been rewritten—today the consumer wears the crown." (Jeff Zucker, CEO of NBC Universal, at the 2008 NATPE Conference).

Throughout most of the history of electronic media, radio and television program distributors had complete control of what programming audiences received and when they received it. For example, in the late 1930s fans of the popular radio drama *The Shadow,* featuring Orson Welles in the title role, knew that their only chance to hear the latest episode required them to tune in to their Mutual Radio Network affiliate station on Sundays at 5:30 P.M. If they missed it, there was no chance to hear it again some other time. Likewise, the popular mid-1970s comedy block of *The Mary Tyler Moore Show* and *The Bob Newhart Show* was aired on the CBS Network on Saturday evenings. Consequently, many ardent admirers of those programs chose to stay home and watch their favorite programs rather than going out on Saturdays. The media controlled the content and its timing, and audiences were forced to adjust their schedules to hear or see their favorite programs.

These were also the days before the widespread introduction of the remote control. In order to change channels or turn off the set, the viewer or listener had to go to the receiver. This, combined with the scheduling realities discussed previously, meant that there was no easy way to avoid commercials. While it is true that many audience members used commercial time to grab a snack or take other necessary breaks, most of the time viewers and listeners sat through the commercials, which in part helped make radio and television such effective advertising vehicles.

All this began to change in the late 1970s with the growing popularity of **video cassette recorders (VCRs).** For the first time television viewers could tape their favorite programs and view them later, a process known as **time shifting.** Suddenly, viewers were no longer captives to the networks' programming schedules. Most early VCRs did not have remote controls, so time shifters still ended up watching most of the commercials. This too changed as the price of remote control technology declined and more people could fast forward the programs from their seats. Much to the chagrin of the advertising business, the age of **zapping** commercials had begun.

The digital revolution, which we address in many places in this book, further changed the balance of power between the program distributors and audiences. The introduction of **digital video recorders (DVRs)** in 1999 further liberated consumers from the scheduling practices of television networks. Now fans could simply program their machines to record their favorite programs whenever they happened to be telecast, no longer to be bothered by having to check their local listings for air times. Research showed that DVR owners skipped commercials even more than VCR owners had. Consumers had taken control of their televisions. Networks and advertisers scrambled to come up with new ways to reach their audiences.

Today we live in a truly customizable media universe, controlling the reception of our media in ways that seemed unimaginable even a decade ago. We watch our favorite programs and listen to our favorite music whenever, and increasingly wherever, we choose. We listen to podcasts on our MP3 players, and watch television on our cell phones. Television networks routinely make programs available via the Internet after their network debut. All this has led Vint Cerf, one of the men who helped develop the technology that led to the Internet, to predict that we are nearing the end of television as we know it (Johnson, 2007). He suggests that most of our television will be recorded for later viewing, and what was once known as **appointment television** will apply only to sporting events and news coverage.

The Effects of Government Policy

As we begin our study it is important to consider how government policies have dramatically affected every aspect of media in the new century. For years, government policy severely limited both the number and type of media companies a single owner could control, but gradually ownership rules were relaxed. That gradual trend continued until passage of the Telecommunications Act of 1996, a law that dramatically reduced media ownership restrictions. Supporters said the legislation was necessary to encourage competition and the development of new media technologies.

Response to the act was immediate and dramatic. Eighteen months after the act's passage, one company, Clear Channel Communications Inc., controlled the programming on more than 160 U.S. radio stations (and on more than 1,200 stations by 2001). Early in 1999, the FCC approved the acquisition of what was then the nation's second largest cable system operator, Tele-Communications, Inc., by AT&T, the largest long distance telephone company. The next year, the FCC approved the merger of Viacom with CBS Corporation. Viacom was already a media colossus and CBS Corporation was itself a media giant. Then, in November 2002, the FCC approved the acquisition of AT&T's cable systems by Comcast, another large cable operator. In May 2004, NBC combined with Vivendi Universal, partnering NBC's television assets with the studio and theme park holdings of Universal Studios. These are only the largest and most widely publicized deals during the decade following passage of the 1996 act. There were hundreds of other sales and mergers involving smaller organizations.

Ten years after the act's passage, critics were complaining that most ownership changes were resulting in large media companies becoming even larger, just as they had predicted (see Exhibit 1.a). They claimed the new law had produced little of the competition promised and, in some ways, had discouraged the technological development the act was supposed to promote. They claimed that the act, combined with the actions of the FCC and other regulatory agencies, too often encouraged huge companies to grow even larger and more profitable by expanding their traditional businesses rather than moving into risky new areas. Critics were concerned about all media channels and control over programming falling into the hands of a few corporate giants.

Supporters of the act, of course, saw things differently. They pointed to stations still on the air that, they claimed, would not have survived had they not been allowed to merge with a larger organization. According to its defenders, without the consolidation allowed by the act, many TV stations would be unable to afford the mandated conversion to digital transmission without cutting back on quality programming or increasing advertising prices. Supporters also noted the number of new cable networks created since 1996, saying these fledgling operations required subsidies to sustain them initially when advertising and subscription dollars were scarce—subsidies only large, financially secure, companies could provide. Rather than stifle diversity of expression as the critics charged, supporters asserted that the act had not

Exhibit 1.a

How Big Is Big? Media Holdings of Disney, News Corp., and Time Warner

Disney

Studio Entertainment: Walt Disney Pictures (Walt Disney Animation Studios, Pixar Animation Studios, Disney Toon Studios), Touchstone Pictures, Hollywood Pictures, Miramax Films, Walt Disney Studios Motion Pictures International, Walt Disney Studios Home Entertainment, Disney Theatrical Productions, Disney Live Family Entertainment, Disney on Ice, Disney Music Group (Walt Disney Records, Hollywood Records, Lyric Street Records).

Parks and Resorts: Disney Cruise Line, Disney Vacation Club, Disneyland Resort, Walt Disney World Resort, Tokyo Disney Resort, Disneyland Resort Paris, Hong Kong Disneyland.

Disney Consumer Products: Disney Toys, Disney Apparel, Disney Food, Disney Home, Disney Stationery, Disney Publishing Worldwide (Disney Libri, Hyperion Books for Children, Jump at the Sun, Disney Press, Disney Editions), Disney Interactive Studios, disneyshopping.com.

Media Networks: Disney-ABC Television Group (ABC Television Network, Disney Channel, ABC Family, SOAPnet, ABC Studios, Walt Disney Television Animation, Disney-ABC Worldwide Television, Walt Disney Television International, Disney Radio Network), ESPN, Inc. (ESPN on ABC, ESPN, ESPN2, ESPN Classic, ESPNEWS, ESPN Deportes, ESPNU, ESPN HD and ESPN2 HD, ESPN Regional Television, ESPN International (31 international networks and syndication), ESPN Radio, ESPN.com, ESPN *The Magazine*, ESPN Enterprises, ESPN Zones, ESPN360.com, ESPN Mobile Properties, ESPN On Demand, ESPN Interactive, and ESPN PPV).

Walt Disney Internet Group: Disney.com, ESPN.com, ABC.com, ABCNEWS.com.

News Corporation

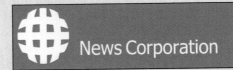

Filmed Entertainment: 20th Century Fox, 20th Century Fox Español, 20th Century Fox Home Entertainment, 20th Century Fox International, 20th Century Fox Television, Fox Searchlight Pictures, Fox Studios Australia, Fox Studios Baja, Fox Studios LA, Fox Television Studios, Blue Sky Studios.

Television: Fox Broadcasting Company, Fox Sports Australia, Fox Television Stations, FOXTEL, MyNetwork TV, STAR.

Cable: Fox Business Network, Fox Movie Channel, Fox News Channel, Fox College Sports, Fox Sports Enterprises, Fox Sports En Español, Fox Sports Net, Fox Soccer Channel, Fox Reality, Fuel TV, FX, National Geographic Channel United States, National Geographic Channel Worldwide, Speed, Stats Inc.

Direct Broadcast Satellite Television: BSkyB, Sky Italia.

Magazines and Inserts: Big League, Inside Out, donna hay, ALPHA, News America Marketing, Smart Source, The Weekly Standard, Gemstar – TV Guide International Inc.

Newspapers—Australasia: Daily Telegraph, Fiji Times, Gold Coast Bulletin, Herald Sun, Newsphotos, Newspix, Newstext, NT News, Post-Courier, Sunday Herald Sun, Sunday Mail, Sunday Tasmanian, Sunday Territorian, Sunday Times, The Advertiser, The Australian, The Courier-Mail, The Mercury, The Sunday Mail, The Sunday Telegraph, Weekly Times.

---

only preserved but actually increased the number and diversity of media voices, providing consumers greater choice. Further evidence that the act promoted competition can be found in the fact that, beginning in the 21st century, cable operators increasingly offered telephone services, and telephone companies returned the favor by delivering television programming.

The recently completed conversion of broadcast transmission from analog to digital provides yet another example of the role government plays in the affairs of media industries and consumers of their products. The multi-billion dollar conversion, which required all television broadcasters to replace their old analog equipment with new digital capability, and which spurred the development of new digital television receivers, was not done voluntarily but was mandated by the government. The conversion process took more than a decade to complete, and its ramifications for both broadcasters and consumers are still being felt.

We will consider many other examples of government policy in Chapters 11 and 12. For now, this much should be clear: Government policies have had and will continue to have significant effects on media businesses and consumers.

1.2 The Players

In spite of constantly advancing technology, shifts in government policies with their sometimes unintended consequences, and economic uncertainties, media leaders must cope with each new challenge and take

United Kingdom: News International, News of the World, The Sun, The Sunday Times, The Times, Times Literary Supplement.

United States: New York Post, The Wall Street Journal, Dow Jones.

Books: HarperCollins, Zondervan.

Other Assets: Broadsystem, Fox Interactive Media, MySpace, IGN Entertainment, Rotten Tomatoes, AskMen, FOXSports.com, Scout, WhatIfSports, kSolo, Fox.com, AmericanIdol.com, Spring Widgets, Milkround, National Rugby League, NDS, News Digital Media, News.com.au, FoxSports.com.au, CARSguide.com.au, careerone.com.au, truelocal.com.au, News Outdoor.

TimeWarner

AOL: AOL, ADTECH, Advertising.com, AIM, CompuServe, GameDaily.com, ICQ, Lightningcast, MapQuest, Moviefone, Netscape, Relegence, Spinner.com, TACODA, Third Screen Media, Truveo, Userplane, Weblogs, Winamp, Xdrive.

HBO: HBO, HBO on Demand, Cinemax, Cinemax on Demand, HBO Video, HBO Mobile, HBO Independent Productions, HBO Domestic and International Program Distribution, HBO On Demand International (Israel, United Kingdom), HBO Mobile International (United Kingdom, Ireland, Belgium, Netherlands, Germany, Austria, Switzerland, Italy, Spain, South Africa, South Korea).

New Line Cinema: New Line Cinema, New Line Distribution, New Line Home Entertainment, New Line International Releasing, New Line Marketing, New Line Merchandising/Licensing, New Line Records, New Line New Media, New Line Television, New Line Theatricals, Picturehouse.

Time, Inc.: 125 magazine titles worldwide, including Entertainment Weekly, Fortune, Golf Magazine, Money, People, Sports Illustrated, and Time.

Turner Broadcasting System: Adult Swim, Boomerang, Cartoon Network, Cartoon Network Asia Pacific, Cartoon Network Europe, Cartoon Network Latin America, Cartoon Network Studios, Williams St. Studio, CNN/U.S., CNN Airport Network, CNN en Español, CNN en Español Radio, CNN Headline News, CNN Headline News in Latin America, CNN Headline News in Asia Pacific, CNN International, CNN Mobile, CNNMoney.com, CNN Newssource, CNN Pipeline, CNN.com, CNNRadio, CNNStudentNews.com, CNN to Go, Court TV, Game Tap, NASCAR.com, PGA.com, Pogo, TBS, TCM Asia Pacific, TCM Canada, TCM Europe, TCM Classic Hollywood in Latin America, TNT HD, TNT Latin America, Toonami, Turner Classic Movies, Turner Network Television.

Warner Bros. Entertainment: Warner Bros. Pictures, Warner Bros. Pictures International, Warner Independent Pictures, Warner Bros. Television Group (Warner Bros. Television, Warner Bros. Domestic Television Distribution, Warner Bros. Domestic Cable Distribution, Warner Bros. International Television Distribution, Warner Bros. Animation (Looney Tunes, Hanna-Barbera), Telepictures Productions, The CW Television Network, Kids' WB, Warner Bros. Home Entertainment Group (Warner Home Video, Warner Bros. Online, Warner Bros. Digital Distribution, Warner Bros. Interactive Entertainment, Warner Bros. Games, Warner Bros. Technical Operations, Warner Bros. Anti-Piracy Operations), Warner Bros. Consumer Products, Warner Bros. International Cinemas, Warner Bros. Studio Facilities, Warner Bros. Theatre Ventures, DC Comics (Mad Magazine, Vertigo, Wildstorm).

Sources: Official Disney logo courtesy of Newscom; official News Corporation logo courtesy of Newscom; official TimeWarner logo courtesy of Time Warner, Inc.

advantage of the opportunities unique to each industry. Although the trends discussed in the previous section make a view of the playing field increasingly blurry, it is still helpful to begin our study by briefly examining several major media industries and communications technologies separately to consider their particular challenges and advantages.

Broadcasting

Many assume that any program or message transmitted over the air, or even over cable, constitutes "broadcasting." But to qualify as broadcasting, programs or messages must pass specific tests. As defined legally, to broadcast means to send out sound and pictures by means of radio waves through space for reception by the general public. The phrases "by means of radio waves through space" and "reception by the general public" are crucial: Cable television systems do not broadcast through space, but rather they send programs through cable. And scrambled over-the-air direct broadcast satellite services delivered on a subscription basis are not intended for the "general public," but are meant to be received only by paying subscribers.

Communication "by means of radio waves" includes many nonbroadcast services, such as CB radio, police calls, taxi dispatching, beepers, and mobile telephones. However, these services operate point-to-point (from a source to one intended recipient) or point-to-multipoint (from a source to more than one specific recipient). Anyone with a suitable receiver can intercept such transmissions, but they are not intended "for reception by the general public" and therefore do not count as broadcasting.

The verb **broadcast** was adopted in the 1920s to distinguish the new radio communication method from the previous point-to-point orientation of radiotelegraphy and radiotelephony. Broadcasting expresses the idea of scattered dissemination to anonymous, undefined destinations (listeners or viewers). The term comes from the farmer's act of hand-sowing grain by casting it broadly. The sower lets seeds fall where they may. (Students should be careful to remember, by the way, that the past tense of the verb broadcast is also broadcast—not broadcasted.)

The number of people receiving television programming directly off the air is only a small fraction of the total number of viewers, but the programs carried by broadcast television stations still attract television's largest audiences. Cable and **direct-to-home (DTH)** satellite programming may sometimes collectively attract a large audience during primetime, but no single cable or DTH channel has a larger audience than any of the major broadcast networks. The broadcast networks remain the principal providers of national news, several major sporting events, and broad-based entertainment, as well as the best way for national advertisers to reach a critical mass of consumers. In most markets, broadcast television enjoys a dominant position compared to its rivals in the area of local news programming, in spite of the growth of national cable news channels and local or regional cable news services.

The recently completed conversion to **digital television (DTV)** transmission also promises to enhance broadcast television's competitive position. Digital transmission allows broadcast stations to offer dramatically improved picture and sound quality, putting broadcast television on a technical par with newer program delivery media such as the **digital video disk (DVD)**. The transition to digital transmission also allows broadcasters to offer multiple programs simultaneously, providing broadcasters the opportunity to appeal to a wider range of viewers. Yet another potential benefit of the DTV transition is the ability to broadcast digital data in addition to and simultaneous with regular television programming.

Unlike cable and DTH satellite services, television broadcasters must depend on advertising revenue alone for income. Cable and satellite service providers can count on a steady flow of subscriber fees as well as income from the sale of advertising. Broadcasters also have somewhat less freedom regarding the content they provide compared to cable and satellite services. Broadcasters are held to a much higher standard regarding indecency, and more is expected in terms of public service programming and programming specifically addressing the needs of children.

The enhanced pictures and sound, the multichannel programming, and the data distribution opportunities promised by conversion to DTV may help traditional broadcasters, but when and how much remains uncertain. Broadcasters must also struggle with the fact that broadcasting is inherently a one-way-only medium that does not fit easily into a converged, multichannel, interactive future.

The future of broadcast radio is clouded by many of the same factors that trouble broadcast television executives. The greater number of radio stations compared to TV stations in a particular market has traditionally required radio executives to be highly competitive in attracting both advertisers and listeners. Today's radio broadcasters face somewhat less competition within their ranks, thanks to consolidation, but more competition than ever before from other media. Radio broadcasters must now compete with satellite-delivered subscription audio services. Equally, if not more, troubling for radio broadcasters is the competition for listeners created by the Internet. Music is a staple of radio broadcasting that has long been the medium's primary appeal, but listeners are increasingly downloading tunes directly from Internet sources. New technology allows listeners to hear only what they want to hear, and hear it exactly when they want it, and without commercial interruptions.

Radio broadcasting is currently converting to digital transmission, although on its own schedule. This transition will provide radio many of the same opportunities promised for television: higher fidelity sound, less interference, and the opportunity to distribute more than one program stream. However, some broadcast leaders think the transition to digital radio and television transmission will, at most, only help level the playing field with other media, not provide broadcasting a resounding competitive advantage.

Some people believe that broadcasting's salvation lies not with new technology, or even massive consolidation, but rather with a renewed commitment to two of the medium's founding concepts:

Localism. Lifestyles today are not what they were in earlier times, and people tend not to "put down roots" as deeply. But stations can serve the unique needs of their communities far better than a national program delivery system can. The popularity of local TV newscasts and the growth of regional cable networks indicate there is a demand for community-centered programming. There is some doubt, however, that broadcasters are placing greater emphasis on localism. Although the data are inconclusive, some radio listeners feel there has been a shift toward cookie-cutter programming controlled by corporate officers far distant from the local audience.

Free universal access. For decades Americans were accustomed to getting entertainment and information over the air at no additional direct expense once they purchased a radio or TV set. Broadcasting's appeal as a "free" service is still strong, and, for many Americans, any delivery system charging a subscription fee is comparatively less attractive. Broadcasters have used the mantra of "free service" effectively in gaining political support, although only about an eighth of U.S. households now receive TV signals directly from broadcast stations.

Cable

About 58 percent of U.S. households receive television programming via cable compared to only about 12 percent watching TV programming off the air. Part of cable's appeal is the greater diversity of programming on cable compared to over the air, and today cable systems are adding new digital channels that dramatically increase the number and types of programs available. But that's only part of cable's appeal. Many cable companies operate interactive systems that permit subscribers to order movies or TV program reruns whenever they want **(video-on-demand; VOD),** to play video games, and to order merchandise without calling a toll-free number. Many systems incorporate **digital video recorders (DVRs)** that allow subscribers to pause programs and resume them as they wish, to record multiple programs simultaneously, and to skip through commercials with the push of a button.

In addition, cable operators are increasingly offering high-speed broadband Internet access and telephony in an effort to become the single-source provider of electronic media services to the American home. Cable's ability to provide video programming, broadband Internet access, interactive features such as video on demand, and telephone service all through one wire into the home is impressive technologically. Even more important, cable companies can bundle these various services in ways that make cable economically attractive. And many consumers may simply like the convenience of having only one company to deal with when they have a service or billing problem.

As explained in Chapter 3, cable initially developed as a technology solely devoted to redistributing crisp, clear broadcast television signals where broadcast signals could not reach. Cable still has that advantage, but today the inherent two-way transmission path provided by cable is emerging as one of its greatest advantages compared to its competitors. Another competitive advantage, compared to broadcasting, is cable's dual revenue stream. Cable system operators collect hefty subscriber fees for each of their services, but in addition

can sell advertising on many of the TV programming channels it carries as well as on the web sites it maintains as an Internet access provider.

Cable certainly has many advantages, but it has sometimes been the victim of its own popularity. In many markets, a single cable operator enjoys a practical monopoly as the community's subscription-based video program provider. Although government at several levels regulates the cable industry, critics say cable's monopoly has sometimes encouraged operators to treat subscribers poorly. Many subscribers have complained of difficulty getting cable installation initially, poor quality pictures once they get connected, and slow responses or rude behavior by service technicians when they request assistance. Even more consumers have complained about their cable bill growing year after year at a rate much faster than that of inflation generally. Disgruntled cable subscribers once had limited options, but today direct-to-home satellite television providers and some telephone companies offer an attractive alternative. The percentage of U.S. homes subscribing to cable decreased between 2000 and 2008, while the percentage of satellite and telephone subscribers increased substantially.

Direct-to-Home Satellite Television

Direct-to-home satellite service (also called **direct broadcast satellite, DBS**) is an increasingly important player in the delivery of popular television programming. Although lacking cable's established market position and a direct, physical connection to the home that encourages interactivity, satellite delivery offers exceptional picture quality and many more program options than some cable systems. Satellite delivery is, of course, most attractive in areas not served by cable.

However, many cable subscribers, unhappy with cable service and lured by both attractive programming packages and lower subscription costs, migrated to DBS in the early years of the new century. By 2008, there were about 20 million DBS subscribers in the United States, and many of them were former cable subscribers.

DBS initially suffered in comparison with cable because it did not provide local broadcast signals as an integral part of the service. By 2008, however, DirecTV and The Dish Network (Dish) were providing local broadcast TV stations to their subscribers in more than three-quarters of the nation's 210 television markets. In addition, thanks to government policy, both DirecTV and Dish can offer broadcast network programming to viewers who are not within the signal coverage area of a terrestrial TV station.

Clearly, DBS is a major player, but it has its limitations. DBS technology theoretically can provide two-way communication. However, DBS providers have been unable to match cable or the telephone industry's ability to provide high-speed two-way Internet access at a competitive price. Rather than compete in the broadband market, both DirecTV and Dish partner with phone companies or other Internet access providers to provide high-speed interactive services.

Newspapers

Talking about newspapers in a book titled *Head's Broadcasting in America* may seem ironic, but in our modern, converging media environment newspapers are playing new roles. And newspapers have always been, and continue to be, major competitors to broadcasting for advertising dollars.

Some people say that no electronic device can ever duplicate the convenience and utility of the newspaper, and they may be right. Millions of Americans wouldn't feel normal if they didn't start their day with a cup of coffee in one hand and a newspaper in the other.

However, the Newspaper Association of America reported that the number of U.S. daily newspapers declined from more than 1,600 in 1990 to 1,400 in 2008. Daily newspaper circulation dropped from about 62 million to slightly more than 52 million in the same period. Even more troubling for newspapers are statistics showing that young adults are much less likely to read a daily newspaper than their grandparents. Given these trends, it is little wonder the newspaper industry has embraced electronic technology to offset losses in traditional print circulation.

The amount of content newspapers make available online, and what they expect in return, has changed since the 1990s. Newspapers initially put much of their print content online at no cost to users, although the content was often smothered by blinking banner ads. By the turn of the century, this model was in trouble. Many newspaper readers began canceling their newspaper subscriptions because they found the free content available online adequate, further adding to the decline in circulation. Competing web sites for classified advertising, a large revenue source for local newspapers, started appearing with prices lower than newspaper ads.

Realizing they were "giving away the store," newspapers began to adjust the model. Many newspapers continued to offer headlines and snippets from their print publications free online, but increasingly charged for full-text access. Access to news archives and popular features, such as *The New York Times'* crossword puzzles, also became a pay-for-content proposition. In addition, newspapers began creating special content for distribution online, some of it available only through subscription. In some cases the "fee" for access to content was not currency but information. Newspapers began asking visitors to "register" before being given access. Registration allowed the web site operator to collect valuable marketing information about the user. The operator could then use that data to sell additional products to the user, or the operator could sell the data itself to other marketers, or do both.

The type of content available on-line from newspapers has also evolved. Early web sites featured text, graphics, and still photos. Today visitors find that kind of content, but also streaming audio and moving images. Much of that audio and video comes from a co-owned or affiliated television station or network. This is not surprising because many media companies that own newspapers also own broadcasting stations or cable news operations.

Newspapers remain largely a traditional mass medium based on the distribution of a physical object (the printed newspaper) using a technology for the final leg of the journey not far removed from that employed by the Pony Express. But if hard-copy circulation continues to decline, newspapers will likely become even larger players in the converged electronic media environment.

Telephone

If a discussion of newspapers initially seemed out of place, a section on the telephone may seem even more so. As you will learn in Chapter 2, however, the telephone company has been a major player in mass media since the birth of broadcasting. But in the 21st century, the telephone is morphing into a far different creature than it was at its birth in the 1800s, or even a few decades ago.

Until fairly recently, telephone companies in the United States were considered **common carriers** and were regulated as such. As common carriers, telephone companies supply communication facilities without assuming any responsibility for what is normally transmitted on those facilities. A telephone company may neither edit conversations nor restrict those who makes use of its facilities. The public can demand, as a right, equal access on equal terms to a common carrier. The government, however, usually controls common carrier profit levels and the fees they charge their customers.

As regulated monopolies guaranteed a profit, for most of their history telephone companies were limited in terms of what products and services they could provide. For example, in an effort to spur the growth of a new cable television industry, government regulations prohibited telephone companies from building cable systems in the areas where they already provided telephone service. All that began changing in 1992 when the FCC began relaxing restrictions on telcos (telephone companies), allowing them to provide video services over their networks in competition with cable companies.

Four years later, Congress passed the Telecommunications Act of 1996, eliminating all restrictions on telcos providing cable services in their local service areas. But telcos, legally freed to compete with cable and other multichannel video providers, began having second thoughts. The economic risks of entering a new market area, unexpected technical difficulties with transitional video delivery systems, and renewed interest in expanding telephony services combined to slow expansion into video delivery. Although renewing their commitment to offer a full range of video and interactive services, telcos acknowledged that these services would evolve more slowly as they upgraded their telephone networks by deploying high capacity fiber optics. Consequently, the telephone companies did not begin offering cable-like video services on a widespread scale until the middle of the new century's first decade.

As telephone companies increasingly move to the delivery of entertainment programs and information services—both their own and those of others—they become less and less distinguishable from cable systems. Indeed, telcos have the characteristics of both common carriers (when delivering switched voice services) and electronic mass media (when delivering cable-like video services).

Computers and the Internet

Regardless of whether program delivery is by cable system, DBS, or telephone company, computers play a central role in producing and distributing what we see and hear. The electronic media have employed computers in a variety of ways for many years. Audio and video editing is done with computers. The amazing special effects we take for granted in today's programming would not be possible without the computer. High volume video servers that store and release programs for video-on-demand are computers. Indeed, there is hardly any function performed by broadcast stations, cable systems, direct broadcast satellite operators, or telephone companies that does not involve computer power.

Computers in various forms are also increasingly apparent at the consumers' end of the communications process. For example, the familiar set-top converter box that facilitates multichannel cable is a computer-based device. So is the receiver that converts DBS signals for display on a TV screen. These computer-like devices, and others that now select, store, and reproduce audio and video, are becoming more complex. Their software can determine the kind of programs a person prefers, then search the list of available programs and automatically record those programs without specific instructions. One can only wonder what capabilities the descendents of these devices may have in the future.

Although these devices actually perform computer-like tasks, they are not what most of us think of as a "computer." That term is usually reserved for a stand-alone unit incorporating a display screen, a box full of electronic components that "processes" information, and some device—usually a keyboard or mouse—that allows us to tell the box of stuff what we want it to do. For most consumers that unit is a PC, a "personal computer" that uses Microsoft's Windows operating system, or a Macintosh running Apple Computer's software.

The home computer has changed dramatically since its introduction in the 1970s. Early home computers, what we now call PCs, performed only a single function or two, such as word processing. Since the early 1990s personal computers have been capable of handling audio, video, and data. Now the PC is merging with the television (and the radio receiver as well) to combine broadcast, cable, and DBS reception, plus Internet browsing, with traditional computing functions in a single appliance. Today, consumers use PCs to send and receive e-mail that includes text, video, and audio. They look at and listen to real-time and archived radio and TV programming. They purchase or exchange popular music and video that may be stored on the PC as well as downloaded to a portable player. They read the daily newspaper and purchase everything from dog food to new cars on-line.

Some say all communication and information functions—telephone, fax, radio, television, multimedia disk-based players/recorders, even home security and utility management—will merge into a single system. Other observers, however, believe that people will prefer having a greater number of less expensive, more specialized, and easier-to-use communication appliances rather than a "loaded" PC. Manufacturers today are responding to consumer interest by offering a variety of computer-based communication appliances that provide specialized services in a smaller, more portable, less expensive, and easier-to-use package than the conventional multifunction PC.

It is likely, of course, that consumers will want it all: a big-screen, **high-definition television (HDTV)** set in the living room as part of a home multimedia center (see Exhibit 1.b), a basic PC/TV in the bedroom, a high-powered PC/TV with a full array of computer peripherals in the home office, and many less sophisticated communications appliances scattered throughout the house, as well as in their vehicles, purses, briefcases, and book bags.

1.3 | Back to Basics

Given all this, one might well argue that this book's title, *Head's Broadcasting in America*, is misleading. As already indicated, its content certainly isn't limited, in precise terms, to broadcasting. Electronic sources of information and entertainment have grown so varied that, quite frankly, no single word describes them all. Nor is this book limited to America, but rather it examines other national systems as well. The increasing globalization of media mandates a broader focus.

Broadcasters, cable and DBS operators, telephone companies, even computer hardware and software manufacturers want to build the technological pathways that bring programs and services to the public and control the content that travels over these pathways. But, in the final analysis, corporate successes in the information age will be determined not by *how* but rather by *what* they deliver. Most people simply have no interest whatsoever in whether they receive information and entertainment through a wire (provided by a cable system or a telephone company) or over the air (by traditional broadcast or by direct broadcast satellite), or whether the picture appears on a traditional television receiver, on a computer screen, or a hand-held device's display. What they *do* have an interest in is

> the variety and quality of the programs and services they receive,
> how easy it is to receive them, and
> how much they have to pay for the package.

The student of electronic communication, however, must understand how it has developed, how it works, how it is controlled, how it affects and is affected by its many audiences, and—as we will see in the next chapter—how it all began.

Exhibit 1.b

The Well-Equipped Multimedia Home

The well-equipped multimedia home may contain many of the items pictured here, plus devices that we can now hardly imagine. The potential size of the projection, wall-mounted HDTV video screen (five feet across or even more), as well as the capacity of digital multitrack sound systems, could force multimedia use to take over an entire room. The home multimedia center features an integrated and fully digital set of devices to offer multiple video and audio inputs through integrated decoders at the flick of a universal remote button. An important part of any such room will be interactive audio and video services allowing consumers to "talk back" to program producers and advertisers.

Source: Photo © William Casey/Alamy.

From Radio to Television

chapter 2

"History is more or less bunk." (Henry Ford, interview with Charles N. Wheeler, *Chicago Tribune*, May 25, 1916)

The groans teachers often hear when assigning a chapter detailing events occurring before 1990 (or even 2000) suggests that many young people share Ford's opinion of history. Many of us are sympathetic. It's challenging enough keeping up with what's happening *now* without the burden of learning about stuff occurring in the distant past. Although acknowledging the success of Henry Ford in spite of his jaundiced view of history, we tend to agree with Ford's contemporary, philosopher George Santayana, who said, "Those who cannot remember the past are condemned to repeat it" (*The Life of Reason*, Volume 1, 1905).

This chapter briefly reviews the historical development of radio and television broadcasting. The next chapter deals with "newer media" that developed to challenge broadcasting in the latter part of the 20th century and beyond. We believe a knowledge of broadcasting's early development helps us better understand these "newer media" because broadcasting established the cultural, economic, technological, and regulatory foundations on which they are based. As you study this chapter, we hope you will begin to understand that many of the things we take for granted, such as a privately-owned and advertising-supported media infrastructure, were not inevitable, but evolved over time in response to a complex mix of forces. We also hope you begin to notice that history does tend to repeat itself as new media take over the functions of the old, and the old media must reinvent themselves if they are to survive.

Hundreds of scholarly articles and dozens of books have chronicled the development of broadcasting during the last century. This chapter must, therefore, touch on only the highlights, many of them listed in the timeline printed on the inside front cover of this book.

As we begin, it is important to recognize that today's electronic media are based on cultural and technological precedents that predate World War I and even the 19th century discoveries that led to the birth of broadcasting.

2.1 Cultural Precedents

Public appetite for mass entertainment developed decades before radio. Popular newspapers, home phonographs, and motion-picture theaters all encouraged a mass media habit, making it easier for broadcasting to achieve success in a very short time.

Urbanization

These older media grew out of fundamental social changes encouraged by the Industrial Revolution (roughly 1740–1850). For centuries, most people worked on farms or in related agricultural roles. But industry, based initially on steam power, increasingly drew people away from the land to live and work in cities.

These urban populations became the target of what we now call **mass media**—technology-based means of communication that reach large numbers of people, delivering news and entertainment that most people find interesting and at a price they can afford.

Penny Press

Urban concentration and increasing literacy and leisure time all helped to transform newspapers. Originally aimed primarily at a wealthy and educated elite, they became a product for the masses. The "penny press" signaled this transformation when, in 1833, the *New York Sun* began a trend toward mass-interest, mass-produced papers. Copies sold for a penny, first in the thousands and eventually in the hundreds of thousands. Much like today's popular radio and television programming, the penny press exploited news of everyday events, sensational crimes, gossip, human-interest stories, sports, and entertaining features—all presented in a breezy style that contrasted with the flowery essay approach of the past. By the 1890s, some popular newspapers, appealing across lines of class, gender, age, political party, and cherished beliefs, had circulations of more than a million.

Vaudeville

Vaudeville was a popular form of entertainment featuring "variety" acts in which performers sang, danced, played musical instruments, and did comedy routines. The first U.S. vaudeville house opened in Boston in 1883, and vaudeville remained immensely popular well into the 1920s, at its peak selling more tickets than all other forms of entertainment combined. New York City alone once had 37 vaudeville houses. The development of motion pictures, especially the "talkies" in the late 1920s, spelled the end of American vaudeville.

But vaudeville developed an audience for forms of entertainment that reappeared later in network radio programming. Vaudeville also served as a training ground for early radio performers such as Jack Benny, Gracie Allen, George Burns, and Milton Berle, all of whom also migrated successfully from radio to television. Many elements of early radio shows were direct descendents of vaudeville routines, routines that differ little from today's comedy sketches and stand-up acts, except for the language restrictions required for early broadcast audiences.

The Phonograph

Around the turn of the century, owning a phonograph (often housed in a handsome wooden cabinet) accustomed people to investing in a piece of furniture that brought entertainment into the home. By the end of World War I, on the eve of radio's introduction, some 200 phonograph manufacturers turned out more than two million players each year. Like vaudeville, the phonograph helped create a popular demand for music that radio then supplied, contributing to radio's rapid growth after 1920.

Motion Pictures

Like the phonograph industry, silent movies were well established by the time broadcasting began in the 1920s. Moviegoers returned weekly for serial dramas, which eventually had their counterparts in broadcasting. "Talkies" began in earnest in 1928, with several rival sound systems competing for acceptance. One of these sound-on-film systems had been developed by the Radio Corporation of America (RCA), the owner of the National Broadcasting Company (NBC), the first national radio network. RCA's executive officer, David Sarnoff (see Exhibit 2.e) joined with Joseph P. Kennedy (father of the future president) to form Radio-Keith-Orpheum Corporation (RKO). RKO became a motion-picture production and distribution company that released films under the trademark "Radio Pictures." These "Radio Pictures" began with a logo showing a radio tower radiating little electromagnetic lighting bolts perched atop Earth. The RCA–RKO alliance is only one example of the many links between broadcasting and motion pictures in the 1920s, long before television brought the two visual media into an even closer relationship, and long before "convergence" became a 1990's buzz-word.

Motion pictures also helped establish the "visual grammar" later adopted by television. Shooting and editing techniques developed by motion-picture pioneers such as Edwin S. Porter, David Wark Griffith, Sergei Eisenstein, and many others not only helped shape popular tastes regarding visual presentations, but also provided a ready guide for early TV producers. Many of the cinematic conventions in today's TV programs date back to the birth of the motion-picture industry.

2.2 Technological Precedents

The "penny press," the phonograph, and the motion-picture industry evolved from technological advances in mass communication, but broadcasting's technological precedents focused on point-to-point communication, which may have delayed broadcasting's development. It is also worth noting that broadcasting's technological precedents were electronic, whereas earlier mass media—newspapers, phonographs, and motion pictures—employed mostly mechanical technologies.

The Telegraph

The British first developed electrical telegraphy in the 1820s as an aid to early railroad operations, but these early devices were clumsy and prone to break down. An American artist/inventor, Samuel F. B. Morse, conducted extensive telegraph experiments in the 1830s—at a time when westward expansion put a high premium on rapid communications over long distances. Morse made significant telegraph improvements, including increased durability and a receiver that recorded messages on strips of paper. He and a partner devised the American Morse code to translate numbers and letters into the dots and dashes of telegraphic language.

In partnership with the federal government, Morse installed the first operational U.S. telegraph line from Washington to Baltimore in 1844. Three years later the government sold its interest to private investors, retaining only the right to regulate telegraphic services. By the end of the Civil War, Western Union had emerged as the dominant telegraph company.

The importance of the government's decision to sell, or privatize, the telegraph is difficult to stress too strongly. The government's decision to only regulate, but not own, the first electronic medium became the precedent for the private ownership of electronic media that we accept today as normal and started the United States on a telecommunications path different from that of most other countries (see Chapter 13).

Communications over transatlantic telegraph cables began in 1866 (after a short-lived attempt in 1858), enabling the exchange of information between Europe and North America in minutes instead of weeks. Newspapers immediately seized on both submarine and land telegraph as a means of sharing information in ways not previously possible. The telegraph had a revolutionary influence because it allowed communication with distant locations at a pace literally millions of times faster than anything before it. The shrinking of the Earth into an electronically interconnected "global village" began with the telegraph.

The Telephone

Investigators worked simultaneously in many nations on developing what became the telephone. Several appeared on the verge of a solution when Alexander Graham Bell delivered his designs to the U.S. Patent Office in 1876, beating fellow American Elisha Gray by only a few hours. Bell organized the original Bell

Telephone Company a year later, when he secured a second essential patent. Though control over Bell's patents soon passed to others who went on to develop the company known today as AT&T (until 1994, American Telephone & Telegraph Company), Bell's name still means "telephone" to many people.

AT&T initially built local telephone systems (known as local exchanges) and then developed a "long lines" network connecting local exchanges with one another. In 1913, AT&T ensured its supremacy in long distance by acquiring a license to a crucial electronic invention, the Audion (see Section 2.3), which made coast-to-coast telephone service possible. AT&T's control of long-distance voice communication by wire had an important bearing on broadcasting, which after 1927 depended on such wire links for network operations.

2.3 Wireless Communication

Simultaneous with the development of the telephone, other inventors were working on wireless systems. Many early experimenters succeeded by "accident," but lacked the understanding of scientific principles required for systematic development of their discoveries.

Hertzian Waves

In 1873, Scottish physicist James Clerk Maxwell published a paper in which he theorized that an invisible form of radiant energy—electromagnetic energy—must exist. He described it mathematically, foreseeing that it resembled light radiating out from a source in the form of waves.

In 1888, German physicist Heinrich Hertz reported his brilliant laboratory experiments that proved conclusively the validity of Maxwell's theory. Hertz generated electromagnetic waves, transmitted them down the length of his laboratory, detected them, measured their lengths, and showed that they had other wave-like properties similar to those of light. In effect, Hertz demonstrated radio. But he sought only to verify a scientific theory, not to develop a new way of communicating. It remained for other experimenters to communicate with what they called Hertzian waves.

"The Right Releasing Touch"

Although many inventors were experimenting with wireless systems, a young Italian experimenter, Guglielmo Marconi, is credited with developing wireless as a viable means of communication. He supplied "the right releasing touch," as a Supreme Court justice put it in upholding Marconi's primacy in a later patent suit (US, 1942: 65). Stimulated by Hertz's paper, Marconi experimented with Hertzian wave signals in

the early 1890s, first sending them across the space of an attic, then for greater distances on the grounds of his father's estate.

It was characteristic of Marconi's aggressive personality that he decided his work was "ready for prime time" when he succeeded in transmitting Hertzian waves a mere two miles. He patriotically offered it to the Italian government, which couldn't see the potential. Still only 22, Marconi next went to England, where in 1896 he registered his patent. He soon launched his own company to manufacture wireless-telegraphy equipment and to offer wireless services to ships and shore stations.

To a remarkable degree, Marconi combined an inventor's genius with that of a business innovator. As inventor he persisted tirelessly, never discouraged even by hundreds of failed attempts at solving a problem. In 1909, Marconi shared the Nobel Prize in physics with Germany's Ferdinand Braun for achievements in wireless telegraphy. As a business manager, Marconi demonstrated a rare entrepreneurial talent plus a flair for effective public relations.

In the early 1900s, to prove his system's value, he repeatedly staged dramatic demonstrations of wireless to skeptical officials, scientists, investors, and equipment buyers. Exhibit 2.a shows Marconi with some of the equipment used in these demonstrations. Realizing the valuable publicity that bridging the Atlantic with radio signals would create for his company, Marconi established a receiving station on Signal Hill, 600 feet above the harbor of St. John's, Newfoundland. On December 12, 1901, he heard three short dots—Morse code for the letter S—transmitted from England.

Among his business ventures, Marconi's American branch had a decisive influence on the development of broadcasting in America. Founded in 1899, American Marconi developed a virtual monopoly on U.S. wireless communication. Marconi's wireless extended the telegraph principle—point-to-point communication between ships and shore stations, between ships at sea, and to a lesser extent between countries. This limited application of radiotelegraphy dominated the early years of radio service because the relatively crude Marconi equipment could transmit only Morse code dots and dashes. Methods had not yet been found to impress sound onto radio waves.

The Vacuum Tube

The solution to this and related radio problems came with the development of an improved **vacuum tube,** capable of electronically amplifying the changing volume and pitch of speech. American inventor Lee de Forest followed up on research leads suggested by Edison's 1883 electric lamp and the original two-element vacuum tube **(diode)** that Ambrose Fleming, a member of Marconi's research staff, patented in 1904.

Exhibit 2.a

Guglielmo Marconi (1874–1937)

Marconi is shown here with some of the early wireless apparatus he used to demonstrate his "miraculous" invention. He is holding a paper tape in his right hand on which a radiotelegraphic message is inscribed in Morse code, a recording technique borrowed from wire telegraphy. Marconi was quick to borrow ideas from other inventors if doing so improved his devices. He was equally quick to patent whatever he could and then to aggressively defend his patents.

Source: Photo from AP Photo/Wide World.

De Forest's crucial improvement consisted of adding a third element to a vacuum tube, turning it into a **triode.** He positioned his new element, a tiny grid or screen, between the diode's existing filament and plate. A small voltage applied to the grid could control, with great precision, the flow of electrons from filament to plate. Thus, a weak signal could be enormously amplified, yet precisely modulated. De Forest first experimented with his triode, or **Audion**, in 1906. It took more than a dozen years to develop the Audion and the new circuits to go with it—and much of the necessary work was done by others.

The Audion marked a great leap forward into the modern age of electronics. Electrons (particles of energy smaller than atoms) could be controlled. This transforming ability to manipulate electrons would revolutionize not only communications, but also virtually all science and industry.

Commercial Uses of Wireless

Into the 1920s, wireless firms made money by supplying telegraphic communication among ships, between ships and shore stations, and between continents. Overland wireless-telegraphy services had less appeal because telephone and telegraph lines satisfied existing needs.

Wireless offered unique advantages to maritime commerce. In fact, Marconi chose international yacht races for some early public wireless demonstrations. Wireless also gained invaluable publicity from its life-saving role in maritime disasters, one as early as 1898. Each year the number of rescues increased. Exhibit 2.b describes the most famous of them all.

Radio had commercial possibilities as a long-distance alternative to submarine telegraph cables, which were fragile and enormously costly to install. On the eve of the U.S. entry into World War I, General Electric's Ernst Alexanderson developed a device called an **alternator**, a new type of transmitter, to send transatlantic messages reliably—a major improvement in long-distance radio communication. But Alexanderson's alternator was a huge and inefficient device compared to tubes. During the 1920s, vacuum-tube transmitters displaced alternators, and radio became a strong competitor of submarine telegraph cables.

Military Wireless

Naturally, navies took an interest in military applications of wireless from the outset. The British Admiralty used Marconi equipment as early as 1899, during the Boer War, but with little success. Technology advanced rapidly during the next decade, however, and wireless telegraphy became an important military weapon. In April 1917, as America entered World War I, the U.S. Navy saw wireless as a threat to national security. Enemy spy agents could (and some did) use radio to send information about ship movements, for example. Therefore, the U.S. Navy took over all wireless stations in the country, commercial and amateur alike.

To mobilize America's wireless resources for war more rapidly, the U.S. Navy placed a freeze on patent lawsuits over radio inventions. This allowed manufacturers to pool their patents and use any patent needed. Patent sharing and the pressure of war encouraged companies to move forward with innovations they might not have risked during peacetime.

By the end of the war, big business had developed a stake in wireless and was ready to branch out into new applications. AT&T had added wireless rights to its original purchase of telephone rights to de Forest's Audion. General Electric (GE) owned patents for its powerful Alexanderson alternator and had the ability to mass produce vacuum tubes. Westinghouse, also a vacuum tube producer, joined in seeking new ways to capitalize on wireless. But before any of these firms could move forward, they had to come to terms with the U.S. Navy, which also had claims on wireless.

Exhibit 2.b

The Titanic Disaster, April 1912

The photo on the left shows the *Titanic* embarking on its maiden voyage. To the right is a photo showing the *Titanic* wireless room.

A luxury liner advertised as unsinkable, the *Titanic* struck an iceberg and sank in the Atlantic on her maiden voyage from Britain to the United States in April 1912. One heroic Marconi radio operator stayed at his post and went down with the ship; the second operator survived. Some 1,500 people died—among them some of the most famous names in the worlds of art, science, finance, and diplomacy—in part because each nearby vessel, unlike the *Titanic*, had but one radio operator (all that was then required), who had already turned in for the night. Only by chance did the operator on a ship some 50 miles distant hear distress calls from the *Titanic*. It steamed full speed to the disaster site, rescuing about 700 survivors.

Radiotelegraphy's role as the world's only thread of contact with the survivors aboard the rescue liner *Carpathia* as it steamed toward New York brought the new medium of wireless to public attention as nothing else had done. Subsequent British and American inquiries revealed that a more sensible use of wireless (such as a 24-hour radio watch) could have decreased the loss of life. Because of such findings, the *Titanic* disaster influenced the worldwide adoption of stringent laws governing shipboard wireless stations. The *Titanic* tragedy also set a precedent for regarding the radio business as having a special public responsibility. This concept carried over into broadcasting legislation a quarter of a century later.

Source: Photos © Bettmann/Corbis.

2.4 Birth of Broadcasting

In 1906, Canadian-born Reginald Fessenden made the first known radiotelephone transmission resembling what we would now call a broadcast. Using an ordinary telephone as a microphone, Fessenden made his historic radiotelephony transmission on Christmas Eve from Brant Rock, on the Massachusetts coast south of Boston. He played a violin, sang, read from the Bible, and played a phonograph recording. Ship operators who picked up the transmission far out at sea could hardly believe they were hearing human voices and musical sounds from earphones that previously brought them only the monotonous drone of Morse code.

In 1907, hard on the heels of Fessenden, de Forest made experimental radiotelephone transmissions from downtown New York City. Some of his equipment appears in Exhibit 2.c

By 1916, de Forest had set up in his Bronx home an experimental transmitter over which he played phonograph recordings and mentioned products made by his own firm, announcements de Forest later claimed were the first radio commercials. De Forest even aired election returns in November of that year, anticipating by four years the opening broadcast of KDKA, which is usually credited as the historical beginning of U.S. broadcasting.

Government Monopoly Avoided

Though World War I ended in November 1918, the U.S. Navy did not relinquish control of radio facilities for another 18 months. The critical decisions made at

Exhibit 2.c

Lee de Forest (1873–1961)

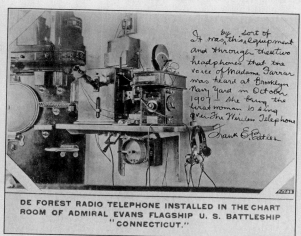

It was, by this sort of equipment and through these two headphones that the voice of Madame Farrar was heard at Brooklyn Navy Yard in October 1907. She being the first woman to sing over the Wireless Telephone

Frank E. Butler

DE FOREST RADIO TELEPHONE INSTALLED IN THE CHART ROOM OF ADMIRAL EVANS FLAGSHIP U. S. BATTLESHIP "CONNECTICUT."

De Forest's invention of the amplifying vacuum tube, the Audion, was critical to the development of modern electronic communication, including broadcasting. The shipboard receiver also pictured is typical of the type used to receive

de Forest's experimental radiotelephone transmissions in 1907.

Sources: De Forest photo © Bettmann/Corbis; transmitter photo from Smithsonian Institution, negative #79-11558.

this time profoundly affected the future of broadcasting in America.

The U.S. Navy thought radio was too vital to entrust to private hands and it supported a bill in Congress late in 1918 proposing, in effect, to make radio a permanent government monopoly. Despite strong arguments from U.S. Navy brass at the hearings, the bill failed. Thus, radio took the road of private enterprise in the United States, though in many other countries governments remained in charge as radio expanded in the postwar years. For decades the United States stood virtually alone in turning over its radio (and later TV) communication system to private enterprise, and only recently has the global trend been toward privatization of at least some aspects of broadcasting.

Origin of RCA

The restoration of private station ownership in 1920 would have meant returning most commercial wireless communication facilities in the United States to British Marconi (parent of American Marconi). Disturbed at the prospect of foreign control, the U.S. Navy strongly opposed the deal.

American wireless manufacturers simply feared Marconi would renew aggressive legal actions to protect patents shared during the war, limiting their ability to maximize profits in a booming postwar economy. Caught in a squeeze play between the U.S. government and the

giants of American industry, the British-based company could neither expand nor effectively operate. With tacit government approval, Owen Young, head of GE's legal department, quietly negotiated the purchase of all American Marconi stock in a "semi-friendly" takeover.

In October 1919, GE created a subsidiary to take over and operate American Marconi—the Radio Corporation of America (RCA)—shortly to become the premier force in American broadcasting. Under RCA's charter, all of its officers had to be Americans, and 80 percent of its stock had to be in American hands.

Westinghouse and AT&T joined GE as investors in the new corporation. In 1922, GE owned about 25 percent of RCA's stock, Westinghouse owned 20 percent, AT&T held 4 percent, and the remainder was owned by former American Marconi shareholders and other investors. AT&T sold its interest in 1923, but RCA remained under GE and Westinghouse control until 1932, when an antitrust suit forced them to make RCA an independent corporation.

Peacetime Patent Pooling

RCA and its parent companies each held important radio patents, yet each found itself blocked by patents the others held. From 1919 to 1923, AT&T, GE, Westinghouse, RCA, and other minor players worked out a series of cross-licensing agreements, modeled after the navy-run wartime patent pool. Under these

Exhibit 2.d

Conrad's 8XK and Its Successor, KDKA

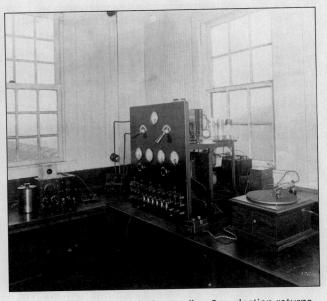

Dr. Frank Conrad (left) and his amateur radio setup typified the improvised wireless stations operated by inventors and experimenters. It contrasts with the first KDKA transmitter facilities (right), with which the Harding-Cox election returns were broadcast on November 2, 1920.

Source: Photos © Bettmann/Corbis.

agreements, each company had its own slice of the electronics manufacturing and services pie. Each parent company and RCA could build equipment for its own use, but AT&T got exclusive rights to build transmitters for sale to "outsiders." Both GE and Westinghouse held exclusive rights to build receivers sold through RCA. Within a few years these carefully laid plans fell into disarray because of the astonishingly rapid growth of a new use for radiotelephony—broadcasting.

The First Broadcasting Station

Stations in many nations claim to be the world's oldest broadcasting station. In the late 19th and early 20th centuries, inventors and experimenters throughout the industrialized world were experimenting with wireless. Which of these experimental stations was the first to adopt the characteristics we now associate with "broadcasting" remains a debatable question. When the question is narrowed to North America, some scholars say Canadian station CFCF in Montreal was the first broadcast station and cite evidence showing the station began regularly scheduled broadcasts as early as December 1919. Certainly, following World War I there were also stations in the United States transmitting forms of information and entertainment we now consider broadcasting. But these stations typically operated sporadically and often the "program" was just something to make a noise, the real purpose of the transmission being to test the equipment.

Many believe the first broadcasting station, at least in the United States, began as 8XK, an amateur radiotelephone station operated in a Pittsburgh garage by Westinghouse engineer Dr. Frank Conrad. Dr. Conrad's equipment (Exhibit 2.d) was crude, with various components connected by a jumble of exposed wires.

In the fall of 1919, Conrad fell into the habit of transmitting recorded music, sports results, and bits of talk in response to requests from other amateurs. These informal transmissions (hardly "programs" in the formal sense) built up so much interest that newspapers began to comment on them.

Managers at the Joseph Horne Company, a Pittsburgh department store, noticed a growing public interest in wireless and decided people might buy receiving sets to pick up Conrad's "broadcasts." They installed a demonstration receiver and ran a newspaper display ad in September 1920: "Air Concert 'Picked Up' by Radio Here . . . Amateur Wireless Sets made by the maker of the Set which is in operation in our store, are on sale here $10.00 up."

Horne's ad caught the eye of Westinghouse vice president H. P. Davis, who immediately saw a novel merchandising tie-in: The company could increase demand for its receivers and promote Westinghouse's name by regularly transmitting programs. Westinghouse adapted a transmitter, installed it in a makeshift shack on the company's tallest building in East Pittsburgh, and at 6:00 P.M. on November 2, 1920, began broadcasting as KDKA.

Because KDKA's opening coincided with Election Day 1920, the maiden broadcast reflected public interest in presidential vote results. KDKA offered brief news reports of election returns, fed to the station by telephone from a newspaper office, alternating with phonograph and live banjo music. The announcer, Leo Rosenberg from Westinghouse's public relations department, repeatedly asked anyone listening to contact the company. After the election, KDKA began a regular daily hour-long schedule of music and talk.

KDKA met five criteria that qualify it as the oldest U.S. station still in operation, despite many other claims based on earlier experiments. KDKA (1) used radio waves, (2) to send out uncoded signals, (3) in a continuous, scheduled program service, (4) intended for the general public, and (5) was licensed by the government to provide such a service (Baudino & Kittross, 1977). However, no broadcasting licenses as such existed at the time; KDKA had the same kind of license as ship-to-shore radiotelegraphic stations.

Westinghouse created KDKA to spur demand for Westinghouse receivers, but many early listeners tuned in on homemade sets. As early as 1906, experimenters discovered that certain minerals (crystals) had an amazing ability to detect Hertzian waves when touched in "hot spots" with a thin metallic wire, popularly called a "cat whisker." Almost anyone could assemble a complete "crystal set" for about $10. Best of all, crystal sets required no electrical power for their operation, making them popular with rural families.

In its first year of operation, KDKA pioneered many types of programs that later became standard radio fare: orchestra music, church services, public-service announcements, political addresses, sports events, dramas, and market reports. But KDKA lacked one now-familiar type of broadcast material—commercials. Westinghouse paid KDKA's expenses to promote sales of its own products. The company assumed that each company wanting to promote its wares over the air would operate its own station.

2.5 Broadcasting Becomes an Industry

Westinghouse did not have the field to itself for long. Department stores, newspapers, educational institutions, churches, and electrical equipment dealers all soon operated their own stations. In early 1922, the new industry gathered momentum; by May more than 200 stations had been licensed, and the number passed 500 early in 1923.

Receiver ownership increased dramatically and consistently. In 1922, about 60,000 households had a radio; only two years later, more than one million had radios.

The Radio Group; The Telephone Group

RCA entered the field in 1921, purchasing WJZ, a second station that Westinghouse built to reach the New York market. WJZ assumed responsibility for producing its own programs, as had KDKA. But when AT&T put WEAF on the air in New York City in 1922, it took a different approach. The telephone company explained that it would furnish no programs whatsoever. AT&T perceived broadcasting as another **common carrier**—merely a variation of telephony. In a 1922 press release about WEAF, AT&T explained its approach:

> Just as the [telephone] company leases its long distance wire facilities for the use of newspapers, banks, and other concerns, so it will lease its radio telephone facilities and will not provide the matter which is sent out from this station. (Quoted in Banning, 1946: 68)

Strange as it seems today, AT&T could not see the difference between a telephone booth and a broadcasting station. It soon became clear, however, that filling radio schedules entirely with leased time would not work. As with print media, advertisers would have to foot the bill. Advertisers initially, however, had no idea how to prepare programs capable of attracting listeners. To fill its schedule, the telephone company found itself getting into show business after all—a decidedly uncomfortable role for a regulated monopoly bent on maintaining a serious and dignified public image.

Soon the industry broke into two conflicting groups with different ideas about the way broadcasting would work. The "Radio Group" consisted of Westinghouse, GE, and RCA; the "Telephone Group" was made up of AT&T and its Western Electric subsidiary. In the end, it turned out that each group was partly right. The Telephone Group correctly foresaw that economic and technical limitations made it impractical for every company wanting to communicate with the public to operate its own radio station. Instead, each station would need to make its services available to many different advertisers. AT&T miscalculated, however, in emphasizing primarily those interested in sending messages instead of those receiving them. Public goodwill had to be earned with listenable programs to pave the way for acceptance of advertising. Here the Radio Group's strategy of providing a program service prevailed.

The First Commercials

AT&T's WEAF called the sale of commercial time **toll broadcasting**, an analogy to telephone long-distance toll calls. It first leased facilities for a toll broadcast in

August 1922 when a Long Island real estate firm paid for 10 minutes of time to extol the advantages of living in an apartment complex in New York. AT&T would not allow mentioning anything so crass as price.

Advertising on something as "personal" as radio was considered a bit scandalous. Many radio pioneers, including Lee de Forest and David Sarnoff, initially abhorred the practice. Potential advertisers must have had similar thoughts, because WEAF's net income from advertising after four months was only about $5,000. In 1923, the first weekly advertiser appeared on WEAF, featuring a musical group the sponsor called "The Browning King Orchestra"—which ensured frequent mention of the sponsor's name, although the script carefully avoided mentioning that Browning King sold clothing. By 1928, under pressure of rising station operating costs and advertiser demand, more blatant advertising had become acceptable.

Unlike most modern advertisers, early sponsors did more than simply advertise—they also owned the programs that served as vehicles for their advertising messages. Later on, during the height of network radio's popularity, advertisers and their agencies controlled most major entertainment shows.

Conflicts

AT&T found a long-lasting broadcast role in its interpretation of the RCA cross-licensing agreements, claiming exclusive rights to interconnect radio stations with its telephone lines. Thus, at first only AT&T-owned WEAF could set up a network. It began in 1923 with the first permanent station interconnection—a telephone line between WEAF in New York City and WMAF in South Dartmouth, Massachusetts. By October 1924, AT&T had a regular network of six stations and assembled a temporary coast-to-coast hookup of 22 outlets to carry a speech by Calvin Coolidge, the first president to address the nation by radio. In broadcasting's early years, it was common practice to call interconnected stations carrying the same program a chain. The terms **chain** and **network** mean the same thing.

New Arrangements

The growing demand for broadcasting equipment, especially receivers, upset the careful balance that the cross-licensing agreements among Westinghouse, GE, AT&T, and RCA had created. The agreements had not included broadcasting, which was seen to be of only minor importance. Further, a federal suit alleged that the cross-licensing agreements violated antitrust laws by aiming to control the manufacture and sale of all radio equipment. At the same time, AT&T concluded that its original concept of broadcasting as a branch of telephony was mistaken.

Accordingly, in 1926 the partners in the cross-licensing agreements redefined the parties' rights to use their commonly owned patents and to engage in the various aspects of the radio business. Briefly, AT&T refocused on telephony, selling WEAF and its other broadcasting assets to the Radio Group for $1 million, agreeing not to manufacture radio receivers. RCA won the right to manufacture receivers while agreeing to lease all network relays from AT&T. It may appear that this concession was small compensation for AT&T, but such was not the case. Radio, and later television, networking became a highly profitable business, a business monopolized by AT&T for many decades.

This 1926 agreement had a defining influence on the future of broadcasting in America. As long as two powerful groups of communications companies fought over basic concepts, broadcasting's economic future remained uncertain. The 1926 agreements removed that uncertainty.

Birth of NBC

A few months after the 1926 settlement, the Radio Group created a new RCA subsidiary, the National Broadcasting Company (NBC)—the first American company organized specifically to operate a broadcasting network. NBC's four and one-half-hour coast-to-coast inaugural broadcast in late 1926 reached an estimated five million listeners and was reported to have cost $50,000 to produce. It took another two years, however, for coast-to-coast network operations to begin on a regular basis.

In 1927, RCA expanded NBC into two semiautonomous networks, the Blue and the Red. WJZ (later to become WABC) and the old Radio Group network formed the nucleus of the Blue; WEAF (later to become WNBC) and the old Telephone Group network formed the nucleus of the Red.

History suggests NBC's networks took their names from the red and blue lines drawn on a map showing interconnecting links among affiliates. Of the two networks, NBC-Red was predominant, with more powerful stations, more popular programming, and a larger income from advertising. NBC-Blue affiliates were weaker stations, or those in less populous cities, and the Blue network offered more public-service programming. NBC's simple Red and Blue designations provide an example of product "branding" long before the concept became a staple of modern broadcast marketing.

Birth of CBS

In 1927, soon after NBC began, an independent talent-booking agency, seeking an alternative to NBC as an outlet for its performers, started a rival network. It went through rapid changes in ownership, picking up the

Exhibit 2.e

Sarnoff and Paley: Giants of Early Broadcasting

Both network broadcasting pioneers came from immigrant Russian families, but there the similarity ceases. Sarnoff (left) rose from direst poverty, a self-educated and self-made man. In contrast, Paley (right) had every advantage of money and social position. After earning a degree from the Wharton School of Business at the University of Pennsylvania in 1922, he joined his father's prosperous cigar company. The differences between Sarnoff and Paley extended to their personalities and special skills. Sarnoff was a "technician turned businessman, ill at ease with the *hucksterism* that he had wrought, and he did not

condescend to sell, but Bill Paley loved to sell. CBS was Paley and he sold it as he sold himself" (Halberstam, 1979: 27). Sarnoff had been introduced to radio by way of hard work at the telegraph key for American Marconi, Paley by way of leisurely DX (long-distance) listening. Both men were highly competitive and pitted their companies against each other for 40 years before Sarnoff's retirement in 1969. Sarnoff died in 1971; Paley lived until 1990.

Source: Photos © Bettmann/Corbis.

---

name Columbia Phonograph Broadcasting System (CBS) as a result of a record company's investment. In September 1928, William S. Paley purchased the "patchwork, money-losing little company," as he later described it. When he took over, CBS had only 22 affiliates. Paley quickly turned the failing network around with a new affiliation contract. In his autobiography a half-century later he recalled:

> I proposed the concept of free sustaining service. . . . I would guarantee not ten but twenty hours of programming per week, pay the stations $50 an hour for the commercial hours used, but with a new proviso. To allow for the possibility of more business to come, the network was to receive an option on additional time. And for the first time, we were to have exclusive rights for network broadcasting through the affiliate. That meant the local station could not use its facilities for any other broadcasting network. I added one more innovation which helped

our cause: local stations would have to identify our programs with the CBS name. (Paley, 1979: 42)

Paley's shrewd innovations became standard practice in network contracts. From that point on, CBS never faltered, and Paley eventually rivaled Sarnoff as the nation's leading broadcasting executive (see Exhibit 2.e).

2.6 Government Regulation

One final piece remained to complete the structure of broadcasting in America—national legislation to impose order on the new medium. With the inception of telegraph systems in the 1840s, most governments recognized the need for both national and international regulation to ensure their fair and efficient operation.

The first international conference devoted to wireless communication issues took place in Berlin in 1903, only six years after Marconi's first patent. It dealt mainly with the Marconi company's refusal to exchange messages with rival maritime wireless systems. The conference emphasized the importance of subordinating commercial interests during emergencies. Marconi's aloof style of operation, aggressive commercial practices, and obvious desire to achieve a wireless monopoly had not made his company popular in international circles. Three years later another Berlin Convention reaffirmed the 1903 provisions, encouraged maritime nations to require wireless equipment on more ships, and established SOS as the international distress call.

1912 Radio Act

Congress confirmed American adherence to the Berlin rules with a 1910 wireless act requiring radio equipment and operators on most ships at sea. Following the April 1912 *Titanic* disaster, Congress modified the wireless act to require at least two operators on most ships. A few weeks later, Congress passed the Radio Act of 1912, the first comprehensive American legislation to govern land-based stations, requiring federal licensing of all radio transmitters. Specifically, the act required the secretary of commerce to grant licenses to U.S. citizens on request, leaving no basis to reject applications. Congress had no reason to anticipate rejections; it presumed that all who needed to operate radio stations could do so.

The 1912 act remained in force until 1927—throughout broadcasting's formative years. The law worked well enough for the point-to-point services it was designed to regulate. Point-to-multipoint broadcasting, however, introduced demands for spectrum space never imagined in 1912. Unregulated growth of broadcast stations in the mid-1920s soon created intolerable interference. Secretary of Commerce Herbert Hoover called on licensees to restrict themselves to certain frequencies, limit their transmitter power, and operate only at certain times.

An ardent believer in free enterprise, Hoover hoped that the new broadcasting business would discipline itself without the need for government regulation. To that end, he called a series of four annual national radio conferences in Washington, DC. At the first in 1922, about 20 broadcast engineers attended; by the fourth in 1925, the number of participants had increased to 400 and included station managers and attorneys. Each year, however, interference grew worse, and, to Hoover's frustration, broadcasters increasingly demanded he impose regulations the industry was unable to impose on itself. Recognizing that broadcasting could not survive without greater discipline imposed by someone, Hoover agreed, although he said he found it remarkable that any industry would request greater government regulation.

Not all broadcasters welcomed more regulation and better enforcement, however. Aimee Semple McPherson,

a controversial and charismatic evangelist of the 1920s, was one of the most outspoken opponents of Secretary Hoover's efforts to regulate broadcasting, as discussed in Exhibit 2.f.

Opposition by critics such as McPherson notwithstanding, in 1926 things finally came to a head when a federal court ruled that Hoover had no right (under the 1912 act) to establish regulations. He had tried to sue Chicago station WJAZ for operating on unauthorized frequencies at unauthorized times. The court found in favor of the station, remarking that, lacking specific congressional authorization in the law, Hoover could not "make conduct criminal which such laws leave untouched" (F, 1926: 618). In less than a year, 200 new stations took advantage of the government's inability to enforce licensing rules. President Coolidge urged Congress to pass a new law to regulate broadcasting. As he put it, "the whole service of this most important public function has drifted into such chaos as seems likely, if not remedied, to destroy its great value" (Coolidge, 1926). Early in 1927 Congress finally complied.

1927 Radio Act

The importance of the 1927 Radio Act is difficult to exaggerate. Although modified by subsequent legislation and court decisions, the fundamental principles established in this law continue to guide federal regulation of broadcasting even today. The concept that the radio spectrum belongs to "the people" rather than individual licensees; that broadcasting, like print, is a form of expression protected by the First Amendment, yet it is a unique medium requiring separate recognition and treatment; that (contrary to the philosophy of the 1912 Radio Act) not everyone can have their own channel and, thus, there must be special qualifications for those who do; and, most importantly, that the spectrum must be used to serve the "public interest, convenience, or necessity" all spring from the 1927 Radio Act.

The 1927 act established the Federal Radio Commission (FRC) to bring order to broadcasting. The FRC's first duty was to eliminate chaotic interference among broadcasting stations. The FRC quickly closed stations operating on frequencies reserved for other nations under international agreements and eliminated portable broadcasting transmitters. It specified transmitter power, frequency, and operating hours for the remaining stations, and increased the number of frequencies available for AM broadcasting. The FRC also established "clear channel" frequency assignments, greatly reducing interference while ensuring that people without a local station could enjoy radio programs at night, when signals on these frequencies travel long distances.

These actions would have been ineffective without the muscle to back them up. The FRC stepped up its inspections of stations and began checking broadcast

Exhibit 2.f

The Secretary and the Evangelist

An example of the bizarre regulatory problems facing the secretary of commerce was the station owned by Aimee Semple McPherson, a popular evangelist of the 1920s. She operated a pioneer broadcast station that "wandered all over the waveband" from her "temple" in Los Angeles. After delivering repeated warnings, a government inspector ordered the station closed down. Secretary Hoover thereupon received the following telegram from the evangelist:

> Please order your minions of Satan to leave my station alone. You cannot expect the Almighty to abide by your wave-length nonsense. When I offer my prayers to him I must fit into his wave reception. Open this station at once. (Hoover, 1952: II-142)

Evangelist McPherson, after being persuaded to engage a competent engineer, was allowed to reopen her station.

Sources: Herbert Hoover photo from Hulton Archive/Getty Images; Aimee Semple McPherson photo from Culver Pictures, Inc.

signals closely for technical violations. As both broadcast and nonbroadcast use of radio increased, the government built facilities around the country to monitor the airwaves and ensure licensees were following the new regulations.

The courts also helped by interpreting the Radio Act language requiring stations to operate in the "public interest, convenience, or necessity" in ways that allowed the fledgling FRC to act decisively. These factors combined to reassure investors and advertisers that broadcasting would develop in an orderly fashion.

2.7 Depression Years, 1929–1937

Two years after passage of the 1927 act, the Depression settled on the nation. A third of all American workers lost their jobs. National productivity fell by half. None of today's welfare programs existed then to cushion the intense suffering that unemployment, poverty, and hunger caused. Given the depressed state of the economy and the FRC's housecleaning, the number of radio stations on the air actually decreased (see Exhibit 2.g).

Role of Broadcasting

In these difficult years, radio entertainment came into its own as the only free (after one owned a receiver), widely available distraction from the grim daily struggle to survive. Listener loyalty became almost irrational, according to broadcast historian Erik Barnouw:

> Destitute families, forced to give up an icebox or furniture or bedding, clung to the radio as to a last link of humanity. In consequence, radio, though briefly jolted by the Depression, was soon prospering from it. Motion picture business was suffering, the theater was collapsing, vaudeville was dying, but many of their major talents

Exhibit 2.g

Growth in Number of Radio Stations, 1920–2008

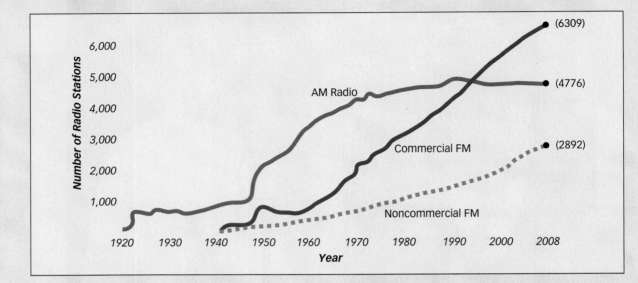

Note that downtrends in the growth curves occurred in 1930s' AM, when the FRC imposed order on the pre-Radio Act chaos, and in 1950s' FM, when the FCC relocated the FM band. The sharp upward trend in AM growth in the late 1940s occurred after the removal of World War II restraints on consumer goods. In the mid-1990s, the number of commercial

FM stations first matched, then surpassed, the number of AM stations.

Source: Adapted from *Stay Tuned: A History of American Broadcasting*, 2nd ed., by Christopher H. Sterling and John M. Kittross, © 2002 by the authors. Published by Routledge. Reprinted by permission of the authors.

flocked to radio—along with audiences and sponsors. (Barnouw, 1978: 27)

Roosevelt and Radio

President Franklin D. Roosevelt, coming into office in 1933, became the first national politician to exploit broadcasting to its full potential in presidential politics. His distinctive delivery soon became familiar to every listener who tuned in to his "fireside chats," the term used to suggest the informality, warmth, and directness of these presidential radio reports to the people (see Exhibit 2.h).

Roosevelt made a significant impact on communication regulation as well. In 1934, the president asked Congress to establish a single communication authority to pull together separate federal responsibilities for regulating both wire and wireless media. After making its own study of the situation, Congress passed the Communications Act of 1934. It created a new regulatory body, the Federal Communications Commission (FCC), one of many agencies set up in the flurry of New Deal government activity. The Communications

Act of 1934 created relatively little change in broadcast regulation because the philosophies of the 1927 act were incorporated into the 1934 legislation. The FCC simply assumed the duties of the FRC, plus new responsibilities for interstate and international wire communication.

Network Developments

During the Depression, CBS tried to chip away at NBC's privileged position as the first network. Big advertisers and star performers usually selected the bigger NBC over CBS when given a choice. It did little good for CBS to build up successful programs: "We were at the mercy of the sponsors and the ad agencies," wrote Paley, because they owned the programs. "They could always take a successful show away from us and put it on NBC" (Paley, 1979: 174).

Another network, the Mutual Broadcasting System (MBS), began in 1934 with a premise different from that of CBS or NBC. In 1934, WGN-Chicago and WOR-New York formed a cooperative network organization with WXYZ-Detroit and WLW-Cincinnati. The four stations pooled some of their own programs,

FDR: Master Broadcaster

President Roosevelt's "fireside chats" helped buoy the spirits of Americans reeling from the effects of the Great Depression. According to historian David Halberstam, "[i]t was in the most direct sense the government reaching out and touching the citizen . . . Roosevelt was the first professional of the art" (Halberstam, 1979: 15).

Source: Photo from AP/Wide World Photos.

most notably *The Lone Ranger*, to form the nucleus of a network schedule. But MBS attempts to expand into a national network were frustrated because most stations had already committed themselves to NBC or CBS. MBS complained to the FCC about this virtual monopoly of the older networks.

The FCC began an in-depth investigation of network practices. After three years of study, the Commission issued its *Chain Broadcasting Regulations* in May 1941. The FCC gave network affiliates more control over their own schedules and the networks less clout. NBC and CBS argued the new rules would devastate the industry. Though the networks fought the rules all the way to the Supreme Court, in 1943 the Court upheld the FCC—a watershed ruling affirming the constitutionality of the commission's rule-making powers (US, 1943).

The decision forced NBC to sell the weaker Blue network, which became the American Broadcasting Company (ABC) in 1945. Thanks to the new regulations, MBS expanded rapidly after the war, but most affiliates were in small markets or were small stations in larger markets. Over the years, various companies owned MBS. During one three-year period in the 1950s, MBS changed ownership six times. In April 1999, the last owner, Westwood One, abandoned the

MBS label and began delivering MBS's services under the CNN Radio banner, thus ending the network's 65-year struggle for survival.

2.8 Early Radio Programs

As detailed in Section 2.1, early radio drew on familiar sources for program material, especially vaudeville acts, some of which proved readily transferable to the new medium.

Comedy

The first network radio entertainment program to achieve widespread popularity was an early 1930s prime-time, five-days-a-week situation comedy, *Amos 'n' Andy*. Charles Correll ("Andy") and Freeman Gosden ("Amos") came to radio from vaudeville as a typical song-and-patter team. The two white performers struck a responsive chord in prevailing American culture when they developed a black-dialect show featuring the ups and downs of the "Fresh Air Taxicab Company of America, Incorporated." Though controversial from its inception, due to what some considered its racist stereotypes, *Amos 'n' Andy* became radio's first big network hit. Traffic stopped across the country and movies halted in midreel at 7:00 P.M. for the nightly 15 minutes of chuckles over the antics of Amos, Andy, the Kingfish, Lightnin', Madam Queen, and a host of minor characters, most of whom the versatile Correll and Gosden played themselves.

Comedy–variety programs and situation comedies reached their greatest popularity near the end of the Depression, just before the beginning of World War II. Comedy became a kind of general anesthetic to ease the pain caused by years of economic hardship and the growing specter of global conflict. Many popular programs featured real-life husband-and-wife combinations: Jack Benny and Mary Livingstone (*The Jack Benny Program*), George Burns and Gracie Allen (*Burns and Allen*), Jim and Marian Jordan (*Fibber McGee and Molly*), and Fred Allen and Portland Hoffa (*The Fred Allen Show*). Ventriloquism and radio may seem incompatible, but NBC had a successful comedy–variety program featuring popular ventriloquist Edgar Bergen and his dummies.

Daytime Drama

Drama became a staple of daytime network programming in the 1930s. Many of these dramas were called "soap operas" for their typical sponsors. Soaps targeted female listeners, and scripts relentlessly reflected the social values and gender roles of the period. "Adventurous" women working outside the home were often depicted as glamorous but sadly unfulfilled. According to the scripts, true happiness came only to dutiful wives, mothers, and homemakers. Program titles such as *When a Girl Marries* and *Young Widder Brown* suggest the general themes. Racial and ethnic stereotyping occurred mercilessly, even down to the naming of characters. Heroes usually had sturdy Anglo-Saxon names, but those given to villains had a "foreign" ring.

News

News depends both on outside sources of supply and on technology. Most news came from press associations or wire services (so called because they distributed news by telegraph for years). Fearing the immediacy offered by radio, newspapers calculated that they could limit radio's competition by denying broadcasters access to major news agencies. NBC had inaugurated regular 15-minute nightly newscasts by Lowell Thomas in 1930 on its Blue network—a sign that radio might soon seriously compete with newspapers.

In late 1933, newspaper publishers, hoping to limit radio news, forced the networks (which were ill-prepared to gather their own news) to accept use of a special Press-Radio Bureau designed to funnel just enough news to radio to tempt listeners to buy newspapers for more details.

The Press-Radio Bureau never worked effectively. In 1935, United Press broke the embargo on unrestricted release of news to radio, joined soon by International News Service (these two merged in 1958 to form United Press International [UPI]). The Press-Radio Bureau finally expired, unmourned, in 1940 when the Associated Press (AP) began to accept radio stations as members. The press associations later acquired more broadcasters than publishers as customers and began offering services especially tailored for broadcast stations, including audio feeds ready to go directly on the air.

Music

Radio relied heavily on music from the beginning. In its early years, CBS devoted a quarter of its entire schedule to music. By the mid-1930s more than half of all radio programming consisted of music, three-quarters of it carried on a sustaining (nonsponsored) basis.

Large stations often hired their own musical groups, while networks supported symphony orchestras. Besides having their own large studios in which groups could perform, networks and some stations aired performances originating live outside the studios. Often these "big band remotes" originated in the ballrooms of famous metropolitan hotels. NBC began regular broadcasts of the Metropolitan Opera in 1931 and hired Arturo Toscanini out of retirement to head the NBC Symphony Orchestra in the late 1930s.

Live Performance vs. Recording

The networks and large stations could afford to broadcast live performances exclusively. Musicians and composers welcomed such opportunities, but many stations could afford only recordings. But playing recordings rather than broadcasting live performances alarmed music creators and performers. The musicians' union tried to keep recordings of all kinds off the air, and copyright holders demanded big bucks for performance rights.

Under copyright law, playing a record in public for profit (as in a broadcast) constitutes a "performance." As such, it obligates the user (in this case, a radio station) to pay copyright holders for performing rights. These music copyright holders rely on music-licensing organizations (also called performance rights organizations) to act on their behalf in monitoring performances and collecting copyright fees for the use of both live and recorded music. The first such U.S. organization, the American Society of Composers, Authors, and Publishers (ASCAP), dates back to 1914.

Almost simultaneously with broadcasting's birth, ASCAP began demanding substantial payments for using musical works in its catalog, whether broadcast live or from records. These demands threatened stations with an unexpectedly heavy financial burden. In 1923, they formed the National Association of Broadcasters (NAB) to negotiate ASCAP's demands on an industry-wide basis. Over the years the NAB has successfully championed the broadcasters' position, especially on the regulatory front in Washington, DC. The NAB continues this role in the new century.

In 1937, when ASCAP announced yet another fee increase, broadcasters decided to boycott ASCAP music and later created their own co-operative music-licensing organization, Broadcast Music, Inc. (BMI). Eventually, BMI built up a comprehensive library. Competition from BMI moderated ASCAP demands, but music licensing and other copyright conflicts have been a cause of lawsuits ever since.

Musicians were not alone in opposing recordings. In 1922, the U.S. secretary of commerce prohibited large stations from using recordings, arguing that records only duplicated programming listeners could receive without radio. Five years later, the FRC issued orders that all stations identify as "mechanical reproductions" any programming on phonograph records to avoid having the public think the program was live.

In spite of government concerns about recorded material, this did not prevent its use, especially by smaller stations. As early as 1928 some programs were being provided to individual stations in recorded form and program syndication via phonograph recording became increasingly commonplace during the 1930s.

Networks banned recordings because they considered their ability to distribute live broadcasts a unique asset, but made exceptions for especially newsworthy events, such as Herb Morrison's emotional description ("Oh, the humanity . . . ") of the fiery *Hindenburg* crash in 1937. The networks also expressed concerns about recorded audio quality, especially for entertainment programming, although this may have been more an excuse than a legitimate complaint.

Recording's Triumph

World War II swept away network opposition to recorded news programming. This opened the door for recorded network programming generally. ABC dropped its recording ban in 1946 to lure Bing Crosby, perhaps the most popular entertainer of the period, away from powerful NBC. Crosby hated the tension and risks of real-time broadcasting, which were compounded by the need to repeat each live program in New York a second time for the West Coast to compensate for time zone differences. Crosby invested in a little-known company, Ampex, which developed magnetic-tape recording based on German wartime technology. As soon as broadcast-quality audiotape recorders became available, ABC agreed to let Crosby break the network ban by recording his weekly prime-time program. The other networks soon followed ABC's lead, appreciating the flexibility and control recording technology offered.

Content Regulation

Reducing interference, a technical issue, initially spurred the government's entry into broadcast station regulation. However, the Congressional mandate to ensure that broadcasters serve "the public interest" lured the FRC, and later the FCC, into content areas.

In the early 1930s, the FRC kicked Milford, Kansas, broadcaster "Dr." John Brinkley off the air for prescribing sex-rejuvenation surgery and drugs of his own fabrication over KFKB ("Kansas First, Kansas Best"). Brinkley's "medical practice" was questionable, but especially so because he was not a licensed physician. About the same time, the FRC also jerked the Los Angeles license of the Reverend Dr. Robert Shuler, a fire-and-brimstone crusader who often would broadcast personal attacks against his critics.

Orson Welles is best remembered today for his classic movie, *Citizen Kane*, but in October 1936 he created a panic with a live CBS network drama in which killer Martians invaded the United States. What made the broadcast so devastating was that the program reported the Martians' "progress" in news bulletin format. People tuning in late—and many did—thought they were hearing legitimate live news reports. Thousands panicked, thinking they faced vaporization by the Martians' "heat ray." The FCC investigated, but declined to take action, deciding Welles and CBS intended no overt deception. Even so, the FCC's "raised eyebrows" put broadcasters on notice that they should be careful.

2.9 That Little Black Box—The Development of FM Radio

For its first quarter-century, broadcasting simply meant AM radio. But the amplitude modulation signals used by radio stations in the 1920s had one serious drawback—they were subject to significant levels of interference. This interference led to much crackling and hissing at the radio receiver. The problem disturbed RCA head David Sarnoff so much that he allegedly told his friend and inventor, Edwin Howard Armstrong (see Exhibit 2.i), that he wished someone would invent a "little black box" that would eliminate the static. Armstrong went to work.

After 10 years of experimentation, in 1933 Armstrong patented a much-improved alternative method of audio transmission using frequency modulation (FM). In December of 1933, he invited Sarnoff and several RCA engineers to his laboratory where he displayed his new invention. Skeptical of the results, Sarnoff offered RCA's transmitting space atop the Empire State Building for a field test. A receiver was placed in a house 70 miles from the transmitter. When Armstrong transmitted a signal via AM, there was significant static. When Armstrong switched over to his FM system, the static disappeared. In fact, the receiver picked up low notes from an organ that the AM signal, with its narrow bandwidth, could not even carry. In addition to high-fidelity sound, later tests with Armstrong's FM system proved the possibility of sending more than one signal simultaneously—a process known as **multiplexing**.

Armstrong tirelessly promoted the superiority of FM, thinking he had the support of his friend David Sarnoff. But Sarnoff's RCA was making good money with AM, expected to make even more with television, and devoted little attention to the development of FM. About 50 stations made it on the air before the United States entered World War II. At the close of the war, however, the FCC shifted FM from its prewar channels to its present location at 88 to 108 MHz in the VHF band. This 1945 move made obsolete the half-million FM receivers that had been built to operate on lower frequencies.

Exhibit 2.i

Edwin Howard Armstrong (1890–1954)

Edwin Howard Armstrong is perhaps the most tragic figure in broadcasting's technical history. Born on December 18, 1890, Armstrong grew up in Yonkers, New York, where the new science of wireless fascinated him even as a child. By age 14 he was experimenting with wireless gear in the attic of his home and erecting antennas higher than 100 feet. He later attended Columbia University, graduating with a degree in electrical engineering in 1913. Before graduating, Armstrong had struck on the idea of the feedback, or regenerative, circuit, the first of his four major inventions. The regenerative circuit dramatically increased the ability of Lee de Forest's Audion vacuum tube to amplify weak radio signals. In developing the circuit, Armstrong explored the Audion's operation thoroughly, and in 1914 he published a technical article on the Audion. In the article he presented a more cogent explanation of the tube's theory of operation than had its inventor. This article and his regenerative circuit immediately established Armstrong's reputation among scientists and engineers.

In 1917, Armstrong entered military service as a captain in the Army Signal Section. During this period he patented his second major invention, the superheterodyne receiver, a system superior to the earlier regenerative circuit. Returning to his civilian career, Armstrong, in 1922, revealed his third major invention, the super-regenerative circuit. Meanwhile, Lee de Forest had sued Armstrong over the regenerative circuit patent, claiming that he had invented the circuit years earlier. A vicious battle, both in the courts and beyond, raged between de Forest and Armstrong for more than 20 years. In 1934, to the astonishment of the engineering community, the U.S. Supreme Court ruled in favor of de Forest. Armstrong's patent for the superheterodyne circuit was also overturned because of a French inventor's prior claim.

While still fighting for his earlier patents, Armstrong began looking for a static-free broadcast technology, a search that led him to frequency modulation, or FM. Armstrong was contractually obligated to give RCA first right of refusal for any new invention. He demonstrated his FM system to his friend David Sarnoff and other RCA officials but received little encouragement. Sarnoff was simply stalling, convinced the next major development would be television, not a new radio service competing with AM. By 1936 Armstrong realized he must develop FM without RCA's help. He built an experimental FM station, W2XMN, in Alpine, New Jersey, where regular FM broadcasting began on July 18, 1939. He began licensing manufacturers to build FM receivers and created the Yankee Network of FM stations. Things were looking up until the United States entered World War II and consumer manufacturing ended. After the war, the FCC moved FM broadcasting from 44–50 MHz to its present allocation, 88–108 MHz, instantly making half a million prewar receivers and about 50 stations obsolete.

Armstrong resumed his efforts to promote FM broadcasting and began receiving royalties from the makers of FM receivers, but not from RCA. In 1948, he sued RCA for infringing his FM patents. The years battling de Forest, his feelings of frustration and betrayal by David Sarnoff, and his disappointment in seeing FM languish while television exploded, took their toll. In 1953, his wife of more than 30 years left him, and on February 1 of the next year, he jumped 13 floors to his death.

Interestingly, Armstrong seemed to get more attention after his death than before. In 1956, *Harper's* magazine ran an article outlining Armstrong's many contributions to modern electronics. Eighty-two-year-old Lee de Forest immediately fired off a four-page rebuttal, chastising *Harper's* for having credited Armstrong with inventions he claimed were his. Even death could not end the old rivalry. Today FM radio reigns supreme, and Edwin Armstrong is unquestionably its inventor.

Source: Photo from Brown Brothers.

2.10 The War Years

During World War II, which the United States entered in 1941, radio escaped direct military censorship by complying voluntarily with codes. For example, broadcasters avoided live man-on-the-street interviews and weather reports; the former could risk transmission of a secret code and the latter would be useful to potential enemy bombers. Radio had a role to play internationally in psychological warfare, and in 1942 President Roosevelt appointed well-known newscaster Elmer Davis to head the newly created Office of War Information (OWI). The OWI mobilized an external broadcasting service that eventually became known as the Voice of America, which still broadcasts to foreign countries today.

Wartime restrictions on civilian manufacturing, imposed from 1942 to 1945, all but eliminated station construction and receiver production. Manufacturers of consumer goods devoted their capacity to military needs, but continued to advertise their peacetime products to keep their names before the public. The government allowed them to write off these advertising costs as business expenses even though they had no products to sell.

Entertainment Programming

Programming during the war years followed the general pattern established during the Depression, but with some changes. Programs reflected the fact that the nation was fully mobilized for war with tens of millions of men and women in uniform at home and abroad or working as civilians in industries directly related to the war effort. People in all walks of life were involved and patriotic themes were emphasized without reservation or embarrassment.

Released from the normal competitive pressures to sell products by support of mass-appeal material, some advertisers invested in their public image by supporting high-quality dramatic programs of a type rarely heard on American radio, though such programs were common in Europe.

Radio developed playwrights such as Norman Corwin and Arch Oboler, who won their chief literary fame in broadcasting. CBS commissioned Corwin to celebrate the Allied victory in Europe with an hour-long radio play, *On a Note of Triumph*, in 1945. This emotional program climaxed an extraordinary flowering of radio art—original writing of high merit, produced with consummate skill, and always live, for the networks still shunned recordings. With the end of the war years and the artificial wartime support for culture, competitive selling resumed, and this brief, luminous period of radio drama and comedy creativity came to an end. These types of programs began their migration to television in the late 1940s and, by the mid-1950s, radio programming consisted mostly of recorded music.

Wartime News

As the threat of European war loomed in the mid-1930s, NBC began developing European news operations to

Exhibit 2.j

Edward R. Murrow (1908–1965)

First employed by CBS in 1935 as director of talks in Europe, Murrow came to the notice of a wider public through his memorable live reports from bomb-ravaged London in 1939–1941, and later from even more dangerous war-front vantage points. Unlike other reporters, he had a college degree in speech rather than newspaper or wire-service experience. The British appreciated his realistic and often moving word-and-sound pictures of their wartime experiences, and American listeners liked the way he radiated "truth and concern," as William Paley put it (1979: 151).

Widely admired by the time the war ended, Murrow became the core of the postwar CBS news organization. He served briefly as vice president for news, but soon resigned the administrative post to resume daily newscasting. As an on-the-air personality, he survived the transition to television better than others, going on to appear in *See It Now* and in often highly controversial documentaries.

But Murrow's TV career was personally disappointing. Although he achieved almost mythic journalistic stature through his serious reporting, CBS also used him as host of *Person to Person*. Each week on *Person to Person*, Murrow "tele-visited" the home of some celebrity, quizzing the famous person about his or her household furnishings and home life. Murrow found it professionally and personally embarrassing. Increasingly despondent about eroding values in broadcast journalism, he resigned from CBS in the early 1960s to direct the U.S. Information Agency under President John F. Kennedy.

Even after leaving CBS, Murrow continued to influence broadcast journalism at the network and elsewhere. Decades after his death, a panel of experts assembled by the New York University Department of Journalism and Mass Communication, ranked Murrow's 1940 reports from London and his 1954 investigation of controversial senator Joseph McCarthy among the top 10 examples of excellence in American journalism.

CBS news reporter Edward R. Murrow, shown here during World War II, often broadcast from the BBC's Broadcasting House in downtown London. He and other American reporters used a tiny studio located in a sub-basement. Once, when the building took a hit during a German bombing raid, Murrow continued his live report as stretcher-bearers carried dead and injured victims of the raid past the studio to the first-aid station.

Source: Photo © Getty Images.

cover rapidly developing events. To counter NBC, Paley decided on a bold CBS stroke—a half-hour of news devoted to the 1938 Nazi incursion into Austria, originating live from such key cities as London, Paris, Rome, Berlin, and Vienna.

The network's objections to the use of recorded material created tremendous problems of coordination and timing for the complex production. But in that historic half-hour, featuring Robert Trout, William Shirer, Edward R. Murrow (see Exhibit 2.j), and others, radio arrived as a full-fledged news medium. Thereafter, on-the-spot radio reporting from Europe became a daily news feature.

Thanks to CBS's early start, Paley's enthusiastic support, and a great staff of reporters and editors, CBS set a high standard for broadcast journalism during the war years, establishing a tradition of excellence that lasted into the 1980s. Then corporate takeovers, competition, and cutbacks began to accelerate the erosion of news standards initiated in those pioneer days.

2.11 Radio Responds to Television

At this point in radio's story, television began a spectacular rise that was soon to affect the older medium profoundly. Television's "takeoff" year of 1948 marked both a high-water mark and the doom of full-service network radio. In that year, radio networks grossed more revenue than ever before, excluding profits from their owned-and-operated stations. For more than 15 years, radio networks had dominated broadcasting, but television was about to end their rule. We pick up the full story of television's rise in Section 2.12.

Radio Network Decline

Sponsors of major radio network programs and stars hastened the decline in radio network fortunes after 1948. As television captured its first audiences, it lured away major radio advertisers—and with them went star performers and their programs. By the early 1950s the radio networks were reeling. CBS's William Paley recalled that

> although [CBS's radio] daytime schedule was more than 90 percent sponsored, our prime-time evening shows were more than 80 percent sustaining. Even our greatest stars could not stop the rush to television. (Paley, 1979: 227)

The ultimate blow came when radio stations began to decline network affiliation—a startling change, considering that previously such an affiliation was a precious asset. But program commitments to the networks interfered with the freedom to put new, tailor-made,

post-television radio formulas into effect. By the early 1960s, only a third of all radio stations still held network affiliations. Networks scaled down service to brief hourly news bulletins, short information features, a few public-affairs programs, and occasional on-the-spot sports events.

Today's dozens of audio networks are possible because there are more stations and cheaper point-to-point satellite distribution to affiliates, and because each modern service or network specializes in a specific kind of programming. But this kind of radio networking differs greatly from that of the 1930s—and perhaps foreshadows the future of network television.

Rock to the Rescue

With the loss of network dramas, variety shows, and quiz games, radio programming shrank essentially to music and news/talk, with music occupying by far the majority of the time on most stations—just as it had in the 1920s. Only this time the music was off records rather than live, broadcasters' aversion to recorded programming having passed into history years before. Fortunately for radio, this programming transition coincided with the rise of a new musical culture, one that found radio an ideally hospitable medium.

Southern stations such as WDIA in Memphis and WLAC in Nashville pioneered key elements of a strange new sound, and early in the 1950s Cleveland disc jockey (DJ) Alan Freed gained national recognition by playing music, which

> combined elements of gospel, harmony, rhythm, blues, and country. He called it "rock and roll." And people everywhere began to listen. . . . It transcended borders and races. . . . Rock and roll sang to the teenager; it charted his habits, his hobbies, his hang-ups. (Drake-Chenault Enterprises, 1978: 1)

Radio proved to be the perfect outlet for this new form of expression as stations in many markets converted to a "Top 40" format in the late 1950s. The format name referred to the practice of rigidly limiting DJs to a prescribed playlist of current best-selling popular recordings. Top 40 specialists frequently reprogrammed bottom-ranked stations and lifted them to top ratings in a matter of months.

The announcer took on a much more important role in the Top 40 format. Before Top 40, announcers typically were wallpaper figures providing continuity between programs. After Top 40, listeners could hear the same songs on many stations, so an important distinguishing attraction became the personality of the DJ. Top DJs commanded high salaries, and even those in small markets sometimes achieved local cult hero status.

A second ingredient in Top 40's success was an equally single-minded dedication to constant promotion and advertising. Call letters and dial position were indelibly imprinted on the listener's mind, usually by endless repetition and promotional gimmicks, in an effort to ensure proper responses to rating surveys.

FM's Rise to Dominance

Postwar interest in FM stations, mostly as minor partners in AM/FM combinations, peaked in 1948, with more than a thousand stations authorized. But as television's rapid climb to power began and the FCC relocated the FM band, FM faded into the background. Total station authorizations declined during most of the 1950s. However, in 1958 FM began to recover, not only because of greater audience interest in improved sound quality, but also from the lack of spectrum space for additional AM stations.

A new pro-FM FCC policy also helped. For example, in 1961 the FCC approved technical standards for FM stereophonic sound. From 1965 to 1967, the FCC adopted a nonduplication rule that required AM/FM owners, first in big cities and then in smaller markets, to program their FM stations independently of AM sister stations. These measures proved effective in moving FM out of AM's shadow and created FM as an independent service with its own formats. Increased listener interest galvanized manufacturers into making FM receivers more widely available, more portable, and at a lower cost. By 1974, the majority of sets included FM, and two years later so did most car radios. By the 1980s, some radios were marketed with FM-only tuning, and 75 percent of all radio listening was to FM outlets.

AM's Struggle

AM experienced a crisis as FM became the preferred service of both listeners and advertisers. The situation became so grim that when the FCC dropped its program nonduplication rules in the 1980s, some FM stations allowed struggling AMs to duplicate their programming. Thirty years earlier many FM stations survived by airing programs originating on AM. Some people thought AM stereo would save AM, or at least allow it to compete with FM on a more equal footing. The FCC unfortunately refused to adopt an AM stereo standard, instead "leaving it to the marketplace" to determine which of several competing and incompatible technologies would be used. By the time the FCC did adopt an AM stereo standard, it was too late to help AM.

AM radio had to save itself. Much as rock saved AM in the 1950s against TV, talk-based programming saved AM against FM in the 1980s. AM radio found an eager audience for a variety of talk formats, many focusing on sports or political commentary, especially appealing to males. AM may have smaller audiences than FM, but loyal AM listeners are often persons hard to reach through other media and are highly valued by advertisers.

2.12 Early TV Development

Television experimentation took place for decades before it developed into a mass medium. Early television produced crude pictures without sound, interesting only as curiosities. Public acceptance awaited pictures with sufficient resolution (detail) and stability (absence of flicker) for comfortable viewing—a standard at least as good as that of the home movies then familiar to wealthier consumers.

Mechanical vs. Electronic Scanning

Inventors long sought a way to break down pictures rapidly into thousands of fragments for transmission bit by bit, and then to reassemble them for viewing. Two incompatible methods of accomplishing this developed simultaneously, one based on a mechanical approach and the other entirely electronic. The mechanical approach initially showed the most promise, but the equipment was large, required almost impossibly precise synchronization between transmitter and receiver, and lacked the picture resolution needed for public acceptance.

No single inventor can claim a breakthrough in electronic television, for television was a corporate rather than an individual achievement. However, two inventors are remembered for solving specific parts of the puzzle. Philo T. Farnsworth, a self-taught American genius, devised an **image dissector**—a device for taking pictures apart electronically for bit-by-bit transmission. His patents required RCA, the corporate leader in American television development, to secure licenses from him to perfect its own system.

Vladimir K. Zworykin immigrated from Russia in 1919 and worked as an engineer for Westinghouse. In 1923, he invented the **iconoscope,** the first electronic camera pickup tube suitable for studio operations. As David Sarnoff focused RCA's resources into a drive to perfect television as early as 1930, he hired Zworykin to head a television research group that was based in Camden, New Jersey. Entrusted with the task of producing a marketable television system, Zworykin's "Camden team" tackled technical concerns, as well as the subjective problem of developing picture-quality standards sufficient to win full public acceptance. (See Exhibit 2.k for more information about Zworykin and Farnsworth.)

Exhibit 2.k

Zworykin and Farnsworth: TV Pioneers

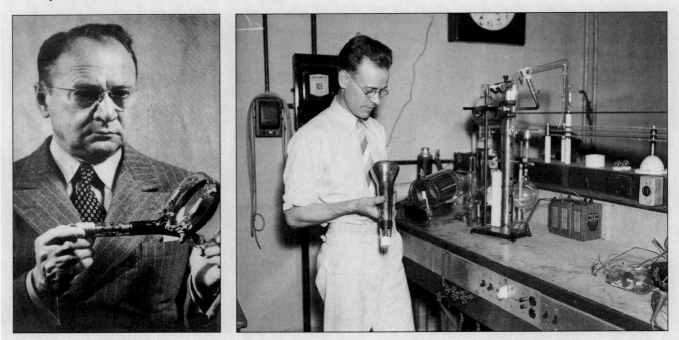

Vladimir K. Zworykin (photo on left) was born in Russia in 1889. In 1906, he enrolled at the St. Petersburg Institute of Technology, where he studied under Boris Rosing, a man whose experiments with cathode-ray tubes greatly influenced Zworykin's later work. He also studied at the College de France in Paris and later earned a Ph.D. in physics from the University of Pittsburgh. He began working on television while still employed at the Russian Wireless Telegraph and Telephone

Company. When he moved to the United States in 1919, he brought his ideas about television with him.

A year later he began working for Westinghouse. Television was not a high priority at Westinghouse at the time, but the company did file for an initial patent on Zworykin's camera tube, which he called the **iconoscope**, in 1923. In 1930, RCA assumed control of GE's and Westinghouse's radio research, and Zworykin moved to RCA, where its leader and Zworykin's

TV's Debut

RCA and others had experimented with television for many years, but it was not until 1939 that David Sarnoff was ready to display his company's product publicly. Sarnoff at the time was maneuvering to have the FCC adopt the RCA system and wanted maximum publicity. He achieved it by introducing RCA's TV system during the New York World's Fair opening ceremonies. The demonstration was successful, and RCA began acting as though its system were already the national standard adopted for telecasting, an attitude that alienated competing manufacturers and members of the FCC.

In July 1941, the FCC adopted technical standards for black-and-white television transmission. The 1941 standards adopted were largely those originally proposed by RCA. They remained essentially unchanged

until the FCC adopted digital TV standards in December 1996.

Within a year of the 1939 RCA demonstration, wartime needs halted production of most consumer electronics. During World War II six experimental stations remained on the air—two in New York City and one each in Schenectady (New York), Philadelphia, Chicago, and Los Angeles. They devoted their few hours of airtime a week primarily to civilian defense programs. Perhaps 10,000 receivers were in use, half of them in New York City.

Postwar Pause

The end of the war in 1945 did not, as some expected, bring an immediate upsurge in television activity, despite a backlog of 158 pending station applications.

fellow Russian immigrant, David Sarnoff, was enthusiastically pushing television's technical development. Sarnoff was so impressed with Zworykin that within a few months he had his own lab at RCA headquarters in Camden, New Jersey. In 1929, Zworykin presented a paper to the Institute of Radio Engineers in which he described the **kinescope**, or picture tube. By 1933 he had dramatically improved his original iconoscope, which, along with the kinescope, formed a workable all-electronic television system.

Philo T. Farnsworth (photo on right) was born near Beaver, Utah, in 1906 but grew up on a ranch near Rigby, Idaho. While still a boy, he began reading about electrical devices and radio, and he became especially fascinated with the photoelectric cell and cathode-ray tube. As early as 1922 he astonished his high school instructor by revealing a diagram for an all-electronic television system based on these devices. Four years later he lined up investors willing to support his work, and in 1927 he filed his first patent for his television system. The following year he demonstrated an all-electronic television system publicly in San Francisco. Development costs continued to mount, however, and in 1931 Farnsworth accepted the financial backing of the Philadelphia Storage Battery Company, better known as Philco. Philco was a leading manufacturer of radios and one of RCA's major competitors in the race to develop television. Farnsworth found it difficult to work within a large organization, however, and he left Philco in 1933.

In 1934, Farnsworth filed a patent interference suit against RCA, based on his original 1927 patents. He claimed that RCA's improved "image iconoscope" incorporated features covered in his patents, while Zworykin claimed that his 1923 disclosures provided him legal priority. Zworykin had visited Farnsworth in 1930, when Farnsworth was still in San Francisco, and the controversy continues regarding whether Zworykin's work was influenced by that visit and to what degree. In any case, Farnsworth's claim was upheld in 1934 and again in 1936 on

appeal. RCA could not move forward with its inauguration of a commercially viable television technology without settling with Farnsworth over the image iconoscope issue. Accordingly, RCA agreed to a nonexclusive cross-licensing agreement with him. Farnsworth later won another fight involving RCA's use of other technology patented by him.

After 1940, both Zworykin and Farnsworth moved on to other projects, but with somewhat different degrees of success. Farnsworth bought an Indiana company and began manufacturing various types of entertainment equipment. By the late 1940s the company was facing bankruptcy. Farnsworth then conducted research on missile guidance systems, nuclear fusion, and other projects for International Telephone and Telegraph. In the late 1960s, Farnsworth moved to Utah, established a small company, and continued his nuclear fusion research until he lost government funding and the company folded in 1970. Farnsworth had suffered ill health since the 1940s, and he died in 1971.

Zworykin, in contrast, continued his successful career with RCA. He worked on many important military projects during World War II, including the development of radar. He became an RCA vice president in 1947, continuing as an honorary vice president even after his retirement. He lectured widely, spent his winters in Miami, and generally lived the good life. He was honored with the National Medal of Science in 1967 and was inducted into the Inventors Hall of Fame a decade later. Zworykin basked in the honors his contribution to the technical development of television brought him, but he—like many other broadcast pioneers—was disappointed with the programming. When asked what he considered to be his greatest contribution to television, he is reported to have said the "off" switch. Zworykin died in 1982.

Many experts believed that all-out development should have awaited adoption of a color system. And potential investors wondered whether the public would buy receivers that cost many times the price of radios—or if advertisers would pay for expensive television time.

2.13 TV Takes Off

By mid-1948, public demand and broadcaster interest inaugurated the long-anticipated television gold rush, the transition from mere experiments to true mass medium. Sixteen stations were on the air at the start of 1948—and nearly 100 two years later. The number of cities that television served grew rapidly. The audience expanded in one year by an astonishing 4,000 percent. Regular network service to a few eastern cities began.

Major advertisers started experimenting with the new medium, and regular programs were launched.

Growing Pains

In spite of these advances there remained a list of things yet to be resolved that included increasing the number of channels available, adopting a color system, and establishing truly national networks.

Given the many channels available to us today through cable and satellites, it's difficult to imagine how limited the choices were during the early days of broadcast television. Recognizing the scarcity of available channels, and the need to serve as much of the nation as possible, the FCC struggled to dole out the licenses as best it could.

In approving commercial television in 1941, the FCC had made available only 13 channels (later reduced to 12) to serve the entire United States. As more and more stations applied to go on the air, it became obvious that demand would soon exceed the supply of channels. And interference among the few stations on the air was growing because of a miscalculation of the distance needed to separate stations assigned to the same channel.

The Freeze and *Sixth Report and Order*

In September 1948, the FCC abruptly froze further processing of television license applications pending solution of these problems. The freeze had no effect on applicants whose permits had already been approved. The FCC held a lengthy series of hearings to settle the complicated engineering and policy questions leading up to the freeze. The much-anticipated decision, the basic charter of 20th-century American broadcast television, came on April 14, 1952, in the FCC's historic *Sixth Report and Order* (FCCR, 1952).

After more than three years of deliberation, the FCC combined four separate frequency bands to obtain sufficient spectrum space for TV. The new rules relocated some of the original 12 VHF (very high frequency) channels to reduce interference and added 70 new channels (14–83) in the UHF (ultrahigh frequency) band. Exhibit 4.g summarizes their location in the spectrum and current TV channel numbers. In a highly controversial move opposed by commercial interests, the Commission, at the insistence of Frieda Hennock, the first female Commissioner, also reserved several hundred television allotments across the country for noncommercial educational broadcast stations. These allocations ultimately led to the public television broadcast system that we know today.

The *Sixth Report and Order*, however, did not settle every issue. New disagreements flared, for example, over **intermixture** (assignment of both VHF and UHF channels in the same market), the distance needed between stations on the same channel to minimize interference, and the importance of adopting color standards.

Channel-Allotment Plan

The new UHF channels and the VHF channels not already in use allowed, at least in theory, the FCC to license more than 2,000 TV stations. The FCC increased the number of communities allotted a TV channel from 345 to almost 1,300.

The number of on-air stations more than tripled in the first postfreeze year, as shown in Exhibit 2.l. Nevertheless, the new channel-allotment plan had

serious defects. For one thing, there were still too few channels to give viewers in every market the same range of choices. Some had only one channel, some two or three, and so on. Viewers in any given market needed access to at least five channels to be able to choose among the three networks, an independent (non-network) station, and an educational outlet. For another, the FCC's decision to make both VHF and UHF allotments in many localities placed UHF stations in such markets at a serious disadvantage.

UHF Problem

Experience with radar on UHF frequencies during World War II suggested that stations assigned to UHF channels could not cover as great an area as stations on VHF channels, given equal transmitter power and antenna systems. The FCC tried to ensure equal coverage for both VHF and UHF stations by authorizing UHF to use higher power. Yet even if added power could have helped, years passed before maximum-power UHF transmitters became available. And long after UHF television service began, set manufacturers still built VHF-only receivers, forcing viewers in markets with UHF stations to buy difficult-to-use UHF converters and often poorly performing UHF antennas.

The FCC addressed this inequity in 1962 when it persuaded Congress to require manufacturers to equip all receivers with built-in UHF tuners. UHF continued to languish, however, and viewer frustration over limited program options caused by the FCC's allotments spurred the growth of cable and other substitutes for over-the-air reception.

Ironically, the development of cable television benefited UHF stations because cable technology eliminated the VHF–UHF coverage inequities inherent in over-the-air reception. As more people turned to cable, UHF stations prospered. By mid-1994, UHF commercial outlets on the air (594) had surpassed VHF (559).

Compatible Color

A battle began in the 1940s between CBS and NBC/RCA over a technical standard for color TV that came to a head during the freeze. CBS proposed a system based partly on mechanical scanning technology, while NBC/RCA advocated an all-electronic system. Interestingly, the FCC approved the CBS system in 1950, in the middle of the freeze. The next year, five East Coast CBS stations hooked up to broadcast the first commercial colorcast, to a very small audience. However, the major equipment manufacturers, led by RCA, simply refused to make TV receivers using the CBS system, in spite of the FCC decision. Finally, in 1953 all parties agreed to an electronic system

Exhibit 2.1

Growth in Number of TV Stations, 1948–2008

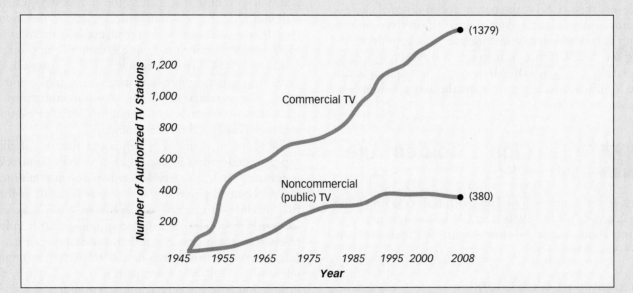

The modern TV era started in 1948, with 16 stations on the air. Only 108 stations had been authorized when the 1948–1952 freeze imposed a temporary ceiling. After that the number shot up, reaching 400 by 1955. Growth began to slow down at that point but has never actually stopped. Noncommercial stations developed more slowly, starting with the first two in 1954. Not included in this chart are the more than 2,300 low-power TV stations or approximately 4,000 TV translators.

Source: Adapted from *Stay Tuned: A History of American Broadcasting*, 2nd ed., by Christopher H. Sterling and John M. Kittross, © 2002 by the authors. Published by Routledge. Reprinted by permission of the authors.

patterned closely on RCA's. An important argument in its favor was that it had compatibility—black-and-white sets already in use could pick up the newly approved color signals and display them in monochrome. The CBS system was not compatible with monochrome sets already in consumers' hands.

Color telecasts on a large scale developed slowly. Five years after the 1953 adoption of color standards, only NBC offered programs in color. Full network color production in prime time finally arrived in 1966. By 1972, nearly two decades after the adoption of color standards, only half of the country's homes had color TV sets.

TV Networking and Recording

Full-scale national network operations had to await completion of AT&T's coaxial cable and microwave relay links, which joined the East and West Coasts in 1951 and enabled the start of live network interconnection.

Until the cable reached them, affiliates had to use kinescopes of network programs—films of television programs photographed as they were displayed on the face of a receiver tube—syndicated films, and their own live productions.

In 1956, the Ampex Corporation demonstrated a successful videotape recorder, which saw its first practical use that fall on CBS. In a rare spirit of cooperation, competing manufacturers put aside rivalries and agreed on a compatible professional videotape standard. Videotape doomed the era of live production, as related in Section 2.12.

Ceiling on Networks

The FCC's 1952 *Sixth Report and Order* effectively limited television to three national networks because there were too few cities with four channels to allow a fourth network to compete nationally on an even footing.

Nevertheless, there have always been pressures to create a fourth national television network. MBS, the fourth radio network, lacked the money to branch into television. From 1946 to 1955, however, a fourth chain did exist—Du Mont Television Network, founded by Allen B. Du Mont, a developer of the cathode-ray tube (CRT), the parent technology of the TV picture tube. The Du Mont network survived only as long as lack of interconnection facilities kept networking in check. Once interconnection relays became generally available, Du Mont could not sign up sufficient affiliates to compete with the larger, older, and richer networks.

2.14 Television's Golden Age, 1948–1957

Just as some people look back with nostalgia on radio's "golden era" of the 1930s and 1940s, some people reminisce about television's first decade as a mass medium, 1948 to 1957.

Programs as Motivators

In that decade, the networks put first priority on stimulating people to buy TV sets. Only attractive programs could do that:

> It was the only time in the history of the medium that program priorities superseded all others. If there was an abundance of original and quality drama at the time . . . it was in large part because those shows tended to appeal to a wealthier and better-educated part of the public, the part best able to afford a television set in those years when the price of receivers was high. (Brown, 1971: 154)

Most programs, local and network, were necessarily live—a throwback to the earliest days of radio. Videotape recording was uncommon, especially at the local level, until the late 1950s. Original television plays constituted the best artistic achievements of television's live decade. "Talent seemed to gush right out of the cement," pioneer *New York Times* critic Jack Gould observed years later.

It would be misleading, however, to suggest that all "golden age" programming achieved high artistic status. NBC's enormously popular *Texaco Star Theater*, for example, featured slapstick routines borrowed almost directly from vaudeville. Such programs appealed to less well-to-do, less elitist viewers, people for whom the purchase of a TV set was a major investment. Without such popular programs the cost of receivers would have remained high, and the growth of TV as a mass medium could have been slowed.

TV vs. Hollywood

Television programs could, of course, have been recorded from the very beginning by filming them (and some were—witness the continuing reruns of the early 1950s' *I Love Lucy*, a series shot using film cameras at an additional expense absorbed by the show's stars, Lucille Ball and Desi Arnaz). Economic, technical, and industrial barriers delayed widespread use of this solution. Hollywood's traditional single-camera method of production was slow and cumbersome, costing far too much for general television use; and it took time to adapt film production to the physical limitations of television, with its lower resolution, smaller picture, and more restricted contrast range.

In addition, many critics opposed the use of film, expecting television to escape Hollywood's straitjacket in favor of a new, live, and less trite mass-entertainment genre. The two points of view were as far apart as their two production centers—television in New York and film in Los Angeles. But the economics of both industries drove them closer together. Inevitably, as technical barriers to producing filmed television programs fell, and as Hollywood accepted use of videotape, the production base for entertainment programs shifted to the West Coast by the late 1950s.

Hollywood's old-line feature-film producers saw television as a threat, much as publishers had feared that radio would undermine newspapers. Producers and distributors refused to release their most recent feature films to television for a dozen years. By the early 1960s, however, movie producers realized that audiences would not stop buying theater tickets just because they could see movies on television. And the networks were ready to pay big money to show more recent films—movies that in most cases had little or no residual value for theatrical release. Eventually, feature-film producers found they could profit even more from delayed release to cable television and the VCR and DVD market, as well as broadcasting.

Competitive Strategies

In terms of program formats, many important ideas in television's first decade sprang from the fertile imagination of Sylvester "Pat" Weaver, who became NBC's vice president for television in 1949, leaving NBC six years later as board chair. Disregarding conventional wisdom about established viewing habits, Weaver occasionally replaced regular series with one-time **spectaculars**, 60 or 90 minutes long. Weaver also foresaw that the single-sponsor show (a hallmark of network radio) simply could not last in prime-time television, as costs soon exceeded what single advertisers could afford. Instead, NBC introduced **participating sponsorship**, which enabled several different advertisers to share the costs of a program. NBC's long-running *Today* and *Tonight* shows are further testimony to Weaver's lasting impact.

Despite Weaver's NBC innovations, CBS steadily gained in the audience ratings race. Much of CBS's success is attributable to William Paley. In the late 1940s, Paley capitalized on a loophole in the tax laws that allowed him to entice talent from NBC and ABC by offering large-income performers deals they could hardly refuse. In 1955, CBS achieved the number-one place in the ratings, a rank it would hold undisputed for 21 years. Meanwhile, the third network, ABC, found itself in somewhat the same position that CBS had occupied in the early days of network radio. Top advertisers and performers automatically chose CBS or NBC, turning to ABC only as a last resort.

A corporate breakup helped rescue ABC. When a Justice Department antitrust suit against the big Hollywood film studios forced them to sell off their extensive theater chains, one of the spun-off companies, Paramount Theaters, merged with ABC in 1953. Paramount injected much-needed funds and established a link with Hollywood that eventually paid off handsomely, helping ABC to achieve status equal to that of CBS and NBC.

In 1954, Walt Disney, the first of the major studio leaders to make a deal with television, agreed to produce a series of programs for ABC called *Disneyland* (1954–1957), later continued on NBC. The deal built ABC audiences and gave Disney free television promotion for his developing California theme park, as well as for Disney feature films.

2.15 Looking Back, Looking Forward

From the mid-1920s until the mid-1970s radio and television broadcasting dominated American popular culture in a way that persons born less than a quarter century ago can hardly imagine. Although alternative news and entertainment delivery systems such as motion pictures and vinyl disk audio recordings existed, broadcasting had no serious competition. Photos from the 1930s and 1940s show the entire family huddled around the home's single radio receiver. Pictures from the 1950s and 1960s look very similar, only the radio is replaced by a television.

Everything changed for radio in the 1950s when television began its ascendancy. Television adopted the types of programming previously found on radio and eventually became the primary source of family news and entertainment and a major socializing agent (see Exhibit 2.m on p. 40), while radio transformed into a more personalized medium with a narrowed range of programming, much of it music targeting younger persons.

By the mid-1970s television broadcasting, too, began to feel the effects of competition from newer media. The growth of cable gradually broke broadcasting's monopoly on video entertainment in the home, helped along by home video recorders that first hit the market in 1975 and, later, satellite-to-home video programming and the Internet. Just as radio before it, TV broadcasting transitioned from the dominant news and entertainment medium to one of many available to viewers during the last two decades of the 20th century.

Broadcasting today continues to evolve in the face of new technologies and increasing competition. On February 17, 2009, television broadcasters turned off their analog transmitters and began a new era of exclusively digital broadcasting. As explained in more detail elsewhere, digital broadcasting provides improved quality and great programming flexibility. For the first time, terrestrial broadcasters now have the ability to broadcast up to six separate program streams at the same time. Digital television also enables the transmission of programming in high definition formats, for a viewing experience similar to theatrical movies.

Radio broadcasters are also moving to digital broadcasting. Marketed as "HD Radio," digital radio permits the transmission of multiple program streams and much improved audio quality; FM digital radio equals CD quality, while AM digital sound is similar to that of traditional FM transmissions.

Even given all the competition from new media, as discussed in the next chapter, broadcasting continues to adapt, offering more services and enhanced technical quality. Don't count broadcasting out just yet.

Exhibit 2.m

Television: The National Hearth

(A)

(B)

Much as radio had been during the Great Depression and World War II, by the 1960s television had become a major socializing agent in the United States. People watched television as families and the next day discussed what they had seen the night before with their co-workers and classmates. Television scenes of great despair and great hope brought the country together, as if we used television as a giant, comforting fireplace hearth, around which we symbolically gathered to share our joy and grief. We sat in profound sadness as we watched President Kennedy's funeral cortege **(A)** and shared a sense of national pride as Apollo 11

(C)

(D)

astronauts Neil Armstrong and "Buzz" Aldrin deployed the U.S. flag on the moon **(B)**. Many argue that television images of the Vietnam War **(C)** helped turn public opinion against the conflict. Though the power of television has eroded, the horrifying images of September 11, 2001, **(D)** brought us together again, at least for a moment.

Cable and Newer Media

As we saw in Chapter 2, radio suffered when the TV boom began in the late 1940s and had to reinvent itself to survive. Television broadcasting prospered into the 1980s, little changed from a decade or two earlier. But new multichannel delivery systems developed in the late 1970s and expanded rapidly in the 1980s and 1990s, dramatically affecting broadcasting's dominance in the media marketplace. During the last quarter of the 20th century, broadcasters went from being "the" source of TV programming to simply "a" source. Indeed, today fewer than one in eight American homes receive all their TV programs directly from over-the-air TV stations. Traditional (terrestrial-based) radio broadcasters also face additional challenges from new competitors.

This transformation is the product of relentless audience demand for more options, along with breathtaking technical progress and important changes in government policies. In this chapter, we examine the newer media that continue to challenge broadcasting such as cable, direct broadcast satellite (DBS), and the Internet. We also briefly examine the technologies underpinning these new media and the winding path of government regulation, although both topics are addressed in greater detail in later chapters.

3.1   Emergence of Cable

Ironically, the first **multi-channel video programming distributor (MVPD)** to challenge broadcast television's dominance emerged from attempts to improve TV station coverage. The FCC's 1952 television channel-allotment plan (the *Sixth Report and Order* described in Section 2.13) left many "white areas"—places where people could not receive television service. Even in the biggest cities viewers might receive only five to eight channels. Most people received three or four, and virtually everyone wanted more.

Extending TV Coverage

Low-power **repeater** transmitters initially met some of the demand by extending station coverage into fringe reception areas and places cut off from normal reception by hills or mountains. The most common type repeater, called a **translator**, transmits on a different channel from the originating station so as not to interfere with the originating station's signal.

CATV

Another signal extender, **community antenna television (CATV)**, originally worked something like a translator, repeating the signal of one or more nearby stations. Instead of transmitting signals over the air,

however, a CATV system delivers them by wire from a "community antenna" on a hilltop or high tower to individual subscribers. Unlike translators, a CATV system using **wide-band** cable can deliver signals from several stations simultaneously, giving subscribers more program choices.

CATV systems began appearing in rural areas of both Oregon and Pennsylvania in 1948, just as regular broadcast television began. And, like radio years earlier, CATV's original economic motivation was to sell receivers. Appliance dealers who built the first systems could market television sets to consumers who otherwise would not buy them because they could not pick up over-the-air signals. Early CATV systems carried only five or six channels, all of them nearby TV stations. Most systems served from a few dozen to a few hundred subscribers.

Program Augmentation

CATV operators soon began enhancing—or augmenting—their services in various ways, as illustrated in Exhibit 3.a. Some systems began delivering programs from more distant TV stations using terrestrial microwave relays. And some systems began to offer nonbroadcast programming—feature films, sports, special events, and even their own locally produced programs.

These new program offerings marked a fundamental change for CATV. Instead of merely extending the coverage of nearby over-the-air broadcast signals it became a business offering programming from a variety of sources. As program augmentation expanded, CATV began to emerge as a competitor for TV viewers. As it matured, the term *CATV* faded out, replaced by **cable television.** But in spite of program augmentation, CATV/cable grew slowly. In 1970, the percentage of homes receiving programming by wire was still under 10 percent (Exhibit 3.b).

Broadcaster Fears

Television broadcasters welcomed CATV as long as it acted merely as a **redelivery service**, enlarging their audiences by extending signals to unserved areas, beefing up fringe reception, and overcoming local interference. Even better, broadcast audiences grew as more systems carried their signals. But, as CATV transformed into what we know today as cable, attitudes changed.

In spite of its anemic growth, by the mid-1960s broadcasters began to worry about cable as a potential competitor. The growing cable practice of importing signals from distant cities tended to fuzz normally fixed boundaries of broadcast markets. A network affiliate might find its programs duplicated in its own viewing area by a cable-delivered distant station affiliated with

Exhibit 3.a

Changing Roles of Cable

Cable has slowly expanded its programming sources, and thus the number of channels offered, since beginning in the late 1940s as a means of extending the viewer's home antenna. In the 1990s, cable began rebuilding its physical plant to accom-

modate new services. In the 21st century, cable is aggressively marketing digital television and a wide range of interactive services, including broadband Internet access, video on demand, and telephony.

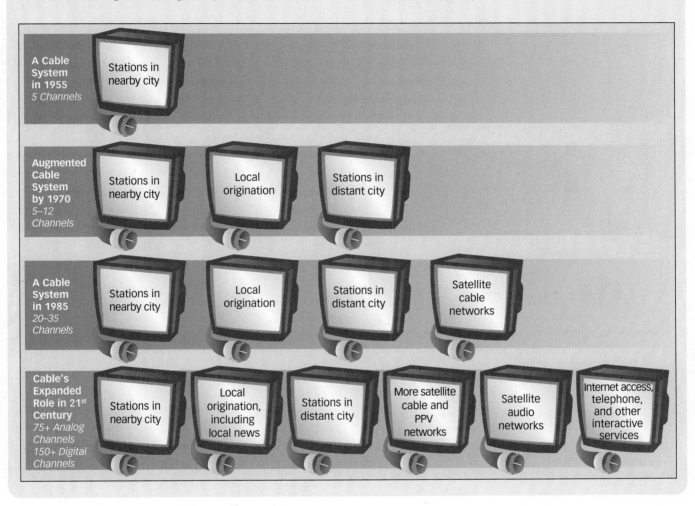

the same network. This undermined the concept of market exclusivity, under which broadcast programs had usually been distributed. Broadcasters feared this program duplication would fragment their audiences, leaving them with lower ratings and, thus, less appeal for advertisers. Broadcasters became even more alarmed as cable began to expand into big-city suburbs, no longer merely serving people unable to receive off-air service.

Cable Regulation

Government can either promote development of a new medium or retard it by the policies it adopts. Cable regulation is discussed in greater detail in Chapter 12, but

a brief overview here may help to explain why cable may appear to have developed in jumps and spurts.

Cable systems remained a local concern in the 1950s. Regulation, if any, came from municipal governments that granted cable operators franchises, permitting them to string cables on utility poles or bury them along public rights of way. The FCC initially adopted a hands-off policy regarding cable regulation, noting that cable operators did not transmit signals over the air.

But, as cable's economic impact grew, broadcasters pressured politicians to encourage the FCC to take action. In 1962, the FCC began to use microwave relay licenses as a justification for regulating cable systems that imported distant station signals. Four years later the Commission extended regulation to all cable systems.

Exhibit 3.b

Cable Growth Indicators, 1960–2008

As cable grew, system size and channel capacity both increased. After 1975, pay cable spurred basic cable growth. The number of cable households continued to increase through the 1990s, but pay cable subscriptions as a percentage of cable households began declining in the mid-1980s. Recent figures show a sharp decline in the percentage of households subscribing to cable, signaling the migration of many subscribers to satellite and telephone video systems.

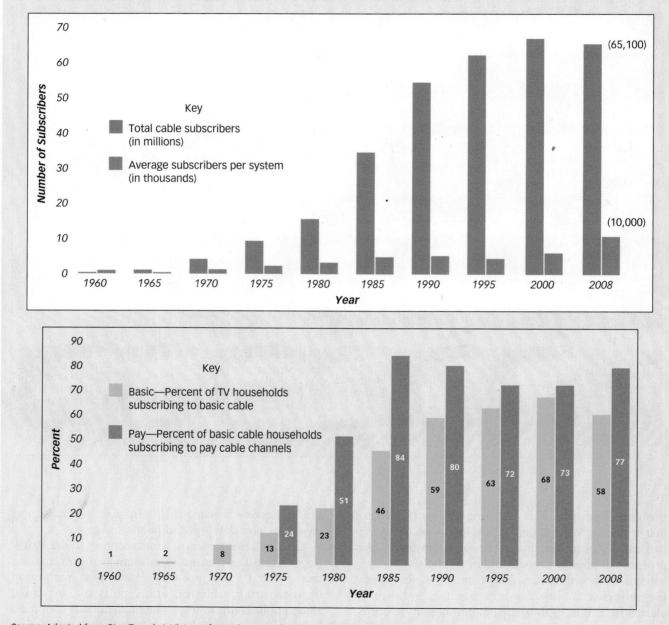

Source: Adapted from *Stay Tuned: A History of American Broadcasting*, 2nd ed., by Christopher H. Sterling and John M. Kittross, © 2002 by the authors. Published by Routledge. Reprinted by permission of the authors.

The FCC soon required cable to carry all TV stations within each system's areas of coverage (the **must-carry rule**) and to avoid duplicating network programs on the same day a network offered them. No new signals could be imported into any of the top 100 TV broadcast markets without a hearing on probable economic impact on existing TV stations.

Continued pressure from broadcasters resulted in the FCC's adopting additional cable regulations in 1972 (FCCR, 1972b). This would be the high-water mark of cable regulation, however. Over the next 12 years, the FCC reversed course on much of its regulatory scheme for cable, and several court cases struck down other regulations (e.g., F, 1977: 36). Congress contributed to the deregulation with the passage of the Cable Communications Policy Act of 1984. What followed was a spirit of *laissez-faire* that prevailed until Congress, prompted by complaints about high subscription fees, poor service, and the arrogance of cable system operators, imposed new regulations with passage of the Cable Television Consumer Protection and Competition Act of 1992. Four years later, Congress again reversed course and passed the Telecommunications Act of 1996, a law significantly reducing restrictions on cable and other electronic media.

 ## 3.2 Cable's Ascendancy

Advancing technology, increased original programming, and supportive government policies combined in the late 1970s and early 1980s to make cable a major player. At the center of this vibrant growth in cable was the communications satellite.

Domsats and TVRO Antennas

Since the 1960s, communication satellites had been used for international broadcast relays, but demand for **domestic satellites (domsats)** lagged. In 1972, the FCC stimulated domsat demand by adopting an "open-skies" policy, allowing any adequately financed and technically qualified business firm to launch satellites for domestic use (FCCR, 1972a). Many American domsats operate as common carriers—point-to-point, rate-regulated communication services for program distributors or brokers who resell short-term access to users, such as TV news departments.

Few cable systems used domsats, however, until after 1979 when the FCC deregulated **television receive-only (TVRO)** antennas used to pick up programs relayed by satellite. This opened the way to widespread satellite use for relaying program services to cable systems—and soon to broadcast stations as well. In 1977, fewer than 200 cable systems owned their own TVROs, but within a decade some 8,000 systems used them.

Turner and Superstations

Domsats and TVROs gave cable systems a more efficient and less expensive way of obtaining new national program services with which to attract subscribers, but programs themselves still remained in short supply. However, when a demand exists, suppliers soon appear.

In 1970, Ted Turner, an innovative entrepreneur with an almost mystical faith in cable's future, bought low-rated Atlanta UHF TV station WJRJ (which he changed to WTCG for Turner Communications Group and later still renamed WTBS for Turner Broadcasting System). Turner loaded the station's schedule with movies and sports, then uplinked the signal for satellite distribution to cable systems throughout the country (see Exhibit 3.c). Turner initially charged nothing for his programs, making his profit from higher advertising rates on WTBS that were justified by the nationwide cable audience watching his "superstation."

Several other TV outlets, most notably Chicago's WGN and New York City's WOR, also became superstations with schedules of films, syndicated fare, and sports, but by the mid-1990s economic factors placed superstations at a competitive disadvantage with other cable program providers. In the late 1990s, Turner separated the programming on his Atlanta TV station from the programming uplinked to cable systems, but the superstation concept was an innovative and provocative source of programming for cable systems before "pure" advertiser-supported cable networks became commonplace.

HBO and Pay Cable

Home Box Office (HBO) led the development of another major programming innovation, **pay (or premium) cable.** In 1972, HBO introduced an advertising-free channel of (primarily) feature films for which subscribers paid an additional monthly fee over and above the charge for advertising-supported channels (later called the **basic tier**).

Progress was slow, however, until 1975, when HBO began uplinking programming to a domsat. This made HBO programs available to any cable system in the country with a TVRO antenna. Satellite delivery reduced distribution costs and enabled simultaneous reception throughout the country—an essential condition for national promotion of the service.

Turner's superstation and HBO demonstrated that domsats allowed the creation of economically viable networks reaching a nationwide audience via cable, the kind of audience only large broadcast networks could reach previously. Many others followed their example.

Cable Programming

Satellite distribution created an increase in the number of cable program providers, but much of the programming

Exhibit 3.c

Turner Pioneer Satellite Relay

When HBO and Ted Turner turned to domsats for distribution of their signals in the mid-1970s, they blazed a trail for hundreds of satellite-delivered cable networks. This exhibit shows how Turner initially distributed programming on his Atlanta-based

UHF TV station to cable subscribers nationwide, making it the first "superstation." A changing cable market persuaded Turner to convert the service from a superstation to a cable network in 1998.

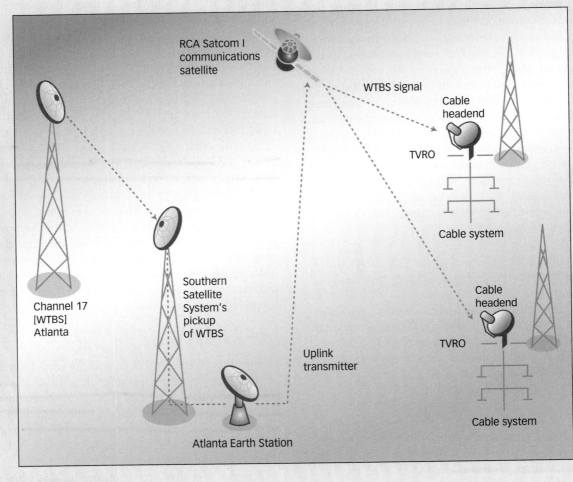

Source: Turner Broadcasting System, Inc.

available on cable was also available elsewhere. Until about 1980, cable remained basically parasitic, feeding off existing broadcast programs and motion pictures. In the 1980s, however, cable began to flex its programming muscle. HBO led the way with cable-specific productions—programs made especially for cable. It taped special on-stage performances, obtained rights to sports events, and commissioned original programs. The cable industry in 1979 collectively began a full-time, public-affairs cable service, Cable-Satellite Public Affairs Network (C-SPAN), aimed at cultivating good public relations for the cable industry. Also that year, ABC and some other

investors launched ESPN, the first network devoted exclusively to sports programming.

Ted Turner made a second major contribution to the development of cable in 1980 by introducing Cable News Network (CNN), a 24-hour schedule of news and news-related features that many broadcast critics dismissed as the "chicken noodle network" for its low budgets, compared with broadcast network news departments. Turner spun off CNN Headline News, another 24-hour service, 18 months later. In 1982, The Weather Channel started providing 24-hour weather and environmental programming. Over the next two decades, other networks appeared featuring mostly original programs devoted to a variety of topics. In 2004, cable networks, exhibiting their programming expertise, for the first time won more prime time Emmy Awards than the broadcast networks. Some cable-original programming is now seen later on a broadcast network, reversing the traditional flow from broadcast networks to cable.

3.3 Advanced Cable Services

From the 1970s through the 1990s, cable typically offered groups—or tiers—of channels from which subscribers selected when purchasing cable services. They could get a basic tier of channels, or for more money, they could receive an expanded number of channels. For an additional fee they could receive premium commercial-free channels, such as HBO. Today, cable subscribers have much more control over the video programming entering the home. Cable also now offers services other than traditional video and audio programming.

Interacting with TV

Cable visionaries in the 1970s foresaw interactivity as a logical next step in evolving home communications. Customers could talk with others on the cable—teachers could interact with students, and the public could more fully communicate with stores, banks, public utilities, and safety agencies—all without leaving home.

Warner Cable gave this type of interactive service a thorough trial beginning in 1977 on its Columbus, Ohio, system. Called Qube, it offered 10 channels over which viewers could respond by means of a touchpad. Though the experiment generated a lot of media coverage, Qube failed to attract sufficient subscribers to warrant its high cost, and after three years of mounting losses Warner closed it down.

Similar viewer apathy greeted later two-way experiments, including one operated by GTE in Cerritos, California, in the early 1990s. After a brief initial fascination, viewers either lost interest or were unwilling to pay the price necessary for the service.

The success of the Internet and the interactivity it provides, however, suggests that there was a dramatic shift in public interest during the middle and late 1990s. Today, there is a growing market for interactive services, available in the home, for sending and receiving text, audio, and video. Although some people will have little interest in particular features of the information superhighway, many are increasingly interested in doing more than simply viewing information on-screen.

Cable provides a large pipeline into millions of homes, and cable operators are rebuilding their systems to accommodate two-way transmission of digital information of all kinds. Conversion to provide digital video programming and increasing system channel capacity to compete with satellite systems are major goals, but delivery of interactive services is also extremely important.

Pay-per-View

First appearing in 1984, **pay-per-view** (**PPV**) allowed viewers to order individual programs from the cable company for a one-time fee. Movies, many of them "adult," have accounted for a large number of PPV requests. "Events," predominantly boxing and wrestling, have been another important source of PPV revenue.

Widespread use of PPV depends on **addressability**—an efficient means for the cable system office to receive program orders and address individual PPV decoders. PPV customers on more advanced cable systems used a touchpad to communicate with a computer called a **video server** at the cable headend. The video server interacted with the customer's decoder and carried out recordkeeping and billing operations. Subscribers on less capable systems had to order PPV programming by calling the cable system operator or program provider.

Digital Cable

Between 1996 and 2008, the cable industry invested more than $100 billion in infrastructure improvements. The money was spent not simply to upgrade PPV performance, but to allow cable to offer a variety of new digital services. By 2008, more than 90 percent of the homes passed by cable had access to digital services and more than 35 million households subscribed to programming on the new digital service tier. Some of these channels offer programs in wide screen high definition format (HDTV). Receiving the HDTV programs requires a HD set-top box and a wide-screen high definition display device, in addition to a digital cable subscription.

In addition to HDTV programming, digital cable subscribers have access to many more channels, in some cases more than 250, with special interest programming not available on the analog tier. Digital cable service also provides many audio channels covering a wide range of music formats.

Video on Demand (VOD)

Another advanced service available to many digital subscribers is **video on demand** (**VOD**). VOD allows digital cable subscribers to access programming stored on the cable system's video server instantly and to control it (pause, rewind, fast-forward) just as they would a tape or DVD. Some systems charge subscribers a fee for each program accessed, but some offer **subscription VOD (SVOD)**, allowing subscribers unlimited access for a monthly fee. As more people subscribe to digital cable and VOD becomes more widely available, the convenience and interactive control offered by VOD makes it a logical replacement for pay-per-view movies and other recorded programming.

Broadband Internet Access

Broadband Internet access is another advanced service available to cable subscribers thanks to the upgraded systems. Cable offers "always on" high-speed access. Some cable companies claim speeds of 3 to 10 million bytes of data per second (Mbps). By 2008, more than 33 million households received Internet access using cable's broadband service.

Cable Telephony

Some cable systems have offered telephone service for years, but the upgrade to digital cable allows cable systems to offer "digital phone" service using **Voice over Internet Protocol (VoIP)**. VoIP turns voice into digital packets that travel over the Internet. VoIP interfaces with the conventional telephone system so subscribers can call people not connected to the Internet. Most systems offering VoIP service allow subscribers to call anyone anywhere in the United States and talk as long as they wish for a fixed monthly fee. Cable VoIP has grown rapidly since a few cable system operators introduced it in 2003. The number of subscribers to cable telephone service grew from less than 3 million in 2003 to more than 16 million in 2008.

Higher Costs: Fewer Owners

Thanks to dramatically enhanced program choices and advanced services, such as high speed Internet access, video on demand, and telephone service, cable is well positioned to compete with its rivals. These services are not free, however. A look at any cable system's menu of products and prices shows that subscribers wanting most or all of the available services will pay a hefty bill each month.

Building the cable infrastructure to support these new services and then developing the services required the investment of billions of dollars. It is little wonder that many small- and medium-sized cable operators were unable to make the capital investments required and were swallowed by huge companies operating multiple local cable systems. As a result of consolidation during the last decade, today more than 80 percent of all cable subscribers receive service from just six **multiple system operators (MSOs)** and the largest two serve more than half the total cable market.

3.4 Programs via Satellite

Until the mid-1990s, broadcasters and cable operators had a virtual monopoly on the delivery of video programming to the home. Today, only about 12 percent of the nation's households watch broadcast television exclusively. Cable has, by far, the majority of viewers, but cable no longer exercises a monopoly in the **multichannel video program distributor (MVPD)** market; in fact, cable's share of the market is steadily dropping (see Exhibit 3.d).

Big Dish TVROs

When cable program providers began using domsats to distribute their product in the mid-1970s, many individuals in underserved areas purchased or built their own TVROs. The law at that time did not address the legality of receiving these signals that were intended solely for cable system operators. Taking advantage of this legal vacuum, some unscrupulous operators began "mini-cable systems" by distributing the satellite-delivered programs throughout large apartment complexes and charging occupants a monthly fee. There were also reports of TV stations outside the United States taking the satellite feeds and broadcasting the programs over the air.

The cable industry looked to Congress for help. Congress responded by passing new laws indicating that receiving un-encrypted signals was legal, but receiving signals that were scrambled required payment. Program distributors responded by encrypting their signals. This helped curtail rampant piracy, but many otherwise law-abiding citizens became enraged when they could no longer watch programs they had been receiving free. Programming was initially distributed on C-band frequencies that required expensive "big dish" antennas measuring yards, not inches, in diameter. In addition, these huge antennas required a steering mechanism because the desired programming might be on several satellites at different locations. Encryption forced big dish owners to buy descrambling equipment and also pay a fee to the program provider. In 1995, about 2.3 million U.S. households received cable programming using C-band TVROs, but today the number is closer to 200,000.

Direct-to-Home Satellites

The FCC authorized commercial operation of the first direct-to-home (DTH) satellite system in 1982. Critics questioned whether DTH service, primarily of interest to small and scattered audiences in uncabled rural areas (as elsewhere it must compete with cable and established program sources), could recoup its costs. The

Exhibit 3.d

Competition for Multichannel Video Subscribers

Throughout the 1970s and 1980s and into the early 1990s, cable dominated the multichannel video market. Cable's share began to drop in the late 1990s with the introduction of

direct-to-home satellite systems. Market shares of both cable and satellite are likely to drop in the next decade as telephone companies expand their multichannel video offerings.

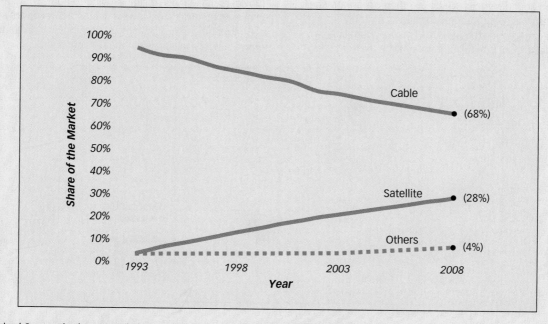

Sources: Federal Communications Commission, National Cable and Telecommunications Association.

---

critics were right—the first American operation (using a Canadian medium-power satellite requiring a smaller TVRO dish than necessary for cable operators) was short-lived because it attracted few subscribers.

Despite the dismal first round, however, interest in direct-to-home satellite service revived less than a decade later. Improving technology created more powerful satellites operating on higher frequencies (Ku-band) which allowed the use of smaller receiving dishes (see Exhibit 3.e). Better technology and better business planning led to the birth of modern **direct broadcast satellite (DBS)** service.

The short history of DBS has been turbulent. Since 1991, no fewer that eight separate DBS services have been launched. Most of them failed to achieve enough market penetration to succeed. Consolidation of the remaining operations resulted in further reductions in service providers. Today, only two serious competitors remain in the DBS market, DirectTV and The Dish Network (Dish). Early in the 21st century the two companies announced they would merge, but the U.S. Department of Justice nixed the idea, citing antitrust concerns.

In spite of the DBS industry's stormy past, enough consumers continued to sign up for service to make DBS a serious competitor to cable. In 1993, almost 95 percent of MVPD subscribers received their service from cable, but by 2008 less than 70 percent were cable subscribers. Most of cable's lost subscribers moved to DBS, and many of those were highly valued customers who subscribed to premium channels and frequently ordered PPV programming.

DBS Programming

Until recently, DBS offered a far greater number of program channels than did cable, thanks to the fact that DBS has long been a digitally based service. Both DirecTV and Dish offer nearly 300 program channels to subscribers located anywhere in the nation. In addition, since 2000 both DBS providers have been authorized to deliver local broadcast stations into local markets, which is called **local-into-local service**. Before 2000, cable operators stressed the fact that DBS subscribers could not receive their local broadcast stations without an external antenna (or a cable subscription!), but today

Exhibit 3.e

Satellite-to-Home Viewing

Satellite delivery of programs directly to viewers' homes, whether by DBS systems intended for such reception or by home pickup of relay signals designed primarily for cable system use, depends on a reliable means of scrambling the video and sound signals, which are then descrambled by devices supplied only to homes that pay monthly subscription charges for the service. The descrambling device is a set-top box installed between the viewer's TVRO antenna and the television set or other display and recording devices.

The smaller, less expensive antennas used by DBS and the wide range of program packages available from DBS service providers make these digital satellite-to-home systems popular with tens of millions of viewers. Many DBS receivers also come with digital recording technology that allows viewers to record programming available from the DBS provider.

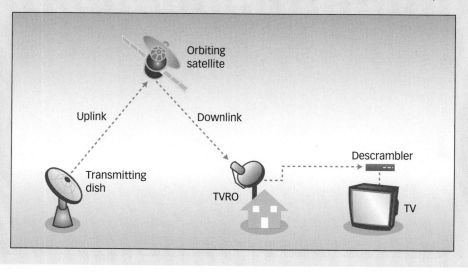

DirecTV and Dish provide local-into-local service in more than three-fourths of the nation's 210 TV markets.

DBS providers have also been leaders in offering high definition (HD) programming. In addition to music channels such as MTV and CMT (Country Music Television), DBS offers dozens of CD-quality audio channels featuring a wide range of music formats. Both DirecTV and Dish also offer a variety of Spanish language channels, plus international channels in many languages, including French, Italian, Russian, Korean, Chinese, and Hindi.

DBS providers promote their service through several "package plans" at various prices that include a collection of channels, as do cable operators. Subscribers may then add premium channels, international channels, high definition channels, sports programming packages, and a variety of other extra-cost products to suit their interests.

Advanced DBS Services

Neither Dish nor DirecTV currently provide satellite-based interactive services such as broadband Internet access and VoIP that depend on having a high-speed "return path" (from subscriber to service provider). Instead, both companies have formed cooperative marketing agreements with major telephone companies, independent Internet Service Providers (ISPs), and independent satellite services to provide "bundled packages" of video programming (via DBS) and broadband Internet access. Consumers may purchase the bundled video programming/Internet access services from either partner forming the agreement.

Satellite Radio

In 1997, the FCC auctioned two bands of frequencies for use by satellite radio broadcasters. On September 25, 2001, XM Satellite Radio began commercial operations using one of the two bands, offering subscribers 29 channels of news, sports, and variety talk and 71 music channels, more than two dozen of them commercial-free. XM Radio attracted only about 140,000 subscribers its first year, but reached the million subscriber mark after two years.

The user of the other frequency band, Sirius Satellite Radio, launched its service on February 14, 2002. Sirius Radio began with about 30,000 subscribers and, almost two years later, still had only about 150,000.

In March, 2007, XM and Sirius announced that the companies would merge into a single operation. The merger required the approval of both the Department of Justice (DOJ) and the Federal Communications Commission. One year later, the merger was approved by the DOJ. Several months later, the FCC approved the deal and the merger was completed on July 29, 2008. The new company, Sirius XM Radio, boasts more than 18.5 million subscribers and offers more than 300 channels of programming, about half of them commercial free.

Sirius XM Radio offers its service by subscription on-line so consumers can access its programming without using a satellite radio receiver. The service also provides local traffic and weather information for selected major markets.

Satellite radio offers advantages to consumers willing to invest in special satellite radio receivers and pay a subscription fee. Digital transmission guarantees nationwide high-quality audio reception and a greater variety of program formats than are available from terrestrial broadcasters in even the largest markets. Many channels are commercial-free, a feature appreciated by many listeners. In addition, satellite programming is uncensored, a major reason for shock jock Howard Stern's move from terrestrial broadcasting to Sirius Radio in 2006.

3.5 Niche Services

In addition to cable, DBS, and satellite radio, several alternative modes of program delivery have arisen to supplement mainstream broadcast services. Each provides programming by subscription that is similar to or the same as that of cable, DBS, or satellite providers.

Wireless Cable/Broadband Radio Service

The term **wireless cable** refers to systems that use terrestrial microwave radio signals to distribute cable programming to subscribers. Because the systems use radio waves rather than wires and provide the same programming as cable, the term is paradoxical but descriptive.

Wireless cable appeared first as the **multichannel multipoint distribution service** (**MMDS**) operating on frequencies in the 2 Ghz band. MMDS's location in the electromagnetic spectrum limits its coverage to about 15 miles using analog transmission techniques. Home antennas must be within the line of sight of the transmitting antenna. The first MMDS system began operating in Washington, DC in 1985.

The economic advantages of distributing programming without the expense of running cable to each subscriber's home are obvious, but wireless cable has not been a serious competitor in areas served by cable.

Wireless cable hit a peak of 1.2 million subscribers in the mid-1990s, but its popularity has plummeted since. By 2008, less than 200,000 households subscribed to wireless cable.

Responding to the failure of wireless cable as a serious competitor in the MVPD market, the FCC in 2004 renamed the portion of the spectrum allocated to MMDS the **Broadband Radio Service** (**BRS**). New licensees in the BRS are using the frequencies for a variety of broadband applications, including high-speed Internet access.

MATV/SMATV

Another niche service meets TV service requirements of a building or group of buildings on a single piece of property. **Master antenna television** (**MATV**) and **satellite MATV** (**SMATV**) are special, limited-area types of cable television. An MATV installation combines a master television antenna on the roof of a building with coaxial or fiber cable feeding programs to each unit. Modern multiple-dwelling units and commercial multiple-tenant units, including hotels and office buildings, usually come with suitable cabling already installed.

Satellite MATV adds a TVRO antenna to the installation, enabling the system to pick up satellite-distributed services. Because SMATVs operate entirely within the boundaries of private property and thus do not cross public rights of way, they are also called private cable systems and are exempt from most cable and broadcast regulations. Private cable systems serve about 1.1 million subscribers, about 1 percent of the MVPD market.

Utility Companies

Over the years, a few gas and electric utility companies have provided video programming for consumers not served by cable. Utilities have some advantages as video program providers, including access to public rights of way, name recognition, and an established relationship with consumers. However, utilities providing voice, video, and data services have done so using the same technologies as cable and wireless cable, not their own power lines into the home.

Electric utility companies for years have used certain broadband capabilities within their systems to help them manage the distribution of electrical power. Now some of these companies want to extend these broadband capabilities directly to their customers. In 2004, the FCC adopted new regulations that encourage the development of **broadband over powerline** (**BPL**). This technology allows the use of ordinary power lines to carry high-speed broadband services "the last mile" into the consumer's home. Most utility companies showing initial interest in BPL focused on providing high-speed Internet access, but some indicated an interest in eventually offering video programming.

Critics of BPL technology say it will create horrendous interference to certain radio services, and FCC regulations require utilities to accommodate radio services harmed by BPL interference. The American Public Power Association also notes that about a dozen states have regulations preventing or discouraging public power companies from offering broadband services. And, of course, utilities face the same crowded MVPD market as other niche providers. How important audio and video program distribution via BPL will become is unknown, given these considerations. But any industry with the capacity to provide high-speed broadband services to consumers cannot be ignored as a potential player.

3.6 Telephone Companies

Throughout the 1990s, broadcast and cable leaders alternated between fear and relief as the telephone industry sent conflicting signals about its interest in becoming a competitor in the distribution of programming.

By the mid-1990s, court decisions had removed most of the regulatory restrictions on telephone companies that had prevented them doing anything more than providing traditional telephone service, and the Telecommunications Act of 1996 (discussed in Chapter 11) opened the field further. Both broadcasting and cable saw expansion of **plain old telephone service (POTS)** into information and entertainment as a threat, although cable foresaw how its own broadband capacity could carry new services in competition with telcos.

In the mid-1990s it appeared the telcos would move aggressively into direct competition with cable by providing interactive television. The telcos found, however, that interactive television technology was extremely expensive, and, in spite of their enormous technical resources, they had problems getting it to work. Meanwhile, the Internet shifted interactivity from the television to the computer, and competition for local and long-distance phone service intensified. The telcos scaled back their earlier plans significantly, but continued to expand and improve their fiber-optic networks.

Over the next few years, several telephone companies offering local service, what the FCC calls **local exchange carriers (LECs),** began expanding their services. At this time they had both a better network infrastructure (more fiber-optic cable closer to consumers' homes) and newer technologies. These improvements facilitated the delivery of high-speed Internet service, providing direct competition to cable

modem service. By 2007, AT&T, Verizon, and a number of smaller LECs were using these newer technologies to provide video programming in selected markets, delivering up to 200 channels, many in high definition. In areas where these wireline broadband services are not yet available, several LECs partner with DirecTV and The Dish Network to sell DBS service. The ability to offer broadband video, telephone service, high-speed Internet, and cell phone service as a bundled package positions the telephone companies as serious competitors to the local cable operators.

3.7 The Internet

Some would argue that the Internet could be considered another "niche service" because it does not operate as a direct competitor to broadcasting, cable, and DBS in the video program distribution market. However, widespread use of the Internet has changed the way people communicate with each other and also the way they view all other forms of communication. People increasingly want all media to provide the same two-way interactivity they enjoy using the Internet. No discussion of newer media is complete without an examination of the Internet because Internet-based technologies and protocols are also an inherent part of the technological changes taking place in other media.

Internet Origins

Many historians say the Internet began in the late 1950s with the creation of the Department of Defense's Advanced Research Projects Agency (ARPA). ARPA was tasked with promoting American scientific research and development in the wake of the Soviet Union's 1957 launch of the first man-made satellite. Among ARPA's employees in the early 1960s was J. C. R. Licklider, a psychologist and computer scientist who was fascinated by the interaction between humans and computers. While many people in the "hard sciences" thought of computers as super calculating machines, Licklider looked at computers as communications devices. Licklider foresaw a virtual "intergalactic community" of human communicators connected through time-sharing computers, a vision that describes today's Internet. But much work was needed to allow computers from a variety of manufacturers to "talk" to each other and even more work was needed to interconnect computers in distant locations.

Another ARPA employee, Larry Roberts, worked on making ARPA's various computers talk to each other. In 1969, Roberts succeeded in linking computers in four locations (University of California Los Angeles, Stanford Research Institute, University of California Santa Barbara, and University of Utah). This was the birth of ARPANET. In developing ARPANET, Roberts depended heavily on the work of Paul Baran. Baran was an electrical engineer who developed the concept of distributed networks and packet switching, two concepts critical to the operation of today's Internet.

ARPANET's function was to allow exchange of scientific data files, but people working on the project needed to communicate with each other individually and collectively. E-mail had been sent previously within a single computer, but in 1971 Ray Tomlinson wrote an e-mail program that allowed e-mail to be shared among computers on a network. Soon persons associated with ARPANET began exchanging text messages using Tomlinson's program until, some reports indicate, e-mail became the dominant traffic on the network, just as e-mail remains today the most popular use of the Internet. Tomlinson's program used the login name of the person and the host computer's name, separated by the @ symbol. Tomlinson says he chose the @ symbol because the message was going to someone "at" (logging into) a particular host computer. The symbol was also selected because it was not widely used in programming languages and would not cause computers to crash or do strange things.

Other computer networks rapidly appeared after the creation of ARPANET, but these networks could not interconnect. It was not until the mid-1970s when Vinton Cerf (along with Robert Kohn) developed a system (what they called **transmission control protocol** or **TCP**) that allowed information-sharing among different computer networks. Cerf's TCP (later developed into TCP/IP) is what allows differing computer networks to interact, to form the Internet: a network of networks. Because of his critical contribution to computer networking, Cerf is often acknowledged as "the father of the Internet."

The infant Internet, however, remained the servant of computer scientists and researchers because users had to type in arcane command sequences. In the late 1980s and early 1990s, Tim Berners-Lee, while working at the European Particle Physics Laboratory (CERN) in Geneva, Switzerland, developed the **Hypertext Transfer Protocol (HTTP),** a language computers use to jump from one hypertext document on the Internet to another. A hypertext document is one with words or images that link to other hypertext documents. Berners-Lee saw these links as forming an "information web" that, using the Internet, connected hypertext documents stored on computers around the world: a World Wide Web (www). He also developed a browser, a software program that makes using the web easier, but Berners-Lee's browser was not truly "user friendly" for anyone other than a computer geek. In 1993, Marc Andreeson, a student at the University of Illinois and a part-time employee at the National Center for Supercomputing Applications, developed his web browser, Mosaic, and offered it free to the public. Mosaic featured a **graphical user interface** that allowed easy point-and-click web navigation. Mosaic became an instant success. Andreeson later developed Mosaic commercially as Netscape, the most popular commercial browser until Microsoft captured the browser market with Internet Explorer.

Many others contributed to the creation of the Internet and the world wide web, but Licklider, Roberts, Baran, Tomlinson, Cerf, Berners-Lee, and Andreeson stand out for their pioneering efforts.

The number of computers connected to the Internet increased dramatically following the government's lifting of all restrictions on commercial use of the nation's Internet backbone in 1991. Between 1990 and 1992 the number of computers connected to the Internet increased from about 100,000 to more than a million. The World Wide Web and availability of a graphical browser made millions more take an interest in the Internet. By 2008, an estimated 70 percent of the U.S. population was on-line. Exhibit 3.f tracks the growth of Internet use in the United States.

Internet Activities

Researchers at The Pew Internet & American Life Project use a hierarchy of colorful metaphors to describe the Internet. They say it is first and foremost a mail pigeon, then a library, then an amusement park, and finally a shopping mall. They note that the order of this hierarchy has remained constant over the Internet's history (Pew, 2005).

Young people may take issue with this hierarchy because many use the Internet to download music, share files peer-to-peer, or participate in social networking sites such as Facebook and MySpace. Pew survey research indicates that more than half of Internet users ages 18 to 29 listen to music on-line and about 30 percent download music and share files. These activities are likely to be even more popular with persons who are younger than 17, as parents of teens can attest. As evidence, Pew research indicates that more than 50 percent of children aged 12–17 use social networks and have created on-line profiles (Pew, 2007). Internet users 30 and older, in contrast, reported using the Internet much less frequently for these activities.

Traditional media owners can take mixed comfort from 2007 Gallup Poll research showing that by a wide margin people of all ages seeking news still turn to traditional media, such as local television stations and newspapers, more often than the Internet. Only about 22 percent of the population reported checking web news sources daily, as contrasted to 55 percent who watch local television news and 44 percent who read a local daily newspaper (Gallup, 2007). The report also

Exhibit 3.f

The Growth of the Internet

Used primarily by researchers in its early years, the Internet began attracting the attention of the general public with the development of easy to use web browsers in the early 1990s.

Broadband penetration in the United States lags behind many other developed countries, but continues to show steady growth.

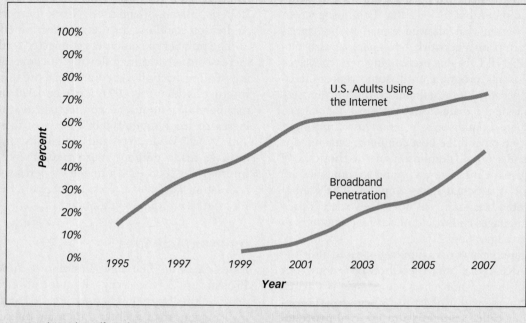

Sources: Pew Internet and American Life Project; Internet World Statistics; National Telecommunications and Information Administration.

indicated that use of Internet news sources was increasing, though the rate of increase had declined in the past couple years. All other news sources, both print and electronic, showed declines.

These reports, and others, suggest that the Internet has not yet emerged as a direct competitor to traditional media in the same sense that the traditional media are competitors to each other. The effect of the Internet, however, cannot be dismissed. The Internet allows anyone to become a producer/provider of music and video (and other forms of content), not just a passive consumer. Unlike traditional media, the Internet does not require a government license or a large capital investment to become a "webcaster" operating an "Internet radio station" with, at least theoretically, a world-wide audience. Internet content also is largely unregulated, another factor that has great appeal to many younger users.

Technical limitations have played a part in the failure of the Internet to become a strong competitor in the delivery of video programming and, to a much lesser degree, audio programming. Streaming audio and video

provides the experience most similar to broadcasting, cable, and DBS. Streaming audio and video plays continuously in real-time as the signal reaches the user's computer. This contrasts with downloading an audio or video file and storing it for later playback.

The quality of streamed audio and video depends greatly on the bandwidth of the consumer's Internet connection, the traffic load on the network at the time, and other factors. For consumers still connected to the Internet using conventional voice-quality telephone lines and modems rated at 56.8 kilobits per second or less, audio quality can be good for voice and adequate for music, but hardly excellent by modern audio standards. Video is restricted to a small part of the screen, the images lack resolution, and the motion is jerky. Real-time delivery of high-quality audio and video via the Internet requires a larger pipeline—broadband access—into the home.

The Federal Communications Commission defines "basic" broadband as service with upstream (customer to provider) and downstream (provider to customer) speeds from 768 kilobits per second to 1.5 megabits per second. Most broadband providers, primarily telephone companies and cable systems, regularly provide downstream service at speeds from 1.5 to 10 megabits per second. These speeds permit very high quality audio and video streaming, as well as downloading times measured in seconds rather than minutes. By 2008, more than 66 million subscribers received broadband Internet service. (See Exhibit 3.f for the growth of broadband penetration in the United States.)

The growth of broadband capability has led to increased distribution of video programming on the Internet. In 2005, Internet portals Yahoo! and Google added video to their popular search engine menus of searchable databases. And high-quality video distribution was crucial to the success of the exceedingly popular YouTube site. Traditional programming providers are also increasingly making their products available via the Internet, as the major broadcast and cable networks now allow viewers to access their favorite programs from the networks' web sites. For example, in 2007 NBC announced that it would make its prime-time schedule available for downloading the week following its network airing.

Other factors driving Internet video are the increasing number of portable devices capable of making a wireless connection to the Internet and the number of locations both public and private offering free (or almost free) wireless Internet access. Modern laptop computers come configured for wireless Internet access or can be upgraded for it using an adaptor card. Rapidly advancing cell phone, **personal digital assistant (PDA),** and other mobile computer-based technologies are also allowing greater wireless Internet access. People often use these portable devices "on the go" and are willing to sacrifice image and audio quality for the convenience of receiving programming in places where it would not otherwise be available at all.

The history of media suggests that few older media are replaced entirely by a new one. More often, a new medium assumes some of the functions of older media and the older media reinvent themselves to accommodate the new reality. One accommodation traditional media have had to make is acknowledging they no longer enjoy quasi-monopolistic control over the sources of information and entertainment available to consumers. Traditional radio broadcasters are painfully aware of the vast amount of music available for nothing or minimal cost on-line, and TV broadcasters fear the same will happen to video programming in the future.

Another example of the impact of the Internet on the operation of traditional media is the growing number of **blogs** (web logs). Blogs allow anyone to become a pundit and also allow everyone with Internet access to contribute new information or insight on any topic to a blog site. By the end of 2007, 39 percent of Internet users regularly read someone else's blog, while 8 percent

wrote their own. Evidence suggests, however, that most blogs are not long-lived, with 60 to 80 percent of blogs being abandoned within a month of their first entry (Caslon Analytics, 2007).

The Internet continues to grow and assume some of the functions previously considered the exclusive domain of other media. Older media are attempting to incorporate features of the Internet to make themselves more competitive. The Internet is relatively young and what it may become, and how older media will adjust to it, promises to be interesting.

3.8 Electronics Revolution

The sweeping changes taking place in electronic media today are made possible by a fundamental shift from analog to digital technology. Digital technology makes all forms of communication content—sound, images, and text—electrically equivalent. The original form of the information no longer matters to the equipment used to produce, distribute, or store it. This basic commonality of content is at the heart of the changes taking place in mass media and was made possible by the development of solid-state microelectronics.

Transistors

The "crystal and cat-whisker" detector employed in radios during broadcasting's infancy was the first solid-state electronic device, but it was not capable of amplification. Fleming's vacuum tube detector, de Forest's Audion, and Armstrong's regenerative circuit eclipsed the crystal detector and dominated electronics for almost 50 years. But vacuum tubes were hot, bulky, fragile, and power-hungry, and, worst of all, had a limited life. In 1947, a trio of Bell Laboratories engineers developed the transistor, a three-element, solid-state tube replacement that had none of these weaknesses. The engineers received the Nobel Prize in 1956 for their invention, a fitting distinction considering their transistor became the foundation on which all modern electronics is based. One of the first mass-produced transistor-based products on the consumer market, a tiny portable radio, appeared in 1954 and began the trend toward miniaturization depicted in Exhibit 3.g.

Transistors also made possible the development of that prime artifact of the late 20th century, the computer. Only computers could manipulate billions of information bits with the speed and intricacy needed for digital processing. In 1945, the first large experimental electronic computer used some 18,000 vacuum tubes plus miles of wire. The tubes generated so much heat that attendants had to stand by to replace them as they blew out. Transistors solved the heat and size problem while reducing costs and enormously increasing computer speed and memory capacity.

Exhibit 3.g

Changing the Definitions of "Portable"

(A)

(B)

(C)

(D)

(A) Edwin Armstrong, the "father of FM radio," shows off an early "portable" radio that required either large batteries or household electric power; **(B)** This photo highlights the relative sizes of a 1950s vacuum tube, a 1960s transistor, and, by today's standards, a fairly large integrated circuit; **(C)** Transistors began to replace vacuum tubes in the 1960s, leading to small, inexpensive portable radios; **(D)** Today integrated circuits provide two-way wireless communication of voice, data, and video from almost any location.

Sources: Photo (A) © Bettmann/Corbis; photo (B) courtesy of AT&T Archives and History Center, Warren, NJ; photo (C) © H. Armstrong Roberts/ClassicStock/Corbis; photo (D) from Comstock.

The Chip

Tiny computers and other devices remained impractical, however, as long as hundreds of separate transistors had to be meticulously wired together with hand-soldered connections. True miniaturization came with the invention of the **integrated circuit (IC)** or computer chip.

Chips are made of crystalline wafers on which microscopically small electronic components are etched. A modern chip may contain many thousands of transistors and other components. This miniaturization makes it possible to crowd all the electrical circuits needed to construct entire radios and other electrical devices into a single chip. The integrated circuit chip is responsible for such dramatic developments as inexpensive multifunction digital watches, hand-held calculators, laptop computers, and cellular telephones.

3.9 Consumer Media

Solid-state technology made possible many new consumer products that widened viewer and listener options. Some have been dramatically successful.

Audio Cassettes and CDs

Introduced by Philips in the 1960s, the audio cassette's popularity boomed following the introduction of Sony's Walkman in 1980. Consumers bought the Walkman and its imitators by the millions, and in their heyday some combination AM/FM/audio cassette players sold for less than $20.

Although the analog audio cassette enjoyed great popularity, other audio cassette formats were much less successful. Compared to an analog audio cassette, a digital audio cassette, or **digital audio tape (DAT)**, provides superior sound quality. Although DAT enjoyed some popularity among professional and semi-professional musicians, a variety of factors combined to keep consumer interest low.

In dramatic contrast to DAT, the digital audio **compact disc (CD)**, introduced in 1983, is one of the most successful products in consumer electronics history. The CD's audio quality, size, and durability make it popular for use at home, in cars, and with personal portable players.

MP3 and MP3 Players

In the second half of the 1990s, many computer owners began using an audio compression algorithm called MP3 to record music from CDs and other sources to their computer hard drives. MP3 (MPeg Audio Level 3) is one of several compression standards developed by the Moving Picture Experts Group (MPEG), an international group of experts working to standardize compressed video and audio. Software programs can extract raw digital audio data from a CD and convert it to an MP3 file (or other file types). MP3 is especially popular because it can reduce the size of a CD audio file by a factor of 12 without significantly affecting the original audio quality. Because of its ability to shrink audio files, and thus speed up the transfer process, MP3 quickly became the most popular file format for distributing music on the Internet.

Music file sharing took on new dimensions in the late 1990s when manufacturers cashed in on the popularity of MP3 by offering portable MP3 players. Early MP3 players allowed users to download MP3 files from a computer to a solid-state memory card. Solid-state storage provided advantages, such as small size, light weight, and immunity to skipping, but could hold only a small number of tunes. The first MP3 player using a small hard disc, the Personal Jukebox, was introduced in 1999. The Personal Jukebox could store about 1,200 tunes compared to the dozen or so available on players using solid-state storage devices.

Apple Computer entered the MP3 arena in 2001 when it introduced the first iPod, which came with a 5 gigabyte hard disc that could also hold more than 1,000 songs. Apple upgraded the iPod during the next several years and it rapidly became the dominant portable MP3 player.

The iPod also popularized a form of **RSS (really simple syndication)** software that searches the web for the latest audio feeds to which the user has subscribed and automatically transfers the files to the consumer's player when the player is connected again to the user's computer. Although it works with other devices, the term **podcast** has come to mean time-shifted audio files that are downloaded and later transferred automatically from the users' computer to a portable player. The fact that the software performs both these functions automatically has increased the amount of Internet audio being downloaded and encouraged more people to produce materials for podcast distribution.

MP3 Music Wars

The recording industry has historically viewed any consumer recording device as a means of pirating copyrighted music. The appearance of MP3 files and portable MP3 players created enormous concern. Concern turned into full-blown panic in 1999 when 18-year-old Shawn Fanning created Napster, a peer-to-peer (P2P) file sharing service for the exchange of music files stored in MP3 format on computers around the world. Napster did not store any music files; it only provided an index to music files on computers that users could then transfer directly computer-to-computer.

Several major recording companies immediately moved against Napster for violation of copyright laws. The recording companies were successful and, in 2002, the original Napster was bankrupt. Other firms followed in Napster's footsteps, but the recording companies pursued them as well.

In mid-2003, the Recording Industry Association of American (RIAA) switched tactics and announced it would go after the computer users themselves, not just the companies. The practice continues, with the industry especially targeting college students who have broadband access through their universities.

Today, there are many Internet sites, including a reconstituted pay-for-play version of Napster and the popular iTunes, offering legal downloads of copyrighted music for modest fees. However, pirated music remains widely available on the Internet and many people still consider the threat of legal action by the RIAA to be worth the risk of downloading and sharing copyrighted music.

VCRs: Giving the Viewer Control

The **video cassette recorder** (**VCR**) was a revolutionary invention because it gave consumers greater control over what they would watch and when. The VCR broke the broadcasters' control over viewers' behavior as had nothing before it.

Marketing of home videotape recorders began in 1975, when Sony introduced its Betamax VCR at an initial price of $1,300. Sony's monopoly ended in 1977 when Matsushita introduced its technically incompatible Video Home System (VHS). By offering longer recording times and lower prices, VHS gradually monopolized consumer VCR markets.

Sony had promoted Betamax's ability to record TV programs for later viewing, a practice called **time-shifting**, as its major feature. TV networks and major movie studios, whose products appeared on the networks, thought off-air recording was illegal pirating of their copyrighted products, not just a convenience to viewers. But in 1984, the Supreme Court ruled that viewers would not violate copyright law by recording programs broadcast over the air for their personal noncommercial use.

Hollywood distributors eventually recognized that the VCR provided a new market for their products. Renting and selling movies on cassette became a big business. Distributors soon discovered that consumers not only wanted recent releases, but also would rent or buy old movies, providing additional unexpected profits. Producers today make far more from the rental and sale of movies on tape and disc than from theater receipts.

At the height of their popularity at the turn of the century, more than 90 percent of TV homes had VCRs.

But despite its ubiquity, the VCR is in decline, succumbing to newer recording and playback technologies such as **digital video discs (DVDs)** and **digital video recorders (DVRs),** discussed later in this section.

Video camcorders are increasingly popular and prices continue to fall even as performance improves. Camcorders replaced 8-millimeter film cameras for shooting home movies. They produce pictures good enough that broadcast stations and networks encourage viewers to send in footage for possible use in newscasts, a practice that raises ethical questions among traditional journalists. Camcorders also contribute to entertainment programming. In the 1990s, ABC was among the first to use consumer-quality camcorder video, filling an hour of prime time with *America's Funniest Home Videos*, a show featuring amateur recordings of people doing goofy or embarrassing things. The popular web site YouTube most likely owes its existence to the popularity and declining prices of camcorders.

Most early consumer camcorders used the half-inch VHS format and several other analog formats, but in recent years the trend has been toward camcorders that record information digitally using small format tapes and disc-based media. The use of chips and digital storage media allow manufacturers to pack features into small camcorders that were once available only to professional videographers.

Relatively inexpensive but sophisticated video editing software allows consumers to create programs using techniques similar to professional video producers on their home computers. Such creative power in the hands of consumers was simply unimaginable two decades ago (see Exhibit 3.h).

Videodisc Players

One of the first attempts to move away from tape to disc-based consumer devices for video was the videodisc. In the early 1980s, both RCA and Magnavox marketed videodisc players for the home. Neither maker's machine could record video or play discs designed for the other. VCRs arrived slightly earlier, and they could, of course, both record and play back. The videodisc had limited appeal for most consumers, and in the mid-1980s both companies pulled out of the videodisc business.

Digital Video Disc

Introduced in the United States in March 1997, and sometimes called the digital versatile disc, the **digital video disc (DVD)** provided up to 25 times as much storage space as a conventional audio CD. Because of its huge capacity, DVD is an ideal medium for distributing full-length movies in wide-screen format with surround sound audio. Indeed, DVDs often store not only the

Exhibit 3.h

Camcorder Evolution

(A)

(B)

(C)

Early camcorders such as the Panasonic shown here **(A)** were heavy and bulky, but large enough to use a full-sized VHS cassette. Newer versions **(B)** are much smaller, and with easy-to-use editing programs, professional looking video production can be as easy as child's play **(C)**.

Sources: Photo (A) courtesy of Michael A. Mc Gregor; photo (B) © Jeff Greenberg/PhotoEdit; photo (C) © David Young-Wolff/PhotoEdit.

movie itself, but also outtakes, dialog in several languages, commentary by the producers, and other supplementary information not available to a theater audience.

The DVD got off to a slower start than some predicted. At the end of 1997, there were only about 350,000 DVD players in the United States. However, monthly DVD player sales exceeded 1 million units for the first time in September 2000. By 2008, DVD players could be found in approximately 84 percent of U.S. households, many of them in combo units housing a VCR as well.

PVR/DVR

Introduced in 1999, the **personal video recorder (PVR)** or **digital video recorder (DVR)** is a device

that records TV programming on a large computer hard drive. DVRs give viewers much greater control over when and how they view TV programming. The disc-based DVR is the logical replacement for the tape-based VCR.

Consumers can record enormous amounts of programming using their DVR, then control the playback using standard commands (pause, rewind, etc.). Viewers often use DVRs to record the program as they are watching. This allows viewers to pause the program, replay previous parts of the program, and skip over commercials even as the DVR continues to record the remainder of the program. DVR/PVR technology also allows users to program the machines to download programming to the hard drive at any time.

 Broadcasting: Changing Course

Development of cable and other delivery and recording options gave people their first real electronic media choices beyond traditional broadcasting; the impact of those choices soon became evident. Dramatic changes in the fortunes of the Big Three broadcast television networks provide one means of assessing such an impact. In the 1980s all three changed hands, and new networks appeared.

FCC Studies Networks—Again

From 1978 to 1980, the FCC conducted its third investigation of broadcasting networks (FCC, 1980b). The Justice Department had previously signed agreements with all three networks requiring them to loosen control over independent programmers and cease serving as sales representatives for their affiliates.

The FCC study concluded that FCC network rules developed during the previous two decades merely restricted legitimate business interaction between networks and their affiliates without actually protecting the stations from network dominance, or improving service to consumers. The study specifically blamed the FCC's own 1952 channel-allotment decision for the continued dominance of ABC, CBS, and NBC. Because few markets had more than three VHF channel allotments, any fourth network faced a hard time in obtaining a competitive line-up of affiliates.

New Player: Fox

This barrier did not deter Rupert Murdoch, an international publishing tycoon with immense resources (see Exhibit 3.i). He launched his Fox network in 1985, the first serious attempt at a fourth national television network since the demise of the DuMont Network in the 1950s.

Initial limitations on the Fox network's size actually worked to its advantage. Fox escaped the FCC's financial-interest rule that restricted ABC, CBS, and NBC in producing their own entertainment programs. This technicality gave Murdoch freedom to use his 20th Century Fox movie studio as a source of programs for the network. Fox made major investments in programming, especially sports programming. During the last week of October 1996, Fox's weekly ratings topped the other networks' for the first time in new season, prime-time, head-to-head competition.

Networks Change Hands

After more than three decades of stable ownership, all three established networks changed hands within a two-year period. This abrupt break with a 30-year tradition coincided with the retirement of long-time leaders, declining ratings in the face of cable competition, weak financial performance, and concern about increasing future multichannel competition.

ABC went first. In 1985, Capital Cities Communications (Cap Cities) announced that it would acquire American Broadcasting Companies, parent of the ABC network, in a friendly deal valued at more than $3.5 billion. The combined firm had to shed its cable interests and several TV stations to meet FCC ownership rules (discussed in Section 11.10)

Within weeks after the Cap Cities/ABC announcement, Ted Turner revealed plans for an unfriendly takeover of CBS. The network managed to thwart Turner by repurchasing nearly a fifth of its own stock from the public. The battle left CBS deeply in debt and torn by internal dissension. Laurence Tisch, chairperson of the entertainment and investment conglomerate, Loews, purchased nearly 25 percent of CBS's stock and became chief executive. Despite CBS's initial ratings success in the 1990s, however, Tisch seemed to tire of the broadcasting business and began considering potential buyers.

NBC's turn came in December 1985. Its parent company, RCA, weakened by years of inept management and huge losses from failed computer and videodisc ventures, welcomed a friendly buyout offer from General Electric. RCA and its NBC subsidiary sold for $6.28 billion.

And Change Again

For several years after the takeovers, news from all three networks went from bad to worse. Profits fell, audience shares continued to slip, and thousands of employees lost their jobs as the networks slimmed down to cut costs and compete more effectively. Competition from Fox, cable, and independent stations lessened the Big Three networks' once dominant role.

By the 1990s, however, stabilized audience levels, growing advertising expenditures, and the approaching demise of financial interest and syndication rules (see Section 8.2) had restored to television networking much of its former luster. Two new national networks, The WB and UPN, premiered in January 1995. And later that year two of the Big Three disclosed that they would once again change ownership.

On July 31 of that year, the Walt Disney Company announced that it would acquire Capital Cities/ABC in a deal valued at $19 billion, combining the most profitable TV network and its ESPN cable service with Disney's Hollywood film and television studios, its theme parks, and its Disney Channel.

The next day, CBS said it would abandon its nearly 70-year legacy of corporate independence by accepting

Exhibit 3.i

Rupert Murdoch: Media Magnate

In 1985, Australian publisher Rupert Murdoch became a U.S. citizen almost overnight to acquire Metromedia's six independent major-market television stations and one network affiliate for $2 billion. Having purchased half-ownership of Twentieth Century Fox Film Corporation in 1984 for $250 million, Murdoch acquired the remaining half in 1985 (after the Metromedia deal) for $325 million. He thus gained complete control over a company with an extensive film library (including such hits as *Cocoon* and *Aliens*) and rights to numerous television series (*L.A. Law* and *M*A*S*H*, for example). In 1985, Murdoch announced plans to form a new national television network, Fox Broadcasting Company.

In its first season, Fox averaged between 2 percent and 6 percent of the national audience. Fox programs typically

Source: Photo © Reuters/Corbis.

languished at the bottom of the Nielsen list, although some fared better.

The quality of the Fox affiliate line-up posed a problem. More than 120 stations carried Fox programming, but most were UHF, some only low-power outlets, and nearly all were the weakest stations in their markets. The network lost about $80 million in its first year of operation, but Murdoch marched on. He concentrated both on programming and on improving his affiliate line-up. Before long, Fox had become a major—and profitable—force in network competition, with some shows (*Married . . . With Children* and *The Simpsons*, for example) appearing on Nielsen's list of top-rated programs. With the help of 22 owned and operated stations reaching almost 35 percent of the nation's homes, Fox programming by 1997 often tied, and sometimes beat, at least one of the three older networks on several nights of the week.

In 1996, Murdoch launched the Fox News Channel (FNC), a cable network intended to compete with newcomer MSNBC as well as the firmly established CNN. FNC made immediate waves by hiring 23-year ABC News veteran Brit Hume, a recognized star. Murdoch also paid cable system operators large upfront fees to ensure FNC's access to a national audience. The same year, Murdoch kicked off FOX Sports Net, a group of regional sports networks.

During the late 1990s, News Corporation's subsidiaries produced some of the most popular entertainment available, including network TV programs such as *The Practice*, *The X-Files*, and *Ally McBeal*. Somewhat belatedly, Murdoch realized that other major media firms had moved ahead of News Corporation in capitalizing on the Internet, and he began taking corrective steps. He also continued expansion of News Corporation's nonmedia holdings. In 1998, he acquired the Los Angeles Dodgers and, for a record $1 billion, Great Britain's largest soccer franchise.

Never content to stand still, Murdoch increased his media holdings in 2007 by acquiring the Dow Jones company, publisher of the prestigious financial daily newspaper, *The Wall Street Journal*. Although some critics of the acquisition argued that Murdoch controlled too much media already, government officials reviewing the sale had no serious qualms about approving the deal.

a $5.4 billion buyout offer from the broadcasting and industrial conglomerate Westinghouse Electric Corporation. Together they would own 15 television stations and 39 radio stations, as well as program production and distribution facilities.

The original Big Three networks continued to lose prime-time audience share to cable, DBS, the newer broadcast networks, and the Internet during the second half of the 1990s. Rumors of sales or mergers continued, especially regarding General Electric's NBC. But it was CBS that, in 1999, announced it would merge with Viacom in a deal estimated to be worth about $36 billion. The merger placed another major TV network and a Hollywood production studio under combined corporate control. It also dramatically enhanced CBS's involvement in cable through Viacom's MTV Networks. Consequently, General Electric remained the only owner of an original Big Three network without a major

Hollywood production studio. That changed in May 2004, when GE merged with Vivendi Universal Entertainment to form NBC Universal. GE also increased its cable holdings by acquiring the USA Network and the Sci Fi Channel as part of the deal.

Throughout this period, questions arose about the continued viability of the newer broadcast networks, UPN and The WB. Unable to attract sufficient audiences to survive on their own, the parent companies of The WB and UPN combined forces in 2006 to create The CW Network, the only television network to target young adults aged 18–34.

Network Programming Strategies

The once-dominant television networks responded to the increased competition by changing their programming strategies. In search of a different image, ABC in the 1970s began to pay more attention to shows appealing to young, urban, adult viewers. Less concerned than other networks with traditional program balance, ABC leaned heavily on action, sex, and violence in much of its prime-time programming.

In the 1990s, Fox, The WB, and UPN tended to test the limits of taste in their effort to distinguish themselves from the well-established Big Three. The CW continues the trend in the 2000s. They were, and continue to be, criticized for this, as well as for targeting and sometimes pandering to minority urban audiences. CBS, on the other hand, found increased success by programming to an older audience.

Four additional broadcast networks target America's rapidly growing Hispanic population by providing programs in Spanish. Univision is king of the hill and the fifth-largest U.S. broadcast network, typically outperforming the other Spanish-language networks by a wide margin. Telemundo, owned by NBC Universal/General Electric, traditionally has been Univision's strongest competitor. In January 2002, Univision Communications, Inc. launched its second network, TeleFutura, a network targeting Spanish-speaking viewers who often watch English-language television. A fourth Spanish-language network, Azteca America, is a U.S. subsidiary of Mexican broadcaster TV Azteca, one of the two largest producers of Spanish language programming in the world.

Television in Transition

TV broadcasters face many challenges, but their toughest, the inauguration of an exclusively digital signal transmission system on February 17, 2009, is mostly behind them.

In 1996, the FCC adopted technical standards for **digital television (DTV)** after eight years of discussion. Because the old analog standard and the new digital standard were technically incompatible, the Commission devised a 10-year transition plan during which broadcasters would deliver both analog and digital signals. In this way, consumers could still watch television using their existing analog sets, and those who bought new digital sets could view the new digital signals as well. To accomplish this, the FCC assigned each television station a second channel to begin digital broadcasting. According to the Commission's original schedule, all analog broadcasting would cease on December 31, 2006. The spectrum no longer being used for analog broadcasting would then be auctioned for other uses.

Concerned that many citizens would not be able to afford new digital television sets before the 2006 deadline, Congress passed legislation instructing the FCC to allow a station to retain its analog channel until 85 percent of the station's viewers could receive its digital signal over the air, by satellite, or via cable. The 85 percent standard created little incentive for consumers to purchase, or retailers to offer, digital television receivers, and sales remained sluggish. Hoping to increase digital receiving ability, in August 2002, the FCC mandated that all TV receivers with screens 13-inches or larger, as well as interface devices such as VCRs and DVRs, manufactured after July 2007, must have DTV tuners. Still the transition languished.

Upset by the lack of progress and anxious to collect the billions of dollars that would be realized from auctioning the spectrum used for the second broadcast channel, Congress changed course again by abandoning the 85 percent reception requirement and setting a firm transition deadline for February 17, 2009. Concerned over the possibility that some consumers would still not have digital receivers, Congress also allocated $1.5 billion to fund a program that provided $40 vouchers to consumers to help pay for analog-to-digital converter boxes.

[*Author's note:* This book went to press before the conversion deadline of February 17, 2009. Thus, today's reader knows more about the success of the transition than we, the authors, knew as we were writing this! Based on what was supposed to happen, how well do you think the transition went?]

A continuing challenge facing TV broadcasting is competition with cable and DBS for high quality popular programming. Since the 2003–2004 TV season, nonbroadcast programming has attracted a larger share of the audience both in prime-time and all-day (24-hour). Each of the major TV broadcast networks still draws a larger prime-time audience than any single cable network, but the era of broadcast television's stranglehold on viewers is long past. With a declining audience, broadcast television is having greater difficulty paying for the increasing cost of quality programming.

Yet another issue confronting both radio and television broadcasters is the dramatic growth of two-way communication services offered by competitors. Traditional one-way delivery of programming, the fundamental business of broadcasters, is a mature market, while two-way interactivity is viewed as a major growth area in the new century. To benefit from the growth in two-way interactive services, broadcasters must develop new business models that take advantage of changes in technology and consumer preferences. For example, broadcasters already make programming available on their web sites, and sales of broadcast programming on various Internet sales sites are becoming increasingly popular. Finding ways for viewers to interact with their favorite programs may be broadcasting's next big challenge.

Radio in Transition

Despite intense competition, the number of radio stations continued to climb after 1970, dividing listeners into ever-smaller segments. FM station numbers rose to match AM by the 1990s as FM's audience appeal overcame AM's former attraction. FM's popularity with audiences grew, prompting the FCC to squeeze in more than 700 channel allotments to allow still more FM outlets.

Meanwhile, looser FCC technical oversight, combined with a growing number of stations on the air, had weakened AM's already-inferior signal quality. Under pressure from AM interests, the FCC adopted several technical and ownership rule changes in an attempt to halt AM's decline. But when the FCC approved AM stereo in 1982, it opted against specifying a technical standard, arguing that "the marketplace" could resolve that issue. Although five competing systems soon dwindled to two, the resulting confusion among manufacturers and consumers led to few stations adopting stereo by the early 1990s. Congress finally required the FCC to pick a standard in 1993, but this seemed a decade too late to help AM reverse its downward spiral.

The FCC also added 10 new channels to the top of the AM radio band. This expanded AM band, located between 1605 and 1705 kHz, to some extent reduced AM interference by moving selected AM stations to the new frequencies.

More important than technical improvements to radio in the 1990s were changes in the rules governing ownership. In the early 1990s, many owners operating only one station—especially an AM station—were destined for bankruptcy. In late 1992, the FCC loosened its rules to allow a single owner to operate two AM and two FM stations in markets with at least 15 stations. The Telecommunications Act of 1996 further lifted radio's fortunes by eliminating the national cap on radio station ownership, although restrictions on the number owned in a single market remain. As noted in Chapter 1, the effect of these changes was to slightly increase the number of radio stations on the air, but dramatically reduce the number of radio station owners.

Although much stronger and more profitable than in the early 1990s, the radio industry still faces challenges. One challenge will come from an increasing number of radio stations competing for the listening audience. In 2004, the FCC held the first open auction of FM radio frequencies and awarded construction permits for almost 260 new stations. Similar auctions are planned for the future. In addition, FM broadcasters face the addition of thousands of **low power FM (LPFM)** stations to the FM band, further fragmenting the radio audience. There also will be increased competition from audio services delivered by cable, DBS, the Internet, satellite radio, and self-programmed MP3 players.

One way in which radio broadcasters are meeting these challenges involves the conversion to digital transmission. As explained more fully in other sections of this book, digital signals can match the quality of CD sound and enhance revenues through the distribution of digital data. Digital stations also can provide several program streams simultaneously, thus reaching multiple target audiences at the same time.

Radio continues to reach about 94 percent of the U.S. population aged 12 and over each week, with men and women aged 25 to 54 listening more than other age groups. However, the time spent listening to radio has generally declined, from more than 22 hours weekly in 1997, to about 18.5 in 2008. Consolidation and economies of scale have allowed radio broadcasters to compete successfully in an increasingly fragmented marketplace, but radio faces even more intense competition both within the broadcasting fraternity and from new delivery technologies in the years ahead.

3.11 Sorting It Out

The development of new delivery systems and dramatic changes in older services has placed enormous pressures on manufacturers, broadcasters, competing systems, and policymakers. In the past two decades, even sympathetic trade publications used terms such as "merger mania" and "feeding frenzy" to describe the wild scramble among media industries trying to position themselves in an unpredictable environment in which plans made one month often seemed foolish the next.

These struggles have produced some interesting contrasts. Today, consumers have more media channels available than ever before. In the United States, there are more than 13,000 terrestrial radio stations, satellite radio subscription services, more than 3,750 TV stations (including more than 2,000 low-power stations), and upwards of 500 national and regional television programming networks delivered by cable, telephone systems, and direct broadcast satellite. And, of course, the Internet offers thousands of audio and video sources. The array of choices seems staggering.

Looking a little deeper, however, reveals that many of these program sources are actually owned or controlled by relatively few companies. Although there are more radio stations now than in the mid-1990s, there are fewer radio station owners. As noted earlier, only a handful of cable operators dominate the industry. The consolidation of media ownership, even as the diversity of media choices appears to increase, is an important trend to consider when attempting to understand what is happening. The Internet remains the only program distribution system not dominated by a relatively few media giants, yet many of the most popular web destinations are owned by a combination of Internet giants such as Google and Yahoo! and the same cast of characters that controls the more traditional media.

For Better or Worse?

Some observers argue that consumers win when there are more choices. It is hard to argue that consumers have not enjoyed an ever-growing menu of channels or that it is not to consumers' advantage that they can now get news, sports, and weather 24 hours a day rather than having to wait until the local broadcast station gets around to it. It is much easier for individuals today to find programming that suits their particular interests than at any time in history. But critics say this bonanza of choices is not without its flaws.

In the scramble to attract viewers in a crowded marketplace, critics say programming standards have suffered. Critics acknowledge that competition, even controlled competition among divisions of the same corporation, is desirable if it improves the diversity of media content and its quality. But they suggest the opposite has occurred. They say that although there are exceptions, much of what the new channels offer is lacking in innovation. If technology and competition only produce 100 new ways to view the same episode of the latest inane comedy that was a shameless copy of last year's inane comedy, what is accomplished? If they make possible a 24-hour *Championship Bean Bag Toss* channel, is this progress? What about repeating the same tawdry details of the celebrity *du jour's* indiscretions hour after hour simply because cable networks have plenty of time to fill and airing the dirty laundry of the rich and famous will attract a certain audience? The critics charge that competition for ratings in a fragmented media environment too often encourages producers to use violence, sex, and foul language to make their programming stand out in a crowded field.

Few Americans want to turn back the clock to the time before the arrival of cable, DBS, and the Internet but the changes have brought with them costs as well as benefits.

How Electronic Media Work

Technology largely determines both the potential and the limitations of electronic media. Where and how far signals will travel, how much information they can carry, their susceptibility to interference, and the need for technical regulation—all of these factors depend primarily on the signal's physical nature.

The digital revolution is well underway and transforming electronic communication. Americans still get most of their radio programming through analog broadcasts, but full-power television is now an all-digital system. This chapter focuses on the basics of the electromagnetic spectrum and provides discussion of both the analog and digital transmissions that comprise today's system of broadcasting. We begin with some basic concepts.

4.1 Electromagnetism

A basic natural force, **electromagnetism** makes possible a host of communication services. All forms of electromagnetic energy share three fundamental characteristics:

▶ They radiate outward from a source without benefit of any discernible physical vehicle.
▶ They travel at the same high velocity.
▶ They have the properties of waves.

Radio Waves

Visible waves that ruffle the water when a stone is dropped into a pond radiate outward from the point of disturbance caused by the stone. Unlike water waves, radio waves have the ability to travel through empty space, going in all directions without benefit of any conductor such as wire. This "wirelessness" gives broadcasting its most significant advantage over other ways of communicating. Radio waves can leap over oceans, span continents, penetrate buildings, pass through people, and go to the moon and back. Students learn in elementary school that the "speed of light" is about 186,000 miles per second. Radio shares this characteristic with light energy, as do all forms of electromagnetic radiation. This means a radio signal can circle the Earth more than seven times in one second. Radio waves also share two other characteristics with other forms of electromagnetic energy, *frequency* and *wavelength*.

Wave frequency refers to the fact that all electromagnetic energy comes from an oscillating (vibrating or alternating) source. The number of separate waves produced each second determines a particular wave's frequency. Differences in frequency determine the varied forms that electromagnetic energy assumes.

Wavelength is measured as the distance from the origin of one wave to the origin of the next. Waves that radiate out from the point of disturbance—the stone in the water or the radio transmitter—travel at a measurable velocity and have measurable frequencies and lengths.

Frequency Spectrum

A large number of frequencies visualized in numerical order constitute a spectrum. The keyboard of a piano represents a sound spectrum. Keys at the left produce low-pitch sounds (low frequencies). Frequency (heard as pitch) rises as the keys progress to the right end of the keyboard. Exhibit 4.a diagrams the electromagnetic spectrum and some of its uses.

As frequency goes up, the practical difficulty of using electromagnetic waves for communication also increases. Frequencies suitable for radio communication occur near the low end of the spectrum, the part with the lower frequencies and longer wavelengths.

Communication satellites employ the highest frequencies currently useful for broadcasting, mostly in the range of 3 gigahertz (3 *billion* oscillations per second) to 31 GHz. Even these frequencies are nowhere near as high as those of light.

As Exhibit 4.a illustrates, only a relatively small part of the electromagnetic spectrum is suitable for radio communication with the current technology. This makes the threat of interference among stations a serious problem, especially in the crowded AM and FM radio broadcast bands. The demand for more space for new services makes efficient spectrum management critical. New digital and compression technologies are, however, making possible more efficient use of the spectrum. The government also is turning over more of the usable spectrum to the private sector for commercial applications.

4.2 Radio and Audio Waves

A burst of radio energy consists of a series of waves radiating from an antenna, much like waves radiate outward on the surface of a pond when a rock falls into the water. Exhibit 4.b depicts basic wave motion and wave characteristics. From a smooth surface (zero in illustration (A) in Exhibit 4.b), the wave of energy goes to a maximum positive peak, back down through the zero point, to a maximum negative peak, then back to zero. This complete process is a **cycle**. If it takes a second to complete the cycle, the wave has a *frequency* of one cycle per second, or one *hertz* (Hz), named in honor of the German scientist Heinrich Hertz, who proved the existence of radio waves. If an electrical current in a wire goes through these cycles increasingly rapidly, the

Exhibit 4.a

Electromagnetic Spectrum Uses

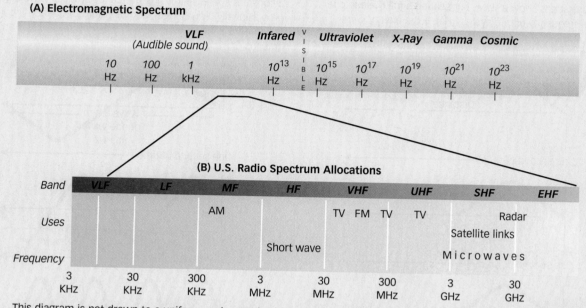

(A) Electromagnetic Spectrum

| | | VLF (Audible sound) | Infared | VISIBLE | Ultraviolet | X-Ray | Gamma | Cosmic |

| 10 Hz | 100 Hz | 1 kHz | | 10^{13} Hz | | 10^{15} Hz | 10^{17} Hz | 10^{19} Hz | 10^{21} Hz | 10^{23} Hz |

(B) U.S. Radio Spectrum Allocations

| Band | VLF | LF | MF | HF | VHF | UHF | SHF | EHF |

Uses: AM, TV FM TV, TV, Radar, Satellite links

Short wave

Microwaves

Frequency: 3 KHz, 30 KHz, 300 KHz, 3 MHz, 30 MHz, 300 MHz, 3 GHz, 30 GHz

This diagram is not drawn to a uniform scale—as the frequencies rise, the scale gets smaller (otherwise it would be impossible to show this much spectrum in a single diagram). The usable radio spectrum with which we are concerned **(B)** is but a small part of the larger electromagnetic spectrum **(A)**. The higher the frequencies, above the usable radio spectrum, the more potentially dangerous the output of electromagnetic radiation can become (infared and ultraviolet rays), though even these can be useful (X-rays).

The radio spectrum is divided into bands by international agreement. Low-frequency radio, a long-distance form of AM broadcasting, is used in Europe but not the United States. Though not shown here, virtually all usable spectrum space is assigned to some use (aviation, land mobile, ship-to-shore, CB radio, cellular telephone, satellite uplinks and downlinks, and military applications). There is no unallocated spectrum, meaning that new services have to move older services aside (and usually upward) in the spectrum. See Exhibit 4.g later in the chapter for more detail on broadcast service allocations.

Changes in frequency nomenclature avoid awkwardly long numbers. Thus, 1 kilohertz (kHz) = 1,000 Hz (hertz, or cycles per second); 1 megahertz (MHz) = 1,000 kHz; 1 gigahertz (GHz) = 1,000 MHz.

electrical energy eventually begins to leave the wire as electromagnetic radiation. If frequency increases enough, almost all of the electrical energy is radiated and the wire becomes a transmission antenna.

Notice that the distance the wave travels, its *wavelength*, depends on how fast the wave moves and the number of new waves created each second. Because the speed of radio energy is constant (about 186,000 miles a second), *frequency* alone determines wavelength. The more waves created each second, the shorter the wavelength. Either wavelength or frequency can be used to distinguish one radio wave from another. Initially, the common practice was to describe a radio wave in terms of its length, and many international broadcasting stations still use wavelength to describe their signals. Modern practice in the United States is to use

frequency. Bands of frequencies have names such as MF (medium frequency), HF (high frequency), and VHF (very high frequency). Exhibit 4.a shows the various frequency bands and their associated designations.

Because radio frequencies involve very large numbers of hertz, it is convenient to use abbreviations: (k)ilo instead of 1,000; (M/m)ega instead of 1,000,000; and (G)iga instead of 1,000,000,000. Thus, a radio wave with a frequency of 650,000 Hz becomes 650 kHz (650 X 1,000).

Radio waves lose their energy as they radiate outward, a phenomenon known as **attenuation**. How quickly a radio wave loses its energy depends on its frequency and the physical characteristics of obstacles encountered along the way. As a rule, high-frequency waves are more easily absorbed and reflected by objects

Exhibit 4.b

Wave–Motion Concepts

These illustrations show a wave completing a full cycle in one second, a frequency of one cycle (1 Hz). If the energy were traveling at the speed of light, the wavelength would be 186,000 miles. Because electromagnetic energy travels at a constant speed, increasing frequency reduces wavelength proportionally. Wavelength, and therefore frequency, is critical to the way a radio wave behaves once it leaves an antenna.

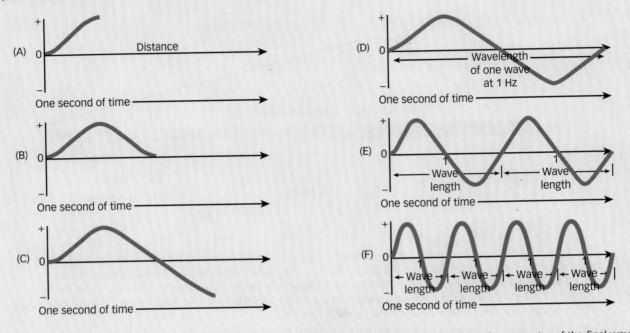

(A) Starting at zero, energy moves up to a positive peak. This represents one-quarter of a full cycle and one-quarter of the final wavelength. **(B)** Passing the peak, energy moves down to zero, the point at which the wave began. This represents one-half of a full cycle and one-half of the final wavelength. **(C)** Having gone to a positive peak, energy falls to a maximum negative value. This represents three-quarters of a full cycle and three-quarters of the final wavelength. **(D)** Starting at the negative peak, energy moves up to the zero point, the point of origin. This completes a full cycle, and the distance the wave travels is one full wavelength.
(E) The effect of doubling the frequency to 2 Hz is illustrated. Note that the wave now completes two cycles (2 Hz) in a period of one second. Doubling the frequency has caused the wavelength to be half as long, "only" 93,000 miles. **(F)** As frequency is doubled again (4 Hz), the wavelength is again halved, making it one-quarter as long as when the frequency was 1 Hz.

in their path. This was one reason Marconi tried to use the lowest possible frequencies during the infancy of wireless communication.

Scientists have known for years that X-rays and other electromagnetic waves with much higher frequencies than those used for radio communication can have hazardous effects on human tissue. In 1985, the FCC established guidelines for limiting radio frequency exposure, recognizing the possible health effects of non-ionizing radiation such as that produced by broadcast stations. The threat to public health created by broadcast stations is considered minimal, but stations must take precautions to protect employees whose duties require that they work near the transmitter and antenna system.

Radio Frequencies and Channels

Broadcasters know most people are not interested in terms like *kilohertz* and *megahertz* when they want to hear their favorite song or watch *American Idol*. Still, people must know where to tune their receivers, and usually that means remembering a number. Most stations simplify the number as much as possible and associate it with a promotional phrase. For example, an AM radio station featuring country and western songs may use the slogan "Real Country 66." The number 66 really means 660 kHz, the station's frequency. The same is true for FM radio stations. The government allots each AM and FM radio station a range of frequencies, or **channel**, in which to operate. The nominal frequency, such as 660 kHz, is the center of the frequency range in which the station can broadcast. Designation by channel rather than frequency is typical of TV stations and accurate because, for example, a station assigned to "Channel 6" operates within a band (a channel) of frequencies ranging from 82 to 88 MHz.

The center frequency of a radio station's channel is the **carrier wave**, so named because it conveys information (sound) superimposed on it, much as a road carries traffic. Although transmitters produce most of their energy at the carrier frequency, they also produce undesirable **harmonics**, weaker signals at multiples of the carrier frequency. Harmonic energy can interfere with services on higher frequencies if it is not suppressed before it reaches the antenna.

Audio Waves

Radio and audio (sound) waves differ in that sound waves propagate mechanically and require a medium, such as air or water, while radio waves propagate electromagnetically, allowing them to travel through a vacuum and many physical materials. The two kinds of waves also travel at vastly different speeds. Sound waves typically travel only about 1,100 feet per second. Otherwise, radio and audio waves share many characteristics such as frequency, amplitude, and attenuation. Objects in the propagation path may absorb, reflect, or refract both radio and sound waves. However, if a microphone converts a sound wave to an electrical current—a process known as **transduction**—the energy travels through the wire at the speed of light.

4.3 Information, Formats, and Modulation

The information transmitted by a station can be in either analog or digital format. Analog techniques have long been the standard in broadcasting, but in 2009 full-powered American TV stations shifted to entirely digital transmission and some radio stations have added one or more digital signals to their assigned channel.

Analog and Digital

Analog techniques impose a pattern on the carrier wave that resembles (is *analogous* to) the wave pattern of the original information (sound or picture). When, for example, radio waves carry words in analog form, they consist of **amplitude patterns** (loudness) and **frequency patterns** (tones or pitches). When a person speaks, air molecules form pressure waves in response to the amplitude/frequency patterns of the words. A microphone responds to air-pressure patterns,

transducing (converting) them into corresponding electrical patterns. The microphone outputs a sequence of waves with amplitude and frequency variations that approximate those of the sound-in-air patterns.

Ultimately, those **audio frequency (AF)** electrical variations are superimposed on a transmitter's **radio frequency (RF)** carrier, causing its oscillations to mimic the AF patterns. The result is a radio wave containing patterned variations analogous to the original sound. To recover the information, it is necessary to detect the sound by "stripping away" the RF carrier, leaving the wave pattern of the original sound.

Digital techniques, in contrast, first encode the wave patterns of the original sound or picture into a series of numerical values that represent the original wave patterns but are not analogous to them (see Section 4.8, p. 79). Digital encoding reduces all forms of information to numbers for transmission; everything takes on the same form. As long as the transmission system can accommodate the large stream of numbers pushed through it, the original form of the information makes no difference. To recover the information, it is necessary to decode the numerical information conveyed, converting it back to what it originally represented, whether it is audio, video, or data. Converting information to digital form prior to modulation is beneficial because of the advantages digital provides during storage and transmission.

AM vs. FM

Modulation refers to ways of imposing meaningful variations on a transmitter's carrier wave to enable it to carry information. Broadcasting transmitters use either amplitude or frequency modulation. Exhibit 4.c shows how they work. Conventional analog television used AM for picture signals and FM for sound. Today's digital TV system uses a complex form of AM called **8-VSB** (vestigial sideband modulation with eight discrete amplitude levels). See Section 4.12 for additional information about digital TV transmission.

Interference caused by lighting or electrical machinery has more effect on the amplitude of a radio wave than on its frequency. This is why such interference causes listeners to hear **static** on AM stations, but not on FM stations. Overlapping signals from more distant stations on the same channel also easily distort AM radio signals. Although DTV (digital television) uses AM, the information is in digital rather than analog format and contains error-correcting coding to reduce the effects of interference. A portion of the data stream used to broadcast DTV consists not of picture and sound information, but of special digital codes that help the receiving set minimize the effects of transmission errors and interference.

Exhibit 4.c

How AM and FM Differ

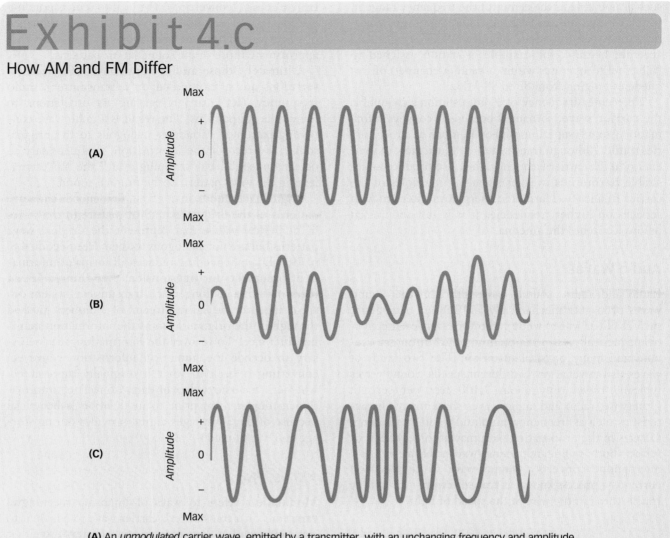

(A) An *unmodulated* carrier wave, emitted by a transmitter, with an unchanging frequency and amplitude pattern. **(B)** An AM carrier wave, modulated by a pattern of *amplitude* changes representing information. **(C)** An FM carrier wave, modulated by a pattern of *frequency* changes representing the same information.

Source: From *Signals: The Telephone and Beyond* by John R. Pierce. Copyright © 1981 by Henry Holt & Company. Used with permission.

Sidebands

A specific radio frequency, not a channel or band of frequencies, identifies a station's carrier wave. For example, an AM station at 600 on the dial has a carrier wave of 600 kHz (600,000 cycles per second). If the station transmits no audio, the only energy radiated is the 600 kHz carrier wave. When the station begins transmitting sound, energy radiates not only on the carrier frequency but also on **sideband** frequencies both above and below the carrier. For AM stations, the audio frequencies being broadcast determine the width of the sidebands. Here is where AM radio has a problem. Because each AM channel is 10 kHz wide, the upper and lower sidebands are each 5 kHz. Popular music contains audio frequencies well above 5,000 Hz, the limit at which the sidebands

start spilling over into other AM stations' channels. AM stations have the unpleasant option of either broadcasting the music's full audio range and risking interference or filtering out the music's higher frequencies, making it sound muffled. To avoid interference, AM broadcasters must settle for the latter option.

The sidebands above and below the carrier frequency are identical, and, technically, no "information" is lost if a station transmits only one sideband. However, this is not always an attractive solution because a **single-sideband (SSB)** signal requires a special, more expensive receiver.

But some services do economize on spectrum usage by suppressing one sideband, thus allowing for more channels. In both analog and digital TV transmission, one TV signal sideband is largely suppressed. Together with compression technologies (see Section 4.8, p.81), single-sideband transmission make it much more spectrum-efficient.

Bandwidth

Just as the quantity of water a pipe delivers depends on the pipe's diameter, the channel's bandwidth limits the capacity of a communication system. The bandwidth needed depends on the application. A taxi dispatch service needs little bandwidth because simple intelligibility, not sound quality, is necessary. Video is an infamous "spectrum hog" requiring much more bandwidth than audio. Bandwidth becomes critical when it is necessary to transmit lots of information "right now," in real time.

Government policy usually dictates providing the minimum bandwidth required to achieve a particular goal at the time of allocation. Allocating AM stations 10 kHz channels made sense at the birth of broadcasting because the goal was to license the maximum number of stations, not broadcast high-fidelity audio. But today, broadcasters face competing program distributors with much larger "pipes." Finding ways to push more product down the same channel is a critical concern.

Multiplexing and Compression

Multiplexing is a process that conserves resources by combining related functions into a single entity. Multiplex theaters, for example, conserve money by offering several movies simultaneously within the same building. Electronic media use several kinds of multiplexing. One form of multiplexing involves modulating two or more separate carriers in the same channel, a process known as **frequency division multiplexing**.

In the 1990s, **compression**, a technique popular in the computer industry, became extremely important to all communication industries struggling with bandwidth limitations. Rather than adding new information to the channel, compression seeks to eliminate all information not essential to the communication task being undertaken. Section 4.8, p. 81, explains compression in greater detail.

4.4 Wave Propagation

Modulated signals are piped from a transmitter to an antenna, the physical structure from which signals radiate into surrounding space. The traveling of signals outward from the antenna is called **propagation**.

Coverage Contours

In theory, an omnidirectional (all-directional) antenna would propagate signals over a circular coverage area.

In practice, coverage patterns often assume uneven shapes. Physical objects in the transmission path, interference from electrical machinery and other stations, and even the time of day can affect propagation distances and patterns. The sun also influences propagation. **Sunspots**, blotches on the sun's surface that increase and decrease over an 11-year cycle, dramatically influence some radio frequencies.

The higher the frequency of waves, the more the atmosphere absorbs their energy and, therefore, the shorter the distance they can travel. Objects wider than a wave's length tend to block propagation. VHF, UHF, and still higher frequency waves (used for microwave relays and satellites) have such short lengths that relatively small objects can interfere with their propagation. Even raindrops can block the shortest waves. Digital television can suffer from multipath signal interference caused by delayed reflected waves. If not corrected by the television receiver, multipath interference can result in the complete loss of DTV reception or, in less severe cases, the pixelization or temporary freezing of the picture.

Because many variables affect wave propagation, broadcasters define their coverage areas in terms of reception probability. Ideally, engineers measure the signal strength at various distances from the transmitting antenna. They then plot these measurements on a map and draw lines connecting those having a minimal strength level, as defined by the FCC. The result is a map showing the station's **coverage contour**. More often, engineers use FCC-approved formulas for calculating the coverage contour rather than determining it by taking measurements.

Questions about coverage contours have become more common with the arrival of DTV. In most respects, propagation of digital TV signals is very similar to analog signals, although digital signals are more affected by physical impediments like hills and buildings. DTV brings with it a change in the way information is formatted and compressed for transmission and, for some broadcasters, a move from a VHF to a UHF channel. Based on field-testing and theory, the FCC established channel-allotment tables, transmitter power levels, and antenna configurations to ensure that most broadcasters achieve essentially the same coverage with DTV that they had with analog transmission. However, unlike an analog TV signal, where various forms of interference may cause only picture degradation, interference to a transmitted digital signal may translate to no picture at all. The condition of receiving either an excellent picture or none at all is known as the **cliff effect**.

Frequency-related propagation differences divide waves into three types: direct, ground, and sky. Each type has advantages and disadvantages that must be considered in matching frequency bands with service needs.

Exhibit 4.d

Ground-, Sky-, and Direct-Wave Propagation

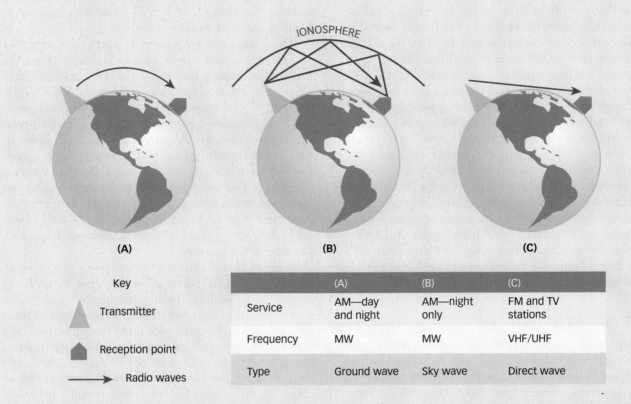

	(A)	(B)	(C)
Service	AM—day and night	AM—night only	FM and TV stations
Frequency	MW	MW	VHF/UHF
Type	Ground wave	Sky wave	Direct wave

Key

Transmitter

Reception point

Radio waves

Because of their location in the spectrum, radio and TV services have different signal propagation paths.

AM radio is most complicated because its *medium-frequency* spectrum location gives it two different means of wave propagation: ground waves in the daytime **(A),** and both ground and sky waves at night. Ground waves travel along the surface of the Earth. Given good soil conductivity and sufficient power, ground waves outdistance direct waves, reaching well beyond the horizon. As discussed in the text, sky waves **(B)** bend back toward the Earth when they encounter the ionospheric layer of the atmosphere at night. Sky waves may bounce off the Earth and back to the ionosphere several times, and different frequencies are affected at different times of the day

and night. In short, they are unpredictable and thus cause more interference than they provide useful service. Because of potential sky-wave interference, some AM stations leave the air at night. *Shortwave* international services make use of sky waves, changing frequencies to best match predicted ionospheric effects on sky waves.

FM radio and *TV stations*, because of their *VHF* and *UHF* spectrum location, are subject only to direct line-of-sight wave propagation at any time of day or night **(C)**. These waves are sent out from elements on top of antenna towers and directed downward toward the reception area, blocking off radiation that would otherwise scatter upward and out into space. The "horizon" limit, of course, depends heavily on local terrain.

Direct Waves

At FM radio and TV frequencies in the VHF and UHF bands, waves follow a line-of-sight path. They are called **direct waves** because they travel directly from transmitter antenna to receiver antenna, reaching only about as far as the horizon, as shown in Exhibit 4.d. Line-of-sight distance to the horizon from a 1,000-foot-high transmitting antenna propagating over a flat surface reaches about 32 miles. The signal does not

cease abruptly, but after reaching the horizon fades rapidly.

Engineers locate direct-wave antennas as high as possible to extend the apparent horizon. Raising the height of the receiving antenna also extends the horizon limit.

Ground Waves

AM radio broadcast stations in the United States use medium-frequency (MF) waves. Waves in the MF band travel as **ground waves**, propagated through and along the surface of the Earth. They can follow the Earth's curvature beyond the horizon, as shown in Exhibit 4.d.

Ground waves can cover wider areas than direct waves. In practice, however, a ground wave's useful coverage area depends on several variables, notably **soil conductivity**—the degree to which soil resists passage of radio waves—which varies according to dampness and soil composition. Soil with a high moisture content will conduct ground waves much better than dry, sandy soil. The area in which the ground wave provides a signal free of objectionable interference and fading defines an AM station's coverage contour.

Sky Waves

Most radio waves that radiate upward dissipate their energy in space. However, waves in the medium-frequency band (AM radio) and the high-frequency band (shortwave radio) when radiated upward tend to bend back at an angle toward the Earth when they encounter the ionosphere (See Exhibit 4.d).

The ionosphere consists of several atmospheric layers located from about 40 to 600 miles above the Earth's surface. Bombarded by high-energy radiation from the sun, these layers take on special electrical properties, causing **refraction** (a gradual type of reflection, or bending back) of AM and short-wave signals. Refracted waves are called **sky waves**.

Sky waves can produce some interesting situations. For example, listeners in Florida may hear a Chicago radio station that listeners in St. Louis cannot, in spite of St. Louis being closer to the station's transmitting antenna. St. Louis is in the **skip zone**, the area between where the Chicago station's ground wave ends and its sky wave returns to Earth.

Under the right frequency, power, and ionospheric conditions, returning sky waves bounce off the surface of the Earth, travel back to the ionosphere, bend back again, and so on. Following the Earth's curvature, they can travel thousands of miles, as depicted in Exhibit 4.d.

The ionosphere's effectiveness varies with time of day and frequency. AM broadcast stations produce sky waves only at night. Sky waves can extend a station's coverage area, but often they have an opposite effect. Sky waves from stations on the same carrier frequency may arrive simultaneously, or sky waves from a distant station may compete with ground waves from a local station. The resulting interference effectively decreases the coverage of all stations on that frequency.

Shortwave stations, however, are not limited to using a single carrier frequency as are AM broadcasting stations. They can switch frequency several times throughout the day to take continuous advantage of the ionosphere's changing refractive abilities. These stations must be careful to tell listeners where to tune when they change frequencies. Shortwave broadcast stations estimate propagation conditions weeks or months in advance and publish the frequencies they plan to use. They also announce, on-air, the new frequency to which they are moving.

Antennas

Whichever type of propagation may be involved, antennas are needed, both to transmit signals and to receive them. Antenna size and location can have a critical influence on the efficiency of transmission and reception.

Small antennas built into receivers can pick up strong AM and FM signals. The higher the frequency, however, the more elusive the signal and the more essential an efficient antenna becomes—for radio, perhaps an outdoor antenna. In the case of digital TV signals, unless the receiver is in relatively close proximity to the transmitting antenna (10–15 miles) an outdoor directional antenna—possibly with a rotor to allow change in its orientation—may be necessary, even in strong signal areas.

Transmitting antennas (see Exhibit 4.e) vary in size because for them to work efficiently their length must be mathematically related to the length of the waves they radiate. For example, channel 2 (VHF) TV transmitters radiate 20-foot waves, but channel 48 (UHF) waves are less than 2 feet long.

Directional Propagation

A flashlight or an auto headlight focuses light into a beam. A reflector creates the beam by redirecting light rays that would otherwise radiate backward or sideways, thus reinforcing the rays that go in a forward direction. Transmitting antennas can also be designed for **directional propagation**—beaming reinforced signals in a desired direction. Directional propagation has value both for increasing signal strength in a desired direction and for preventing interference between stations.

Concentrating radio waves by means of directional propagation increases their strength. This increase, called **antenna gain**, can be many-thousandfold. Gain, however, is not always easily achieved. Concentrating radio waves in a particular direction sometimes requires large or complex antenna designs. AM radio stations need physically large antennas because of their long carrier waves. A directional system requires at least two tall towers, often more, so a directional AM broadcast antenna requires more land and is expensive. AM stations need directional antennas more than FM and TV stations, to reduce sky-wave interference.

Receiving antennas are also directional; this is easily demonstrated by turning a portable AM radio in different directions. Signals from a given station come in

Exhibit 4.e

Transmitting Antennas

(A)   (B)   (C)

Antennas differ depending on the service for which they are built.

(A) AM antennas use the entire steel tower as a radiating element. For efficient propagation, the height of this tower must equal one-quarter the length of the waves it radiates. Propagation of ground waves depends on soil conductivity, among other things. Heavy copper ground cables (not shown) are buried in trenches radiating from the tower base to ensure good ground contact. **(B)** Shortwave antennas are very complex. Each transmitting site has many antennas to feed different frequency signals, along with other suspended wires that act as reflectors to beam signals in specific directions to reach designated overseas target areas. The Voice of America uses scores of antennas like this one. **(C)** FM and TV broadcasters often mount transmitting antennas atop tall buildings and mountains, providing the height needed for effective signal propagation without the expense of building supporting towers.

Sources: Photo (A) © David Frazier/Corbis; photo (B) courtesy of Voice of America, Washington, DC; photo (C) © Joel Gordon.

most strongly when the radio's built-in antenna points in the direction of that station's transmitter. Outdoor antennas used for TV (and FM radio) reception also display directional characteristics. Reception of signals arriving from several directions often requires antennas mounted on rotatable masts.

4.5 Mutual Interference

Mutual interference between stations limits the number of stations that can be licensed to operate in any particular community.

Co-Channel Stations

The primary troublemaker, **co-channel interference**, comes from mutual interference between stations operating on the same frequency. Co-channel stations must be located far enough apart geographically to prevent their coverage contours from overlapping. Separation rules must take into account that signals too weak for useful reception by an audience may nevertheless cause co-channel interference. A station's **interference zone** therefore extends far beyond its service area.

In keeping with U.S. policy of allowing as many local communities as possible to have their own stations, the FCC makes co-channel separation rules as liberal as possible. Changing daytime versus nighttime coverage areas of AM stations, caused by sky-wave propagation at night, complicates the problem. The FCC seeks to prevent such sky-wave interference by requiring many AM stations to sign off or use lower power at night. Relocating some stations in the expanded AM band (see Section 4.6, p. 75) will help reduce these interference problems.

Adjacent-Channel Stations

Engineers design TV and radio receivers to be selective, to tune in one station and reject those operating on different frequencies or channels. But building highly selective receivers would be expensive, so set manufacturers balance *selectivity* against cost. The result is that receivers sometimes pass not only the desired signal, but also those of strong stations on adjacent channels, those just above and below the desired station. To reduce **adjacent-channel interference** the FCC avoids placing analog stations on adjacent channels in the same market.

Maximum-power FM stations using antennas high above the ground must be about 180 miles apart to avoid co-channel interference and 150 miles apart to prevent adjacent-channel interference. Because of sky-wave propagation, AM radio stations can suffer both co-channel and adjacent-channel interference from stations many hundreds of miles away.

Adjacent-channel interference was seldom a problem in the analog TV environment, but became a concern as more digital TV (DTV) stations went on the air. During the transition to digital, many markets had many more TV signals on the air than were allowed previously. Digital and analog signals differ greatly, so an analog TV tuned to an analog station did not notice a DTV station on a nearby channel. A strong digital signal on an adjacent channel, however, sometimes overpowered the analog set's selectivity circuits and created interference. The FCC spaced digital and analog stations to avoid mutual interference, but some broadcasters experienced some adjacent-channel analog/digital interference during the transition period. The digital TV system in use today is generally less susceptible to interference than our previous analog TV system, allowing some relaxation of channel spacing requirements.

4.6 AM Stations

As a broadcast station class name, AM is somewhat misleading because the term means simply **amplitude modulation**, and many services other than AM radio broadcasting use such modulation.

Band and Channels

For years the government assigned AM broadcast stations to frequencies ranging from 535 to 1,605 kHz. This band provided 1,070 kHz of spectrum in which to assign stations. Each AM station received a channel 10 kHz wide, so there were 107 channels (1,070 divided by 10) on which AM stations could operate. In 1988, an international agreement expanded the U.S. AM broadcast band to 1,705 kHz. This expansion made available 10 new regional channels.

Rather than adding new stations in this expanded band, the FCC decided to use the space to reduce AM broadcast station interference by moving existing stations. Using a complex formula, the FCC in 1997 identified 88 AM stations for "migration" to the new frequencies. Stations allowed to move had five years in which to do so, and during that period, could transmit on both their old and new frequencies. This helped listeners follow these stations up the band. AM stations will still operate in a restrictive 10 kHz channel, but spreading them out has somewhat reduced co-channel and adjacent-channel interference. In early 2008, 68 stations were operating in the extended AM band.

Channel and Station Classes

The FCC has a rather complex method of categorizing AM stations according to the type of channel assigned and their class. There are three types of channels: clear, regional, and local. Clear channels provide stations assigned to them a considerable degree of freedom from interference, allowing them to cover large geographical areas. Regional channels cover smaller areas, and local channels typically serve only a single community.

There are four classes of AM stations, ranging from Class A to Class D. Class A stations have the most "privileges" in terms of maximum transmitting power and permissible hours of operation, while Class D stations have the least. There is considerable overlap, and the FCC rules devote several paragraphs to explaining the differences (see 47 CFR 73.21). Exhibit 4.f outlines the method of categorizing AM stations in greater detail.

Transmission

High AM radio transmitter power improves efficiency of both ground-wave and sky-wave propagation, providing greater coverage and overcoming interference. Daytime power authorizations for domestic U.S. AM broadcasting range from 250 watts to a maximum of 50,000 watts, as indicated in Exhibit 4.f. AM radio stations have wavelengths about 550 to 1,800 feet long, depending on their exact carrier frequency. Because antennas at least a quarter-wave long are necessary, AM stations must use vertical steel towers several hundred feet tall to radiate their signals.

In choosing sites for AM antennas, engineers look for good soil conductivity, freedom from surrounding sources of electrical interference, and distance from aircraft flight paths. Ground waves are critical to the coverage provided by AM stations, so the station's antenna system must include an effective ground system. Much of an AM radio station's antenna consists of many buried copper wires radiating from the base of the vertical steel tower. Engineers often have trouble convincing station owners that the expensive buried parts are no less important than the tower above ground.

Exhibit 4.f

AM Radio Station Classification Structure

AM Radio Stations and Channel Classes				
Station Class	Channel Class	Number Channels in Class	Power Range (kW)	Percentage in Each Channel Class
A, B, D	Clear	60	.25–50	34
B, D	Regional	51	.25–50	44
C	Local	6	.25–1	22

AM Radio Stations by Station Class		
Station Class	Number of Stations*	Percentage of Total Stations†
A	74	2
B	1,773	37
C	1,045	22
D	1,938	40

*Data provided by FCC. The numbers vary as new stations sign on and others leave the air.
†Percentages do not add up to 100 percent because of rounding.

Class A stations operate unlimited schedules only on clear channels with powers ranging from 10 to 50 kW. Class A stations are protected from other stations on the same or adjacent channels.

Class B stations operate unlimited schedules on clear and regional channels with powers ranging from .25 to 50 kW. Class B stations in the extended AM band (1,605–1,705 kHz) operate with a maximum power of 10 kW.

Class C stations operate unlimited schedules only on local channels with powers ranging from .25 to 1 kW.

Class D stations operate either daytime, limited time, or unlimited time with nighttime power less than .25 kW. Daytime powers range from .25 to 50 kW. Nighttime operations of Class D stations are not protected from interference, and Class D stations must protect all Class A and Class B stations from nighttime interference.

Low-power AM signals can be fed into building power lines or steam pipes, which serve as distribution grids. The signals radiate for a short distance into the space surrounding these conductors, usually enough to cover the interior of the building. Services using this propagation method are called **carrier-current stations**. Colleges and universities often use carrier-current stations, which require no licensing. **Travelers Information Service (TIS)** is a licensed application of carrier-current sometimes used to help motorists navigate in congested areas, such as busy airports. Roadside signs tell drivers where to tune their AM radios to get helpful information.

AM Stereo

Because of its narrower channel, AM took longer to develop stereo than did FM. AM stereo uses a **matrixmode** that melds left and right channels in a way somewhat similar to the two channels of FM stereo, but without the full high-fidelity benefit. The few AM stereo stations in existence in the early 1990s had mostly chosen the Motorola *C-QUAM* standard finally adopted by the FCC in 1993. Early excitement regarding AM stereo had largely dissipated by the mid-1990s. Few listeners were aware of its existence, and programming on many AM stations benefited little from being offered in stereo. In 2008, about 300 AM analog stations were broadcasting in stereo. Today, AM digital radio broadcasts can also provide one stereo stream (see Section 4.9, p. 82).

Shortwave AM

Shortwave broadcasting, which also uses AM, has been allocated parts of the high-frequency (HF) band between 6 and 25 MHz. The ionosphere refracts waves in this band both day and night, enabling round-the-clock coverage in target zones thousands of miles away from the originating transmitter.

The U.S. public makes little use of shortwave broadcasting. However, some foreign countries use short waves extensively for domestic services. A few privately operated American HF stations, mostly evangelistic religious outlets, broadcast to foreign audiences. Short waves are used extensively for international diplomacy.

4.7 FM Stations

FM's inherently superior quality has enabled it to forge ahead of AM in numbers of both listeners and stations.

Band and Channels

U.S. frequency-modulation broadcasting occupies a 20 MHz block of frequencies running from 88 to 108 MHz in the VHF band. This 20 MHz block allows for 100 FM channels of 200 kHz (.2 MHz) width. Exhibit 4.g

shows their spectrum location in relation to other broadcast channels.

The FCC numbers FM channels 201 to 300, but licensees prefer to identify their stations by their mid-channel frequency (in megahertz) rather than by channel number (88.1 for channel 201, 88.3 for channel 202, and so on). The lowest 20 FM channels (88.1 to 91.9 MHz) are reserved for noncommercial use. The analog FM channel width of 200 kHz is generous—20 times the width of the AM channel.

Transmission

The coverage area of an FM station depends on the station's power, the height of the transmitting and receiving

Exhibit 4.g

Summary of Broadcast Channel Specifications

Service	AM Radio	FM Radio	Digital Television
Frequencies	535–1705 kHz (MF band)	88–108 MHz (VHF band)	54–72 Mhz (channels 2–4) 76–88 MHz (channels 5 and 6) 174–216 MHz (channels 7–13) (VHF band) 470–608 MHz (channels 14–36) 614–698 MHz (channels 38–51) (UHF band)
Total channels	117	100	12 VHF 37 UHF
Bandwidth (signal station)	10 kHz	200 kHz (equivalent to 20 AM channels)	6,000 kHz (equivalent to 600 AM or 30 FM Channels)
Classes of stations and power limits	Class A 10–50 kW Class B .25–50 kW Class C .25–1 kW Class D <.25–50 kW	A .1–6 kW; about 15 miles B >6–50 kW; about 30 miles C 25–100 kW; about 60 miles	Up to 1,000 kW
Educational allocation	None	88–92 MHz (20 channels)	383 specific station assignments
Factors affecting station coverage and signal quality	Frequency Power Soil conductivity Day/night (sky wave) Thunderstorms Many directional antennas	Antenna height Power (to a degree) Unlimited time Few directional antennas High fidelity Little static Line-of-sight range	Antenna height Frequency Power Rigid spacing Line-of-site range Unlimited time Local noise enviornment

This table pulls together information scattered throughout the text to allow comparison of the major channel specifications of radio and TV services. Note especially the allocation of TV channels into five separate frequency allotments in two different bands. DTV will use only channels 2–51. The spectrum occupied by UHF channels 52–69 has been reassigned to other services.

antennas above the surrounding terrain, and the extent to which obtrusive terrain features or buildings block wave paths. In any event, FM uses direct waves, which reach only to the horizon.

Once determined by these factors, an FM station's coverage remains stable, day and night. This stability is one reason the FCC had an easier time preventing FM interference than it did AM interference.

The FCC divides the country into geographic zones and FM stations into three groups according to coverage area: Classes A, B, and C, defined by power, antenna height, and zone. Classes B and C are further subdivided, but generally the maximum coverage areas for FM stations by class are as follows: Class A about 15 miles; Class B about 40 miles; Class C about 60 miles. The maximum power/height combination permits 100,000 watts (twice the maximum AM station power) and a 600-meter (almost 2,000-foot) antenna elevation.

In January 2000, the FCC, at the urging of then Chairman William Kennard, created two new classes of noncommercial **low power FM (LPFM)** stations. The FCC established a new LP100 class station operating with a maximum power of 100 watts and an antenna no higher than 30 meters (98.4 feet) to provide an approximate service radius of 3.5 miles. A second class, called LP10, provides for stations operating with 1 to 10 watts and antennas no higher than 30 meters to serve a one or two mile area around the station.

Frequencies used for FM broadcasting are much higher than those of AM stations, so they have proportionally shorter wavelengths and much smaller antennas. FM stations use tall towers only to place their small antennas high above the ground, not to actually radiate the signal, as do the towers of AM stations. FM stations take advantage of this by mounting their antennas on mountains or tall buildings. FM stations depend on direct, not ground, waves to provide primary coverage and do not need expensive buried radial systems. Finally, the small size of FM antennas allows engineers to design radiating systems that exhibit **antenna gain**. Using an FM antenna with gain increases the station's **effective radiated power (ERP)**, as does boosting transmitter power, but over time it is much less expensive than a larger transmitter's monthly electric bill.

Reception

FM receivers with quality loudspeakers can reproduce the audio frequencies essential for high-fidelity sound. In addition, FM radio has greater **dynamic range** (the loudness difference between the weakest and strongest sounds) than does AM, making for more realistic reproduction of music.

FM's inherent immunity to static and interference gives FM radio a significant quality advantage over AM radio. FM's static-free reception is particularly noticeable in the southern part of the country, where subtropical storms cause much natural interference. FM also has an advantage in large cities, where concentrations of electrical machinery and appliances cause static. Large buildings in urban areas can, however, create reception problems for FM stations because they reflect FM radio's VHF signals.

FM Stereo

The left and right channel audio off stereo tapes, audio file servers, and CDs pass through the FM radio station's equipment as entirely separate signals until they reach the station's stereo generator, a subsystem of the transmitter. Here the two audio channels combine with supersonic (above the range of human hearing) pilot and subcarrier signals. The result is a composite signal that modulates the station's carrier wave. FM receivers designed to reproduce stereo audio use the subcarrier and pilot signals to separate the two audio channels once again. Just as it is possible to watch color TV signals on a monochrome (black-and-white) set, a monaural FM radio reproduces the audio in full fidelity, minus the separation between audio channels required for stereophonic effect.

Subsidiary Communications Service (SCS)

FM stations can also **multiplex** additional information on an unused portion of their frequency channel to provide a nonbroadcast service that can be received using special equipment. This multiplexed analog signal most frequently provides background ("elevator") music to stores and offices, or a reading service for the blind. SCS can accommodate a wide range of other applications, including distribution of market and financial data, detailed weather reports, and traffic information. SCS may also provide station promotional information (such as music format, call letters, or location) in a visual format on special receivers. Such multiplexed signals may also be used in digital audio broadcasting, as discussed in Section 4.9 on p. 82.

After long debate, both broadcasters and consumer electronics manufacturers, working through an industry group, the National Radio Systems Committee (NRSC), agreed on technical standards for a **radio broadcast data system (RBDS)**, transmitted on an analog FM station's subcarrier for receivers equipped with a special microchip. Stations provide promotional information (such as song title, call letters, or location) in a visual format on special receivers.

RBDS transmits a digital signal—an ad slogan, identification of the station's format, or other information—that can be displayed in a special receiver panel. The system also makes it possible for an RBDS-equipped car to tune stations by format, with the receiver jumping to a different but more powerful signal when the tuned signal becomes weak. And in an emergency situation (e.g., an approaching tornado), RBDS can be used to turn on a receiver to deliver a warning message.

4.8 Digital Signal Processing

Electronic communications systems increasingly speak a digital language. Although radio broadcasting continues to operate mainly in the analog world, most audio and video recording and transmission have moved into the digital domain. Broadcast television, direct broadcast satellites, DVDs, MP3 players, and the Internet are all anchored in the digital realm. Analog processing imitates nature. For example, the continuously rotating hands of a clock imitate the movement of shadows on a sundial. A digital timepiece, however, tells time directly in numbers, jumping from one number to the next. Digital signals bear no resemblance to natural forms because they consist entirely of digits—simple strings of numbers.

Sampling

Digital processing can be likened to cutting up a sound wave (the analog signal) into thousands of tiny pieces, selecting every other piece, assigning a number to each of those pieces representing its amplitude, transmitting the numbers, and then using the numbers to reassemble the wave with every other piece missing. If the pieces are tiny enough, the absence of the missing pieces will not be noticed.

Cutting up an original analog signal and leaving out some pieces is done by high-speed sampling, using a process known as binary **pulse-code modulation (PCM)**. Each sample consists of a short pulse of energy, proportional in strength to the original signal's amplitude at that point. Each energy pulse is then **quantized**—labeled with a number representing the level of momentary amplitude from the analog wave. The quantized sample is then converted to binary form.

Encoding

The numbers attached to each sample are encoded by converting them from the decimal number system (0, 1, 2, 3 . . . 9) into the binary (two-part) number system (0 and 1 only). Computers have made the binary system familiar, along with the term **bit**, which stands for **binary digit**. Numbers expressed in binary digits consist of nothing more than strings composed of only two digits. They are conventionally expressed as "zero" and "one" but can also be regarded as equivalent to "on" and "off."

As an example, the output of a microphone consists of an analog signal, continuously varying electrical amplitude (i.e., voltage). A digital processor samples this continuous amplitude pattern, breaking it down into a series of small, discrete amplitude values. Each value is quantized by assigning it a number representing its level of momentary amplitude that is then encoded to binary form. The digitized output consists of a string of "power-off" signals (zeros) and "power-on" signals (ones). Exhibit 4.h expands on digital signal processing.

Bit Speed

Capacity of a digital channel is measured by **bit speed**—the number of bits per second that one channel can handle. Digitally processed signals inherently need wider channels than do the same signals in analog form. Sampling takes place many thousands of times per second. Those thousands are in turn multiplied by the number of binary digits it takes to represent each quantized value. Exhibit 4.h shows how expressing a three-digit decimal number digitally results in 12 binary digits. An analog telephone channel requires a bandwidth of only about 3 kHz. When converted to digital code, however, a telephone call requires a 32 kHz transmission channel to accommodate its bit speed of 64,000 bits per second (8,000 samples × 8 bits per second).

In essence, digital processing converts a continuous signal into a series of samples that are given numerical values encoded as binary numbers.

Advantages

The extreme simplicity of digitized signals protects them from many extraneous influences that distort analog signals. A digital signal cannot be distorted or misunderstood as long as the elementary difference between "off" and "on" can be discerned. In contrast, each new manipulation of analog signals lowers their quality. Recording, relaying, and other processing of analog information inevitably introduce noise, causing quality loss. However, each new digital copy of a digitally encoded sound or picture produces a perfect replica of the original, a characteristic triggering concerns over piracy.

Because digitally processed information exists as binary digits, the stored signal can be taken apart and reassembled at will in infinitely varied forms. The possibilities for manipulation are endless.

Spectrum Disadvantages

Digitally processed signals need wider channels than do the same signals in analog form because a string of binary digits is needed to identify each tiny sample. The first communication modes to use digital processing, therefore, were those with relatively simple signals that made no great demands on the spectrum (e.g., data processing and telephone calls).

Exhibit 4.h

More on Digital Signal Processing

Digital signal processing has become so pervasive in contemporary life that it's worth a little effort to learn how it works.

Actually, digital signal processing began with the first electrical communication system, the 19th-century telegraph. In that system, telegraph operators sent messages in Morse code by means of an on/off key that controlled electricity going down the telegraph wire. The code consists simply of varying lengths of "on" and "off," presented to the ear or eye as dots, dashes, and spaces, which in turn represent letters of the alphabet, punctuation marks, and numbers.

Modern digital signal processing also employs simple on/off signals. They represent the elements of a binary code, a two-digit number system that requires only two code symbols, conventionally written as 0 and 1. All communication content can be reduced to nothing more than strings of zeros and ones.

A system that communicates digitally needs to make only one elementary distinction. "On" and "off" differ so obviously that they leave little chance for ambiguity. That simplicity makes digital signals extremely "rugged"—able to withstand external interference and imperfections in transmission and copying systems.

The familiar 10-digit decimal system (0 through 9) is used in everyday life. In that familiar system, the values of digits depend on their positions relative to one another, counting from right to left. Each new position increases a digit's value by a multiple of 10.

Thus, the number 11 means (counting from right to left) one 1 plus one 10 (1 + 10 = 11). The binary code also relies on position, but each digit's position (again counting from right to left) increases by a multiple of 2. Thus, in binary code the decimal number 11 becomes 1011, which means (counting from right to left) one 1 plus one 2 plus no 4 plus one 8 (1 + 2 + 0 + 8 = 11). Here's an example converting the three-digit number 463 to binary coded decimal (BCD) form:

Multipliers   8   4   2   1
Binary numbers

$$0100 = 0 + 4 + 0 + 0 = 4$$
$$0110 = 0 + 4 + 2 + 0 = 6$$
$$0011 = 0 + 0 + 2 + 1 = 3$$

As the examples indicate, it takes more digits to express a number in the binary system than in the decimal system. Thus, although the simplicity of digital transmissions makes them less subject to error, they need larger channels than analog transmissions.

Conversion of an analog signal to a digitized signal involves rapidly sampling an analog waveform and assigning a number that represents the monetary amplitude (quantizing). That number is then converted to a binary numerical value.

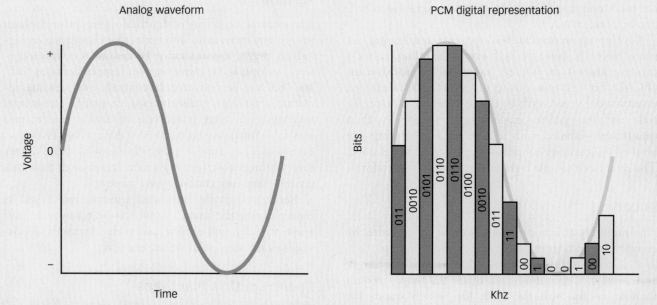

Analog waveform   PCM digital representation

The left figure shows an analog waveform. The waveform on the right indicates the points at which the wave's amplitude is sampled and quantized. The higher the sampling rate, the greater the fidelity of the digitized signal. There is an equation for calculating the sampling rate necessary to avoid distortion; it usually calls for sampling thousands of times per second.

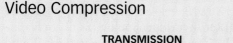

Video Compression

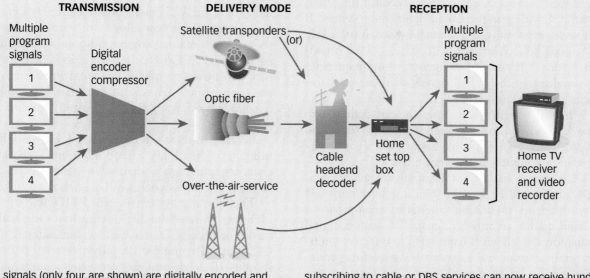

Multiple signals (only four are shown) are digitally encoded and compressed for transmission by satellite, optical fiber, or over-the-air services. The compressed signal is decompressed by an intermediary (such as a cable system headend decoder before passing the signal on to a household subscriber), by circuitry in digital home TV receivers, or by set-top boxes. Viewers subscribing to cable or DBS services can now receive hundreds of channels; viewers watching over-the-air TV on digital sets may receive dozens of additional channels, depending on the number of stations in the market and programming being broadcast on local stations' digital subchannels.

The need for high-capacity channels delayed the application of digital methods to broadcast transmission and reception. However, there were dramatic advances in compression technologies during the 1990s. Digital compression now enables broadcasters, cable operators, and direct broadcast satellite (DBS) providers to transmit multiple programs in the same size channel required for one analog signal. Exhibit 4.i illustrates how this is accomplished.

Compression

Digital signals' hunger for bandwidth efficiency drives the ongoing development of **signal compression**. Compression involves determining those portions of the original digital data that are necessary for adequately reconstructing the analog wave. Often there are sequences of repeated information, and one or a few symbols saying "Do this x number of times" can substitute for many individual bits of data that do the same thing over and over. Since all of the original information is reconstructed during reception, this is called **lossless compression**.

Some portions of an original audio or video analog wave contain information that humans do not consciously perceive. Compression techniques can delete this information without it being missed, a process known as **perceptual coding**. This is **lossy compression** because the deleted parts of the original are not restored during reception. If lossy compression is taken too far, however, audio and video quality is degraded so much that consumers can begin to notice a difference. There is a tradeoff between quality and conservation of channel bandwidth.

Some early experiences with compression proved less than "picture perfect." The process proved unable to handle some scenes that involved rapid motion. Basketballs passed from player to player, for example, looked like comets with long orange tails. But continuing dramatic improvements in compression technology are at the core of the digital revolution. Better compression techniques allow the transmission of constantly increasing amounts of information through the same bandwidth channels and permit more data to be crowded into each unit of storage capacity.

For digital TV broadcasters, video compression offers the opportunity for multichannel delivery services (multicasting) and is central to squeezing high-definition TV's (HDTV) massive information load into an existing 6 MHz channel. Compression technology continues to improve. Popular **c**ompression–**dec**ompression (codecs) programs include MPEG-2, MPEG-4, and VC-1.

4.9 Digital Audio Broadcasting

Digital audio broadcasting (DAB), launched in 2002, ultimately promises (or threatens, depending on one's point of view) to replace analog radio broadcasting, both AM and FM, with a single new all-digital radio system. If such a widespread transition does take place, it will likely follow a long period during which stations would broadcast in analog AM and FM on their existing frequencies while simulcasting their DAB signals on those same frequencies (thanks to new multiplexing technology). Under such a hybrid system, radio listeners can continue to receive AM and FM analog signals with their older radio receivers. When enough people have DAB receivers, stations would cease their analog transmissions.

A DAB system has a number of advantages. Digital signals transmitted by an FM station deliver near-CD quality sound; an AM station's digital signal approaches the sound quality of an FM signal. FM station digital transmission also allows broadcasters to transmit multiple program streams and a variety of datacasting services. While radio broadcasters hope to boost station revenues using their digital capacity, the technology also presents an opportunity for expanded public interest programming, such as traffic safety and weather alerts, foreign language broadcasts, and educational and cultural programming targeting underserved audiences.

DAB Spectrum Needs

By the early 1990s, about 10 different technologies for achieving DAB existed, all of which fell into one of two categories. Some required additional spectrum to achieve true digital sound quality, whereas others would operate in the present combined AM and FM bands, though with wider channels.

DAB Progress

The radio broadcasting industry, represented by the National Association of Broadcasters (NAB), was a strong advocate of offering a hybrid DAB system known as **in-band, on-channel (IBOC),** allowing existing terrestrial stations to add digital carriers to their currently assigned frequencies while simultaneously maintaining their analog service. In 1992, the FCC granted experimental authority for testing in-band, on-channel DAB.

DAB Launches

In 2001, the National Radio Systems Committee (NRSC) recommended that an IBOC DAB system for FM stations developed by iBiquity Digital Corporation

be authorized by the FCC; a similar recommendation was made for digital AM service in spring 2002. Rejecting the idea of assigning an entirely new band of frequencies for DAB, the FCC in its 2002 *First Report and Order on DAB*, selected iBiquity Digital Corporation's IBOC hybrid technology as the only digital system for U.S. radio broadcasting stations. Radio broadcasters were now allowed to simulcast digital signals of their analog programming on an interim basis. In 2005, the FCC reiterated to stations that they could seek permission to split their digital signals into multiple channels on an experimental basis, an important issue for broadcasters seeking to profit from multicasting services.

Because of limits on channel capacity, only FM stations have the ability to add additional programming channels, although a method to split an AM digital channel into two signals was being reviewed in 2007.

The iBiquity system is called HD Radio, but the HD doesn't stand for high definition. Originally, HD stood for Hybrid Digital/analog, but today is simply a trademarked name for iBiquity's system. Because the iBiquity IBOC system uses protected patents, software, and trademarks, stations adding digital technology must pay a one-time basic licensing and usage fees, estimated at $25,000 per station in summer 2008. Additional fees are required for separate multicast channels and some datacasting services, using a formula based on the incremental net revenue derived from these services. iBiquity also receives payments of $5–$6 for each HD receiver sold.

In a *Second Report and Order* issued in 2007, the Commission granted permanent authorization for IBOC DAB, and adopted a flexible bandwidth policy permitting radio stations to transmit high-quality audio, multiple-program streams, and datacasting services at their discretion. A radio station must continue to simulcast its analog programming service on its main digital signal and is required to provide at least one free digital over-the-air audio broadcast service that is comparable to or better in audio quality than that of their current analog service (usually the digital simulcast of the analog signal). The FCC also allowed nighttime digital operations for AM stations after concluding that there was little potential for substantial interference due to sky wave propagation. However, the Commission refused to either set a date for requiring stations to begin digital broadcasting or a timetable for conversion to all-digital radio broadcasting.

DAB Today

In November 2008, about 1,819 radio stations (out of a total of nearly 14,000) had begun digital broadcasting throughout the United States. Over 800 stations offer one or two multicast program channels separate from their analog content. In spring 2007, approximately 85 percent of the IBOC stations on the air were FM stations, mostly located in the top 50 markets in the country.

Consumer adoption has been slow, in part because of a lack of awareness of DAB, confusion over the technology, and the relatively high cost of receivers—about $50 for the cheapest desktop model. There has also been sluggishness on the part of automobile manufacturers to offer the sets as standard equipment or even as an option. Although the transition to digital radio may be inevitable, other technologies, such as MP3 players, satellite radio, and streaming-only (broadband) "radio" may pose challenges to its commercial success.

How DAB Works

IBOC DAB requires doubling the radio broadcaster's existing channel bandwidth (from 10 kHz to 20 kHz for AM stations; 200 kHz to 400 kHz for FM stations) to accommodate placing of the digital signals onto the upper and lower sidebands surrounding the analog signal. This channel expansion is possible because of the FCC's channel spacing requirements, which set a minimum distance between stations operating on the same channel or on the first-, second-, and third-adjacent frequencies. Although the possibility for interference is increased in some situations, the much lower power used to transmit the digital signals in the sidebands usually offers sufficient protection against interference with another station. Exhibit 4.j illustrates the channel

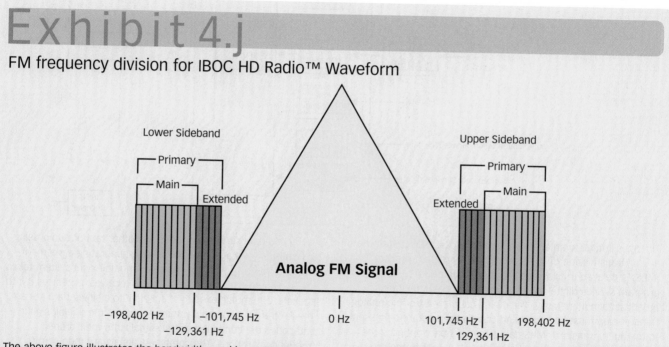

Exhibit 4.j

FM frequency division for IBOC HD Radio™ Waveform

The above figure illustrates the bandwidth used by an FM station for hybrid analog/digital transmission in the same channel. Note that the analog FM signal occupies its assigned 200 kHz channel (actually, a bit more: –101,745 Hz to +101,745 Hz from the carrier wave). Almost 200 kHz of additional bandwidth in the lower and upper sidebands (–198,402 Hz to –101,745 Hz and +101,745 Hz to +198,402 Hz from the carrier wave) is used for digital transmission.

Given the FCC's 200 kHz allocation for FM channels, a station's digital signal extends into the adjacent channels both above and below its allocated frequency. However, the emissions generated in the digital sidebands are so much lower in transmitted energy that they are unlikely to cause interference with stations operating on adjacent frequencies. Additionally, in most markets, stations are normally not permitted to operate on adjacent channels.

A digital modulation scheme known as orthogonal frequency-division multiplexing (OFDM) is used. The colored bars indicate comb-like frequency partitions, closely spaced subcarriers used to transmit the data.

A station operating in extended hybrid mode, as shown above, will use its main partitions—with a capacity of about 96 kilobits per second (kbps)—to transmit a digital simulcast of its analog signal and usually one or two additional audio channels of programming. Approximately 45 kbps is also available in the extended partitions. As long as broadcasters transmit a digital simulcast of their analog programming, and at least one digital program stream equal or better in quality to their analog signal (which may be the digital simulcast), they may use their remaining digital capacity however they wish.

Source: Reproduced with permission from iBiquity Digital Corporation.

Exhibit 4.k

In-Band, On-Channel (IBOC) Digital Audio Broadcasting System

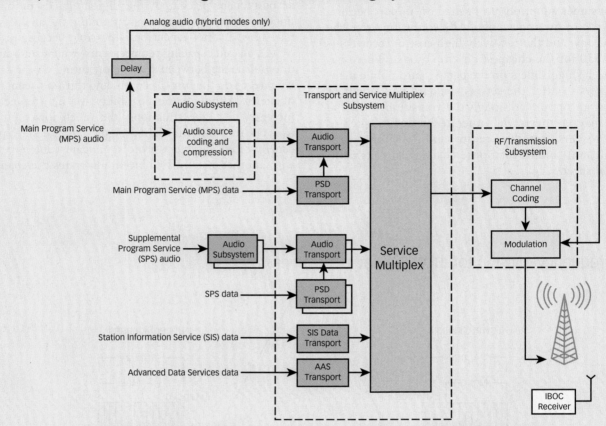

Timing is critical to an analog/digital simulcast. Notice that the analog transmission of the station's main program service (MPS) is delayed to allow for the processing of the main program service digital signal before being combined and broadcast simultaneously. The digital counterpart of the analog transmission must be coded and compressed before being sent to the audio transport. MPS data (such as text identifying the song title, artist, and album being played) is sent to the program service data (PSD) transport then to the audio transport. The supplemental program service (SPS) audio and SPS data represent secondary channels of digital programming and related data. The station information service (SIS) data includes such things as the station's call letters, slogan, and the time.

Advanced data services includes any other text or audio being transmitted, perhaps under a revenue-generating agreement with a third-party. The transport and multiplex subsystem takes the audio and data information that it receives, organizes it into packets, and multiplexes the packets into a single data stream. The RF/transmission subsystem modulates the analog signal and codes the combined digital signals into their proper frequency partitions. The combined signals are then sent to the antenna.

Source: In-band, on-channel digital audio broadcasting system. From National Radio Systems Committee, *In-Band/On-Channel Digital Radio Broadcasting Standard* (April 2008): p. 13 (modified). © 2008 Consumer Electronics Association and National Association of Broadcasters.

architecture of an FM HD radio station operating in the extended hybrid mode.

As shown in Exhibit 4.k, a station's digital audio signal (and possibly textual information) is compressed before being combined with the analog signal and sent to an HD transmitter and antenna where the signals are broadcast. HD receivers receive both the analog and digital signals, while older radios receive only the analog signal.

An HD radio receiver will initially acquire the station's analog signal in mono, then in stereo, and finally the station's digital simulcast signal. This **blending** process allows the receiver to automatically revert back to an analog-only signal if the digital signal is lost, avoiding any disruption in listening caused by the so-called *cliff effect* common to digital transmissions where a signal suddenly drops out completely. Such blending, of course, is only available with the station's digital stream that is simulcasting the analog signal; it is not available on additional digital programming channels the station may be broadcasting. If blending is to work properly, station engineers must carefully time the digital signal to match the analog signal and be sure that audio levels are closely matched to avoid having listeners experience annoying changes in signal loudness.

4.10 Digital TV Begins

Digital technologies made great progress in the acquisition, editing, and storage of TV programming during the 1980s and early 1990s. In the distribution area, however, the calendar often seemed stuck at 1941, when American TV broadcast standards for black-and-white transmission were developed by the National Television System Committee (NTSC). Movement toward more modern standards was slow. The major impetus for change emerged from a desire for TV pictures and sound rivaling that found in movie theaters. The initial goal was a **high-definition television (HDTV)** system providing a larger screen, vastly improved picture resolution, and multichannel sound. What has emerged is a new **digital television (DTV)** broadcasting environment in which HDTV as originally conceived is an important, but not an exclusive, component.

Engineers in Japan, beginning in the 1960s, made the first significant progress with HDTV, developing a 1,125-line picture with a wide-screen, 16-to-9 aspect ratio. This primarily analog system, called MUSE, required 36 MHz channels—six times wider than the 6 MHz U.S. standard. Japanese engineers later developed a broadcast MUSE version using a 9 MHz channel.

By late 1991, the Japanese were providing, eight hours a day, satellite delivery of MUSE service to selected viewing sites in Japan. However, the initial cost of receivers (about $18,000) drastically limited HDTV penetration. By the mid-1990s, Japanese analog HDTV sets were still twice as expensive as ordinary sets, and fewer than 350,000 households had HDTV receivers. The transition to digital HDTV via satellite in Japan began in 1996 with PerfecTV, a pay-per-view service, followed closely by DBS providers JSkyB and DirecTV Japan.

America's Response

In 1988, the FCC began to consider U.S. HDTV standards to ensure U.S. terrestrial broadcasting's ability to keep up with Japanese and European efforts in the race toward improved television. Also, nonbroadcast services (domestic cable and DBS), not being subject to the NTSC's 6 MHz channel constraint of broadcast television, could forge ahead with their own versions of HDTV without waiting for a compatible broadcast version to emerge.

The FCC Advisory Committee on Advanced Television Service (ACATS), established to compare HDTV systems and recommend one to the Commission, sparked creative thinking among many domestic and foreign companies. The term "advanced," rather than "high-definition," in the committee's title was prophetic. The original goal was development of HDTV, but the focus changed in the early 1990s when several companies began concentrating on rapidly developing digital technologies. Rather than continuing to work as competitors in isolation, in May 1993 the developers formed a "Grand Alliance" and merged their ideas to accelerate the development and approval of a workable digital system.

Although continuing to claim HDTV was the ultimate objective, broadcasters began urging Congress to allow them to use digital transmission technology for other services, such as interactive television, pay services, and high-speed data transmission. This shift in emphasis raised new questions and occasioned fierce debate regarding the transition from an analog to a digital broadcast service. It was not until mid-1996 that the FCC authorized three stations to begin broadcasting digital signals experimentally.

Just as a final transmission standard seemed ready for adoption, objections from leaders in the entertainment, computer, and cable industries once more delayed the decision. They claimed that some parts of the proposed standard interfered seriously with the smooth convergence of television and computer-based technologies. A compromise in late November 1996 allowed the FCC to adopt a digital TV broadcast standard on Christmas Eve. Reflecting the compromise, the FCC chose not to impose a single picture format for all digital broadcasting. The Commission allows broadcasters to use any picture format they wish, but only a few of the DTV formats recommended to the FCC by the Advanced Television Systems Committee (ATSC) have been adopted widely. The ATSC formats vary in their aspect ratio (relationship of image width to height), number of vertical lines scanned, number of picture elements (pixels) per horizontal line, type of scanning (interlaced or progressive), and number of frames transmitted each second.

Moving from NTSC to Digital

One of the most difficult decisions facing the FCC amid all this fast-moving technical change was how best to handle the transition from existing NTSC receivers and production and transmission equipment to the selected digital standard.

Simultaneous with the development of transmission standards for digital broadcasting, the FCC wrestled with the issue of how best to move stations from their NTSC analog channels to their new digital channels. Knowing the transition would take years, the FCC needed to give stations new digital channels while allowing them to continue analog broadcasting on their old channels.

Early in 1992, the FCC decided on a 15-year transition period following adoption of a digital transmission standard. Broadcasters were to receive a second 6 MHz channel in the UHF band for digital broadcasting while continuing conventional analog transmission on their respective existing channels. Broadcasters would have to begin digital (at that time meaning high-definition) operations six years after the FCC's selection of a digital standard. At the end of the transition, when presumably a substantial portion of TV homes would have digital receivers, stations and networks would convert to digital operations exclusively. All TV broadcasting would be on UHF channels, the broadcasters having given up their old NTSC broadcast channels for reallocation to other services.

In 1996, the FCC revised its transitional plan dramatically by announcing a new channel-allotment scheme. Rather than move terrestrial broadcasters to all UHF digital channels, the Commission proposed packing most of the new digital licenses into a "core spectrum" comprising channels 7–51. Upon completion of the estimated 15-year transition to digital, 23 channels formerly used by broadcasters (channels 2–6 and 52–69) would be auctioned to other users providing other services. Broadcasters immediately countered that the entire range of TV channels (2–69) was necessary to avoid interference and maintain existing signal coverage patterns during the transition.

When the FCC finally assigned the new digital channels in 1997, the plan had changed again: The FCC made initial digital assignments on all available TV channels (2–69). Then, in 1998, it announced that stations would eventually be assigned to a "core" DTV spectrum of channels 2–51. The FCC also sharply accelerated the phase-in period for DTV. Rather than allowing stations six years to begin digital broadcasting, the FCC required that at least three network-affiliated DTV stations be on the air in the top 30 markets by November 1, 1999. The mandate was designed to ensure DTV's availability to more than half the nation's TV households by the year 2000. More than two dozen stations failed to make the deadline, however, because of equipment delivery delays or problems acquiring access to usable antenna sites. The FCC also shortened the transition period to digital-only transmission from 15 to 10 years, until the end of 2006.

In early 2006, Congress changed the timetable yet again, setting February 17, 2009, as the "hard" deadline for the DTV transition of all full-powered TV broadcasters. In August 2007, after a multistep channel election process that began in 2004, the FCC released its final *DTV Table of Allotments* for all digital TV operations. The final plan maintained core DTV spectrum on channels 2–51, freeing up 108 MHz of spectrum formerly assigned to UHF TV channels 52–69 (18 channels of 6 MHz each). Exhibit 4.g on p. 77 shows a summary of digital TV channel specifications.

In early 2008, about $20 billion were bid by telecommunication companies interested in providing advanced wireless services, including wireless broadband, for 62 MHz of the newly freed spectrum. Portions of the reclaimed spectrum will also be used for wireless communication systems for police, fire fighters, paramedics, and other first-responders. Broadcasters were pleased that the plan did not require them to pay a spectrum fee for their new digital channels.

4.11 Digital TV (ATSC) vs. Analog TV (NTSC)

Despite a number of notable improvements—including the introduction of solid-state technology and microelectronics—from the late 1940s until February 2009 the basic structure of an analog TV station remained the same. Cameras and microphones converted sounds and pictures into electrical signals, which were fed to a transmitter, where they modulated RF carrier waves radiated from an antenna.

A DTV station is much the same. The major difference involves the way stations encode the information and modulate the transmitter. Although modern TV receivers rely on their digital tuners, many households will need digital-to-analog converter boxes to display video images on their older **cathode ray tube (CRT)** TV sets.

Camera Technology

From the 1940s until the early 1990s, tube-type cameras dominated the broadcasting industry. It was not until the 1980s that broadcasters began using cameras with a solid-state **charge-coupled device (CCD)** rather than a camera tube which used magnets to guide an electron beam to convert light energy to an electrical signal. The video produced by these early "chip" (CCD-equipped) cameras relegated them mainly to shooting news footage, where picture quality is less critical. Solid-state technology advanced dramatically in the 1990s, and cameras using CCDs capable of excellent picture quality have replaced tube-type cameras in both the consumer and professional market. CCDs offer the usual advantages of solid-state devices compared to tubes: less weight and bulk, longer service life, greater reliability, and reduced energy consumption.

Exhibit 4.l shows a photo of older camera pick-up tubes, a CCD chip, and a simplified functional diagram of the CCD operations in modern cameras.

Scanning and Frame Frequency Standards

The technology of tube-based display devices required that the video information be transmitted in a pattern that allowed the receiver to "paint" images on-screen one line at a time using a moving electron beam. The NTSC analog system employed a standard of 525 lines of video information to be painted in horizontal rows from top to bottom to create the image on the TV screen. The number of lines making up the image helps determine the **resolution**—the clarity of the image. The more lines, the greater the resolution. However, not all 525 lines of the U.S. analog standard were used to convey pictures. Some time, and thus some lines, were devoted to the auxiliary signals used by the receiver to control the scanning. Transmission standards called for 483 active video lines, those providing specific picture information, in the 525-line analog system.

The analog TV system exclusively used a method called **interlaced scanning** to paint the image on the screen, while the new digital standard allows broadcasters to use either interlaced or **progressive scanning**.

Exhibit 4.m show examples of both scanning methods. With interlaced scanning, all the odd-numbered lines are scanned first, followed by the even-numbered lines. Each of these scans constitutes an odd or even **field**. Two fields combine to make a complete **frame** of video. This odd-even scanning structure was a way to prevent the image from appearing to flicker without having to increase the channel bandwidth required for TV transmission. The U.S. analog TV system painted the screen with 30 complete frames (60 fields) every second. The human eye and brain cannot distinguish individual images flashed in rapid succession. This **persistence of vision** causes viewers to see a smoothly moving image rather than a series of individual frames of video.

Progressive scanning display devices paint the lines on the screen one after the other, in numerical sequence. Computer monitors use progressive scan-

Exhibit 4.l

Camera Pick-Up Tubes and CCD Chip

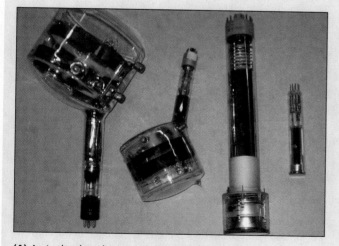

(A) As technology improved, tubes became smaller. Commercial broadcasters first used the *iconoscope*, the two odd shaped tubes on the left. Then, *image orthicons*, with 3-inch and 4.5-inch faces, replaced iconoscopes. Smaller tubes, such as the *vidicon* (far right) in turn replaced the image orthicon.

(B) In the 1990s, smaller, more rugged and energy efficient chips largely replaced tubes as imaging devices for cameras. Charge-coupled devices (CCDs) are image sensors that use hundreds of thousands of tiny light-sensitive elements to convert (transduce) light to electricity. The electrical charge depends on the intensity of the light striking the light-sensitive element, so the CCD creates a pattern of electrical charges analogous to the bright and dark portions of the image. Each transducer produces a picture element (pixel) that combines with others to form the complete image. The advanced CCD chip shown here progressively scans 1,080 lines each containing 1,920 pixels (1920 × 1080) at a rate of 60 frames per second.

(continued)

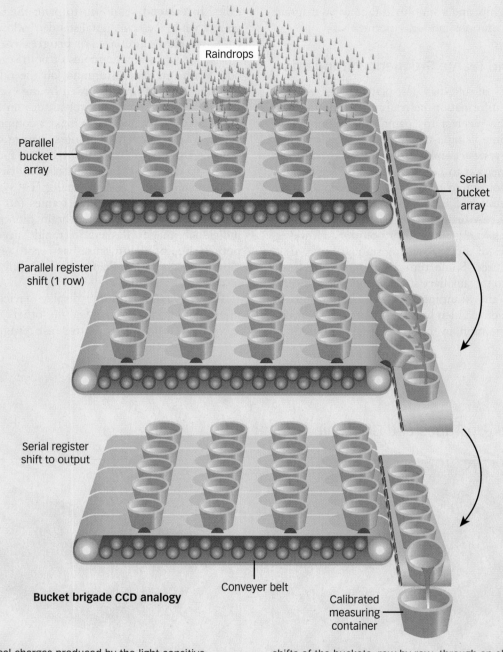

Parallel bucket array

Serial bucket array

Parallel register shift (1 row)

Serial register shift to output

Bucket brigade CCD analogy

Conveyer belt

Calibrated measuring container

(C) The electrical charges produced by the light-sensitive transducers are transferred and stored in another part of the CCD and, finally, read out in a line-by-line order. The bucket brigade analogy, shown above, helps to visualize the operation of a CCD. The "raindrops" falling with different intensity, represent light striking the photosensitive pixels shown as "buckets" on a conveyer belt. Light energy is transduced (through photon interaction) to an electrical charge proportional to the intensity of the light. The charge-transfer process begins with parallel

shifts of the buckets, row by row, through an electrode network built into the chip. The individual charges are then transferred to a special row of pixels at the edge of the chip know as the serial register. From there, each individual charge is measured in a "calibrated container." In digital cameras, the stream of amplitudes is converted into a stream of digital values using an analog-to-digital-converter then passed through a video compressor for storage or transmission.

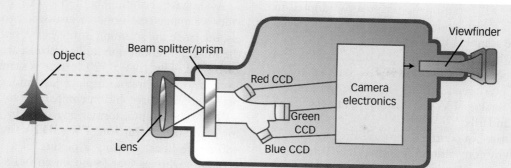

(D) As shown above, today's broadcast-quality cameras use three CCDs and are called "three-chip cameras." An optical beam splitter is used to separate the scene into three image planes. Thin color film filters attached to a mirrored prism direct each of the primary colors of light (red, green, blue) to a corresponding CCD. When combined, the output from each chip can produce all the colors we see on television. Consumer-quality cameras typically have only a single CCD with the necessary color filtering dyed onto the chip itself. One-chip cameras deliver a less crisp color image, but one that is still amazingly good considering their price.

Sources: Photo (A) courtesy of the Early Television Museum; photo (B) courtesy of Kodak Corporation; (C) Copyright © Molecular Expressions. Reprinted with permission of Florida State University Research Foundation. All rights reserved; (D) from Joseph R Dominick, Fritz Messere, and Barry L. Sherman, *Broadcasting, Cable, the Internet, and Beyond,* 6th ed. Copyright © 2008 by McGraw-Hill. Reprinted by permission of McGraw-Hill. All rights reserved.

Interlaced and Progressive Scanning

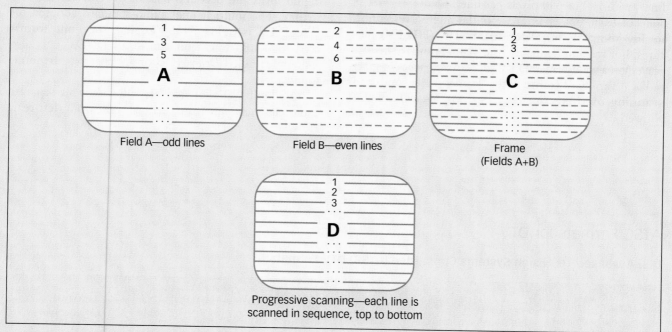

Analog television uses interlaced scanning. Several of the DTV picture formats recommended by the ATSC also use interlaced scanning. In interlaced scanning a complete electronic picture, or frame, is made up of two fields, each of which makes up half the picture definition. One field **(A)** scans the odd-numbered lines, and the other **(B)** scans the even-numbered lines. Together, the lines of the two fields "interlace" to make up a complete frame. **(C)** With progressive scanning formats **(D)** each line is traced one at a time, top to bottom, in sequential order. Each scan produces one complete electronic picture, or frame. Computer screens use progressive scanning. The computer industry supports progressive scanning formats for DTV, eliminating the need to convert an interlaced signal for display on the progressively scanned computer monitor.

ning, and the DTV transmission standards adopted in 1996 allow DTV display devices to use either interlaced or progressive scanning methods.

In analog broadcasting the scanning format and frame frequency standards were fixed. Stations transmitted using interlaced scanning and 30 frames per second, and all analog TV sets displayed images using these same standards.

A DTV station, in contrast, may use any picture format, although by convention the format used is normally one of those recommended by the ATSC. At the consumer's receiver, however, the displayed image format need not be the same as that broadcast. Many people will initially watch DTV transmissions on analog receivers by using a set-top box to convert the digital signal, in whatever format, to the only format the set can display: an interlaced 30-frames-per-second image. The decision of the FCC not to link the receiver's scanning format and frame frequency to that being broadcast is an important difference between analog and DTV transmission standards.

As shown in Exhibit 4.n, the ATSC standard for DTV allows TV receivers to display a variety of active lines featuring a set number of **pixels**, or picture elements, per line: 1,080 lines (with 1,920 pixels per horizontal line), 720 lines (with 1,280 pixels per line), or 480 lines (with 704 or 640 pixels per line). Digital transmissions of 1,080 or 720 lines are of the highest resolution quality known as **high-definition TV (HDTV)** pictures. For maximum quality, the pictures should be displayed on a wide-screen DTV set featuring a 16:9 aspect radio. A variety of **frame rates** (frames per second) and **scanning methods** (interlaced or progressive) are also allowed.

As shown in Exhibit 4.o, the 1920 x 1080 format provides an image resolution of just over two million pixels, but since the scanning is interlaced, only one-half of the image, or about one million pixels, are displayed in each field. The 1280 x 720 format is scanned progressively and each frame displays just under one million pixels, an image resolution comparable to 1080i.

The other digital format approved by the ATSC is for **standard-definition TV (SDTV)** which displays 480 active lines, yielding a picture of about the same general quality as that found on an NTSC receiver. If the receiver displays 704 pixels per line, the transmission may be in either the 16:9 or 4:3 aspect ratios. If only 640 pixels per line are displayed, the aspect ratio is 4:3 (see Exhibit 4.o).

TV Sound

U.S. analog television used FM sound placed on a separate carrier in the 6 MHz TV channel. The analog sound channel was designed to respond to a sound range from 10 to 15,000 Hz. It also had room for subcarriers that enabled multiplexing stereophonic sound and a secondary audio program, such as an alternative-language soundtrack, within the channel.

With DTV, the sound, like the picture, is encoded in digital form and becomes part of the transmitted data stream. The multichannel audio standard adopted for U.S. DTV is called Dolby Digital; the same format used for audio tracks on almost all DVDs. It is also sometimes called *Dolby AC-3* or 5.1 channel surround-sound audio.

The Dolby Digital standard allows for six separate audio channels: left front, center, right front, left rear,

Exhibit 4.n

ATSC Formats for DTV

U.S. Advanced Television Systems Committee (ATSC) DTV Formats

Format	Active Lines	Horizontal Pixels	Aspect Ratio	Picture Rate*
HDTV	1,080 lines	1,920 pixels/line	16:9	60I, 30P, 24P
HDTV	720 lines	1,280 pixels/line	16:9	60P, 30P, 24P
SDTV	480 lines	704 pixels/line	16:9 or 4:3	60I, 50P, 30P, 24P
SDTV	480 lines	640 pixels/line	4:3	60I, 60P, 30P, 24P

* In the picture rate column, "I" indicates interlace scan in *fields*/second and "P" means progressive scan in *frames*/second.

Source: ATSC data as presented by Peter B. Seel and Michel Dupagne, "Digital Television," in August E. Grant and Jennifer H. Meadows (Eds.), Communication Technology Update and Fundamentals (11th ed.) (Boston: Focal Press, 2008), p. 80.

Exhibit 4.0

High-Definition Systems

(A) NTSC—483 active lines, analog audio

(B) HDTV—1,080 or 720 active lines, digital audio

American HDTV, compared to the NTSC standard, has many more scanning lines for improved picture definition, a much wider screen size, and both digital audio and video signal generation. The diagrams compare **(A)** NTSC television with its 4:3 picture aspect ratio as approved in 1941 (and modified with color in 1953) with **(B)** HDTV with its 16:9 aspect ratio.

Source: Diagram based in part on Mark Long, ed., *World Satellite Almanac: The Global Guide to Satellite Transmission and Technology,* 3rd edition. © 1993 Access Intelligence. Reprinted by permission of Access Intelligence. All Rights Reserved.

right rear, and a limited-bandwidth low-frequency (subwoofer) channel. The ".1" refers to the subwoofer channel that handles only very low frequency sounds, the center channel is for dialogue audio, and the remaining channels provide the surround-sound effect. Producing programs with surround sound is a complex and costly process. It is likely that most programs produced for transmission in wide-screen high-definition format will fully utilize the capabilities inherent in Dolby Digital audio.

An additional advantage of the audio standard adopted is that it allows for multiple streams of audio, which can be used, for example, to deliver a separate audio program, dialogue in several different languages, program-related commentary, or specially enhanced audio for the hearing impaired. Unlike analog TV sound, DTV sound requires synchronizing audio with its associated video in the data stream. Some early DTV transmissions featured sound that did not match the lip movement of people on-screen.

TV Color

The signal specifications for analog color television provided for compatibility with black-and-white (monochrome) receivers. A color subcarrier was interleaved with the main video carrier for transmitting black and white information (luminance information). The color subcarrier added a color component without expanding the 6 MHz TV channel. RCA developed this color system and, with NTSC approval, the FCC adopted it in 1953.

Color information in a DTV transmission is, like the sound, digitally encoded and included in the data stream rather than being added to the channel by a separate color subcarrier. DTV will not suffer from image artifacts (abnormalities introduced by the transmission process itself) caused by adding color to an existing analog black-and-white TV system through multiplexing. However, DTV may sometimes exhibit image artifacts caused by excessive compression.

Channel Width and Resolution

The U.S. DTV standard calls for a 6 MHz TV channel, the same bandwidth previously used with analog television. A 6 MHz channel is 600 times the width of an AM radio broadcast channel (10 kHz) and 30 times the width of an FM channel (200 kHz). Indeed, *all* AM and FM broadcast channels together occupy less spectrum space than only four television channels.

Although HDTV is a centerpiece application providing a vast improvement in picture resolution, broadcasters continue to confront a tradeoff between picture quality and the available spectrum space in their 6 MHz digital channels. Compression technology allows DTV to increase dramatically the resolution possible while occupying less spectrum space than standard analog television. But within the DTV realm, a higher-resolution image requires more spectrum space than a lower-resolution image.

A broadcaster's digital transmission has a capacity of up to 19.39 million bits per second (Mbps). Given current compression technology, broadcasters can basically multicast one HDTV channel, requiring between 6 and 18 Mbps depending on program content, and one to two SDTV channels of lower-resolution programming. When not transmitting an HDTV signal, a broadcaster can offer many more lower-definition programs in the same channel bandwidth. Advances in compression technology are predicted to greatly expand broadcasters' ability to offer additional digital services, including sending information and video content to mobile and hand-held devices, including cell phones.

4.12 DTV Transmission

Exhibit 4.p shows a diagram of the basic components of a TV station transmitting a digital signal. Much of the work necessary to transmit a digital signal occurs just ahead of and within the transmitter itself. The goal is to minimize the data needed to represent a standard of high quality audio and video. First, bit-rate reduction is accomplished by encoding and compressing the video and audio signals (and ancillary and control data) using the ATSC-approved compression algorithms—the **MPEG-2 standard** for video and the **Dolby Digital/AC-3 standard** for audio. Next, the digital streams are divided into "packets" of information with unique identifying "tags," (packet headers) and multiplexed into a single digital data stream. With DTV, transmission of ancillary information, such as closed captioning, goes within the data stream itself.

A highly compressed MPEG-2 serial data stream exits the transport subsystem at a data rate of 19.28 Mbps. Additional information, as well as a **pilot signal**, is added to help the receiver reconstruct the original information in proper form and to compensate for errors caused by problems in transmission and propagation.

The transmitted data stream contains millions of data segments. Beginning each data segment there is a **segment sync signal**, which basically tells the receiver where to begin and end each horizontal line of video. Although the scanning format, frame frequency, and other image characteristics (such as the shape of the displayed image) can be altered by the receiving equipment to accommodate the display device, receivers still need to synchronize information to function properly.

The total data stream is then used to amplitude modulate a radio wave using a modulation system called **8-VSB (eight-level vestigial sideband)**. The modulated signal is then amplified and passed to the station's antenna system.

Like analog TV, DTV uses the same 6 MHz channel. Unlike analog transmission, all of the needed information is combined into one data stream; there are no separate carriers for video, audio, and color information. To conserve spectrum space, only the upper sideband is transmitted, much as with analog TV transmission. A pilot signal is located 310 kHz up from the lower edge of the channel, which is unique to DTV transmission. The pilot signal helps the receiver lock onto the incoming signal and begin decoding, even in the presence of multipath interference and high noise levels.

Propagation

The FCC allows DTV stations to use from 50,000 to one million watts effective radiated power (ERP) to propagate their signals. In setting TV power limits, the FCC uses a formula that takes antenna height into consideration. The FCC assigns each DTV station a power level and antenna height calculated to duplicate, or almost duplicate, the station's analog coverage contour. A DTV station's coverage distance and the shape of its coverage area thus depend on several factors: transmitting and receiving antenna height and efficiency, obstructive terrain features, transmitter frequency, and effective radiated power.

Engineers elevate TV transmission antennas as high as possible—on mountain peaks, roofs of tall buildings, or the tops of tall steel towers. The antenna towers themselves do not radiate signals as do AM towers. As is true of FM stations, they only support the radiating elements, which are relatively small, in keeping with the shortness of television's VHF and UHF waves. Television (and FM radio) station antennas provide **beam tilt**. Beam tilt concentrates the radiated energy downward so little of it skims over the line-of-sight horizon to be lost uselessly in space.

Exhibit 4.p

Digital TV System Components and Signals

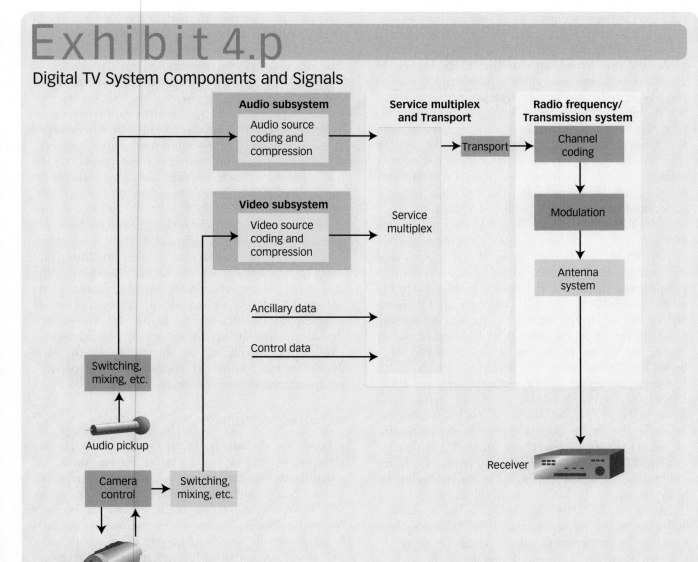

In some ways, the DTV station is similar to the analog station. In both analog and digital stations, audio and video are picked up by microphones and cameras, switched and mixed, combined with graphics, and otherwise manipulated in the production process. At this point in a DTV system, the audio and video are encoded and compressed in audio and video subsystems. The audio and video data stream is then divided into discrete "packets" with individual identifying data added. In the radio frequency transmission system additional information needed by the receiver is added. The final data stream then modulates the transmitter using the 8-VSB (eight discrete amplitude level vestigial sideband) technique mandated by the FCC. The signal is then transmitted to receivers, where the process is reversed to re-create the original analog sound and picture.

Source: Reprinted with permission of Advanced Television Systems Committee. All Rights Reserved. Please check the ATSC web site for updates at www.atsc.org.

4.13 DTV Reception

DTV reception is the inverse of the transmission process. The receiver must tune to the frequency of the signal, isolate the digital data stream, and then decompress and decode it back into its original form. These functions can be performed by circuitry built into a DTV receiver or by a set-top box for subscribers to cable or DBS service. Consumers watching television over-the-air on an NTSC analog receiver will be able to use digital-to-analog converter boxes to continue their viewing, including broadcasters' multicast channels.

Most of the approximately 114 million TV households in the United States should experience a seamless transition to the new digital TV system. At least 86 percent of TV households subscribe to a multi-channel video programming distributor (MVPD), usually a **cable** or **direct broadcast satellite (DBS)** service. In 2008, the FCC required cable systems to continue to carry both the analog and digital feeds of full-powered TV stations for three years following the digital transition, with some possible exceptions for systems with very limited bandwidth capacity. Although the decision sparked a lawsuit from cable programmers fearing they would be removed from the cable line-up to make room for the additional analog signals, the cable industry announced plans to comply with the regulation.

Since 1999, DBS carriers have had the right to provide subscribers with local market TV stations' signals directly from their satellite feeds. If one full-powered station in the local market is carried in this way, all other full-powered stations in the market may also demand carriage. In fall 2008, about 95 percent of all TV households could watch their local TV stations by subscribing to a DBS service, albeit with a small additional monthly charge. Since these transmissions are already carried in digital form, no additional steps need to be taken.

Feared disruption of TV service, therefore, would affect only households receiving their TV signals over-the-air. Of course, any analog TV sets in households that subscribe to cable or DBS that are not physically connected to the service would also be affected. Additionally, cable and DBS services are presently required to carry only the primary broadcast signal so stations' multicast channels may not be available to all subscribers.

In spring 2008, the National Telecommunications and Information Administration (NTIA), a branch of the U.S. Department of Commerce, began offering $40 coupons (two per household) that could be applied toward the purchase of digital-to-analog converter boxes available at electronics retailers. These converters will allow digital over-the-air TV signals to be displayed on analog-only TV sets. The estimated 13 to 15 million households that watch television directly from over-the-air signals, and do not have a TV set equipped with a digital tuner, can either purchase a converter box or subscribe to a cable or DBS service if one is available.

Signal Interference

For over-the-air DTV viewers, signal obstructions can affect reception. In the analog TV system, receivers would sometimes display "ghost images" caused when waves reflected off objects like buildings, mountains, or even trees. These reflected waves traveled a longer path to reach the TV receiver, and arrived a fraction of a second later than the direct waves that reached the receiver unimpeded.

DTV also suffers from this phenomenon, known as **multipath signal interference**. If not corrected, multipath interference can result in the complete loss of DTV reception rather than the displaying of ghost images. DTV receivers have adaptive equalizer circuits that help to correct for errors caused by delayed reflected waves and help to prevent signal loss. DTV set makers are continually improving the ability of receivers to cope with multipath problems and other sources of interference.

Another DTV interference concern has emerged from proposals to allow unlicensed radio frequency devices to operate on unassigned and unused digital TV channels. Each of the 210 TV markets in the United States will have some of these vacant channels (see 47 CFR 73.622 for the DTV Table of Allotments). Proponents wishing to use these so-called "white spaces" claim that their equipment, which may be used to provide wireless broadband and other services, will have the ability to automatically detect a DTV transmission and select a frequency that will not create co-channel or adjacent channel interference. Broadcasters are highly skeptical of such devices, claiming that widespread interference is likely. Despite broadcasters' objections, in November 2008 the FCC voted to approve the use of such equipment on these frequencies.

Receiving Antennas

A **receiving antenna** is a metal apparatus for capturing electromagnetic waves over a range of frequencies. TV antennas are designed to capture either VHF or UHF frequencies, or both, and feed the signal to a TV receiver. Simple indoor antennas often suffice if the receiver is in close enough proximity to a station's transmitter. Some viewers had trouble receiving DTV signals using indoor antennas with early-generation DTV receivers because of multipath signal interference. Many over-the-air viewers will probably need an antenna to watch all the DTV stations in their market.

Antennas operate at maximum efficiency on only one frequency, so antennas used for receiving many channels require a compromise. Even so, the short wavelengths used for television allow receiving antennas to be highly efficient and directional. Like outdoor FM radio antennas, TV antennas must point toward the station, and if stations are at widely different points of the compass, the antenna must be rotatable.

4.14 Low-Power TV (LPTV) and Translators

It is a common misconception that all analog TV transmissions ended in February 2009. The FCC has not set a deadline for a digital transition for almost 2,900 **low-power TV (LPTV)** stations, many of which continued with analog operations beyond the 2009 transition.

LPTV stations serve viewers in both rural and urban communities, often carrying programming for minority and ethnic populations.

In 1982, the FCC gave final approval for LPTV service. LPTV stations operate on the same VHF and UHF channels and have the same technical characteristics as other analog TV stations, but they use greatly reduced power, from 10 to 1,000 watts. Coverage under ideal conditions is only about 10 miles, but in urban areas is often much less. LPTV stations were considered secondary services and, provided they did not cause interference to full-power TV stations in the area, could operate on any channel.

LPTV's secondary status became a serious liability when the FCC began assigning channels for DTV. In announcing the DTV rules, the Commission made some concessions and pledged continuing efforts to accommodate LPTV, but the service's future in a digital world remained uncertain.

In November 1999, President Bill Clinton signed a law creating a new protected class of LPTV stations. To be eligible for the new Class A status and the protection it offers, an LPTV station had to have been broadcasting at least 18 hours a day since September 1999, including a minimum of 3 hours of locally produced programming each week. In addition, no LPTV station could achieve Class A status if its signal posed an interference threat to an existing full-power station's planned DTV coverage area. In effect, the law protected LPTV stations against new high-power stations wanting to take their frequencies, but offered little protection against established full-power stations wanting to maximize their DTV service areas at the expense of LPTV. The FCC has promised to assist displaced LPTV stations move to other frequencies.

At the end of 2007, there were approximately 560 Class A stations and over 2,300 other low-power stations, most of which continued to broadcast an analog signal after the 2009 transition. A number of proposals have been suggested, including setting a 2012 hard date for an LPTV transition to digital and publicizing the need for consumers who view LPTV stations to purchase only converter boxes that will "pass through" the analog signals of LPTV stations in addition to converting digital signals to analog.

In spring 2008, FCC Chairman Kevin Martin proposed that Class A LPTV stations be given full-power status when they go digital, entitling them to mandatory carriage on their local cable systems. The cable industry opposes the plan. Martin has also suggested that full-power TV stations carry LPTV signals on their digital subchannels, a proposition strongly disfavored by some broadcasters.

A close cousin to the LPTV station is the TV **translator**, which rebroadcasts the signal of a full-power station. Over 4,000 translators are in use, mostly in remote areas, to provide signals to viewers living too far from the transmitter to receive a usable over-the-air signal and in areas where uneven terrain disrupts the signal. Stations may use multiple translators to distribute their signal. In order to reduce multipath interference, translator stations rebroadcast the full-power station's signal on a separate channel.

Although neither the FCC nor Congress has set a deadline to convert to digital, by early 2008 more than 2,100 LPTV and translator stations have been authorized to construct digital plants and some are already on the air.

4.15 Your TV Set

The Consumer Electronics Association estimates that there are 285 million TV receivers in use in households in the United States. Most TV receivers in use still rely on the **cathode ray tube (CRT)** for picture display, although the transition to a digital TV system has prompted many people to purchase solid-state, flat-screen receivers capable of displaying wide-screen high definition images in a 16:9 aspect ratio. In fact, many electronics retailers have ceased selling CRT sets.

All color TV receivers, regardless of display type, construct pictures by illuminating thousands of individual picture elements or *pixels*. Each pixel consists of three subpixels matching the primary colors of red, green and blue. Illuminating the pixel to various intensities creates hues perceived as different colors by the eye. Pixels may take different shapes such as dots, squares, or rectangles, but all rely on the same color principles to display an image.

Cathode Ray Tube Displays

Exhibit 4.q illustrates how a CRT works. The viewer looks at the front end of the tube as the receiver "screen." On the inside face of the CRT, pixels, consisting of phosphorescent dots, glow when bombarded with electrons. Within the neck of the CRT reside three electron guns that shoot beams of electrons carrying red, green, and blue video information toward the face of the tube. Guided by external deflection coils, the electron beam "paints" an image on the screen (actually the inner face of the tube).

The electron beam stimulates pixels that glow with varying intensities, depending on the beam's strength. It lays down an image, line-by-line, field-by-field (when using interlaced scanning), and frame-by-frame (when using progressive scanning). Codes in the digital data stream, processed through a digital-to-analog converter, provide the necessary synchronization signals, keeping the receiver scanning in proper sequence. Although most of the CRT receivers still in use are capable of displaying

Exhibit 4.q

Cathode Ray Tube

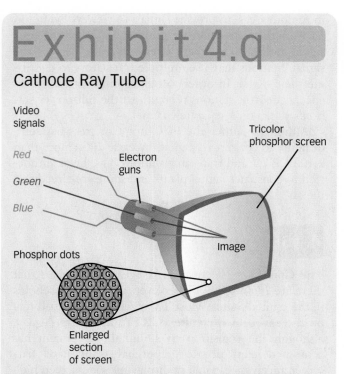

Video signals

Red

Green

Blue

Electron guns

Tricolor phosphor screen

Image

Phosphor dots

G R B G
R B G R B
B G R B G R
G R B G R
B G R B G
G B G R

Enlarged section of screen

Some receiver tubes use three electronic guns and tricolor phosphor dots. Varying amplitudes in the modulated currents fed to each of the electron guns cause the dots to glow with varying intensities; though only the red, green, and blue primary colors appear on the tube face, the eye blends them together to make all the various hues.

Source: Adapted from Paul Davidovits, *Communication* (New York: Holt, Rinehart & Winston, 1972), p. 114. Used by permission of the author.

only the analog NTSC 525-line format, a number of manufacturers have produced HDTV and SDTV receivers using cathode ray tubes. The CRT screen may be curved or flat, but the need to place an electron gun in the receiver means the cabinet is normally very deep. CRT receivers feature very bright pictures, but larger units are quite heavy. As older sets are retired, consumers will likely purchase new receivers without a CRT.

Liquid Crystal Displays

Researchers have developed several all solid-state electronics technologies for producing flat screen TVs that can be hung on a wall. Flat screens initially appeared in tiny, portable TV receivers and in laptop computers. Flat-screen displays are also replacing conventional CRTs as viewfinders in camcorders. Most flat-screen devices currently available use some form of **liquid crystal display (LCD)** technology. This technology employs a liquid crystal fluid sandwiched between two plates of glass. When voltage is applied to the individual subpixels, the liquid crystal molecules twist on or off. A backlight, mounted behind a polarized filter,

either blocks or allows light to pass through each sub-pixel, which has a red, green, or blue color filter. The quantity of passed light varies, depending on how much the subpixels have twisted or untwisted.

The sheets of glass between which the liquid crystals are trapped carry thin films of connected transistors etched onto their inner surfaces. Each tiny transistor is, in effect, a switch that can be turned rapidly on or off to polarize the liquid crystal at that point, and hence let light through (see Exhibit 4.r). The backlighting is usually produced by a fluorescent tube, but light emitting diodes (LEDs) are now being used in more expensive sets. Three transistors are needed to create a single pixel capable of displaying a range of colors.

LCDs are colorful, bright, and flicker-free, and they provide contrast comparable to that of a CRT. Improvements in technology and marketplace competition are reducing the cost of LCD TV receivers significantly. The small space requirements, reduced power consumption, and elimination of high-voltage electrical currents (with their associated electromagnetic radiation) make LCDs an attractive alternative.

Plasma Displays

The **plasma display panel (PDP)** is an increasingly popular flat-screen technology. A PDP uses a grid of tiny channels (pixels) filled with gas, usually a mixture of neon and xenon. An electrical charge causes the gas to change to a plasma state, generating ultra violet (UV) light, which, in turn, reacts with red, green, and blue phosphors to produce visible light. PDPs provide bright images that do not wash out under most ambient light conditions (see Exhibit 4.s). PDPs provide viewing angles of about 160 degrees, so even people sitting off to the side get a clear view, a problem experienced with early LCD sets. PDPs are relatively lightweight compared with other displays of similar size, and they are also very thin, allowing them to be hung on walls.

Digital Light Processing Displays

A third type of TV receiver popular today is based on a digital micro-mirror device that employs a technique known as a **digital light processing (DLP)**. Developed by Texas Instruments, DLP sets contain an optical semiconductor chip that contains up to two million, hinge-mounted, tiny aluminum mirrors that reflect light to make a picture. Each mirror is one-fifth the width of a human hair, and represents one pixel.

The number of mirrors used determines the resolution of the picture. The semiconductor chip reads an incoming data stream and electrostatically tilts each tiny mirror either toward (on) or away (off) from a light source up to 5,000 times per second in response to the bit stream information entering the chip. Mirrors facing

Exhibit 4.r

Liquid Crystal Display

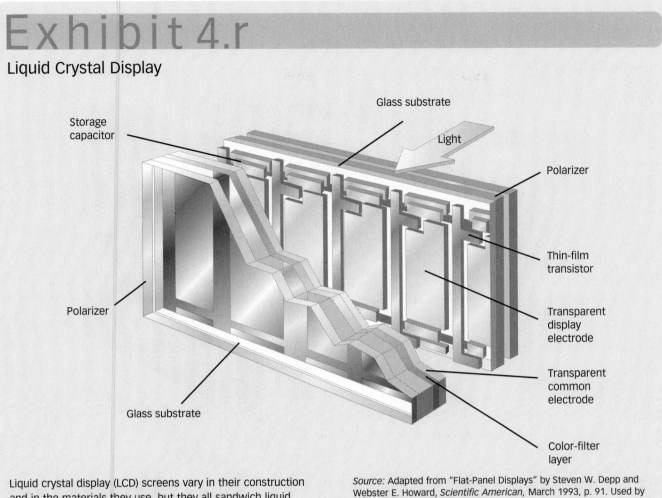

Liquid crystal display (LCD) screens vary in their construction and in the materials they use, but they all sandwich liquid crystals between two plates of glass.

Source: Adapted from "Flat-Panel Displays" by Steven W. Depp and Webster E. Howard, *Scientific American,* March 1993, p. 91. Used by permission of Michael Gordman.

toward the light source frequently produce light-gray pixels, while those frequently facing away from the light source are dark gray. A white light source passing through a color wheel strikes the mirrors and produces color information. The picture is then projected through a lens onto the screen. Consumer DLP sets are normally cheaper than LCD or plasma receivers, although 3-chip DLP projection units that use a prism to separate a white light into its red, blue, and green components are very expensive.

Improvements in Display Technology

Scientists continue to work on improving receiver displays. For example, **organic light-emitting diodes (OLEDs),** which rely on inks with light-emitting properties, may eventually replace today's LCD displays and eliminate the need for back-lighting while delivering ultra-thin screens. **Liquid crystal on silicon (LCoS),** a micro-projection device similar to DLP, uses highly reflective liquid crystals rather than mirrors to form the image. LCoS receivers are available in the marketplace, but are in very limited distribution.

Converging Display Technologies

Just as flat-screen displays first used in laptop computers migrated to TV sets, other computer-oriented technology is merging with TV receiver technology. Digital-analog incompatibility initially delayed progress, but $300 digital set-top boxes appeared in the mid-1990s, enabling viewers to use their TV sets to surf the Internet and view web pages. Concurrently, add-on circuit boards selling for around $150 became available for personal computers that effectively turned the computer into a TV/radio receiver. Appliances like the Apple TV, Sony's Bravia Internet Video Link, and D-Link MediaLounge can wirelessly transmit movies and TV

Exhibit 4.s

Plasma Display Panels

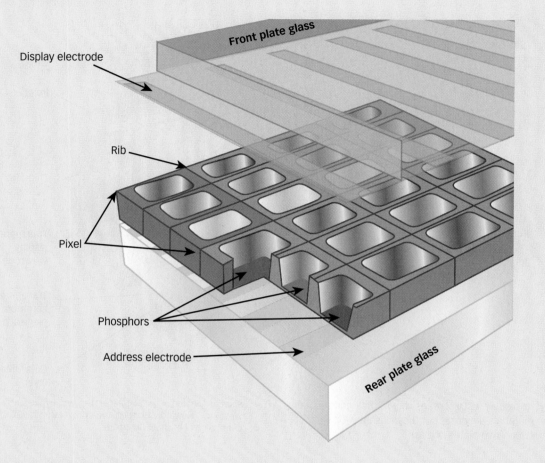

Display electrode

Front plate glass

Rib

Pixel

Phosphors

Address electrode

Rear plate glass

Introducing an electrical voltage through electrodes that crisscross the screen excites the atoms in thousands of tiny, colored, gas-filled compartments, causing them to fluoresce. A computer chip determines when electrical charges should be applied. One red, one green, and one blue compartment make up each pixel.

Source: Reprinted with permission of DTV City. All Rights Reserved.

shows downloaded from the web by a computer to a wide-screen TV set. These and other developments reflect the evolutionary convergence of the TV receiver and the computer into a single device that can perform the functions of both. However, accelerated progress toward setting compatible technical standards and improvements in broadband speeds is needed before the computer and the TV receiver are seamlessly integrated in the home, especially when it comes to providing TV programs in high definition. Eventually, the web–TV link may revolutionize the way audio and TV programming is distributed.

Distribution by Wired Relays, Wireless Relays, and over the Internet

Advances in telecommunication technology, and the supremacy of digital over analog transmission methods, are producing an electronic media system that many think will soon offer consumers access to whatever media content they want, whenever they want, and wherever they want. The interaction of technology, content, and the consumer is transforming existing media structures into new and unfamiliar forms where traditional business models no longer seem to apply. It is an exhilarating time for those with the creativity and vision to exploit the opportunities presented by new technology, and a time of grave peril for media businesses that stand still. This chapter examines both the established nonbroadcast distribution technologies that underpin today's electronic media system and the new technological applications that are shifting its very foundation.

Transmission media used in relaying information include those that use physical interconnections (copper wire and fiber-optic cable) and those that operate over the air using radio frequencies (satellite, microwave, and other wireless systems). Some connections combine both physical and wireless transmission media, such as sending an e-mail from your home computer connected to a wired broadband (high-speed) network to a friend's wireless cellular telephone. Any point-to-point or point-to-multipoint linkage, whether by wire or radio, can function as an information relay. A relay's channel bandwidth determines how much information the channel can handle in a given instant, which in turn determines which types of content the relay can distribute most efficiently.

5.1 Wire Relays

Early broadcasters tried using telegraph lines in the 1920s when the telephone company refused to lease lines for networking. But telegraph lines lacked the needed bandwidth. Voice transmissions required lines designed for that purpose. In turn, lines designed for voice were inadequate for the demands of television's full-motion real-time video signal. Internet users faced similar limitations when they tried using analog modems and the thin copper wire used by the telephone service to send and receive video via the Internet. The primary wire connections used for delivering TV programs, telephone service, and broadband Internet access to the home are shown in Exhibit 5.a.

Fiber-Optic Cable

The high capacity of fiber-optic conductors makes them ideal for handling digitally processed information. In a **fiber-optic cable,** hair-thin strands of extremely pure glass (or plastic for shorter distances) convey modulated light beams with a bandwidth over 1,000 Megabytes per second (MBps). Ordinary light will not travel efficiently through an optical fiber. Instead, **lasers** (light amplification by stimulated emission of radiation) or **light-emitting diodes (LEDs)** must be used to generate light consisting of a very narrow band of frequencies. Fiber-optic cables have many advantages as relay links, especially for very heavy traffic. Little signal loss occurs from attenuation, reducing the number of amplifiers required. Fiber-optic cables are small, lightweight, and insensitive to temperature. They neither radiate energy to interfere with electrical circuits nor receive interference from the outside. Fiber-optic cables have been permanently installed on heavy-traffic telephone routes and the main distribution lines of most cable systems.

Coaxial Cable

A special form of transmission line known as **coaxial cable** remains a primary method for relaying TV programs by wire. Coaxial cable's outer conductor provides a barrier that both confines the signal within the cable and protects it against external electromagnetic interference. Attenuation still occurs when signals are relayed via coaxial cable over long distances, but amplifiers inserted at intervals compensate for the loss. Coaxial cable's broad bandwidth is useful not only for television, but also whenever it is desirable to relay lots of data from point to point rapidly.

Twisted Pair

A third form of wired transmission line is the twisted pair. These are the same pairs of copper wires the telephone companies have used for decades to connect households for plain old telephone service (POTS), the original circuit-based landline telephone networks built out since the 1940s. Technological innovations in networking and switching digital signals have now unleashed the power of the twisted pair to provide not only phone service, but Internet broadband and even subscription TV services on par with cable (see Section 5.2, p. 103). While the main advantage of twisted pair is its wide availability in the telephone infrastructure, its bandwidth is far more limited than coaxial cable or fiber-optic cable.

5.2 Cable and Telephone Distribution Networks

Today, it is increasingly difficult for the consumer to distinguish between a traditional cable TV provider and a telephone company because both seek to extend their offerings into the other's core business. The cable TV

Exhibit 5.a

Wired Relays

(A) Coaxial Cable The name *coaxial cable* derives from its two conductors with a common axis: a solid central conductor and a braided copper shield conductor. Radio energy travels within the protected environment between the two conductors through the white plastic (or foam) insulator. The cable is covered with a tough outer sheath made of plastic. Coaxial cable is sometimes made from metals other than copper. Cable television relies on this type of conductor, as do many terrestrial relay links that convey TV signals, telephone calls, data, and other types of information.

(B) Fiber-Optic Cable *Fiber-optic cable* consists of hair thin glass or plastic strands each able to carry some 50,000 telephone calls—or hundreds of TV signals—transmitted on beams of laser light. Capacity is limited not by the small size of the fibers, but rather by the speed of the lasers that generate the information-bearing light beams, as well as the light detectors at the receiving end.

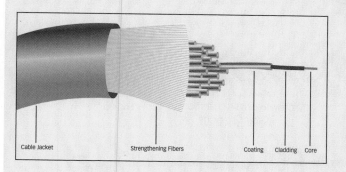

Cable Jacket | Strengthening Fibers | Coating | Cladding | Core

(C)
Each fiber-optic cable has extensive insulation and holds many bundles of fibers, each of which can carry many signals.

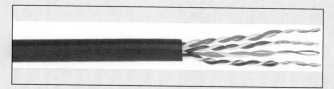

(D) Twisted Copper Pairs
Telephone companies normally use twisted-pairs networks to provide landline voice service. Today the twisted-pair running to a home may also be used to provide broadband Internet service. The pairs of copper wire are twisted to prevent cross talk and electromagnetic interference. Twisted pair wiring is available in a variety of grades and may be shielded or unshielded depending on the application. Telephone network trunk cables may contain thousands of twisted pairs.

Sources: (A) Coaxial cable photo from GIPhotoStock/Photo Researchers, Inc.; (B) fiber-optic cable photo from Photodisc/Punchstock; (D) twisted copper pairs photo courtesy of Extron Electronics.

industry continues to provide subscription TV services to over 64 million households, but today it also offers customers additional services, like telephone, broadband Internet connections, and multiple channels of audio programming. For their part, telephone companies, facing sharp declines in the number of subscribers to POTS lines, have moved aggressively into offering broadband Internet connections and are now rolling out subscription TV service. Although both traditional cable

operators and telephone companies are competing to offer the so-called "triple play" of services (TV, broadband Internet, and telephone), each industry remains dominant in its historical specialty. In 2008, almost 60 percent of all U.S. TV households were served by cable operators, while fewer than 2.5 million homes received their TV service from a phone company. Similarly, cable runs far behind the telephone companies in phone customers, about 16 million households.

System Designs

At the cable system's **headend** (sometimes called a "super hub" in telephone industry jargon), the system operator aggregates TV programming from various sources and delivers them via cable to subscriber homes. Besides reception facilities, a headend contains equipment for reprocessing incoming signals, equalizing and feeding them to modulators for transmission over the system's delivery network, and assigning each program source to a specific cable channel.

Older cable system designs, like the one shown in Exhibit 5.b, use a **tree and branch architecture,** where **trunk cables** branch to thinner **feeder cables** that carry the signals to streets, where still thinner **drop cables** carry the signals to individual households. This configuration allows a headend to feed programs over a radius of 5–10 miles; covering wider areas requires secondary headends that receive the programs via fiber-optic cables or microwave relays.

Today, most cable companies have widely deployed **hybrid fiber-coaxial (HFC)** networks that send signals over fiber-optic lines from the company's headend to an **optical node** located in the customers' neighborhood, a design known as **fiber to the node (FTTN)** or **fiber to the neighborhood**. At the node, the light signals are converted back to electrical signals that run through

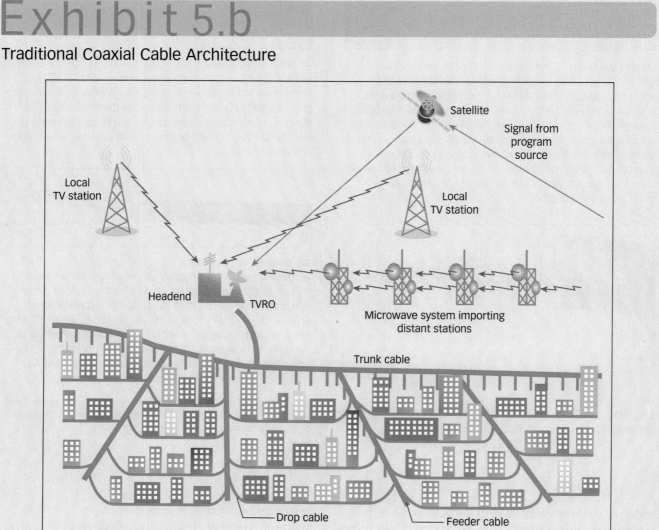

Exhibit 5.b

Traditional Coaxial Cable Architecture

The cable system headend receives off-the-air TV station signals picked up by special antennas, and possibly also signals from more distant stations fed by microwave relay. The most important antennas are usually several TV receive-only (TVRO) antennas for picking up satellite signals relayed from a variety of program sources. Trunk and feeder distribution cables, shown mounted on poles in the sketch, are often run underground within urban areas. Newer cable TV networks that also provide high-speed data, digital video, and telephony service often employ fiber rings with hubs that connect to nodes in the neighborhood service area.

Exhibit 5.c

A Hybrid Fiber-Coaxial (HFC) Network

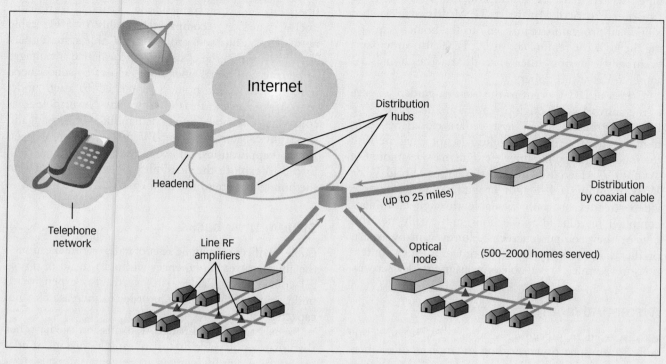

Most cable systems have installed fiber-optic backbones that increase bandwidth, allowing more TV channels and interactive services, such as Internet access and Voice over Internet Protocol (VoIP) telephone. The ring architecture connecting the headend with multiple distribution hubs provides backup protection in case of line failure.

coaxial cable to the customers' homes. The use of fiber-optic cable reduces the length of coaxial deployed between the customer's home and the headend, resulting in fewer amplifiers being needed to transport the signal. A typical node serves between 500 and 2,000 homes. Exhibit 5.c shows a headend with an HFC configuration.

Early telephone entrants to the subscription TV business have embraced two different network designs for distributing TV channels. Verizon, best known for its cellular telephone operations, has begun to deploy its FiOS network, which brings optical **fiber to the home (FTTH)**. Though more costly than other designs, running fiber directly to the customer's home adds tremendous capacity and, like a traditional cable system, all of the TV channels are carried simultaneously into the home using the same modulation scheme employed by cable systems. From the FiOS central office (or headend), a fiber-optic cable carrying a downstream wavelength of light brings the video signals into a neighborhood where an optical splitter duplicates the signal onto multiple fiber strands that run directly to homes or

businesses. Coaxial cable is used to link the fiber at the home to a **set-top box (STB),** which the consumer then uses to switch TV channels. The FiOS network uses a different standard, known as **Internet Protocol TV (IPTV)** to provide customers with access to its Video on Demand (VOD) content. IPTV uses Internet technology, such as Transmission Control Protocol and Internet Protocol (TCP/IP), originally developed for use in computer networks (see Section 5.4, p. 115). Similar to using the Internet, a customer makes a request for specific VOD content that is then delivered to the home. IPTV capability is also built into the set-top boxes used in the FiOS network. Exhibit 5.d shows how the FiOS network is deployed.

AT&T's digital U-Verse system, a second large telephone company venture into the subscription TV business, is a full-fledged IPTV network. By pushing fiber closer to the consumer's home and using TCP/IP, the U-Verse system can deliver hundreds of TV channels to the consumer over traditional twisted-pair wiring running to the home. Since copper phone lines already run to homes and businesses, there is a major cost advantage. Like the Internet, the U-Verse network delivers to the home only the content (TV channels) actually requested by the consumer, thereby overcoming the inherent bandwidth limitations of the small-pipe twisted pair. A routing technique, known as **Internet Protocol Multicast (IP Multicast),** switches individual program streams only to the homes requesting them via the remote control. AT&T also anticipates eventually running fiber directly to the homes of some U-Verse subscribers.

Critics of IPTV point to the "walled garden" nature of the networks. Although programs are delivered using Internet Protocol, IPTV systems are closed networks that, in order to ensure reliability, do not integrate with the much larger public Internet. The massive amount of "Web-TV" video available on the larger World Wide Web, including full-length programs and continuous video streams, are only available through customers' computer broadband connections and usually viewable only on their computer screens. However, many experts predict that it is only a matter of time until such content becomes seamlessly available on consumers' TV screens.

System Advantages

As discussed in preceding sections, TV broadcasting suffers from spectrum crowding and interference inherent in any over-the-air communication. Cable systems avoid these problems by sending signals through the artificial, enclosed environments of fiber-optic, coaxial, and twisted-pair cables.

If properly installed and maintained, cable TV is a closed system preventing signals from radiating beyond the cable and blocking external signals from over-the-air services from getting in. This signal isolation means that cable can use many frequencies denied to broadcasting and other over-the-air services that would otherwise cause interference. The extremely wide range of available frequencies allows cable systems to offer viewers hundreds of channels compared with an over-the-air station's single primary channel and a few additional multicast channels. But keeping cable a closed system requires constant vigilance, because damage by weather and rodents or inept in-house wiring by subscribers can compromise the system's integrity. Cable operators spend large sums annually to maintain their systems.

Another increasingly important advantage of cable is its physical connection to the home, which can deliver high-speed, two-way data flow. Though initially designed as a one-way delivery system for TV programming, cable technology inherently provides an easier and less expensive transition to two-way communication than does broadcasting, direct broadcast satellite (DBS), or wireless broadband systems. Cable can offer a full menu of interactive services, including telephony, Internet access, and VOD, all over a single wire.

Running fiber directly to the home also brings substantial benefits. A single glass strand to the home has potentially thousands of times the information carrying capacity of coaxial cable, depending on the equipment on either end of the fiber-optic cable. While a direct fiber link delivers tremendous capacity, it remains unclear whether it compares favorably to HFC cable networks as a business proposition. Cable system operators must weigh the costs and performance advantages of placing additional fiber nodes closer to subscribers' homes, with fewer homes connected to each node, against their present HFC networks. Nevertheless, as consumers become more demanding of broadband spectrum capacity for their TV, VOD, telephone, and Internet applications, cable operators may ultimately be forced to explore the possibility of bringing fiber into the home, in spite of the high cost.

System Drawbacks

Cable sacrifices the unique asset of radio communication—the ability to reach audiences without the aid of physical connections. Cable systems are also expensive to build, and to rebuild later in order to increase channel capacity.

Signals traveling through transmission media other than fiber-optic cable attenuate rapidly, making it necessary to re-amplify signals at frequent intervals, thus increasing costs. Cable companies must usually pay to mount cables on existing utility poles. And within cities, cables are often buried underground in conduits and tunnels at even greater expense.

Traditional cable operators are also constrained by the need to provide service to about 26 million households that subscribe to analog-only programming packages despite efforts to move them to all digital packages, which usually carry a higher price. Cable operators would like to reclaim the analog channels since each one takes up 6 MHz of system capacity on the coaxial cable, enough bandwidth to digitally deliver two channels of HDTV programming. Unlike the switched all-digital systems like U-Verse, traditional cable operators must send parallel analog and digital channels on the coaxial cable to the home to service analog customers. A Fall 2007 FCC ruling required most cable operators to continue to supply analog-only customers with local TV signals for three years after the February 2009 switch to digital TV broadcasting. While most operators convert local TV stations' digital signals into analog at their system headend, some cable operators are examining the possibility of switching to all-digital cable systems and providing analog-only customers stripped-down digital-to-analog converter boxes (rather than the more expensive digital set-top boxes that provide enhanced services like interactive program guides, VOD, and HDTV programming).

Exhibit 5.d

Verizon's FiOS System in the Home

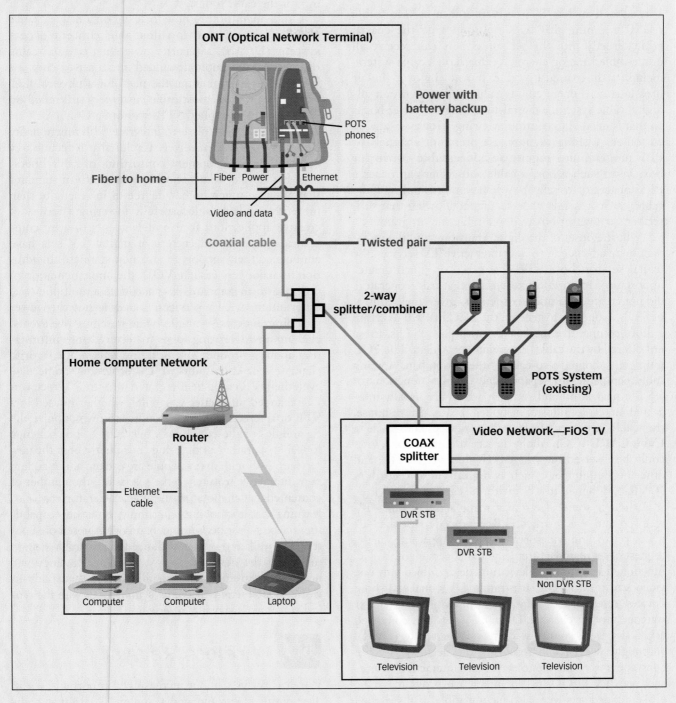

There are a number of possible wiring configurations for FiOS depending on the bundle of services ordered and the home's existing wiring. In this example, a strand of fiber optic cable runs to an optical network terminal (ONT) mounted on the exterior or interior of the residence. The ONT converts light waves from the fiber optic cable to electrical signals carried by copper wires. Plain old telephone service (POTS) is provided by twisted pair over the home's existing wiring. Digital video signals and broadband data are carried by a coaxial cable into a two-way splitter/combiner. One of the coaxial strands runs to a router to deliver Internet service to the home's computer network. The other coaxial feed runs to another splitter that connects to the set-top boxes (STB) on each TV receiver. While all the regular TV channels are carried simultaneously through the fiber/cable, the system's program guide and video on demand (VOD) offerings—including pay-per-view movies—are delivered on request using Internet Protocol. A battery backup unit provides up to 8 hours of telephone service during a power outage.

Cable Set-Top Boxes and Interactive Services

Virtually all analog TV receivers still in use are "cable ready," meaning that by simply plugging the coaxial cable directly into the set subscribers can receive all unscrambled analog channels offered on a cable system, including those used by cable, but not by over-the-air broadcasters. For an analog cable customer on an all-digital cable system, a digital-to-analog converter box is all that is needed to continue viewing. However, analog customers wishing to purchase premium channels or PPV programming require an **addressable converter box.** With such a box, a cable subscriber can order a PPV program (usually by phone or on-line) and the cable headend sends a special signal allowing that subscriber's converter box to descramble the program.

With the onset of the digital transition and the introduction of advanced two-way interactive TV services, the digital **set-top box (STB)** has taken on much greater importance. In an effort to ensure that cable operators did not create innovation bottlenecks given their control of STBs, Congress instructed the FCC in 1996 to create a more competitive market for third-party STBs, those not offered by the cable (or satellite) providers. The FCC ultimately adopted a so-called "integration ban," forcing cable companies to separate the two key functions of a STB: navigation and security, which are usually integrated in cable-industry supplied boxes. In response, the cable industry developed a device known as a **CableCARD (CC).** About the size of a credit card, CCs could be inserted into digital TV receivers, STBs, and other host equipment, such as **digital video recorders (DVRs),** designed to work with the cards.

Although some electronics manufacturers built TV receivers and retail market STBs equipped to use the CC, it has yet to find widespread support. Apparently at the request of set manufacturers, the initial version of the CC functioned as a one-way device and descrambled only one video stream at a time, frustrating DVR makers whose devices often record one program while the viewer watches another channel. Digital TV sets that contained a CC slot were known as **digital cable ready (DCR).** Although successful in removing the need for a STB, consumers were unable to access any interactive services such as PPV, VOD, or an interactive program guide. CC-equipped sets were also incompatible with switched digital video technology, like IPTV. Specifications for a two-way version of the CC were announced in 2005, but the cards have not been widely deployed.

Beginning in July 2007, the FCC began to enforce its integration ban requiring any consumers getting a set-top box from the cable company for the first time, or existing customers getting a new set-top box, receive one that is CC ready. By the end of 2007, about 2.25 million CC-ready boxes had been deployed; a small number compared to the over 38 million digital cable TV households, but nonetheless an expensive undertaking for the cable industry.

Cable operators are now focusing on a new software solution, known as a **downloadable content access system (DCAS),** a security program that each cable operator could simply download into a set-top box (or TV receiver), eliminating the need for a physical CC. However, in 2008, most cable customers still relied on cable-operator supplied STBs without a CC.

Today, there are plans to integrate STB functionality right into the TV receiver. CableLabs, a technology research and development consortium of cable operators, has developed a national open platform standard that allows a much higher degree of interactivity than presently available and hopefully fostering a variety of creative applications from independent software companies. Large manufacturers of digital TV sets have announced their support for the new standard. In addition to major services like VOD, the implementation of open platform standards may facilitate a multiplicity of other interactive TV services, such as letting the viewer pick different camera angles while watching live events, clicking on advertising logos to receive more information about a product, or voting by remote for favorite characters or contestants in TV programs. Some day, even the DVR could be integrated into the TV receiver.

Expanded interactive capability, whether housed in a STB or the receiver itself, promises to revolutionize the capabilities of the consumer's television. The challenge for cable operators is educating consumers about the new services. Although many people are excited about adding new interactive features to the television, the number of contented couch potatoes is huge. Operators are also learning that it is not enough simply to put new capabilities in the subscriber's home, hand over the remote control, and walk away. Users will need considerable help in mastering the new technology, or the technology will need to be extremely user-friendly, before the wondrous world of interactivity becomes synonymous with the typical consumer's viewing experience.

5.3 Wireless Relays

Wireless relays play an increasingly important role in distributing electronic media content. A variety of technologies, some long-established and others just being introduced, are contributing to the information revolution now occurring throughout the world.

Distribution by Microwave

Terrestrial microwave networks have been around since the 1950s and remain a crucial part of the communication system in the United States and around the world.

Exhibit 5.e

Microwave Relay Antennas

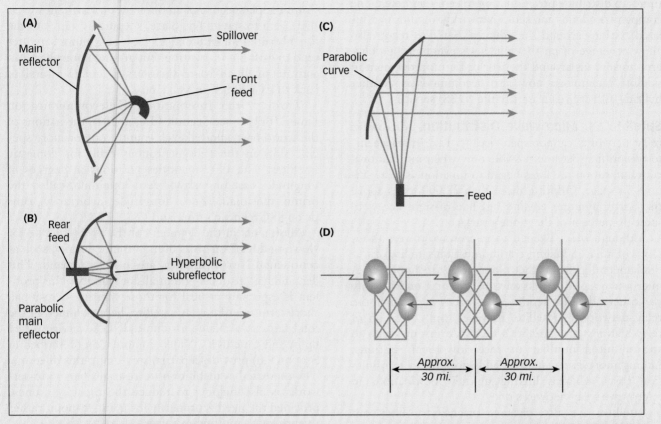

(A) An outlet positioned in front of the dish-shaped parabolic reflector delivers the radio waves, which are then reflected outward in a narrow beam resembling that of a searchlight.

(B) A variation of the parabolic reflector directs the energy from the center of the reflector toward a small subreflector that sends the waves back to the main reflector for transmission.

Source: From Graham Langley, *Telecommunications Primer*, 2nd ed. © 1986. Used by permission of Pitman Publishing.

(C) Dish-shaped reflectors lose efficiency because the feed tube or subreflector cuts off part of the outgoing beam. The horn reflector avoids this problem.

(D) Microwave relay towers can be seen throughout the United States, with all of these antenna types mounted at various heights, providing trunk communication to companion antennas about 30 miles distant.

Microwaves can carry large amounts of information at high speeds from point-to-point links using highly focused beams of radio waves. All kinds of information may be carried, including video, music, telephone calls, and web pages.

Microwave frequencies have very short wavelengths, ranging from one meter to one millimeter (300 MHz to 300 GHz), which begin in the UHF band. Terrestrial microwave relays use UHF waves that attenuate rapidly in the atmosphere and can travel only to the horizon. Higher transmitter powers and antennas that concentrate the energy into a narrow beam (see Exhibit 5.e) compensate to a considerable degree for losses from atmospheric attenuation. Increasing the height of the transmitting and receiving antennas extends the line-of-sight path over which microwaves can travel, but there are practical limits on tower heights.

Because of atmospheric attenuation and height limitations, relay towers are typically spaced about 30 miles apart. Repeater equipment on one tower receives transmissions from the previous tower, amplifies the signals, and retransmits them to the next tower in the series. It takes more than 100 towers to span the continental United States from coast to coast. Local TV stations make extensive use of microwave links to send live news reports from the field back to the station.

Distribution by Satellite

Like coaxial cable, satellites first served a limited relay function and only later began to deliver programs directly to consumers. Today, the satellite industry continues to distribute programming to cable and telephone company headends and sends network programs to affiliated stations around the country. Satellite relays also allow coverage of on-the-spot news events to be delivered to stations around the world. But improvement in satellite technology now also accommodates another hybrid—direct broadcast satellite (DBS) services.

Satellite vs. Microwave Distribution. Microwave relay networks cannot span oceans. Live transoceanic television first became possible only when international communication satellites began to function as relay stations in space. Orbiting more than 22,000 miles above the Earth, a single satellite has line-of-sight access to some 40 percent of the globe's surface.

Although often likened to microwave towers thousands of miles in height, communication satellites differ fundamentally from the older relay technology. A microwave repeater links one specific location with only two others: the next sending and receiving points in the relay network. A satellite, however, links a group of relay stations (the satellite's receive/transmit units) to an unlimited number of receiving Earth stations. Adding more Earth stations adds nothing to transmission costs, whereas linking up new destinations in microwave relay networks does.

Satellites are also distance insensitive. They can reach Earth stations at any distance within the satellite's **footprint** (coverage area). Distance adds no transmission expense, as it does with microwave networks. In addition, microwave signals lose quality as they go through scores of re-amplifications in being passed on from one repeater station to the next. But satellite relays amplify a signal only once before sending it down to Earth stations.

Geostationary Orbit. Early satellites moved across the sky like the sun and moon, requiring huge receiving antennas with costly tracking mechanisms to keep them pointing toward the moving signal source. But today's satellites can be positioned so that they remain stationary with respect to their target area on the Earth below. Once a receiving antenna has been adjusted to point in the right direction, it needs no further attention.

Satellites that appear to stay in one location above the Earth operate in **geostationary** (or **geosynchronous**) **orbit**—an orbital position directly above the equator at a height of about 22,300 miles. At that height, objects revolve around the Earth at the same rate that the Earth turns on its axis. Moreover, the centrifugal force tending to push a satellite outward into space cancels the gravitational force tending to pull it back to Earth, keeping it suspended in space for years.

The geostationary orbit consists of an imaginary circle in space. Satellites in that enormous orbit actually move through space at about 7,000 miles per hour. From the perspective of an observer on Earth, however, they seem to stay in one place, keeping in step with the Earth's rotation. In practice, geosynchronous satellites tend to drift out of position, but ground controllers can activate small on-board thrusters to nudge a satellite back to its assigned orbital slot.

Through the International Telecommunication Union (ITU— see Section 13.4, p. 283), the nations of the world have allotted each country one or more specific slots in the geosynchronous orbit for domestic satellites. The ITU identifies positions in degrees of longitude, east or west of zero longitude, called the prime meridian. Zero longitude arbitrarily runs through Greenwich, England.

Allotments in the segments of the orbit suitable for "looking down" on areas of high traffic density, such as continental North America, are in high demand. This demand has created a potential slot scarcity. This problem is especially critical for those wanting occasional, short-term use of a relay satellite, because much of the total capacity available for domestic U.S. service is tied up by full-time users. Video compression (described in Section 4.8) provides a partial solution to this dilemma. The increased availability of terrestrial fiber-optic networks is also helping to reduce the capacity crunch, provided the need is primarily for point-to-point rather than point-to multipoint relays.

Spectrum Allocations. Like Earth-based transmitters, satellite transmitters need internationally allocated transmission channels. Satellites used in broadcasting transmit on microwave frequencies in the 3–7 GHz region (C band), the 11–15 GHz region (Ku band), and the 17–31 GHz (Ka band). Ku- and Ka-band satellite transmissions, intended primarily for direct reception by small home and business antennas, normally transmit with much more power than C-band satellites. Capturing low-power C-band satellite transmissions requires the use of a much larger dish. Portions of the Ku- and Ka-band frequencies are also used for terrestrial-based services.

In areas of heavy terrestrial microwave usage, ground-based services often interfere with Earth stations receiving C-band signals. Ku- and Ka-band signals escape this drawback. But Ku- and Ka-band wavelengths are so short that raindrops in heavy downpours can interfere with their propagation, commonly called rain fade, a phenomenon well known to many DBS subscribers.

Each satellite needs two groups of frequencies, one for **uplinking** (on-board reception) and one for

downlinking (on-board transmission). These frequency groups must be far enough apart in the spectrum to prevent interference between uplink and downlink signals. Thus, satellite frequency allocations come in pairs—4/6 GHz, 12/14 GHz, and so on—with the lower frequencies used for downlinking. The downlink frequency bands must be large enough to accommodate a number of different channels for simultaneous transmission by the satellite's *transponders*—combination receive/transmit units. Some satellites combine both C-, Ku-, and Ka-band transponders for maximum flexibility. For example, Telesat's Anik F2 satellite, built by Boeing and launched in 2004, carries 38 Ka-band transponders, 32 Ku-band transponders, and 24 C-band transponders, and provides a wide variety of services. Using digital transmission and advanced compression technologies, today's satellites are capable of carrying hundreds of channels of TV programming. The increasing proportion of high-definition TV channels, which require approximately four times the bandwidth of SD channels, continues to drive demand for additional satellite capacity.

Transmission/Reception.

Satellite transmitting antennas focus their output into beams to create footprints of varying size. Exhibit 5.f shows an example. The narrower the beam, the stronger the signal within the footprint, because directionality causes signal gain.

A satellite downlink beam is strongest at its center, growing progressively weaker at reception points farther out. Earth stations located near the margins of footprints therefore need larger-diameter antennas than those closer to the center. Besides being on the margin of the continental footprint, stations near the poles have an additional problem using geostationary satellites. The receiving antenna of an Earth station must be pointed toward the satellite in orbit over the equator. For stations near the poles, this requires that the antenna be pointed almost parallel to the Earth's surface. This, in turn, increases the likelihood that the Earth station will pick up interfering signals from land-based transmitters. Special spot beams are sometimes used to help boost signals in these areas.

The diameter of Earth antennas varies from more than 100 feet to less than 1 foot. The large antennas of receive-only satellite Earth stations, such as those shown in Exhibit 5.g, have become familiar sights. Round or square antennas about 18 inches in diameter have become the standard for direct broadcast reception in homes.

The signals captured by a satellite-receiving antenna are extremely weak. They therefore need beefing up by a special high-quality amplifier—a **low-noise amplifier (LNA)**. LNAs magnify the incoming signal strength by as much as a million times. Even this enormous amplification is inadequate if the antenna's efficiency is decreased by snow or ice collecting in the dish. Manufacturers design dishes to minimize the effects of ice and snow, sometimes including built-in heating elements, but Earth station dishes located in the nation's snowbelt sometimes must be swept out. The LNA feeds the satellite signal to a **down-converter,** which translates the high satellite frequencies into the lower-frequency range that TV receivers use. Many systems use a **low-noise block converter (LNB),** which combines the functions of amplification and frequency conversion in a single device.

Satellite Construction.

Communication satellites need five essential groups of hardware components (see Exhibit 5.h):

▶ **transponders,** the receive/transmit units that pick up programs, amplify them, and transmit them back to Earth
▶ **antennas** for receiving uplink signals and transmitting downlink signals (both program material and telemetering information)
▶ **power supplies,** consisting of arrays of solar cells and storage batteries
▶ **telemetering devices** for reporting the satellite's vital signs to, and receiving instructions from, the ground controllers
▶ **small thrusters** for moving the satellite, orienting it, and holding it in its assigned position, activated on command from ground controllers

Orientation is vital to a satellite because its antennas must always point in the target direction and its arrays of solar collectors, located on the satellite's body or on extended wings, must be positioned to receive direct rays from the sun. These solar collectors provide electricity to operate the satellite. They also charge on-board batteries that take over during periods when the Earth's shadow interrupts sunlight.

Satellites operate at low power relative to terrestrial relays. Power per transponder varies from about 5 watts to 250 watts (the higher power for Ku- and Ka-band satellites designed for direct-broadcast reception). Most satellite transmitters use no more wattage than ordinary electric light bulbs, though their power is focused by directional antennas.

It seems paradoxical that, despite atmospheric absorption, satellites send signals such great distances with so little power. However, for most of their 22,300-mile journey, satellite signals travel through the near vacuum of space. When at last they encounter the Earth's relatively thin atmospheric envelope, they pass almost straight down through it, experiencing little attenuation. Terrestrial radio signals, in contrast, travel nearly parallel to the Earth, impeded by atmospheric absorption along their entire route.

Exhibit 5.f

Satellite Footprints

The higher numbers on the C-band and Ku-band coverage map show where the downlink beam is strongest and most easy to receive. In the center of the beam a smaller receive dish on the ground is required. As you move farther away from the beam peak, the beam becomes less powerful and a larger dish may be required. The numbers indicate the power of the received signal (effective isotropic radiated power) measured in dBW, or decibel watts. Note the higher signal strengths in the Ku-band footprint.

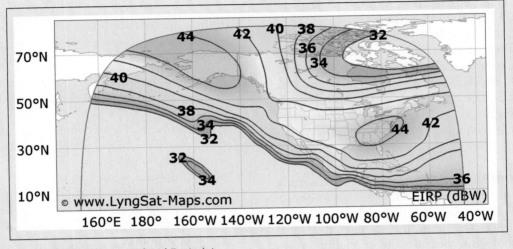

(A) Galaxy 13/Horizons 1 C-band Footprint

Launched in 2003, this geostationary satellite contains **(A)** 24 C-band transponders (Galaxy 13 service) that distribute cable channels in the United States and **(B)** 24 Ku-band transponders (Horizons-1) offering digital video feeds, Internet, and other data services. The satellite is located at 127 degrees west latitude.

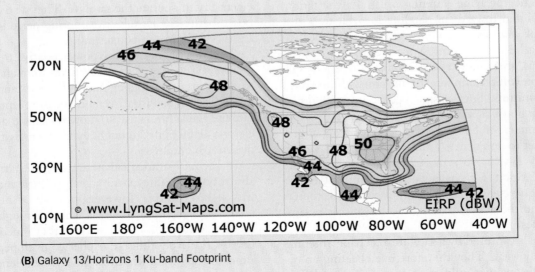

(B) Galaxy 13/Horizons 1 Ku-band Footprint

Source: Maps courtesy of www.lyngsat.com.

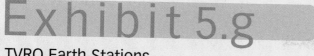

TVRO Earth Stations

Each of the relatively expensive television receive-only (TVRO) Earth stations (antennas) shown here concentrates the weak satellite signals into a narrow beam directed at a small second reflector mounted on the tripod. This secondary reflector beams the signal into a horn at the center of the TVRO dish, from which it is fed, still as a very weak signal, to a low noise amplifier (LNA) or low noise block converter (LNB).

Source: Photo © Carl and Ann Purcell/Corbis.

Satellite Launching. Launching involves two phases: A powerful rocket vehicle overcomes the initial drag of gravity and air resistance, carrying the satellite into low orbit. After being released from the rocket, the satellite's own, less powerful on-board rockets propel it into the high, geostationary orbit. Exhibit 5.i llustrates the sequence of events.

Direct Broadcast Satellite Services. Cable TV systems, broadcast stations, and other satellite-relay users can afford relatively large, expensive TV receive-only antennas (TVROs). Large antennas compensate for the low power of C-band satellite transponders. An unexpected bonanza for TVRO manufacturers came when people hungry for video programs, but beyond the reach of either TV stations or cable, began buying TVROs. They found they could intercept C-band satellite-relay signals with somewhat smaller, less expensive backyard dishes.

Today, almost all C-band households have abandoned their large dishes and subscribe instead to one of the Ku- and Ka-band DBS services designed specifically for home reception. The extremely short wavelengths and the high power of the DBS transponders allow for use of receiving antennas mounted on private dwellings—in most cases only 18 inches in diameter, but in all cases not more than 3 feet.

One of the technical innovations leading to a dramatic increase in DBS subscriptions was the use of spot-beam satellites to deliver a local market's over-the-air TV station signals to DBS subscribers directly from the satellite, eliminating the need to switch from the satellite feed to an over-the-air antenna to watch local programming. Using spot beams, a satellite can direct different signals to various limited geographic areas. The development of DBS TV systems in the United States is discussed in Section 3.4 (p. 48).

Satellite Set-Top Boxes. The core function of a satellite STB is to process the incoming feed and output audio and visual signals that can be used by the display device. Satellite boxes are also configured to authorize content and receive the electronic programming guide information. If needed, the STB will convert the digital satellite signal to analog for display on an older set.

DBS service offers a good alternative to wired cable systems for the one-way delivery of TV channels. However, it is unlikely to ever offer interactive applications or on-demand services at the same level of its wired competitors. The connection from the home back to the DBS provider is normally an analog modem in the set-top box that is connected to a regular phone line. This link allows for the purchase of PPV programming corresponding to the multiple start times the program is scheduled to be distributed via the satellite. Customers can also order PPV programming on-line.

One DBS operator, DIRECTV, is attempting to mimic cable by offering true VOD to their customers, delivering requested programs not by satellite but through customers' broadband connections. If a customer's connection speed is sufficient, the program stream could be watched almost immediately; if not, the program can be downloaded into the customer's DVR for later viewing. In either case, a DVR and a broadband connection are needed to use the service. The link between the customer's computer and the satellite STB can be wired (with an Ethernet connection) or wireless. DBS provider DIRECTV launched its On Demand product in Spring 2008, but HDTV offerings for this service were not available. It remains to be seen if such a system can deliver the quality, speed, and ease of use that consumers have come to expect. One potential roadblock is the increasing practice by broadband providers of limiting the amount of data that can be downloaded each month and adding surcharges for customers who exceed their limits.

Exhibit 5.h

Satellite Components

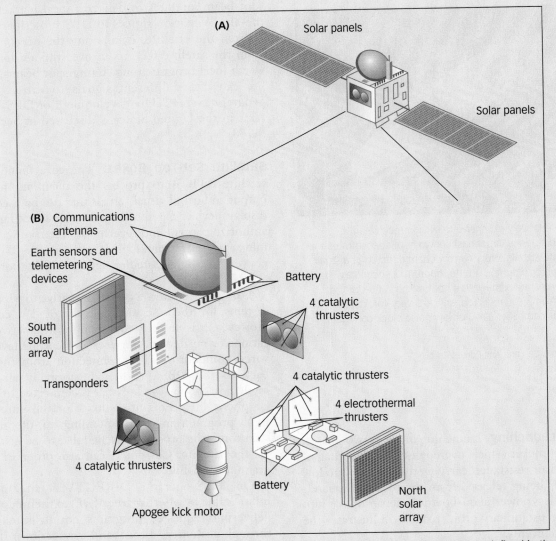

(A) Solar panels

Solar panels

(B) Communications antennas

Earth sensors and telemetering devices

Battery

4 catalytic thrusters

South solar array

Transponders

4 catalytic thrusters

4 electrothermal thrusters

4 catalytic thrusters

Battery

North solar array

Apogee kick motor

(A) The largest part of most communication satellites is an array of solar panels (which power on-board batteries)—in this case two huge wings on either side of the electronic core of the satellite.

(B) The major parts of a satellite as defined in the text: transponders, antennas, power supplies (batteries and the "wing" solar panels, shown here folded up for launch), telemetering devices, and thrusters for minor orbit adjustments.

Source: Mark Long, Ed., *World Satellite Almanac: The Global Guide to Satellite Transmission and Technology*, 3rd ed. © 1993 Access Intelligence. Reprinted by permission of Access Intelligence. All rights reserved.

Satellite Radio Service. Subscription-based **satellite digital audio radio services (SDARS)** offer customers an alternative to traditional radio broadcasting, with an average of 150 channels of audio programming. It is especially popular in areas severely underserved by regular radio stations. Strong digital satellite signals eliminate the need for a dish; programming is delivered directly to mobile- and home-based receivers. Ground-based repeaters are used to fill-in coverage gaps caused by large buildings and other obstructions. Satellite radio in North America is located in the 3.2 GHz, Super High Frequency band. See Section 3.4, p. 50 for a discussion of satellite radio services.

Exhibit 5.i

Satellite Launches

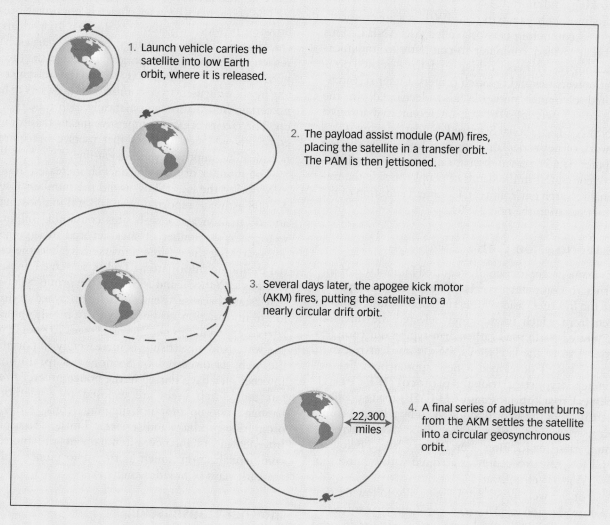

1. Launch vehicle carries the satellite into low Earth orbit, where it is released.

2. The payload assist module (PAM) fires, placing the satellite in a transfer orbit. The PAM is then jettisoned.

3. Several days later, the apogee kick motor (AKM) fires, putting the satellite into a nearly circular drift orbit.

22,300 miles

4. A final series of adjustment burns from the AKM settles the satellite into a circular geosynchronous orbit.

A critical moment in the life of every satellite occurs when it first leaves the Earth. An enormous, unmanned launch rocket is needed to (a) overcome gravity and atmospheric resistance, (b) attain escape velocity, and (c) place the satellite in an initial low orbit. The fragile satellite starts its journey as a mere passenger, protected within a nose cone. Only after it reaches an altitude of about 200 miles does a satellite ignite its own rocket engines to loft itself—by stages as shown in the diagram—into its 22,300 mile-high geosynchronous orbit.

Source: Mark Long, Ed., *World Satellite Almanac: The Global Guide to Satellite Transmission and Technology*, 3rd ed. © 1993 Access Intelligence. Reprinted by permission of Access Intelligence. All rights reserved.

5.4 Distribution by the Internet

Some people believe that the Internet *is* the information superhighway. For them, the Internet, especially the World Wide Web, is the quintessential convergence technology combining text, audio, and video into a new medium that will, eventually, replace most traditional electronic media. Although many people think that is unlikely, the Internet has remained a critical component in the digital revolution.

Today, the Internet offers an array of applications, many of which will continue to shape, supplement, and perhaps even replace the structure and operations of traditional electronic media industries around the world. Typical applications include search, e-mail, web surfing, e-commerce, instant messaging, podcasting, Internet radio, Internet telephony, Internet TV, social networking, and more.

The Internet began in the late 1960s as a government-sponsored computing network called ARPANET. This network provided computer-to-computer communication among researchers working on defense-related projects at universities and research centers. Other research-oriented computer networks also developed. In the 1980s, these networks became interconnected through the NSFNET (National Science Foundation network), a "network of networks" or inter-net. Interest in sharing computer data increased dramatically with the proliferation of computers in the hands of people outside the traditional research environment. Commercialization of the Internet began in the mid-1990s.

The World Wide Web

The arcane protocols initially required limited use of the Internet to computer experts. There were attempts to make the Internet easier to use, such as providing a menu screen from which users simply selected the function they wanted performed rather than typing out complex instructions. In the late 1980s, a Swiss nuclear research center (CERN) developed a new approach to linking computers; **hypertext transfer protocol (HTTP)** and **hypertext markup language (HTML)** made possible the creation of the World Wide Web by allowing computer users to access files residing on any other type of computers in any location. Tim Berners-Lee, a fellow at the CERN research center, is credited with writing the World Wide Web software.

Use of the web increased dramatically following the 1993 introduction of *Mosaic*, a revolutionary software program providing network navigation aids and featuring the icons and point-and-click features familiar to users of Apple Macintosh or Microsoft Windows computers. The Mosaic graphical user interface opened the door to computer-based communication for millions of people. Similar browser programs offering additional features and greater power appeared later, two of the most popular being Netscape Navigator and Microsoft Internet Explorer.

Long-running "browser wars" erupted in the late 1990s when competitors claimed that Microsoft had gained an unfair advantage by bundling the Internet Explorer browser with Windows, its ubiquitous operating system software. In 1999, a federal judge ruled that Microsoft had illegally used its monopolistic power to reduce competition in the software market. Microsoft's legal problems, however, appeared to have little effect on its browser business. In spring 2008, according to one global source, Internet Explorer remained the browser of choice for about 78 percent of all users, with Firefox (formerly Mozilla Firefox) in second place with about 16 percent. Google entered the browser wars in September 2008, launching a test version of its Google Chrome web browser for Microsoft Windows.

The consumer's browser choice is important because browsers provide the gateway to the web. Individuals can change their "home" destination, but many start each web session by visiting the site programmed into the browser by its maker. Designers also try to develop consumer loyalty by allowing users to customize their browsers to bring up certain information automatically each time they log on. The race to remain competitive means that browsers constantly add new features that users can acquire by downloading improved versions on-line.

The number of sites on the web increased dramatically during the late 1990s, as did the number of users. A 2008 estimate reported over 168 million host names and 68 million active web sites containing billions of web pages. A number of sites devoted to aggregating and searching the on-line universe have become essential to finding information. Today, search engines such as Google, Yahoo!, and MSN are the prime cyberspace real estate because users go to them when trying to locate information on-line. They are highly valued by advertisers trying to get their messages to people using the web. And advertising is increasingly important on the web, as discussed in Section. 6.6 (p. 140). The Internet may have started in the noncommercial realm, but today web users are exposed to a plethora of banners, pop-up graphics, jiggling icons, and videos promoting products and services. Those who used the Internet in its infancy often lament the increasing commercialization, much as the radio pioneers did in the early days of broadcasting.

Internet Transmission

The physical infrastructure of the Internet is made up of thousands of individual, mostly privately owned networks, that are interconnected with one another, similar to a road system or a spider web. Large central hubs, sometimes called gateways, are necessary for all of the networks to interconnect with one another. In 1995, four **national access points (NAPs)** were created to connect the major national backbone networks (three of which were owned by telephone companies). Regional networks connected to the national backbone networks and, in turn, smaller networks connected to regional sites.

Additional large central access points eventually emerged to serve the thousands of networks connecting to the Internet. Most networks seek multiple connections in order to continue operating if a particular connection fails, adding to the complexity. Today, there are hundreds of **Internet exchange points (IXPs)** around the world serving as giant central hubs for Internet traffic.

The physical interconnection between separate Internet networks is based on "peering" agreements to route traffic traveling on one network across a different company's network, usually without a charge. This sometimes leads people to say that the Internet is free, but peering agreements are between networks at similar levels: national networks do charge regional networks (and regional networks charge local networks) for the right to interconnect. Ultimately, the consumer pays an **Internet service provider (ISP)** for access to the larger Internet. A strict set of technical rules for routing data across different networks, called the **border gateway protocol (BGP),** are followed by ISPs.

Data flowing across the Internet follows a strict set of rules known as transmission control protocol (TCP), an advanced packet-switching technology that digitizes information, compresses it, and breaks it up into small bytes, known as packets. Delivery of the packets is accomplished using Internet protocol (IP). Each digital packet contains header information that allow switching devices called routers to send the individual packets first to the correct network address, and then onward to its final destination. The packets representing the original information typically travel many different paths, but eventually they arrive at their destination and are reassembled using TCP to form the original message. The most popular applications on the Internet use this combination of TCP/IP protocols.

Packet-switching technology is a great improvement over the traditional circuit-switching used in POTS, where two people are connected to a circuit that continues unbroken until the people finished talking. If the two were only sighing every 10 seconds or so, the connection remained constant even between sighs. Nobody else could use the network resources dedicated to this conversation. This was inefficient. If the sighs and long silences were broken up, the circuits could be rapidly switched during the silent periods so that two other people could get a few words in between sighs. Four people rather than two could use the same resources simultaneously, and system efficiency would be doubled. If the switching was done at the proper times and quickly enough, nobody would realize that the network resources were being shared.

Packet switching allows the number of people using the same network resources, and the amount of information conveyed, to increase dramatically without an apparent loss in service quality, provided the packets move through the network rapidly enough for the application. Some applications, such as transmission of a web page, can tolerate considerable delays in packet transmission, but others, such as voice and full-motion video, cannot.

Packet switching is also used in telephone services known as **Voice over Internet Protocol (VoIP).** Many large cable operators, AT&T's U-Verse network,

Voice over Internet Telephony

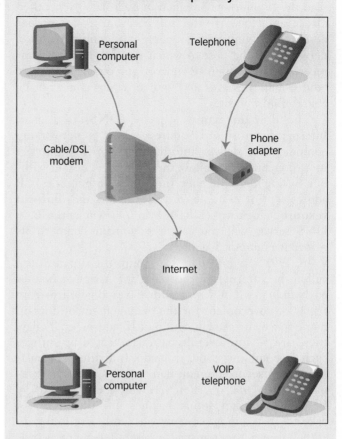

VoIP converts analog telephone signals into a digital data stream that can travel over the Internet. Spurred by the explosion in high-speed broadband Internet connections and improvements in technology, VoIP is beginning to capture the interest of consumers. The cost of VoIP is generally lower than traditional landline telephone service and often includes a rich variety of features like voice mail, caller ID, call waiting, and call forwarding. Mobile phones equipped with VoIP software allow users to connect to wireless Internet networks, saving their cellular phone plan minutes. Calls can also be completed from laptop computers containing VoIP software.

There are a number of drawbacks to VoIP service depending on the provider. A failed Internet connection means no telephone service. During power outages consumers without a backup battery connection will also be without service. There may also be problems reaching emergency 911 services.

Source: Federal Communications Commission, www.fcc.gov/cgb/consumerfacts/voip.html

and independent phone companies, like Vonage, deliver VoIP phone services to their customers over broadband connections using Internet technology. Exhibit 5.j illustrates how a VoIP service works.

Domain Name System

The Internet is like a post office in that an address is required to send and receive information. As data travel over the Internet, computer devices known as routers read the IP address contained in each data packet then direct and forward the information to its proper destination. Numerical IP addresses identify both the network and the host to which data are being sent or received. Without an IP address, you could not receive your e-mail messages and your browser would not be able to find web sites.

The **domain name system (DNS)** is a giant Internet directory of IP addresses used by networking equipment to deliver information. For the Internet user, domain names allow travel on the Internet without having to remember thousands of numerical IP addresses. For example, if a user enters the **uniform resource locator (URL)** http://www.miami.edu, a DNS server will translate the domain name to its respective numerical address, 129.171.32.100.

In 1998, an international nonprofit organization called the Internet Corporation for Assigned Names & Numbers (ICANN) assumed responsibility from the U.S. government for the management of domain name space and the allocation of IP addresses. Today, there are 14 top-level domains, indicated by suffixes such as .com, .org, .gov, and .edu. Individuals or businesses can secure domain names from registrar companies (or one of their resellers) accredited by ICANN to assign domain names. In 2008, ICANN relaxed its naming conventions and, beginning in 2009, allows the registration of almost any words users wish as top-level domain names. Businesses and large organizations, especially those with trademark and intellectual property rights to their names, will be given first priority.

Names of web sites may take on great commercial value since domain names are used to identify and locate specific sites on the web. Registered domain names can also be transferred, which led many people to register particular domain names in hopes of reselling them for a large profit. In 1996, "tv.com" sold for a reported $15,000. High-price transactions for domain names, often conducted by auction, include: sex.com ($12 million, 2006); porn.com ($9.5 million, 2007); vodka.com ($7.5 million, 2006); and bored.com ($4 million, 2008). The typical domain name purchase price for an existing site, however, is less than $1,000. While generic domain name speculation is a legal activity, **cyber-squatters**—those who register a domain name (or close variation) of an existing business whose identity is protected by trademarks, service marks, or other intellectual property laws—are likely to lose the domain name in a legal challenge.

Internet Access

An April 2008 study by the Pew Internet and American Life Project estimated that 65 percent of adult Americans had access to the Internet in their home, with only 10 percent relying on slower dial-up service. The most frequent way households connect to the Internet is through cable modems (35.3 million), followed closely by **digital subscriber line (DSL)** service (29.7 million). Over 5.5 million residences go on-line using a mobile wireless connection and about one-half million residences each connect using satellite or a fixed wireless link. Although fiber-optic cable is quickly becoming the dominant medium for the network backbone of telephone and cable operators, only about two million households connect through optical fiber running directly to the home (FTTH).

About 15 million homes still rely on a painfully slow analog dial-up connection for Internet access. Using regular phone lines, the maximum speed is about 56 kbps, but may be improved somewhat with data compression techniques, albeit at a loss of quality in graphics. Not surprisingly, access to the Internet at home and the purchase of a high-speed connection are positively correlated to household income, since both require paying a fee to an ISP with higher charges for a faster connection. All of the services use a modulation/demodulation device known as a modem to send data from the provider to the user's computer.

Cable Modems. Cable systems are offering "always on" high-speed Internet access in many communities. In fact, high-speed modem service is available to 96 percent of all households where cable TV is offered. Cable's broadband speed depends on several factors, including the bandwidth allocated by the system operator to data transmission and the amount of noise or interference in the system.

A state-of-the-art cable network can download data at speeds between 100 and 160 megabits per second (Mbps). However, the speed available to the consumer is less, usually much less, because cable broadband capacity is a shared resource and speed drops as the number of subscribers simultaneously using the system for downloads increases. For example, the highest advertised broadband speed offered by one major cable provider in 2008 was up to 16 Mbps downstream.

Upstream speed is typically much slower because a smaller slice of bandwidth is devoted to the upstream connection. This limited upstream capacity can place significant stress on network resources when networks or file sharing programs like BitTorrent are used, since they often require large upstream capacity. In 2008, maximum upstream speed, shared by all users on the node, was about 80 Mbps. Faster upstream speeds were forecast to become available in 2009. At least for now, by applying advanced standards, cable operators have the ability to deliver broadband Internet at speeds that allow them to compete with fiber-optic providers, like Verizon's FiOS system.

Digital Subscriber Lines. A telephone-based technology called **digital subscriber line (DSL)** has also found widespread success in providing broadband access to the home. In 1988, the potential of the copper twisted pair was finally unleashed with the development of DSL technology that separates the lower frequencies used for voice transmission from higher frequencies that can be used to carry digital information. Filters are employed to keep the high frequencies out of the user's telephone, allowing the phone and the Internet link to be used simultaneously.

DSL is actually a family of technologies offering a range of performance, the most popular for residential customers being the **asymmetric digital subscriber line (ADSL),** which provides much greater downstream than upstream capacity. The **symmetric digital subscriber line (SDSL)** provides a more balanced upstream and downstream capacity required for applications like two-way video conferencing.

DSL technology is distance-sensitive, and the data rate drops as distance between the user and the nearest telephone switching office increases. Telephone companies can extend the distance by utilizing fiber-optic cable in their backbone.

Full-rate residential ADSL provides downloads at about 6 Mbps and back-channel (upstream) rates of around 512 kbps. The next generation of DSL services is expected to deliver speeds up to 25 Mbps and higher depending on how close the home is to a telephone company central office.

The major advantage of DSL technology is that it uses the existing twisted-pair copper wires that already provide telephone service to most homes. Telephone companies can offer DSL service by simply installing new equipment in the subscriber's home and at the central office. Once installed, the same line used for normal voice communication can be used for data transmission simultaneously. This is an important consideration for heavy Internet users who previously paid for two phone lines into the home, one for dial-up Internet access and one for voice. DSL also provides the same "always on" convenience of cable modems. Unlike cable modems, DSL's bit rate does not decrease as more people use it, because DSL does not share capacity among users. The subscription plans of many DSL providers are tiered with higher monthly charges for consumers wanting faster download speeds.

Optical Fibers. While most of the large ISPs deploy fiber-optic cables to carry traffic along some portion of their networks, only Verizon's FiOS service and a host of smaller providers offer FTTH connections. Verizon's FTTH network offers Internet access with maximum speeds of up to 50 Mbps downstream and up to 20 Mbps upstream to all 10 million homes and businesses presently within its reach. However, the cost of such blazing speed is high, averaging over $100 per month. In 2008, most of Verizon's 1.8 million FiOS Internet subscribers selected slower and lower-priced offerings.

Satellites. For homes and businesses unable to access broadband service using a wired or terrestrial wireless connection, satellite offers a potential solution. For many rural households, the only connection to the Internet may be through an analog modem, if service is available at all. Today, small dishes mounted on the subscriber's home can communicate directly with a satellite which relays the signal to a company operations center connected to the wired Internet. The requested data are routed back to the customer's home from the operations center, again via satellite. While much faster than dial-up service, the biggest drawback is cost. One of the largest satellite broadband companies charges $80 per month for maximum speed of 1.5 Mbps downstream and 200 Kbps upstream, warning that the speed is about half as fast during peak times. The monthly charge does not include equipment and installation costs. Much faster broadband speeds are available by satellite, but the cost of such service is prohibitive for the home user.

Other Wireless Connections. The FCC estimated that in June 2007, over 35 million mobile wireless devices capable of accessing the Internet were in use, with mobile wireless broadband service available to 82 percent of the U.S. population. Wireless local area networks (LANs) and wireless wide area networks (WANs) allow users to access the Internet without the constraint of plugging in a wire. Cellular telephone services have also become serious players in the broadband market.

Wi-Fi. Wireless LANs, more commonly known as Wi-Fi or IEEE 802.11 networks (based on standards certified by the Institute of Electrical and Electronics Engineers) allow computers and other devices equipped with an appropriate network card to connect wirelessly to an access point that itself has a wired connection to the Internet. Wi-Fi "hotspots" can be found in buildings, college campuses, airports, coffee shops, and a variety of other locations. Both free and fee-based Wi-Fi services are available. The popular home wireless network, which lets multiple users share the home Internet connection and allows for mobile computing around the house, also uses Wi-Fi technology.

Exhibit 5.k

Municipal Wi-Fi Networks

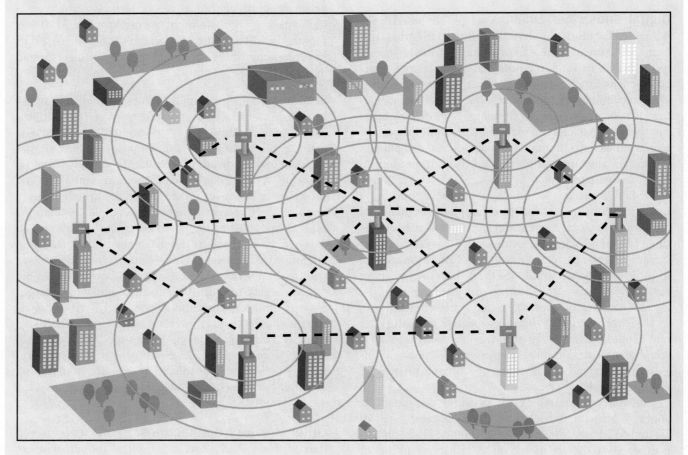

Many cities around the world have deployed municipal Wi-Fi networks. Multiple Wi-Fi routers can be meshed together to provide wireless broadband service to metropolitan areas. Data traffic is handed off from router to router using radio frequencies and software that determines the most efficient route. Ultimately, the signal reaches a wired Internet gateway.

In addition to using WiFi connections for routine computing tasks, like checking e-mail and surfing the web, WiFi enabled telephones can now be used to place and receive calls using VoIP.

One drawback to Wi-Fi is that service range is limited, due to FCC power restrictions. Depending on the particular standard used, maximum outdoor coverage is about 600 feet. This limitation can be overcome by meshing together multiple access points, creating a "cloud" of connectivity for the user, an approach that has been adopted on many large college campuses.

Some municipalities, including some large cities, have installed meshed Wi-Fi networks and provide broadband access to residents and visitors either free of charge or by subscription (see Exhibit 5.k). However, many large-scale deployments have been aborted when local governments are confronted with the expense of building large networks.

WiFi service uses an unlicensed portion of the electromagnetic spectrum in the 2.4 and 5 GHz frequency bands using fixed 20 MHz channels. Maximum download speed is about 54 Mbps, but speeds from

200 to 600 Mbps are anticipated using new standards. Of course, the average connection is much slower, since available speed decreases as more users begin to share the network. Obstacles, such as walls and doors, can limit the practical range of indoor Wi-Fi reception as well.

WiMax. A wireless wide area network known as WiMax generally works much the same way as WiFi, but covers a much greater area, up to 30 miles. WiMax towers can connect to one another using line-of-sight microwave links allowing them to function as backhaul feeds that connect ultimately to the wired Internet. Broadband speeds using WiMax technology can reach 75 Mbps downstream under ideal conditions. WiMax technology has been primarily deployed as a backhaul feed for cellular telephone systems or in tandem with Wi-Fi meshes to provide services to large areas. WiMax operates on a number of licensed and unlicensed frequencies in the 2–5.8 GHz bands, with flexible channel widths. A WiMax mobile standard, approved in 2005, has been used by some companies to build out regional and national networks capable of delivering broadband to their customers throughout the country. In 2007, Sprint Nextel announced plans to spend $5 billion to build a nationwide network based on the mobile WiMax standard.

Cellular Broadband Networks. Cellular telephone companies employ a variety of mobile data standards as they seek to entice users to connect their portable computers, personal digital assistants (PDAs), mobile phones, and other devices to broadband Internet connections on their networks. Compared to fixed wireless services such as Wi-Fi, it is a much greater technical challenge to provide broadband service while the user is actually moving.

Developed through the ITU, the most popular standard for mobile phone and data transmission in the world is the **global system for mobile communications (GSM)**. In the United States, GSM services use the 850 MHz and 1900 MHz bands. The GSM standard encompasses a number of different distribution standards.

The third-generation of GSM standards (3G) allows cellular providers to offer a wide range of advanced digital services, including mobile broadband wireless connections capable of delivering video streams. Networks supporting a 3G standard will be able to provide a broadband connection almost everywhere a person can acquire cell service. Depending on the network, a 3G device may be able to deliver up to 3.1 Mbps upstream and 1.8 Mbps speeds downstream. Already in the works is the next generation of the GMS standard, 4G, which could boost downstream rates to 20 Mbps.

5.5 Mobile DTV Services

Delivery of TV programming to mobile devices is one of the newest frontiers in the continuing electronic media revolution. The first mobile TV network was launched in 2005 in South Korea. It was introduced in the United States over the Sprint network in 2006. IP-based technology has now made it possible to stream digital video to mobile handsets, laptop computers, automobile displays, and other devices.

Initial forays into mobile TV services, made by telephone companies over their cellular phone networks, resembled little more than a selection of video clips customized for the small screen. Today, mobile TV customers can not only access video residing on the Internet, but also watch live simulcasts of certain network entertainment programs and sporting events.

Cellular telephone carriers are the dominant players in mobile TV today, but broadcasters are anxious to break into a market that may someday be worth billions of dollars in advertising revenues. The National Association of Broadcasters (NAB) anticipates $2 billion in incremental advertising revenue annually from mobile TV and possibly more from subscription fees.

Control of the wireless video pipe to hand-held and other mobile devices has yet to be determined. Although the telephone companies gained a head start by providing mobile TV service, broadcasters' plan to transmit mobile TV signals using their existing digital spectrum and infrastructure may ultimately be a key advantage. Start-up costs are low and engineers believe that local TV stations will be able to carry multiple streams of mobile video within their 6 MHz of digital spectrum. TV broadcasters across the country also control a key piece of content: local programming, especially local news.

The Advanced Television Systems Committee (ATSC) is expected to set a broadcast mobile TV standard in early 2009. Broadcasters hope to launch service later that year. Early trials suggest that broadcast mobile TV is technically feasible. In one trial, conducted in Las Vegas in late 2007 and early 2008, 24 channels of TV programming, mostly national cable channels, were made available to a sample of residents. In addition to the technical success, research also showed that viewers were willing to watch program-length shows rather than simply video "snacking." Researchers were also surprised to find that a lot of "mobile" viewing is actually done in the home.

Another possibility for delivering TV programming to mobile devices is via satellite. Satellite delivery would provide a national footprint that could be supplemented with terrestrial transmitters operating on the same frequency to fill in any gaps in reception.

Such a satellite–terrestrial hybrid network could someday be integrated with broadcasters' mobile efforts.

5.6 The Future

Technological change and its tumultuous effect on electronic media distribution show no signs of deceleration. While the Internet may someday become the principal delivery vehicle of electronic mass media, traditional distribution systems have evolved, adapted, and continue to dominate the delivery of audio and video programming to the home.

The growing availability of attractive content accessible through the Internet, such as video programs, music, and games, stimulated a tremendous appetite for speed and bandwidth on the part of consumers. The introduction of high-definition video on the web will unquestionably increase the consumption of digital bytes. It remains to be seen if the increased bandwidth that new technology may be able to supply can be offered at prices consumers are willing to pay. In fact, ISPs are just beginning to discourage so-called "bandwidth hogs" by slowing Internet connections to their heaviest users or levying a surcharge for exceeding the bandwidth cap offered with a particular monthly plan. While the ISPs argue that such measures ensure fairness to users and generate additional revenues needed to upgrade their networks, content providers claim that a change from today's flat-rate pricing structure or a throttling back of network throughput could cause users to reduce their on-line activities and possibly derail the advertising-based business model that supports video on the web.

In summary, the impact of the Internet on existing media distribution systems has been profound and will continue to play a principal role in the development of our electronic media system.

Commercial Operations

Commercial electronic mass media in the United States are businesses. Their primary motivation is to make money. And as in any business, the way to make money is to offer a worthwhile product or service to an interested buyer. The essential business of broadcasting is the sale of audiences to advertisers. Advertising's dominant role in financing most broadcast media has had a profound impact on the types, number, and variety of program services offered to audiences. Cable and similar technologies rely mostly on subscriptions for their support, although advertising plays an increasing role in generating revenue for those media as well. Advertising on the Internet has grown explosively in recent years and will probably continue to do so as consumers adopt high-speed Internet access technology. In fact, radio and TV broadcasters and cable operators are growing their individual audiences by expanding into on-line program content. This chapter focuses on commercial operations and their underlying business models.

6.1 The Basics

People sometimes use the terms **local station** and **local cable system**, but, in fact, *all* stations and systems are local in the sense that each is licensed or franchised to serve a specific local community. An exception to the local outlet model, **direct broadcast satellite (DBS)** systems market their services directly to consumers on a nationwide basis. Similarly, a growing number of "virtual" radio stations are using the Internet to reach national and international audiences.

Despite the localism of station licenses and cable franchises, media ownership and program production tend not to be local, but rather owned and operated by large corporations that can offer cost savings through what economists call **economies of scale**, meaning that large business often can be more efficient than a small business. For example, no single TV station in the country could afford to produce million-dollar episodes of a prime-time program, such as *Law and Order*, however, the NBC network can afford to do so by distributing the program to over 200 "affiliate" stations operating throughout the country. Still more efficiency comes from vertical integration—common ownership of production, distribution, and delivery facilities (see Section 6.4). The "delivery facilities" in reality are local broadcast stations and cable system franchises. All of these concepts will be discussed in more depth later in this chapter.

As presented in Chapter 4, technological convergence has blurred the once familiar distinctions among not only broadcast television and cable, but all kinds of mediated communication. There is an understandable confusion among audiences about programming delivered over-the-air versus over-wire, versus over satellite, and versus over the Internet. The challenge for the student of electronic media is understanding the differences among the technological, regulatory and economic *components* underlying these systems.

6.2 Broadcast Stations

In the United States, the traditional commercial broadcast station can be defined as an entity (individual, partnership, corporation, or nonfederal governmental authority) that:

▶ holds a license from the federal government to organize and schedule programs for *a specific community* in accordance with an approved plan
▶ transmits those programs *over the air*, using designated radio frequencies in accordance with specified technical standards
▶ carries commercial messages that promote the products or services of profit-making organizations, for which the station receives compensation

Within limits, an individual owner may legally control more than one station, but each outlet must be licensed separately to serve a specific community. Moreover, each license encompasses both transmission and programming functions. A station therefore normally combines three groups of facilities: business offices, studio facilities, and transmitter (including an antenna and its tower). Usually, all facilities come under common ownership, although in a few cases stations lease some or all of them.

Station Functions

Exhibit 6.a offers examples of **tables of organization** (sometimes called **organization charts**) for both a television and a radio station. These vary widely from facility to facility, but all outline the station's personnel structure and indicate who reports to whom.

All commercial stations need to perform four basic functions: general and administrative, technical, programming (including promotion and news), and sales.

General and administrative functions include the services that any business needs to create an appropriate working environment—services such as payroll, accounting, housekeeping, and purchasing. Services of a specialized nature peculiar to broadcasting usually come from external organizations, such as engineering consulting firms, audience research companies, and program syndicators. For a network affiliate, the main such external contract is with its network.

Technical functions, usually supervised by the station's chief engineer, center on transmitter operations, which must follow strict FCC rules, and the maintenance and operation of studio and news-gathering equipment. Tied in with almost all technical systems used by broadcasters (and cable operators) are computers. Many facilities maintain special departments or personnel dedicated exclusively to keeping the station's many computers working properly.

Programming functions involve planning and implementation. Major program planning decisions usually evolve from interplay among the programming, sales, and management heads. Because most stations produce few non-news programs locally, many stations have now dispensed with that Program Director title, leaving program decisions to the general manager or combining the function with that of the promotion department.

Promotion (increasingly called **creative services** or **marketing**) includes making its potential audience aware of a station's programs and special events through advertising, on-air announcements called **promos**, newspaper listings, and even T-shirts and bumper stickers. Some stations have a separate unit dedicated strictly to **sales promotion** aimed at helping the sales department attract advertisers.

News, though a form of programming, usually constitutes a separate department headed by a news director who reports directly to top management. This separation of news from entertainment makes sense because of the timely nature of news and the unique responsibilities news broadcasting imposes on management.

Sales functions divide into local and national aspects. Station sales departments have their own staff members to sell time to local advertisers. To reach regional and national advertisers, however, a station usually contracts with a national sales representative firm that acts for the station in out-of-state business centers. In addition to placing commercials on the station's regular broadcast programming, stations now use their dedicated web sites for additional advertising opportunities.

One job straddles the programming and sales functions—that of the traffic department. This department coordinates sales with program operations, preparing the daily program **pre-log** (usually called simply the **log**), which schedules programs and announcements.

New technologies influence station functions by enabling several stations to share duties. As will be discussed in the next section of this chapter, most radio and TV stations today are group-owned, meaning that they are owned by a company that operates several licensed stations. In recent years, the development of highly sophisticated computer-driven automation devices have allowed group owners to consolidate several individual station functions, such as traffic and master control, "under one roof." Many radio stations now receive live programming each day from studios situated at their corporate headquarters located thousands of miles away, thus eliminating the need for local program directors and announcers. The underlying motivation to invest in these new technologies, of course, is cost-savings, including the reduction of the number of full-time employees.

Some new technologies have had a reverse effect on station employment, in particular the growth of station web site services, which has stimulated the hiring of additional employees. As web-based technology has become more sophisticated and consumers have eagerly upgraded their home computers and adopted high-speed Internet access, on-line programming, promotion, and sales opportunities are on the rise.

Station Groups

Today, many important station management decisions are made on a group or corporate level. These include group purchases of supplies, equipment, consulting, accounting, legal services, syndicated programs, and group affiliation renewals with the networks. Some group owners operate stations affiliated with the same network, while others own stations affiliated with a variety of networks. The most powerful group owners are the networks with their **owned-and-operated (O&O)** stations licensed to the country's biggest broadcast markets.

For reasons of public policy, the FCC places limits on the number of radio and TV stations one owner may control (see Section 11.10, p. 249, for details). Still, within those limitations, the trend is toward greater concentration of control. Congress assisted that trend by passing the Telecommunications Act of 1996, which removed all national limits on the number of stations any one company may own, although there are still limits on the percentage of TV households (currently 39 percent) that any one TV group owner may cover. Also, there are limits on the number of stations one entity can own per local market. Radio was also given the green light to increase the number of owned stations operating in the same market to as many as eight, depending on the size of the market.

A consequence of this relaxation of ownership rules was a flurry of station-buying activity in the late 1990s that eventually resulted in several group owners acquiring hundreds of stations. The original motivation for granting increased multiple ownerships was to rescue struggling radio stations from financial ruin. By being absorbed into a larger *consolidated* operation, many station functions could be shared. Similar to the fallout from introducing automated technologies, consolidating station ownership has enabled broadcast station owners to cut costs and operate individual stations more efficiently. Again, this has resulted in a dramatic reduction in the number of individuals that work in radio. For example, most consolidated radio sales departments sell commercial time on all stations owned by the parent company. In addition, programming, promotion, and news duties typically are shared across all stations. For television, ownership within the same market in most cases is restricted to no more than two stations—what is called a **duopoly**—and, therefore, the impact of ownership consolidation on local TV markets has not been as dramatic as that of radio.

Interestingly, at the same time Congress allowed for such increased concentration, it also ordered the FCC

Exhibit 6.a

Broadcast Station Tables of Organization

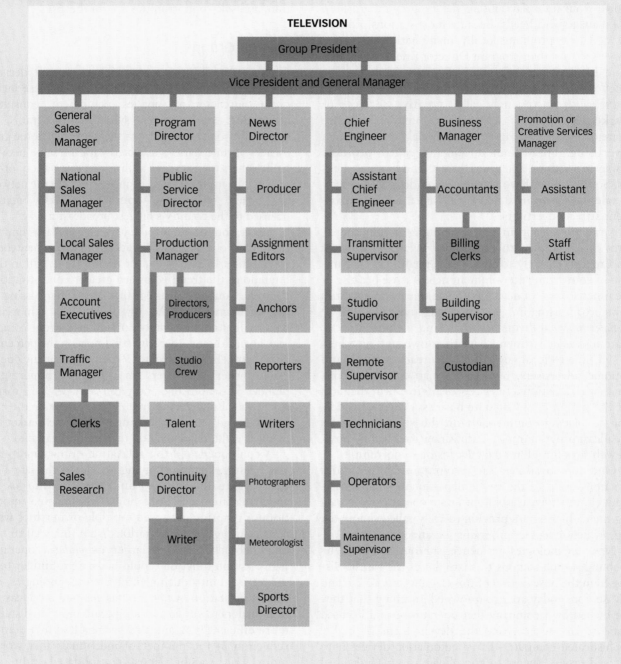

TELEVISION

Group President

Vice President and General Manager

General Sales Manager	Program Director	News Director	Chief Engineer	Business Manager	Promotion or Creative Services Manager
National Sales Manager	Public Service Director	Producer	Assistant Chief Engineer	Accountants	Assistant
Local Sales Manager	Production Manager	Assignment Editors	Transmitter Supervisor	Billing Clerks	Staff Artist
Account Executives	Directors, Producers	Anchors	Studio Supervisor	Building Supervisor	
Traffic Manager	Studio Crew	Reporters	Remote Supervisor	Custodian	
Clerks	Talent	Writers	Technicians		
Sales Research	Continuity Director	Photographers	Operators		
	Writer	Meteorologist	Maintenance Supervisor		
		Sports Director			

to find new ways to promote the ownership of media by small businesses, presumably in an effort to diversify electronic media ownership. Now that more than a decade has passed since the introduction of the 1996 Telecommunications Act, the results remain controversial. Advocates for the emphasis on ownership *deregulation* maintain that the broadcast industry desperately needed the relaxation of rules in order to compete in the brave new world of unprecedented competition from cable, satellite, telephone, and the Internet. On the other hand, critics worry about the loss of content diversity and true "localism."

Competition Changes Everything

The underlying stimulus for most recent changes in the structure, operations, and ownership of broadcast media has been competition. For instance, for over

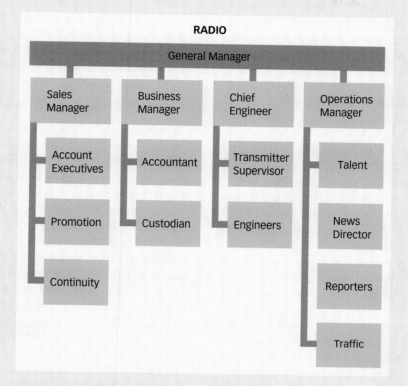

RADIO

General Manager

- Sales Manager
  - Account Executives
  - Promotion
  - Continuity
- Business Manager
  - Accountant
  - Custodian
- Chief Engineer
  - Transmitter Supervisor
  - Engineers
- Operations Manager
  - Talent
  - News Director
  - Reporters
  - Traffic

No single table of organization fits all stations. Structures, functions, and job titles vary widely throughout the industry. These are examples to illustrate how one TV station and one radio station might organize their personnel.

three decades a three-network oligopoly of ABC, CBS, and NBC dominated the TV industry and audience-viewing habits. By the mid-1980s, the competitive picture began to change when Fox became a legitimate network player. Later UPN and The WB would make things more interesting, but the biggest competition for audiences and advertisers has come from the enormous growth of cable, satellite, and Internet services. So far, conventional television has managed to survive by providing popular program content that proportionately delivers to advertisers much bigger audiences at any point in time than these other electronic media.

6.3 Broadcast TV Networks

As presented in earlier chapters discussing the history of broadcasting, the concept of networking made economic sense right away. National advertisers were eager to reach audiences nationwide and local stations desired quality programming, plus the opportunity to insert local commercials inside network programs. From a technological perspective, the only means of achieving this national exposure was to create partnerships with hundreds of stations, each broadcasting over the air to a designated geographical market. The FCC from the beginning has been reluctant to have too many of these connected stations actually owned by the networks themselves. Instead, the Commission wanted these stations to be somewhat autonomous. This long-standing posture has led to a vast station system in the United States consisting of network *affiliated* stations. Today, most of the major TV networks have over 200 affiliates.

Except for a small number of network O&Os, the relationship between a TV station and a TV network is purely contractual and subject to all kinds of legal issues involving programming obligations, compensation fees, commercial opportunities, and most importantly, affiliation renewals. Since the 1980s, several dozen stations have switched networks and a few have actually abandoned any network affiliation and opted to become *independent*. The duration of most network affiliation contracts has ranged from 3 to 10 years.

This technological and economic interdependency between networks and stations has lasted for several decades but, as presented in more detail elsewhere in this book, new distribution technologies, particularly cable, satellite, and the Internet, have caused the networks to reevaluate their relationships with their once exclusive partners. This rising tension is particularly evident within the TV industry and to a lesser degree within radio.

Although the term **television network** means one of the major national commercial networks to most people, in fact there are many TV networks in operation. Some are national, some regional, and some exist only for the purpose of distributing one or two programs. The rules dealing with affiliation agreements between networks and their affiliate stations define network, or "chain," broadcasting as "simultaneous broadcasting of an identical program by two or more connected stations" (47 USC 153[p]).

For years only three major national commercial television networks existed—ABC, CBS, and NBC. From 1948 to 1955 the Dumont Network struggled to be a viable competitor, but eventually failed. Over 30 years would elapse before the Fox network premiered in 1986, providing audiences with a viable fourth national network. In 1994, Fox made enormous strides toward parity with the Big Three when it entered into an agreement with New World Communications Group, whereby New World would switch affiliations of its major-market stations to Fox. The move created a domino effect as the major networks scrambled to line up new affiliates. Fox moved to near parity with the established networks by gaining the network rights to NFL Football and by developing a network news service, Fox NewsEdge. Each of the Big Three plus Fox now have about 200 affiliates, through which they can reach virtually all U.S. households.

In 1995, The WB network (owned by Warner Brothers), the United Paramount Network (UPN), (owned by Paramount Studios, and eventually CBS), began operations. A seventh broadcast network focusing on family programming, PAX TV, debuted in 1998. Like Fox before them, these networks began with limited hours of programming, but had aspirations of becoming fully competitive national broadcast TV networks. In 2005, PAX TV changed its name to i: Independent Television and two years later in 2007 changed its name again to ION Television.

After struggling for sizable audiences and experiencing huge costs in creating competitive programming, in 2006 The WB and UPN networks merged to form a single "new" network called the CW network. The letter "C" in the network's brand name refers to CBS, the parent corporation of UPN; the "W" refers to Warner Brothers. Obviously, shrinking from two affiliates to one affiliate per market resulted in many stations losing a network partner to provide programming. Responding to the crisis, NewsCorp, which owns the Fox network, quickly assembled the MyNetworkTV (sometimes written My Network TV) to fill the void.

Spanish language networks began to offer real competition beginning in the 1990s, in particular Univision and Telemundo (owned by NBC) have achieved almost complete nationwide coverage with affiliated stations.

In addition to the previously mentioned national networks, more than 100 regional and part-time networks are in operation, providing mostly sports and special event programming. Like stations, networks vary in their organizational structure, yet each must fulfill the same four basic functions of administration, programming, technical engineering, and sales.

The Affiliation Agreement

Today, most full-power commercial TV stations affiliate with one of the major networks. Most function as a **primary affiliate**—the only affiliate of a given network in a given market. **Secondary affiliates**, typically those in markets with only two stations, share affiliation with more than one network. Recall that affiliation does not mean that a network owns or operates the affiliated stations. Instead, the networks contract with hundreds of stations, agreeing with each to offer exclusive broadcast rights to network programs within a station's licensed market. This notion of **market exclusivity** is an important factor for acquiring syndicated programming as well as network offerings. The station in turn agrees to *clear* time for all or portions of the network schedule. However, it has the right to decline to carry any specific program, or it may offer to carry the program at a time other than that of network origination (a **delayed broadcast,** or **DB**); the network may or may not agree to this last option.

Under the conventional affiliation agreement, the affiliated stations received free programming in exchange for providing national distribution for network commercials. To enhance the deal, the affiliated stations also were given (a) cash compensation (often abbreviated as **network comp**) for the right to use the station's time, and (b) opportunities to insert local commercials within network programming, often referred to as **adjacencies**.

The amount of network compensation paid to affiliates varies from station to station, reflecting differences in market size, station popularity, and other factors. The total compensation package typically is divided into hourly rates based on the time of day. For example, compensation rates will be higher for programs airing in prime time than those scheduled for late-night exposure. Compensation represents a surprisingly small percentage of the gross revenues of network-affiliated stations—on the average, less than 5 percent, although small-market stations may depend on compensation for as much as 25 percent of their total revenue. But stations measure the value of affiliation less in terms of compensation than in terms of the audiences that network programs attract. In recent years, the networks have attempted to eliminate or cut back station compensation.

For decades stations rarely changed affiliations and when changes did occur, they were prompted usually by a network seeking a more powerful station. In the 1950s, the FCC expanded the number of available operating channels from a small handful of VHF (very high frequency) frequencies to dozens more UHF (ultra high frequency) frequencies. For years to come, UHF stations would have a terrible time getting good reception on ordinary home TV sets. As a result, when networks looked for new or better affiliate stations, UHF operators were the least attractive candidates. During the late 1970s, when ABC finally reached prime-time ratings parity with CBS and NBC, there was a flurry of affiliation changes in which many stations abandoned their old network partnerships when ABC tempted them with huge cash compensation deals. A similar situation occurred in the early 1990s, when the burgeoning Fox network went searching for successful VHF stations to bolster its station line-up. Of course, one station switch inevitably fosters at least one other switch in the same market. That is, the losing network must find a new affiliate, which in turn stimulates yet another switch, similar to a row of falling dominos.

The real revenue opportunities for affiliate stations are in the sale of local commercials the network leaves open for affiliate station breaks in each prime-time hour of network programming and the seven or eight minutes made available at other times of the day. Moreover, the stations' own programs (whether locally produced or purchased from syndicators) benefit from association with popular and widely promoted network programs.

Clearance

Networks and their affiliates experience a somewhat uneasy sharing of power, complicated by political and economic factors too subtle for contracts to define. In one sense the networks have the upper hand. Affiliation plays a vitally important role in an affiliate station's success. However, without the voluntary compliance of affiliates, a TV network amounts to nothing but a group owner of a few stations rather than the main source of programming for some 200 stations.

The complex relationships between networks and their affiliates hinge on the act of **clearance**—an affiliate's contractual agreement to keep clear in its program schedule the times the network needs to run its programs. An affiliate might fail to clear time or might preempt already cleared time for several reasons. Network public affairs and other nonentertainment offerings usually get low ratings and therefore most often fail to get clearance. Sometimes stations skip low-rated network programs in favor of syndicated shows simply to keep audiences from flowing to the competition. Often a station wants to increase the amount of commercial time available. It can run more commercials than the network allows by substituting a syndicated program or a movie.

Networks rely on affiliates not only to carry their programs, but also to carry them *as scheduled*. Delayed network broadcasts erode national ratings. Networks also need simultaneous coverage to get the maximum benefit from promotion and advertising. In practice, affiliates accept over 90 percent of all programs offered by their networks as scheduled, most of them on faith. Stations can request advance screening of questionable programs, but usually feel no need to do so, even though, as licensees, stations rather than networks have the ultimate legal responsibility. Because most TV programs come in series, affiliates know their general tone, so the acceptability of future episodes can usually be taken for granted. Thus, affiliates have little or no direct influence over the day-to-day programming decisions of their networks. In the long run, however, they have powerful leverage. Network programming strategists take serious note of the feedback that comes from their affiliates.

Network Multicasting Opportunities

Anticipating the move from analog to digital broadcasting and, in particular, the opportunities for multicasting, all the major TV networks approached their affiliated stations with novel proposals for using their standard digital TV (SDTV) subchannels as vehicles for new secondary national networks. These programming ideas typically include 24-hour movie channels and news offerings. The individual stations probably would be offered some type of network compensation either in cash and/or opportunities for local commercial insertion. While these network proposals may seem attractive, a major legal roadblock has been the reluctance of the cable industry to carry this programming without some type of compensation. To date, despite the pleadings by the NAB for required carriage of all digital channels, the FCC has sided with the cable industry's position that these new networks should compete for cable carriage in the same way that any other program content provider would approach a cable system. In order to achieve nationwide coverage, the network would need carriage agreements with 200 or more affiliated stations and the affected cable companies within each TV market.

Changing Network–Affiliate Relations

Starting in the late 1980s, when rising costs and increasing competition combined to weaken ABC, CBS, and NBC, the traditional network–affiliate relationship began to crack under the strain. Both parties believed they were being abused by the other. Affiliates felt that network compensation failed to reflect the true value of their time to their networks. When the networks increased the amount of commercial time to sell within its programs, they refused to increase the number of local adjacency commercial slots for the affiliated station to sell. The networks clashed with affiliates over program **repurposing**—the reuse of network programming on other media, such as cable networks. Affiliates argued that this repurposing undermines the importance of the broadcast outlet. As a result, network program preemptions by stations reached all-time highs, costing the networks millions of dollars in lost revenues. On the other side of this two-way tension, the networks complained of excessive program development costs of which the affiliated stations shared none of the risk and none of the debt. With some prime-time programs costing over a million dollars per episode to produce, regardless of whether the program would be a ratings hit or a ratings flop, the broadcast networks wanted some help from their partner stations. The increased cost of network programming and the networks' declining revenues forced them to seek new arrangements. Fox, for example, convinced its affiliates to pay a share of the network's royalties to the National Football League.

Over a period of five years or so the networks increased the pressure on their affiliate stations with the following business strategies:

1. A dramatic decrease or outright elimination of cash compensation to stations.
2. The introduction of so-called "reverse compensation" schemes in which some stations pay the network a fee to have the privilege of being an affiliate.
3. A reduction or "give-back" of local avails (i.e., adjacencies) in certain network programs or dayparts, enabling the network to acquire more commercial revenue.
4. Insisting on long-term affiliation renewals (typically 10 years), in effect squelching any temptations to "shop around" for a more agreeable network parent.
5. Instituting severe penalties for program preemptions by affiliate stations.
6. Insisting on having the right to repurpose programming to cable.
7. Forcing stations to broadcast promos for cable networks owned by the parent network (called **cross-promotion**).

But affiliates are not helpless in this struggle with the networks. Technology has freed many affiliates from their former, almost total dependence on networks for nonlocal news. Using satellites and mini-cams, stations can now cover not only local, but also national and even international news. In fact, the roles are partially reversed, making the networks dependent on affiliates for coverage of local stories of national significance.

The often rocky relationship between stations and networks will not lessen as new technologies enable networks to distribute their programming via non-broadcast means, such as cable and the Internet. A student of contemporary mass media needs to remember that the parent companies of the major broadcast networks are heavily invested in competing media. For example, the Walt Disney Company owns not only the ABC network, but also most of ESPN and a sizable portion of A&E, plus several other media enterprises. Similarly, NBC Universal obviously owns the NBC network, but also several cable networks, including USA, Bravo, and Sci Fi, not to mention the Hispanic broadcast network, Telemundo. Rupert Murdoch's News Corp owns the Fox broadcast network, the Fox News cable channel, and a significant share of the National Geographic cable network. The aforementioned are just a few examples of the deep equity investments large media corporations have in all types of media content creation and distribution, some of which compete against each other under the same corporate banner. A quick example would be ABC network sports and ESPN, each airing sports programming simultaneously. The first is distributed nationally through ABC-affiliated TV stations, while the second is distributed nationally through local cable systems (sometimes referred to as cable "affiliates").

Ironically, the one thing that seems to keep the networks from bolting to other media altogether is the fact that they own many successful TV stations. To date, these O&Os are highly profitable, especially those licensed to big city markets, such as New York, Los Angeles, and Chicago. Furthermore, the networks like the idea of duopolies, in which one company can own two stations in the same market.

Competition from Independents

A small number of TV stations, most of them UHF, are known as **independents**. They have no full-service network affiliation, although they may have a partial affiliation with a major network or one of the regional networks. In the context of American broadcasting, largely defined by networked stations, independent stations had three obstacles to overcome. The first was the ability to have a clear signal reception, particularly UHF reception. Cable helped by making the signal quality of UHF independent stations equal (for cable subscribers at least) to that of VHF affiliates. The second obstacle was the ability to obtain programming at a reasonable cost and in spite of competition from richer affiliate stations in the same local market. The third obstacle was related to national advertising, the life-blood of the American broadcasting industries. For decades, national advertisers ignored independent stations and routinely placed national commercials with the networks and their affiliated stations that could deliver the huge mass audiences. Most independent stations, except those licensed to big city markets, had to depend on local advertising for their livelihood. As years passed, the number of true independent stations dwindled, particularly after the introduction of the Fox network in the late 1980s and early 1990s, which converted close to 200 independent stations to Fox-affiliated stations. With the eventual emergence of more networks, such as CW, ION Television, and MyNetworkTV, few TV stations today are true independents, demonstrating that affiliation with a national network remains one of the most valuable assets a TV station can have.

Network Regulation

Unable to control the networks directly (because it does not license them), the FCC regulates them indirectly through rules governing the stations they own and the contracts affiliates make with them.

The FCC's network regulations were originally intended to ensure station autonomy and to prevent the networks from becoming the overwhelmingly dominant force in broadcasting. For example, regulations prevent network contracts from forcing stations to clear time for network programs. However, as network power waned with the increasing strength of competing media, the FCC became less concerned with network dominance. Nevertheless, the FCC still prohibits the national broadcast TV networks from preventing an affiliate from accepting programs from other networks, nor may an affiliate prevent its network from offering rejected programs to other stations in the affiliate's market.

6.4 Cable

Cable/Broadcast Comparison

The economic organization of cable TV systems and networks differs substantially from that of broadcast stations and networks. Cable systems depend primarily on subscriber fees, not advertising, for their revenue. A cable system therefore owes allegiance only to the TV households in its franchise area that choose to subscribe. A commercial broadcaster, in contrast, depends almost entirely on advertisers and has a legal obligation to serve the total audience in its market area, which is usually much larger than that of a cable system. Large cities often divide their municipal areas into several different cable franchises. Cable systems outnumber commercial TV stations about 3 to 1. Whereas most viewers can tune in a number of local radio and TV stations, almost without exception they can subscribe to only a single cable system.

Cable television (also called CATV or community antenna television) was developed in the late 1940s for communities unable to receive TV signals because of terrain or distance from TV stations. Cable TV system operators located antennas in areas with good reception, picked up broadcast station signals, and then distributed them by coaxial cable to subscribers for a fee. During these early years of cable's development, TV broadcasters appreciated the signal boost provided by this new technology, but in subsequent years, as cable began to acquire dozens of specialized program networks, over-the-air TV broadcasters began to feel threatened and this love–hate relationship has continued to this day.

System Organization

Today, over 6,600 **cable systems** (the basic units of the industry) serve about 64.8 million subscribers in the United States, with essentialy all cable subscribers having access to 50 or more channels and more than half accessing more than 100 channels. In addition, cable companies now provide broadband Internet access to more than 33 million customers. Exhibit 6.b shows how a typical system structures its organization. Whether small, with a few hundred subscribers, or large, with thousands, each cable system performs the same four basic functions as do broadcast stations, as described in Section 6.2. However, a cable system's *technical* functions differ from those of a broadcast station. Broadcast technicians' jobs end when the signal leaves the transmitter—listeners/viewers are on their own when it comes to arranging for reception. Cable technicians must be concerned with the integrity of both the sending and the receiving aspects of the system. Often this division of responsibility results in a distinction between inside- and outside-plant personnel.

The inside group operates and maintains studio facilities, as well as the complex array of equipment at the **headend**, which receives programs by various means from program suppliers and processes the signals for delivery via coaxial and fiber-optic cables to subscribers. The outside group installs and services subscriber cable connections and equipment. As for the *programming* function, cable systems start with a more level playing field than broadcasters because the distinction between network affiliates and independents does not exist in cable. Nor does broadcasting's elaborate symbiotic relationship between an affiliate and its sole network exist for cable.

Typically, cable systems fill their multiple channels with programs from both broadcasting stations and cable networks. In fact, typically more than half of all TV viewing in prime time occurs among a small handful of *broadcast networks*, even among cable households that can receive 200 or more channels. The general

Exhibit 6.b
Cable System Table of Organization

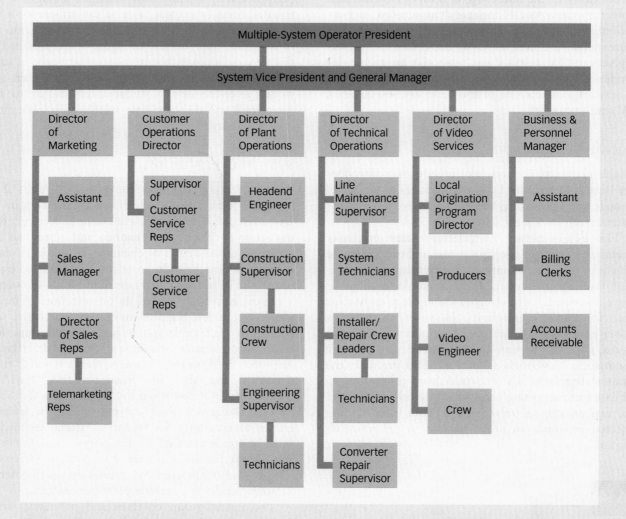

As is the case with radio and TV stations, every cable system designs its own table of organization to meet its individual needs. This is one example.

manager of smaller systems makes program decisions, usually in consultation with the marketing director. Some cable systems carry local programs, often on channels programmed by community or educational organizations. Although a few cable companies have made a commitment to locally produced news, most systems defer to broadcast radio and television in this expensive and personnel-intensive area.

Cable system *sales* operations might better be called *sales and marketing*. Although some systems sell commercial time on some of their channels, marketing the cable service to subscribers ranks as the all-important function that brings in most of the revenue in the form of monthly subscriber fees. The cable system marketing department tries to convince nonsubscribers to subscribe and current subscribers not to disconnect. These personnel also encourage existing subscribers to purchase additional service tiers and premium channels. The marketing department's customer service representatives interface with the public, answering telephones for eight or more hours a day, responding to complaints from subscribers and questions from potential customers. A system's ability to handle these contacts promptly and skillfully can have a profound effect on its financial success and, in extreme cases, on whether it keeps or loses its franchise.

In recent years, among large cable systems operating in large metropolitan areas, advertising sales has become an important source of revenue. Today, many prominent advertisers allocate substantial advertising dollars to both conventional broadcast television and cable. Offering commercial opportunities within programming aimed at specialized "targeted" audiences, the cable industry has evolved from a media industry relying almost exclusively on a subscriber-based business model to one that can increase its bottom-line revenues and profits through an advertising-based model.

System Interconnection

Often several cable systems in a large market *interconnect* so that commercials (or programs) can be seen on all of them, rather than only one, providing combined advertising coverage equivalent in reach to that of the area's TV stations.

System interconnection may involve physically linking the systems by cable, microwave, or satellite (**hard** or **true interconnections**), or it may depend simply on the exchange of videotapes (**soft interconnections**).

Multiple-System Operators (MSOs)

Firms large enough to make the capital investments necessary to build, buy, or improve cable systems are not likely to be attracted by the limited potential of a single franchise. Thus, a trend emerged toward **multiple-system operators (MSOs)**—firms that gather scores and even hundreds of systems under single ownership. Such firms have the resources to bid for high-cost, politically intricate cable franchises in metropolitan areas. Not until the 1992 cable act were any efforts made to establish cable ownership limits.

In the 1990s, the trend toward mergers and consolidations increased. In fact, the five largest MSOs now serve almost two-thirds of all cable subscribers nationwide, and the top 25 MSOs serve 90 percent of all U.S. cable customers. Nonetheless, hundreds of smaller MSOs operate in the United States. The era of the relatively small, locally owned "Ma and Pa" cable systems has given way to big companies buying out little companies and consolidating resources. The primary reason for most of these business takeovers has been economics. The enormous costs involved in upgrading cable's technical infrastructure to digital essentially forced smaller operators to get out of the business. In addition, these large MSOs have attempted to purchase or trade for systems that are close to one another geographically to form what the industry calls system **clusters**. Logically, clustering encourages interconnects and other cost-saving practices in which many systems can be managed from one central location, similar to radio station consolidation discussed earlier.

Vertical Integration

In addition to ownership consolidation of individual systems, cable television often involves ownership links with related businesses such as program production, distribution, and delivery. This type of linkage is called **vertical integration** and the cable industry increasingly resorts to it. Time Warner, by virtue of its acquisition of the Turner Broadcasting System, offers an excellent example. Time Warner operates the nation's second-largest MSO, serving millions of subscribers. It also has partial ownership of the CW network (a merger of the former Warner Brothers WB and UPN networks), several film and TV production companies, and nearly 20 cable TV networks, including CNN, Home Box Office (HBO), TNT, and Turner Classic Movies. Although not all cable networks are owned by MSOs, the trend toward vertical integration is always attractive to media businesses.

The notion of competition is difficult to define in an age of media consolidation, cross-media ownership, and vertical integration. As mentioned earlier, radio consolidation has resulted in one company owning up to eight "competing" stations in a single market. Similarly, all the major broadcast TV networks have equity investments in all sorts of "competing" cable networks. Along this same line of thinking, several media conglomerates, such as Time Warner and News Corp (i.e., Fox) own production studios that sell programs to competing networks that they do not own. For instance, Warner Brothers Studios is more than happy to produce a sitcom that will air on Fox in direct competition to programming on its half-owned CW network. In one sense, we can see a certain conflict of interest among the different components of a large media company. Some media analysts have referred to this phenomenon as economic "cannibalism," implying a kind of self-defeating consumption of one's own audiences and customers.

Enter the Telcos

For much of the history of the cable TV industry, telephone companies were prohibited from providing cable TV services in the same area they provided local telephone services. The Bell telephone companies were prohibited from providing cable services altogether. This changed dramatically with the passage of the 1996 Telecommunications Act, by which Congress, attempting to stimulate competition in the cable TV industry, allowed telephone companies to begin delivering cable services—both within and outside their local telephone service areas. According to the legislation, telephone companies can offer video programming services in a number of different ways: over the air, as do wireless cable operators; as common carriers; by obtaining franchises and operating as a traditional cable system; or through a hybrid operation known as open video systems, which combines aspects of common carriage and the cable TV model of operation.

As detailed in other chapters, telephone companies such as AT&T, Verizon, and others are now using their fiber optic networks to provide multi-channel video services in direct competition with cable companies. By the end of 2008, local telephone companies provided these services to roughly one million subscribers, but industry analysts expect that number to grow exponentially in coming years.

6.5 Cable Program Services

The channel capacity of a cable system makes it possible for a cable TV system operator to provide many services. In addition to over-the-air TV broadcast signals, most systems also offer diverse program services, including, for example, news, weather, business information, movies, sports, special entertainment features, and programming designed for specific audiences such as children, women, and ethnic and racial groups. Within the past few years, some cable systems have begun offering a full-range of telecommunications services, including video on demand, high-speed Internet access, and local telephone service.

Some cable operators also create their own local programming and provide access channels for public and institutional uses. They also provide leased access channels for "rent" to those wishing to show specific programs. Electronic banking, shopping, utility meter reading, and home security are some of the home services that are possible using the two-way transmission capabilities of cable TV systems.

Cable systems typically carry most broadcast TV stations whose signals cover their franchise areas. Beyond that, they draw on three main types of centralized program providers: basic-cable networks, superstations, and pay-cable/pay-per-view networks. Despite ever-increasing channel capacity, most cable systems are unable to carry all of the program services available to them. As the major cable networks began programming multiple channels rather than only one, competition for carriage intensified. Today, over 500 national video programming services compete for cable carriage and audience attention.

Basic-Cable Networks

The 1992 cable act requires cable operators to offer subscribers a **basic service tier** (or level) of program sources, including, at a minimum, local TV stations and all public, educational, and government access (PEG)

channels. (See Section 11.8, p. 246, for TV stations' *must-carry* and *re-transmission consent* options.) A cable operator may add other channels of programming to this minimum, or **lifeline**, service. Subscribers pay a monthly fee to receive the basic tier.

The 1992 cable act defines **cable programming service** as all video programming provided over a cable system except that provided on the basic service tier. This includes programming from such cable networks as USA, ESPN, and MTV, nearly all of which are advertiser supported. Some cable systems include such networks in the basic service tier, others on what they call an **expanded basic tier**. Many systems have expanded further by offering an advanced **digital tier**, requiring another bump up in subscriber rates. Some systems have specialized content tiers, such as movies, sports, and comedy, each for a separate fee.

For virtually all basic-cable network programs a cable system pays a monthly **per-subscriber fee** directly to each network that it carries. Fees range from just a few cents up to several dollars, depending primarily on the popularity of the network. Home satellite providers negotiate similar deals on a national distribution basis. Note how this business model is essentially opposite to that found in over-the-air broadcasting, in which historically the networks have paid fees to their affiliated stations for program carriage. As competition for channel space has increased, some new cable networks are forced to reverse this model and actually pay the cable operators up-front cash payments to secure carriage on the system's basic or enhanced basic channel tiers. This practice may well continue as the number of new cable networks increases. The worst situation for a new struggling cable program network is to be deposited on a system's advanced digital tier, which typically has fewer subscribers. As will be discussed in more detail later in this chapter, basic-cable program networks sell commercial spots to national advertisers, but also withhold about two minutes of advertising time each hour for local cable systems sales. The broadcast term *network affiliate* gradually has been incorporated into the vocabulary of the cable industry, characterizing local systems as similar to local broadcasting stations "affiliating" with a program network. Also, another source of confusion in terminology is that millions of households receive the same program content not from a cable, but from direct broadcast satellite (DBS), but these satellite providers still refer to their program offerings as "cable channels."

Obviously, popular basic advertising-supported cable networks have an advantage over many smaller nonbasic networks in that they receive substantial revenue from per-subscriber fees and national advertising.

Superstations

The **superstation** is a paradoxical hybrid of broadcasting and cable television—paradoxical because, although the FCC licenses each broadcast station to serve only one specific local market, superstations also reach hundreds of other markets throughout the country by means of satellite distribution to cable systems (see Exhibit 3.c, p. 46).

Cable operators often include superstations in one of their basic packages of channels, paying a few cents per subscriber per month for the service. The station gets most of its revenue through higher advertising rates, justified by the cumulative size of the audiences it reaches through cable systems. Before superstations altered the rules, copyright holders selling syndicated programs to individual stations had based their licensing charges on the assumption that each station reached a limited, fixed market. For example, syndicators formerly licensed programs to WTBS to reach only the Atlanta audience. But once WTBS achieved superstation status, its programs reached audiences in hundreds of other markets, in many of which TV stations may have paid copyright fees for the right to broadcast the very same programs.

Responding to complaints about the inequities created by duplicate TV program distribution on superstations, the FCC reemployed its **syndicated exclusivity (syndex)** rule in 1988. Syndex requires each cable system, at a local TV station's request, to delete from its schedule any superstation programs that duplicate programs for which the station holds exclusive rights. The rule spawned a new industry: companies that supply programs cable systems can insert on a superstation channel to cover deleted programs. WTBS, meanwhile, worked out a **blackout proof** schedule, free of syndicated programs subject to exclusivity clauses.

In 1996, the role of the superstation began to change. WWOR, a popular superstation from New York, stopped its nationwide distribution, and Ted Turner announced that WTBS would cease operations as a superstation. Turner replaced WTBS with a similar cable network called TBS Superstation. These events leave WGN in Chicago as the most prominent and popular superstation still in operation.

Some cable systems also carry **radio superstations**, notably Chicago's Beethoven Satellite Network (WFMT-FM), a classical music station. Listeners pay an extra fee to the cable system operator to receive such radio stations, as well as other audio services, which go through a special cable connection to their home high-fidelity stereo systems. Subscribership to premium audio services has never exceeded 3 percent of cable households.

Pay-Cable Networks

Subscribers pay their cable systems an additional monthly fee to receive **pay-cable**, or **premium, networks**. In exchange, the subscriber gets programs (recent movies, sporting events, music concerts, etc.) without commercial interruption. The cable operator negotiates the fee with the program supplier, usually splitting proceeds 50/50.

Included under pay cable are **pay-per-view (PPV) networks**. Instead of paying a monthly fee, PPV subscribers pay a separate charge for each program they watch, much as they would at a movie theater. Although their programs resemble those of regular pay-cable networks, PPV services usually offer recent theatrical releases before they are available on other channels, as well as special events that regular pay-cable networks decline to carry because of the high price tag. Professional wrestling and boxing matches typically draw the largest PPV audiences. Like other program services, PPV networks take advantage of multiplexing, offering their fare on several channels. This allows them to offer more programs and to schedule them more times each day. New, highly sophisticated technologies have made some program content available at any time, creating a new type of pay-per-view called **video on demand (VOD)**.

6.6 Advertising Basics

Unlike cable television, broadcasting in America operates primarily as an advertising medium. Dependence on advertising colors every aspect of broadcast operations. Except for direct mail, broadcast television ranks as the largest *national* advertising medium, though newspapers surpass television in total advertising volume. Radio comes in fourth in *total* advertising dollars, after television but ahead of magazines and the Yellow Pages. Advertising on cable and the Internet, although rapidly increasing, remains small relative to advertising on other electronic media.

Commercial broadcasting in the United States uses a two-phase business model in which stations and networks develop business strategies that address two distinct target "customers," namely *audiences* and *advertisers*. While audience-based business strategies are aimed primarily at the general public, advertiser-based business strategies concentrate on a much smaller audience of business decision makers—people who actually *buy* what the media are selling, namely audiences. As a result, the media first must attract and retain audiences and then sell these audiences to interested advertisers.

The long-standing advertising-based business model used by most electronic media is based on the important assumption that audiences will tolerate the interruption of program content to present marketing messages called commercials or **spots**. The media sell specified units of time within programming called **avails** (shorthand for availability), which can vary in duration from as short as 10 seconds to as long as two minutes. For television and cable, the most common length is 30 seconds, but radio prefers 60-second announcements, although all media have utilized at one time or another 45-, 15-, 10-, and even 5-second spot announcements. The total number of avails per program that can be sold is referred to as the program's **inventory**. These avails are clustered into program interruptions called **breaks** or **pods**. The number and duration of these breaks can vary greatly, depending on the format of the program and the demand by advertisers for commercial time. For example, during certain months of the year, particularly those leading into the traditional Christmas shopping season, local stations and national networks often will add breaks and avails to many programs to accommodate increased demand. Conversely, during slow months these same media operators may decrease the number of commercial interruptions.

The scheduling of commercial interruptions with program content has certain logical limitations in that there is a supposed threshold beyond which audiences will no longer tolerate these intrusions and tune out. Consequently, a station's or network's commercial inventory is *limited*. In addition, the surrounding program content is time-bound by air date and time of day. As a result, we can conclude that this limited inventory is also *perishable*. Given these dual constraints, an essential job of sales management is to maximize revenue through commercial pricing for a limited and perishable inventory. For many contemporary businesses, the coordination of pricing and inventory has been called **yield management**, a concept taken originally from agriculture studies investigating methods to earn the most income from perishable crops. Today, the notions of yield management are applied to myriad business models that must wrestle with limited and perishable inventories. For example, the airline industry is often used as an exemplar for yield-management case studies because they must reconcile the pressures of seating capacity, flight schedules, and competitive pricing by rival companies. Another example would be managing the pricing of a limited number of hotel rooms. By selling too cheaply, the hotel may be deprived of greater revenue but, on the other hand, excessive pricing may leave the hotel with empty rooms at the end of an evening generating no revenue at all! In both scenarios, competition can play a major role. Do you own the only hotel in town or do you have a dozen competitors operating on the same street as your business? In a similar manner, broadcasters and cable operators must reconcile the interrelated pressures of a program's commercial capacity, the scheduled air date, and competitive pricing by rival companies. Inventory and pricing factors included within yield management are interrelated in that commercial pricing is adjusted continually in response to the available spot inventory. Ultimately, these decisions determine a company's sales revenue. The term *yield management* has become part of the vocabulary of radio, television, and cable sales management systems. The introduction of sophisticated yield-management computer software has enabled sales managers to quickly adjust inventory and pricing strategies based on market demand.

In recent years, the amount of time allocated to commercials and promotional announcements in general has increased substantially, stimulating much criticism and accusations from advertisers about the negative impact of "commercial clutter" on the desired effectiveness of commercials. To date, cable networks appear to generate more commercial clutter than broadcast networks.

From Mass Media to Niche Media Thinking

Although the notion of a mass audience still exists, as demonstrated by the huge audiences broadcast network programs attract each week in prime time, the dramatic expansion in recent years of multichannel delivery systems, such as cable, satellite, and the Internet, has fostered a serious interest in more **niche** content that focuses more on specialized "target audiences" rather than on a singular, homogeneous mass audience. In addition, many advertisers are more than willing to purchase commercial time within programs that attract a certain *type* of audience that matches their desired customer profile.

Niche thinking has its origins in survival. That is, in order to survive and prosper in a highly competitive marketplace, individual firms must *differentiate* themselves from their competitors by creating unique and desirable niches. The lack of highly differentiated consumer products in a marketplace leads to the undesirable situation that brand-management researchers call **equivalent substitutes**, in which a customer finds two or more brands equally satisfying and therefore easily substituted. This lack of **brand differentiation** often leads to mutually destructive "pricing wars" among competitors, where the only victor is the buyer.

Looking at the history of electronic media, we can see how radio was the true pioneer in creating niches in the form of specialized format programming aimed at specific demographic groups. From hip hop, country and gospel, to news/talk, oldies, and jazz, each format is intended to nurture a particular niche audience that will be of value to advertisers looking for potential customers for their products and services. Later, cable adopted similar niche strategies by creating specialized program networks such as MTV, Nickelodeon, ESPN, CNN, Spike, and Oxygen; each catering to the interests of certain types of audiences that may be of interest to potential advertisers. Broadcast TV stations and networks tend to take a broader cut with their programming by offering a variety of program niches throughout the broadcast day. For example, a typical network-affiliated TV station during daytime hours may cater to young stay-at-home women with soap operas and talk shows, but later in the day aim its programming at young males with a prime-time football game. The diversity of audiences attracted by typical broadcast stations and networks allows their sales departments to approach an equally diverse group of advertisers. On the contrary, cable program networks tend to be more consistent in their programming throughout the day and night hours. Cable networks deliver relatively small audiences compared with the major broadcast networks and therefore advertisers are likely to place commercials on several different networks, which can be a bothersome task. Time-buying organizations, such as Cable One, solve this problem by negotiating deals on behalf of advertisers for spots on any combination of cable networks.

Types of Advertising

Radio, television and cable advertising can be divided into four categories: **network advertising**, **local advertising**, **national spot advertising** and **syndicated barter advertising**. These types of advertising are discussed in the following paragraphs.

Network advertising includes commercials placed by major advertisers on the broadcast and cable networks intended to reach a nationwide audience. Although the commercials will be seen on hundreds of stations (i.e., network affiliates) in local markets, the stations themselves do not share in any of the commercial revenue. As part of their affiliation agreement, the networks do offer their local stations the opportunity to insert commercials called **adjacencies** (i.e., implying that the local commercials are scheduled adjacent to network programming). Each broadcast TV network maintains its own sales department, typically headed by a vice president, usually with offices in New York and Los Angeles, and sometimes in other cities such as Chicago and Dallas. They tend to organize into specialties such as prime time, late night, news, sports, and so on, and they deal almost exclusively with advertising agencies.

Ad-supported cable networks and superstations also have sales departments. Advertisers who wish to place orders with several networks often do so through time-buying organizations, which negotiate buys on their behalf for spots on a combination of cable networks.

Cable system interconnects differ from cable networks. A network may deliver its programs to thousands of systems throughout the nation, but interconnects involve mostly the placement of commercials on a number of systems within a geographic region. The area covered by such a group of systems can vary greatly depending on the location of cities and cable franchises.

Local advertising includes commercials placed by businesses or advertising agencies located in the same market as the TV station or cable franchise. For example, a local car dealer in Boston will purchase commercial time on a TV station licensed to the Boston TV market or Boston cable franchise area. In this situation, the local station or system retains all the advertising revenue. Local advertising comes mostly from fast-food restaurants, auto dealers, department and furniture stores, banks, food stores, and movie theaters.

Often, local retailers participate in a cost-saving exercise with product manufacturers known as **cooperative advertising**, or just **co-op**. The manufacturer or distributor will offer to pay a percentage of the advertising costs. In general, radio stations, especially small-market radio stations, are more dependent on local advertising than their television counterparts. For many local TV stations, almost half of the station's total revenue comes from our next advertising category, called national spot.

Most TV station sales departments employ a general sales manager, a local (and sometimes also a national) sales manager, account executives, and support staff. The number of account executives (a fancy name for salespersons) varies from station to station. About six usually suffice for a medium-market outlet. At some stations a sales assistant or even a secretary does all the support work; some stations include research specialists and commercial writers on the sales staff.

Sales managers hire, fire, and train salespersons, assigning them a list of specific advertisers and ad agencies as contacts. Beginning salespeople sometimes start without benefit of such an account list (other than, by industry tradition, the Yellow Pages). They must develop their own accounts, making **cold calls** on potential new advertisers.

Salespeople usually work on a commission basis, keeping a percentage of all advertising dollars they bring into the station. This arrangement gives them incentive to make more sales to raise their income.

National spot advertising is an alternative to network advertising in which a business wishes not to reach the entire country but prefers to advertise in only selected geographical areas of the country. For example, a company that sells snow blowers would be interested in reaching people living in New England, but certainly not the Deep South. National spot advertisers bypass the networks and purchase commercial time from local stations or cable systems. Typically a **national rep firm** acts as an intermediary or broker between an advertising agency and the station. National-spot advertising enables advertisers to capitalize on audience interest in local programs, something the network advertiser cannot do. The largest national advertisers use spot and network advertising in combination to achieve better coverage than either could yield on its own.

A rep firm contracts with a string of stations, or MSOs, acting as an extension of the stations' own sales staffs in national and regional markets. Reps perform many services other than sales. Their national perspective provides client stations or systems with a broader view than that of local markets. Reps often advise clients on programming, conduct research for them, and act as all-around consultants. In return for their services, reps collect a commission of 8 to 15 percent on spot sales they make for their clients.

The size of the market in which a radio, TV station, or cable system operates is an important factor in determining how many national spot dollars are spent by advertisers over the course of a year. A simple rule of thumb is that large markets tend to attract more national advertising than small markets, regardless of a station's ratings performance. The smaller the market, the more dependent stations are on local and regional advertisers.

Barter syndication advertising is defined as commercials placed by national advertisers inside various syndicated programs airing on local TV stations around the country. This will be discussed in greater detail in Chapter 8.

Barter-syndicated programs are purchased by individual broadcast stations with the understanding that some commercial opportunities are turned back to the syndicator to sell to national advertisers. Local stations do not share in this "bartered" revenue, but can still sell the remaining open commercial avails to local advertisers or national spot clients.

A national advertiser using this method must be aware that, unlike network advertising, a specific syndicated program currently may not air in every market in the United States. Also, the advertiser cannot be assured that the program airs at the same time of day in every market where it is cleared for broadcast.

Today, most stations are members of the Radio Advertising Bureau (RAB) or the Television Bureau of Advertising, commonly TVB. Cable companies have their own sales organization called the Cable Advertising Bureau (CAB). These not-for-profit trade associations provide members with a variety of research and sales training resources. Although some items are available only to paying members, others are available free to interested advertisers, students, and the general public.

Managing Spot Placement within Programs

The sales management team and the traffic department work together in deciding where commercials are placed. Students often become confused when comparing the types of advertising, which were just discussed, and the *types of programs* in which these commercials are placed. For example, looking at the situation from a TV station perspective, we understand that sales revenue can be taken in from both local and national spot advertisers. These commercials can be inserted within several different types of programs airing on the station, namely *local*, *syndicated*, or *network* programs. This means that a **nationally produced commercial** can be inserted within local programming, such as a local newscast. Later in the day, the same commercial may be placed in a syndicated program (such as *Jeopardy* or *Entertainment Tonight*) and even later, inserted in a network program (such as *Desperate Housewives*). Conversely, a **locally produced commercial** can be inserted in the same programs just mentioned.

In addition to commercials, stations and networks also schedule promotional announcements called **promos.** The standard procedure is for unsold avails to be turned over to promos and occasionally to public service announcements. Another option, depending on the flexibility of the program content, is to simply eliminate unsold avails and give the surplus time back to program content. Live, unscripted programs, such as newscasts and talk shows, can readily accommodate this extra time, but recorded or scripted programs, requiring a rigid predetermined commercial format, must run something in these designated voids.

In some instances, stations and networks deliberately withhold some avails from their total inventory in order to schedule important promotional spots intended to attract audiences to upcoming programming. The most well-known example of this is the annual Super Bowl in which the breaks feature not only expensive commercials, but also an array of network promos.

In addition to accommodating advertisers that purchased avails within specified programming, the traffic department also must deal with product category and brand **separation guidelines**, in which direct competitors are not supposed to be scheduled side-by-side within the same break. For example, a traffic department will not schedule two competing retail furniture store commercials back-to-back within the same break. In addition, many broadcasters offer clients a rotation of insertion positions within breaks or *pods*; the theory being that the first position is the most valuable. In some instances this separation simply cannot be achieved, especially when dealing with dozens of automobile and truck advertisers who all want to have commercials in the same program.

Cable-system operators face more complexities than do broadcasters when inserting commercials in their programs. They have to deal with many channels, each with different requirements for advertising insertions. Modern systems use computer programs triggered by electronic signals originated by cable networks to insert locally sold commercials automatically into cable/network programming. Advertiser-supported cable-networks and superstations include commercials within programs, in the same way broadcast networks do.

After commercials have aired, advertisers and their agencies need evidence to show that contracts have been carried out. This process is called **proof of performance**. Broadcast stations log the time, length, and source of each commercial when broadcast. These logs provide documentary proof of contract fulfillment. Broadcast business offices rely on logs when preparing proof-of-performance affidavits to accompany billing statements. At many stations, computers do the logging automatically. Some stations also make slow-speed audio recordings of everything they air as backup evidence in the event of a dispute, retaining the tapes for three to six months. Cable systems rely mostly on equipment that not only inserts commercials into various cable programs, but also provides verification of proper performance.

Advertisers and agencies can get independent confirmation of contract fulfillment by subscribing to the services of companies such as Competitive Media Reporting (CMR).

The Relationship between Commercials and Program Content

In simple terms, stations, cable operators, and networks want to introduce the maximum number of commercial spots without jeopardizing the appreciation of the program content for audiences or the effectiveness of commercials for advertisers. The number and duration of commercial breaks influence writers, producers, directors, and on-air talent who accommodate these intrusions by creating compelling program segments and transitions in and out of breaks so that audiences will be reluctant to tune away. Radio has always faced the challenge of station switching during breaks. For television, the issue of commercial avoidance or **zapping** has become exacerbated in recent years with the popularity of remote control devices and digital video recorders, such as the popular TiVo systems.

The Art and Science of Pricing and Inventory Control

The skill of commercial unit pricing and inventory control, often referred to as *yield management*, is both art and science in that sales managers must rely on not only hard sales data, but also intuition about the future. That is, most commercial avails on radio, television, and cable typically are sold weeks, if not months, in advance of actual air dates. Of course, there is certain predictability to advertising demand in that toy stores will always want to attract shoppers for Christmas and theme parks will always want to attract vacationers during the summer, but many other intervening factors make accurate predictions a difficult task.

Sales managers must balance several factors, including current sales activity, expected ratings performance of programs, overall economic conditions for the market, and anticipated moves by the competition. For networks and large-market stations and cable systems, the media essentially promise a certain minimum audience delivery reflected in Nielsen ratings and Arbitron ratings. If, in fact, the program or daypart does not deliver what was promised, the media often are obliged to compensate for this shortfall by offering additional free commercials called **make-goods** (i.e., making good on a promise). Although make-goods may satisfy advertisers, these unexpected free commercials interfere with the current inventory of avails intended to be sold to cash customers. After a disappointing ratings sweep, in order to handle the extraordinary demand by irate advertisers for make-goods, broadcasters sometimes will add avails to existing breaks or even add entirely new breaks to their current programming. Some of the factors contributing to accusations of excessive commercial clutter involve the need to provide an excessive number of unexpected make-goods to clients.

The essential steps in a buyer/seller transaction are the following. For the broadcaster or cable operator, the ultimate goal is to achieve maximum pricing for a limited and perishable inventory without driving business away to competitors. For the advertiser, the goal is to obtain the maximum commercial exposure at the lowest price possible without the media walking away.

Step 1. The advertiser or media buyer submits a **request for avails** informing the network or station of the desired target audience, size of budget, and air dates of campaign. In addition, buyers may stipulate desired audience ratings, plus data on the expected demographic *reach* and *frequency* of audience exposure to the commercial.

Step 2. The network or station responds to these requests with a proposed **sales plan** or **submission of avails** that hopefully will accommodate the audience needs of the advertiser or media buyer. This plan includes **projected ratings** and commercial pricing for each recommended program or daypart.

Step 3. The media and potential buyer negotiate a final plan. For some situations, such as the network "upfront" season, these deals are consummated months in advance of actual air dates.

Step 4. After all the commercials have aired, the two parties involved in this transaction look at the audience promised versus the audience delivered (based on ratings) and, if necessary, appropriate make-goods are scheduled. Finally, the advertiser is sent an invoice for services rendered by the media.

Factors Influencing Advertising Rates The following factors influence commercial pricing.

1. *Overall advertiser demand for the medium.* Media compete for advertisers among not only their own kind, but also among other types of advertising-based media. For example, TV stations invest much time and energy in attempting to persuade retailers to shift advertising budget dollars away from newspapers. Similarly, television views cable as a prime competitor. Advertisers typically design their budgets according to the type of advertising media they wish to use (i.e., radio, television, cable, newspaper, magazines, Internet, billboards, etc.). Within this context, pricing can be an important factor in diverting budget dollars from one medium to another. A disappointing economy often forces media of all types to compete ruthlessly for dwindling advertising budgets.

2. *Advertiser demand for target audiences.* Some audiences are more attractive to advertisers than other audiences. Certain age and sex demographics, such as the much-coveted 18–34-year-old young adults, can command higher commercial rates than say an older-skewing audience.

3. *Audience delivery.* Closely related to the desirability of certain audiences is the capacity of the media to deliver these audiences in the form of program ratings. Consequently, the commercial unit pricing can vary greatly across program segments. As discussed earlier, broadcasters often are compelled to forecast ratings' performance and then provide make-goods for insufficient audience delivery.

4. *Discounted pricing for large contracts.* Advertisers willing to spend substantial dollars with a network or station will receive "bulk rate" pricing discounts.

5. *Competitor pricing.* Few media operate in a business vacuum in which there are no direct competitors attempting to win over the same advertisers. Earlier in this chapter we discussed the impact of "pricing wars" in which all competitors are perceived by buyers as essentially the same in terms of product benefits. If no brand within a product category, from beverages to broadcasts, is believed to be superior to other brands, then the lowest price becomes the determining factor in making a purchase.

Unit Pricing

Most large advertisers make their electronic media buys based on **ratings**, the statistical measurement of audiences exposed to a product's commercials (Chapter 9 addresses audience measurement in detail). In particular, they order spot schedules designed to achieve a predetermined number of **gross rating points (GRPs)**;— that is, to reach an overall number of viewers, or **target rating points (TRPs)**, to reach audience subgroups such as teens or women 18 to 49 years of age.

The industry uses **cost per thousand (CPM)** to compare relative advertising costs among competing media. CPM is the cost of reaching 1,000 (represented by the Roman numeral M) households or other defined targets. CPM is calculated by dividing the cost of a commercial by the number of homes (in thousands) that it reached. Another common measure is **cost per point (CPP)**, which is calculated by dividing the cost of the commercial by the number of ratings "points" that the program earned. These points can be based on total households or narrower demographic ratings. These calculations enable advertisers to compare the cost of advertising on one medium with the cost on another, one station with another, and one program with another. These and similar measurements also enable a station or network to guarantee a specific audience in advance. Advertisers whose commercials fail to reach the promised viewer level usually receive additional commercials— make-goods—at no cost. On rare occasions, networks have been known to provide cash rebates.

Factors Influencing Inventory Management The following factors influence control of commercial inventory.

1. *Program commercial format (local, syndicated, or network).* Syndicated and network programs have a prescribed break structure that cannot be changed easily. For example, the number of local commercial opportunities available in most network programs, particularly prime time, is considerably less than the number found in local or syndicated programming. The formatting of some local programming, particularly local newscasts, can be adjusted within certain limits, but excessive commercial "clutter" can drive away both audiences and advertisers.

2. *Barter syndication avails.* These avails are the exclusive property of the program syndicator and sold to national advertisers. Depending on the contractual licensing agreement between the station and the syndicator, the number of these nonrevenue producing "barter avails" can range typically from 10 to 50 percent of all avails within a program. While barter may reduce a station's cash outlay for acquiring program content, it also reduces the number of selling opportunities.

3. *Guaranteed or "fixed" avails for promos.* Recognizing the value of their own air time for promoting program content and community image, most stations reserve a number of guaranteed avails for promotion. Rather then merely filling in slots of unsold commercial time, avails are permanent or "fixed" in the schedule and cannot be used by the sales department.

4. *Make-goods.* As discussed earlier, these "no-charge" commercials are offered to advertisers when originally scheduled commercials are preempted or promised ratings' delivery is not achieved.

5. *Length of commercials.* Obviously a 60-second commercial will occupy an avail "space" that could accommodate two 30-second commercials. Conversely, two 15-second announcements can supplant one 30-second spot.

The inventory and pricing factors described are interrelated in that commercial pricing often is adjusted continually in response to the degree of **inventory sell-out**. Logically, as a program's air date approaches and the program's inventory of spot positions becomes smaller, individual commercial pricing typically will rise. Conversely, the opposite situation would feature inventory that is wide open due to low demand as the air date approaches, thus forcing commercial pricing to fall.

Sales departments monitor their performance using various daily, weekly, and monthly reports, often referred to as **pacing reports** that compare current pricing and inventory sellout with historical benchmarks. In addition, these reports look at forecasted sales budgets in relation to current performance. In summary, these reports look at how well the sales department is "pacing" with the same period a year ago and how well it is pacing with what it promised (i.e., forecasted) it would sell at this point in time.

As will be presented later in this chapter, and in Chapter 9, many advertisers are taking advantage of the Internet to reach potential customers and the manner in which advertisers pay for these services is still a work in progress. The earliest "unit pricing" was based on the total number of web site "hits," but now media buyers are more demanding and insisting on data that includes "click-throughs" to specific pages or sections or even the number of "transactions" in which the web site visitor requests something.

Alternative Ad Buys

Some types of ad-buying techniques used by both broadcasters and cable operators fall outside normal rate practices.

▶ In a **trade deal** (also called a **tradeout**), a station or cable system exchanges commercial time for an advertiser's goods or services.
▶ **Time brokerage** refers to the practice of selling time in blocks to brokers, who then resell it at a markup.
▶ **Per-inquiry (PI)** buys commit the advertiser to pay not for advertising time, but for the number of inquiries or the number of items sold in direct response to PI commercials. Many Internet-based companies have adopted this pricing model.

Product Placement as a New Business Model

Research indicates that with the introduction of electronic devices, such as remote controls and DVRs, audiences are "zapping" commercial matter at alarming rates. One result has been the rapid growth of a new business model that ignores program interruptions, called **product placement** or **product integration**. Although the concept is not new, the degree to which it has been used in recent years has been remarkable. Several companies have emerged within the advertising community that work exclusively with product placement or brand logo placement within network and syndicated programs. Unscripted "reality programs" appear to be the most commonly used program genre using product-placement tactics. A relatively new practice involves the digital manipulation of images, tricking viewers into thinking they are seeing something that is not really there. Networks now routinely inject digital advertising messages into sports programs, creating billboards and display ads that show up on the TV screen but do not exist at the ballpark or racetrack.

Product placement has received its share of criticism from both outside and inside the industry. Consumer advocates are concerned about the lack of disclosure for unsuspecting audiences that do not realize that a portion of the program content is a "commercial." These critics maintain that audiences have an ethical right to be notified in some fashion that subtle marketing messages are embedded within program content. Within the industry, creative people, including producers, writers, and directors, object to the idea that they must include unnecessary products and brand logos within the context of the program content and fear that these contrived additions can hurt the audience appreciation of the program. Unlike the conventional advertising-based model in which commercials are inserted long after the program episodes have been recorded, product placement requires that the "commercial" be included during the planning, writing and recording of the program, often months before it is aired. A major exception would be live programming, such as sports coverage.

The actual buying and selling of product placements usually includes a conventional spot buy within the program and sponsor participation on the program's audience web site. Rather than breaking out the exact price of a product placement, the network or syndicator will "package" all three components into a single, all-inclusive price for the entire season.

Local TV stations have been reluctant to use product placement a great deal because most local programming today is news and there is a concern about the ethics of merging journalism with commercialism. Of course, all newscasts have commercial breaks and many news segments receive sponsorship mentions (e.g., "Today's weather forecast is brought to you by _____"). According to critics, the problem with product placement is that it "crosses the line" from a brand message to a brand endorsement.

Advertising on the Internet

One of the hottest areas of advertising growth involves the Internet. The interactive nature of Internet marketing offers unique marketing advantages that conventional electronic media, such as radio and television, cannot replicate. Interactive advertising affords the marketer the ability to engage the consumer in a direct and personal way. Another major advantage of on-line advertising is the content is not limited by geography or time. In addition, the results for advertisement campaigns may be monitored in real-time. Essentially all of the leading 100 national advertisers in the United States have begun advertising on the web.

Conventional electronic advertising media, such as radio, television, and cable, have embraced the Internet as a programming, promotion, and sales tool. Almost all broadcast stations and their networks have dedicated web sites. Furthermore, most individual programs have their own "on-line extensions" to audiences, providing all sorts of information and activities. From a sales perspective, web sites have evolved from being merely a promotional tool to attract and hold audiences, to a revenue-generating tool that can help a company's bottom line. In the beginning, web site opportunities were used as a kind of bonus or "value-added" inducement to get an advertiser to purchase commercial time on the primary medium, such as a station or network. However, media executives are now insisting that web site sales be a separate, stand-alone operation that can bring in advertising clients that may or may not be involved with a conventional spot buy.

Among the many advertising techniques being experimented with today, **web banner advertising** is the most popular among serious advertisers. Banner advertising functions the same way as traditional advertisements in that the goal is to notify consumers of the product or service and present reasons why the consumer should choose the product brand in question. The web banner is displayed when a web page that references the banner is loaded into a web browser. This event is known as an **impression**. When the viewer clicks on the banner, he or she is directed to the web site advertised in the banner. This event is known as a **click through**. When the advertiser scans their log files and detects that a web user has visited the advertiser's site from the content site by clicking on the banner ad, the advertiser sends the content provider some small amount of money (usually around five to ten U.S. cents). This payback system is often how the content provider is able to pay for the Internet access to supply the content in the first place. Since exposure, response, and overall efficiency of Internet media is easy to track, Internet marketing can offer a greater sense of accountability for advertisers.

Internet measurement still presents several challenges, as will be presented in Chapter 9. Traditional media rating services, such as Nielsen, are attempting to measure the audiences on-line, but developing a reliable and useful measurement has been a challenge. First, what is the basis for the value? The mere impression or the more active click through? Advertisers ask, "Was the banner seen by 1,000 people or one person 1,000 times?" In an effort to be more engaging with visitors, web site operators have become more aggressive with advertising opportunities, such as interrupter pages, and pop-up advertising. Some have created software or web browser enhancements which also deliver advertising. Because users have been caught unaware of the link between the software and advertising, the derogatory term "adware" has been used to refer to these products.

Most web browsers are designed to accommodate an enhancement called a **cookie**. The cookie takes space on the user's computer to store information that web services can retrieve and use later. Cookies have been used by web advertisers to track individual users and their activities. This means a web service can track the pages visited, user preferences, and provide services such as shopping carts across several pages. Web services may also use the cookie to help count individual impressions and provide evidence of accumulated (cume) audiences over time. The cookie is commonly used to track users across different web sites. The goal is to offer advertising most likely to get a positive response from the user. Thus, if the cookie detects the user is visiting car sites, the cookie might cause banner advertisements to be automobile related. While privacy advocates object, the technique is gaining acceptability among advertisers.

Current conventional wisdom holds that as more video moves to the Internet, advertising will follow but the industry is still experimenting as to the number of commercial breaks and the ideal commercial unit length. Preliminary research indicates within broadband programming, audiences are less tolerant of interruptions and long commercials. As a result, the total inventory of commercial matter (i.e., avails) is considerably smaller than that found in conventional television programs. Many broadcast networks and stations merely "bundle" broadband avails within their broadcast inventory, but more aggressive companies are beginning to insist that broadband avails be priced separately.

Perhaps one of the most effective implementations of interactive advertising is so-called **viral marketing**. This technique uses images, texts, web links, flash animations, audio/video clips, and so on, passed from user to user chain letter-style, via e-mail.

Person-to-person transfer is most effective if started in appropriate Internet groups and social-networking sites. Companies have been known to plant users in a social site to encourage a viral campaign. In addition, videos that look home-made are released on sites such as YouTube.com. What is thought to be an authentic home video becomes very popular and is later revealed as an advertisement. For example, "spoiled rich girl" video showed a teenage girl berating her father in 2006. The dad had purchased an expensive sports car for the daughter in the wrong color. A later video shows the daughter selling the car to purchase a Domino's pizza.

Broadcasters are starting to see the Internet as a viable means to distribute products. As broadband adoption grows, users have an ever-increasing ability to enjoy full motion programs delivered via the Internet. Currently, the most popular use is to support and promote on-air programs by distributing clips, outtakes, and additional material via the Internet. However, most national broadcasters are also distributing entire video programs online. Programs include advertisements which, unlike DVR and taped programs, cannot be skipped. Some even require a user click before the advertisement is dismissed and the program continues. On-line viewing, while still a minor proportion of the audience, is becoming more popular despite the advertisements.

Mobile Advertising

Another burgeoning area for advertisers is mobile wireless. As mobile phones outnumber TV sets by over 2 to 1, and Internet users by nearly 3 to 1, and the total laptop and desktop PC population by over 4 to 1, mobile media are evolving rapidly. While mobile phones will continue to be the mainstay, other types of wireless communication devices surely will be included. Many conventional media, such as radio and television, are beginning to expand their services to mobile audiences,

such as sponsored news, sports, and weather alerts. This type of advertising is most commonly seen as a **mobile banner** (top of page banner) or a **mobile poster** (bottom of page banner). The effectiveness of a mobile ad campaign can be measured in a variety of ways, including number of impressions (views) and click-through rates. Types of mobile advertising are expected to change as rapidly as technology.

Advertising Agencies

All regional and national advertisers and most large local advertisers deal with media through advertising agencies. Agencies conduct research; design advertising campaigns; create commercials; buy time from cable systems, broadcast stations, and cable and broadcast networks; supervise implementation of campaigns and evaluate their effectiveness; and, finally, pay media on behalf of the advertisers they represent.

Agencies become intimately familiar with each client's business problems, sometimes even assisting in the development of new products or the redesigning and repackaging of old ones. Ad agencies that handle large national accounts determine the best **media mix** for their clients, allocating budgets among the major media.

For decades, ad agencies traditionally received a 15 percent commission on **billings**—the amount the advertising media charged. That is, an agency would bill its client the full amount of advertising time charges, pay the medium 85 percent, and keep 15 percent as payment for its services. Today, fewer than half of all agency arrangements use this scheme. Some agencies now accept less than 15 percent or charge fees in addition to commission, some work on a straight-fee basis, while others work on a "cost-plus" basis.

In any event, that media allow a discount on business brought to them by agencies creates an odd relationship: The agency works for its client, the advertiser, but gets paid by the medium in the form of a discount on time charges. The travel business operates similarly. A travel agency works, at least theoretically, for the traveler, but gets paid by the hotel or airline in discounts on charges.

6.7 Advertising Standards

Advertising raises touchy issues of taste, legality, and social responsibility. Both legal and voluntary self-regulatory standards influence what may be advertised and what methods may be used.

Government Regulation

Section 317 of the Communications Act requires reasonably recognizable differences between radio/TV commercials and programs. A station must disclose the source of anything it puts on the air for which it receives payment, whether in money or some other "valuable consideration."

This **sponsor identification rule** attempts to prevent deception by disguised propaganda from unidentified sources. Of course, anonymity is the last thing commercial advertisers desire. But propagandists who use **editorial advertising** (sometimes called **advertorials**) may not always be so eager to reveal their true identities, nor do those who make under-the-table payments to disc jockeys or others for on-the-air favors wish to be identified. Outright deception in advertising comes under Federal Trade Commission (FTC) jurisdiction.

Contrary to popular opinion, neither Congress nor the FCC has set a maximum number of commercial minutes per hour of programming—by broadcast or on cable. Limits have been set on advertising content in children's shows, however.

Program-Length Commercials

The FCC once prohibited **program-length commercials**—productions that interweave program and commercial material so closely that the program as a whole promotes the sponsor's product or service. The FCC lifted the ban on program-length commercials in 1981 for radio and in 1984 for television. They are still illegal when directed toward children. A flood of program-length commercials, known also as **infomercials**, ensued, often touting merchandise of questionable value. Ads for nostrums, kitchen gadgets, astrology charts, and the like overran both broadcast and cable. Despite the aura of sleaze surrounding infomercials, some began to achieve respectability. Many struggling TV stations and cable networks find infomercials a vital source of revenue to keep the company in the black.

Taboo Products

Some perfectly legal products and services that appear in print and on billboards never appear in electronic mass media. This double standard confirms that special restraints are imposed on broadcasting and, to a lesser degree, on cable because they come directly to the home, accessible to all. Nevertheless, canons of acceptability constantly evolve. Not until the 1980s, for example, did formerly unthinkable ads—such as those for contraceptives and those showing brassieres worn by live models—begin to appear.

Congress banned the broadcasting of cigarette ads in 1971 and later extended the ban to include all tobacco products. Up until 1996, the most conspicuous example of self-imposed advertising abstinence involved the industry's refusal to accept hard liquor ads. Broadcasters were concerned that carriage of such ads would provoke opponents of all alcoholic beverages to begin an assault on beer and wine ads. In 1996, however, several TV stations began accepting advertising from Seagrams for two of that company's hard liquor products. By the end of the decade, more than 300 radio stations and more than 100 TV stations and cable networks were airing Seagram's commercials. As feared by many in the industry, critics of such advertising, both inside and outside the government, called for the ads to be banned, much as cigarette ads had been 25 years earlier. Congress, the FTC, and the FCC began considering the issue, at least informally. The FCC subsequently declined to initiate a formal inquiry, leaving that task to the FTC.

Prior to 1999, federal law prohibited broadcast advertising of gambling casinos. Responding to a challenge brought by a group of TV broadcasters, the Supreme Court unanimously ruled the statute unconstitutional. According to the Court, it is the job of advertisers and broadcasters, not the government, to assess the value of truthful information about lawful conduct (US, 1999).

Self-Regulation

The ban on liquor ads is an example of the voluntary self-regulation once codified by the NAB. Its radio and TV codes, though full of exceptions and qualifications, set nominal limits on commercial time. For example, the NAB allowed radio 18 minutes of commercial time per hour, and it allowed network TV affiliates 9.5 minutes in prime time, 16 minutes at other times. In 1984, the Justice Department charged that the NAB standards, even though voluntary, violated antitrust laws by urging limits that reduced competition. The NAB promptly disbanded its Code Office, apparently relieved to be rid of a thankless task.

Meanwhile, the TV networks, and some group broadcasters, had begun dismantling their individual program and advertising codes. The networks had separate departments, variously called Continuity Acceptance, Broadcast Standards, and Program Practices. In the late 1980s, ABC and CBS sharply cut back the number of employees assigned to standards and practices departments. Advertisers, agencies, and others expressed fears that these moves might result in an overall lowering of standards. Adverse public reaction, they felt, could be followed by attempts at governmental intervention.

Unethical Practices

Aside from issues of advertising length and content, four specific types of unethical advertising practices in broadcasting have proved particularly troublesome. In the past they triggered both FCC and congressional action. A conflict of interest occurs when a station or one of its employees uses or promotes on the air something in which the station or employee has an undisclosed financial interest. Called **plugola**, this practice usually results in an indirect payoff. A disc jockey who gives unpaid publicity to his or her personal sideline business is an example. Direct payments to the person responsible for inserting plugs usually constitute **payola**. It typically takes the form of under-the-table payoffs by recording-company representatives to disc jockeys and others responsible for putting music on the air.

Local cooperative advertising sometimes tempts stations into **double billing**. Manufacturers who share with their local dealers the cost of local advertising of their products must rely on those dealers to handle cooperative advertising. Dealer and station may conspire to send the manufacturer a bill for advertising higher than the one the dealer actually paid. Station and dealer then split the excess payment.

Clipping occurs when affiliates cut away from network or barter-syndication programs prematurely, usually to insert commercials of their own. Clipping constitutes fraud because the networks compensate affiliates for carrying programs in their entirety with all commercials intact.

As discussed earlier, some people question the ethics of the increased use of product placement within programming, claiming that the practice violates the accepted tradition of enabling audiences to distinguish commercial content from program content. Critics argue that this practice is more sinister than program-length commercials because few adults would mistake the overriding purpose of an infomercial, while product placement can be far more subtle.

6.8 Subscription-Fee Revenue

Cable-Fee Regulation

In sharp contrast to broadcasting, cable television, wireless cable, and DBS systems rely on subscription fees for most of their revenues. If a graph could chart the history of cable TV rate regulation, it would resemble a very wild roller coaster. Regulation of cable rates was at the discretion of local franchising authorities during cable's early history. When the FCC established its comprehensive cable regulatory scheme in 1972, it *required* local governments to regulate basic-cable rates, only to rescind that requirement several years later. At the height of the deregulatory movement in the mid-1980s, Congress effectively deregulated cable rates for the vast majority of systems. This led to a period of rapidly rising prices and increasing consumer complaints. The number of households subscribing to cable TV systems increased, as did the channel capacity of many cable systems. However, competition among distributors of cable

services did not increase, and, in many communities, the rates for cable services far outpaced inflation. Responding to these problems, Congress enacted the Cable Television Consumer Protection and Competition Act of 1992. Congress enacted legislation that again required the FCC to assume supervisory responsibility over most cable rates. The Commission responded in early 1993 and again in 1994 with a series of rulings that not only limited most cable-subscriber fees, but also required some cable systems to reduce their prices and even make refunds. By 1996, the regulatory pendulum had begun to reverse direction, and Congress moved to end most cable TV rate regulation. In adopting the Telecommunications Act of 1996, Congress noted that it wanted to provide a pro-competitive, deregulatory national policy framework designed to accelerate rapidly private sector deployment of advanced telecommunications and information technologies and services to all Americans by opening all telecommunications markets to competition.

Cable Service Tiers

Some cable systems charge a single monthly rate for their service. But most divide their product into several levels of program service, called **tiers**, with a separate fee for each level. Most modern systems offer a **basic service** that includes local TV stations, one or more distant superstations, and some advertiser-supported cable networks. The monthly fee for this basic package can vary from a few dollars to $25 or more. Some systems break their basic service into two or more tiers. For example, they may pull several of the more popular ad-supported networks (such as MTV and ESPN) out of the basic package and offer them separately as an **extended** or **expanded basic service** at extra cost.

At first in anticipation of, and later in reaction to, a provision in the 1992 cable act calling for governmental rate regulation of the basic program tier, some systems restructured their service. Many now offer a **broadcast basic** or **lifeline tier** limited to local stations and public access, educational, and government (PEG) channels. They then offer ad-supported networks and superstations only on one or more expanded tiers. Some systems also offer *a la carte* program options, charging subscribers a per-channel fee for individual ad-supported program services, or for groups of services that are **bundled** together.

The next level of service includes **pay-cable**, or **premium channels**, such as HBO, Showtime, and Cinemax. Today, almost three-fourths of all cable households subscribe to pay cable. Usually, subscribers pay a separate fee for each pay service they select. Some cable operators require that their customers subscribe not only to the basic, but also to an expanded-basic tier before they can buy any premium services.

Pay-Per-View Programs

Cable systems with *addressable* converters dedicate one or more of their channels to **pay-per-view (PPV)** programs. A one-time PPV charge allows viewers to see a single program, either a movie or a special event, such as a boxing match or a rock concert. PPV programs come in one of two ways. First, individual cable systems—so-called *stand alones*—negotiate directly with producers for PPV movies and events. Much more commonly, national program services, such as Viewer's Choice, acquire PPV rights to programs and distribute them to cable systems under an arrangement that splits revenues between the program service and the cable system.

As video compression produces greater cable channel capacity, more and more systems are devoting multiple channels to PPV. Some also are beginning to experiment with two-way, interactive **video on demand (VOD)**, a PPV technology that will compete with neighborhood VCR rental operations by permitting subscribers to order their choice of movies at the touch of a button.

Satellite-to-Home Services

In 1994, two high-power DBS services, Hughes DIRECTV and United States Satellite Broadcasting (USSB), began active marketing to potential subscribers. Both DBS providers used the same high-power satellite to deliver their services to subscribers, although their program packages were different. Both companies offered an exclusive selection of cable TV networks for a fee. As many industry analysts predicted, the two services merged in 1999 when DIRECTV acquired USSB.

Because they were nationally distributed, none of these DBS systems could initially include signals of local TV stations. Customers had to either switch between satellite and rooftop antenna or subscribe to basic cable to fill this void. This limitation put DBS at a disadvantage compared to cable systems, which carry both cable networks and local broadcast stations. To overcome this competitive barrier, Echostar, after acquiring additional satellite channel capacity in 1998, began beaming selected local TV signals into several local markets—a service that became known as **local into local**. Local broadcast stations and cable system operators objected, arguing that the service should have to deliver *all* broadcast signals in each market. Today, almost all TV markets have local-to-local service.

6.9 Personnel

The number of people employed in an industry usually gives some indication of its importance. According to that yardstick, electronic media have relatively little importance. However, their social significance lends them far greater weight than their small workforce suggests.

Employment Levels

Many specialized creative firms support media, producing materials ranging from station-identification jingles to prime-time entertainment series. Such firms offer more opportunities for creative work than do the media themselves—performing, writing, directing, designing, and so on. Other media-related jobs are found in nonprogram areas. These include jobs in advertising agencies, sales representative firms, program-syndicating organizations, news agencies, common-carrier companies, and audience-research organizations.

Aside from the major TV networks, most broadcast and cable organizations have small staffs. The number of full-time employees at radio stations ranges from fewer than 5 for the smallest markets to about 60 for the largest, with the average being 15. TV stations have between 20 and 300 employees. A typical network affiliate employs about 90 full-time people, and an independent station about 60. Cable systems average about 30 full-time employees, but range from family-run systems in small communities (with perhaps 5 or 6 employees) to large-city systems with staffs of more than 100. Cable MSO headquarters units average about 55 full-time employees.

Salary Levels

The huge salaries reported in *People* magazine and on *Entertainment Tonight* go to top-performing and creative talent and executives who work mostly at network headquarters and the production centers of New York and Hollywood. Average salaries for jobs at most stations and cable systems rank as moderate at best. Typically, those working in sales earn the highest incomes at broadcasting stations. They are the ones who, quite simply, bring revenue directly to the enterprise so that bills—and salaries—can be paid. At the department-head level, general sales managers usually make the most money and traffic managers the least. Program directors fall somewhere in between. Exhibit 6.c offers a more detailed salary analysis.

Typically, TV stations pay higher salaries than radio stations or cable systems for comparable positions, although in the late 1990s the salaries of radio general managers matched and then exceeded the salaries of their TV counterparts. Presumably, this is a result of local radio consolidation; local radio managers may be running up to eight stations per market. Fewer general managers are doing more work and are getting paid handsomely. Basic laws of supply and demand come into play throughout the compensation structure. Because fewer people want and are technically qualified (e.g., to be TV weathercasters than want to be sportscasters), salaries for the former group tend to exceed those for the latter. Salaries for radio talent reflect the relative importance of various dayparts.

Diversity

When media companies consolidate in the hands of fewer and fewer owners, the diversity of viewpoints, cultures, and voices to which we're exposed can dramatically decrease. Ethnic minorities make up about one-third of America's population, but own fewer than 4 percent of America's broadcast licenses. Numerous studies show that minority employment in the media industry does not reflect the diversity of our country. Using government sanctions to correct these problems sometimes has created more problems. For example, in 2001 a federal appeals court struck down FCC rules that encourage recruitment of women and minorities by television, radio, and cable-TV companies. The court claimed that the rule put official pressure upon broadcasters to recruit minority candidates, thus creating a race-based classification that is unconstitutional.

Rather than turning to government, the media industries themselves have attempted to rectify these imbalances. For example, the NAB established the Education Foundation in 1994 in part to address the need to increase diversity at all levels in broadcasting. Since that time, the Foundation provided career advancement opportunities for people of color and women, offering a full range of education and training programs, from entry level through ownership. The stated mission of American Women in Radio and Television (AWRT) is to advance the impact of women in the electronic media and allied fields by educating, advocating, and acting as a resource to its members and the industry. Other examples of special interest organizations with similar agendas, particularly in the field of news, include the National Association of Black Journalists (NABJ), National Association of Hispanic Journalists (NAHJ), Asian American Journalist Association (AAJA), and the Native American Journalist Association (NAJA).

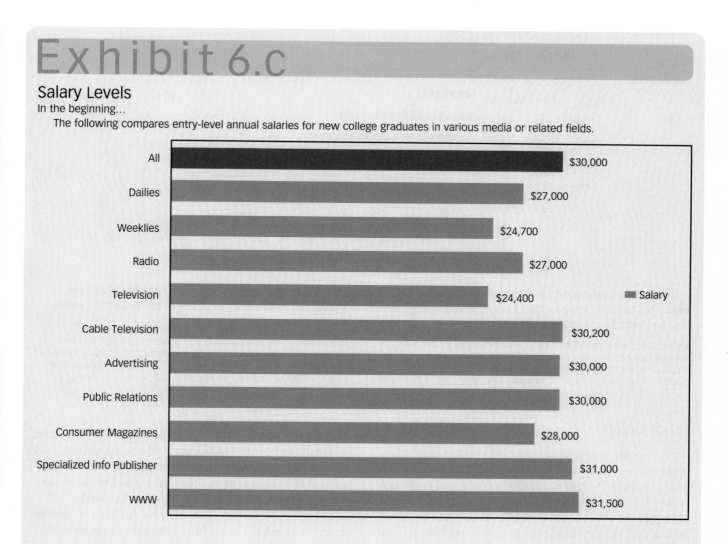

Exhibit 6.c

Salary Levels
In the beginning...

The following compares entry-level annual salaries for new college graduates in various media or related fields.

Field	Salary
All	$30,000
Dailies	$27,000
Weeklies	$24,700
Radio	$27,000
Television	$24,400
Cable Television	$30,200
Advertising	$30,000
Public Relations	$30,000
Consumer Magazines	$28,000
Specialized info Publisher	$31,000
WWW	$31,500

(continued)

Continued from p. 145

And *on the average...*
As they moved from entry-level to top-level positions,

electronic media employees in radio and television stations, earned the following annual salaries along the way.

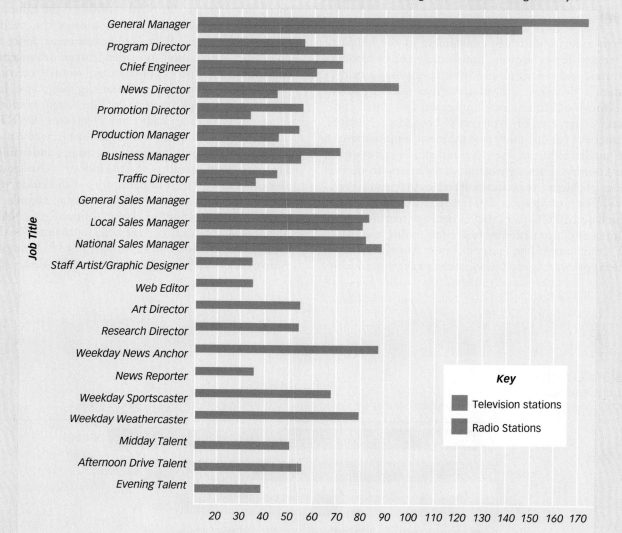

Dollars in Thousands

Key
Television stations
Radio Stations

These are only *averages*. Salaries paid by organizations in large cities tend to run higher than those in smaller communities. And because averages typically rise each year, the above

data prove most useful in comparing compensation levels for the various positions rather than in studying specific salaries themselves.

Source: Salary levels data from *Annual Survey of Journalism and Mass Communications Graduates,* www.grady.uga.edu/annualsurveys/. Reprinted by permission. All rights reserved. Radio station data from "Radio Stations Salaries: 2004," compiled by Miller et al. Table 1. Copyright

Labor Unions

At networks, national production centers, and most large-market network TV affiliates, unionization generally prevails. Not so at smaller stations and cable systems. The fragmentation of the industry into many units, each with a small staff, makes unionization impractical. In small operations, staff members often have to handle two or more jobs that in a union shop might come under different jurisdictions. For example, a small radio station cannot afford to assign two employees to record an interview, paying one as a technician to operate equipment and another as a performer, when the job can be done by one person.

The biggest factors impacting media labor unions in recent years have been breakthroughs in automation, digital convergence, and ownership consolidation. As discussed earlier in this chapter, stations, networks, and cable systems have introduced several sophisticated automation devices that can accomplish many daily routine tasks that in the past had to be done by people. In addition, breakthroughs in digital technology enable "cross-platform" duties, such as providing graphics for a TV station's on-air newscasts and its web site. Finally, as mentioned earlier, consolidation of ownership typically leads to a centralization of duties and a reduction in jobs. In combination, these factors all have resulted in a smaller, more agile workforce in which fewer people are asked to accomplish more.

Electronic mass media unions draw on types of personnel first unionized in older industries—electrical work, music, motion pictures, stage, and newspapers. Thus, the American Federation of Musicians represents every kind of professional musician, from pianists in bars to drummers on television. People who work in broadcasting and cable can be grouped into two broad categories: the creative/performing group and the craft/technical group. Unions divide along similar lines; those representing the former usually avoid the word **union**, calling themselves **guilds**, **associations**, or **federations**.

The first pure broadcasting union, the American Federation of Television and Radio Artists (AFTRA), began (originally as AFRA) in 1937, representing that universal radio performer, the announcer. Most creative/performing unions, however, began with stage and motion-picture workers. Examples include the Writers Guild of America (WGA), the American Guild of Variety Artists (AGVA), and the Screen Actors Guild (SAG). A technical union, the International Alliance of Theatrical Stage Employees and Moving Picture Machine Operators of the United States and Canada (IATSE), expanded into television from the motion-picture industry.

In 1953, NBC technicians formed an association of their own that ultimately became the National Association of Broadcast Engineers and Technicians (NABET). Later, the union changed the word *Engineers* to *Employees* to broaden its scope. Recently, NABET has been negotiating with the broadcast networks about the status of new jobs in the digital era. NABET argues that the new jobs should be union positions; the networks counter that they need the flexibility to hire nonunion employees for certain positions.

There will always be a certain "give and take" in union/management negotiations. Most labor unions recognize that they cannot stop the march of progress, but they can make these transitions fair and equitable for employees.

Job Opportunities

Surveys of students enrolled in college electronic media programs indicate that most want to work in the creative/performing area, especially in on-camera or on-mike positions. The oversupply of candidates makes these the least accessible jobs for beginners. Broadcast stations and cable systems usually delegate creative work to outside production companies, which means that such work is concentrated in a few major centers, where newcomers face fierce competition and unions control entry. News, the one field in which local production still flourishes, offers an exception to the scarcity of creative jobs at stations and systems. Nearly all TV stations and some cable systems employ news specialists, and although there are typically more applicants than openings for on-air jobs such as news reporters and anchors, job notices for qualified news producers often go unanswered.

Sales offers another employment area likely to expand. All commercial networks and stations, as well as a growing number of cable systems, employ salespeople. Ambitious job seekers should also note that top managerial positions have historically been filled by sales personnel, although in recent years more general managers have come from news. Advertising agencies and national sales representative firms offer entry-level employment opportunities. Nevertheless, personnel directors frequently complain that college-educated job applicants fail to understand or appreciate the financial basics of the industry.

As technologies proliferate and competition intensifies, so does the need for creative and effective promotion. Stations, systems, and networks have to promote themselves and their products to potential audiences and advertisers. Cable networks use promotion extensively to persuade cable systems to buy their offerings. About two-thirds of all jobs in cable are technical, but marketing, market research, and advertising also have high priority. The need for creative people will also increase as more cable systems provide public-access and local-origination programming.

Corporate Video

Applicants who look only to broadcasting and cable for entry-level jobs unnecessarily limit their employment options. Virtually every large organization that has contact with the public uses electronic mass media in one form or another. Opportunities for production and writing jobs exist in business; religious, educational, and health organizations and foundations; government agencies; the armed services; and specialized production companies.

Many such organizations make extensive in-house use of satellite-fed, closed-circuit television. This rapidly growing field of corporate video applies broadcast techniques to job skills training, management development, sales presentations, and public relations. Such nonbroadcast uses of television require trained personnel for production, direction, writing, studio operations, program planning, and similar functions. Regardless of the specific type of company an individual may work for, computer skills are essential. From designing web sites and producing commercials or promos, to analyzing ratings and preparing sales presentations, the reliance on computers and digital know-how will only increase in years to come.

6.10 The Cost of Doing Business

While most of this chapter so far has focused on how electronic media earn money, we must not forget that this income doesn't become *profit* until the costs of doing business are factored into the business equation. In addition to paying employees, the electronic media industries require high capital investments to construct new facilities or acquire and maintain existing ones. Radio station construction costs range from $50,000 for a simple, small-market AM or FM outlet, to several million dollars for a sophisticated station in a major market. Full-power, major-market TV facilities may cost tens of millions of dollars. Upgrading operations with new technologies such as satellite news gathering (SNG) vans, helicopters, and newsroom computer systems calls for additional capital outlays in the hundreds of thousands. The transition from analog to digital transmission has cost TV stations, networks, and production companies hundreds of millions of dollars for a technology that, in all likelihood, will neither increase a station's or a network's audience nor expand its advertising revenue. On a per-home-served basis, a cable system costs even more to construct because each home must be physically connected to the headend. New or upgraded cable systems can cost between $10,000 and $15,000 per mile. Industry experts estimate that start-up costs for DBS systems begin at around $500 million.

The previously mentioned costs have not included the expenses involved in producing or acquiring *content*. Upcoming chapters addressing programming and promotion will reveal the huge costs and high risks involved in trying to win the hearts and minds of audiences. Whether a media company makes use of an advertising-based, subscription-based, pay-per-play based, or pay-per-click business model, the all important common denominator is the need to attract audiences with compelling content. Indeed, programming is a cost of doing business along with technology.

Cutting Costs by Getting Bigger

For any business, one way to offset costs is to become bigger through acquisition of new properties, mergers with competitors, or the creation of brand new businesses. Deregulation and digital convergence have also stimulated investment in all types of electronic media that in the past would have been technologically impossible or legally forbidden.

The economic notion of **economy of scale** maintains that as a company gets bigger its costs of doing business are reduced relative to the "output" of what the company sells to customers. For media companies this output typically is audiences obtained through content. For example, large group-owned broadcast stations can get significant discounts on purchasing syndicated programming and technical equipment by buying "in bulk" and sharing these resources with other stations within the group. Broadcasting, and to a large extent cable, have reached the point where investment in new facilities has come to a halt. Now the more likely route to ownership is through the purchase of existing facilities. Factors such as market size and location, format (in the case of radio), network affiliation (in the case of television), and competitive position in the market all influence asking/offering prices for stations. As discussed earlier, the 1996 telecommunications act stimulated a huge number of media ownership transactions and consolidation of operations, but the pace has slowed significantly.

Despite periodic downturns in the general economy, ever-changing technology and often brutal competition, the future of electronic media as a dynamic, profit-making enterprise appears bright.

6.11 Bottom-Line Mentality

In the early 1920s, the founders of American broadcasting decided that radio, and later television, would be privately owned *businesses*. Unlike most of the rest of the world in which the development of electronic media was placed in the hands of government, the United States would rely on business entrepreneurs to grow these industries. For good or bad, financial profit became a primary factor in managing these operations. This free-enterprise philosophical approach is not new to this country. As far back as the American Revolution, print media in the form of newspapers and magazines were given the freedom to charge subscription fees and sell display advertising.

As revealed in earlier chapters of this book, throughout the history of electronic media the government on occasion has stepped in to rectify problems which free enterprise appeared unable to solve. In some cases, government agencies such as the FCC enacted rules to protect broadcasters from unfair competition, such as early restrictions on the growth of cable. In other cases, the Commission took a totally different stance and enacted rules that were intended to encourage competition, such as the 1996 communications act. Other rulings ventured into employment practices and content regulation. Regardless of the individual decision making by the government, the underlying policy has always been to generate the least amount of regulation necessary to properly sustain the business of media.

From the public-interest standpoint, stations, cable systems, and networks need to earn profits. When they operate at a loss, their public-service programs tend to suffer first. Moreover, the lowering of standards by money-losing firms can be contagious: Their rivals tend to match lower standards to compete in the marketplace. But obsessive concern for short-term profits has its dangers, too. Critics have charged that federal deregulation and permissive interpretation of antitrust laws have encouraged too many media acquisitions, mergers, takeovers, and consolidations. They claim that these transactions focus so single-mindedly on profits that they produce a **bottom-line mentality**— a preoccupation with profit-and-loss statements to the exclusion of all else. While the profit motive has been the underlying force behind the incredible innovations in electronic media, there is a need for caution. For example, some concerned media observers believe that cable television, not explicitly required to operate in the public interest, has made little or no effort to modify profit-driven goals beyond such services as C-SPAN and Cable in the Classroom. Broadcasting, which does have a public-interest mandate, has fallen increasingly under the control of conglomerate officials with no broadcasting background. In particular, many industry commentators are worried about the future of American journalism. For example, the owners and managers of broadcast networks and local stations expect their news divisions to be profitable, while maintaining high journalistic standards. News personnel are learning to do more with less and still get the story to the public.

One thing is certain: The technology, the structure, and the business of the electronic mass media will continue to change rapidly. Only by keeping up with such change and adapting to it can existing media companies hope to survive. Looking at the future, one can argue that the bottom-line mentality presents both promises and perils.

Noncommercial Services

Most of this text deals with commercial electronic media. But many Americans believe that profit motives alone cannot be counted on to fulfill all the national cultural, educational, and informational needs that electronic media ideally could serve. Hence, arose the concept of **noncommercial** broadcasting—motivated by public-service goals rather than by profit. As noble as these goals seem, noncommercial broadcasting for decades has experienced criticism from politicians, citizens groups, columnists, and audiences. Two intertwined issues have been (a) defining exactly what noncommercial program content should be, and (b) determining the best means to fund the creation and distribution of this content. In recent years, with the enormous expansion of program options now available via commercial cable, satellite, and broadband, some critics maintain that conventional public broadcasting is no longer as essential to Americans as it was a couple of decades ago, when content choices were so meager. Defenders of the system claim that new technologies have enabled noncommercial media to become more valuable to the American public than ever before. This chapter examines the origins, current posture, criticism, and future of this unique service.

7.1 From Educational Radio to "Public" Broadcasting

Today's **public broadcasting** began as a more narrowly defined service devoted explicitly to education. When radio boomed in the 1920s, educational institutions joined in the rush. Most of these pioneer not-for-profit stations operated on a shoestring for only a few hours a week.

AM Radio

With broadcasting's growing financial success in the late 1920s, commercial interests began to covet AM channels tied up by educational licenses. Some schools surrendered their licenses in return for promises of airtime for educational programs on commercial stations—promises that faded with the rising value of commercial time.

Many stations that held on found themselves confined to low-power, inconvenient hours (often daytime only, of limited value for adult education), and constantly changing frequency assignments. In 1927, 98 noncommercial AM stations were in operation, but by 1945 they had dwindled to about 25.

Reserved Channels

The decline in educational AM stations confirmed what critics had said from the start: Educational interests should not be expected to compete with commercial interests for broadcast channels, and the government should have set aside a certain number of AM channels exclusively for educational use.

When the Federal Communications Commission (FCC) came into being in 1934, it reviewed the proposal to reserve AM channels. But the Commission accepted commercial owners' assurances that they would give ample free time for education. As stations that gave up their licenses for promises of time had already discovered, such promises never seemed to work out in practice.

The FCC finally endorsed the **reserved-channels principle** when it had an opportunity to allocate a brand-new group of channels in 1941—those for FM radio. In its final FM-allotment plan in 1945, the Commission reserved the lower portion of the FM band exclusively for educational use—20 channels (of the 100 total) running from 88 to 92 MHz.

The first noncommercial educational FM stations depended almost totally on local programs. They had neither a well-developed system of program exchange nor a network to help fill out station schedules. Their experience, of course, repeated that of commercial stations in the early 1920s—local resources alone simply could not provide adequate programming. Networking was as essential for noncommercial as for commercial broadcasting.

The arrival of television in the late 1940s stimulated a new campaign for reserved channels. It was considerably more intense than previous radio campaigns, because television attracted more attention. Educators and foundations foresaw far greater possibilities for educational television than they had for educational radio.

During the FCC's 1948–1952 freeze on new TV station applications, some commercial interests made a concerted effort to block the educators' campaign. But a wide spectrum of educational and cultural groups combined into a counter lobby: the Joint Committee on Educational Television (JCET). As part of its pro-reservations exhibits, JCET prepared a content analysis of existing TV programming (fewer than 100 commercial TV stations were then on the air). Analysis showed conclusively that commercial stations and networks did little to put television at the disposal of education and culture. JCET sounded a warning: If the forthcoming channel allotments failed to reserve channels for educational use, a once-in-a-lifetime opportunity would be lost.

The FCC took notice. Its *Sixth Report and Order*, which ended the freeze in 1952, provided for 242 reserved educational television (ETV) channel allotments, 80 VHF, and 162 UHF. Many more were added in later years, bringing the total allocation to about 600, of which some 240 remain unused.

ETV Constituency

Educational radio leaders had kept the faith over many lean years, largely ignored in the seats of power. During the fight to achieve educational TV channel reservations, however, the noncommercial broadcasting constituency grew larger and more diversified. Television's glamour attracted national educational, cultural, and consumer groups that previously had taken little notice of educational radio broadcasters.

Various enthusiasts developed conflicting views about the form ETV should take. Some held "educational television" to mean a broadly inclusive cultural and information service. Others took it to mean a new and improved audio-visual device, primarily important to schools and formal adult education. Some, following the model of commercial broadcasting, favored a strong centralized system and a concern for national audiences. Others, expressly rejecting such a model, focused on localism and service for more limited, specialized audiences. Some wanted to stress high culture and intellectual stimulation. Others wanted to emphasize programs of interest to ethnic minorities, children, and the poor. These differences would plague public television when it appeared in the late 1960s.

A New Beginning

For its first dozen years, ETV developed slowly, long on promise but short on performance. The few stations on the air depended on underfunded local productions and filmed programs of limited quality and interest. Their broadcast day lasted about half the length of commercial station schedules.

In 1959, many stations formed a program cooperative, the National Educational Television (NET). It provided five to ten hours a week of shared programs, delivered to the cooperating stations by mail. Though it was a step in the right direction, NET still fell far short of meeting the enormous program needs of full noncommercial service.

In the mid-1960s, a nonprofit foundation stepped into this bleak picture, hoping to transform it with a dynamic vision. The Carnegie Foundation felt that ETV needed well-articulated national goals, top-notch public relations, and leadership at the federal level. To generate highly visible recommendations for achieving these goals, the foundation set up the Carnegie Commission on Educational Television (CCET). The Carnegie Commission comprised nationally known figures from higher education, media, business, politics, and the arts. In its watershed 1967 report, *Public Television: A Program for Action*, the Carnegie Commission proposed that Congress establish a national "corporation for public television."

The Carnegie Commission deliberately used the word *public* rather than *educational* to disassociate much of its proposals from what many had come to regard as the "somber and static image" projected by the use of the word "education." It also chose the word *public* to emphasize its recommendation for an inclusive service embracing not only formal instruction and classroom television, but also a broad cultural/informational service intended for the public.

Six months after the 1967 Carnegie Commission report was published, its basic recommendations were enacted into law as part of President Lyndon Johnson's Great Society legislative program. The system it created survives to this day.

7.2 National Organizations

The transformation of ETV into a national public TV system succeeded in bringing it to public attention. In solving some problems, however, the Carnegie Commission created others. Public TV stations were often highly individualistic. They made uneasy, sometimes even acrimonious, partners with their allies in Washington, DC.

Corporation for Public Broadcasting

Congress set the Carnegie Commission's keystone recommendation in place with the Public Broadcasting Act of 1967 (*broadcasting* because Congress added radio at the last minute). The new law became part of the 1934 Communications Act. It created the Corporation for Public Broadcasting (CPB), a quasi-governmental organization whose key role is to provide a funding mechanism for individual public broadcasting stations, but not subject these stations to political influence or favoritism.

The Carnegie Commission had recommended that the president of the United States nominate only half of the CPB board. Congress, however, gave the president all the nomination power. The President appoints each member, who, after confirmation by the Senate, serves a six-year term. The Board, in turn, appoints the president and chief executive officer, who then names the other corporate officers. Congress also declined to legislate the long-term federal funding that the Carnegie Commission had recommended. These two departures from the plan left CPB at the mercy of presidential and congressional politics.

The Public Broadcasting Act gives CPB such tasks as the following:

▶ making grants and contracts for obtaining and producing high-quality programs from diverse sources
▶ helping to set up network interconnection
▶ encouraging the development of new public broadcasting stations
▶ conducting research and training

CPB itself may not own or operate stations. Congress emphasized that the stations should retain local autonomy, remaining free to select and schedule programs according to local needs. The last thing Congress wanted was to create a centralized, federal broadcaster.

The act directs CPB to do its job "in ways that will most effectively assure the maximum freedom . . . from interference with or control of program content or other activities." Nevertheless, some stations regarded the very existence of a distant agency dispensing federal funds as a threat. The Public Broadcasting System (PBS), National Public Radio (NPR), and Public Radio International (PRI) do not receive any direct appropriations from CPB. Instead, all of the appropriated money goes directly to member stations (i.e., affiliates) of these organizations. The issue of local versus centralized or national control has continually stirred up controversy between CPB and the stations.

Public Broadcasting Service (PBS)

CPB launched its network in 1969–1970, calling it the Public Broadcasting Service (PBS). PBS was deliberately fashioned to differ considerably from the commercial network model. Over the years, however, these differences have diminished. PBS schedules and operates the interconnection facilities and gradually has increased its control of the all-important task of program selection.

A weak national network had in fact been a Carnegie Commission recommendation. Though the report stressed the vital importance of network interconnection, it also warned against tight centralization of program control. Public broadcasting was expected to have "a strong component of local and regional programming" to "provide the opportunity and the means for local choice to be exercised upon the programs made available from central programming sources" (CCET, 1967: 33).

As time proved, it was unrealistic to limit PBS's programming role, even though doing so was desirable to avoid the over centralization typical of commercial networks. The Carnegie Commission failed to anticipate the practical problems of asking PBS to lay out a smorgasbord of programs from which affiliates would pick and choose at will. (Public broadcasters tend to avoid the term *affiliate* because of its commercial connotations—*member station* is preferred—but it is used here for convenience.)

Commercial experience had shown that a network needs the strong identity that can come only from a uniform national program schedule—identical key network programs available to everybody in the nation at the same time of day. But stations zealous to protect their local identity, operating under varied ownership and funding patterns, and profoundly suspicious of political interference from Washington, resisted that type of network. They sided with "their" organization, PBS, against CPB in the battles over program philosophy that followed.

As a means of continuing service while the philosophical debate continued, PBS program selection from 1974 until 1990 occurred through a complicated mechanism called the **Station Program Cooperative (SPC)**. Member stations (whose executives actually voted for which programs they would carry and help finance) praised SPC for its democratic participation. But SPC was also criticized for limiting program innovation, as stations nearly always voted and paid for programs successful in the past, rarely investing scarce dollars in new ideas.

Under pressure from a Congress concerned about SPC's decentralized and argument-ridden decision making, PBS stations concluded that the democratic SPC system had outlived its usefulness. They dissolved SPC and centralized all programming decisions under one PBS officer—much like the traditional commercial network model.

When former FCC Commissioner Ervin Duggan became PBS president in 1994, he designed a new three-division management organization. The new structure returned more choice to individual stations, allowing them to buy less from the national program service and to select more single programs or series from a new unit, PBS Syndication Services. The revised plan was intended in part to address what cost-conscious members of Congress and others called the "overlap" problem—several PBS stations that serve the same metropolitan area spending money on essentially the same program.

PBS Operations

PBS differs from the commercial networks in that it carries only programs that others produce. Member stations (affiliates) contract with PBS, agreeing to pay dues determined by their respective budget and market sizes. Rather than the network paying for use of their time (long the case with commercial television network affiliates), public stations pay PBS for programs—an arrangement closer to a cable system's relationship with the many cable networks, or to program syndication in commercial broadcasting. At present, PBS serves virtually all public TV stations on the air. Its 35-member board consists of professional station managers and members of the public drawn from station boards. The PBS staff totals about 300 in Alexandria, Virginia (near Washington, DC), New York, and Los Angeles. While the term "broadcasting" encompasses both radio and television, PBS only covers television; public radio in the United States is served by National Public Radio and other content providers.

Today, PBS serves 355 public noncommercial TV stations and reaches nearly 73 million people each week through on-air and on-line content. With the goal of providing diverse viewpoints to television and the Internet, PBS provides high-quality documentary and dramatic entertainment. PBS is also a leading provider of digital learning content for pre-K–12 educators, and offers a broad array of other educational services. PBS' premier kids' TV programming and web site, PBS KIDS Online, continue to be parents' and teachers' most trusted learning environments for children. More information about PBS is available at www.pbs.org.

PBS is not responsible for all programming carried on public TV stations; in fact, stations usually receive a large portion of their content (including most pledge-drive specials) from third-party sources, such as American Public Television, NETA, and independent producers. This distinction is a frequent source of viewer confusion.

Political Pressure

Since its inception in the 1970s, insulating PBS from politics has been a frustrating challenge. Section 398 of the Communications Act, added by the 1967 Public Broadcasting Act, tries to prevent political influence by expressly forbidding any "direction, supervision, or control" over noncommercial broadcasting by officials of the U.S. government. This legal detail has not stopped most administrations from manipulating CPB for their own ends. The usual premise for such interference has been the alleged liberal-leaning content found in public

broadcasting programs. In addition to merely complaining about certain programs, the White House has used its considerable political leverage to deny or postpone funding. Congress has often added its support to these maneuvers. For example, soon after the Republican Party took control of Congress in 1994, House Speaker Newt Gingrich (R-Ga.) issued a call to "zero out" all federal funding for CPB. In subsequent years, calls for investigations, hearings, and cutbacks have threatened the long-term planning and growth of public broadcasting in the United States. During difficult economic times, when the government decides to reduce debt and run more efficiently, public broadcasting inevitably is brought up as a likely target for cost cutting. Exhibit 7.a provides a financial breakdown of where public TV stations receive revenue support.

The consequences of all this pressure has been programming that is culturally enriching, but not necessarily controversial or provocative. Instead, audiences typically are presented with critically acclaimed but somewhat inoffensive product that seldom "rocks the boat." For instance, the most acclaimed prime-time programming in recent years have been multipart historical documentaries about the Civil War, baseball, jazz, and World War II. Some media scholars assert that the relentless threat to funding has had a chilling effect on public broadcasting's willingness to criticize government. Of course, one can find exceptions to this attribution, such as *Frontline*, a show that often takes a hard look at government policy, or an occasional investigative documentary, but in general, most programming on noncommercial broadcasting is rather tame.

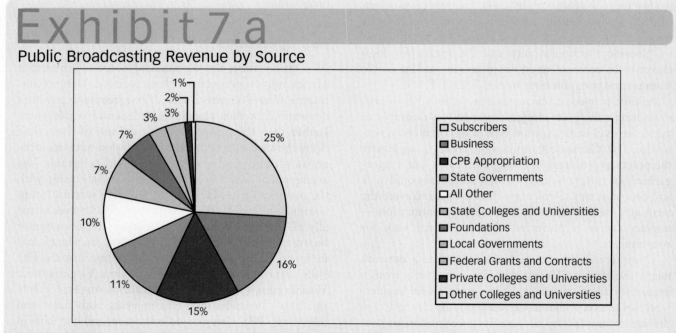

Exhibit 7.a

Public Broadcasting Revenue by Source

- Subscribers — 25%
- Business — 16%
- CPB Appropriation — 15%
- State Governments — 11%
- All Other — 10%
- State Colleges and Universities — 7%
- Foundations — 7%
- Local Governments — 3%
- Federal Grants and Contracts — 3%
- Private Colleges and Universities — 2%
- Other Colleges and Universities — 1%

Programming Services

The following are the primary services PBS provides to its member stations.

National Programming Service (NPS). The National Programming Service (NPS) provides the documentaries, arts, children's, and news and public-affairs programming. In prime time, PBS presents signature series like *Frontline*, *American Experience*, *NOVA*, *Nature and American Masters*, as well as a wide range of high-profile miniseries and specials. The NPS distributes the PBS Ready To Learn Service, which provides hours of children's programming every day.

PBS Plus. This service is intended to complement the National Program Service, which provides the national program schedule to PBS member stations. PBS PLUS consists entirely of fully underwritten continuing series, limited series, and specials in a variety of genres.

PBS via Satellite. PBS also offers two full-time satellite channels: the PBS National Satellite Service for C-Band, which is transmitted to the backyard (TVRO) audience; and the PBS National Satellite Service for DBS, which is transmitted on DIRECTV and DISH Network. All satellite services are made possible by viewer support of local PBS stations.

National Public Radio (NPR). In 1970, CPB created National Public Radio (NPR) both to interconnect stations (like PBS) and to produce some programs (unlike PBS). NPR provides its member stations, which do not have to carry any set amount of network programming, with about 22 percent of their daily schedules. NPR also coordinates satellite interconnection with 24 uplinks and more than 300 downlinks. Satellite distribution (the world's first satellite-delivered radio network) began in 1980 with four audio channels, which has now increased to 24.

CPB radio program funds go directly to NPR member stations, which support the network by paying a flat fee and then subscribing to morning and afternoon news services, NPR's musical and cultural programs, and Public Radio International programs. Stations pay anywhere from $25,000 to more than $300,000 annually, depending on market size, for NPR's program service, providing more than half of NPR's operating income.

7.3 Public Stations

Both public radio and public TV stations vary enormously in size, resources, goals, and philosophy. Though all are licensed by the FCC as "noncommercial educational" stations, some flirt with commercialism and many play no discernible formal educational role.

Television

In general, four classes of owners hold public TV station licenses. The four groups differ and even conflict in their concepts of noncommercial broadcasting.

States and municipalities hold about 40 percent of the licenses. Many belong to state educational networks, usually programmed by the station located at the state capital or other key origination points. Many southern states in particular chose this means of capitalizing on educational television.

Colleges and universities own about 25 percent of the stations. They often complement educational radio stations of long standing and sometimes closely tie to college curricula.

Public-school boards hold licenses for about 3 percent. Their stations naturally focus on in-school instructional programs, many produced by and for the local school system. The low number of such stations reflects the inability of public television to live up to its early promise as a major adjunct of formal education. In fact, as school budgets became tighter, several school stations left the air or transferred to other licensees. As will be presented later in the chapter, this situation may change radically with the introduction of new digital technologies, enabling stations to simultaneously reach students as well as the general public.

Community foundations control one-third of the outlets. The licensees are nonprofit foundations created especially to operate noncommercial stations. They recruit support from all sectors—schools, colleges, art and cultural organizations, foundations, businesses, and the public. Usually free of obligations to local tax sources, they tend to be politically more independent than stations that depend on revenue from local or state tax dollars. Among the best-known community stations, because they produce much of what appears on PBS, are WNET in New York; WETA in Washington, DC; KQED in San Francisco; KCET in Los Angeles; WGBH in Boston; WTTW in Chicago; and WQED in Pittsburgh.

Digital Opportunities

Just as commercial networks developed multiple distribution platforms for digital content when airwaves go all-DTV, so public broadcasters have recognized the need to make content available from a variety of sources including MP3, cell phone, and Internet stream, as well as conventional television. For example, in 2008, Apple launched iTunes U, a dedicated area within the iTunes Store, featuring free content such as course lectures, language lessons, lab demonstrations, sports highlights, and campus tours provided by top U.S. colleges and universities. In addition, the site offers downloads of many popular PBS programs.

As presented in prior chapters, the historic transition from analog to digital television has provided all TV stations, including noncommercial stations, with the opportunity to **multicast**. Multicasting allows stations to air four or more standard-definition (SDTV) program streams at the same time, and/or various data and audio channels. Public TV stations generally expect to multicast during the day and do HDTV at night. Many public TV stations have created, or are planning to launch, new and differentiated programming via their digital channels. Among the options for content are:

▶ repeats of the best PBS programs
▶ instructional and teacher-training programs on channels devoted to education
▶ Internet-like content for rural areas where on-line access is limited, as in a new Texas project
▶ local and state public affairs programming that typically is not available on the main public TV channels
▶ other specialized genres, such as cultural or Spanish-language programming

One example of a move to digital programming has been the launching of PBS World, a repository for the public broadcaster's documentary, news, and public affairs programming. Distributed by WGBH Boston and New York's Thirteen/WNET, in association with American Public Television (APT) and the National Educational Telecommunications Association (NETA), PBS World offers second runs of popular PBS programs including *American Experience*, *Frontline*, *History Detectives*, *Nature*, *The NewsHour with Jim Lehrer*, *NOVA*, *Scientific American Frontiers*, and *The Tavis Smiley Show*.

According to several surveys, in coming years education is likely to be the purpose of much of public TV's digital output. One can see a certain irony here in that the creators of public broadcasting in the 1960s deliberately wanted to avoid the term "educational" in their plans. This increased interest in education is discussed at the conclusion of this chapter.

In addition to new programming opportunities, revenue generation seems a likely byproduct of the DTV transition for financially strapped stations. The FCC decided to let public television use "excess" capacity in its digital transmissions to make money. The ruling will not permit commercials on broadcast channels, but these channels could be leased for data transmissions and other services. However, the FCC still insists that this additional capacity primarily be used for nonprofit, noncommercial, educational broadcast services. The Commission said it would not establish a bright line test to define the term "primarily," but will instead define it

as a "substantial majority" of a station's entire digital capacity, measured on a weekly basis. The Commission has further ruled that stations must pay a fee of 5 percent of gross revenues generated by ancillary or supplementary services provided on their DTV service.

Alternative Distribution of Programming

Unlike their counterparts in commercial television, the cable industry has welcomed all noncommercial TV offerings, including new digital channels. In 2005, the Association of Public Television Stations (APTS) and the National Cable and Telecommunications Association (NCTA) created the Public Television Digital Cable Carriage Agreement, ensuring that local public TV stations' digital programming will be carried on cable systems serving the vast majority of the nation's cable subscribers.

In addition to cable opportunities, digital public broadcasting has found its way onto satellite distribution. Continuing its expansion of high-definition services, DIRECTV has agreed with APTS to include local high-definition (HD) feeds of public TV stations in its long-term HD roll-out plans that began in 2008. DIRECTV, APTS, and PBS also have agreed to work together to develop video on demand offerings to make local and national TV programming to DIRECTV's customers anytime they wish. In addition, the satellite service will carry two national standard-definition channels of public TV programming.

Of course, PBS has had a presence on the Internet for many years, but new broadband technologies are offering more complex interactive offerings on its popular web site (www.pbs.org). In addition, PBS programming has become available on several commercial video sites. For example, Hulu, a joint video downloading venture of NBC Universal and News Corp, has added PBS shows, including *NOVA*, *Wired Science*, and *Scientific American*.

Radio

CPB built its national noncommercial radio network, NPR, around a cadre of professionally competent, full-service stations (referred to as "CPB-qualified"). These stations had to meet certain standards involving factors such as power, facilities, budgets, and number of employees. Today's standards for what are now called "CPB-supported" stations are much less rigorous: minimum hours of operation (12 or 18, depending on the level of financial support sought) and program schedules that do not advocate a religious or political philosophy or consist primarily of in-school or in-service educational instruction.

Stations that carry NPR programming do not necessarily have to be CPB-supported, although nearly all of them are. By the year 2000, more than 600 non-commercial stations were NPR members (like PBS, NPR does not use the term *affiliate*). A much larger group of more than 1,000 noncommercial stations either do not qualify for NPR membership or choose not to join the network. In 2000, the FCC authorized a new class of low-power noncommercial FCC station. Once implemented, this action gave hundreds of community groups and non-profit organizations access to the airwaves.

7.4 Economics

Ask any noncommercial broadcaster to name his or her most serious problem, and the answer will almost always be "not enough money." Compared with those in many other countries, America's noncommercial system, on a per-person basis, is woefully underfunded. Exhibit 7.a on p. 154 shows the diversity of public television's funding sources. But diversity has a price: Each source brings different obligations with its funding, and each has its biases.

Government Support

Local and state governments supported educational FM from its inception in the 1940s, and many states expanded into educational television over the ensuing decades. By the mid-1960s, state tax funds provided about half of all public broadcasting income. In the face of rising budget shortages, however, both state and local support had declined substantially by the 1990s.

At the onset, the federal government gave no financial assistance at all. Federal legislative recognition came first with the Educational Television Facilities Act of 1962. It granted up to a million dollars of federal money to stations in each state, subject to their matching federal dollars with money from other sources. Extended and revised, this act continues to support equipment and facilities purchases for public broadcasting. This program is administered by the National Telecommunications and Information Agency (NTIA), an arm of the U.S. Department of Commerce. As with CPB, federal funding of NTIA also is under attack, and there is considerable argument over whether this funding should continue.

Long-Range Funding

Attempts to fund CPB for longer than the usual federal one-year budget cycle failed until 1975 when Congress finally authorized funds for a three-year period. Although similar multiyear appropriations have followed since, Congress has sometimes rescinded appropriations to which it had already agreed, and there have even been attempts to halt federal funding entirely. This uncertain commitment by Congress, and several state governments as well, has made it difficult for public broadcasting to plan, let alone pay, for the future.

Foundation Grants

Foundations provide substantial support for noncommercial broadcasting. Without the backing of the Ford Foundation, early educational television might not have survived its first decade. Carnegie Foundation money paid for two important studies, the first of which shaped public broadcasting.

In 1981, the largest single gift ever made to public broadcasting to that date came from Walter Annenberg, then publisher of *TV Guide*. He donated $150 million, spread over 15 years, to fund a project to create innovative college-level courses and programs. The Annenberg/CPB project shifted focus in the early 1990s, in part because of changes in tax laws, to support programming for primary and secondary schools rather than university-level audiences.

Corporate Underwriting

Through a limited form of sponsorship called **underwriting**, businesses provide program producers funds to cover at least some production costs for specific projects. FCC regulations allow companies brief identifying announcements at the beginning and end of such programs. After 1981, the FCC also allowed corporations to display logos or trademarks. Some critics worry that excessive corporate underwriting may influence the content of noncommercial programming; a fear similarly arose regarding advertisers and commercial broadcasting.

Commercial Experiment

Seeking alternative or additional revenue sources for public broadcasting, Congress established the Temporary Commission on Alternative Financing for Public Telecommunications (TCAF) in 1981 to supervise an experiment with commercials as a means of support. The TCAF found that most public TV stations would not carry ads because of labor union contract requirements, local economic considerations, or concerns about advertising's impact on the character of and other financial support for public broadcasting (TCAF, 1983). The experiment ended in mid-1983, and outright commercials remained taboo.

Creeping Commercialism?

Influenced by TCAF recommendations, the FCC in 1984 authorized **enhanced underwriting**, leading stations to carry what former PBS President Bruce Christensen called "almost commercials" (Smith, 1985). The FCC tried to balance station and public needs: Stations may sell announcements up to 30 seconds long and mention specific consumer products, but may sell no more than two and a half minutes between individual programs.

The line between "enhanced underwriting" and commercial spots has now become increasingly blurred. Critics deplore public TV's increasing commercialization. After all, public broadcasting's primary justification is that it furnishes *alternatives*—programs not likely to appeal to advertisers, but nevertheless useful and desirable. To the extent that pleasing advertisers motivates *both* services, the argument for public broadcasting is weakened. Still, the notion resurfaces from time to time, particularly when conservative Republicans are in the White House or dominate Congress.

The phrase "creeping commercialism" has been used by some critics to denote the temptations public broadcasters face when approaching businesses for financial support. Over the decades, the "identification" of corporate underwriters has become ever more commercial in on-air execution. Potential underwriters and their advertising agencies continually push the creative boundaries as to what is acceptable audio and video content. Financially desperate public stations often are tempted to offer more than they should.

Local Contributions

Federal appropriations (and often national foundation grants) trickle down only when stations match federal grants. The desperate scramble to match federal money forces local fund-raisers to push membership/subscription drives to the saturation point. Polls indicate that many viewers detest marathon fund-raising drives (derisively called *begathons* by critics). On-air auctions of donated goods and services (most of them from commercial sources) promote the givers so blatantly as to amount to program-length commercials. However, as Exhibit 7.a (on p. 154) demonstrates, these efforts are vital to the survival of noncommercial stations: Nearly 25 percent of public broadcasting's revenue comes from individual viewers and listeners.

Other devices used (in some cases merely proposed) to raise funds locally, and to some extent nationally, include:

- selling commercial rights to market merchandise associated with programs (the Children's Television Workshop defrays a large part of *Sesame Street*'s production costs from such sources)
- selling newly produced programs to commercial television or pay cable for initial showing before release to public television (proposed)
- renting station facilities (usually studios) to commercial producers

- selling books, videotapes, and other items to viewers
- trading a reserved educational channel for a less desirable commercial channel for a price (such channel reclassification requires FCC approval)
- acquiring assured tax-based revenue by charging commercial broadcasters a tax on profits, a receiver licensing fee, or a spectrum-use fee (proposed)
- selling access to the FM subcarrier or TV vertical blanking interval for commercial use
- selling excess channel capacity

In sum, public broadcasting executives have to serve too many masters and spend an inordinate amount of time on fund-raising. The year-to-year uncertainties of congressional appropriations, corporate underwriting, and local membership drives make it impossible for public broadcasters to plan rationally for long-term development. As a result, in the mid- and late 1990s some prominent legislators began calling for the establishment of a public broadcasting trust fund, the proceeds of which could provide predictable long-term funding. Interestingly, this is exactly what the Carnegie Commission suggested in its initial report in 1967. As of the publication of this text, these proposals have yet to become a reality.

Public television's funding uncertainties became especially urgent as the 2009 deadline for conversion to digital broadcasting approached. The Association of Public Television Stations estimates that the conversion will have cost close to two billion dollars. Despite special government funding for the transition, most public stations today are still searching for ways to offset this huge investment. Of course, from a long-term perspective, the move to digital will prove to be a wonderful advantage, but the short-term problems of paying for the initial changeover are daunting. As a result, station operators have been temporarily distracted by acquiring new technology hardware rather than focusing on generating new program content.

7.5 TV Program Sources

Although noncommercial broadcasting's basic purpose is to supply an alternative to commercial services, program overlap does occur. Noncommercial stations often show feature films and syndicated series obtained from the same distributors that commercial stations use. On the other hand, noncommercial outlets do more local production and experimental programming than do their commercial counterparts.

TV Network Business Model

Unlike the model of America's commercial TV networks, in which affiliates give up portions of their local advertising airtime in exchange for network programming, PBS member stations pay substantial fees for the shows acquired and distributed by the national organization. This relationship means that PBS member stations have greater latitude in local scheduling than their commercial counterparts. Scheduling of PBS-distributed series may vary greatly from market to market. This can be a source of tension as stations seek to preserve their localism and PBS strives to market a consistent national line-up. However, PBS has a policy of "common carriage" requiring most stations to clear the national prime-time programs on a common schedule so that they can be more effectively marketed on a national basis.

Stations as Network Producers

A handful of major-market producing stations act as primary producers for PBS. In the 1990s, they provided more than a third of national programming, with another 10 percent or so coming from lesser public TV stations. Major producer stations, such as WGBH-Boston, have long histories of creative innovation in public television. They tend to develop specializations, such as WETA (Washington, DC), for news and public affairs, and WGBH for science, documentary, and drama presentations.

Foreign Sources

By the turn of the century, nearly a fifth of all PBS series contained some overseas material, while others came straight from sources such as British commercial and BBC TV series. Best known are the long-running *Masterpiece Theatre* and *Mystery!* series, both co-produced by WGBH.

Independent and Syndicated Production

Under pressure from producers who claimed PBS largely ignored their output and abilities, Congress in 1988 required CPB to fund an Independent Production Service, separate from CPB, to encourage more independent program sources.

Easily the best known of these is the nonprofit Children's Television Workshop, which won international fame for *Sesame Street* and subsequent children's series. The *Sesame Street* series began in 1969 with initial funding from government and foundation grants. By the late 1980s, ancillary commercial ventures, such as merchandising items using the program name and characters, defrayed well over half of its budget.

Local Production

The amount and quality of local production among public stations is a matter of market size. Stations licensed to large markets tend to have larger operating budgets and therefore produce more ambitious programming. In some instances, local stations operating in the same state or same geographical area will combine efforts to generate programs of regional interest. Because production and distribution costs are shared among the participating stations, the final program product typically will be more impressive than a single station effort. Locally produced programs consist mainly of news and public affairs, along with some educational/instructional material telecast during daytime hours for in-school use. Daily newscasts are rare among public TV stations due to high operating expenses. Most are associated with major universities offering degrees in journalism, allowing students to learn news-gathering skills in a real world environment. The least costly local programming involves in-studio interviews or "talking heads" that have dominated public broadcasting since its inception.

Although localism has always been a key component of the noncommercial broadcasting philosophy, local production is often one of the first things to go when budgets are cut. Even simple in-studio productions typically require paid technical employees and on-air talent. As discussed earlier, converting from analog to digital transmission has been costly and this includes the conversion of studio equipment, such as cameras and video switchers.

Cable Alternatives

Just as cable has increasingly taken on many functions of traditional broadcasting in entertainment, it has also done so in education and public affairs. C-SPAN, in addition to its extensive public-affairs programming, offers C-SPAN in the Classroom, a free educational service that allows teachers to tape material for instructional use. Today, the majority of schools in the country are supplied with free cable service, most by local cable systems as a part of their franchises. Cable in the Classroom, a free service of the commercial cable industry, provides some national coordination. The service provides about 500 hours of commercial-free programming per month, supplied largely by over 30 cable-delivered networks.

Cable television also provides noncommercial alternatives through its access channels—channels set aside for public, educational, and governmental use. Many communities have vital cable access operations, providing one or more channels of local entertainment, educational, and government programming. Public access channels provide a forum for residents to showcase their artistic (though in some cases that is certainly open to argument) talents on television, a proposition too expensive for most people to pursue on a broadcast station. Some cities use their government access channels to transmit council meetings, school board meetings, and various other local government activities, providing their citizens with greater access to local decision making.

DBS and the Internet

In the cable act of 1992, Congress imposed a requirement on all DBS operators that they reserve from 4 to 7 percent of their channel capacity, as determined by the FCC, "exclusively for noncommercial programming of an educational or informational nature." This does not necessarily mean that these programs originate with PBS. On the contrary, all kinds of educational programmers have applied to the DBS operators for carriage of their channels. According to the FCC's rules, DBS operators may charge the educational programmers half of the direct costs they incur in carrying the channels. The regulations also limit carriage to only one channel per programmer.

Increasingly, the Internet is providing significant amounts of educational "programming" to a global audience. Many universities offer courses and even entire degree programs on-line. With the push to reach nontraditional students through "distance education," the Internet is unique in its ability to deliver interactive instructional programming to widely dispersed audiences.

With so many content providers and so many distribution platforms available today, conventional public broadcasting is experiencing something that for several decades was not a burning issue—competition.

7.6 Noncommercial TV Programs

The following section provides a brief overview of the types of programs typically found on noncommercial TV stations. Some are provided by PBS, but others are acquired through other networks or syndication program services. The longevity of many popular programs is remarkable, featuring some that are into their third or fourth decade. On one hand, this consistent performance can be applauded, but some critics see extreme program longevity as a sign of creative stagnation, a kind of prime time "mustiness" as one critic calls it. Of course, the final evaluation should be made by audiences and, despite unprecedented media competition, noncommercial programming is still watched by millions of people every day.

News and Public Affairs

In contrast to commercial networks, PBS found its affiliated stations receptive to long-format (more than half-hour) newscasts. *The NewsHour with Jim Lehrer* (and its immediate predecessor, *The MacNeil/Lehrer*

NewsHour) has consistently been acclaimed as one of TV's best news and information programs, featuring in-depth interviews and analyses of current news stories. *NewsHour* provides a significant alternative to the comercial-based network newscasts. Despite critical praise, *NewsHour* has failed to build a large following, even by noncommercial standards. Still, its loyal audience has kept the program on the air for more than 25 years.

PBS and other program providers offer a steady diet of other public affairs programs as well, including *Washington Week in Review with Gwen Ifill*, *Nightly Business Report*, *The McLaughlin Group*, *Charlie Rose*, *Frontline*, and most recently the return of Bill Moyers from doing occasional specials to a weekly program, entitled *Bill Moyers' Journal*.

History

Occasionally, documentaries attract viewers who do not normally watch the noncommercial service. Public television's provision of such programming goes back more than two decades. The multipart *Civilization*, a review of world history and cultural development featuring Sir Kenneth Clark, ran in PBS's first season and helped to introduce the companion book marketing idea. In the 1980s, *Vietnam: A Television History*, co-produced by Boston's WGBH and French television brought howls of protest from conservative groups and unprecedented audience ratings. In recent years, this multipart documentary category is exemplified by *The Civil War*, *The West*, *The History of Jazz*, *Baseball*, and *The War*, which have won widespread praise and viewership—and helped sell thousands of copies of a handsome companion book and videotape copies of the series, proceeds from which helped meet the program's production costs. *The American Experience* has served as host vehicle for a series of historical documentaries on American history and key historical figures—with such varied programs as those on the building of the Brooklyn Bridge, the impact of rigged TV quiz shows, immigration, and several studies of American presidents (Exhibit 7.b highlights the contributions of Ken Burns).

Part adventure, part history lesson, and part treasure hunt, *Antiques Roadshow* debuted in 1997 and has become one of PBS's most popular series. Hosted by antiques expert Chris Jussel, the show brings antiques specialists together with citizens seeking information about their possessions.

Performing Arts

All of the performing arts—drama, dance, music—find a home in public television. Among public TV evening programs, *Masterpiece* is probably best known. The Sunday evening hour-long staple provides British-made drama, ranging from short series built around

Exhibit 7.b

The Extraordinary Ken Burns

For five consecutive nights in September 1991, some 14 million viewers watched *The Civil War* unfold, making it the most-watched series in the history of public television. It earned an average national rating that was four times the normal PBS audience. The creator of this groundbreaking series was Ken Burns, who had done earlier documentary programs for PBS, but this was different—an 11-hour series that brought the 1861–1865 struggle to life as most viewers had never seen or thought about it before. Combining the creative use of period music, live shots of battlefields, quotes from experts, and old photos, this multidimensional approach to producing a TV documentary was extraordinary. Many media observers would assert that there is no way that *The Civil War* could have been produced anywhere but on public television. The series proved financially valuable, too. Viewer contributions to local stations rose sharply, a companion book sold more

than 750,000 copies, and related video and audio recordings also sold well.

The Civil War series set the stage for many more highly successful series on PBS using essentially the same production techniques. Here are just a few of the critically acclaimed historical series Ken Burns has produced in only a few years.

▶ **2007** *The War* tells the story of the Second World War through the personal accounts of a handful of men and women from four American towns.

▶ **2005** *Unforgivable Blackness: The Rise and Fall of Jack Johnson* describes the ordeal of the first African-American boxer to win the most coveted title in all of sports and his struggle, in and out of the ring.

▶ **2003** *Horatio's Drive: America's First Road Trip* recounts the story of America's first transcontinental road trip, a truly unforgettable experience crossing the nation's vast landscape.

▶ **2002** *Mark Twain* is an illuminating and touching portrait of Mark Twain, born Samuel Clemens, one of the greatest writers in American history.

▶ **2001** *JAZZ* looks at the development of a type of music that is uniquely American.

▶ **1997** *Thomas Jefferson* examines the life and times of the author of the Declaration of Independence, who ironically was also a lifelong owner of slaves.

▶ **1997** *Lewis and Clark: The Journey of the Corps of Discovery* tells the remarkable story of a voyage of danger and discovery from St. Louis to the headwaters of the Missouri River.

▶ **1996** *The West* chronicles the epic saga of America's most vast and turbulent region, beginning before European settlement and continuing into the 20th century.

▶ **1994** *Baseball* is a saga spanning the quest for racial justice, the clash of labor and management, the transformation of popular culture, and the unfolding of the national pastime.

Ken Burns' stature as a creator of outstanding TV documentaries is unparalleled in recent history and noncommercial broadcasting has been the beneficiary of his extraordinary talents.

Source: Photo from AP/Wide World Photos.

historical events, famous novels, or contemporary views of the human condition. Another popular program since its first broadcast in 1980 is *Masterpiece Mystery!* hosted first by Vincent Price and then by Diana Rigg. Viewers of this program watch as their favorite sleuths—Miss Marple, Hercule Poirot, Inspector Morse, Sherlock Holmes, Rumpole of the Bailey—solve crimes and other mysteries in often humorous and intellectually stimulating ways.

Music and dance appear regularly on three PBS programs that began in the mid-1970s and are still going strong: *Great Performances*, *Austin City Limits*, and *Live from Lincoln Center*.

Science and Nature

One of the first programs dealing with science and nature aired in the 1970s. *The Ascent of Man* featured philosopher Jacob Bronowski's view of developing mankind in a multipart series and yet another useful companion volume. Since then PBS has offered the eight-part series, *The Brain*, as well as the multipart *Cosmos*, with famous astronomer Carl Sagan introducing many Americans to the wonders of astronomy. The long-running series *Nature* and some of the most popular public TV documentaries, such as the *National Geographic Specials* and *National Audubon Society Specials*, proved that Americans could also produce and enjoy top-notch nature films.

Over the last two decades, *NOVA*, the longest-running nationally broadcast science series, has presented on PBS more than 400 different hour-long science programs, each devoted to a single topic. Each week the program typically attracts the largest audience of any PBS weekly series.

Children

Public broadcasting has a clear mandate to provide constructive, imaginative children's programs. Accordingly, many public TV stations fill a large portion of their daytime hours with in-school programs (paid for by school districts) and schedule additional special programs for children both early in the morning and again in the afternoon.

No series on either commercial or public television has ever been given as much scheduled airtime as has *Sesame Street*, which now has taken on classic status as the preeminent program for preschoolers. The Children's Television Workshop (CTW) brought all

the technical resources of television, as well as all the capabilities of educational research, to bear with its 1969 premier of *Sesame Street*. A wonderfully original group of large-scale puppets, the Muppets, became the program's hallmark. Research showed that children who watched *Sesame Street* learned to read more quickly than did other children (see Exhibit 7.c). From 1968 to 2001, in another long-running children's program, millions of young children heard and sang along to the soothing words of Fred Rogers as he began each episode of *Mister Rogers' Neighborhood*.

Education and Instruction

Since 1977, CPB has funded more than 20 instructional television (ITV) series for use in classrooms, providing texts and other support for each series. Since 1981, PBS has offered the Adult Learning Service (ALS), a cooperative effort with local stations that provides college-credit TV courses for viewers at home. Many of these courses reach colleges directly by means of the Adult Learning Satellite Service, which began in 1988

Exhibit 7.c

The All-Powerful *Sesame Street*

Ask someone to name a program on public television and the odds are very good that the most mentioned program title will be *Sesame Street*. Many of today's adult parents not only watch the daily program with their children, but most likely watched the antics of "Big Bird," "Elmo," and "Cookie Monster" as children themselves. For 40 years, *Sesame Street* has delighted preschool children and their families. Using songs, music, animation, live action "street scenes," and short films, along with a cast of lovable human and Muppet characters, *Sesame Street* makes learning fun. In addition to the academic skills of learning

language and numbers, other instructional goals have been basic life skills, such as how to cross the street safely, proper hygiene, healthy eating habits, and social skills.

Most media observers would agree that *Sesame Street* by far is the most recognized programming on public television in the United States and one of the primary motivators for individuals—especially parents—to donate money to public broadcasting. Winning more than 100 Emmy Awards, few TV series have matched its level of international praise. Although public broadcasting provides an impressive array of long-standing, prestigious adult programs, from *Masterpiece Theater* to *Nova*, the all-powerful *Sesame Street*, aimed at preschoolers, is at the core of the PBS brand.

Because of its brand strength, *Sesame Street* is also known for its extensive merchandising, which includes many books, magazines, video/audio media, and toys. Although a percentage of the money from any Sesame Street Workshop product goes to help fund *Sesame Street* or its international co-productions, critics accuse the program of crossing the line from a purely noncommercial venture to something that seems disturbingly commercial.

Over the decades, *Sesame Street* occasionally has stirred up some controversy. For example, the program faced hostility in the southern United States when it first aired because it portrayed people of various races mingling peacefully. In recent years, many unsubstantiated rumors have circulated about the series, including that "Bert" and "Ernie" are a gay couple. Perhaps much of the concern about the program is rooted in its enormous popularity, which in turn is rooted in its willingness to break new ground.

Source: Photo courtesy of Sesame Workshop.

and serves some 2,000 institutions of higher learning. In parallel fashion, PBS coordinates the distribution of programs for elementary and secondary schools. In carrying out their classroom instruction mission, public TV stations draw on several large libraries of instructional materials from companies that act as syndicators. Notable examples include the Agency for Instructional Television (AIT) in Bloomington, Indiana, innovative producers of interactive videodisc programs for children; the Great Plains National Instructional Television Library (GPN) of Lincoln, Nebraska, producers of well-known classroom series for children; and the Annenberg/CPB Project, producers of several prime-time adult learning series.

Not all of the educational and information programming from PBS is intended solely for the classroom. Many of the most popular PBS series feature how-to themes. Programs such as *This Old House*, *The New Yankee Workshop*, and *The Victory Garden* deliver entertaining instructional content to do-it-yourselfers across the country.

7.7 Noncommercial Radio Programs

Typical public radio stations affiliated with National Public Radio (NPR) and/or Public Radio International (PRI) fill about two-fifths of their weekly total airtime with programs from these networks and other syndicated sources. In addition to conventional over-the-air reception, much program content is available for personal iPod downloads.

National Public Radio (NPR)

A privately supported, not-for-profit membership organization, NPR serves a growing audience of 26 million Americans each week in partnership with more than 800 independently operated, noncommercial public radio stations. Each NPR member station serves local listeners with a distinctive combination of national and local programming. With original on-line content and audio streaming, www.NPR.org offers hourly newscasts, special features, and 10 years of archived audio and information. NPR's first continuing success was its weekday late-afternoon news-and-feature program, *All Things Considered*, which began in 1971. The program quickly won every radio program award available and became a listening addiction for its loyal fans. NPR took the same approach to news on *Morning Edition*, which premiered in 1979, and *Weekend Edition*, which debuted in 1985. While other news organizations downsized over the past several years, NPR News added reporters, correspondents, and offices worldwide, and now gathers and produces content from some 36 locations around the world.

In addition to news programs, NPR distributes a series of talk, cultural, and informational programs to its affiliates. One particularly popular talk show is the Peabody Award-winning *Fresh Air* with Terry Gross. This weekday magazine of contemporary arts and issues features in-depth interviews with prominent cultural and entertainment figures, plus criticism and comment. Perhaps the most unlikely NPR offering—though one of the most popular and financially successful for stations that carry it—is *Car Talk*, featuring the Magliozzi brothers, whose answers to called-in car-maintenance questions are spiced with jokes, word play, and a general sense of fun. *Wait Wait ... Don't Tell Me!* is NPR's weekly hour-long quiz program. Each week on the radio, listeners can test their knowledge against some of the best and brightest in the news and entertainment world while figuring out what's real news and what's made up.

Public Radio International (PRI)

A second national public radio service, Public Radio International (PRI), began as American Public Radio (APR) in 1983. Formed by Minnesota Public Radio, it first served chiefly as a distribution channel for the popular *A Prairie Home Companion* (now distributed by American Public Media), featuring Garrison Keillor (see Exhibit 7.d). By the early 1990s, it was the largest distributor of public radio programming. In 1994, it changed its name to reflect its increasing global emphasis on news and other programming.

PRI's stated mission is to serve audiences with distinctive programming that provides information, insights, and cultural experiences essential to understanding a diverse, interdependent world. Partnering with public media's most talented producers and hosts, PRI offers distinctly global voices on *The World* and *BBC World Service*. The service also provides voices of culture, contemporary American life, and artistry on *The Tavis Smiley Show*, *This American Life*, *Studio 360 with Kurt Andersen*, and *Sounds Eclectic*. Unlike NPR, PRI provides programs to only one station per market. Also, unlike NPR, it does not produce programs, but rather acquires them from member stations.

Formats

The primary appeal of public stations is that they offer content usually heard nowhere else—jazz, opera, local public affairs, folk music, and the like. Recently, a growing number of stations, especially in larger radio markets with multiple noncommercial licensees, have shifted their formats from music to all-talk. The single largest format is religious/gospel programming, reflecting the large number of noncommercial stations licensed to religious organizations.

Public stations tend to differ most from their commercial counterparts in that many vary their content

Exhibit 7.d

The Mythical World of Garrison Keillor

If the mandate for noncommercial radio is to provide genuine alternative program content not available on commercial radio, then *A Prairie Home Companion* hosted by Garrison Keillor is the perfect example. Nothing on American radio comes close to the music and zany homespun humor generated every Saturday night from 5:00 to 7:00 P.M. Central Time. Created by Minnesota Public Radio and distributed today by American Public Media, the program usually originates from the Fitzgerald Theater in St. Paul, Minnesota, although it is frequently taken on the road. Today, *A Prairie Home Companion* is heard by more than four million listeners each week on some 580 public radio stations, and abroad on America One and the Armed Forces Networks in Europe and the Far East. Over the years, the program has cultivated an almost fanatical listenership who cannot wait for Keillor's comedic storytelling segment, "News from Lake Wobegon."

More than 1,000 live broadcasts over a span of more than 30 years testify to the popularity of *A Prairie Home Companion*. In 1987, the program ended for a while. Garrison thought it was a good idea at the time, but only two years later, the show was back, based in New York and called *American Radio Company of the Air*. But there's no place like home. So, in 1992 it was back to Minnesota and, soon after, back to the old name: *A Prairie Home Companion*. The program's appeal centers on Keillor and a cast that includes "The Guy's All-Star Shoe Band" and a sound effects expert, Tom Keith. The live variety show runs for two hours and features comedy sketches, and music heard nowhere else. The radio program inspired a 2006 film of the same name starring Keillor, Meryl Streep, and Kevin Kline. Robert Altman directed the film, which is a fictional representation of behind-the-scenes activities on a long-running radio show that has unexpectedly been cancelled.

Source: Photo from Chuck Fadley/Miami Herald/Newscom.

Several hundred noncommercial FM stations and a growing number of low-power AM stations (and a few cable-only FM services) provide one or more types of community radio. (College stations operating on student fees could be considered a type of community radio.) In the 1960s, reacting against rigidly formatted radio and dissenting from establishment values, some small stations began the **underground** or **free form** radio format.

Such radio is now lumped under the **progressive** format, which mixes live and recorded music and talk, usually at the whim of the presenter. Community stations often feature, if not progressive music, a classical, jazz, or diversified format. Small, low-salaried staffs supplemented by volunteers mean low overhead, enabling such outlets to present formats that would not be commercially viable. (See Exhibit 8.e, p. 185, for a closer look at noncommercial radio formats.)

7.8 Changing Roles

With their small but generally upscale audiences, noncommercial stations are concerned with survival in the new century in at least two areas: financial support and competition from other services. But they face an even more basic dilemma as well: Can they successfully continue to justify their very existence? It is important to note that most of the concern has been aimed at television rather than radio. Criticism of noncommercial radio's program content and funding practices has been minimal over the decades. In fact, in recent years the audience ratings for NPR radio have risen and the service has received mostly positive evaluations by media critics and audiences. Furthermore, because radio program content is so inexpensive to produce compared to TV content, noncommercial radio has not attracted a great deal of financial scrutiny. On the other hand, noncommercial television continues to receive negative criticism. For example, after 40 years of service to American audiences, a column in the *New York Times* in 2008 featured the provocative headline "Is PBS Still Necessary?" Indeed, this columnist has not been the only vocal critic of the noncommercial service. While in the past the primary attacks involved notions of political bias and creeping commercialism, the common argument heard these days is that the development of alternative media, especially cable, has weakened the major rationale for public television. Programs for children, good drama, science and history, and other cultural programming—once the nearly exclusive domain of public broadcasting—now appear on several cable networks delivered via DBS as well as cable systems.

The counterargument, of course, is that these newer distribution technologies are subscription-based and many people who might otherwise want these services cannot afford them, while more than 98 percent of the U.S. population has access to at least one over-the-air

considerably each day rather than consistently hewing to a single format. They come close to the "middle-of-the-road" or "something for everybody" formats that traditional radio stations provided in the 1940s and 1950s.

public TV signal. Further, audience research shows that viewership is relatively high compared to most cable offerings. Some 80 million people in almost 50 million households watch public television during an average week. Over a typical month over 133 million people tune into public television, representing 67 percent of American households. Also, the increasingly widespread use of VCRs, DVDs, and CD-ROMs for educational material makes public broadcasters more aware of the need to specify clearly what role they will play amid a wider variety of viewer choices. But it remains just as clear that, for the foreseeable future, newer media cannot provide noncommercial system-type services to all who want them.

Critical Views

In addition to citing an increasing variety of media options providing educational and cultural fare, critics in recent years have broadened their attacks on the current system of noncommercial broadcasting on several related but distinct fronts:

▶ The funding shortage always cited by public broadcasters is largely a matter of evasion: Lack of sufficient audience appeal (and thus support) lies at the root of their problem.

▶ Public participation in public television is in too many cases a sham because professional managers make most of the decisions, just as they do in commercial operations.

▶ Public television has little public appeal. Its vaunted fine arts and high culture merely serve privileged groups that are easily able to afford other sources of such material without resorting to publicly supported broadcast channels.

▶ Conservatives have long targeted public broadcasting as being too liberal in news and documentary programs, presenting a one-sided view of American life—this despite regular appearances by such alternative spokespersons as the late William F. Buckley and John McLaughlin.

Outlook

Some of these criticisms reflect the deregulatory philosophy that dominated discussions of U.S. media policy during the conservative political ascendancy of the 1980s. Similar attacks on public broadcasting surfaced in other countries, also stimulated by a market-oriented, *laissez-faire* approach to media regulation. Even a service so widely esteemed as the BBC came under attack as elitist and lacking in the fiscal responsibility that, according to deregulatory theory, only the "discipline of the market" can impose.

In Europe, as in the United States, these attacks raise a basic question: Should all broadcasting be regarded strictly as an *economic* undertaking, with programs treated as ordinary consumer goods? Or should at least some part of any national electronic media system be regarded as a cultural undertaking, with programs treated as a significant aspect of national life? Must everything depend on that slogan of free marketers, "consumer choice"? Not everyone chooses to attend great museums, galleries, and libraries that public funds support—often in locations not far from festering slums. Yet few would advocate dismantling all such cultural treasures and diverting their government grants to public housing.

As discussed earlier in this chapter, the funding for public broadcasting increasingly is shifting to nonfederal sources, as federal tax dollars now represent less than 15 percent of total public broadcasting revenues. Many stations report that fund-raising appeals based in part on reduced federal funding are effective. Further, additional noncommercial sources of programming are available and are slowly increasing. While the future of public broadcasting might not necessarily be considered bright, these developments suggest that noncommercial services are important to the public and that the public, when faced with a diminution of those services, will respond with increased financial support in an attempt to retain them.

From "Public" Back to "Educational"

Perhaps the future of noncommercial broadcasting, particularly for television, is a renewed emphasis on education. Recall that in the early development of this service the founders wanted to digress from the notions of educational TV (ETV) and pursue broader objectives that included more culture and public affairs content. The term "educational" was downplayed in favor of "public." Now, after recognizing the changing media landscape, the Corporation for Public Broadcasting is pushing education. In 2008, a comprehensive national survey of all PBS television stations entitled "Public Television Stations: A Trusted Source for Educating America" did not ask about the programs aired by these stations, but rather the off-air educational services that they provide to their communities. In most cases these activities involved partnerships with local schools, universities, museums, libraries, and community organizations. From a technological perspective, the term "broadcasting" seems outdated because stations are making use of all sorts of new media technology to multiple audiences with a broad array of available content. In an effort to redefine itself in a media environment of abundant choice, public broadcasting eventually may adopt the signature of *educational media*.

Programs and Programming Basics

chapter

This chapter looks at the creating, selecting, scheduling, and evaluating of program content. Whether viewed from the perspective of radio, television, cable, satellite or the Internet, the overriding purpose of commercial programming is either to attract advertisers by delivering audiences of sufficient size and appropriate composition or to attract audiences who pay subscription fees, pay-per-play fees, or a combination of these business models.

8.1 It's Always About the Bottom Line

Business is always about the bottom line. Programs must be both affordable and relevant to the programming goals of particular schedules. Programmers never end their search for what they refer to as usable **product**—a term derived from the motion-picture industry, that gives a hint of the programmer's neutral point of view as to program quality. Looking at the essentials of the advertising-based business model, we can see that the core business transaction is not the selling of programs, but rather the selling of **audiences**. Programming basically is the cost of doing business; that is, the cost of creating and distributing a product that will be appreciated by audiences. Later in this text we will examine in detail how program ratings are so important to this model and how audience **rating points** are treated in a sense as commodities that are bought and sold in a competitive marketplace.

A media enterprise can be both costly to operate, but also enormously profitable. For example, a broadcast network may invest hundreds of millions of dollars in acquiring the exclusive television rights to the Olympics, but eventually, if the predicted ratings come true, the network will still reap substantial profits. On the other hand, a much smaller investment by a media enterprise may generate equally impressive profit margins. For example, on a network level, unscripted **reality programming** typically is far less expensive and quicker to produce than scripted programs, and yet they often deliver comparable or even larger audience ratings than expensive scripted programs that take much longer to produce. On a local market level, a struggling radio or TV station may eliminate an expensive syndicated program from its schedule, knowing that the station probably will lose ratings, but also knowing that less costly programming still may enhance the station's profits.

For media utilizing an advertising-based business model, the ultimate goal is to generate program content for the *least cost* that attracts the *biggest audiences* that in turn can be sold to the *most advertisers* at the *highest commercial rates*. This is no easy task in today's highly competitive media marketplace. We begin this chapter with an overview of economic forces at work that influence programming and ultimately a media company's bottom line.

Audience Targeting and the Notion of the Niche

Achieving an acceptable bottom line means knowing at what audiences a program should be aimed. As the numbers of stations, cable systems, satellite-delivered program services, and networks have grown, many program services have given up aiming at the mass audience that for decades was the original target of radio and television broadcasting. In recent years, the terms **narrowcasting** and **niche services** have come into vogue, suggesting a different audience goal. The decades-old assumptions surrounding the notion of mass communication have fragmented into the far more complex world of satisfying esoteric needs of audiences. As the number of media competitors has increased dramatically, the old homogenous "mass audience" is becoming divided and subdivided into an ever-changing array of new demographic and psychographic categories. For example, cable networks such as CNN, MTV, Nickelodeon, and the Home Shopping Network deliberately limit their appeal to specific audience segments. Radio stations adopt rigid music formats; a particular radio format may repel most listeners but nevertheless prove irresistible to a narrow audience segment.

In addition to increased media competition, advertisers have encouraged the trend toward narrowcasting because typically they are looking for the ideal potential customer, exhibiting special attributes. The need to target people willing and able to buy products and services, whether as advertisers or as subscribers, has led to **audience targeting** throughout all electronic media. Researchers often use the term **segmentation** to denote the dividing or slicing of an audience into all types of geographic, demographic, and lifestyle categories. In a real-world media business situation, the target audience usually is determined *first*; then, the creative people are invited to come up with program content that will attract this desired audience.

Bigger Often Is Better

The bottom line often is influenced by the relative size of the business venture. While niche programming may be attractive to audiences and advertisers, the notion of *niche* typically implies *small* and small is seldom an advantage in any business, including electronic media. Even in this age of slicing the economic pie into ever-smaller pieces, size still matters. Excessive niche programming can lead to a point of diminishing returns in which audiences become so small that advertising or subscription revenue derived from targeted audiences cannot offset the cost of doing business. From a commercial sales perspective, the burning question is how high a premium price will advertisers pay to reach a small but highly desirable audience?

Long before broadcast television and cable had to cope with massive competition, American radio had for many years dealt with the promises and perils of the niche. Radio has further refined the process of targeting extremely narrow subsets of the potential radio audience. Radio usually segments audiences in both demographic and psychographic terms (e.g., teenagers who want to hear only hit songs or 25- to 44-year-old adults who prefer the music of the 1980s).

Audience segmentation makes attracting an economically desirable audience of adequate size more difficult. Consequently, many media owners believe that it is essential to control not one but multiple program niches that satisfy the needs and desires of several types of audiences. Greatly relaxed ownership restrictions during the late 1990s have allowed individual stations to target ever smaller segments, while still attracting a large total audience for a particular owner. That is, a single owner can now operate up to eight stations within a designated market, permitting eight different audiences to be served by the same consolidated company.

Taking advantage of size is common in electronic media. Looking back at prior chapters in this text, we can recall that today most local radio and television stations are group-owned. In addition, the parent companies of most television networks have major investments in cable networks. Most local cable systems are owned by huge media corporations that are investing in Internet access and telephone services. Most successful Internet web sites typically are associated with other media enterprises and so on. While entrepreneurs and investors may be encouraged to know that many successful big businesses began as small businesses, the sobering downside is that most small businesses fail within the first few years of their existence. In a fiercely competitive marketplace, growing bigger is a prerequisite for long-term prosperity.

Consumer research for years has found that big brands have disproportionate advantages over small brands. As competition becomes more intense due to the increasing number of media players, a kind of natural selection occurs, favoring the larger more efficient organizations. From the financial advantages of **economies of scale** in reducing costs to the benefits of cultivating customer loyalty, bigger is usually better. For example, even though conventional TV broadcasting has lost substantial audiences to cable and other competing media, it remains the best way to reach large audiences quickly and efficiently. Even on a local level, most TV stations continue to reveal handsome profit margins derived from advertisers who want to place commercials in fairly broad-based programming such as

Oprah, *Dr. Phil*, *Entertainment Tonight*, *Jeopardy*, and most importantly, local newscasts. Each of these programs has a programming niche (i.e., talk show, entertainment news, game show), but each niche is *big enough* to attract sizable audiences.

The 80/20 Principle

The bottom line of most companies is determined by many factors, but typically some factors are far more important than others. For example, the lopsided distribution of audiences and advertising revenue among most electronic media in a competitive market can be explained by means of a common business phenomenon known as the **80/20 Principle** or **(80/20 Rule)**. In 1906, Italian economist Vilfredo Pareto created a mathematical formula to describe the unequal distribution of wealth in his country, observing that 20 percent of the people owned 80 percent of the wealth. After Pareto made his observation, many others observed similar phenomena in their own areas of expertise. For businesses, the principle means typically that roughly 20 percent of the products sold are responsible for 80 percent of a company's profit.

This disproportionate 80/20 pattern is found to some degree among all electronic and print media in that, within any given market, only a small handful of large media firms control the bulk of advertising dollars spent. Comparing the television and cable industries as an example, one can see readily that despite all the doomsday rhetoric aimed at the broadcast TV networks, the four major TV networks (ABC, CBS, Fox, and NBC) still manage to control almost half of all television viewing and more than half of all advertising dollars spent on television and cable advertising in the United States. The remaining 100 or more cable networks must scavenge for the remaining advertising dollars, and even within this fragmented market the 80/20 rule again applies. That is, roughly 70 to 80 percent of all cable viewing occurs among 20 percent of all available channels. Consequently, these dozen or so program networks attract most of the available advertising allocated to cable.

In addition, this phenomenon can be seen in most radio markets throughout the country, regardless of the number of stations involved. Whether the market has over 70 licensed stations, such as Los Angeles, or less than a dozen stations, such as Carbondale, Illinois, the 80/20 rule in general reveals itself in attracting audiences and advertisers.

Taking a narrower view of this phenomenon on an individual station or network level, we can see that typically only a few hours of the day and a small handful of programs have the greatest impact on the bottom line. For instance, a radio station may be on the air 7 days a week, 24 hours a day, but most of its advertising revenue will be derived from program content offered Monday through Friday during morning and afternoon drive times. Naturally, these are the times that generate the largest available audiences for radio listening. Television presents a more complicated version of the 80/20 Principle, in that the cost of programming for prime time is so high that other times of the day, exhibiting lower audience levels than prime time, actually become the major profit centers. Remember, the 80/20 Principle applies to profits, not overall revenue. A good example for television is the early morning programming, such as *Good Morning America* and *Today*, that generate huge profits in the tens of millions of dollars for relatively little investment compared to expensive prime-time offerings.

Limited research on Internet activity appears to reinforce the same notion that most web users and web advertisers are drawn to a relatively small number of sites, considering the thousands that are available. In addition, commercial web sites offering many program services, such as downloading content, interactive activities, and blogs, in general, will find that visitors usually gravitate toward a limited number of content offerings that become the "20 percent" that keeps the web site in the black.

80/20 and the Psychology of Too Much Choice

The bottom line of a media venture can be affected dramatically by the way human beings make decisions. One important psychological result from what some media scholars call "abundant choice" is the overloaded human mind desperately seeks out ways to reduce the number of realistic choices and simplify decision making. Most people do not want to deal with 200 choices of anything! For electronic media, the consequence has been that as the number of program content options has skyrocketed, the number of such options *actually used* regularly is surprisingly small. Several studies conducted by Nielsen and other research companies indicate that for an average American household, there is a viewing threshold of approximately a dozen or so heavily viewed channels. Even in homes where 200 or more channels are available, the number actually viewed is less than 20. Several media researchers have adopted the concept of **channel repertoire** to describe this limited array of channels from which audiences select television programming.

Narrowing a focus even more, the 80/20 Principle can be applied to the previously-mentioned repertoire in that the amount of time allocated to these chosen items is not distributed equally. In general, one could say that a person spends roughly 80 percent of his or her media time with only 20 percent of the content items contained within an already small repertoire.

Radio audience behavior replicates the same behavior as television and cable in that in a typical local market, people listen on a regular basis to only a small handful of available stations. Also, satellite radio services, offering hundreds of channels, experience the same phenomenon. Internet user activity is no different. Although people may "surf the net" at random on some occasions, most of the time people stay within the boundaries of a handful of stored or "bookmarked" web sites that receive repeat visits and even within these specially identified web sites, the amount of time dedicated to each is not the same.

New "Long Tail" Media Economics Versus the 80/20 Rule. The internet has introduced a new style of economic model that in a sense contradicts the long-standing 80/20 model of business success. The "long tail" refers to a portion of a graph that compares popularity with inventory. The conventional way of doing business is to match one's inventory with high demand products and services. This creates the high point of a distribution curve while less popular items, of which there can be many, are revealed in the long tail of the curve that travels further away from the highpoint of the curve. The underlying assumption has been that less popular items are not cost efficient to produce. For example, publishing only a few copies of a book or manufacturing only a few copies of a CD typically will cost a company more than it can ever hope to recapture in consumer sales. Only when items are produced in large quantities, coinciding with high demand, can the business become profitable—at least that is how it used to be, but new digital technologies have challenged these assumptions.

The distribution and inventory costs of many new Internet-based businesses allow them to realize significant profits out of selling small volumes of hard-to-find items to many customers, instead of only selling large volumes of a reduced number of popular items. Long Tail theory argues that products that are in low demand or have low sales volume can *collectively* make up a market share that rivals or exceeds the relatively few current bestsellers and blockbusters, if the store or distribution channel is large enough. In addition, if the product can be produced electronically, such as a downloaded book, song, movie or TV program, the cost of reproduction is almost nothing. For example, a publishing company does not need to make a tangible copy of a book that is now out of print, instead, the publisher can scan pages electronically for hardly any cost and sell them to only a small handful of buyers and still make a profit. Multiply this same profit margin over thousands of low-demand but easily-replicated books (or programs or songs, etc.) and suddenly the long tail becomes an important profit center for the company.

In recent months, all the major TV networks have begun to offer broadband streaming and downloads of dozens of old TV programs that have been stored for decades in their archives, no longer popular enough to be in syndication but sufficiently attractive to a small group of fans who are willing to pay a modest fee or accept a few commercial interruptions.

Taking Advantage of Economies of Scale

The bottom line of a media enterprise can be enhanced by taking advantage of economies of scale, particularly in exploiting the cost-effectiveness of distributing expensive programming over many different venues. This is best illustrated by the networks, which enable the same programs to appear on hundreds of different stations and cable systems all over the country. Such sharing by stations and systems spreads high costs among many users. The sharing does not stop there, because network entertainment programs reappear in syndication (the mechanics of which are explained later in this chapter); this enables further sharing worldwide among stations, cable systems, and networks. On a local level, stations in many markets also share their newscasts with local cable systems or reuse source materials to produce another version of the newscast for cable distribution or for broadcast on another station. In recent years, stations and networks have taken the same content and made it available via Internet streaming and downloading.

The Zero Sum Market Phenomenon

The ability of a media enterprise to pull audiences away from its direct competitors can have a major impact on its bottom line. We sometimes forget that, despite the massive increase in program options available from all kinds of media, there are still only 24 hours in a day and people have obligations other than interacting with electronic media devices all day, including work, school, and household demands. Many studies have found that the amount of time spent with all media has changed little in decades. As a result, the real battle for audiences is two-fold. The first factor involves one medium *displacing* another. For example, several studies have found that younger audiences today spend more time on the Internet than watching television. A second and equally important factor is that *within* each medium, whether it is radio, television, cable, or the Internet, the number of available content options in recent years has far outstripped the number of available audiences intending to watch, listen, or read. The result is what business researchers call a **zero sum market**, meaning that despite the number of brand offerings for a product or service, the total number of customers desiring that product or service remains unchanged (i.e., zero). Consequently, the only way to increase market share for your brand is to wrestle customers away from your

competition. One simple example is morning drive time on radio. Regardless of the number of new stations that enter the market, the total number of people listening to the radio will remain unchanged. The obvious challenge is not to find new radio listeners in the morning, but rather to persuade current listeners to *switch stations*. The same can be said for local television newscasts in which some markets have up to five or more stations all airing a newscast each day at 6:00 P.M. Common sense would dictate that adding another newscast at 6:00 P.M. probably will not increase the total number of people interested in local news. Instead, the result is more choice for the existing target audience and a more competitive, and sometimes more ruthless, battle for market share by rival stations.

The Repeatability Factor

The financial success or failure of a media enterprise often depends on how often its content can be exposed to audiences. When a program product is presented to audiences for the first time, it is designated as **first-run**. Examples can range from a once-per-week police drama presented on a broadcast network, to a daily, syndicated talk show presented on a local station. A **repeat** or **rerun**, as the name implies, denotes program content that is presented to audiences repeatedly. For television and cable, this can range from one or two repeat exposures in prime time on a network, to seemingly endless repeat exposures in daily syndication, in which programs such as *M*A*S*H* and *I Love Lucy* have survived on the airways for decades. Audience acceptance of repeat program content has been crucial to the success of many program content providers. For example, dozens of cable networks, such as TV Land, FX, USA, and TBS are dependent on program product that has aired sometimes hundreds of times and yet still attracts an audience. In some cases, an audience member may be viewing an episode for the first time, but more often, the episode has been seen and appreciated several times by the viewer.

Radio programming tends to be first-run in terms of live presentation of on-air talent, either local, network, or in syndication, but we cannot forget that most of the music content presented is highly familiar to radio audiences. Listeners seldom tire of hearing their favorite songs and artists over and over.

History has shown that some program content "repeats" better than others. For example, one of the negative business aspects of most reality programs is that they typically do not do well in syndication, unlike scripted sitcoms and dramas. These programs have a limited lifespan in which the producers and the media distributers make most of their profits off first-run exposure. On the contrary, as will be presented in more detail later in this chapter, some programs possess an afterlife that can go on for years in which most of the true profits from a program are derived from its repeatability.

The Art and Science of Scheduling

Maximizing the value of program content often means scheduling it in the right place. Regardless of whether a program is created on a local level, network level, or syndicated level, scheduling can have a direct impact on a media company's income. Whatever their program content, stations and networks strive to structure their selections into coherent schedules.

In addition to specific programs, electronic media often deal with **dayparts**, which are blocks of time in which several programs may be scheduled or one consistent type of program content may be offered. Radio programmers generally divide the day into **morning drive**, **midday**, **afternoon drive**, **night**, and **overnight** segments. The morning and afternoon drive periods, with commuters traveling to and from work, provide the largest audiences for most radio stations. Radio program directors schedule most on-air personalities by daypart coinciding with the same type music or talk format. In addition, radio audience ratings provided by the Arbitron Company present most of their listening data by daypart.

Television programmers divide the day into specific dayparts as well (see Exhibit 8.a). **Prime time**, the most important segment, commands the largest audiences. **Access time**, the prime-time hour preceding network programming, often delivers the most revenue for network affiliates. In most situations, more than one program is scheduled within the daypart. Nielsen Media Research offers its clients audience ratings based on both individual program performance and by longer dayparts. As discussed in Chapter 6, sales departments for these media operations, including web sites, often establish advertising rates based on daypart.

Typically, a broadcast or cable program is scheduled in a daily **stripped** manner, (such as a daily soap opera or talk show) or in a once-per-week **checkerboard** manner (such as a prime-time drama or sitcom). Of course, many former once-per-week prime-time network programs are rerun in syndication in a stripped format. Also, while most broadcast networks and TV stations halt daily strip programming by 8:00 P.M. (EST), many cable networks continue to strip programs throughout the evening. Most often these programs are reruns of former broadcast network hits that over several years have accumulated hundreds of episodes. Compared to television and cable, radio program scheduling is easy to understand because almost all of radio programming is stripped, with the only exceptions being specialty programs scheduled typically on weekends.

Exhibit 8.a

TV Dayparts

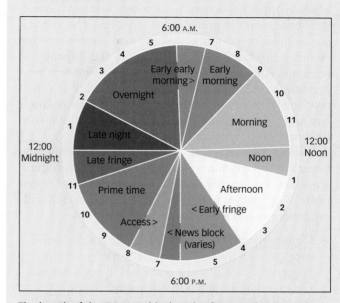

The length of the TV news block varies from market to market and station to station, running as long as two or three hours on some major-market TV stations and as short as an hour elsewhere.

The practice of stripping reruns of network TV programs led to an enormous demand for television series with many episodes already "in the can." Stripping ideally requires 130 episodes for a half-year run. Off-network series that have generated such large numbers of episodes have, by definition, earned good ratings on a network over more than one season. They therefore command the highest prices among syndicated series.

Schedulers try to draw audience members away from rival stations or networks and to prevent rivals from enticing away members of their own audience. These audience attraction and retention efforts focus on controlling **audience flow**—the movement of viewers or listeners from one program to another. Flow occurs mostly at the junctions between programs or, on radio, after one block of songs ends and before the next begins. Audience flow includes both **flowthrough** (on the same stations or channel) and **outflow** or **inflow** (to or from competing programs).

Audience research can measure the extent and direction of audience flow. Such data give programmers guidance on how to adjust schedules and program types to retain audience members and gain new ones at the expense of competing channels. However, remote-control channel selectors and VCRs, now in more than 90 percent of all households, have made tracking television-audience flow more difficult. A special vocabulary has evolved to describe how some audience members use these devices: they **surf** or **graze** through the available channels, **zap** the sound of unwanted commercials, **jump** between pairs of channels, **flip** around to see what is happening on nearby channels, and **zip** through the boring parts of prerecorded cassettes. The increasing popularity of more sophisticated personal video recorder products also contributes to the difficulty of tracking audience flow and controlling it through programming strategies. The growing availability of video-on-demand as cable systems convert to digital technology will further erode the ability to control audience flow with programming strategies.

Taking into account the line-ups on competing channels, programmers adjust their own program schedules, fine-tuning them to take advantage of opponents' weak points. Following are some typical scheduling strategies to exploit audience flow.

- ▶ **Counterprogramming** seeks to attract the audience to one's own station or network by offering programs different from those of the competition. For example, an independent station might schedule situation comedies against evening news programs on the network affiliates in its market.
- ▶ **Block programming** tries to maintain audience flowthrough by scheduling programs with similar appeal next to each other; for example, by filling an entire evening with family-comedy programs.
- ▶ A strong **lead-in** attempts to attract the maximum initial audience by starting a daypart with a particularly strong program in the hope of retaining the audience for subsequent programs.
- ▶ **Leading out** with a strong program may similarly attract viewers to the program that precedes it.
- ▶ **Hot switching** fine-tunes the previous lead-in strategy through the use of "seamless," commercial-free transitions from one show to another. Running crunched-together credits at warp speed while viewers are enticed to stay tuned by promotions occupying two-thirds of the screen further enhances a seamless transition.
- ▶ A **hammock** tries to establish an audience for a new program, or to recover the audience for a show slipping in popularity, by scheduling the program in question *between* two strong programs. Flowthrough from the previous (lead-in) program should enhance the initial audience for the hammocked program, and viewers may stick with the weak (or unfamiliar) show in anticipation of the strong (lead-out) program that follows it.
- ▶ **Tent-pole** is just the opposite from hammock. Here the strategy is to place your most popular program at the center of your schedule, hoping that the audience will gravitate to either side of "the pole," capitalizing on the notions of *lead-in* and *lead-out*.

- ▶ **Bridging** attempts to weaken the drawing power of a competing show by scheduling a one-hour (or longer) program that overlaps the start time of the competing show.
- ▶ **Repetition**, a pay-cable strategy, makes it convenient for viewers to catch a program, such as a movie, because repeat showings are scattered throughout the schedule. Local stations may also repeat syndicated talk or reality-based programs during the same day.
- ▶ **Stunting** seeks to keep the opposing networks off balance in the short term by tactics such as making abrupt schedule changes, opening a new series with an extra-long episode, and interrupting regular programming frequently with heavily promoted specials.

Two general theories sometimes get in the way of these scheduling strategies. One suggests that no matter what is offered, viewers will watch the **least objectionable program (LOP)** in the time period. The other, **appointment television**, holds that successful programs may be scheduled anywhere because serious-minded fans will follow wherever they go.

Another increasingly popular practice also conflicts with these scheduling strategies. Some programmers try to extend their control over the audience by diverting them to a related information source at the program's conclusion. Many programs now invite viewers to visit their associated web site to learn more about the topic, interact with the program's performers or production staff, comment on the show, enter a contest, or explore the topic in greater detail through links to other web pages. This **extended viewing period** allows the program sponsors additional opportunities to present their messages. This strategy has obvious advantages for sponsors, but it is antithetical to the scheduling strategies just discussed, which attempt to hold viewers through a series of shows. While diversion helps prevent audience flow to a competing channel, it also diverts the audience from the next program on the same channel. At least this is true for those viewers who do not, or cannot, use the Internet while watching television.

While network-affiliated stations are obligated contractually to air network programming at specified times, programmers at **independent stations** have charge of their total schedules. Their chief stratagem, counterprogramming, capitalizes on the inflexibility of the affiliate's schedule because of its prior commitment to network programs. For example, an independent station can schedule sports events at times when affiliates carry major network shows. Networks can afford to devote prime time to only a few top-rated sports events of national interest. Independents, however, can schedule sports events of local interest, even during prime time.

Radio stations use counterprogramming, stripping, and blocking strategies even more than television stations do. Most radio stations schedule their program elements, whether songs or news items, in hourly rotations, creating 60-minute cycles. As the day progresses, the hourly pattern is altered by daypart to match changing audience activities. Exhibit 8.b shows an hourly plan for a Top 40 format. Radio stations pay special attention to their programming during drive-time hours, the periods when stations reach the largest audiences and commercials command top dollar.

Scripted vs. Unscripted/Live vs. Recorded

The bottom line success of a program depends on how well an audience appreciates the content, but often this content is somewhat "out of control" depending on how it is created. Today, many prime-time television programs are totally or partially unscripted, relying on the spontaneous actions of the program's participants.

In recent years, unscripted so-called "reality programming" has become hugely popular, not only among audiences but also program producers, because this type of content can be created quickly and inexpensively compared to complex, scripted programming. Although newscasts and special reports usually deal with the "real" world, the industry so far has excluded news and sports reporting from its definition of reality, and instead has used the term to encompass primarily entertainment content. Network and syndicated game shows are a type of semi-scripted content in which the game format is strictly enforced but the players are given wide latitude in their behavior while on camera.

Scripted and unscripted program content can be divided further into **live** versus **recorded** material. Historically, most daily radio programs were presented live to audiences with no formal scripts, but today many radio hosts prerecord their shows—a process known as **voice tracking**. Most TV reality competitions such as *Survivor* and *The Great Race* are completely spontaneous, but nonetheless are recorded and edited before airing. Late night talk shows such as *The Late Show with David Letterman* are presented unscripted to a live audience, but are recorded earlier in the evening and played back with little if any editing. A few live, scripted TV programs still exist, the most well known being *Saturday Night Live* on NBC. Today live, unscripted programming is dominated by sports coverage. Again, there is a certain lack of control in that the producers cannot be guaranteed of having an exciting contest.

8.2 Reaching Audiences Through Local, Syndicated, and Network Distribution Paths

This section of the chapter is rather complex because all kinds of program content can be presented to audiences via several unique distribution paths and sometimes highly successful programs are distributed several different ways simultaneously. For instance, for a brief period, the producers of the hit sitcom *Friends* were creating fresh episodes to air in prime time on the NBC broadcast network, while at the same time, they were providing repeat episodes to the TBS cable network, and also providing additional rerun episodes to scores of local TV stations through syndication: One program—three distribution paths.

The simplest way to understand the three primary ways programming is distributed among electronic media is to place yourself in the position of a broadcast or cable system operator. Throughout the day and night, you can acquire program content from three basic distribution sources: **local**, **syndicated**, and

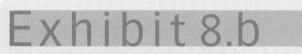

Exhibit 8.b

Radio Station Format Clock

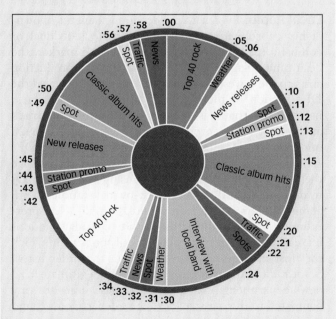

Beginning with the music revolution in the 1950s, radio programmers planned their schedules hour by hour, drawing a circle around a 45 rpm record and dividing the circle into segments to indicate where program elements would air. Many continue to use this concept, employing computer programs that adapt to audience activities in various dayparts by incorporating changes in both content and tempo of presentation. The example given here represents a typical afternoon drive-time clock for a commercial station.

network. All of the bottom-line factors discussed in the prior section can be applied to the distribution process.

Local Programming

Locally originated programming is the simplest to understand because by definition it is created at the local station or local system level. All the necessary resources are acquired by the local operation, including personnel, such as on-air talent, producers and director, and technical facilities, such as studios, cameras, and web sites. Many radio stations still do live local programming at least during certain dayparts, but the temptation to substitute network or syndicated program content has increased in recent years as stations become ever more cost-conscious.

Local Television. For television stations, almost all relevant local programming takes the form of live daily newscasts often beginning as early as 5:00 A.M., continuing throughout the day at various times, and concluding with a late evening newscast at 10:00 or 11:00 P.M. Aside from providing a community with much-needed information about local issues, weather, and sports, this type of local programming has proven to be highly profitable. In some cases, among large-market stations, up to 50 percent of all sales revenue can be attributed to commercials airing in local newscasts. Needless to say, this has become a hugely competitive arena with stations investing millions of dollars in equipment, vehicles, news services, studio sets, reporters, anchors, research, and promotion activities.

The most obvious downside to going local all the time is the cost of production. Unlike networks that can offset their costs by charging hundreds of thousands of dollars for the nationwide exposure of their commercials, local stations soon reach a point of diminishing returns, in which revenue from commercials cannot keep pace with money spent on overly elaborate productions with limited distribution.

To increase their audience reach and offset production costs, some stations produce special newscasts for, or rerun their regular programs on, independent stations or cable systems. They also offer the audio portion of their newscasts to local radio stations. Some TV stations produce weather reports for local insertion into cable networks such as The Weather Channel. Others provide local radio stations frequent weather updates voiced by their highly promoted on-air meteorologists, expensive talent many radio stations cannot afford.

Aside from news, local television stations produce relatively few programs. Affiliates generally schedule local talk and public-affairs shows on weekday or Sunday mornings. During election years, or at times when important local issues arise, they may increase local production, but they normally avoid scheduling local shows in valuable time periods such as early fringe, access, or prime time. Affiliates that produce regularly scheduled local non-news/public-affairs shows usually choose a magazine/talk program for women, scheduled on weekday mornings. Non-network magazine shows, though actually syndicated, may give the appearance of local productions. In fact, syndicated formats sometimes acquire local color by providing for live or recorded inserts by local personalities.

Local Cable. About a third of the cable systems in the United States originate local programs other than automated services such as time, weather, and channel guides. Those that do produce such programs mostly offer either commercial **local-origination (LO)** channels, controlled and programmed by the cable operators themselves, or noncommercial **public-access** channels, programmed by private citizens and nonprofit institutions such as schools and municipal governments.

Although some cable systems occasionally originate coverage of local sporting events, cable systems rarely undertake the expense required to produce regularly scheduled half-hour newscasts. Many do, however, produce local news inserts in CNN Headline News. An increasing number of large-market cable systems devote one channel full-time to regional news services.

Local Radio. Even with the economic benefits of ownership consolidation, in which a single individual or company can own several stations in one market, the desire among most operators is to keep local production costs to the lowest possible level. Increasingly, even the DJ's portion of the broadcast is recorded. Managers have learned that it is possible for a DJ to **voice track** an hour of on-air programming in perhaps 15 or 20 minutes. An automation system then melds the DJ's recorded material and the recorded music to produce the show. Group owners are also using one popular DJ to do shows heard on several co-owned stations. Until about 25 years ago, at least some DJs could select pretty much whatever music they wanted. Today, stations increasingly set up strict **playlists** of songs from which the host must select or even play in the order listed. Some radio stations attempt to maintain legitimate local news departments, but in general these units are tiny compared to the massive local news departments found at most local television stations.

Syndicated Programming

The FCC defines a **syndicated** program as any program sold, licensed, distributed, or offered to radio and television stations in more than one market within the United States for noninterconnected (i.e., no network) television broadcast exhibition, but not including live presentations. In practice, programmers classify as syndicated all **nonlocal** programs not currently licensed to a network, including movies, and even some live presentations.

There are two types of syndicated programming: **first-run** and **off-network**. First-run syndication refers to fresh programming that typically has never been on a network. *Entertainment Tonight, Oprah, Jeopardy,* and *Wheel of Fortune* are examples. In addition, first-run syndication rarely gets involved with repeat episodes, though a program may exhibit a few repeat episodes while the hosts and crew are on vacation or hiatus. On the other hand, off-network syndication is totally about repeats. As the term implies, off-network refers to program content that began on one of the major broadcast or cable networks before being made available in reruns to stations. Repeats of *Seinfeld, Friends, The Simpsons,* and *Frasier* are examples of this type of syndication.

Whether first-run or off-network, the local station is not responsible for the cost of production. Instead, the syndicator picks up these expenses, which can be sizable. A syndicated transaction involves the station purchasing the **exclusive broadcast rights** for the program in that designated broadcast market. This is a contractual agreement for a specified period of time, typically two to five years. At the conclusion of the contract, and assuming the program is still popular with audiences, the station management and the syndicator can negotiate a **renewal agreement** for one or more subsequent years. If the program is a big hit, the syndicator naturally will demand a substantial increase in broadcast rights fees. If these two parties fail to negotiate an acceptable agreement, the program is then available to be auctioned off to other stations licensed to the same market, similar to a professional athlete becoming a "free agent." Popular syndicated programs typically lead to bidding wars in which more than one station would like to own the program property. Essentially, the syndicator is offering the program to the highest bidder. Sometimes this results in a popular syndicated program abruptly switching stations in a market, much to the confusion of loyal audiences.

Exclusive broadcast rights are sold to individual stations based on not only the number of **episodes** produced, but also on the number of allowable repeat airings or **runs** per episode. Unlike first-run syndicated programs, in which episodes are almost always new, off-network syndication contracts typically deal with several runs for each episode over many years. For example, the total price for acquiring the broadcast syndicated rights for three runs of each episode of an off-network program (or movie) would be less expensive than acquiring similar rights for five runs. Negotiating runs is important because audiences seem never to tire of watching episodes of their favorite old network programs.

Cash–Barter Deals. The purchase of almost any syndicated program today involves not only a cash payment to the syndicator, but also what the industry calls a **barter** arrangement in which the syndicator is permitted to sell a specified number of commercials within the program to national advertisers. This commercial time cannot be used by the local station's sales department and none of the derived revenue goes to the station. Consequently, the forfeiture of these commercial opportunities is part of the overall "cost" of the program. These types of transactions are called **cash–barter deals**. The **barter syndication** practice began in the 1970s as a device to help lower the cash cost of syndicated programming for stations, but over the years it has mutated into merely a second source of impressive profits for syndicators. Today, stations have little choice but to relinquish these avails and often pay out big cash payments as well.

Negotiating Factors. When negotiating the purchase price of a syndicated program, the station must weigh several crucial factors. First, the station must predict the program's audience attraction (i.e., expected ratings) and its expected long-term performance over several years. This analysis involves looking at (a) when the program will be scheduled, (b) its lead-in and lead-out programs, and most importantly, (c) the type of competition it may face from other stations during that time period. Rarely does the introduction of a new program increase substantially the total number of listeners or viewers available in a specific time period. Instead, the programmer must assume a zero sum market, in which ratings and revenue must be taken away from direct competitors.

The process can be far more art than science, especially for new syndicated properties, in which there is little or no audience research (i.e., ratings) evaluating the program's competitive performance in similar markets. For newly released off-network programs, prior network ratings can be examined, but this is no guarantee of similar performance in syndication because essentially all off-network syndicated programs were scheduled in prime time once-per-week, while most syndicated programs are scheduled on stations during daytime hours on a Monday through Friday stripped basis. The **audience composition** of the time period may be radically different than in prime time. The syndicated programming landscape is strewn with familiar titles, such as historic sitcoms *All in the Family, Murphy Brown,* and *Frasier,* that were huge hits in prime-time network TV and equally huge flops in local station syndication. On the contrary, the original *Star Trek* enjoyed only a modest three-season network run, but went on to become a successful off-network syndicated program, in addition to launching a series of theatrical features and TV series using the same theme. Buyers and sellers of programming continue to price product based on its network performance because this remains the best predictor of success in syndication.

Many syndication contracts contain **upgrading** and **downgrading** provisions in which the cost per episode will vary according to the time period in which the program is scheduled. For instance, if a program is rescheduled from early afternoon to late night, the broadcast rights fees probably would decrease. Conversely, if a program is highly successful in a lesser time period and the station wants to upgrade it to a more lucrative time of day, the syndicator may demand a higher rights fee. Occasionally, syndicated contracts will stipulate certain **ratings thresholds** in which the rights fees can be altered either up or down, depending on audience delivery reflected in Nielsen ratings.

Based on calculated expected audience levels, the second step in the negotiation process is to determine beforehand how much the station plausibly can earn from owning the rights to this program, often referred to as a program's **revenue potential**. In other words, how much can the station charge for commercials? Again, this step can be more art than science, requiring some educated guessing about the business climate and the competition. An overriding factor is the value of the program's target audience. As alluded to earlier, some audiences are more valuable to advertisers than others. For example, winning the time period in total households may not be a sufficient reason to increase commercial rates if the demographic composition of that audience is not in high demand by media buyers. By multiplying the number of commercial insertion opportunities (i.e., avails) by the projected commercial rate, the station management arrives at a revenue potential figure.

Step number three is to compare the revenue potential of the program with its anticipated *cost* (i.e., the syndicated broadcast rights). Obviously, this is all dependent on the program delivering its promised ratings and economic forecasts being accurate. An important factor that must be included in these calculations is the number of **barter avails** provided to the syndicator. Too many barter avails can interfere with the revenue potential of a program in that the station cannot take full advantage of its commercial inventory. In some instances, syndicated programs take as much as 50 percent of the program's commercial inventory.

The 80/20 Principle can be applied here in that over the course of 24 hours, seven days a week, some time periods (typically 20 percent or so) are more valuable than others, and consequently, the investment in programming must coincide with its intended place on the schedule. For example, a TV station is willing to invest more money in syndicated programming designed to air weeknights at 7:00 P.M. than at midnight, regardless of the popularity of the show. Cable and radio are

essentially in the same situation, as they must spend money on programming in time periods that will generate the greatest return on investment (ROI). Conversely, one cannot squander money on syndicated program content that might assure ratings success but revenue failure—paying a huge syndicated rights fee for *Friends* and then scheduling the program at 2:00 A.M. for instance. You probably would win the time period handily, but you also would go broke.

Once the revenue potential of a syndicated program has been calculated, the station management can then enter negotiations with a good idea as to how much the program rights are worth fighting for. Assuming outlets in big markets can charge more for commercials and therefore earn more revenue than outlets in smaller markets, a station located in Syracuse, New York, would not pay nearly as much for the broadcast rights to a syndicated program as a station licensed to New York City.

One can find scores of cases in which television stations paid far too much for a syndicated program that never fulfilled ratings and revenue expectations. Often these disappointing programs are downgraded to less important time periods, such as late night hours, where they live in a kind of purgatory until the contract finally expires. The station cannot "ask for its money back" as we might ask with a purchased product or service that did not live up to expectations. Of course, eventually the station can refuse to renew the contract, but the renewal date may be years way. Meanwhile, the station must keep making cash payments to the syndicator and honoring its commercial barter agreements. Downgrading can present stations with a barter dilemma. A station that carries a barter program typically agrees that, if the program is downgraded to another, less desirable time period, the station will continue to air the syndicator's barter commercials in the original time period. This could mean that the replacement show, if it too were on a barter deal, would be filled with both syndicator's commercials, leaving little if any time for station sales.

Group Deals. The bigger is often better theme presented earlier resonates with the notions of purchasing syndicated programming. Today, most radio and television stations are group owned and therefore a common practice is for the group owner to negotiate a multistation deal in which the syndicator offers a substantial discount on the total price. From an accounting perspective, the parent company distributes the cost among all stations according to the relative size of their markets. Of course, the assumption with these group deals is that the individual stations can make good use of the program. As a result, many stations owned by the same company tend to have highly similar syndicated program schedules, especially when they are affiliated with the same network.

NATPE. Television syndicators showcase new productions at annual meetings of the National Association of Television Program Executives (NATPE) and at other national and international program trade fairs. Each year several thousand TV professionals attend the annual NATPE convention to discuss programming issues and preview new syndicated offerings. For many years deals were consummated in person at the conference, but gradually the negotiation process has moved to other venues, such as station group headquarters. Many times the transaction is accomplished through e-mail, cell phones, and faxes without the old-fashioned handshake to signal a "done deal." In addition to domestic syndication, NATPE is also a showcase for international syndication. Similar to the motion-picture industry, real profits often are found in overseas markets.

Broadcast Network Involvement in Syndication. For years ABC, CBS, and NBC owned relatively few off-network syndicated programs—the result of an FCC regulation and an antitrust consent decree. Designed to prevent network domination of program production and distribution, the **financial interest and syndication (fin/syn) rules** severely limited network freedom to participate in production and ownership of prime-time programs or in their domestic syndication. At the time, the Commission and the Justice Department were worried about the powerful control the three networks exerted over the creation and distribution of program content. The fin/syn rules attempted to dilute this power by forcing the networks to purchase programs from independent studios and production companies that retained ownership of the program property, including the right to syndicate the program on a station level.

With the introduction of new multichannel media options, such as cable, satellite, and the Internet, offering hundreds of program choices, rather than just three, as was the case in the 1970s when the rule was enacted, the networks eventually persuaded the FCC to rescind the rules in the early 1990s. Later, a federal judge lifted the consent decree, removing the last barrier to full participation by the networks in program ownership and syndication. As expected, the networks moved rapidly to take advantage of their new opportunities. Today, over half of all network programs and made-for-TV movies are produced in-house by the networks. When a product is successful on the network, the parent company turns it over to a syndication unit that sells it to individual stations or cable networks.

A source of some confusion among students of programming is that programs that go into **off-network syndication** end up on stations with a completely different network affiliation. For example, *Seinfeld*, after many successful seasons airing on NBC, became available for station syndication. Around the country, stations affiliated with not only NBC but all other networks bid on the program with the intention of stripping it in the afternoon or late night time periods.

Radio Syndication. Essentially, all the buying and scheduling strategies for syndication already discussed can be applied to radio. Throughout a typical broadcast schedule a radio programmer can chose to do local programming or opt to purchase any number of available syndicated programs. Of course, off-network syndication in radio does not exist, but otherwise the discussion concerning the types of agreements and negotiating procedures are the same. Syndicators use satellites to relay news, sports, and entertainment material to stations. Programmers distinguish between **syndicated formats** and **syndicated features**. A station might buy the use of a ready-made syndicated country music format, for example, supplementing it with syndicated news and entertainment features from other sources. Thus, stations can create unique programming mixes from commonly available syndicated elements. Radio feature material is often bartered, whereas syndicated formats are usually cash deals.

Cable "Syndication." For decades the term "syndication" referred to the purchase of programming by individual broadcast stations, but in recent years the phrase **cable syndication** has entered the lexicon of programming, and describes the movement of programs from broadcast networks to cable networks, essentially bypassing conventional station syndication. Over time, these programs may become available for station purchase, but initially they remain exclusively on one or more cable networks, typically stripped Monday through Friday during prime-time hours. This phenomenon occurs most often among hour-long dramatic series, such as *ER* and *Law and Order*, that were expected not to perform well in station syndication.

The confusion with using the term cable syndication is that students sometimes presume that individual local cable systems or multiple system operators (MSOs) are purchasing these programs for their franchise areas in a manner similar to that used by local TV stations purchasing syndicated rights for their individual markets. On the contrary, these former network broadcast programs are purchased by the major **cable networks**. In reality, local cable systems rarely become involved with true market-by-market syndicated programming, although they certainly could from a legal perspective. That is, a local cable system could purchase the syndicated rights to a popular program that typically is distributed through local TV stations around the country. The cable operator also could negotiate for market exclusivity, denying any repeat exposures on nearby TV stations. Again, this is all possible, but to date, no cable system has made a serious effort to get into the syndicated programming business.

Network Programming

The third source for programming for a station is a network. Whether we are addressing a **television network**, **radio network** or **cable network**, the essential business model is the same. A program network produces or acquires program content that it distributes through various "affiliates" operating throughout the country. As discussed in depth in prior chapters of this text, the networks sell advertising time to national advertisers and also offer affiliates (either broadcast stations or cable systems) the opportunity to sell local and regional advertising.

Unlike syndicated programming, radio and TV stations usually receive network program content for free and sometimes receive some kind of cash compensation, although the compensation has dropped dramatically in recent years. On the other hand, cable systems usually must pay a monthly **per-subscriber fee** to a cable program network in order to carry its programming.

As discussed earlier, the broadcast TV networks themselves own several stations in large markets, but the majority of participating stations in a network are affiliates owned by other companies. For several decades, with only ABC, CBS, and NBC operating full-scale national networks, many stations in the United States had no network affiliation and were designated as **independent** stations, relying on local and syndicated programming to attract audiences. In the late 1980s, Fox became a major network player. In recent years, a number of broadcast networks have attempted to compete with "The Big Four." A more detailed discussion of network affiliation is provided in Chapter 6.

Despite a decline in their combined audience share, the broadcast television networks still draw the most massive audiences of any media. The best-known and most popular programs appear on television broadcast networks in prime time. They consist mostly of light entertainment—comedy and drama. Prime-time entertainment network programs come as weekly series, with a sprinkling of movies and occasional one-time specials. A series can run for an indefinite number of episodes. Those designed typically with three to eight episodes are known as **miniseries**.

As with syndicated programming, the local broadcast station or cable system does not participate directly in the cost of producing the program content, which can amount to many millions of dollars. As a result, the local affiliated stations are given only a small portion of the available commercial time within each program—far less than what most cash–barter syndicated programs offer to stations. From a bottom line perspective this can be troublesome for a station since typically its most popular programming (i.e., prime time) may not generate as much revenue as lesser time periods in which the station schedules locally produced programming (i.e., newscasts) or syndicated product, both of which present better inventories for commercial placement.

Radio Networks. A radio network is a network system which distributes programming to multiple stations simultaneously, for the purpose of extending total coverage beyond the limits of a single broadcast signal. Radio networks often pay compensation to major-market affiliates, but radio syndicators usually charge for their programs. Stations can choose from dozens of specialized networks catering to every conceivable audience interest. For example, Westwood One is a major provider of network music. Stations can choose from among formats such as Adult Rock & Roll, Bright Adult Contemporary, Soft Adult Contemporary, Adult Standards, Hot Country, Mainstream Country, and two oldies formats.

The major networks supply news, sports, and specials, or all-talk or all-music, relaying programs to affiliates by satellite, accompanied by national advertising. The availability of music programming from the networks and through syndication allows individual stations (or, increasingly, a group of co-owned stations) to adjust their formats rapidly as listener or advertiser preferences shift in local markets. Because of industry consolidation, there is increasing pressure on stations to use the music programs offered by co-owned networks and syndication organizations.

Direct-to-listener, subscriber-based **satellite radio** hopes to become a major competitor of conventional broadcast radio, particularly of network radio. Offering hundreds of nationally distributed program "channels" of original programming, satellite radio cannot be defined as a network provider in the strict definition because it has no "affiliates," such as a station or cable system, to act as an intermediary between the content provider and the audience member. This is also true for satellite television, but to date, the TV satellite services do not provide any original program content. Instead, they merely offer subscribers the traditional array of cable networks. Another point of distinction is that the majority of program offerings on satellite radio are commercial-free.

The Impact of Digital on Program Distribution

Prior chapters of this text addressing other topics have touched on the distribution opportunities of digital broadcast television in the form of **multicasting** by local TV stations. These subchannels are available for local, syndicated, or network program content and permit the broadcaster to consider more niche marketing to targeted audiences in demand by advertisers. By 2008, close to a dozen companies were developing new networks to be affiliated with digital, multi-cast channels. Assuming the TV broadcasters can get retransmission carriage on local cable systems, the potential for creating additional revenue has many TV broadcasters excited about the future.

In a somewhat similar fashion, the cable industry has taken advantage of digital technology to create more channels on local distribution systems. Many established basic program networks, such as Discovery and Animal Planet, have expanded into what cable operators call **digital tiers**. Subscribers often must pay a higher subscription fee in order to access these tiers, but nonetheless these extra channels do offer extra opportunities for program content development.

Internet Distribution of Content

The Internet has become an important distribution tool for conventional media, such as radio, television, and cable, and also for original content. As individuals abandon analog modems connected to conventional phone lines and adopt broadband technology, the quality of program video and sound will increase dramatically. Mass media managers recognize the opportunity to expand their audiences by both creating new content and repurposing programming produced as part of their traditional operations for distribution via the Internet.

Internet content often duplicates what the provider already offers through other distribution systems. Many radio stations, for example, stream their on-air signals. Radio broadcasters are finding that there are more computers than radio receivers in the workplace. Streaming their on-air signals expands their audiences by reaching people outside the home or automobile, the traditional locations for radio listening. Similarly, TV stations and networks also stream programming in real time or provide it for downloading so it can be viewed at a later time.

Although an increasing amount of video is streamed live as it is distributed over the air or on cable, most is content that was previously distributed through other media and available via the Internet on demand. Short-format programming predominates, but less expensive storage capacity is prompting producers to offer longer programs for those with the time and interest to watch them. In recent years, both broadcast and cable networks have begun to provide large inventories of old program episodes that can be downloaded to a home computer or portable laptop for a small fee or free with inserted advertising.

Podcasting is the method of distributing multimedia files, such as audio programs or music videos, over the Internet for playback on mobile devices and personal computers. The term podcast, like radio, can mean both the content and the method of delivery. The host or author of a podcast is often called a podcaster. Usually a podcast features one type of show, with new episodes released either sporadically or at planned intervals, such as daily or weekly.

An offshoot of a podcast is a **blogcast**, which is simply the combination of a blog and podcast into a single web site. A blog is a weblog, or journal, that is available on the Internet. A podcast is an audio file that is shared with visitors or subscribers to a site. A blogcast enables participants to freely add text, photos, and music.

Most program producers and distributors use the Internet to repurpose and supplement content provided through other channels and to promote their primary delivery systems. The Internet lets producers showcase more of their content and allows people to select what they want based on their interests and time availability. A rock concert on MTV probably will not include an interview with the producer of the event discussing site selection, booking of performers, and other pre-production planning details. Putting the interview on MTV's web site, however, does not tie up valuable time on the cable channel and allows those with an interest to get "inside" information.

Original Content. Although much Internet content duplicates what is available through the conventional mass media, some content is available only on the Internet. Some media organizations are putting original content on the Internet to test its popularity before migrating it to broadcast or cable. Dozens of media companies are finding the Internet an inexpensive medium for testing content before risking its distribution through conventional channels. Many companies also believe that the Internet is a new medium with unique characteristics and unique audiences that merits original programming reflecting those characteristics. Warner Bros. is among the major media companies developing original programming designed expressly for Internet transmission rather than supplementing or marketing existing programming. All the major broadcast networks and many local broadcast stations are experimenting with original Internet-only programming.

In addition to established media companies and commercial organizations, an unknown number of small groups and individuals are streaming audio and video on the Internet. The low cost of streaming technology and the fact that no license is required make the Internet a popular medium for those wanting to "broadcast." Witness, for example, the widespread popularity of YouTube. User-generated content (UGC) is discussed later in this chapter.

Creating Entertainment Content for Distribution

Broadcast and cable networks acquire entertainment programming from studios and production companies, some of which may be owned by the network's parent company. Giant media mergers, such as Disney with

ABC and Universal with NBC, are intended to keep both program production and distribution under one roof. Before the mid-1990s, nearly all original entertainment programming on the networks was provided by *outside* producers, but the elimination of the fin/syn rules and increased co-ownership of production studios, cable networks, and broadcast networks means there will be more in-house—or at least within conglomerate—production and distribution of entertainment programming in the future. It would be a mistake, however, to assume that a network carries only those programs produced by a co-owned company. It is not unusual for an owner's product to air on a competitor's network.

The increasing control of syndication by a few media giants, however, raises old concerns. Some fear that the consolidation of distribution will make it impossible for independently owned stations to compete for product against those owned by the media conglomerates. The creative community also fears that there will be fewer opportunities to get new ideas accepted when a relatively few corporate executives exercise veto power over any product proposed for syndicated distribution.

For most programs obtained from outside independent producers the television and cable networks introduce what the industry calls **deficit financing**. When considering the adoption of a new program to its schedule, a major broadcast network will ask the program producer to share in the financial risk, at least for the first season. The "deficit" in deficit financing means essentially that the network does not pay in full the total cost of creating a pilot program or the cost of creating a few episodes of a new program. Producers grudgingly agree to these terms with the hope that eventually the program will be a hit and, when the product is up for *renewal* for the additional seasons, the deficit will be offset with a huge increase in licensing fees from the network. A second motivation to accept deficit financing is the hope that over several years the program will accumulate enough episodes (at least 100) to be introduced into off-network syndication, where the profit potential can be enormous. Independent producers range in size from large firms that usually have several series in production simultaneously, to smaller producers with only a single series under contract at any one time.

In recent years, competition made network schedules more volatile. The networks nervously cancel shows at the first sign of weakening ratings. Runs became shorter, building up too few episodes for strip scheduling over the long period needed for best results. This, in turn, means increasing scarcity of, and thus intensified competition and higher prices for, successful off-network syndicated series.

In-house production by stations, cable systems, and networks once consisted mostly of news and sports programs, but now networks increasingly produce entertainment shows as well. In recent years, original program production by the cable networks has increased, although these networks continue to depend heavily on entertainment programming that was originally seen in theaters, on the broadcast networks, or that is widely available in syndication.

In addition to conventional half-hour and one-hour series, feature films are a staple item in broadcast and cable network schedules and even in some individual broadcast station schedules. They have the advantage of filling large blocks of time with material that has strong audience appeal. By definition, theatrical feature films normally reach audiences first through motion-picture theaters. Thereafter, distributors release them successively to video rental stores, cable and satellite pay-per-view services, and other electronic media at intervals governed by windows of availability, as shown in Exhibit 8.c. Increasing co-ownership of studios and networks is making it easier to alter windows of availability in response to market demands. Despite the exhibition priority enjoyed by movie theaters, movie studios make more money from television, cable, videocassette, and foreign rights than from American theatrical exhibition.

Creating News Content for Distribution

A markedly different atmosphere usually surrounds the creation of news programs. By assuming the serious function of conveying news and information, broadcasters, at least initially, took on a more important role than that of merely entertaining. Admittedly, some broadcasters cared little about being part of a great free-speech tradition if doing so interfered with another great American tradition—making money through free enterprise. But in time, news programs changed from money losers into money-makers, ensuring the survival of broadcasting's special role as bearer of information-as-entertainment.

News Agencies. Long before broadcasting and cable, newspapers established news-collecting agencies, the news field's equivalent of program syndicators. Today, more than 100 news services are available to U.S. electronic mass media and many specialize. For example, Bloomberg Business News provides stations with reports on financial matters, while Metro Networks, Inc. is known for traffic reporting in large cities. Major news agencies such as the Associated Press (AP), Worldwide Television News (WTN), and Reuters are international in scope. They supply text, audio, video, and still pictures to subscribing networks and stations for incorporation into their newscasts and other programs.

Network News. The broadcast networks maintain tight control over most news and public-affairs production. ABC, CBS, NBC, and Fox operate news divisions separate from their entertainment divisions, each

Exhibit 8.c

Movie Windows of Availability

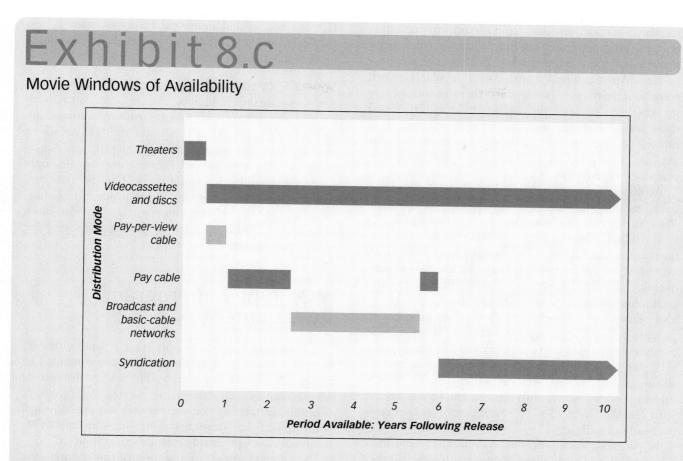

Occasionally, exceptions to this sequence occur. Sometimes distributors withhold highly popular movies from broadcast and cable for many years; sometimes a broadcast network pays extra to step in ahead of the pay-cable window. Some unsuccessful films move directly to syndication, and some movies never appear in theaters or television but go directly to video stores. With increasing vertical integration among producers and distributors, the ability to move a product to the most economically advantageous window has improved.

employing hundreds of people. Each also supports its own foreign news bureaus in the major world capitals, staffed by correspondents with in-depth knowledge of the regions they cover. Fox does not provide its broadcast affiliates the array of news programs provided by the older networks. Fox affiliates can, however, use material provided by Fox NewsEdge, a Fox news service, in their local newscasts.

In addition to the familiar broadcast network news operations, we cannot ignore several cable news networks. For almost 20 years CNN was the only 24-hour cable news outlet in the United States. The Big Three television networks (ABC, CBS, and NBC), despite their decades-old reputations for broadcast journalism, were reluctant to enter the cable news business and challenge CNN's comfortable monopoly. Suddenly, in 1996, two competitors came on the scene, Fox News Channel and MSNBC, followed by CNBC (both outgrowths of NBC), and the race was on.

Ironically, in the late 1990s, as the cable news networks were heating up the competition with expanded operations, the major broadcast networks cut back their news department operating budgets, reduced staffs, and consolidated or closed some of their news bureaus, both overseas and in the United States, relying more than ever on affiliates and outside news agencies. However, the 9/11 tragedy of 2001 and the subsequent invasion of Iraq served as catalysts for a renewed interest by the general public in national and international news. As a result, the broadcast networks responded by reversing the trend and investing again in their news-gathering operations and programming. Both Fox and NBC have taken advantage of merging much of their broadcast and cable news-gathering resources and on-air talent.

Local News. Local TV stations increased the time devoted to news in the 1990s, sometimes dramatically. Today, many stations air four or more hours of local news daily. As discussed earlier in this text, local news is not only good programming but good business. Stations have many sources to call on beyond those of their local staffs and regional news services. Both television and radio affiliates can obtain what amounts to syndicated news services from their own networks. Provided by the networks' news divisions, these services feed hard news and features over regular network relay facilities during hours when these facilities carry no scheduled network programs. Affiliates can record these feeds, selecting items for later insertion in local newscasts. They can obtain the right to record regular network news programs as sources of stories for insertion in local programs.

Affiliates and independents alike can draw on established news agencies, such as AP, Reuters, and others. With the advent of electronic news gathering (ENG) and satellite news gathering (SNG), local television news teams can fill longer newscasts and provide more on-the-scene coverage of both local and distant events. The availability of modern news-gathering technology and satellite uplinking by local stations also allows the networks to call on their affiliates to provide network coverage of breaking news. CNN, though originally a news network only for cable, now acts also as a syndicated news source for television stations, affiliates as well as independents. CNN exchanges news stories with stations and supplies them with *Headline News* in 5- or 30-minute blocks, or continuously overnight.

In addition, images produced by modern consumer camcorders and cell phone cameras provide another news source for local stations and network news organizations—the amateur. Broadcast and cable news operations on a regular basis solicit still pictures and moving video from the general public.

Of course, the Internet continues to play a major role in the everyday activities of television, radio, and cable news divisions. Over the course of a typical day, more people will visit any major network news web site than will actually watch a conventional evening newscast. With the accelerating growth of high-speed Internet access for individual subscribers, capturing and viewing moving video images is no longer a time-consuming ordeal. In addition to simulcasting newscasts or offering news clips on-line, many stations and networks are experimenting with custom-tailored on-line newscasts that can accommodate small screens, such as those found on laptop computers or cell phones.

Creating Sports Content for Distribution

Networks. Except for professional football games, the broadcast networks rely increasingly on production companies that specialize in televising sports. The networks simply pay the cost of national rights to the events and of producing live games, as well as their own announcers' salaries and travel costs. Mega-events, such as the World Series, the Olympic Games, the Super Bowl, and regular-season NFL football, remain exceptions to this trend.

Cable networks and individual broadcast stations also employ sports production companies. ESPN produces most of the games it carries.

Sports Sponsorships. Advertisers gave up most program sponsorship long ago, but the practice has been revived for some lesser sports events. Sponsorship means that the advertiser obtains the rights to broadcast or cablecast the event and controls the program. A network carrying a sponsored sports event supplies only play-by-play and color announcers. The sponsors hire nearby television stations or sports production houses to do the rest of the production work. They also often participate in lining up celebrity guests, promoting the program, and even selling tickets.

8.3 Types of Program Content

The bottom line success of a program depends ultimately on how much an audience appreciates its content. The notions of **format** and **genre** address the substance of what audiences seek. Attempting to categorize programs is always dangerous because inevitably somebody will come up with a program that defies any convenient definition or overlaps already established definitions.

As was used in the prior section of this chapter, one broad manner to define content in terms of substance rather than structure is to place programs into either entertainment or news and information slots. This dichotomy, however, can be overly simplistic. For example, syndicated programs *Entertainment Tonight* and *Access Hollywood* mimic traditional news programs in that they deal with real people and events, but the treatment is more entertaining than informative. Other reality-based shows such as *Cops* and *America's Most Wanted* also deal with real events and people and present the stories in a documentary style. The producers' objective, however, seems more focused on entertaining than informing. The same can be said of most court shows, such as the long-running *Judge Judy*. Although it is possible to learn some things about the justice system from these programs, the cases and the personalities involved seem to be selected for their ability to engage viewers emotionally rather than intellectually. **Infomercials**, long-format commercials that often resemble talk shows, also mix information (or sales pitches masquerading as information) and entertainment.

Given this warning, categorizing program content still can be useful. Programmers identify programming by format or genre as a shorthand way of conveying a great deal of information about its probable length, seriousness, subject matter, visual approach, production method, and audience appeal. It would be impossible to provide lists of all the program titles throughout history that could occupy each category we will address. Instead, our intention is to provide an overview of each with a few representative examples of past and present program successes.

Formats vs. Genres

A program may have a quiz-show format. A cable channel may have a home shopping format. CNN has an all-news format, ESPN an all-sports format, and so on. For our purposes, the term **format** refers to the organization of an entire service. Most radio stations have adopted distinctive formats, such as country, classical music, or all news.

Television stations and broadcast television networks tend not to adopt single formats because they need to appeal to a broad audience. As a single-channel service, a station cannot afford to narrow its audience to followers of one particular format. Cable and DBS can afford such specialization, however, because they are multiple-channel services.

In the context of programs, **genre** (pronounced "zhahn'-ruh") usually denotes a type of content. Familiar entertainment genres include the situation comedy, the game show, the drama, and the soap opera. By combining information presented earlier in this chapter with additional information about content, we can make sense of the often bewildering world of electronic media programming.

Situation Comedies

The origins of situation comedies, or sitcoms, can be found in the early days of radio, when millions of Americans tuned into the exploits of *Amos 'n Andy*, *Burns and Allen*, *Easy Aces*, *Ethel and Albert*, *Fibber McGee and Molly*, and *The Goldbergs*. In the 1950s, the situation comedy disappeared from radio, but became a staple on television. Among TV prime-time series, situation comedies have always had an important role. Hit sitcoms attract huge audiences and, in general, tend to earn higher ratings than do hour-long dramas. Writers of situation comedies create a group of engaging characters who find themselves in a particular situation—often a family setting. Plots spring from the way characters react to a new source of tension injected into the situation week by week. The characters have marked traits—habits, attitudes, and mannerisms—that soon become familiar to the audience.

Early TV sitcoms, such as *Ozzie and Harriet* and *Father Knows Best*, portrayed only stereotypical modular family units—with a handsome middle-class father, loving mother/homemaker, and adorable kids—and emphasized idealized "wholesome" values. *The Honeymooners* was a little different—temperamental working-class husband, no kids—but was still rather conventional. *All in the Family* broke new ground in the 1970s by dealing with generational conflict, civil rights, racial and religious prejudice, homosexuality, and gender issues. In the 1980s and 1990s, some sitcoms moved out of the living room, and the definition of "family" changed. Hits such as *M*A*S*H*, *Cheers*, and *Murphy Brown* revolved around character interaction in the workplace. This approach has been carried forward to more contemporary hits such as *Scrubs* and *The Office*. Over time, sitcoms increasingly have probed the boundaries of acceptable home viewing. *Empty Nest* featured a motherless family, and *Seinfeld* offered a variety of offbeat plots, including a contest to determine which of the four leading characters could survive the longest without masturbating. *Ellen* created controversy when the lead character, and the actress portraying her, revealed that she was gay. The ensemble hit comedy *Friends* occasionally would touch on issues of race and gender. Exhibit 8.d pays due respect to one of the longest running "adult" cartoon sitcoms, *The Simpsons*.

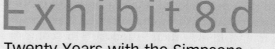

Twenty Years with the Simpsons

Homer, Marge, Bart, Maggie, and Lisa first found their way into the living rooms of America in 1987 in short features on *The Tracy Ullman Show*, one of the Fox Television Network's first critical hits. *The Simpsons* became so popular that Fox began airing a 30-minute version of the show in 1989. Twenty years and more than 425 episodes later, the show, which has won dozens of Emmys and a Peabody Award, still delivers strong ratings and sports a large and loyal fan base. Sharply satirical and willing to lampoon even the most sacred of cows, *The Simpsons* is the longest running sitcom and animated program in United States television history. Pictured here is the creator of the series, Matt Groening, with his famous characters.

Source: Photo © Douglas Kirkland/Corbis.

In the early 1980s, producers began injecting comedy elements, formerly the exclusive province of sitcoms, into action/adventure shows. Series such as *Moonlighting* included lighthearted comic scenes. Critics referred to some of these shows as dramedies—blends of drama and comedy. In 2006, *Desperate Housewives* further blurred the boundaries between comedy and drama.

Crime Dramas

As with the origins of the sitcom, long-form dramas began on radio in the 1920s and 1930s but no longer exist to any real extent on commercial radio. On television, police, courtroom, and detective dramas such as *Dragnet* and *Perry Mason* peaked in the ratings around 1960. In the mid-1980s, a new breed of more authentic crime shows captured top ratings. *Hill Street Blues* and *Cagney and Lacey* began a trend toward crime dramas dealing with tough social issues, using multilayered plots involving many characters. *NYPD Blue* tested the limits of acceptable program content for broadcast networks by using limited nudity and strong language. Although the series enjoyed some success with viewers and received numerous awards and critical praise, many advertisers withheld their support. In contrast, *Diagnosis Murder* featured sanitized homicide mysteries, usually set in upper-class surroundings, with a well-bred, mature physician as the unlikely detective. Several versions of the ever popular *Law and Order* series have kept this genre alive and well on both broadcast and cable networks for over a decade.

Beginning near the turn of this century, the cable industry began investing in several successful made-for-cable dramas such as *The Shield* and *Rescue Me*. Because program content on cable is not as highly scrutinized and regulated by the FCC as that on broadcast television, original cable dramas often address adult themes and sometimes use rougher language. While almost all sitcoms over the decades have been a half-hour in length, the duration of almost all dramas has been one-hour. In recent years, creators have attempted to inject ongoing storylines within the weekly stand-alone episodes of many dramas.

Medical Dramas

For years programs in hospital settings were staple fare on prime-time network television. Shows such as *Ben Casey* and *Dr. Kildare*, exploring the lives of both patients and practitioners, drew millions of viewers every week. In fact, *Dr. Kildare* began on radio. Bowing to the cyclical nature of audience taste, medical dramas disappeared for many years. After some successes, such as *St. Elsewhere*, the genre returned in the mid-1990s with *Chicago Hope* and *ER*, the latter often finding itself at the top of the Nielsen ratings. *City of Angels* appeared

in January 2000 and was unique among medical dramas in that it featured minorities in the leading roles, and also employed many minorities on the production staff. This trend in diversity continued, culminating in the huge prime-time hit *Grey's Anatomy*.

Movies

By the 1970s, the TV networks were paying increasingly astronomical prices for licenses to exhibit hit feature films. By the 1990s, VCRs and pay cable had devalued network showings of movies to the point that the average network licensing fee dropped to about $3 million per showing. Nevertheless, both broadcast and cable networks still pay huge fees for the movie blockbusters. Typically, a broadcast network's rental fee for a single showing of a major theatrical feature would cover all or most of the $4 million typically required to produce a brand-new, modest-budget, made-for-TV-movie. Often the top made-for-TV movies command higher audience shares than most televised theatrical movies.

Beginning in the mid-1980s, the major pay-cable networks (such as HBO and Showtime), as well as some other cable services (USA and TNT), also plunged into the financing of **made-for-cable** movies. Pay cable still relies on theatrical films as its bread-and-butter entertainment, but original movies are increasingly important components of the schedule.

Movies are also sold to individual TV stations through syndication. Rather than purchasing individual movie titles, syndicators typically bundle several dozen titles into a **package.** Similar to the negotiations for off-network syndication programs, the number of **runs per title** (i.e., the same as runs per episode for a regular program) are part of the deal. Essentially, all syndicated movie titles have already been exposed many times on the broadcast and basic cable networks, plus pay-per-view and DVD rentals.

Music

Because of the overwhelming dominance of music on radio, we begin this section by looking at various music formats. As presented elsewhere in this text, the term radio can be misleading because music is now available from several competing electronic sources, including Internet streaming and downloading, plus direct satellite distribution. Formats based broadly on rock music predominate, as Exhibit 8.e shows. Radio draws more fine distinctions among types of rock than among other musical genres, producing what some refer to as **format fragmentation.** Rock formats include **adult contemporary** (AC, a broad array of popular music and golden oldies); **contemporary hit radio** (CHR) or **Top 40** (playlists sometimes restricted to about 20 to 40

Exhibit 8.e

Top Radio Station Formats by Popularity and Station Type

Format	No. of Stations	AM	FM	Commercial	Noncommercial
Religious*	2880	1125	1755	1460	1420
Country/Bluegrass	2141	633	1508	2102	39
Adult Contemporary	1763	257	1506	1649	114
Oldies/Classic Rock	1710	485	1225	1639	71
News/Talk	1262	1000	262	1069	193
Sports	993	874	119	982	11
Spanish	753	410	343	690	63
Talk	761	602	159	686	75
Rock/Album Oriented Rock+	751	16	735	539	202
News	743	264	479	321	422
Contemporary Hit/Top 40	673	34	639	587	86
Variety/Diverse	666	143	523	340	326
Classical	489	10	479	43	446
Progressive/Alternative	402	9	393	124	278
Jazz	402	15	387	96	306
Urban Contemporary	352	56	296	294	58
Educational	236	18	218	19	217
Middle of the Road	189	141	48	169	20

*Religious includes Christian, gospel, and inspirational.
+Rock/Album Oriented Rock includes Light Rock and Triple A.

Source: Broadcasting & Cable Yearbook (2008), D729–730.

of the most recent hits); **classic rock** (familiar songs from popular albums of the 1960s, 1970s, and 1980s); **oldies** (hits from the 1950s through the 1970s); and **urban contemporary** or simply **urban** (a mix of rap, rhythm and blues, and jazz, favoring black artists). Among these subformats, many of which themselves are subdivided, adult contemporary has been the most successful. The **alternative**, or **progressive**, format featuring avant-garde music not played by conventional commercial outlets became popular on many college stations in the early 1990s. Exhibit 8.e shows that there is some commercial interest in the format, but most stations featuring the alternative/progressive format are noncommercial.

In the aggregate, more stations play **country** or **country-western music** than any other single type except rock, if all rock formats are added together. Though Exhibit 8.e shows country combined with bluegrass as a single format, it has followed rock's trend of subdividing, splitting into urban, traditional, crossover, oldies, and other specialties. After years as a mostly AM format, country music today is more often heard on FM. Religious stations make up the largest overall format, though many of those are not predominately music stations.

As mentioned previously, satellite-delivered radio provides its subscribers with dozens of unique "channels" or "networks" of all types of music and talk formats. The diversity of formats, the digital quality sound, and the lack of commercials among most offerings are the major selling points of this subscriber-based music source.

Music on TV. Except for variety shows and a few programs such as *American Bandstand*, which in the 1950s became one of television's first hits, and *Your Hit Parade*, which aired from 1950 to 1974, television paid little attention to popular music. That changed in 1981 with the formation of the Music Television (MTV) cable network. MTV quickly became a 24-hour rock-video powerhouse that targets teens and young adults ages 12 to 24. A co-owned network, VH1, programs to attract 18- to 49-year-olds. Originally intended to promote record sales, music videos became a television genre in their own right: Performers act out song lyrics, interpret them, or otherwise create imaginative visual images for songs. As promotional tools, videos originally came free of charge to stations and networks, but MTV changed the ground rules in 1984 by *paying* for exclusive rights to Michael Jackson's much-publicized *Thriller* video. MTV now contracts for exclusive early **windows** (periods of availability) for some videos.

Today, there are about two dozen music video channels distributed nationally featuring many kinds of music. For example, Country Music Television (CMT) provides country-western music videos and music-based features, as does Great American Country (GAC).

Variety

Variety programs once played a role both in viewers' habits and in the world of music. Hosted by stars such as Ed Sullivan (who introduced Elvis and the Beatles to America), Judy Garland, Frank Sinatra, Dean Martin, Perry Como, and Sonny and Cher, these programs once brought hours of music into the home, but their popularity faded as production costs increased and as musical tastes changed. By the 1990s, music-based variety programs had disappeared as series from network television, reappearing only occasionally as specials. Today, network and syndicated programs such as *The Tonight Show with Jay Leno*, *Saturday Night Live*, and *Ellen* occasionally feature recording artists and groups and even have their own in-studio bands, but music is not the central focus of these programs.

Reality Programming

In the commercial environment that governs almost all our television, the economics are too attractive to ignore. In virtually every line of the production budget, reality-based programming is cheaper than traditional programming. Reality programs offer the temptation of programming that costs less than $500,000 for an hour or one-third of the cost of an hour of comedy or drama.

From *Survivor* and *Big Brother* to *American Idol* and *America's Most Wanted*, reality programming on television has proven to be an enormously successful genre, but the notion of nonscripted programming is not new. *Truth or Consequences* and *Candid Camera* had their roots in radio and moved to television in the early 1950s. Both of these two pioneering series created artificial realities to see how ordinary people would respond. The reality series of today borrow a lot from these precedents and differ mostly in scope and locale. Perhaps ahead of its time was *An American Family* on PBS in 1973. It was unusual in its focus on a seemingly mundane family named the Louds, who harbored sensational secrets. This series pushed the documentary genre beyond its traditional bounds. The televised decision of the parents to divorce and the on-screen coming out of their gay son shocked audiences nationwide. All of these series share a dominant characteristic of the reality-soap genre: They find compelling storylines in hundreds of hours of video-taped life and, through careful writing and editing, shape the real-life subjects into reality-show characters. An import, *Big Brother*, and a startup, *Survivor*, would break open the genre of staged reality in 2000. These staged reality shows increasingly borrowed from the concept of game shows, which have been a persistent television staple. *The Real World*, *Big Brother*, and especially, *Survivor*, took that idea to a much higher-concept level.

The talent show, another type of reality programming, was first popular on radio. Both Ted Mack and the *Original Amateur Hour* and *Arthur Godfrey's Talent Scouts* began on radio and appeared on television in 1948. The *Original Amateur Hour* started in 1934 (which is almost as early as any programming started) under the leadership of its creator, Major Edward Bowes. Mack had scouted for and directed for Bowes and succeeded him as host after his death. The pure talent show genre persisted in the form of *Star Search* (1983) and now the enormously popular *American Idol* and *Dancing with the Stars*. Televised talent searches have had the same appeal throughout their entire history: seeing a star created before our eyes.

As mentioned in the introduction of this section, court shows represent a type of reality programming that seems to bridge the arbitrary categories of information and entertainment. This program genre has remained a viable piece of competitive programming for many years on local TV stations, mostly in the form of daily stripped, half-hour, first-run syndication. *Judge Judy*, *Divorce Court*, and *Celebrity Justice* are contemporary examples.

Soap Operas

In the early days of radio, soap companies often sponsored daytime serial dramas whose broad histrionics earned them the nickname "soap operas." This genre is a classic case of parsimonious use of program resources.

Notorious for their snail-like pace, soaps use every means imaginable to drag out each episode's story. Most minimize scenery costs, relying heavily on head shots of actors in emotion-laden, one-on-one dialogue. In addition, a typical soap features perhaps a dozen sets depicting the workplaces, living rooms, and bedrooms of the principal characters.

Contemporary soaps have responded to changing public tastes. They include story lines based on once-forbidden subjects such as drug addiction, sexually transmitted diseases, and family violence. Women and members of minority groups began appearing in more varied roles by the mid-1970s. First *General Hospital* and then *The Young and the Restless* stimulated a faddish interest on the part of younger viewers, including males, during the 1980s. Sexual attraction and conflict continue to be key themes in soaps, with bedroom scenes perhaps steamier than ever. In the 1990s, female leads increasingly held positions of financial power, often cast as owners or top-level managers of businesses. Most women portrayed in soaps had careers outside the home and exercised greater control over their lives than female soap opera characters in earlier decades. Responding to criticism of the blatant sexuality depicted, soaps began incorporating at least tangential references to safe sex and sexual responsibility. Alternative lifestyles also are treated with greater sensitivity in story lines.

Even a modestly successful soap generates profits amounting to tens of millions of dollars annually, thanks in large measure to relatively low production cost. However, the audience for soaps dropped dramatically in the second half of the 1990s and has not returned. Observers note that there are more women in the workforce today, and even those who work at home are busier than ever. Competition from cable, DBS, and the Internet also is blamed.

Soap operas have highly successful counterparts on ethnic and foreign-language outlets. Two competing U.S. Spanish-language cable/broadcast networks, Univision and Telemundo, feature imported **telenovelas**. These enormously popular soap operas reach tens of millions of viewers throughout the Hispanic world. In contrast to American soaps, which can endure for decades, telenovelas burn themselves out in a few months. Though primarily entertainment, they often carry educational messages, typically promoting socially approved conduct and family values.

Game Shows

Another inexpensive and popular type of programming is the audience participation game show, which has its origins in network radio more than a half-century ago. Game shows cost little in time, talent, effort, and money once a winning formula has been devised and a popular emcee selected. Talent expenses are limited to the host's salary and, in some cases, fees for show business personalities, who usually work at minimum union scale because of the publicity value of game show appearances. Taping five or more episodes in a single day reduces production costs further. Once a successful game show formula is perfected, a producer can often duplicate that success in foreign markets by hiring a native emcee and perhaps making a few changes to accommodate the local culture.

Opportunities for enhanced commercial content also contribute to the profitability of game shows. The giveaway format justifies supplementing the normal daytime limit of 16 minutes or so of advertising spots with plugs—short paid-for announcements on behalf of advertisers who donate prizes and other services such as transportation and wardrobe items. The prizes come free of charge from advertisers, who write them off as business expenses. Game shows were among TV's most popular programs in the 1950s and remained on the broadcast networks well into the 1980s. But by the mid-1990s, game shows had practically disappeared from broadcast network schedules. In 1999, however, ABC introduced *Who Wants to Be a Millionaire* in prime time, which earned spectacular ratings for a brief time. Subsequently, all the major networks have experimented with prime-time game formats. More recently, *Deal or No Deal* has shown surprising ratings strength.

Game shows such as *Wheel of Fortune* and *Jeopardy!* remain among the most successful programs in first-run syndication. *Wheel* benefits both from the suspense element of the wheel's unpredictable stopping places and from the winning talent combination of emcee Pat Sajack and his assistant, Vanna White. Most games run the half-hour length favored for syndication to enable flexible scheduling in all dayparts. CBS runs *The Price Is Right* in the late morning, a traditional slot for game shows on the broadcast networks. Network affiliates typically purchase first-run game shows to schedule in the hour before prime-time network programming begins.

Part of a game show's appeal is that it encourages viewers to play along with the contestants. The popularity of interactive games available on CD-ROM has not been lost on producers, and they are working to enhance viewer loyalty and involvement by providing ways viewers can participate in a version of the game. Game show producers, of course, are not alone in seeking audience participation. The Internet is a popular vehicle for such activities, and many web sites promoting programming provide varying degrees of interactivity.

Magazine Shows

In the 1950s, programmers began extending network television into hitherto unprogrammed early-morning and late-evening hours, a radical move at the time. For those innovative shows, NBC developed the **magazine**

format—a medley of short features bound together by a personable host or group of hosts. *Today*, NBC's pioneer early-morning magazine show, started in 1952 and continues strong to this day, along with impressive competition magazines such as ABC's *Good Morning America*. In recent years, the 24-hour cable news networks have launched their own versions of early morning magazine programming that has a direct tie with their hard news operations. Later in the day, during the early evening hours, many local television stations offer magazine programs concentrating primarily on the entertainment world, such as the decades-old *Entertainment Tonight*, which attracts large, loyal audiences each night (see Exhibit 8.f).

In addition to daily stripped presentations, the magazine approach can also take the form of a once-per-week prime-time program. *60 Minutes* is generally acknowledged to be the most successful news program—in terms of both ratings and revenues—in television history. It may well be the most successful *of any* program, news or otherwise. It is the only broadcast to have finished in the top 10 Nielsen ratings for more than 22 consecutive seasons, and the only program to be rated number one in each of three different decades. Other prime-time news magazines such as *20/20* and *NBC Dateline* for many years have earned sizable ratings and prestige for their parent network news departments.

The networks favor prime-time news magazines because, compared with most entertainment programs, they are relatively inexpensive to produce. They often use and reuse resources already in place in network news divisions. However, many of them compete for the same

Exhibit 8.f

Entertainment Tonight

Entertainment Tonight (ET) revolutionized the syndication business by proving that inexpensive, original, non-network programs—other than game shows—could be profitable for stations as well as for producers and syndicators. The economics of such an effort are all the more unusual in that each episode is an original—with no reruns to help spread out the cost.

Introduced in the late 1970s, *ET* took off in 1981 when Group W began delivering the topical show by satellite. Mary Hart (right) joined *ET* in 1982 and has worked with several co-hosts since then, most recently Mark Steines (left).

Entertainment Tonight provides a classic example of the constant innovation essential to keep a series from going stale.

Initially, the program capitalized on the audience's appetite for gossip, personality exploitation, and show-biz fluff. Later, the producer countered the lightweight image by introducing brief think pieces, some hard news, and more in-depth stories.

Among the best elements of the show are the contributions of Leonard Maltin, who became a regular contributor in 1982 and obviously knows and loves "the business." His constantly perceptive pieces are as rare on popular commercial television as is an episode of *Entertainment Tonight* that uses neither the word "exclusive" nor the phrase "behind-the-scenes."

Sources: Mark Steines photo from Cliff Lipson/CBS/Landov; Mary Hart photo from AP Photo/Kevork Djansezian.

stories and for the same audience. Often the various episodes of *Dateline, 20/20,* and *60 Minutes* are among the top-rated programs on the broadcast networks. Even when they do not rank among the top 10 or even top 30 programs, their low production costs allow the networks to offer prime-time advertising opportunities at attractive rates while still guaranteeing the network a comfortable profit. And because they are produced in-house, the networks do not face increased demands for higher licensing fees when a show becomes successful.

Talk Shows

Although related to magazine shows, the talk show more closely resembles an essay than a magazine. It emphasizes the talker's personality, which colors the interviews and other segments of the show. NBC's *Tonight* (later called *The Tonight Show,* and now *The Tonight Show with Jay Leno*), a late-night companion to the morning magazine show, started in 1954 as a showcase for the comic talents of Steve Allen. After a series of other hosts, including Jack Paar, Johnny Carson took over in 1962. For 30 years Carson reigned as the "King of Late Night." He hosted some 5,000 shows, talked with more than 22,000 guests, and ran about 100,000 commercials. Carson's reign finally came to a close in 1992. Letterman, who moved to CBS in 1993 to compete directly against the program, had aspired to move up to *The Tonight Show.* But it was Jay Leno who succeeded into the host's chair.

The talk show genre for daytime television also has a rich history going back for decades. Successful daily syndicated shows, such as *Mike Douglas, Merv Griffin,* and *Phil Donahue,* set the stage for later hit programming, such as *The Oprah Winfrey Show,* which is currently the longest-running daytime television talk show in the United States, having run since September 8, 1986, for over 22 seasons and 3,000 episodes.

Cable television also takes advantage of the relatively low production cost and flexibility of talk shows. The Lifetime network, for example, specializes in talk programs, carrying a dozen or so on health, consumer services, and the like. In addition to *Larry King Live,* CNN regularly schedules talk shows on money management, as well as news interviews and discussions. Fox News Channel features many talk shows that focus on news and politics. Religious networks rely heavily on inspirational talk programs, and sports channels depend on sports talk segments and interview shows.

Some interview-discussion programs on cable focus on what is currently happening in the news that week or even that day. Prime-time stripped programs, such as *Hardball with Chris Matthews* on MSNBC, *The O'Reilly Factor* and *Hannity & Colmes* on the Fox News Channel, and *Anderson Cooper 360* on CNN, tend to exhibit more "attitude" in their approaches to both the topics and

guests appearing on the shows. Interviewees frequently became embroiled in heated arguments with each other and with the hosts.

Talk radio occurs primarily on commercial AM stations. It combines call-in and interview programs with feature material and local news. Talk content varies between the extremes of sexual innuendo and serious political or social commentary. In major markets, shock radio deliberately aims at outraging conservative listeners by violating common taboos and desecrating sacred cows. Shock radio's contempt for adult authority and social tradition tends to attract listeners younger than the usual talk radio audience. Howard Stern, probably the best-known practitioner of the shock radio format, had repeated run-ins with the FCC and eventually abandoned broadcast radio and joined a satellite radio service, which is less regulated than broadcast radio. Another often controversial radio host, Don Imus, in 2007 stepped over the line of good taste and lost his job at WFAN, New York for making racist remarks about a college women's basketball team. The incident created nationwide media attention and heated debates for several weeks. Imus has since resurfaced on competitor WABC.

Most talk programs focus on controversial issues, using guest-expert interviews and call-in questions. The two-way telephone call-in show attracts an older and generally conservative group of listeners who have both the time and the strong convictions that incline them to engage in discussions with talk-show hosts. Program directors have to be alert lest a small but highly vocal group of repeat callers kill listener and advertiser interest in telephone talk shows.

Many radio talk shows cater to interests other than politics and current affairs. Dr. Laura Schlessinger, for example, offers culturally conservative advice to callers having relationship problems with spouses, children, in-laws, and bosses, while Bruce Williams specializes in helping callers with financial concerns. There are also shows dealing with computers and the Internet, health and fitness, automobile maintenance, gardening, home repairs, and a variety of other topics.

An interesting twist on talk radio is the simulcast of the program on television or cable. For example, before his sudden departure from WFAN, *The Don Imus Show* was simulcast every morning on MSNBC cable. Another radio/cable example is ESPN's *Mike and Mike in the Morning.* In addition, several local TV stations and local radio stations have formed morning program partnerships.

Home Shopping and E-Commerce

Not all viewers find commercials boring, at least not those that appear on the various home shopping networks. These broadcast/cable operations market consumer items such as clothing, jewelry, home appliances, and novelty ware, claiming that bulk purchasing and low overhead cost result in drastically reduced prices compared with those in stores. A cable system carrying a shopping network receives a percentage of each sale in its service area.

The conversion to digital television is expected to make home shopping an option for viewers during any program. Viewers will be able to click on icons displayed during programs or commercials and actually purchase a product while watching. Alternatively, viewers may click on a "Want to know more?" icon to see a recorded "pitch" for the product, such as those used on traditional home shopping channels. The viewer may prefer to have the set-top box record the information for viewing later. In either case, the viewer will have the opportunity to click on another icon to order the product.

In addition to television and cable home shopping experiences, the Internet now offers a much more intimate means for buying products and services. Two giant examples have been Amazon.com for buying books and eBay.com for auctioning all kinds of merchandise and services. Today, **e-commerce** has become an acceptable means of conducting business to a large number of people. This encouraged networks and stations to increase the commercialization of their web sites. In addition to simply displaying advertising messages for commercial sponsors on their web pages, many stations and networks began offering products for sale directly on-line or added links to their sponsors' web sites. The addition of e-commerce features to a web site makes it more useful and further helps promote audience identification with the station or network.

News and Information Programming

Network News. As presented in prior chapters of this text addressing the history of broadcasting, serious news programming has its roots in radio. World War II stimulated a new interest in the power of electronic journalism. With the introduction of television to the general public in the late 1940s, the major radio networks began to produce brief TV newscasts. In 1963, CBS and NBC expanded their prime-time news programs from 15 minutes to a half-hour. By the 1970s, ABC was a serious player in the network news business and most network-affiliated TV stations were producing local newscasts.

Ted Turner launched Cable News Network (CNN) as a fourth major television news service in 1980. With a 24-hour schedule to fill, CNN can supply in-depth reporting, as well as continuous coverage of breaking news stories. Early doubts about CNN as a serious news service began to disappear when in 1986 it was the only network to carry live coverage of the explosion of the space shuttle *Challenger*. Those doubts dissolved completely in January 1991 as government officials, and even ABC, CBS, and NBC, turned to CNN for its coverage of the war in the Persian Gulf. Turner's companion news service, CNN Headline News, provides news headlines and frequent updates in continuous half-hour cycles. It resembles all-news radio with pictures and reaches more than 72 million subscribers. Other news channels joined CNN on cable in the mid-1990s, including CNN International (CNNI) in 1995. In 1996, News Corporation launched the Fox News Channel, and NBC collaborated with Microsoft to start MSNBC, a cable network with an exceptionally strong Internet presence.

In addition to news, many cable networks provide informational programming. NBC's Consumer News and Business Channel (CNBC) moved to become a major cable player when it acquired its prime competitor, Financial News Network (FNN), in 1991. Also launched in 1995, Bloomberg Information Television provides financial and other news featuring a multiscreen format with a newscaster in the upper corner and text filling the remainder of the screen. The Weather Channel remains one of the "purest," information channels. Many others offering healthy doses of information along with entertainment have either joined in or announced launch dates. These include The Learning Channel, the Food Network, The Travel Channel, Home & Garden Television, and the Hobby Craft Network.

All the major TV network news operations provide some type of radio news programming. For example, ABC Radio Networks has five full-service networks, each targeted to a particular demographic group and each designed to complement the affiliated station's particular program format. The CNN Radio Network provides news, sports, business, and feature reports to about 1,900 affiliated radio stations. CNN Radio Noticias is a full-service Spanish-language network with affiliates throughout Latin America and the United States. Fox News Radio is the newest TV-related network providing radio news services. In addition to news provided by broadcast and cable companies, several news agencies, such as Associated Press Network News, can provide continuous 24-hour news programming in addition to periodic newscasts and features intended for stations not wishing to broadcast news around the clock. Radio networks associated with television networks get the benefit of daily newscasts voiced by well-known television news personalities. Some television journalists anchor radio news bulletins, such as morning-drive reports. Others prerecord news stories for later inclusion in scheduled radio newscasts.

The **all-news format**, which typically includes both local and network news, costs a lot to produce, yet earns low ratings compared with successful music formats. All-news stations count on holding listeners' attention for only about 20 minutes at a time, long enough for listeners to arm themselves with the latest headlines, the time of day, weather tips, and advice about driving conditions. To succeed, this revolving-door programming needs a large audience reservoir that only major markets can supply.

Local News. Audience interest in local television newscasts escalated during the 1970s, converting news from a loss leader into a profit center. It is not unusual for a network affiliate to make up to half its annual profit from advertising during local newscasts. It helps if the affiliate is the top-rated news station in the market, but even a modestly successful news operation attracts sponsors who would not otherwise advertise. In the 1970s, major-market stations developed their own investigative reporting and documentary units. Satellite technology enlarged the reach of local stations even further, minimizing time and distance constraints. By the mid-1980s, large-market stations routinely dispatched local news teams to distant places to get local angles on national news events.

Multimillion-dollar budgets for local television news departments have become commonplace in large markets, enabling stations to invest in high-tech equipment, such as news vans equipped to transmit digital signals back to the station and Doppler radar weather systems. As the new century dawned, local news executives braced themselves for the expensive conversion to digital news-gathering technologies.

Local news departments sometimes capitalize on the availability of home camcorders and, most recently, cell phones, to turn amateur shooters, at least temporarily, into **stringers** (self-employed professionals who sell individual stories to radio and TV stations). This technological trend, coupled with the ease of ordinary people to create their own web sites for distributing content, has led to a new media topic of debate often referred to as "citizen journalism." Today, just about anyone can be a news reporter.

Most network affiliates originate an early-evening newscast and a late-fringe newscast. Affiliates' local evening news shows either lead into network news or both precede and follow it to form a "sandwich." In the Eastern and Pacific time zones, network evening news usually starts at 6:30 P.M., preceded by local newscasts ranging from a half-hour to two hours in length. Late newscasts typically appear at 11:00 P.M. (Eastern time). For years these newscasts lasted a half-hour, but by the 1990s, they had expanded to 35 minutes—a network concession to affiliates' desire for more local advertising time and to the network's own efforts to improve clearances of their programs that followed.

Fox stations often schedule their late newscast an hour earlier than affiliates of other networks. Modern lifestyles make staying up past 11:00 P.M. for the news unappealing, especially when many people can get national news, sports, and local weather anytime from cable or DBS. Fox's early news is a more successful programming strategy on the East and West coasts than in the nation's midsection, where most network stations air late news at 10:00 P.M. local time.

Many affiliates also schedule a half-hour or hour of noon news. Most affiliates originate early-morning newscasts or magazine/talk shows preceding the network morning programs. The network shows provide slots into which affiliates can insert local news segments. Some stations broadcast brief **updates** or **news capsules** during breaks in prime-time programs, many of which actually provide little news, serving mostly as promotions for their late newscasts. Some also offer "news-all-night," a mix of network overnight news programs, CNN Headline News, and other alternative news services, and repeats of the affiliate's own late newscasts.

Many independent stations or stations affiliated with smaller networks that do not provide an entire evening of prime-time entertainment programming will schedule late local newscasts, usually at 10:00 P.M. (Eastern and Pacific times) to counter-program network entertainment on competing stations. Independents also carry national news programs provided by services such as CNN, scheduling them immediately before or after their late local newscasts.

As mentioned earlier in the section addressing program distribution, most local cable systems to date do not produce meaningful local news programming. Similarly, most radio stations—except for those using an all-news format—do not invest substantial resources into local news gathering.

Public Affairs Programs

News and public-affairs programs tend to overlap, but the Federal Communications Commission makes a distinction, defining "public affairs" as local, state, regional, national, or international issues or problems, including, but not limited to, talks, commentaries, discussions, speeches, editorials, political programs, documentaries, mini-documentaries, panels, roundtables and vignettes, and extended coverage (whether live or recorded) of public events or proceedings, such as local council meetings, congressional hearings, and the like. The Commission stressed public-affairs programs because of the traditional view that broadcasters in a democracy have a special obligation to serve the needs of citizen-voters.

Most commercial broadcast television networks and most large stations maintain at least one weekly public-affairs discussion series, sometimes also a news documentary series, and often mini-documentaries within newscasts (especially during sweeps periods). ABC, CBS, Fox, and NBC schedule public-affairs question-and-answer sessions with newsworthy figures on Sunday mornings. NBC's *Meet the Press* started in 1947 and is the oldest continuously scheduled program on network television. CBS launched *Face the Nation* in 1954, and ABC began *Issues and Answers* in 1960, later replacing it with *This Week with David Brinkley*. Brinkley retired in 1996, and the title was shortened to *This Week*. In the mid-1990s, Fox joined the older networks with *Fox News Sunday*.

In 1979, cable developed a unique public-affairs vehicle specifically to cultivate a positive image for its industry. C-SPAN (Cable Satellite Public Affairs Network), a nonprofit corporation, originates a full 24-hour public-affairs service. Together with its companion, C-SPAN II, it offers live coverage of congressional floor sessions, hearings, political conventions, and other informative programs. From a local perspective, cable systems often are obligated through their franchise agreement to provide a certain amount of public affairs programming, such as live coverage of city council meetings or some type of regularly scheduled interview program. Often local systems become involved with nearby universities that provide student-produced newscasts and other programming.

Sports Programming

For true fans, sports are ideal television and radio subjects: real-life events that occur on predictable schedules, yet are filled with suspense. Professional football, basketball, and major-league baseball attract by far the largest audience. The numbers of viewers for other sports fall off rapidly. Super Bowl football and World Series baseball rank among the all-time hit programs because their excitement and spectacle appeal to a broad audience. The Olympic Games are also a major TV sports attraction. For many years the Big Three of ABC, CBS, and NBC dominated network sports coverage. In 1993, Fox made a spectacular entry into sports broadcasting by outbidding CBS for four years of National Football League (NFL) games. The Fox bid topped that of CBS by $400 million, showing the seriousness of Fox's desire to become a power in sports programming.

From a business perspective, program strategists value sports programs because they appeal to middle-class males, an audience not well reached by most other programs. The ability of sports to capture such elusive consumers justifies charging higher-than-normal advertising rates for commercials on sports programs. The proliferation of sports channels on cable and the desire of the broadcast networks to increase sports coverage attest to the importance of the genre.

Perhaps the best demonstration of the rise of sports programming is to track the spectacular growth of ESPN. In 1984, ABC acquired control of ESPN (originally Entertainment and Sports Program Network). The 24-hour all-sports network furnishes full-length coverage that ABC cannot provide, as well as enhanced bidding power for rights to sports events, a significant advantage. ESPN2 was launched in 1993, providing even greater sports coverage, and three years later ESPNews appeared. In 1997, ESPN added ESPN Classic to its roster of cable sports networks. ESPN brand extensions now include merchandise and a string of sports restaurants. It should be no surprise that one of these restaurants is located within Disney World, which happens to be part of the Disney conglomerate that owns ESPN. From a ratings and revenue perspective in recent years, these cable networks typically have generated more profit than the ABC broadcast network.

Following ABC's lead, all the other major broadcast networks have invested in cable sports, usually on a regional basis. Today, the National Cable & Telecommunications Association (NCTA) has identified more than 40 cable networks offering sports exclusively or routinely featuring sports programming. Many cable networks serve only a regional audience. Typical examples are the New England Sports Network, the Empire Sports Network, and of course, about a dozen regional Fox Sports Net services. Most sports networks focus on popular team sports, but others, such as The Outdoor Channel, feature hunting, fishing, camping, hiking, and similar outdoor activities.

In spite of huge increases in fees for major sports rights and smaller more fragmented audiences, a strong demand by media buyers has allowed networks to continually charge higher commercial rates to advertisers. Companies that sell products purchased predominantly by males know that team sports are among the few programs that continue to attract men in significant numbers. For breweries and automobile makers, major sports are a "must-buy." Even if increased advertising rates charged by the networks, affiliated stations, and cable systems do not match the higher costs of sports programming, programmers may still consider sports a wise investment. In addition to attracting hard-to-reach adult male viewers, sports programming is key to providing lead-ins to entertainment programming and establishing a brand-name image for a network.

Pay-Cable and PPV Sports. Increases in rights charges for sports events forced some events to pay cable, which can afford the high costs. Despite its relatively small subscribership, HBO, for example, receives stable, predictable revenue that handily covers the costs of sports rights. Events such as championship boxing and professional wrestling have strong appeal for relatively small but intensely loyal and willing-to-pay audiences. Such events can be profitably scheduled on national pay-per-view (PPV) television. In addition to high-cost sports events, PPV is a viable delivery vehicle for sports programming that lacks the wide appeal necessary for carriage on a broadcast or cable network. PPV programs are seen mostly by means of addressable cable technology in homes, bars, and hotels. The average cable home has access to about a half-dozen PPV channels, but the number will increase as more system operators offer digital services. DBS subscribers also have access to PPV programs.

The growth of cable has obviously had a major impact on the scheduling and financial structuring of sports programming. Unlike the broadcast networks, which must appeal to the largest possible audiences, the cable networks can cater to the special interests of smaller but highly desirable audiences. They have dramatically improved sports coverage not only of professional "big-event" sports, but also of nonprofessional and "minor" sports. Viewers now see a variety of sports once largely ignored by the broadcast networks. Team sports such as volleyball, rugby, and soccer appear frequently. Individual-event sports such as track, gymnastics, tennis, golf, swimming, diving, and skiing receive unprecedented coverage. More automobile, motorcycle, and boat races are available. Even events such as dog and cat shows that many would question as being sports receive coverage.

Cable also merits credit for reducing the gender gap in sports programming. Although sports programming remains firmly focused on male competitors and targeted to male audiences, cable's increasing coverage of women's sports has demonstrated that these sports attract loyal fans of both genders.

Sports Radio. Sports are alive and well on the radio. Again, ESPN has been at the forefront of network-based sports radio, but there are many others, such as CBS-managed Westwood One and its associated radio networks, that offer a wide variety of sports programming. In addition, the industry supports dozens of smaller national and regional networks that provide live game coverage and sports talk programming to local stations. In most cases, the live on-air content is also streamed over a station or network web site, providing enhanced geographical coverage.

Children's Programming

Children have such easy access to television, they consume so much of it, and it exerts such a powerful hold on their attention that society has a special stake in the quality of programs made especially for them. Children's programming encompasses virtually all genres. For decades ABC, CBS, and NBC scheduled several hours of children's programming every week for their affiliates. This programming consisted mostly of Saturday morning animated cartoons. They were joined by the Fox Children's Network, which by 1994 had become the highest-rated supplier of children's programs on weekdays as well as Saturdays. But in the late 1990s, broadcast television's share of this audience declined considerably as new cable networks catering to kids appeared. Today, cable provides over 60 percent of total television hours devoted to children. As noted in the previous chapter, much of the rest is offered by PBS.

Broadcasting. Children's programs earn a relatively small percentage of broadcast television's total advertising revenues, but most run at times that might otherwise go unsold. Toy, candy, and cereal manufacturers have been the traditional sponsors of commercial children's programming.

All the major broadcast networks have begun to phase out their Saturday morning animated cartoon line-up, moving instead to live-action programs that the networks hope will attract a somewhat older audience—so-called teens and "tweens." Also, both the broadcast networks and local stations have recognized opportunities to attract adults audiences on the weekend. This has led to more news and magazine-type programs, similar to those already provided during the week.

Television broadcasters cannot ignore their child audiences, however. As explained in more detail in Chapter 12, federal rules require television licensees to provide at least three hours of educational children's programming per week. Pressure remains on the networks to help affiliates meet the FCC-imposed three-hour minimum, but reaching the kids is increasingly difficult because of competition from video games, social networking sites such as Facebook, and, most seriously, the cable networks.

Cable. Traditionally a strong competitor for young viewers, Nickelodeon became the principal channel for kids in the mid-1990s, accounting for almost 60 percent of TV viewing by kids ages 2 to 11. Nickelodeon targets younger children in the daytime. After 8:00 P.M. (Eastern time) the network runs Nick at Nite, featuring a heavy schedule of classic off-network sitcoms such as *Happy Days* and *The Brady Bunch*. Besides sitcoms, cartoons, and game shows, Nickelodeon also originates high-quality programs that avoid violence as entertainment and feature a broad range of role models. In 1992, Ted Turner launched his 24-hour-a-day Cartoon Network. Many of its programs come from the Hanna-Barbera library, which includes old television series such as *The Jetsons* and *The Flintstones*. Turner also owns about 800 MGM half-hours, including *Tom and Jerry*.

Several cable channels offer children's programs that, while entertaining, have an educational or informational objective. The Disney Channel programs for children in the daytime and for the family in the evenings. The Learning Channel programs commercial-free, nonviolent shows for preschoolers on weekdays. Discovery Communications dramatically increased the number of children's programs on basic cable by launching two new advertising-supported networks: Animal Planet, featuring animal-related programs designed specifically for children, and the Discovery Kids Channel, a 24-hour programming service targeted at young people ages 7 to 14. MTV Networks offers Noggin, a commercial-free digital cable network that targets children ages 2 to 11. Children's programming also is available on the pay-cable channels such as HBO.

Children's Television Issues

Children are a special audience and therefore, concerned children's advocates, parents, professors, and politicians often have advocated more government regulation of program and advertising content that is exposed to children. Advocates of greater control raise issues such as these:

▶ the inappropriateness of much television viewed by children in terms of their needs and vulnerabilities

▶ the negative impact of violent and aggressive program content

▶ the absence of a wide range of suitable role models on television

▶ the exploitation of children by advertisers, especially by those that encourage eating candy and sugar-coated cereals

▶ the shortage of age-specific programs, especially for very young children

Although these concerns are indeed worth investigating and resolving, strong supporters of the First Amendment are concerned with the whole idea of the government becoming more involved with media content regulation.

Congress reflected concern about children in the Telecommunications Act of 1996 by requiring that manufacturers install a V-chip (V for violence) in new TV receivers that parents can use to block programs containing objectionable content. The V-chip senses codes transmitted by the broadcast station or cable network that reflect ratings assigned to each program. The law also requires program distributors to abide by a ratings system developed by the broadcast and cable industry (see Exhibit 8.g).

The Internet Factor

Although the Internet technically is not a format or genre of program content, but rather a means of distribution, we cannot ignore the fact that this technology does influence how content is experienced. Today, essentially all programming presented on radio, television, cable, or satellite, regardless of whether it is locally originated or acquired from a syndicator or network, has a web site associated with it.

Besides providing users with the ability to select the content they want when they want it, the Internet encourages them to interact with it. On-air contests, slogans, and promotions seek to create a sense of "belonging" among audience members, to make them feel "we're your" station, network, or channel. Web site content often extends the opportunities for interaction by offering contest clues or earlier access to promotional materials.

Many radio and television station web sites provide pictures of their on-air staff, along with biographical information. TV newscasts may include pictures and a detailed explanation of how their "exclusive Doppler radar" makes the station's weathercast superior to other stations' in the market. Research indicates, however, that the materials building audience allegiance and promoting the station most effectively are those that

Exhibit 8.g

The TV Program Ratings

The six-category age-based rating system allows programs to be rated both as series and as individual episodes. The ratings apply only to entertainment programs, not news, sports, or home shopping channels. Unedited movies on pay-cable channels are not rated under this system. Instead, they carry the original movie-theater rating assigned by the Motion Picture Association of America (MPAA). Program guides publish the ratings, and they appear superimposed on-air at the beginning of programs for 15 seconds.

The following programs are designed solely for children:

TV-Y Appropriate for all children. The themes and elements in this program are specifically designed for a very young audience, including children ages 2 to 6. This program is not expected to frighten younger children.

TV-Y7 Designed for older children, age 7 and up. This program is appropriate for children who have acquired the developmental skills needed to distinguish between make-believe and reality. Programs in which fantasy violence may be more intense or more combative than in other programs in this category will he designated **TV-Y7-FV**.

The following programs are designed for all members of the audience:

TV-G General Audience: This program is appropriate for all ages. It contains little or no violence, no strong language, and little or no sexual language or situations. Most parents would find this program suitable for viewing by children of all ages.

TV-PG Parental Guidance Suggested: This program contains material that parents may find unsuitable for younger children. The theme itself may call for parental guidance and/or the program contains one or more of the following: moderate violence (V), some sexual situations (S), infrequent coarse language (L), or some suggestive dialogue (D).

TV-14 Parents Strongly Cautioned: This program contains material that many parents would find unsuitable for children under the age of 14. The program contains one or more of the following: intense violence (V), intense sexual situations (S), strong coarse language (L), or intensely suggestive dialogue (D).

TV-MA Mature Audiences Only: This program is specifically designed to be viewed by adults and therefore may be unsuitable for children under 17. This program contains one or more of the following: graphic violence (V), explicit sexual activity (S), or crude indecent language (L).

provide information that people find instantly and personally useful. Weather and traffic updates, information about concerts, opportunities to win free tickets to events, coupons for special discounts on advertised products, and similar items are more likely to bring people back to the station's web pages than photos of the staff. As presented earlier in this section, the Internet often provides opportunities to conduct commerce in which stations and networks now can sell merchandize as well as advertising.

Unlike conventional media, the Internet can provide instant audience feedback on program content. For example, some radio stations test new musical selections by asking web site visitors to listen to short excerpts and rate them. Many television stations and networks encourage audiences to vote on what is the most desired content. For example, for years, *American Idol* has solicited millions of audience votes to determine what contestants will return the following week. From sitcoms, dramas, and game shows, to talk shows, magazine and newscasts, the Internet has become an integral part of the content of any program.

User-generated content (UGC, often hyphenated), also known as consumer-generated media (CGM) or user-created content (UCC) refers to various kinds of media content, publicly available, that are produced by end-users using all types of digital media technologies. For example, YouTube, created in 2005, is a hugely popular video sharing web site using Adobe Flash technology to display a wide variety of user-generated video content, including movie clips, TV clips, and music videos, as well as amateur content. In 2006, Google Inc. announced that it had reached a deal to acquire the company for $1.65 billion in Google stock.

Conventional media companies are always looking for Internet business opportunities. One example is the astonishing growth of a new kind of media content called **social networks** with MySpace and Facebook being the most widely used. Most services provide a collection of various ways for users to interact, such as chat, messaging, e-mail, video, voice chat, file sharing, blogging, and discussion groups. These networks also offer business opportunities in terms of advertising, membership fees, and purchase transactions. Various social networking web sites are being used by millions of people every day on a regular basis and participation is predicted to only increase in coming years. Anticipating this enormous growth, in 2005, Rupert Murdoch, head of News Corp, bought MySpace for the now bargain price of $580 million.

The discussion so far has focused primarily on the supplementary use of the Internet by established electronic media and that is as far as we plan to go. Delving into all the types of self-standing, independent Internet offerings, from giant profit-making ventures to tiny local hobby clubs, is beyond the scope of this text.

8.4 Program Promotion and Brand Management

Having the best programs in the world means little if audiences don't know about them. Therefore, informing and persuading audiences to listen and watch ranks as a major aspect of programming strategies. Within the broadcast and cable television industries, the "selling" of programs to audiences has traditionally been called **promotion**, although in recent years broadcasters have adopted the terms **marketing** or **creative services** to denote the same function. Many operations divide responsibilities between **audience promotion** aimed at potential audiences and **sales promotion** aimed at potential advertisers.

Although stations and the national networks have sizable budgets to win the hearts and minds of audiences using advertising and public relations strategies, such as running ads in *TV Guide* or booking program celebrities on interview shows, their most important promotion asset is their own air time. "Commercials" promoting one's own programming, called **promos**, are produced and scheduled in the same manner as real commercials, only these announcements are free. One could argue that there is a "cost" of sorts in that these promos take up commercial inventory space that otherwise could be allocated to revenue-producing advertising. (See Chapter 6 for more details on the topic of commercial inventory.) Announcements that promote an entire series are referred to as **generic**, while those that highlight one episode in a series are called **specific** or **episodic**. In addition to using one's own air time, most broadcast networks are involved with "sister" cable networks owned by the same parent corporation, enabling **cross-promotion** in which the networks air promos for each other. For example, ABC Sports often promotes its cable cousin ESPN and vice versa.

Aside from using conventional promo spot announcements of varying lengths, stations and networks make use of other tactics to gain the attention of audiences. These include audio-only **voice-over** announcements during final credits of a program urging viewers to stay tuned to what follows. In recent years, video-only animated messages now appear throughout program content, usually positioned at the bottom of the screen and lasting only a few seconds. To promote upcoming newscasts, stations and networks use teasers—brief mentions of upcoming news stories—during the hour preceding newscasts.

The pay-cable networks schedule billboards of upcoming programs as filler between the end of one show and the start of the next. These networks periodically descramble their signals for several days (often over a weekend) so that nonsubscribers can sample their wares. Usually, the networks offer special promotional rates to new subscribers during the free preview periods. Special discounts are often pitched to current subscribers, adding another channel of the provider's multiplexed offerings.

Cable systems and DBS typically dedicate one or more channels entirely to program listings. Some form of on-screen "navigation device" is increasingly important to viewers as they try to find programming of special interest among dozens of available channels. New technologies allow viewers to see program titles on-screen as they graze channels, to search for programs by theme or genre, to call up a program by title, to scan a seven-day program guide organized by channel and time, and even to program their VCRs and DVRs for desired programs, program types, or program characteristics.

Supplementing on-air promotion activities, stations and networks advertise in all kinds of media, including newspapers, magazines, outdoor billboards, and Internet web sites. Radio stations promote television programs, and television stations promote radio stations—sometimes as paid advertising and sometimes as **trade outs**, whereby media exchange airtime with no cash involved. Daily newspapers and Sunday supplements devote considerable space to broadcast and cable listings and typically offer display advertising space for the media. Cable systems mail customized program guides to their subscribers. *TV Guide* is the most popular source of printed program listings in the country and the nation's largest weekly circulation magazine.

In addition to pure advertising, electronic media look for positive public relations and publicity opportunities. For example, stations will sponsor rock concerts, ice shows, charity road races, and give away T-shirts and bumper stickers at the event. Electronic media are always looking for positive "free press" in the form of cast interviews, articles, and reviews by professional critics.

Media Brand Management

A recent trend in electronic media promotion has been the adoption of brand management strategies. Radio and television broadcasters have for decades given unique "brand names" to their stations, networks, and programs, but the decade of the 1990s introduced a much deeper interest in the art and science of brand management. The primary motivation for applying brand management to a consumer product or service is competition. As the number of similar products or services in the marketplace increases, the need for highly differentiated brands becomes more important. It is no secret that the amount of program content available now to audiences is staggering and competition among content providers is fierce.

Brand management has a special role within the larger context of promotion. Some promotion activities may have a branding component, while others may not. In simple terms, branding deals with a product's **reputation**. This encompasses those promotion activities that are intended to distinguish a brand from its competitors by communicating to consumers the brand's unique attributes.

Not all promotion activity is branding. For example, a TV program's ratings success may be more the result of clever program scheduling rather than genuine audience preference. In a similar manner, a "listen and win" radio contest may attract listeners only for the short-lived content and not retain audiences when the contest ends. Effective **media branding** strategies are designed for the long run and require special skills. Today, media branding is the new industry buzz phrase. Media brand consultants have been welcomed by broadcasting professionals looking for long-term competitive advantages. Today, the term media branding is pervasive in industry trade publications, conference seminars, and informal conversations among media executives.

8.5 Programs and the Public Interest

This chapter has examined broadcast and cable programs largely from the industry viewpoint—as vehicles to carry commercial messages or to entice paying subscribers. Here we touch on other perspectives—those of critics and consumers.

The best-known critique of the industry's program performance in public-interest terms came from an FCC chairperson appointed by the Kennedy administration, Newton Minow (1961–1963). In an address to the National Association of Broadcasters in 1961, Minow challenged station owners and managers to watch their own programs for a full broadcast day. They would, he assured them, find a "vast wasteland" of violence, repetitive formulas, irritating commercials, and sheer boredom (Minow, 1964: 52). The "vast wasteland" phrase caught on and became a permanent part of broadcasting lore.

Fundamentally, the viewer/listener perspective asks whether commercial motives should be the primary factor in program choice and quality. Debate has swirled around the issue of commerce versus culture ever since broadcasting began. How should society balance these sometimes conflicting goals? Is it enough for media to treat programs simply as "product"—articles of trade? Some people argue that programs can also be broadly cultural and contribute to the intellectual, artistic, and moral quality of national life. Seen in that perspective, programs should do more than encourage audiences to watch commercials.

Program producers have a difficult task. They face constant pressure to produce a product generating maximum profit regardless of its artistic quality or social impact. On the other hand, the electronic media, especially the licensed media, have a legal and moral responsibility to do more than offer programs that are simply popular and make money. Indeed, they have a responsibility to provide programs that sometimes may be very unpopular.

At least theoretically, ultimate power over programming rests with the audience. Programming must compete for survival as does any other product in a consumer-driven economy, and there are political channels of control available when the marketplace fails to produce culturally acceptable programming. This does not mean that the media do not have a responsibility to strive independently toward a higher standard than the lowest common denominator without being goaded to do so by economic or legislative threats.

In simple terms the debate can be distilled down to a fundamental question: To what degree should the media pander to (a) what audiences *want*, based on demand versus (b) what audiences *need* based on standards other than mere economics? Complicating this debate is the question of when should the government intervene? Other chapters in this text address in more detail the complexities of regulating media in a society that values free market capitalism and free expression.

Popular Taste vs. Bad Taste

Although commercial broadcasters have always catered to **popular taste**, they once refrained from catering to the appetite for downright **bad taste** in programs. In its now-abandoned Television Code, the National Association of Broadcasters (NAB) emphasized the role of television as a family medium, warning that "great care must be exercised to be sure that treatment and presentation are made in good faith and not for the purpose of sensationalism or to shock or exploit the audience or appeal to prurient interests or morbid curiosity" (NAB, 1978: 2). Today, however, graphic—some would say gratuitous—violence pervades many prime-time dramas. Moreover, although containing little or no violent content, sitcoms continue to test the boundaries with their use of language and sexual innuendo. Cable producers, which operate on a standard less strict than that of broadcast, "double-shoot" some programs—one version with topless scenes for the pay-cable network and foreign syndication, and another without for ad-supported cable and domestic station use. Pay-cable "adult" services, such as Playboy's Spice networks, offer full nudity and carefully edited, but nonetheless graphic, movies.

Radio is not exempt from this type of criticism. Far more cases of alleged indecency have been filed against radio stations than television or cable operators. In addition to music lyrics, the ad lib comments by DJs and their guests have caught the attention of many irate listeners who have complained to the FCC.

Criticism Beyond Entertainment Content

Criticism of electronic media content goes beyond entertainment genres. News and public affairs content is essential to a successful democracy and few would argue the importance of a free press devoid of government censorship. But the very fact that in this country journalism is a *business* makes it vulnerable to market pressures that may not always be in the public interest. As the public's primary news source, television has special obligations not always met in a competitive marketplace. Some observers express concern over reduced journalistic diversity resulting from the trend toward media concentration in the hands of a few huge corporations with no direct accountability to the public. Others contemplate the impact of television trial coverage on the rights of defendants and victims. Some say that this coverage makes the public more aware of judicial procedures. Others say that the minute coverage of the trials only confuses, frustrates, and divides people rather than informs or reassures them.

Traditional news programs have come under attack for stressing violence and tragedy at the expense of more far-reaching but less sensational stories. Some critics say that this accounts in part for the relatively low opinion many Americans have of journalism today. The need for visually appealing stories has tempted producers to create **staged news events**. Television also is susceptible to manipulation by persons or organizations who stage dramatically visual **pseudo-events** designed to attract news coverage. TV journalists may sometimes use, but fail to identify, footage from **video news releases (VNRs)** produced by outside sources, such as government agencies and businesses.

Critics also deplore **checkbook journalism**—the practice of paying for interviews. Reputable news organizations seldom pay for interviews, but sometimes their purity is questionable. For instance, networks also use their prestige and the celebrity status of their top reporters and anchors to entice people to grant interviews. It is less likely that a source will refuse an interview request by Leslie Stahl, Barbara Walters, or Larry King than by an unknown reporter.

Challenges for the Future

The new millennium brings with it wondrous new technologies that will dramatically improve the technical quality of programming. The new technology will also usher in a new age of audience control over what they receive, how they will receive it, and when. But there is no guarantee that program content will be the better for these technological advancements. If electronic media are to change for the better, the men and women in these industries will have to make program content more than merely a reactive mirror of the lowest common denominator in the marketplace.

Audience Measurement

9 chapter

Commercial broadcast and cable services compete to win the popularity contest that ratings measure. If people don't watch or listen—as measured by ratings—then advertisers lose interest and programs die to be replaced by others, or stations fail and leave the air. Electronic media managers need unbiased and consistent audience information. For this, broadcasters, cable services (whether delivered via traditional systems or DBS), and advertisers employ independent companies to conduct most day-to-day audience research, using scientific methods for probing into human behavior and attitudes. Measuring audiences has become increasingly complex given the proliferation of distribution platforms used to access electronic media programming. Internet streams, mobile devices, video-on-demand (VOD) services, DVRs, and other distribution methods present challenges to companies that provide the industry with data essential to its advertising-based business model.

9.1 Ratings Business

Practically everyone knows what TV ratings are in a general sense. In the long broadcast TV network battle for ratings dominance, the rise and fall of prime-time programs always make news. But unlike most other industries, broadcasting and cable deliver no physical products. Program "publishing" goes on continuously, with audiences flowing at will from one program to another. The enormous amount of available program content and the growing complexity of audience viewing patterns generate a need for highly specialized research.

Arbitron and Nielsen

Two ratings firms, Arbitron and Nielsen, dominate the ratings business as sources of most audience measurements used by electronic media and their advertisers. Other competitors (e.g., Knowledge Networks/SRI), focus more on limited or specialized types of research. By 1994, Arbitron had ended the TV (and later cable) ratings service it had begun in 1949, leaving Nielsen as the sole provider of audience ratings in those areas. Arbitron continues to dominate radio ratings, but in November 2008 Nielsen announced plans to resume measuring radio audiences after leaving the business over 40 years ago.

The two services' revenues come mainly from subscriptions by cable and broadcast networks, stations, advertising agencies, sales rep firms, program suppliers, and syndicators. Station subscription rates vary, but generally correspond to the size of the local market. Major ad agencies subscribe to both network and local-market ratings reports, with some agencies spending over a million dollars a year for audience research.

Local-Market Ratings

Nielsen gathers and publishes TV data for virtually all TV markets in the United States. Local reports reflect the relative position of each station among its competitors and estimate local audience size for network, syndicated, and locally produced programs.

For all but the largest markets, it costs too much to collect data for local TV ratings continuously. Instead, researchers gather data in short spurts known as **rating periods**.

The Nielsen Local Service, the major Nielsen local TV market measure, covers all 210 TV markets—154 by means of written diaries, the other 56 by Local People Meters or a combination of diary and Set Meters (see Section 9.2). In large markets, Local People Meters have replaced diaries and Set Meters. The company measures all markets four times a year in four-week-long **sweep weeks** (or simply **sweeps**); it measures larger markets up to three additional times per year. Nielsen also publishes additional local reports in 19 markets where there is a significant Hispanic population using a Spanish-language sample. A sample page from a local-market report appears in Exhibit 9.a.

Arbitron is now the primary firm providing radio market ratings, as Nielsen stopped measuring radio use in 1964, and Birch Radio left the business at the end of 1991. Arbitron covers 302 radio markets, about 95 year-round and the rest in the spring and fall. In most markets, Arbitron collects radio listening data using a seven-day paper diary, but has replaced diaries with its Portable People Meters in some markets (see Section 9.2). Exhibit 9.b offers a sample page from a diary used in producing radio-rating reports.

Network Ratings

Broadcast TV networks demand faster and more frequent reporting than do local stations. But in two respects network ratings are easier to obtain: (1) not every market need be surveyed, as a national sample yields a reliable picture of national network audiences; and (2) far fewer broadcast TV networks than stations compete at any one time. One sample is the source of all national TV ratings.

The Nielsen Television Index (NTI) is a report of TV network ratings in what is called a "Pocketpiece" (see Exhibit 9.c). Nielsen's regular network reports use a national sample of about 15,000 People Meter homes. Nielsen also reports on its national Hispanic sample (National Hispanic Television Index), which includes about 1,000 People Meter homes.

Arbitron's *Radio's All-Dimension Audience Research (RADAR)* report provides the only ratings service for national network radio listening. RADAR issues reports four times a year, each covering an average week based on the last 12-month period, reflecting the surveys of

Exhibit 9.a

Local-Market TV Ratings Report

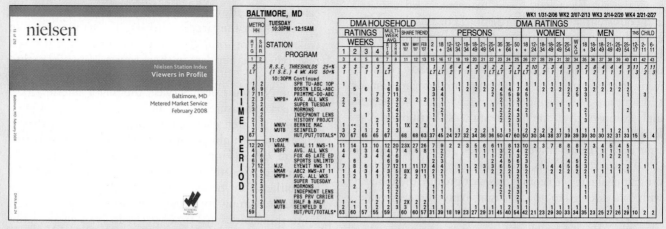

Nielsen uses diaries and household meters to measure 210 local-market TV audiences. Shown here is part of a sample page of late-night ratings and shares for network and syndicated programs in the Baltimore market. This report includes data from four weeks and shows a variety of demographic breakdowns so that station management and advertisers can obtain ratings for, say, women 25 to 49 years of age.

250,000 respondents. Network listening estimates are based on data collected by a combination of paper diaries and Portable People Meters (PPMs) (see Section 9.2) used for local radio market reports. Twice annually, Arbitron also produces *Radio Nationwide*, a network radio report that measures the performance of radio networks on a local and regional basis.

Syndicated-Program Ratings

By using data already obtained for market-ratings reports, Nielsen provides regular analyses on the relative performance of nationally syndicated TV programs.

Nielsen provides detailed audience demographic information for both first-run and off-network syndicated programs, allowing researchers to compare household demographic information for syndicated programs across markets and to collect and measure similar data on both lead-in and lead-out programs. Syndicated program audiences are reported in a variety of published reports that show ratings from local and national markets.

Special Studies

Many supplementary reports, drawing on data gathered in preparing regular ratings reports, are also available. Clients can order special reports tailored to their needs. For example, to help determine when to schedule its news promotion announcements, a TV station might order a special "audience flow" study to discover which of its own programs attract viewers who normally watch a competing newscast. Another might commission a study to find out how much a program appeals to specific audience subgroups.

9.2 Collecting Data

Whatever electronic medium they analyze, researchers use several methods for collecting data on which to base ratings: paper diaries, Set Meters, People Meters, and Portable People Meters (PPMs). Special studies often use other methods and combinations, including telephone contacts. Each has advantages and disadvantages.

Diaries and Set Meters

Arbitron and Nielsen researchers use a written diary method for gathering most local-market data. To obtain radio data, Arbitron sends a separate diary to each person over 12 years of age in every sample household. It asks diary keepers to write down for one week their listening times and the stations they tune to, keeping track of away-from-home as well as in-home listening. Local market reports cover 12 weeks of listening and are issued either twice (spring and fall) or four times a year (spring, summer, fall, and winter). Arbitron publishes local ratings reports electronically in Arbitron "eBooks." Local markets measured with Arbitron's Portable People Meters publish reports every month.

Exhibit 9.b

Local-Market Radio Ratings

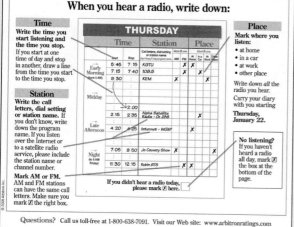

You count in the radio ratings!

No matter how much or how little you listen, you're important!
You're one of the few people picked in your area to have the chance to tell radio stations what you listen to.

This is *your* ratings diary. Please make sure you fill it out yourself.

Here's what we mean by "listening":
Listening is any time you can hear a radio – whether you choose the station or not. You may be listening to radio on AM, FM, the Internet or satellite. Be sure to include all your listening.

Any time you hear radio from **Thursday, January 22,** through **Wednesday, January 28,** write it down – whether you're at home, in a car, at work or someplace else.

When you hear a radio, write down:

Time
Write the time you start listening and the time you stop.
If you start at one time of day and stop in another, draw a line from the time you start to the time you stop.

Station
Write the call letters, dial setting or station name. If you don't know, write down the program name. If you listen over the Internet or to a satellite radio service, please include the station name or channel number.

Mark AM or FM.
AM and FM stations can have the same call letters. Make sure you mark ☒ the right box.

Place
Mark where you listen:
• at home
• in a car
• at work
• other place

Write down *all* the radio you hear. Carry your diary with you starting **Thursday, January 22.**

No listening?
If you haven't heard a radio all day, mark ☒ the box at the bottom of the page.

THURSDAY

	Time		Station	Place					
	Start	Stop	Call letters, dial setting or station name	AM	FM	At Home	In a Car	At Work	Other Place
Early Morning (from 5 AM)	5:45	7:15	KGTU	X	X				
	7:15	7:40	108.5		X	X			
	8:30		KEM	X		X			
Midday		2:00							
	2:15	2:35	Alpha Satellite Radio - Ch 208		X			X	
Late Afternoon	4:20	4:25	Internet - WGRP		X		X		
Night (to 5 AM Friday)	7:05	9:50	Jo Cauvery Show	X		X			
	11:30	12:15	Robin 87.5		X		X	X	

If you didn't hear a radio today, please mark ☒ here. ☐

Questions? Call us toll-free at 1-800-638-7091. Visit our Web site: www.arbitronratings.com

This instruction page from a radio diary illustrates the Arbitron system. Each individual in a household who is at least 12 years old fills out a separate diary.

Source: © 2000 The Arbitron Company. Used by permission.

Except for its Local People Meter markets, Nielsen uses diaries for its local TV ratings. A separate paper diary is used for each set in the home. Diaries are used in local markets to measure TV viewing during the four sweeps months (November, February, May, and July). Participating households fill out their diaries for a one-week period (or eight-day diaries in homes with DVRs). A new panel of households receives diaries for the next week of the sweeps month. Viewing data are aggregated for each week and for the total month of measurement.

Diaries suffer from a serious flaw: People often enter inaccurate information, purposely (to show they have good taste in programs) or not (many sample families fill in a diary in "catch-up" style at the end of the week rather than as listening or viewing takes place). Some also tire of making entries, suffering from **diary fatigue**. Both Nielsen and Arbitron have plans to move from diaries to metering technologies in every market where it is economically practical.

The **Set Meter** (Nielsen's Audimeter) was first used to gather data in 1950. Attached to each TV set in a sample household, the so-called black box automatically records when the set is on and to which channel it is tuned. Researchers refer to the Set Meter as *passive* because no effort is required on the part of the viewer to record its information, and to distinguish it from the newer People Meter. Because it provides no information as to who, if anyone, is actually watching, during sweeps periods Nielsen supplements meter data in local Set Meter markets with written diary data from a separate sample of households to obtain demographic data on actual viewers. Set Meters were phased out of national network ratings use in 1987 with the activation of People Meters, and they are being phased out of local markets as well. In 2007, Local People Meters were in 18 TV markets and will be in all 56 metered markets by 2011, representing about 70 percent of all U.S. TV households.

People Meters

Nielsen uses People Meters for its national TV ratings service, the Nielsen Television Index, and in large TV markets to measure local-market viewing. Like the Set Meter, the People Meter keeps a record of receiver use. It also offers research that formerly only diaries provided by simultaneously collecting demographic data. It does this by requiring each viewer, whenever she or he watches television, to "check in" and "check out" by pushing a special handset button (see Exhibit 9.d). These meters are capable of identifying tuning and playback on cable set-top boxes, DVRs, DBS, and VOD systems. Data on both receiver use and viewer identity go by telephone line to a central computer containing basic household demographic data, stored earlier when the People Meter was installed. The People Meter also allows guest viewers to participate by entering their age, gender, and viewing status into the box. A great benefit of People Meters is the ability to provide viewing estimates and key demographic data 365 days a year.

Nielsen began a three-year test of a People Meter sample in 1983 and started its People Meter-based national network ratings service in 1987. The first deployment of People Meters for local audience measurement was in Boston in 2002.

Arbitron, meanwhile, had developed **ScanAmerica,** a three-pronged single-source system providing ratings, audience demographic data, and—through the use of a *wand* that read universal bar codes—a measure of product purchasing. In 1992, lacking sufficient advertiser interest, Arbitron dropped use of both the wand and the name ScanAmerica and soon after ended all of its broadcast TV and cable ratings activities. Arbitron continues to publish reports useful to the TV industry through its Scarborough Research arm, a joint venture with Nielsen, which produces studies focusing on shopping patterns, media use, lifestyle patterns, and demographics of American consumers.

Exhibit 9.c

Nielsen TV Network Ratings Report

NATIONAL *NielsenTV* AUDIENCE ESTIMATES												EVE.THU. APR.24, 2008		
TIME	7:00	7:15	7:30	7:45	8:00	8:15	8:30	8:45	9:00	9:15	9:30	9:45	10:00	10:15	10:30	10:45
HUT	48.9	50.7	51.7	54.2	58.3	60.2	61.8	63.7	66.2	66.4	67.1	67.2	64.3	62.2	60.3	59.0

ABC TV
← UGLY BETTY → | ← GREY'S ANATOMY-THU 9PM → (9:00-10:02)(PAE) | ← LOST → (10:02-11:00)(PAE)

HHLD AUDIENCE% & (000)				6.5 7,380		6.9*	12.1 13,670		12.6*	8.4 9,460		8.5*
TA%, AVG. AUD. 1/2 HR %				9.3 6.1*		11	15.4 11.5*		19	11.0 8.3*		14*
SHARE AUDIENCE %				11 10*		11	18 17*		14	14 13*		
AVG. AUD. BY 1/4 HR %				6.2 6.1	6.7	7.2	11.8 11.2	12.4	12.7	8.8 7.8	8.4	8.6

CBS TV
← SURVIVOR: MICRONESIA → | ← CSI → (9:00-10:01) | ← WITHOUT A TRACE → (10:01-11:00)(PAE)

HHLD AUDIENCE% & (000)				8.1 9,170		8.4*	11.6 13,090		12.1*	9.7 10,970		9.6*
TA%, AVG. AUD. 1/2 HR %				10.6 7.8*		13	15.3 11.2*		12.4	12.4 9.9*		16*
SHARE AUDIENCE %				13 13*		17	17*		18	16 16*		
AVG. AUD. BY 1/4 HR %				7.7 7.9	8.2	8.6	10.8 11.5	12.4	11.8	9.9 9.8	9.5	9.7

NBC TV
MY NAME IS EARL | SCRUBS | OFFICE (9:00-9:31) | 30 ROCK (9:31-10:01)(PAE) | ← E.R. → (10:01-11:00)(PAE)

HHLD AUDIENCE% & (000)				4.3 4,900	3.8 4,300		5.2 5,920	3.8 4,260	5.7 6,420		5.8*
TA%, AVG. AUD. 1/2 HR %				5.7 4.7		6.6 4.6		7.6 5.6*		10*
SHARE AUDIENCE %				7 6		8 6		9 9*		
AVG. AUD. BY 1/4 HR%				4.3 4.4	3.9 3.8	5.3 5.2	3.8 3.7	5.4 5.7	5.6	6.0

FOX TV
← SMARTER THAN 5TH GRADER (8:00-9:01) → | SMARTER THAN 5TH 4/24-9P (9:01-10:00)(PAE)

HHLD AUDIENCE% & (000)				5.3 5,970		5.8*	5.4 6,080		5.3*
TA%, AVG. AUD. 1/2 HR %				8.1 4.7*		9.2 5.5*		8*
SHARE AUDIENCE %				9 8*		9*		
AVG. AUD. BY 1/4 HR %				4.3 5.1	5.7	6.0	6.0 5.1	5.0	5.6

CW TV
← SMALLVILLE → | ← SUPERNATURAL →

HHLD AUDIENCE% & (000)				2.5 2,780		2.6*	1.6 1,860		1.5*
TA%, AVG. AUD. 1/2 HR %				3.5 2.3*		2.3 1.8*		2*
SHARE AUDIENCE %				4 4*		4* 3*		
AVG. AUD. BY 1/4 HR%				2.3 2.3	2.5	2.7	1.9 1.6	1.6	1.5

UNI TV
← YO AMO JUAN QUERENDON THU (7:00-8:01) → | ← AL DIABLO CON GUAPOS THU (8:01-9:02)(PAE) → | ← PASION THU (9:02-10:02)(PAE) → | ← AMAS CASA DESESPERADS THU (10:02-11:00)(PAE) →

HHLD AUDIENCE% & (000)	1.6 1,800		1.7*	2.4 2,680		2.5*	2.5 2,860		2.6*	1.5 1,670		1.4*
TA%, AVG. AUD. 1/2 HR %	2.3 1.5*		3.0 2.2*		2.9 2.5*		2.1 1.6*		
SHARE AUDIENCE %	3 3*		3	4 4*		4 4*		4	2 3	
AVG. AUD. BY 1/4 HR %	1.4 1.6	1.6	1.7	2.2 2.3	2.4	2.6	2.4 2.5	2.6	2.5	1.7 1.5	1.4	1.4

ION TV
← THURSDAY 8PM MOVIE ONE FLEW OVER CUCKOO'S NEST (R) →

HHLD AUDIENCE% & (000)				0.3 390		0.3*	0.4	0.4	0.4*		0.3*
TA%, AVG. AUD. 1/2 HR %				1.3 0.3*		1*	1	1	1*		1*
SHARE AUDIENCE %				1 1*		1*				
AVG. AUD. BY 1/4 HR %				0.3 0.3	0.3	0.3	0.4 0.4	0.4	0.4 0.3	0.3	0.3

U.S. TV Households: 112,800,000   *Estimates include Live+7*

This ratings report for a weekday evening compares the prime-time appeal of the national broadcasting networks. Shown for each broadcast network program is the rating (bold face), average audience in TV households, percent of total audience (persons) for the hour and half-hour, share of audience, and the average audience rating by quarter-hour.

Nielsen plans to add Internet measurement to its national and local People Meter sample households to better understand and report the relationship between TV viewing, web site usage, and video stream consumption. It also hopes to measure what people are watching on portable devices by placing microchips in mobile display devices and small plug-in meters in MP3 players, like the iPod. It remains to be seen if people will agree to "opt-in" to such comprehensive monitoring of their electronic media use.

Portable People Meters

In the late 1990s, Arbitron began testing a new method of data collection that would lessen some of the difficulties and concerns associated with using paper diaries to collect radio ratings data. Not to be confused with Nielsen's People Meter, Arbitron's Portable People Meter (PPM) is a small cell-phone size meter that is worn throughout the day by individuals participating in local market radio measurement. The device detects

Exhibit 9.d

National People Meter Ratings

The Nielsen national audience reporting system depends heavily on automation, from the home meter through the gathering, analyzing, and reporting processes. The People Meter used for national ratings consists of two parts: the hand-held remote control on which each viewing member of the family and guests can "check in," using individual keys, and the base unit on top of the receiver that stores home-viewing information.

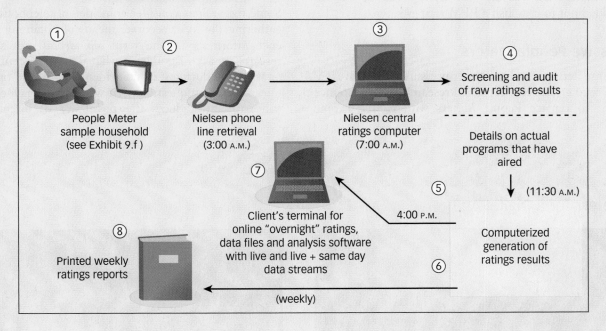

① People Meter sample household (see Exhibit 9.f)

② Nielsen phone line retrieval (3:00 A.M.)

③ Nielsen central ratings computer (7:00 A.M.)

④ Screening and audit of raw ratings results

Details on actual programs that have aired

(11:30 A.M.)

⑤ 4:00 P.M.

⑥ Computerized generation of ratings results

⑦ Client's terminal for online "overnight" ratings, data files and analysis software with live and live + same day data streams

⑧ Printed weekly ratings reports

(weekly)

The Nielsen system begins with the individual sample household (1), whose People Meter base unit results are (2) downloaded over a telephone line (leased by Nielsen) at 3:00 A.M. local time each morning by a computer that sends the viewing results of the sample household into (3) the Nielsen central ratings computers. The collected raw ratings are (4) sent to the screening and audit process, where all ratings materials are assembled and (5) combined with the detailed program information constantly gathered by Nielsen. They are then sent for (6) computer generation of actual overnight ratings. By the afternoon, two sets of national ratings are delivered—Live and Live + Same Day of DVR playback. Data files and software are available to facilitate analysis by (7) clients (agencies, stations, networks) to retrieve by computer and (8) weekly printed ratings reports. Nielsen Local Meter Markets go through a similar process to generate market-by-market reports.

exposure to inaudible identification signals encoded in any broadcast signal. Most radio stations in PPM markets use a special encoder to broadcast their identification signal and Arbitron is field testing a PPM that can identify broadcast signals not carrying identification codes. A motion sensor in the device can determine whether it was actually carried around on any given day.

In addition to measuring analog AM and FM stations, the PPM can also detect HD radio signals and Internet streaming by traditional radio stations. Internet-only radio stations and satellite radio channels (however delivered) are not reported in local market station estimates.

As of August 2008, only two radio markets (Houston-Galveston and Philadelphia) had completely replaced diaries with PPMs to report official radio ratings. An additional 12 markets were on schedule to transition to PPMs by the end of 2008, with 35 more markets to be added by 2010. Arbitron's system is detailed in Exhibit 9.e.

It was expected that Nielsen would join with Arbitron in deploying PPMs to measure TV audiences. Although there was early interest, in 2006, Nielsen decided not to establish a PPM ratings service.

Passive People Meters

Intense network and advertiser pressure to improve TV audience measurement pushed researchers to announce plans to replace People Meters with *passive* People Meters. Using computerized image recognition or having persons wear a personal tag read by the meter, these passive devices presumably could "recognize" regular (family) viewers. Further, the devices eventually could tell when viewers were actually watching the screen rather than doing something else.

A number of variations are under consideration and being tested, including one that counts someone as watching television only if that person is actually facing the receiver. There have been kinks—early demonstrations confused pets with people—but when perfected, the passive People Meter should be able to record electronically regular family members and others, such as guests, tabulating who and how many are watching and when. Although such systems might alleviate the operational problems of active People Meters, they raise other, more troublesome concerns—chiefly viewer privacy; TV viewers may experience severe discomfort knowing that their television is watching back.

Coincidental Telephone Interviews

Some researchers consider coincidental telephone data gathering the most accurate means of obtaining audience information. The term *coincidental* means that researchers ask respondents what they are listening to or watching during (i.e., coincidental with) the time of the call. Putting questions that way eliminates memory concerns and reduces the possibility of intentional

Exhibit 9.e

Meters for a Digital Age

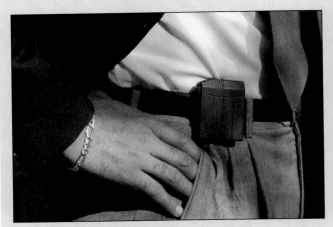

Arbitron's Portable People Meter system requires respondents to carry at all times a meter about the size of a small cell phone. The meter detects all radio signals being heard by the wearer and stores the listening data. At night the meter is placed in a data-collection box in the user's home. While in the box, the battery is recharged and the data are sent via

telephone lines to a computerized collection center. The technology makes out-of-home measurement more dependable and significantly reduces the burden on the survey participant.

Source: Photos © The Arbitron Company. Used by permission.

misinformation. Researchers ask whether respondents have a set turned on at that moment and, if so, what program, station, or channel the set is tuned to, plus a few demographic questions such as the number, gender, and age of those watching or listening.

Because coincidental methods provide only *momentary* data from each respondent ("What are you listening to or watching *now?*"), they require many calls, spaced out to cover each daypart, to build up a complete profile of listening or viewing. Properly conducted, coincidental calls require large batteries of trained interviewers, making the method expensive. Nor can coincidental calls cover the entire broadcast day; information on audience activity after 10:30 P.M. and before 8:00 A.M. must be gathered during more socially acceptable calling hours, when researchers ask respondents to recall programs they listened to or viewed during these nighttime and early-morning hours. Because of these limitations, the telephone coincidental method is seldom used today, although it is sometimes employed to validate data generated by newer measurement methods, such as the People Meter.

Telephone Recall

Tricks of memory make **telephone recall** less reliable than coincidental calls, but it costs less because more data can be gathered per call. The telephone recall methodology is often used to collect information about media use and exposure to and perceptions of advertisements, but is not used to generate ratings estimates.

Personal Interviews

The use of in-person, door-to-door surveys has declined in recent years largely because of dangers implicit in knocking on doors in strange neighborhoods. Typically, interviewers question people on the street or in shopping centers, or, for car radio listening, at stoplights. Data gathered in these ways cannot be projected to the general population, however, because the samples are not at all representative.

9.3 Sampling

Around-the-clock monitoring of all the private listening and viewing behaviors of millions of people is obviously impossible. The task becomes possible only by sampling—studying some people to represent the behavior of all.

Using Samples to Simplify

Sampling simplifies three aspects of ratings research: behavior, time, and number of people.

▶ **Behavioral sampling.** Researchers agreed years ago on a series of minimum measurable behavioral responses—turning on a receiver, selecting a station or programs, and later turning off the set.

▶ **Time sampling.** The second simplification used in ratings takes advantage of repetitive daily and weekly cycles of most broadcast and cable programming. A sample taken every few weeks or months from this continuous program stream suffices for most purposes. Daily measurements occur only for network and major-city audiences.

▶ **Number of people sampled.** The most controversial ratings simplification arises from the use of only hundreds or thousands of people to represent program choices of thousands or millions of others. Nielsen uses about 15,000 homes to represent 114 million TV homes for its national network ratings; fewer households are sampled for local-market measurement. When introducing Local People Meter markets, Nielsen faced strong criticism that minority households were underrepresented as a result of its sampling methodology. Arbitron faces similar criticism with its rollout of Portable People Meters to measure radio listening.

Random Samples

Contrary to what many people believe, small samples *can* give reasonably accurate estimates. The laws of chance, or *probability*, predict that *a randomly selected* small sample from a large population will be representative (within a predictable degree of accuracy) of the entire population. Random selection means that, ideally, *every* member of the entire population to be surveyed has an *equal* chance of being selected. Major defining characteristics of the sample (such as age and gender) will appear in about the same proportion as their distribution throughout the entire population.

However, choosing at random is not as easy as it sounds. Drawing a sample randomly from a large human population requires some means of identifying each member by name, number, location, or some other unique distinguishing label. In practice, this usually means using lists of either telephone numbers or maps of housing unit locations. Such lists are called **sample frames**.

Selecting a Ratings Sample

Nielsen draws its national and local People Meter market samples of TV households, and samples for large TV markets using Set Meters, from U.S. Census maps by a method known as **multistage area probability sampling**. *Multistage* refers to the step-by-step narrowing down of selection areas, starting with census block groups and ending with individual housing units.

Using this method, all households have an equal probability of selection into the sample. For diary-only local-market ratings, Nielsen uses an address-based sampling methodology (ABS). The sample frame is comprised of addresses provided by the United States Postal Service, covering approximately 98 percent of U.S. TV households.

Ideally, each time a company conducts a survey, it should draw a brand-new sample. On the other hand, if the company uses expensive sampling and data-gathering methods, it cannot afford to discard each sample after only one use. Nielsen tries to retain each People Meter household in its national sample for no more than two years, but allows local-market Set Meter families to stay in samples for up to five years. Diaries are only kept for one week. In some markets, a supplemental sample of cell phone-only households is also used.

Arbitron follows similar procedures to generate a random sample, but relies mostly on telephone dialing rather than selecting geographic housing units to recruit participants.

Sample Size

Having established a sample universe, the researcher must next decide how large a sample to choose—the larger the sample, the greater its *reliability* (the consistency of results over time). But reliability does not have a one-to-one relationship with sample size. For example, to double the reliability of a sample using 1,000 homes, you would have to quadruple the sample size to 4,000 homes. Thus, *a point of diminishing returns* soon arrives, after which an increase in sample size yields such small gains in reliability as not to be worth the added cost.

Sources of Error

At its best, sampling yields only estimates, *never* absolute certainties. Thus, the real question becomes how much uncertainty can be accepted in a given sampling situation.

Even when researchers carefully select their samples and sample sizes, two kinds of errors can invalidate research findings. The built-in uncertainty of all measurements based on samples arises first from **sampling error**. No matter how carefully a sample is drawn, that sample will never exactly represent the entire population (or universe) being measured. With the use of statistical techniques, the *probable* amount of statistical uncertainty in ratings (i.e., the amount of sampling error to be expected) can be calculated in advance.

The second possibly invalidating problem—**nonsampling error**—arises from mistakes, both

---

Exhibit 9.f

Nonresponse Errors

Typical nonresponse errors for each of the principal methods of ratings data collection include the following:

▶ **Diaries:** refusal to accept diaries; failure to complete accepted diaries; unreadable and self-contradictory diary entries; drop-off in entries as the week progresses ("diary fatigue"); and failure to mail in completed diaries.
▶ **Set Meters:** refusal to allow installation; breakdown of receivers, meters, and associated equipment; telephone-line failures.
▶ **People Meters:** same drawbacks as passive meters, plus failure of some viewers (especially the very old and very young) to use the buttons to "check in" and "check out," having succumbed to "response fatigue."
▶ **Portable People Meters:** refusal to accept meter; breakdown of meter and associated equipment; telephone-line failure; breakdown of station encoding equipment or stations not encoding signal.
▶ **Telephone calls:** busy signals; no answer; disconnected telephones; refusal to talk; inability to communicate with respondents who speak foreign languages.

---

intentional and inadvertent. Such errors produce **bias** in the results. Bias can come from lying by respondents, as well as from honest mistakes. The wording of questionnaires may be misleading. And mistakes can also occur in recording data and calculating results.

Sometimes reports state sample size as the number of people (or households) the researcher contacted, when the key element should be how many actually *participated*. A 45 percent response rate indicates that only 45 out of 100 homes or individuals contacted actually participated. In practice, a response rate of 100 percent never occurs. Depending on the research method and purpose, a low response rate may be cause for concern.

Notwithstanding a series of incentives and entreaties from the ratings services, nonresponse places a serious limitation on ratings accuracy. Some age groups (e.g., teenagers), have a particularly low response rate for radio diaries. Moreover, those who do return diaries may not represent those who do not. Exhibit 9.f lists typical **nonresponse errors**.

Overall, diary and meter methods yield a usable response rate of about 40 percent ("usable" being variously defined, but meaning "returned on time," plus other measures of how completely the diary is filled in). The number of such usable responses is termed the **in-tab sample**, the sample actually used in tabulating results and producing a given ratings report.

9.4 Determining Ratings and Shares

Defining Markets

A crucial step in ratings research is an accurate definition of the local market to be measured. Advertising depends on a universally recognized, national system of clearly defined, non-overlapping markets.

The most widely accepted system for defining TV markets is Nielsen's **designated market area (DMA)**. A DMA consists of one or more counties in which stations located in a central town or city are the most viewed (see Exhibit 9.g). DMAs usually extend over smaller areas in the East, where cities are closer together, than in the West. Nielsen assigns each of the more than 3,000 counties in the United States to a single DMA, updating the assignments annually. DMAs range in size from No. 1 (New York City, with over seven million TV households) to No. 210 (Glendive, Montana, with fewer than 4,000).

Arbitron reports local radio ratings in the top-50 radio markets corresponding to Nielsen's DMAs. It also reports two other related areas. One, the **metro area**, usually consists of one or more counties around a central city core. The metro area covers an area smaller than the DMA. The other, **total survey area (TSA)**, the largest local region on which Arbitron reports, includes 98 percent of a market's listening audience, thus covering counties outside the DMA and overlapping with adjacent DMAs. Thus, although counties are assigned to only one DMA, they may be shown in more than one TSA, depending on listening in that county. Nielsen takes a similar approach with its TV ratings, defining both metro and station total areas in all markets.

Households

Another preliminary step in ratings research is to define what will count as "one" when measuring audience size. Television viewing has traditionally been a family activity, making the *household* a logical unit of measure, even though a majority of households now have two or more TV sets and much viewing takes place as a solo rather than a family activity. A single diary or meter records the viewing of each TV receiver. Thus, if one family member is watching a program on CBS and another family member is watching a program on NBC on another set in the house, both programs will get credit for delivering that household.

For radio, each listener has a separate diary or meter. Radio researchers prefer to count persons rather than households because (1) radio listening usually occurs as an individual activity, and (2) much radio listening takes place outside the home, especially in autos and workplaces.

Ratings

The term **rating** is widely misused and usually confuses two quite separate industry measures: rating and share (discussed in the next section). Specifically, a *rating* is an estimate of the number of households (or persons, in the case of radio) tuned to a specific channel (station, network, or program), expressed as a percentage of *available* households (or persons). "Available" refers to the entire potential audience, even those who may not have their receivers turned on.

In the 2007–2008 TV season, prime-time shows on the Big Four broadcast TV networks averaged about a 5.5 rating. The most successful nonsports entertainment program of all time, the final episode of *M*A*S*H* in 1983, had a Nielsen rating of 60.2. This means that 60.2 percent of all U.S. TV households watched at least part of that episode. The Super Bowl of 1982 achieved a rating of 49.1, a record for that annual football championship that continues to stand through 2008. By contrast, the most popular cable TV programs—often professional wrestling events—seldom garner ratings higher than 5.

Radio stations and public TV stations—often earn ratings of less than 1 and rarely more than 2 or 3. Such low ratings make no meaningful distinctions among stations; radio, therefore, relies more often on **cumes** (measures of cumulative audiences) and shares.

Network and syndicated radio programs typically do not garner national ratings anywhere near as large as network TV programs because most radio programs do not have full nationwide coverage. A few radio programs that do have national distribution may achieve a rating of 2 or 3, but such figures are very unusual.

Shares

A share is an estimate of the number of households (or persons, for radio) tuned to a given channel, expressed as a percentage of all those households (or persons) *actually using* their receivers at that time. Recall that a rating is based on all those *owning* receivers, not necessarily *using* them.

A station's share of the TV audience is calculated on the basis of **households using television (HUT)**. A HUT of 55 indicates that at a given time an estimated 55 percent of all TV households are actually tuned in to *some* channel receivable in that market; the remaining 45 percent are not at home, busy with something else (screening DVDs perhaps), or otherwise not using television. HUTs vary with daypart, averaging about 25 percent for daytime hours and about 60 for prime time. Because of multiple TV sets in most households, shares frequently sum to more than 100 percent. Each household only counts once toward the HUT, but each program or station viewed is credited with audience share.

Exhibit 9.g

Miami-Ft. Lauderdale DMA® Region

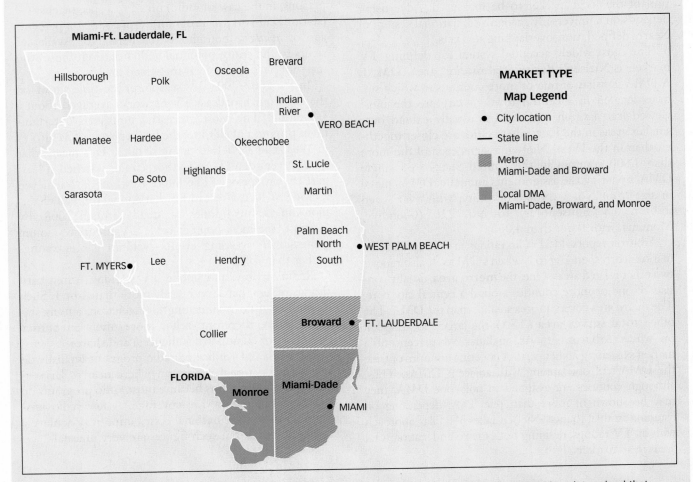

Miami-Ft. Lauderdale, FL

MARKET TYPE

Map Legend

- • City location
- — State line
- Metro
  Miami-Dade and Broward
- Local DMA
  Miami-Dade, Broward, and Monroe

In the Miami-Ft. Lauderdale TV market, the designated market area of stations located in or near Miami extends to three counties—Miami-Dade and Broward (also shown here as the Metro area), and Monroe, which includes the Florida Keys. In practice, viewers often receive programs from stations in two or more markets. In those cases, Nielsen determines which stations are viewed most frequently in the market being defined and designates which counties are to be assigned to which DMAs. For example, in this illustration, when viewers in Broward County receive signals from stations in both Miami and West Palm Beach, Nielsen has determined that most of the time Broward County viewers tune to Miami stations.

No county is assigned to more than one DMA. Nielsen also measures audiences in the station total area, which includes all counties wherever viewership is reported.

Source: Map is Copyrighted information of The Nielsen Company, licensed for use herein. DMA is a registered service mark of The Nielsen Company, licensed for use herein. All rights reserved.

Radio research usually measures persons rather than households. Radio ratings reports usually refer to blocks of time—either individual quarter-hours or cumulative quarter-hours for a day or week—rather than to programs.

Shares are figures based on either HUT or *persons using radio (PUR) data. A station always has a larger share than rating for a given time period.* For example, the 2008 opening ceremony for the Beijing Olympics captured a 25.1 rating, but its corresponding share was a 37. Exhibit 9.h explains how to calculate both ratings and shares.

Television programmers use shares in making programming decisions; salespersons usually use ratings as advertising sales tools. The reason is that shares give programmers a better estimate of their competitive

Exhibit 9.h

Ratings Concepts

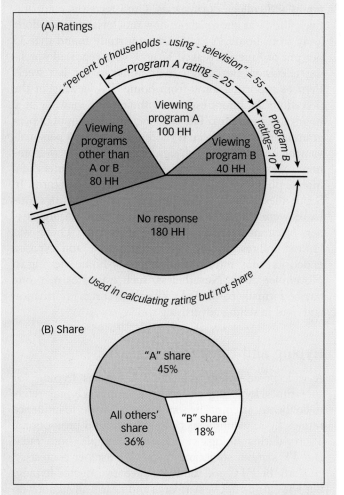

(A) The pie chart shows TV set use information gathered from a sample of 400 households, representing a hypothetical market of 100,000 TV households.

Note that program ratings are percentages based on the entire sample (including the "no-response" households). Thus, Program A, with 100 households, represents a quarter (25 percent) of the total sample of 400. The formula is 100/400 = .25; the decimal is dropped when expressing the number as a rating.

Projected to the entire population, this rating of 25 would mean an estimated audience of 25,000 households. The formula is .25 (the rating with the decimal restored) × 100,000 = 25,000. (B) The smaller pie chart, representing 55 percent of pie A, includes only the households using television, in this case 80 + 100 + 40 households, or a total of 220 (expressed as households using television (or HUT) percentage of 55, as shown in A). Shares are computed by treating the total number of households using television, in this case 220, as 100 percent. Thus, Program A's 100 households divided by 220 equals about .4545, expressed in rounded numbers as a share of 45.

positions within a medium, whereas ratings more readily allow comparison of advertiser exposure on radio or television with that in other media. Also, because HUT levels vary widely during different times of the year (higher in November, lower in May), programmers use share rather than rating to compare a program's competitive performance from one time of year to another. HUT levels also vary by time of day, highest in prime time and lower in the overnight hours.

Because radio ratings are typically very low, radio stations more often than not judge their competitive standing in a market based on audience shares. With few exceptions the top-rated stations in major radio markets, based on listening of people 12 years old and older between 6:00 A.M. and midnight, average between a 6 and 7 share.

Cumes

A radio program reaches a relatively small number of people in any given quarter-hour. *Cumulatively*, however, over a period of many hours, or during the same period over a number of days, it reaches a large number of *different* listeners. *A cume* rating gives an estimate of the (cumulative) number of *unduplicated* persons a station reaches over a period of time. "Unduplicated" means that during a given ratings period, a person who listened several times to a particular station on different days would be counted as only one person in constructing a cume figure. A person listening only once during that period would also be counted as one person, because a cume shows how many *different* people tuned to the station during a given period of time. The terms *reach* and *circulation* usually refer to cume audience measurements. Cumes are useful in commercial radio and television because ads are often repeated. Consequently, the larger the cume for a station, the greater the chance that more listeners have been exposed to the advertiser's message.

Reporting Demographics

Ratings reports detail audience composition by gender and age. These **demographic breakouts**, or simply **demographics**, divide overall ratings into such subgroups as those for men, women, and teens. Adult audience age-group categories typically consist of decade units (such as men 35–44) for radio and larger units for television (e.g., women 18–34 or 25–49), although "persons 12+" serves as the basic category for determining, for example, which radio station in a given market is number one.

Advertising agencies usually buy demographics rather than generalized audiences. Most advertisers would rather have an audience of moderate size with the right demographics for their products than a huge audience containing many members not likely to be interested.

9.5 Use and Abuse of Ratings

Ratings and shares perform a vital function for operators and advertisers—which makes them subject to misuse. Blind consideration of only the numbers could lead to one station getting a disproportionate amount of advertising dollars when the spread between that station and its nearest competitor is less than the sampling error reported. Most users of ratings data understand and accept the fact that the data are estimates. But because everyone uses the same data, users tend to shrug off the data's shortcomings and treat them as being more precise than they really are.

Facing Complaints

In response to complaints and investigations about ratings in the 1960s, the Broadcast Rating Council was established in 1964. Known today as the Media Ratings Council (MRC), it serves as an independent auditing agency representing ratings users. The MRC accredits ratings services that meet its standards and submit to annual auditing paid for by the service provider, not by the MRC. The procedures are sufficiently involved and costly so that many smaller companies do not bother to apply.

Reliability of Ratings

Reliability in research refers to the degree to which methods yield consistent results over time. For example, the drops in broadcast TV network ratings in initial People Meter surveys raised questions about ratings reliability, because those results clearly were *not* consistent with earlier findings. Consistent reports of lower network ratings since the People Meter's introduction suggest that the method is generally reliable, though not necessarily valid.

Validity of Ratings

Validity in research refers to the degree to which findings actually measure what they purport to measure. Ratings purport to measure the *entire* broadcast audience, but in practice they can account for only the broad middle-range majority of that audience. Thus, ratings sometimes underrepresent the very rich, the very poor, the very young, and ethnic minorities, and they are less valid for that limitation.

Television's use of households rather than individuals as its ratings measurement unit also affects validity. Some demographic groups, including younger heads of households and some ethinic groups, can be more difficult to recruit. Sample quality is connected to its ability to accurately reflect the universe it seeks to measure. As a result, controls are used to recruit enough households for the sample to be representative. For those demographics and characteristics closely correlated to TV viewing that are not proportionally represented, a system of statistical weighing may be used to compensate.

Further, measuring only households excludes many other venues for watching television. Not included in the ratings data is viewing from bars, hotels and motels, hospitals, and college dormitories. Until recently, comparatively little was known about how much viewing was done away from home. A 2006 Arbitron study found that 35 percent of Americans aged 12 and older reported watching television away from their home in the last week. Persons reporting away-from-home TV viewing in the preceding 24 hours estimated their away viewing at 2 hours and 7 minutes. The ever-increasing amount of programming being delivered via the Internet and personal-viewing devices could also significantly affect away-from-home viewing rates, especially as more computers and mobile phones come equipped with TV receiver cards. In September 2008, the first out-of-home TV ratings estimates were released by Nielsen and its joint venture partner Integrated Media Measurement, Inc. There was limited interest in the service, however, and Nielsen ended its foray into measuring out-of-home viewing in November 2008. Nevertheless, such estimates may one day be formally combined with other ratings information and used in selling advertising time.

Hyping and Tampering

A widespread industry practice known as **hyping** (or sometimes, **hypoing**) can also bias ratings. Hyping refers to deliberate attempts by stations or networks to influence ratings by scheduling special programs and promotional efforts during ratings sweeps. For example, both radio and TV stations sometimes hype with listener contests.

Both the FTC and the FCC have investigated hyping, but with little effect—networks and nearly all stations do it to some degree. The arrival of 52-weeks-a-year meter ratings for television has reduced the incidence of hyping somewhat, yet many stations continue hyping during sweep weeks. In any case, Arbitron and Nielsen note in ratings reports any exceptionally blatant activities so advertisers can take them into account in market analyses.

Less commonly, ratings can be vulnerable to **tampering**: Someone who can influence the viewing habits of even a few households in a small sample can have a substantial impact on resulting ratings. Ratings companies therefore keep sample household identities a closely held secret. Still, a few cases of outright manipulation of viewers have become public, causing ratings services to junk reports for some programs, and even entire station or market reports for a given ratings period.

Qualitative Ratings

As long as ratings have dominated programming strategies, critics have complained that ratings encourage mediocrity by emphasizing sheer size to the exclusion of qualitative program aspects. Time and again, programs that are seemingly of above-average quality receive enthusiastic reviews and audiences, but fail to meet the rigid minimum-share requirements for commercial survival. Critics question whether programs that are merely accepted by large audiences should automatically win out over programs that attract smaller but intensely interested audiences. **Quantitative** ratings dictate this kind of judgment—the system favors "least objectionable" majority programs over possible alternatives.

The current multichannel environment has changed this situation somewhat, though not entirely. Prime-time network programs today survive with ratings and shares that would have resulted in sure cancellation even five years ago. And because of the proliferation of cable networks eager to find product, programs that are forced off the broadcast networks may find a place on cable. Numbers are still the name of the game for the networks, but shows do not have to be as popular as in years past to survive commercially.

Among the qualitative ratings services in which U.S. commercial broadcasters have shown an interest are those conducted by Marketing Evaluations, Inc. Using questionnaires completed by a random national sample of 1,600 respondents 13 years of age and older, this firm regularly estimates image (familiarity and likability—not necessarily the same thing) ratings of major performers and the popularity of specific programs among various demographic groups. These are commonly known as **Q scores.**

9.6 Broadcast Audiences

Over decades of intensive ratings research, a vast amount of knowledge about electronic media listening and viewing habits has been accumulated. This is surely the most analyzed media activity in history.

Set Penetration

The most basic statistic about broadcast audiences is **set penetration** or **saturation**—the percentage of all homes that have broadcast receivers. In the United States, radio and TV penetration has long since peaked at more than 98 percent. Indeed, most homes have several radios and more than one TV set. In short, for practical purposes, the entire U.S. population constitutes the potential broadcast audience.

Set Use

HUT measurements tell us the average percentage of TV households actually using sets at different times of the day. Television viewing climbs throughout the day from a low of about 12 percent of households at 7:00 A.M. to a high of about 70 percent in the top prime-time hour

of 9:00 to 10:00 P.M. (Eastern time). Audience levels for television change somewhat with the seasons: Viewing peaks in January–February and bottoms out in June, reflecting some influence of weather and leisure activity on audience availability.

On the other hand, radio listening has a flatter profile than television. Radio listening typically reaches its highest peak during morning drive-time hours, recedes through the midday shifts, and climbs again during the afternoon drive-time period. Listening after 6:00 P.M. continually declines through the evening, as more listeners begin watching TV news and then prime-time programming. Unlike TV viewing, radio listening has very little seasonal variance.

TV as Habit

Long-term trends aside, people tend to turn on their TV sets day after day in the same overall numbers, with no apparent regard for the particular programs that may be scheduled. Expressed in terms made famous by Marshall McLuhan, the *medium* matters more than the *message*. Paul Klein, former CBS programming chief, proposed a similar theory, that of the **least objectionable program (LOP)**. He theorized that people stay with the same station until they are driven to another station by an objectionable program. But even if they find *all* programs objectionable, they will stay tuned to the least objectionable one rather than turn off the set. Although such tuning behavior still frequently occurs, the presence of hundreds of TV channels available from cable and DBS services and the strategy of targeting particular demographic groups may be curtailing such actions.

Impact of Remote Controls

A corollary of LOP was **tuning inertia**. Whether because of viewer loyalty to a station or network, or simple laziness before widespread use of remote controls, viewers tended to leave sets tuned to the same station. Tuning inertia still strongly affects radio audiences; in large markets with as many as 40 stations from which to choose, listeners tend to confine their tuning to only two or three favorites.

By the late 1980s, however, remote-control devices (RCDs) for television—and the increased number of available channels—began to modify old patterns. Whereas fewer than 30 percent of households had remote controls in 1985, today they are a ubiquitous household device. One result has been **restless viewers**, or **grazers**—those who use a remote control to switch rapidly among several channels.

Time Spent

The total amount of time that people devote to television serves as a broad measure of its audience impact.

This statistic arouses the most widespread concern among critics: Any activity that takes up more time than sleeping, working, or going to school—as watching television does for many viewers—surely has profound social implications.

In the 1982–1983 television season, average daily viewing per household was 6 hours and 55 minutes (or, more precisely, at least the TV set was turned on for that length of time). By 2007, the average TV household tuned in for 8 hours and 14 minutes. Exhibit 9.i details other average viewing levels by various demographic groups. According to Arbitron, radio use by all people age 12 and over averaged 19 hours per week in 2007, down slightly from previous years (see Exhibit 9.j).

Exhibit 9.i

TV Viewing Trends

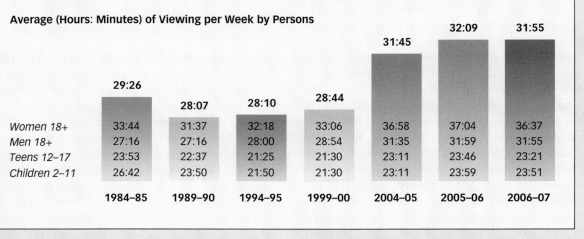

Average (Hours: Minutes) of Viewing per Week by Persons

	1984–85	1989–90	1994–95	1999–00	2004–05	2005–06	2006–07
(Total)	29:26	28:07	28:10	28:44	31:45	32:09	31:55
Women 18+	33:44	31:37	32:18	33:06	36:58	37:04	36:37
Men 18+	27:16	27:16	28:00	28:54	31:35	31:59	31:55
Teens 12–17	23:53	22:37	21:25	21:30	23:11	23:46	23:21
Children 2–11	26:42	23:50	21:50	21:30	23:11	23:59	23:51

The amount of time people spent viewing television has actually remained remarkably stable between the 1984–1985 and the 2006–2007 seasons. Time spent viewing dipped in the 1990s and then recovered to reach new heights during 2005–2006.

During the 2006–2007 season, the amount of time the average viewer spent watching television dipped slightly across all demographic categories.

Average (Hours: Minutes) of Viewing per Week by Households

	1975	1980	1985	1990	1995	2000	2005	2006	2007
Hours: Minutes	43:42	46:06	50:00	48:29	50:42	52:35	57:17	57:39	57:37
Other	8%	15%	16%	18%	19%	21%	23%	23%	24%
Sat.–Sun. Day	15%	15%	15%	15%	15%	15%	15%	15%	15%
Late Fringe	10%	9%	9%	9%	10%	10%	10%	10%	10%
Primetime	32%	28%	27%	26%	25%	25%	23%	23%	23%
Early Fringe	15%	14%	14%	14%	13%	12%	12%	12%	12%
Mon.–Fri. Day	20%	19%	19%	18%	18%	17%	17%	17%	17%

In 2007, weekly TV tuning for the average household was 57 hours and 37 minutes per week, down slightly from 2006. Distribution of tuning by daypart has remained relatively consistent over the past 30 years. Prime-time remains the most viewed single period, followed by "Other" which combines Overnight, Early Morning, and other remaining periods. While there has been some decline in prime-time tuning, other dayparts have remained relatively stable. (Estimates may not add up to 100% due to rounding.)

Source: Tables are Copyrighted information of The Nielsen Company, licensed for use herein.

Exhibit 9.j

Radio Listening Patterns

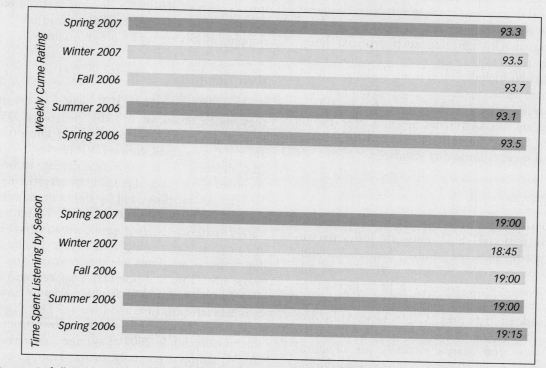

At least 93 percent of all teenagers and adults listen to radio each week. The average radio listener tunes in for about 19 hours per week—that adds up to almost 1,000 hours of listening per year.

These graphs track radio listening for all people aged 12 and older. The top graph demonstrates that more than 93 percent of all radio listeners tune in at least once a week.

The bottom graph illustrates time spent listening to radio in hours and minutes per week, Monday through Sunday, 6:00 A.M. to midnight.

As technology changes and new generations of consumers begin using media, new habits develop. Children may now turn to computers rather than television for entertainment. And many students today choose to listen to their favorite music via MP3 players rather than the radio and watch episodes of their favorite network programs on Internet streams.

 **Cable Audiences**

Researching audiences that subscribe to a cable or DBS service somewhat parallels the patterns familiar in broadcast research, in terms of both methods and findings.

Cable Research

Cable networks determine their potential audience on the basis of households that subscribe to a cable or DBS service and have their networks available to viewers in the subscribing household.

Because of the large number of available channels (with more being added all the time), the total audience subdivides into many small groups, posing some measurement difficulties.

Cable Ratings

Nielsen introduced audience reports for a few national cable networks in 1979, gradually increasing the amount of information provided on basic and pay networks. Based on Nielsen's national People Meter sample, the *Nielsen Homevideo Index* (*NHI*) issues national audience estimates for more than 90 cable networks. Daily overnight reports are produced just as those for the broadcast networks. Among the published reports that track cable audiences are the quarterly *Cable National Audience Demographic Reports* and *Nielsen Cable*

Audience Reports, which provide cable household viewing data in all dayparts for the measured national cable and broadcast networks.

However, local cable audiences are far more difficult to measure than national audiences. Political boundaries define cable franchise areas, which often comprise only a single county or even just part of one; whereas broadcast signals, by ignoring such artificial lines, create larger markets that are more cost-effective to measure. Nielsen includes local cable viewing only in markets where cable audiences reach minimum TV reporting levels, usually a share percentage of 3 or more. Local audience estimates are now reported in *Total Viewing Source* reports that include all stations and channels that meet reportability standards.

Uses of Cable

By the mid-1980s, research had begun to show clear evidence of national cable network influence on audience-viewing patterns. Among households subscribing to cable in the February 2007 sweeps, ad-supported cable networks collectively had a prime-time viewing share of 56 percent, compared with 42 percent for the broadcast networks. Cable viewership now regularly exceeds the collective audience levels of broadcast television across virtually all segments of the viewing day and all demographics, according to analysis of Nielsen data. (*NCTA 2008 Industry Overview*, p. 7). Use of television increases in households with more than one set and as more than one set is connected to cable television.

9.8 Recording Devices

A 2007 study estimated that approximately 95 percent of TV viewing is of live TV (Leichtman Research Group, 2007). But the ability to record programming for later playback is becoming more consumer-friendly, creating challenges for audience measurement.

The original device for time-shifted viewing of TV programs was the video cassette recorder (VCR). From the time VCRs were introduced, programs have been credited with viewing when a program was recorded. The VCR contribution to a program's rating is reported in Nielsen's published reports. Advertisers and advertising agencies have long argued that this inflates ratings. Although once present in about 80 percent of U.S. households, many VCRs are no longer in use, displaced—at least as a playback device—by digital video disc (DVD) players, now found in about 82 percent of households.

In 2007, about 27 percent of U.S. households had a digital video recorder (DVR). The introduction of DVRs has made it possible to credit ratings only for the playback of recorded programs.

On the horizon—if it survives legal challenges—is the remote server DVR (RS-DVR) that would allow cable customers to record and playback TV programs from servers stored at a cable company's headend. Television programmers are attempting to block the introduction of RS-DVRs, fearing that the popularity of such a service could lead to a large increase of ad skipping as viewers replay programming.

DVR Research

Time shifting enables DVR owners to control when they watch broadcast or cable programs. DVRs also facilitate skipping commercials by **zipping** (the avoidance of commercials during DVR playback) or **zapping** (the deletion of commercials during recording). A recorded program (and possibly its advertisements) may be seen several times and by different viewers, or the ads may be seen only once, if at all. To trace all these varied patterns, Nielsen produces audience estimates for time-shifted viewing with DVRs. Program ratings for national programs are reported in three separate ways: Live, Live + Same Day Playback, and Live + 7 Day Playback. Local audience estimates now include two data streams: Live and Live + 7 Day Playback.

Another development that has grown from DVRs is the introduction in 2007 of average commercial minute (ACM) ratings. Previously, national ratings have represented the audience to the average minute of the program—including program content, commercial content, and promotional content. Nielsen's ACM data provides viewing estimates for the minutes with commercial content only. Buyers and sellers of national TV advertising have multiple streams of time-shifted commercial minute data to evaluate and use for negotiating advertising rates. Many have selected Live + 3 Days of DVR playback as the preferred metric, known as "C3." Only minutes with commercial content that are viewed in "Play" mode (not fast forward or rewind) are credited for the ACM calculation.

9.9 Measuring Internet Use

Unlike audience ratings of conventional media, such as radio, television, and cable, that have used essentially the same methodology and terminology for decades, the Internet has generated a flurry of new ways to account for on-line activity. In fact, the term *ratings* is seldom used in the new world of digital interaction. Industry groups, such as the Interactive Advertising Bureau and the Online Publishers Association, have been trying to establish measurement guidelines, but so far the field is so new and unpredictable that rigid guidelines are probably premature. The primary reason for such turmoil is that the Internet is so fundamentally different from conventional media, particularly in the way audiences approach and respond to the medium. The ultimate goal for most of these measurement services is to provide clients with worthwhile information that will enable them to make money through some type of business model, such as advertising, subscriptions, per-download fees, referrals, or some type of retail transaction.

Beginning in the mid-1990s, many companies began to provide some type of "ratings" data. The new buzz phrase **web traffic analytics** refers specifically to looking at the data that comes from user activity on a given web site. In most cases, web data comes from log files, capturing all the requests that users make to the web site's servers. Software then translates the coded requests into tables, charts, and graphs that give a picture of what users are doing on the site. Another type of web measurement tool is an embedded "tag" associated with each page that can be tracked through the server. This data is then pulled into a software program that allows the analyst to interpret the data. Typically, these measurement companies provide summary reports to their clients on a monthly basis. Most reports are divided into two main sections, namely overall **site metrics** and **page-level metrics**. These analyses typically track the anonymous movement of visitors, but there is a third level of analysis offered by some companies that examines important characteristics of the actual users. These user metrics (sometimes called **user-centric data**) track Internet activity by installing a device on the computers of willing volunteers in a fashion not unlike the sample-based audience meters used by Nielsen and Arbitron to measure broadcast and cable audience behavior. In fact, both Nielsen and Arbitron have invested in Internet measuring services, but unlike those companies' almost monopolistic status with conventional ratings, the Internet measurement business has many players.

Recognizing that Internet measurement is evolving quickly and that competing companies are experimenting with a variety of methodologies and jargon, we can consolidate most of their efforts into a list of some fundamental units of measure, which are presented here:

- total number of visitors or "hits"
- number of repeat visits versus "unique visits" (similar to cume for broadcasters)
- average number of page-views per visitor
- most requested pages
- average duration of a visit to the overall site
- average duration of particular page visits
- sequence of pages viewed by visitors from entry to exit
- number of advertisement click-throughs for additional product information
- number of visitor transactions in which something is requested or purchased

- high and low traffic times of day
- source links from other web sites or search engines
- demographic, lifestyle, and purchasing behavior of Internet users

As discussed briefly in Chapter 6, web-based media companies can make money several ways, with the most common being some type of fee for inserting advertising messages or brand logos. The simplest model is based on mere exposure or *impressions* based on the number of page-views. A more demanding model looks only at recorded click-throughs, indicating visitor interest in the ad content. Raising the bar even higher, some models are based only on some type of visitor response, such as a request for additional information or a money transaction. Obviously, the name of the game for success is attracting as many visitors as possible, or **traffic,** as the industry calls it. Web sites often aim to increase their visitor traffic through inclusion on various search engines, which typically want some type of compensation for generating these visits. As opposed to a pay-per-view model, search engine marketing is usually paid monthly or annually, and most search engine companies cannot promise specific results for their fees. Web traffic can also be increased by purchasing non-Internet based advertising, such as TV commercials and magazine ads.

A traffic analysis can help not only advertisers looking for targeted audiences, but also web site owners in making their sites more appealing to users. For example, an operator may want to check web site traffic activity each time a home page is modified or when the navigation schemes within a site are adjusted. This data can provide a better understanding of how web site design affects visitor behavior. The more attractive and user-friendly the web site, the more likely visitors will respond to embedded advertising and other marketing devices intended to generate revenue.

One interesting digression from measuring traditional web sites' traffic is the tracking of Internet radio listening. Today, most radio stations operate a web site that offers streamed audio of their over-the-air programming, plus specialized audio channels. comScore and Arbitron recently formed a partnership to provide traditional broadcast ratings for the on-line radio industry. Not to be outdone, in 2008 the Nielsen Company introduced its own streaming measurement tool called VideoCensus, which is intended to provide audience data for all kinds of streamed audio and video program content.

To capture demographic and consumer attitude information about visitors and to provide clients with comparable information about competitors' web sites, Internet measurement companies must go beyond anonymous traffic data and examine the individuals that make up the traffic. Several companies, most notably Nielsen NetRatings, comScore, and Hitwise, collect data from diverse panels of web users who have installed software on their computers that tracks their Internet use. Scanning tens of thousands of individuals selected randomly over the course of a year, respondents are asked a variety of questions about their Internet use, as well as demographic and lifestyle information. The makeup of the panels, in theory, replicates the universe of Internet users. In short, this is the Internet equivalent of the broadcast ratings discussed earlier in this chapter.

These panels provide clients with the ability to conduct all sorts of survey research intended to reveal many "off-line" behaviors and attitudes about products and services offered on a stand-alone web site or a web site associated with a conventional store, such as a retail outlet. Targeted panel participants can be asked about anything from product usage to brand loyalty. Of course, these panelists can refuse to participate in a particular survey, which may hurt the representativeness of the sample, and there is no way to determine that participant responses are in fact truthful. Another challenge for researchers is the accessing of the Internet from locations outside the home and from mobile devices.

Presenting the full array of specialized client services offered by the dozen or more companies that have surfaced in recent years is beyond the scope of this chapter, but one unique new service is worth noting because its methodology is like no other, at least for now.

Nielsen NetRatings offers a range of proprietary research tools and services to help meet business challenges. One of the most advanced is its Homescan Online, the first service to measure both consumers' on-line activity and off-line purchasing behavior. Integrating product bar codes scanned by cashiers with customer ID cards given to on-line panelists, this tool creates a direct "single source" connection between on-line marketing activity and off-line purchasing behavior. It is interesting to note the similarity between Homescan Online and Arbitron's ScanAmerica—an unsuccessful attempt in the early 1990s to provide a similar service linking TV viewing with purchasing behavior.

In coming years, the number of competing companies offering Internet measurement will probably decrease as some businesses fail to attract a sufficient number of clients or are bought out by larger, more successful firms. The number may even shrink to only a small handful, as did the conventional broadcast ratings business now dominated by Nielsen and Arbitron. The future is uncertain as to who will survive, but there is no uncertainty that the Internet itself, with its millions of users, will survive and prosper for decades to come.

9.10 Other Applied Research

Nonratings research tries to find out what people like and dislike, what interests or bores them, what they recognize and remember, and what they overlook and forget. To study such subjective reactions, investigators usually use *attitudinal* research methods, which reveal not so much people's actions (such as set use) as their reactions—their *reasons* for action, as revealed in their attitudes toward programming and advertisements. Large advertisers are increasingly interested in attempts to measure "consumer engagement," including the mental and emotional connections people have with the programs they view and the possible effects on product and brand perceptions.

Focus Groups

Commercial attitudinal research often makes no attempt to construct probability samples, because it usually does not try to make estimates generalizable to whole populations. Instead, investigators choose respondents informally. They assemble small panels, called **focus groups**, and gain insights about people's motivations through informal discussion interview sessions.

Program concept research, for example, tries out ideas for potential new shows. A focus group's reactions to a one-page program description can help programmers decide whether to develop an idea further, to change details, or to drop it entirely. Advertisers often test concepts for commercials before making final commitments to full production. These tests may use simple graphic storyboards, or they may employ **photomatics**, video versions of original storyboards with camera effects and audio added to make them look and sound something like full-scale commercials.

To test new or changed programs, producers often show pilot versions to focus groups. People watch, give their reactions, and sometimes discuss reasons for their attitudes with a session director. Frequently, producers, writers, and others study reactions by watching these discussions through one-way mirrors or by screening video of the session. Increasingly, web site designers are testing new sites in similar ways.

Program Analysis

Minute-by-minute reactions to a program can be studied using a **program analyzer**—a device first developed in the 1940s and now thoroughly computerized—which enables test-group members to express favorable, neutral, or unfavorable reactions by pushing buttons at regular intervals on cue. The machine automatically sums up the entire test group's reactions, furnishing a graphic profile. A follow-up discussion can then probe for reasons why audience interest changed at given moments in a script, as revealed by peaks and valleys in the graph.

Theater vs. In-Home Testing

The movie industry has long used theater previews to gauge audience response. Several firms specialize in

People have long assumed that spending so much time with electronic media simply had to have some impact, good or bad. Such assumptions take on practical significance when policy decisions are based on imagined or real media impact. For that reason, and because of scientific curiosity, researchers have spent considerable effort exploring media effects. Because many issues surrounding media effects are so emotionally charged, some concerned citizens, advocacy groups, politicians, and even some scientists, may have exaggerated or distorted the findings of studies in the name of a particular agenda. A major objective of this chapter is to not only explain different approaches to the study of media effects, but also to enable the reader to become a more critical consumer of media research.

10.1 Conducting and Evaluating Media Effects Research

Despite many decades of research and hundreds of published studies, the goal of finding important connections between people's consumption of mass media and their resulting behavior has remained a frustrating task. The source of this frustration is that different people can respond in different ways to the same media experience, and therefore, good media effects research, in order to get the best understanding of what is truly going on, needs to analyze not only characteristics of the media, but also characteristics of the **audience** as well. Age, gender, education, race, ethnicity, and dozens of cultural and lifestyle factors, from hobbies to religious beliefs, can all influence the way a person will respond to media exposure. The bottom line is that researchers now strongly believe that the background audiences bring to their use of electronic media is more important to understanding media "effects" than any study of media itself. In addition, despite what some commentators and critics wish to believe, audiences are not always passive, uncritical, gullible receivers of media content, incapable of resisting the manipulations of marketers and politicians.

Of course, to deny absolutely the influence of media on human thought and behavior is equally wrong. Media technology and the content it distributes to audiences are factors that cannot be ignored, but must be understood within the context of many other influential factors.

Research has found that, depending on an array of circumstances, audiences can be primarily passive and easily influenced in a direct way by media or relatively active and critical of media content. Human beings are complex creatures, and as a result, social scientists, including media scholars, have had a difficult time predicting people's attitudes and actions. When asked to make such predictions, the most common response by researchers has been "It depends." This is not a confession of simply not knowing, but rather an acknowledgement of how complicated the study of media effects can be. Before we explore the different ways to understand how electronic media interact within our lives, we first need to think about how we define the terms "media" and "effects."

What Do We Mean by "Media"?

One must examine carefully the definition of "media," as researchers today make a distinction between the effects of media **content** versus the effects of media **technology**. An analogy would be an examination of the influences of *software* (i.e., content) versus *hardware* (i.e., the device that provides the content) on audience attitudes and behavior. For example, the introduction of the cell phone has changed how our society communicates, and consequently, the way people relate to one another. The technology itself, regardless of the content of our phone messages, has had an important "effect" on our culture. In recent years, with the launching of so much new media technology, from cell phones and MP3 players, to satellite radio and high definition television, the study of media effects now encompasses not only words, pictures, and sounds, but also the technological delivery systems. As will be elaborated on later in this chapter, the adage of "The medium is the message" has become more relevant than ever before.

Although the term "media" by definition should include all types of media, in recent decades, media effects research has focused almost exclusively on one prominent mass communication system, namely television. On occasion, researchers have investigated the influence of other mass media, such as newspapers, radio, and motion pictures, but none has captured the ongoing concern and controversy to the degree that the television has. From encouraging violence and obesity among children, to corrupting politics and contributing to illiteracy, television has been blamed for many of society's ills and yet we can't stop watching. Years ago, renowned playwright and screenwriter Paddy Chayefsky saw the irony of America's preoccupation with television when he observed that, "Television is the menace that everyone loves to hate but can't seem to live without." Indeed, despite all the distractions of Internet-based media, Americans today watch more television (including broadcast and cable television) than ever before: The average adult watches more than four hours of television per day, and the average household watches more than eight hours per day. This viewing activity is at an historic high. Of course, audiences today now have extraordinary choice of television content, approaching over 200 channels for many U.S. households.

In fact, the word television has become difficult to define precisely. **Technological convergence**, fostered by the adoption of digital communication, has blurred the once-familiar distinctions among "television" from broadcasting, "television" from cable, "television" from satellite, or "television" from computers. Conventional print and electronic media content can now be **digitized** and offered to consumers through a variety of electronic sources or **platforms**, including over-the-air broadcast, satellite, microwave, cable, telephone, fiber optics, and the Internet. Essentially, content is no longer attached exclusively to any particular delivery device. As a result, looking at media effects in recent years has become even more complicated. For example, are the possible effects of viewing a Hollywood movie different depending on whether an individual watches it in a movie theater, on TV at home, downloaded to a laptop computer, or streamed to a smart phone?

What Do We Mean by "Effects"?

In addition to making sure we know what we mean by media, we must be equally confident that we appreciate the problems in defining effects. Sometimes we take for granted certain common words and their definitions without questioning their influence on how we make decisions and conduct our lives. For example, "effects" often is interpreted as synonymous with "causes." That is, the media are said to cause change in human attitudes and behavior. But much scientific research cannot prove that A causes change in B, but only that A and B appear to change together. People sometimes confuse two things happening together as a direct "cause and effect" relationship, when in truth the two activities may be closely associated, but one does not necessarily cause the other to happen. Instead, another factor may be responsible for the observed change.

Professional researchers and statisticians use the term **correlation** to describe two or more events that appear to occur together in a systematic way, but do not provide evidence that one is the direct result of the other. Misinterpreting *correlation* for *causation* can lead to false conclusions about genuine effects. For example, researchers have found an obvious mathematical correlation between the number of deaths due to drowning and the purchase of ice-cream cones; that is, as one increases or decreases so does the other in a similar fashion. *Therefore, we should not eat ice cream for fear of increasing the chances of drowning*! What makes this recommendation silly? The answer is *summer*. The number of drownings and the number of ice cream cones purchased indeed rise and fall together in a highly predictable way, not because ice cream causes drowning, but because of the season. Would anyone describe this as an "ice cream effects study"? Of course not, but the

results of many scientific studies have been distorted or misinterpreted by sponsoring organizations and the press. Even without a background in statistics or research methods, a student of media, using some common sense and critical thinking, can uncover misrepresentations of causal conclusions. One clue is to see if the researchers conducted a controlled experiment rather than a simple survey. These methods will be explained in more detail later in this chapter.

Another issue surrounding many media effects studies is that by the time the results are released to the general public, the findings or conclusions derived from these findings have been exaggerated. In much social science research, statistical results often are disappointingly small. Regrettably, press releases and other public disclosures will deliberately ignore the statistics and say things such as, "researchers have found a direct connection between A and B" or "studies have found a close relationship between A and B." What is missing is the *strength* of the connection or the *size* of the relationship. Within the social sciences, one can be assured that if enough factors (i.e., variables) are analyzed, just about any study can reveal some correlation. After all, our world is hugely interconnected, but some things are more interconnected or correlated than others. When examining the results of a study, an important question to ask is *how big*? Professional and academic researchers often use the term *effects size* to describe the size or magnitude of one variable influencing another. Media effects studies are notorious for finding tiny effects sizes that somehow become important revelations by the time the information is released to the public.

A research phrase often misunderstood by ordinary people is **statistical significance**. In ordinary conversation the word significance means important or noteworthy, but within scientific circles the term has a special meaning that can be misinterpreted as effects size. In simple terms, questions about statistical significance are not about how big, but rather how reliable. This notion of reliability comes from the fact that most social science research studies, and especially mass communication studies, must depend on **random samples** for acquiring information because it would be impossible to survey every single person in a population. For example, earlier in this text we examined how Nielsen and Arbitron attempt to generate random samples of media markets throughout the country. With random sampling comes **sampling error**, often referred to as margin of error. Using the laws of probability, statistical calculations can determine the sampling error of the results provided from a random sample or a comparison of several random samples. The core issue is whether the results could have occurred by mere chance (due to the randomness of the sample) or do the results "beat the odds," and as a result, can be declared *significant*. In reality, significance is simply a measure of how confident the researchers are that, if they repeated the study using many more random samples, their findings, within a margin or error, would be essentially the same. Consistent results time after time is the definition of reliability.

Problems can arise when the phrase **statistically significant** is used to publicize the findings of a study in that "significant" is misinterpreted as important rather than reliable. Within this context, the results of a study may be statistically significant, but the actual effect may be very small and therefore relatively unimportant. For example, the effects of eating bananas on your mood could very well be "statistically significant," but would be tiny, almost imperceptible, whereas the effect of a death in your immediate family would also be "statistically significant," but obviously much larger in magnitude. Unfortunately, as with our discussion of correlations mentioned earlier, the general public often is presented with news reports about a study boasting of "statistically significant findings" that falsely imply importance (i.e., large effect size), but in reality, this phrase means simply the results went beyond a specified margin of error. Again, many effects studies released to the general public fail to properly explain the unique definition of significance used by the scientific community, and as a result, people can overreact to the results. A savvy critic of a research study will realize the limitations of the term "significant" and look deeper into the findings of the exercise to see whether the data are truly meaningful or trivial.

A student of media should be suspicious of any research that has been "commissioned" or "sanctioned" by an organization that holds an obvious opinion about a controversial issue. Rather than seeking any real insight into an often complex issue, these groups sometimes turn to contrived research studies intended solely to support their already entrenched opinions.

Along with these obvious conflicts of interest among sponsoring organizations, we also must deal with more subtle issues of potential bias in what some researchers call "the people problem." Researchers face the frustrating problem that conclusions about media effects usually consist of people's subjective responses that are hard to verify by direct observation and measuring instruments. Much effects research today relies in whole or in part on questioning people about their subjective experiences—how they think and feel about something—rather than on observing their reactions. Regrettably, these self-reporting research techniques are not altogether reliable. Depending on the topic, people are sometimes unwilling—or unable—to tell the truth about their true opinions or recollections, or they may be forgetful or unaware of their own subconscious motivations. For decades, media scholars and professionals have been forced to deal with the dilemma that audience attitudes are not always good predictors of audience behavior. In other words, what people *say they do* is not necessarily what they *actually do*. For example, the types of TV programs people claim they watch often do not correspond with the viewing behavior data coming out of Nielsen meters.

A final caution concerning the study of media effects is that the notion of effects can be a two-way street because people affect the media too. Many media business professionals would argue that the way audiences respond to program content (such as audience ratings) affect what the media provide. That is, the media simply reflect the needs and desires of the audience, not the other way around. The question of whether the media *mold* or *mirror* human thoughts and actions has fostered an ongoing debate that is at the center of any thoughtful discussion of media effects. Rather than ask whether audiences are easily influenced by the media, it might be better to ask when and under what conditions they are influenced and when they are not. Yes, audiences react to the media, but the media also react to audiences. One could argue that prior chapters in this text that addressed stations, networks, programming, and sales all address examples of "audience effects."

What Do We Mean by a "Theory"?

We began this chapter by calling attention to the need to define exactly what we mean by the terms *media* and *effects*. We also set the stage, hopefully, for you to exercise some critical thinking about how media effects research is conducted and interpreted for public consumption. All good science-based research, regardless of the field of inquiry, from the physical sciences such as chemistry, physics, and biology, to the social sciences, such as sociology, psychology, and mass communication, work with theories. A scientific theory is in simple terms a **causal explanation** of an occurrence. It attempts to explain how and why things happen. No one theory can provide all the answers to big questions, such as media effects. All theories are partial; all theories leave something out. A single occurrence can be understood using a number of theories, each taking a special point of view. Just as a doctor may use several different diagnostic tools, such as heartbeat, blood pressure, temperature, x-rays, and blood analysis to support various theories about the well-being of a patient, so social scientists attempt to understand all kinds of human events by creating plausible theories that are then tested using various research techniques.

Testing Theories Using Research Methods

How do we know how accurate and useful a theory is? The answer is to test it. Investigators usually select one of five major types of research, described in the following paragraphs.

▶ **Sample surveys.** The research strategy most familiar to the public is the sample survey used in opinion polls and audience ratings reports. Such surveys can estimate characteristics of entire populations through the use of very small, but highly representative, samples. Although surveys can provide all kinds of interesting information in terms of how often things occur and how closely associated things can be, surveys tell us nothing about causes, despite what some interpreters of this type of data want to believe. A researcher may ask survey participants to disclose the effects media have on them through self-reports, or the researcher may simply observe participant behavior.

▶ **Content analysis.** Rather than concentrating on audiences, content analysis concentrates on media content. Classification of programs into various categories constitutes one form of content analysis. On a more sophisticated level, content analysis categorizes, counts, and interprets message content. Media researchers have used content analysis to study advertising copy, censors' actions, TV specials, violent acts in programs, and the portrayal of minorities in television dramas. As with the previously mentioned survey technique, the results from any content analysis cannot be linked with causation. In fact, content analysis does not directly address media effects at all. Merely itemizing the number of times a certain item of interest occurs within an entertainment program, newscast, commercial, or magazine story does not provide causal proof of the effects of these items on audiences.

▶ **Laboratory experiments.** Researchers are able to control some experimental factors precisely while excluding others through laboratory experiments. By manipulating independent variables, researchers can get closer to determining causation and genuine "effects." The key to understanding better a proposed "effect," whether it is a study to determine the effect of new medicine or new media, is to be sure that extraneous factors—sometimes referred to as **confounding variables**—do not interfere with the findings of a study. From a scientific perspective, three criteria must be satisfied before the notion of causation between two variables can be supported. First, changes in the two must be closely associated or *correlated*. Second, the timing of these changes must be correct in that the supposed causal changes of the independent variable must occur *before* one observes changes in the dependent variable. Finally, the third criteria demands that all conceivable extraneous factors (i.e., possible confounding variables) are controlled by the researcher. Survey data can satisfy the initial two criteria, but only a controlled experiment can provide the final requirement to provide convincing evidence of "effects" as being truly causal. Unfortunately, lab experiments put people in artificially simplified situations unlike the complex ways in which most of us actually use media.

▶ **Field studies.** Behavior that is recorded in "the real world" without unduly intruding on or otherwise influencing participants is known as field studies. In studying the impact of violent programming, for example, field-study researchers can watch children in their normal home or school environment rather than in a lab setting. However, these experiments require a great deal of time and effort to arrange, and some of their methods can be just as questionable as those used in laboratories. The obvious trade-off between lab studies and field studies is the degree of control the researcher has in designing the study.

▶ **Ethnographic studies.** Here the researcher becomes part of the (usually small) group being studied, and this **participant observation** over extended time periods allows a realistic "window"

Exhibit 10.a

Psychophysiology Anyone? A Typical Lab Experiment

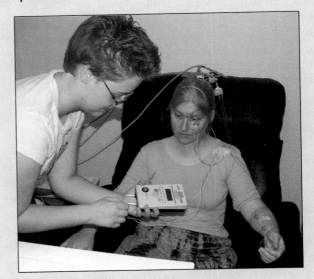

Some researchers employ psychophysiological measures to investigate how media impact variables such as attention and emotional response. Here, a researcher prepares sensors to measure a participant's heart rate, skin conductance, and facial muscles while watching a television program.

Source: Photo courtesy of Michael A. McGregor.

on media consumption patterns to develop, along with some sense of subtle media effects. Ethnographic studies are expensive because of their intensive and time-consuming nature and are not readily generalizable to larger groups in society because of their narrow study-group base.

Regardless of the research method chosen, the selected variables and conditions under which these variables operate are the crucial elements in a meaningful study of media effects. Differences in individual psychology and values, membership in a particular social group, disparities in income, religion, age, gender, and other demographic characteristics can often overwhelm the persuasive power of a mass medium message. A properly constructed research study must recognize differences in what individuals will find of interest and what messages they will choose to be exposed to, how closely they will pay attention to those messages, how those messages will be interpreted, and how those messages will ultimately "affect" them.

10.2 Communication as a Process—A Simple Communication Model

Before looking at media effects theories, we need to understand that communication involves a chain of events, and it is best explained as a *process*. Study of the process can be directed to any one, or any combination, of five different elements: (1) **originators** of messages, (2) **contents** of messages, (3) **channels** through which messages travel, (4) **audiences** that receive messages, and finally (5) **effects** of messages. A pioneer communications researcher, Harold Lasswell, summarized these stages by saying that the objects of research could be identified by posing the question, *"Who says what in which channel to whom with what effect?"* (adapted from Smith et al., 1946: 121).

Communication researchers interested in effects (number 5) typically focus on one of the other four components.

▶ Researchers study the "who" of communication to learn about sources and shapers of media content—those who act as **gatekeepers**. FCC regulation and station or network "clearance" offices are types of gatekeeping, as is the selection, placement, and editing of all content presented.

▶ "What" studies usually consist of content analyses of electronic media programming and thus concern us only insofar as they indicate potential impact—as with measures of the amount and types of violence present in programs of different kinds aimed at different audiences.

▶ As to the "which channel" question, research shows that media channels differ in their psychological impact because audiences form expectations for each medium and interpret what each delivers accordingly. The term "channel" should not be interpreted as a "TV channel," but rather as any type of transmission device or platform.

▶ Ratings are an example of the "to whom" factor of Lasswell's model inasmuch as they detail media use with **media exposure** or **time-spent** data. Breakdowns of audiences into demographic subcategories give further details about the "to whom" of broadcasting. But in researching the "to whom" question, scholars use more detailed personal and social-group indicators to study the composition of audiences than does ratings research. In particular, the child audience has been extensively analyzed, using variables such as race, intelligence, social class, home environment, and personality type. These analyses relate audience characteristics to effects. Researchers ask questions such as, what types of children will be most likely to believe what they see on television, and what types will imitate what they see?

▶ Finally, Lasswell's "with what effect" culminates his question, because communicators, content, channels, and audiences all help determine the ultimate outcomes of communicating. Exhibit 10.b offers another communication model that can be useful.

10.3 Early Research on Media Effects

Early media research on media effects focused on the impact of **mass propaganda** efforts used during World War I (1914–1918), before broadcasting arrived. After the war, the extent of deception by propagandists on all sides showed how thousands supposedly had been manipulated. The postwar advent of radio broadcasting—along with the emergence of the politically threatening new communist regime in Russia—made fear of increased propaganda manipulation more alarming. This led to more research on the social and psychological dynamics of propaganda.

The 1920s' concept of media impact saw messages as so many bullets of information (or misinformation) aimed at passive groups. Because researchers assumed that messages penetrated and caused specific reactions, the concept became known as the **bullet** or **hypodermic-injection** theory.

By the late 1930s, researchers realized the bullet theory was oversimplified in treating message receivers as mere passive, unthinking targets. New and more sophisticated studies discovered that audiences react to messages as individuals. Media effects, therefore, depend on many variables unique to individual audience

Exhibit 10.b

Another Simple Communication Model

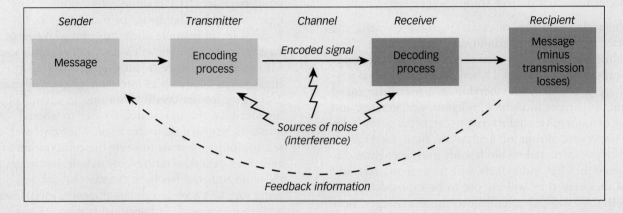

This figure illustrates another simple model of communication, which includes the elements of interference and feedback. The model can be adapted to describe many modes of communi-

cation, from those with no technology (two people talking together) to the most complex (satellite relays of scrambled video signals).

members. Researchers labeled such factors (many not directly observable) **intervening variables** because they come between messages and effects. They vary a message's impact because of each person's previously acquired attitudes, traits, experiences, social situation, and education. Intervening variables explain why an identical message often has a different impact on different people.

One important intervening variable studied in the 1940s was the personal influence of **opinion leaders**, as contrasted with media's *impersonal* influence. One theory suggested that media influence often passes through leaders to followers rather than to all individuals directly. For most people, opinion leaders play a greater role in various decisions than does the direct influence of radio, newspapers, magazines, or books. Other studies confirmed and refined this **two-step flow** hypothesis of media influence (Katz & Lazarsfield, 1955), which had great impact on research for two decades.

Selective Effects

Yet, even opinion leaders are not influenced in direct proportion to the amount of persuasive media content they receive. People pay attention to messages that fit their established opinions and ignore those that don't. Researchers discovered that because of this **selective exposure**, media tend to *reinforce* existing views rather than convert people to new ones. Existing mindsets color how people perceive media they select. Those who select the same message may interpret it in different

ways. Though the stimulus is constant, the response varies. Called **selective perception**, this variable shows that people interpret messages based on their opinions and attitudes rather than receiving them passively (as the old bullet theory had supposed).

Exhibit 10.c summarizes the stages of research development, from the simplistic cause-effect concept of early studies, to our present interest in looking more deeply into the many variables involved in impact.

10.4 A Sampling of Media Effects Theories

Cultivation Theory

Developed by Professor George Gerbner and several colleagues at the Annenberg School for Communication at the University of Pennsylvania in the 1960s and 1970s, **cultivation theory** takes an all-encompassing look at the power of television to influence people's perceptions, attitudes, and values about the world in which they live. In particular, Gerbner's research focused on heavy users of television and how they tend to see the world as television portrays it. For instance, survey results found that heavy users saw their world as more violent and threatening than light users. The term "cultivation" was derived from the notion that the long-term repetition of television's mass-produced messages and images subtly "cultivate" viewers' perceptions of reality. Television is thought to be a substitute for many

Exhibit 10.c

Development of Media Effects Research

Time Period	Prevailing Viewpoint	Empirical Basis
1. 1920s–1930s	Mass media have strong effects	Observation of apparent success of propaganda campaigns
		Experiments show immediate attitude change after exposure to messages
2. 1940s–1950s	Mass media largely reinforce existing predispositions, and thus outcomes are likely to be the same in their absence	Evidence of personal influence—persons are more influenced by others than by the mass media
		Evidence of little influence on voting
		No relationship observed between exposure to mass media violence and delinquent behavior among the young
3. 1950s–1960s	Mass media have effects independent of other influences, which would not occur in the absence of the particular mass media stimuli under scrutiny	Evidence that selective perception is only partially operative
		Evidence that media set the context and identify the persons, events, and issued toward which existing predispositions affect attitudes and behavior
		Evidence that television violence increases aggressiveness in the young
4. 1970s–1980s	Process behind effects so far studied may be more general, suggesting new areas for research	Research finds that under some circumstances TV may influence attitudes and behavior *other than* aggressiveness
		Many agenda-setting studies
5. 1980–today	Individual differences in audience background and needs are found central in defining media impact	Qualitative studies (including ethnographies) of media as one of many social resources

Source: First four segments adapted from George Comstock et al., *Television and Human Behavior.* Copyright © 1978. Used by permission of RAND Corporation.

traditional institutions, such as family, school, and church, in teaching the core beliefs and values of a culture. That is, the way people behave on television affects how people behave in real life. In addition, television produces what has been called a "mainstreaming" effect in which cultural diversity and divergent opinions are suppressed in favor of a more homogenized worldview. Mainstreaming also reinforces stereotypes, versions of reality that are deliberately oversimplified to fit preconceived images, such as the stock characters of popular drama: the mad scientist, the bespectacled librarian, the befuddled father, or the absent-minded professor.

The first step in cultivation research is content analysis: in short, the process of studying the subject matter on television. For example, Gerbner and his colleagues charted the content of hundreds of prime-time and weekend children's television programs. Among their findings was that men outnumbered women three to one on television, and that older people, younger people, African Americans, and Hispanics were underrepresented on television. In addition, crime was 10 times as rampant in the "television world" as it was in the real world, based on government statistics. The second step in cultivation research is the cultural indicators analysis—the process of assessing light users and heavy users of television about what the world is like. For example, an analysis of perceptions about violence might ask respondents about the likelihood of being a victim of violent crime.

Cultivation theory has received both praise and criticism over the years. While calling attention to the power of television to be more than a mere source for entertainment, many of the research results have not been as dramatic as some would want to believe. First, most of the scientific research has been survey-based and not experimental, so that the findings are far more correlational than causal. Second, effects sizes have been small, suggesting that many other factors (i.e., intervening variables) are at play. One of these factors is the type or genre of program viewed. For instance, a heavy user of sitcoms and game shows may respond quite differently than a heavy user of police dramas and professional wrestling. Critics also question the notion of mass cultivation in an era of so much choice, thanks to multichannel video sources, such as cable, satellite, and the Internet. Cultivation theory was developed in a time when most U.S. households had a choice of only a small handful of stations and networks. Today, however, many homes have hundreds of channels and web sites from which to select content. Under these circumstances, the idea of cultural mainstreaming seems far more problematic than in prior decades.

Recognizing the shortcomings of cultivation theory, the concerns about heavy users of any type of media, especially among young people, appear worthy of continued research. No doubt, the electronic media have become major agents of socialization—the all-important process that turns a squalling infant into a functioning member of society. Socialization, though a lifelong process, occurs intensively during the first few years of life, the time when children begin to learn the language, detailed rules of behavior, and value system of their culture. The electronic media can, of course, have both good (prosocial) and bad (antisocial) effects. The make-believe world of the electronic media serves as a model of reality for countless people—especially children. Viewers and listeners identify with heroes, participating vicariously in their adventures. Research indicates that young children tend to believe what they see on television, making no distinction between fact, fiction, and advertising. A final concern is media addiction. Excessive use of any medium, whether it is television, the Internet, or video games, can lead to psychological dependencies.

Social Learning Theory

Social Learning Theory, developed by Albert Bandura, is closely associated with the notions of cultivation in that the theory suggests that much learning takes place through observing and modeling the behavior of others. In particular, social learning theory has been applied to the study of the possible effects of TV violence, which will be discussed in more depth later in this chapter. The premise of the theory is that the "others" that people learn from can be not only immediate family, friends, classmates, and workers, but also people on television, both real and fictional. These effects can range from people learning how to wear a new fashion to learning how to respond to someone who angers them.

The necessary conditions for effective modeling include (a) the degree of attention paid to an event, (b) the ability to properly remember the event, (c) the skills necessary to reproduce the event, and (d) the motivation to want to imitate an event. Bandura believed in **reciprocal determinism**, in which the world and a person's behavior cause each other, while **behaviorism** essentially states that one's environment causes one's behavior. Bandura, who was studying adolescent aggression, found this too simplistic, and so in addition he suggested that behavior causes environment as well. This dependency on what others think and do carries over to our next theory—the spiral of silence.

Spiral of Silence Theory

The **spiral of silence** is a political science and mass communication theory asserting that a person is less likely to voice an opinion on a topic if one feels that one is in the minority for fear of reprisal or isolation from the majority. This theory assumes that the mass media have an enormous impact on how public opinion is portrayed, and can dramatically affect an individual's perception about where public opinion lies, whether that portrayal is factual or not. The media's coverage of the majority opinion ultimately becomes the status quo, and those who disagree become less likely to speak out. One can see the danger of a government that has too much control over media content inventing a false "majority" opinion and forcing citizens with contrary opinions to remain silent. As with cultivation theory, there is an assumption of few choices for audiences and the few that are available all portray the same opinion. Again, in a growing multichannel world of almost infinite choice, the idea of a small oligopoly of media sources concocting a phony majority opinion seems more challenging than in the recent past. Also, as more factors are analyzed, the spiral appears less impressive. For example, studies addressing the degree of people's outspokenness were influenced substantially by variables such as age, education, income, interest in current affairs, and the certainty of one's opinion. We can conclude that the power of spiral of silence effect on audiences, as with most communication theories, is more a function of the type of person processing the message than the message itself. In other words, people are not quite as helpless in the face of public opinion as one might believe. In fact, this concern about how "other people" may be manipulated by the media ties in with our next theory.

Third Person Effect

The **third-person effect** hypothesis states that a person exposed to a persuasive communication in the mass media sees it as having a greater effect on others than on himself. As a result, people will often advocate media censorship, not to protect themselves from the dangers of undesirable media effects, but to protect others (i.e., third persons) who are more vulnerable. A number of scholars have speculated that "experts" are particularly likely to overemphasize the effects of the media on others. The third-person effect has been supported by many studies, including perceptions of political campaign advertising, weight loss programming, and pornography. The findings essentially confirm the idea that, "It won't have any effect on me, but I am worried about the effects on them." This communication theory provides some good insight into the much-publicized concerns people have about the alleged power of the media to manipulate unsuspecting audiences. While most people claim that they are seldom if ever naive victims of media effects, these same people are confident that others are not so perceptive and need to be warned, and in some cases protected, from certain undesirable media influence.

Agenda Setting

Agenda-setting theory concentrates primarily on the power of the news media to determine what issues people think are important to their community and personal well-being. In short, although media may not tell us *what* to think, they do tell us what to think *about*. That is, the choices the media consider newsworthy eventually become the burning issues that people care most about. As a consequence, these issues then become the main topics for politicians to debate and run for office on. In essence, the theory maintains that the media agenda determines the public agenda, which in turn, determines the policy agenda of a community or a country.

Media can report only a tiny fraction of everything that happens in a day. On its way to becoming neatly packaged pieces on the TV screen, raw reporting of events passes through many editorial **gatekeepers**. News directors, news producers, photographers, and reporters open and close gates deliberately, deciding which events to cover in which places and how stories should be written, edited, and positioned in the news presentation. Some gatekeeping occurs inadvertently, depending on accessibility of news events or availability of transportation or relay facilities. Some gatekeeping has an institutional or an ideological bias—or both. Institutional biases can develop from news organization priorities ("If it bleeds, it leads"); ideological biases are drawn from individual political,

social, economic, or religious beliefs ("We don't reveal the names of rape victims"). Television demands pictures. This tends to bias the medium toward covering events that can be visualized. Impacts of this visual bias include a preference for airing stories that have dramatic pictures (fires, accidents, disasters) and a forced effort to illustrate nonvisual stories with often irrelevant shots (as when file pictures of bidding on the floor of the stock exchange illustrate a story on financial trends).

Agenda-setting theory was introduced in 1972 by Maxwell McCombs and Donald Shaw in their groundbreaking study of the role of the media in the 1968 presidential campaign in Chapel Hill, North Carolina. The researchers surveyed 100 undecided voters during the campaign on what they thought were key issues and measured that against the actual media content. The ranking of issues was almost identical. Since then, hundreds of studies have been performed to test the theory. Two basic assumptions underlie most research on agenda-setting: First, the press and the media do not reflect reality, but rather, filter and shape it. Second, media concentration on a few issues and subjects leads the public to perceive those issues as more important than other issues.

The findings from these studies vary greatly depending on several audience factors. For example, an individual's interest in the topic and uncertainty about the issue will influence the "effect" of the news media on setting that person's issue agenda. Another important factor is what researchers called the "obtrusiveness" of the topic, suggesting that an issue is obtrusive if most members of the public have had direct contact with it, and less obtrusive if audience members have not had direct experience. This means that agenda setting is strongest for unobtrusive issues because audience members must rely on media for information on these topics. For example, parents may be very involved in the activities and administration of their children's local school and consequently media news reports would have only a marginal influence on their issue agenda. On the other hand, these same parents may have little or no direct encounters with the government's foreign policy, and as a result, they depend more on the news media to shape their issue agenda. Exhibit 10.d offers one contemporary example of agenda setting.

A valid criticism of agenda-setting theory relates to the fact that news media generally try to be responsive to audience needs and desires. Many large news organizations spend millions of dollars on audience research, desperately trying to find out what viewers, listeners, and readers want from their news sources. Indeed, most news executives would argue that agenda-setting theory does not adequately handle the **reciprocal relationship** between media and audience.

Exhibit 10.d

Agenda Setting: Spotlight on Africa

(A)

The violence in the Darfur region of Sudan had its roots in the 1990s, but escalated to what some have called genocide in 2003. Despite pleas for intervention from groups such as Amnesty International, the U.S. press did not begin covering the story meaningfully until 2004. Coverage began to decline in 2006 when a peace agreement was signed, but the strife continues, as shown by these displaced women and children

(B)

(A). By 2008, the press refocused most of its attention to the violence surrounding the "re-election" of Robert Mugabe in Zimbabwe **(B)**. Is it possible that the U.S. press or the American people can only process one story at a time from Africa?

Sources: Photo (A) from AP Photo/Jose Cendon; photo (B) from AP Photo/Tsvangirayi Mukwazhi.

10.5 The Active Audience Approach

Over time, media effects theory and research began to shift away from a singular focus on the media to a more enlightened focus on how audiences deal with media. Researchers now even avoid talking about *effects* as such. The very word implies an oversimplification of what is now understood to be an extremely complex process. Without denying that specific media content might under specific conditions have specific effects on some specific people, researchers prefer to speak in terms of *associating* certain inputs with certain outputs.

Uses and Gratifications

A result of this increased emphasis on the audience over the media can be observed in a theoretical approach to media consumption called **uses and gratifications (U&G)**. This line of inquiry links need gratifications and media choice clearly on the side of audience members. It suggests that people's needs influence what media they would choose, how they use certain media, and what gratifications the media give them. This approach differs from conventional media effects research in that it regards audiences as active media users as opposed to merely passive receivers of information. Rather than studying "what media do to people" and presuming that all people are essentially the same, the uses and gratifications approach is more concerned with "what people do with media" and recognizes that people seek out specific media to satisfy, or "gratify," needs that may not be the same for everybody. These needs, sometimes defined by U&G researchers as **gratifications sought (GS)** can include such things as information, companionship, emotional release, relaxation, and enhanced family relations. Along these same lines, audience satisfaction with the media content received has been defined as **gratifications obtained (GO)**. Although some media scholars would argue that the uses and gratifications approach can be seen as the direct opposite of media effects, a second look at the theory reveals that the two are not totally contrary to each other in that people actively seek out certain media because of the expected *effects* they will experience. For instance, a lonely individual may turn on a TV program desiring the effects of companionship. Similarly, an individual may turn to a particular newscast anticipating the effects will be knowledge of important issues of the day. As traditional mass media and new media continue to provide people with a wide range of media platforms and content, uses and gratifications is considered one of the most appropriate perspectives for investigating why audiences choose to be exposed to different media.

One of the major criticism of uses and gratifications theory stems from the fact that at times audiences are not particularly active or engaged with the media. Sometimes the stereotype of the "couch potato" staring mindlessly at a TV screen is true. But in other circumstances the same person may be highly alert and captivated by what is on the screen. Some researchers have defined two extremes of media consumption as either (a) **ritualistic**, implying the individual has not invested a lot of thought concerning the media choice and is participating mostly out of habit, or (b) **instrumental**, implying that the individual has invested considerable thought about the media selection and has expectations concerning the outcome of the experience.

The ritualistic or habitual type of TV viewing sometimes can be taken to an extreme in which programs seem of secondary importance as long as something fills the screen. This complete indifference to the specific program content, whether it is a sitcom, police drama, or newscast, has been coined the **glow and flow principle**. In short, the electronic media answer a compelling need of the mass audience simply to kill time painlessly, to fill an otherwise unendurable void. But social critics worry that while we relax with our guard down watching television, violence and other antisocial activities portrayed in many programs may produce antisocial effects.

Elaboration Likelihood Model (ELM)

This issue of audience activity or involvement in a media-related experience has been found to be an important variable in understanding media effects in terms of persuasion. For decades, politicians, marketing professionals and advertising professionals have wrestled with the complex and bewildering challenge of creating "effective" messages that will persuade people to change their attitudes or behaviors. Rather than inquiring about what are the most persuasive types of messages, a better question to ask is under what conditions are people easily persuaded and under what conditions are the same people stubbornly resistant to change?

One popular theory that has attempted to answer this question has been the **elaboration likelihood model (ELM)**, developed in the 1980s and typical of the research effort made to better understand how audiences *process* media content. In simple terms, "elaboration" can be understood as "how hard" someone thinks about a topic (psychologists might use phrases such as cognitive activity to denote the same idea). The ELM distinguishes between two routes to persuasion: the **central route** and the **peripheral route**. Central route processing requires a great deal of thought and careful scrutiny of a persuasive message, such as a speech or an advertisement, to determine the merits of the arguments. Peripheral route processing, on the other hand, does not involve elaboration of the message through extensive mental effort, but instead seeks out simpler ways to evaluate the argument presented. Essentially, people are looking for mental "shortcuts" to make a decision. Under these conditions, factors such as the credibility of the source can be important. This is why many consumer brands use experts or celebrities to endorse their products. In politics, a fairly unknown candidate may find that the endorsement by a popular and respected fellow politician may be far more persuasive in changing voters' minds than expecting the voter to pay close attention to a long, complicated speech.

The two factors that most influence which route an individual will take in a persuasive situation are **motivation**, or how willing the person is to elaborate the message, and **ability**, or how capable the person is to elaborate on the message. For example, returning to our political campaign, a voter may not be interested in a particular election and therefore does have the *motivation* to invest a lot of time and energy in carefully studying each candidate's positions. In another circumstance, the voter indeed may be interested in the election, but is in a hurry or does not have access to a TV set to watch a live debate and therefore, does not have the *ability* to carefully study each candidate's positions. In each of these situations, the ELM would predict that the person would opt for the peripheral route rather than a central route for information processing.

In line with ELM and the wider point of view that audiences process media content in different ways, is the principle of consistency or **congruence**, which holds that a person's internal state of mind is usually in balance or congruence. A message that contradicts or is inconsistent with established opinions causes what some researchers have called "cognitive dissonance" or a lack of congruity or an imbalance. An effort to restore balance (conscious or unconscious) follows. It might take the form of rejecting the message (e.g., saying the source is unreliable), distorting the message to make it fit the existing mindset, or, least likely, adjusting the balance by accepting the new idea. Essentially, consistency or congruity theory is the driving force behind **selective exposure** discussed earlier. Researchers have found time and again that media are far more effective in reinforcing the beliefs that people already have and strengthening their positions, than fostering change.

Brand Marketing Theory

ELM and scores of other communication theories have focused on human persuasion, which, of course, includes advertising. Other than violence, no aspect of electronic media impact has been more measured than advertising. Advertisers demand and receive vast amounts of applied research on the reach and effects of their messages. Electronic media advertising often stimulates widespread demand for goods and services for which consumers may have little real need. Advertising can build overnight markets for virtually useless products or "new and improved" versions of old products. Critics often assume from these successes that advertising can overcome most consumer resistance, but advertising professionals only wish that were true. Failure of a huge number of new products every year belies the accusations that advertising is all-powerful. Not only do many products fail to catch on, but leading products also often give way to competitors. As discussed in the introduction of this chapter, people are complex and persuading them to change their attitudes and behaviors often is a daunting task. Again, depending on many intertwined factors and conditions, people can be easily persuaded or not.

The focus on audience processing of messages found in the elaboration likelihood model can be readily adapted to explain consumer purchase behavior and why **brand marketing theory** is so important to competitive businesses. On a very practical level, consumers like brands because they package meaning. They form a kind of shorthand that makes choice easier. They let one escape from a feature-by-feature analysis of category alternatives, and so, in a world where time is an ever-diminishing commodity, brands make it easier to store evaluations. Aside from easing mental effort, strong brands also reduce risk and uncertainty for consumers. A behavioral outcome of relying on brands is the cultivation of habits. In repetitive decision-making situations, habits save time, energy, and apprehension of decision making. For marketing researchers, habitual purchase behavior is the definition of **brand loyalty**. Using ELM terminology, we can see that brand-loyal customers tend to use the "peripheral route" in purchase decision-making. As a result, the effects of mass media advertising typically are more powerful in reinforcing brand loyalty than persuading consumers to switch brands.

The possible impact of commercials and brand marketing in children's programs raises special issues. Children start watching television early in their lives and often find commercials just as fascinating as programs. Consumer organizations have long believed that commercials take unfair advantage of young children—especially preschoolers, who are not yet able to differentiate between advertising and programs. Psychologists and child-health professionals have questioned the use of psychological techniques by advertisers of children's products. They seek to shield children from such commercial manipulation and exploitation.

For decades advertisers used the media as a branding tool, but in recent years the media themselves have realized that they too are consumer brands. The primary motivation for a business to embrace the principles of brand marketing is **competition**, and while the notions of branding are not new to most American consumer goods, they are relatively new to media brands. It was not until the early 1990s that electronic media, in the form of radio, television, cable, and satellite, began to experience massive competition for the attention of scarce audiences. Today, media brands are scrambling to win the hearts and minds of audiences using brand-marketing techniques. The decades-old assumptions surrounding mass communication have fragmented into the far more complex world of satisfying special needs of narrowly defined audiences. The old homogenous mass audience is becoming divided and subdivided into an ever-changing array of new demographic and psychographic "niche" audience categories. The very fact that audiences today have such variety of media content from which to choose surely must have an "effect" on how they regard their media relationships. With almost limitless media options the mind seeks ways to simplify decision making. One common way is to depend on media brand names to uncomplicate the process. For example, studies have found that cable news networks, such as CNN, Fox News, and MSNBC have substantial brand-loyal viewers. Disney's ESPN brand is so strong that National Football League games televised on the ABC broadcast network are now presented as "ESPN on ABC."

Technological Determinism

A final approach to studying media effects deals with technology, rather than the content. As mentioned earlier in this chapter, new ways to create and distribute content can have an "effect" regardless of the intended message. This concept of what some scholars call **technological determinism** is not new. In the 1960s, media philosopher and writer Marshall McLuhan made popular the phrase "the medium is the message" and offered many provocative commentaries in his classic book *Understanding Media* on how societies and cultures are influenced by the type of media available. In particular, he maintained that electronic media (mainly radio and television in his time) are distinctly different from print media in the way they are physiologically and psychologically used by humans. Researchers have attempted to test some of McLuhan's ideas, but most of his notions are so far-reaching and philosophical in nature that they are almost impossible

Exhibit 10.e

Multi-Tasking Made Easy

(A)

(B)

For audiences, the ultimate consequences of media competition coupled with media convergence are increased choice and convenience. "Multitasking" has become part of the new vocabulary of modern media. Simultaneous media activities **(A)**, such as instant messaging, playing video games, downloading music files, and watching television have become second nature to young people. Furthermore, these simultaneous media experiences are enhanced by the development of media-on-demand technology. Emerging video delivery technology, such as video-on-demand (VOD) and personal video recorders (PVRs) are cultivating a new media market-

place in which audiences can select program content at will, without the shackles of program scheduling or having to drive to a rental store or movie theater. Of course, the interaction with media is no longer relegated to the homestead. Wireless access to the Internet and other multichannel services enable people to remain electronically "connected" regardless of their physical location **(B)**. Without delving into the content, the *technology alone* has become a crucial variable in the future study of what we call media effects.

Sources: Photo (A) from Bill Aron/PhotoEdit; photo (B) from Stockbyte/Punchstock.

to test in a scientific sense. Nonetheless, McLuhan's approach recognizes the potential effects of the hardware, as well as the software, on audiences. Today, with so many new technologies being introduced to our culture, many of McLuhan's opinions have received renewed interest. Researchers are just beginning to explore the many human factors that become entwined with the adoption of new communication devices. Among those factors is the notion of multi-tasking presented in Exhibit 10.e.

10.6 The Effects of Media Violence: A Case Study

The discussion of theories of media effects mentioned in this chapter serves only as an introduction to a much bigger field of communication study. Communication researchers have not yet come up with a single unified theory that will explain adequately the effects of mass communication. Instead, we have a number of theories, each intended to explain a particular aspect. The most recent

and relevant research suggest that many contributing factors must converge in order for an "effect" to occur.

To illustrate in more detail many of the topics covered so far, a case study looking at the effects of media violence seems an appropriate way to conclude the chapter. No aspect of the effects of electronic media on human behavior raises more worry than the amount of violence portrayed on the illuminated screens of TV sets, movie theaters, and computers. But the concern that portrayals of violence and crime might have antisocial effects preceded television by many years. The first systematic research on media violence dates to film studies in the 1930s. Accusations about the potential effects of violence shifted to radio and comic books in the 1950s, and later to television, rock videos, computer games, and the Internet. Along the way, emphasis progressed from merely measuring violent content and deploring its presumed effects toward supporting conclusions about effects with explanatory theories.

Since the 1950s, more than 1,000 studies employing every research method available have been done on the effects of violence in television and movies, with the primary focus on children. The majority of these studies have concluded that children who watch significant amounts of television and movie violence are more likely to exhibit aggressive behavior, attitudes, and values. Children are affected at any age, but young children are seen as more vulnerable to the effects of media violence because they have a harder time distinguishing between fantasy and reality. In addition to television, violent video games supposedly are even more troublesome. Studies claim that children who watch more television and play more video games are not only exposed to more media violence, but are more likely to behave more aggressively. Other studies have concluded that television, movies, and music videos normalize carrying and using weapons and glamorize them as a source of personal power.

As a result of this work, Congress and private groups periodically have pressured the FCC to limit televised violence. Chiefly for fear of violating the First Amendment and because of the trend toward deregulation, the FCC has declined to act. However, in 2007 the FCC concluded that regulating TV violence would serve the public interest, particularly during times when children are likely to be viewers. Notwithstanding the dictates of the First Amendment, the FCC concluded that Congress has the authority to regulate "excessive violence" and to extend its reach for the first time into basic-cable TV channels that consumers pay to receive.

Criticism of Media Violence Effects Research

Although organizations such as the American Academy of Pediatrics and the American Psychological Association have suggested that thousands of studies have been conducted confirming the link between media violence and aggressive behavior in real life, others have argued that this information is greatly exaggerated. They maintain that only about 200 studies have been reported in peer-reviewed scientific journals, and only about half of these found some link between media and subsequent aggression, but none demonstrated a connection with violent crime. This means that the remaining half of the studies found nothing. Critics assert that research findings that do not support media/aggression linkage often fail to be reported to the general public. Not reporting such findings is a problem throughout all areas of science, but may be a particular issue for publicized areas such as media violence.

Criticisms of the media violence link focus on a number of issues presented at the beginning of this chapter, including small effects sizes and the failure to account adequately for other variables, such as gender, heredity, personality traits, and exposure to family violence that may explain both why some people become violent and why those same people may choose to

expose themselves to violent media. Truly competent and ethical media violence researchers seldom if ever claim that media violence effects are the only or most important cause of aggressive behavior. Serious aggressive behavior only occurs when there is a convergence of multiple factors of which exposure to some type of media content can be one. Also, critics claim that even when media violence studies do find significant media-related factors, they usually produce very small, short-term effects that do not translate into large effects in the real world. Some would argue that the biggest problem for this body of research is the lack of a convincing correlation between the rise in media violence and the degree of recorded violent crime, which has been cycling up and down throughout human history, seemingly oblivious to mass media circumstances. In this same vein, critics maintain that media violence researchers cannot explain why many countries with media violence rates similar to or equal to the United States, such as Norway, Canada, and Japan, have much lower violent crime rates.

What Do We Mean by Violence?

For television and motion pictures to serve as serious media for adult audiences, we cannot ban all violence. After all, violence occurs in all forms of literature, including even fairy tales for children. Bodies litter the stage when the curtain falls on some of Shakespeare's tragedies. Writers would face a difficult challenge without resorting to violent clashes between opposing forces.

Perhaps the one issue that is at the core of so much of this debate over the relative influence of media violence on behavior is defining precisely what we mean by violence. For example, as conscientious researchers, should we place the violence we observe in a *Roadrunner* cartoon or a slapstick comedy skit such as *The Three Stooges* in the same category as the violence portrayed in Shakespeare's *Macbeth* or the award-winning war movie *Saving Private Ryan*? Should real-world violence and carnage found in daily newscasts be placed in the same category as fictional violence found in a typical police drama such as *Law and Order*? Should we recognize a difference between justified violence and gratuitous violence in media content? Is televised football a violent sport? Do commercials for the armed services glamorize war? The questions are endless and that is the point. Regardless of all the other possible contributing factors (i.e., intervening variables) that may encourage antisocial behavior, we cannot come up with a simple all-purpose definition of violence. Many media scholars would argue that it is not violence itself but the *context* in which it is portrayed that can make the difference between learning about violence and learning to be violent.

Using Different Theoretical Approaches

The study of the effects of media violence was chosen for a case study because not only is it a burning issue, but also because it can be examined from several theoretical approaches already presented in this chapter. For example, **cultivation theory** addresses the cultural impact on heavy users of TV content and how their perceptions of the world can take on the artificial renderings of TV characters and their actions, including violent behavior. **Agenda setting** takes aim at how the news media determine what is important and, in this case, how parents and educators deem media violence as an important issue needing social action. **Social learning theory** looks at how people, especially children, model their behavior based on observations of characters and noteworthy celebrities in the media. That is, people look to the media for guidance as to what is acceptable behavior. Resorting to violence to resolve conflicts can derive from watching how people behave on television. The **third person effect** proposes that, while most people would not confess that they are susceptible to the influences of the media, such as violent content, they would also maintain the contrary view that other people are highly vulnerable to such exposure. **Uses and gratifications theory** concentrates on how people are not necessarily passive recipients of media content, but rather active participants that seek out specific media to gratify their needs and desires. Within this context, violent program content would be analyzed according to what psychological satisfactions it provides for an individual. The **elaboration likelihood model** acknowledges that audiences are not always highly engaged with a media message. Depending on their motivation and ability to process information, including depictions of violence, people sometimes apply critical thinking about what they are viewing, and at other times they can be barely aware of what is on the screen.

Each of these theories offers a different perspective on the topic of media violence. None can satisfy all our questions. No one theory is necessarily "better" than the others. Instead, each provides a unique frame of reference from which to conduct meaningful research.

Responding to Allegations of Media Effects

What do cigarettes, movies, junk food, video games, alcohol, and comic books have in common? These are all examples of media content that offend or frighten certain citizens, politicians, and public interest groups. The mass media content we see and/or hear on television, radio, film, the Internet, CDs, newspapers, books, and magazines are used by these concerned activists to justify restrictions on what mass media can or cannot portray for public consumption. One highly controversial option is to apply government-sponsored censorship. Another course is to encourage industry self-regulation. Media policy and First Amendment issues are not within the scope of this chapter and, in fact, will be discussed in depth in Chapters 11 and 12, but the complexity attached to the whole topic of media effects must be appreciated by all interested students and citizens. The overriding point of this chapter has been that the study of media effects is a complicated and controversial topic that cannot provide simple answers to what often seem to be simple questions.

The Communications Act, Licensing, and Structural Regulation

chapter

The previous chapter surveyed the social effects of the electronic mass media—some real, some probably only imagined. As long as people believe that effects actually occur, they want to have some control over them. They want to maximize beneficial effects (e.g., from wholesome entertainment and useful information) while minimizing perceived harmful effects (e.g., from pornography and misleading propaganda).

Direct social control comes primarily from government licensing, which determines who is allowed to operate stations, cable systems, and other program outlets. Licensing not only selects operators, but also enables the monitoring and regulating of their performance. Regulation starts with the Constitution, on which all laws and administrative controls are based. These controls, in turn, are embedded in the Communications Act, which defines the role of the Federal Communications Commission.

11.1 Federal Jurisdiction

Specific constitutional justification for Congress's taking control of the electronic media comes from Article 1, Section 8(3), which gives Congress power "to regulate commerce with foreign nations, and among the several states." This **commerce clause** has played a vital role in American history, preventing states from erecting internal trade barriers to national unity. The provision forms a link in a chain of responsibility from Constitution to the stations being regulated, as shown in Exhibit 11.a.

Exhibit 11.a

Chain of Legal Authority

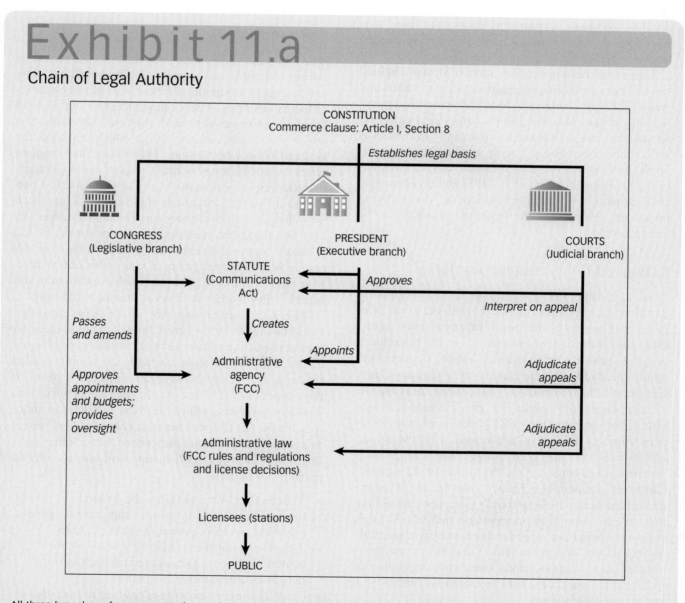

All three branches of government play a role in controlling the electronic media under the general umbrella of the Constitution.

Interstate vs. Intrastate Commerce

The commerce clause gives Congress jurisdiction over *interstate* and *foreign* commerce, but not over commerce within individual states. The law regards radio communications, including all kinds of broadcasting, as **interstate** by definition. Radio (including television) transmissions, even when low in power and designed to cover a limited area within a state, do not simply stop at state boundaries.

Regulation of wireline and cable services, however, differs significantly from that of radio-based services. Local exchange telephone companies and cable systems are usually limited to a specific geographical service area within a state. Because such services are **intrastate**, they are subject to state regulation. States have their own **public utility commissions (PUCs)** that approve changes in in-state telephone rates and services. Long-distance telephone carriers that cross state lines, thus providing *interstate* service, have traditionally needed federal approval for rate and service changes.

Cable (discussed in detail in Section 11.8) is a **hybrid** service. Because a cable system must use city streets and rights of way, it is subject to local and state jurisdiction. A cable system also distributes signals that originate outside the state, so it is subject to federal jurisdiction as well. Once controlled primarily at the state and local levels, cable is now subject to extensive federal regulation. Direct broadcast satellite (DBS) and other services that provide multichannel video or audio using microwave frequencies are regulated exclusively at the federal level.

Delegated Congressional Authority

It is impossible for Congress to dictate regulatory details in all specialized fields. Therefore, it has delegated to a series of **independent regulatory agencies** the authority to oversee such often complex areas as power, transportation, labor, finance, and communication. In the realm of communication, Congress delegated authority to regulate most aspects of the electronic media to the Federal Communications Commission (FCC). Although the president appoints FCC commissioners, with the advice and consent of the U.S. Senate, the Commission remains what some call a "creature of Congress." Congress defined the FCC's role in the Communications Act of 1934, and only Congress can change that role by amending or replacing the Act. Though commissioners have considerable leeway in determining regulatory direction, House and Senate subcommittees on communications constantly monitor the FCC, which must come back to Congress annually for budget appropriations.

Congress gave the FCC the power to adopt, modify, and repeal regulations concerning *interstate* electronic media, with the overarching goal of serving the public interest, convenience, and necessity. These regulations carry the force of federal law, deriving their power from Congress through the Communications Act. An understanding of the Act is vital to understanding the FCC's day-to-day role.

11.2 Communications Act

As described in Section 2.6, the Radio Act of 1927 ended a period of chaotic radio broadcast development. Congress for the first time crafted a statute and created an agency concerned explicitly with broadcasting. The 1927 act gave the Federal Radio Commission the responsibility of defining what the public interest, convenience, and necessity would mean in practice.

Basic Provisions

The Radio Act of 1927 imposed order on broadcasting, but left control of some aspects of radio and all interstate and foreign wire communication scattered among several federal agencies. The Communications Act of 1934 brought interstate wire and wireless communication under the control of the FCC, which replaced the Federal Radio Commission. This change had minimal effect on broadcasting because Congress simply reenacted broadcasting provisions from the 1927 law as a part of the 1934 Act. Although the Act has often been amended, its underlying concepts remain unchanged. Its very first paragraph specifies the reasons for the FCC's creation: "to make available, so far as possible, to all the people of the United States a rapid, efficient, nationwide and worldwide wire and radio communication service with adequate facilities at reasonable charges."

The Communications Act of 1934, as amended numerous times by Congress, provides the foundation for the regulation of the electronic media in the United States. The Act is separated into seven units, called **titles**, which focus broadly on different aspects of regulation. These titles are further subdivided into separate **sections**, which address regulations more specifically. (In this and the next chapter, "Sec." refers to a section of the Communications Act or other indicated law. "Section" spelled out continues to refer to parts of this book.)

▶ Title I of the Act establishes the Federal Communications Commission and provides general guidelines on its organization and operation.
▶ Title II sets out the regulatory framework for communications common carriers, such as the telephone companies.
▶ Title III contains provisions relating to over-the-air communications, including radio, television, and various forms of microwave transmission.

► Title IV focuses on additional procedural regulations covering Commission inquiries and trial-like proceedings.

► Title V outlines penalties for violation of FCC rules.

► Title VI establishes the regulatory framework for cable television.

► Title VII contains miscellaneous provisions, such as the unauthorized disclosure of private communications and telephone service for the disabled.

Specific sections in Title III of the Act formalize broadcasting's role as the "dissemination of radio communications intended to be received by the public directly." This excludes from **broadcasting** any private radio communication service aimed at individuals or specific groups of individuals. Nor is broadcasting supposed to be used for private messages not intended for the general public. People who greet their families over the air during broadcast interviews, for example, technically violate the law—although the practice occurs regularly and without consequences.

The Act forbids **disclosure** of nonbroadcast messages to people for whom they were not intended. Congress, the courts, and the FCC have also made it illegal for people even to intercept some nonbroadcast signals, such as pay cable, unless they are subscribers.

Finally, Sec. 3 of the Act defines **radio communication** as "transmission by radio of writing, signs, signals, pictures, and sounds of all kinds, including all instrumentalities, facilities, apparatus, and services . . . incidental to such transmission." By giving the term *radio* such a broad definition, Congress made it possible for the Act to incorporate television when it became a licensed service nearly 15 years after the adoption of these words in 1927.

As communication technology changes, Congress often finds it necessary to change the law regulating that technology. In 1984, for example, Congress amended the Communications Act by adding a new Title VI and defined cable television as neither a common carrier nor a broadcasting service. Congress left the FCC with little responsibility for cable, far less than it had for broadcasting and interstate wire services, and limited the power of states to regulate cable programming and subscriber rates. But Congress amended the Act again in 1992, reinstating many cable regulatory powers to the FCC and local authorities.

Probably the most significant changes to the Communications Act came with the passage of the Telecommunications Act of 1996. This legislation changed many aspects of how the electronic media industries in the United States are regulated. The law allows companies once permitted to operate certain specified businesses to move into other areas not previously open to them. For example, telephone companies are allowed to provide cable television services in their local service areas. The 1996 act also minimized many of the ownership restrictions that limited the number of radio and television stations any one entity could own. Later amendments to the act addressed the problems of new technologies such as DBS and the Internet. The specifics of these changes are addressed throughout this and the next chapter.

The Federal Communications Commission

The president appoints the five FCC commissioners to five-year terms, subject to Senate confirmation, and designates which of them shall serve as chair. Congress sought to minimize political bias by allowing no more than three commissioners from the same party.

Section 4 of the Communications Act assigns the Commission broad power to "perform any and all acts, make such rules and regulations, and issue such orders . . . as may be necessary in the execution of its functions." Originally, in only a few instances did Congress tie the Commission's hands with hard-and-fast requirements, such as specific station license terms and restrictions concerning foreign ownership of broadcast stations. Then, in the 1990s, as Congress became more involved in the oversight of the electronic communications industries, legislation amending the Communications Act became increasingly specific.

PICON Standard

Congress created a highly flexible yet legally recognized standard—**public interest, convenience, or necessity (PICON)**—to limit FCC discretion. PICON occurs regularly in the Act's broadcasting sections. For example, Sec. 303 begins: "Except as otherwise provided in this Act, the Commission from time to time, as public convenience, interest, or necessity requires, shall . . ." and goes on to list 19 powers, ranging from classification of radio stations to making regulations necessary to carry out the Act's provisions. The PICON phrase similarly occurs in sections dealing with the granting, renewal, and transfer of broadcast licenses. As we shall see, the FCC's discretion in defining the public interest is quite broad.

11.3 FCC Basics

While theoretically an independent regulatory agency, the FCC, as a creation of Congress, acts on behalf of the legislative branch. When it makes regulations, the Commission acts in a quasi-legislative capacity. It functions as an executive agency when it puts the will of Congress and its own regulations into effect. And when the FCC interprets the Act, conducts hearings, or decides disputes, it takes on a judicial role.

Budget and Organization

Over the past few years the FCC's annual budget has hovered around $300 million. This budget makes the Commission one of the smaller federal agencies, employing about 2,000 persons.

Throughout most of its existence, the FCC's budget came out of general tax revenues. In 1989, Congress began requiring the FCC to collect most of its budget directly from the industries it regulates. This money comes from annual regulatory fees and application fees. Fees defray the costs of the Commission's enforcement, policy- and rule-making, user information, and international activities.

Annual fees vary widely, depending on the service. In 2007, for example, Class C AM stations paid as much as $3,800 or as little as $400, depending on the number of homes in their service areas. VHF TV stations in the top 10 markets paid $64,300. DBS operators were assessed a fee of $109,200 per satellite, and cable systems paid 75 cents per subscriber. Clearly, these fees are passed on to consumers as higher rates for subscription services and higher costs of consumer goods stemming from increased advertising costs.

Exhibit 11.b depicts the FCC's organizational structure. The Media Bureau, one of the units of most interest here, has five divisions:

▶ **Audio Division.** Processes applications for construction permits, licenses, and license renewals for radio stations.
▶ **Video Division.** Processes the same for television stations.
▶ **Policy Division.** Handles FCC proceedings that produce new rules concerning broadcast stations, cable systems, and direct broadcast satellites, and handles media related issues involving cable program carriage, political broadcasting, and equal employment opportunity (EEO).
▶ **Industry Analysis Division.** Participates in proceedings regarding media ownership and economic aspects of media and collects, compiles, analyzes, and develops reports on the industry and media markets.
▶ **Engineering Division.** Oversees the technical regulation of cable television systems and other multichannel video programming distributors such as DBS and MMDS.

The **Wireless Telecommunications Bureau** handles most FCC domestic wireless telecommunications programs and policies (including cellular services, paging systems, and amateur radio services, but excluding satellite communications). The Wireless Bureau is also responsible for implementing competitive bidding for spectrum auctions. The newest bureau at the Commission, the **Public Safety & Homeland Security Bureau,** was established in 2006 in response to the terrorist attacks of 2001 and natural disasters such as Hurricane Katrina in 2005. The Bureau is responsible for all FCC activities relating to public safety, homeland security, emergency management and preparedness, and disaster management.

Commissioners

Most of the work of the FCC is done by the staff. Only the most important decisions are made by the commissioners themselves, although they establish overall policy that must be followed by Commission employees.

The five commissioners (seven until 1982) serve five-year terms and may be reappointed. Commissioners must be citizens, may not have a financial interest in any type of communications business, and must devote themselves full-time to the job. In practice, many commissioners never finish their terms of office because other opportunities entice them into higher-paying positions outside the government. There are exceptions, however. James Quello, a Democrat from Michigan, was first appointed to the Commission in 1974 by President Nixon and served until 1997.

The president appoints one commissioner to serve as chair. Although the chair of the Commission has only one vote when the Commission makes decisions, he or she exercises considerable power within the agency by setting the agenda and making important staff appointments.

The first woman commissioner, Frieda Hennock, served from 1948 to 1955. The next woman was not appointed until 1971, but since 1979 at least one commissioner at any one time has been a woman. The first African-American commissioner was Benjamin Hooks (1972–1977), later the head of the National Association for the Advancement of Colored People (NAACP). Hispanics (Henry Rivera, 1981–1985) as well as African Americans have been appointed since, including the appointment in 1997 of William Kennard as the first African-American chair of the FCC. In 1994, Rachelle Chong, a San Francisco-based attorney, became the first Asian American to serve as a commissioner.

Staff Role

References to "the Commission" usually include not only the five commissioners, but also staff members. Staff members handle inquiries and complaints, which seldom come to the commissioners' attention, as well as thousands of letters, applications, and forms from FCC-regulated industries. **Processing rules** spell out which decisions staff members may settle and which must go to the commissioners.

Except for top administrators (bureau and office chiefs), whom the chair appoints, Commission staff members are part of the federal civil service. Many serve for decades, developing in-depth expertise on which the commissioners depend. Because of this

Exhibit 11.b

FCC Organization

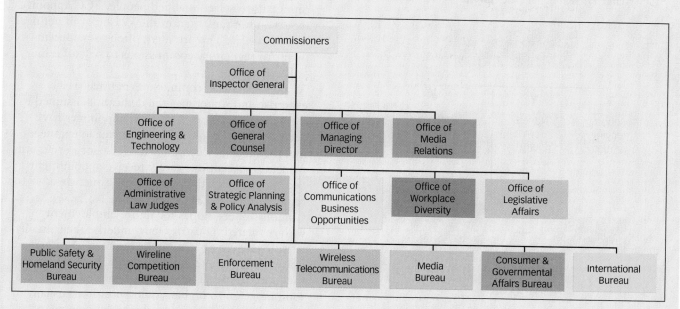

Whereas most FCC employees are located at the national headquarters in Washington, DC, some Enforcement Bureau employees are scattered throughout the country in FCC regional offices. The Office of Inspector General conducts audits and investigations of internal programs and operations of the agency, while the Office of Managing Director handles personnel, budget, and administrative matters.

expertise, the professional staff often exerts considerable influence not only on the day-to-day operations of the Commission, but often on long-term policy as well.

Rule-Making Process

The rule-making function generates a large body of FCC administrative law called **rules and regulations** (there is no difference between the two—the phrase is traditional). Whether the Commission acts on a petition to consider a certain action or acts on its own, it often begins with a **Notice of Inquiry (NOI)** for a subject that needs preliminary comment and research, a **Notice of Proposed Rule Making (NPRM)** when offering specific new rules for public comment, or a combination of both (see Exhibit 11.c). These notices invite comment from interested parties, traditionally attorneys representing affected individuals, stations, companies, or industries. More recently, given the opportunity to comment via e-mail, interested citizens have begun commenting in rule-making proceedings, sometimes in great numbers. For example, when considering a controversial set of ownership rule amendments in 2003, the FCC received more than 500,000 comments from concerned individuals. On rare occasions, proposed rule changes of special significance or of a controversial nature may be

scheduled for oral argument or public hearings before the five commissioners. Several such public hearings were conducted across the country in 2006 and 2007 in relation to Commission proceedings involving broadcast localism and ownership restrictions.

After digesting outside comments, the staff prepares a proposed decision for the commissioners, usually as a recommended **Report and Order** with background discussion explaining and defending the action. Once a proposed Report and Order is adopted, that action becomes subject to petitions to the Commission for reconsideration and/or appeal to a U.S. court of appeals. Increasingly in recent years, one party or another appeals the "final" FCC decision, sometimes delaying implementation by months or years.

Adjudication

A second type of FCC decision making is adjudication, which settles specific disputes—whether between outside parties (e.g., a broadcaster and a political candidate arguing over equal opportunities [see Section 12.6]) or between the FCC and an outside party (e.g., a broadcaster who protests a fine).

The staff may settle simple disputes quickly, but others become the subjects of hearings. Electronic media

Exhibit 11.c

FCC Rule-Making Process

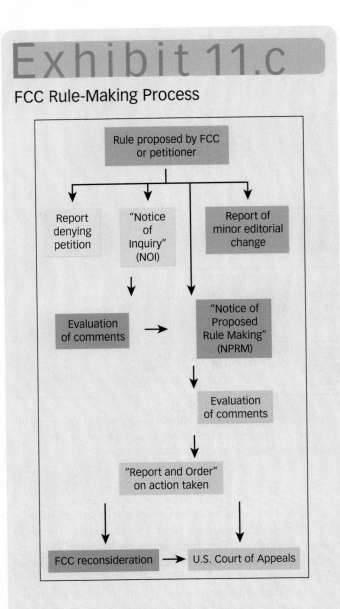

A petition for a new rule or a change of existing rules can come from the public (rare), the regulated industries (common), another part of the executive branch, or a unit within the FCC itself. Parties who are dissatisfied with denials or new rules often appeal for reconsideration by the FCC, and, if they are still not satisfied, to the courts. Each step of the process must be documented in the **Federal Register** so that all interested parties can keep informed of rule-making actions.

owners avoid hearings if at all possible. Such hearings require expensive legal representation and can take months to resolve the contested issue.

FCC Critique

Over the years the FCC has been among the most frequently analyzed and scathingly criticized of all federal regulatory agencies. Past official investigations and private studies of the Commission and its methods have reached negative conclusions with monotonous regularity. A few criticisms have been recurrent.

▶ The political process for choosing commissioners often fails to select qualified people. FCC appointments do not rank high in the Washington political pecking order. The president often uses appointments to regulatory commissions to pay off minor political debts.

▶ As a consequence, commissioners usually lack expertise and sometimes the dedication assumed by the Communications Act. Most appointees have been lawyers. People with experience in engineering, the media, or common carriers—or in relevant academic specialties—rarely receive appointment because they lack the political constituencies required for serious consideration.

▶ Commissioners' hopes for future employment with regulated industries may underlie their usually narrow reading of "the public interest." Not many stay in office long enough to attain great expertise; the more ambitious and better-qualified appointees soon move on to higher-paying positions, usually in private legal practice, specializing (of course) in communications law.

Although some of these criticisms remain valid today, others do not. Most recent Commission appointees have been highly qualified and dedicated public servants from state public-service commissions, legislative staffs, communications law firms, and the ranks of the FCC's staff. With the ascendance of telecommunications as a hot topic in Washington, being named to the Commission is now seen as a prestigious and important appointment.

More recent criticism of the FCC focuses not so much on the competence or expertise of the commissioners, but on the FCC's timing and policy directions. Long-time FCC watchers lament the increasingly partisan nature of Commission decision making, characterized by 3-2 votes along party lines on important policy issues and scathing dissenting opinions criticizing both the policy outcomes and procedures.

However, it is somewhat misleading to speak of *the* FCC. As its membership (along with the administration in Washington) changes, the Commission takes on varying complexions—sometimes reform-minded, sometimes more interested in the welfare of the businesses it regulates than in the public interest.

Moreover, the Commission does not operate in a vacuum; it is under constant and often conflicting pressures not only from the White House, Congress, and the courts, but also from the industries it regulates, lobbyists representing special interests, and the public. Although Congress gave the FCC a mandate in the

Communications Act of 1934 to act on its behalf, it continually holds the Commission accountable if it wanders far afield. In addition to Senate approval of nominations to the FCC and congressional control of federal budgeting, Congress conducts frequent **oversight hearings** on the Commission's performance and plans.

11.4 Broadcast Licensing

The **authorizing of service**—licensing of broadcasting stations—is one of the FCC's more important functions. (State and local authorities that franchise cable systems play a parallel role, as described in Section 11.8.) Most other regulation grows out of this licensing process. The FCC acts as gatekeeper, using its licensing power to offer station operation to some and not others. No one can legally "own" any part of the electromagnetic spectrum. Conscious of both real and potential claims to the contrary, the Communications Act repeatedly codifies the ban on channel ownership.

Finding a Channel

A would-be broadcast licensee applies for specific facilities (channel, power, coverage pattern, antenna location, time of operation). Most desirable commercial channels had been assigned by the 1970s, so a new licensee nearly always had to buy an existing station. Later, several new opportunities developed.

In 1982, the Commission approved low-power television (LPTV), a service limited in power so as not to interfere with full-power television stations. LPTV stations were considered secondary services, which meant that if interference developed between a low-powered station and a full-powered station, the low-powered station would have to resolve the interference or stop broadcasting altogether.

In the mid-1980s, the FCC created nearly 700 new FM allotments, made possible by improved technology limiting interference with stations already on the air. In the early 1990s, the FCC extended the AM band to 1705 kHz, adding 10 new medium-wave channels to which existing AM outlets could migrate, thus cutting down on existing interference. Most recently, the FCC paved the way for the creation of hundreds of new low-powered FM radio stations. These stations, which have service radii of 1 to 3.5 miles, are licensed exclusively to noncommercial groups with local ties.

Application Filing Windows

Before filing a broadcast application with the Commission, would-be broadcasters must first ascertain whether a frequency is available for the area they wish to serve. Assuming an appropriate frequency is available, applicants must wait for the FCC to open a "filing window" before submitting their applications. The Commission opens these filing windows periodically, on no apparent systematic schedule. Several months before a filing window opens the agency announces the opening so that applicants have notice and time to prepare their applications. Applicants who fail to submit their applications during the filing window must wait until the next window opens, which might be a matter of years.

Construction Permit

When the filing window opens, would-be licensees for new facilities apply first for **construction permits (CPs)**. The holder of a CP applies for a regular license to broadcast only after submitting satisfactory proof of performance of transmitter and antenna.

A CP gives its holder a limited time (usually 24 months for television and 18 for radio) to construct and test the station. The CP holder then files a record of technical testing to apply for a regular license. With FCC permission, a permittee may (and most do) begin on-air program testing pending final approval of the license.

Licensee Qualifications

Section 310(b) of the Communications Act forbids foreign control of a broadcast license. Section 308(b) limits licensees to those U.S. citizens, or corporations owned primarily by U.S. citizens, who qualify in these areas:

▶ **Character.** Applicants should have personal and business histories free of evidence suggesting defects in character that would cast doubt on their ability to operate in the public interest. Criminal records and violations of antitrust laws may constitute such evidence. Any misrepresentation to the FCC would be an almost-fatal defect.

▶ **Financial resources.** Applicants must certify that they have "sufficient" financial resources. The FCC has issued varied definitions of "sufficient," but currently it means the ability to construct and operate facilities for 90 days without reliance on station revenue.

▶ **Technical ability.** Most applicants hire engineering consultants to prepare technical aspects of their applications. They show how a proposed station will get maximum physical coverage without causing objectionable interference to existing stations.

Mutually Exclusive Applications

Until the mid-1990s, when two or more qualified applicants sought the same channel, the Act required the

FCC to make a choice among the applicants only after conducting comparative hearings. These hearings took on the appearance of full-blown trials, with attorneys for all parties presenting evidence, calling witnesses, and engaging in cross-examination—an often drawn-out and costly process for all concerned.

In 1993, a federal court declared the FCC's comparative licensing criteria illegal (F, 1993) and the Commission was either unwilling or unable to formulate new criteria. Consequently, almost 2,000 mutually exclusive applications for radio and television stations were put on hold until the Commission figured out another method of awarding contested licenses. Congress then stepped in and ordered the Commission to deal with the log-jam and any new comparative broadcast licensing situations through a competitive bidding, or auction, process. The FCC held the first broadcast auction in September 1999 and began granting construction permits to the winning applicants, after making sure they met the basic qualifications of a broadcast licensee. The auction raised $57 million, all of which went directly to the federal treasury. Since that time, more than 650 broadcast frequencies have gone to the highest bidder at a collective cost of close to $315 million.

In addition to the auctions for new broadcast stations, Congress, as part of its effort to balance the federal budget, required the auction of much of the existing TV spectrum that TV broadcasters gave up after the transition to digital. That auction, conducted early in 2008, raised nearly $20 billion. Most of that spectrum went to bidders hoping to expand their mobile telephone networks.

Services Requiring No License

The FCC requires virtually all spectrum-using electronic mass media and common carriers to obtain licenses to operate. The few exceptions include the following:

- radio station auxiliary services transmitted on sub-carriers and neither related to broadcasting nor decoded by regular radio receivers
- data and closed-captioned services broadcast by television stations
- carrier-current radio stations such as those used on some college campuses
- very low power AM radio stations designed to serve small, discrete areas

The FCC also regulates the manufacture of many nonbroadcast devices that use part of the electromagnetic spectrum (e.g., remote garage-door openers, microwave ovens, and cordless telephones), but does not require that consumers be licensed to use them.

11.5 Operations

Ideally, the FCC should monitor station operations constantly to ensure operation in the public interest. But it simply is not feasible for the Commission to keep watch over all the activities of thousands of stations. In the course of normal day-to-day operations, broadcasters experience little official supervision.

Employment Practices

In 1969, the FCC began monitoring broadcast employment practices, and over the years added equal employment requirements. Under the current **equal employment opportunity (EEO)** regime adopted by the Commission, broadcast licensees, cable system operators, and other multichannel video programming distributors (such as DBS and MMDS operators) are prohibited from engaging in employment discrimination. They are also required to provide broad notice of job vacancies and to undertake additional outreach measures, such as job fairs and scholarship programs. Entities subject to the EEO requirement must document their outreach activities, keep records on job vacancies and applicants, and submit to the Commission annual reports that provide employment information on race, ethnicity, and gender. The annual reports are used by the FCC to compile industry employment trend reports.

Public File

The FCC requires stations to keep license-renewal applications and other relevant documents in a file readily available for public inspection. All stations, commercial and noncommercial, must maintain such a file, which includes the following:

- the station's current license and any pending license application (e.g., for renewal or transfer)
- ownership and annual employment reports
- the pamphlet titled "The Public and Broadcasting—A Procedural Manual," issued in 1974 and updated in 1998
- a record of the disposition of any political-broadcast time requests for the preceding two years
- a quarterly listing of programs the licensee believes provided the most significant treatment of local community problems of public importance
- records required by the Children's Television Act of 1990 concerning programming for and advertising to children
- any time-brokerage agreements in force
- copies of (television) station decisions concerning must-carry and retransmission consent governing its relationship with any local cable systems

▶ letters received from members of the public (to be kept for three years) and any agreement with citizens groups

Although members of the public rarely ask to see it, the file receives a thorough examination when FCC inspectors visit a station.

Keeping up with Washington

Electronic media managers must keep current with changes in FCC regulations. Trade organizations and publications and an army of communications attorneys in Washington—many of whom are members of the Federal Communications Bar Association (FCBA)—help licensees with this task. Personal contacts with FCC staff members enable Washington lawyers to get things done faster than can distant licensees unfamiliar with the federal bureaucracy. The National Association of Broadcasters, National Cable & Telecommunications Association, and other trade associations offer legal clinics and regular publications on FCC rules.

From all of these sources, stations and systems receive continuous advice on what is new and what not to forget. For example, licensees often seem unaware of differing federal or state requirements on things such as employee drug use and over-the-air use of live or recorded telephone conversations. The timely filing of regular ownership, employment, and other reports required by the Commission is a mundane but important aspect of using legal counsel.

Monitoring Performance

The FCC rarely monitors electronic media. Inspectors from the Enforcement Bureau check technical aspects of station and cable system operations, but only occasionally and in random fashion. Questions about programming and commercial practices usually come to FCC attention through complaints from the public, consumer groups, or competing media. Because the FCC now accepts such complaints via e-mail, the Commission often is flooded with comments about inappropriate programming, usually of the sexually explicit nature (see Section 12.5). Such complaints are sometimes influenced by organized letter-writing campaigns spearheaded by special interest groups.

11.6 License Renewals and Transfers

Under the Communications Act, licenses may be awarded for only "limited periods of time," currently a maximum of eight years, and must regularly come up for renewal. Although the FCC renews more than 98 percent of all licenses without asking any searching questions, possible nonrenewal seems always to be lurking in the background. Challenges to renewal applications can come from the FCC, but may also be lodged by dissatisfied citizens in the licensee's community. Even if the incumbent wins a contested renewal (and they usually do), defending it can be both expensive and time consuming.

Application Routes

Section 309 of the Communications Act stipulates that "licenses shall be renewed if the public interest, convenience, and necessity would be served" by renewal. Before deregulation of renewal procedures, applications often required piles of supporting documents showing how the licensee had served or would serve the public interest. In 1981, the FCC began using a simple postcard-size renewal form, later expanded to a still relatively simple five-page form, which most applicants supplement with additional multipage exhibits.

Renewal applications take one of three paths: uncontested, FCC staff contested, and the petition to deny.

▶ Some 98 percent of all renewal applications fall in the **uncontested** category. The FCC staff uses its delegated authority to renew the station almost automatically. In fact, consumer advocates complain that the Mass Media Bureau merely rubber-stamps uncontested applications, no matter how mediocre a station's past performance may have been.

▶ Occasionally, the FCC staff will initiate a proceeding to deny a license renewal if it finds serious or frequent violations of U.S. law or FCC regulations. Allegations of criminal law breaches, antitrust activity, or concealing information from the Commission could lead to such action.

▶ The **petition-to-deny** renewal comes from a citizen group or other party that opposes an incumbent licensee (see Exhibit 11.d). Such groups claim that incumbents have failed to meet public-interest standards. Although the petition process is important in giving citizens the right to challenge licensees who may not be serving the public interest, in practice the petition-to-deny process rarely results in the denial of renewal.

License Transfers

Other than uncontested renewal, the most frequent licensing process is license transfer, which occurs when an owner sells a station to another party. A large majority of station owners have acquired their stations by buying them rather than by securing new stations from the FCC.

All station ownership transfers require Commission approval. After the parties to the transfer agree on the terms of the sale, they submit their transfer application to the FCC. The Commission issues a public notice of the application, and interested parties have 30 days to submit comments. In most instances, no one objects and the Commission staff routinely approves the license transfer. Individuals or groups may, however, file petitions to deny the sale. If the FCC finds that a petition raises serious issues, it will order a hearing to determine whether the proposed transfer would serve the public interest. Such findings rarely occur; in most cases, the Commission dismisses petitions to deny.

Because large mergers involve the transfer of licenses, the FCC must approve them. In reviewing these mergers the Commission often takes into account the antitrust implications (the fear of overwhelming market power) of the transactions as well as their public-interest ramifications. Such comprehensive reviews may take many months to complete. Some members of Congress have criticized the FCC's actions in such cases, arguing that the agency is duplicating the efforts of the Justice Department, which has primary jurisdiction over antitrust matters.

 **Enforcement**

The FCC can impose a variety of penalties on licensees for infractions of its rules. These range from simple letters of admonition to fines, short-term license renewal, or—the ultimate penalty—no renewal at all. When a licensee proves incorrigible, the FCC can either refuse to renew the license or revoke it outright. The FCC prefers the nonrenewal option because it puts the burden of proof on the licensee, whereas revocation places the burden of proof on the Commission. None of these sanctions can be invoked without legal due process, often beginning with a formal hearing.

Due Process

A fundamental safeguard of individual liberties under the Constitution, the Fifth Amendment's **due process clause,** guarantees that government may not deprive a person of "life, liberty, or property without due process of law." Among many other applications, this means that the FCC may not use its powers arbitrarily. Fairness, the goal of due process, requires that applicants and petitioners have ample opportunity to argue their cases under nondiscriminatory conditions and that parties adversely affected by decisions may appeal for review by authorities other than those that made the initial decision. Many due process rights are detailed in the Administrative Procedure Act of 1946, which specifies how agencies such as the FCC must conduct their proceedings to ensure due process for all participants.

FCC Hearings

Senior staff attorneys, called **administrative law judges (ALJs)**, preside over initial FCC hearings. They conduct the proceedings somewhat like courtroom trials, with sworn witnesses, testimony, evidence, and counsel for each side. Appeals of initial decisions of ALJs are reviewed by the commissioners themselves. Procedural rules head off frivolous interventions and intentional delays by carefully defining circumstances that justify hearings and qualifications of parties entitled to standing—that is, the right to participate.

Court Appeals

Even after all safeguards in FCC hearings and re-hearings have been exhausted, the Communications Act gives parties adversely affected by FCC actions still further recourse. The Act provides that all appeals concerning station licenses must go before the U.S. Court of Appeals for the District of Columbia Circuit in Washington, DC. Appeals from FCC decisions in cases that do not involve licensing may be initiated in any of the 12 U.S. courts of appeals. Each serves a specific region of the country and is known as a **circuit court of appeal.**

The court may confirm or overturn Commission actions in part or in whole. It may also **remand** a case, sending it back to the FCC for further consideration in keeping with the court's interpretation of the Communications Act and other laws. From any of the federal circuit courts, final appeals may be sought before the Supreme Court of the United States. A request for consideration by the Supreme Court, called **a writ of certiorari,** is most often turned down ("cert. denied"). If that happens, the appeal process is over. Refusal to hear a case does not necessarily mean that the Supreme Court agrees with lower court findings, but the earlier decision holds nonetheless, though without standing as a compelling nationwide legal precedent.

Loss of License

Since the FCC's creation in 1934, fewer than 200 stations have involuntarily lost their licenses. **Non-renewal** accounts for two-thirds of these losses; outright revocation—not waiting for the current license to expire—about one-third. Though an ever-present background threat, loss of license only rarely becomes a reality among the thousands of stations on the air.

Stations that have lost their licenses have largely been obscure radio outlets whose licensees have accumulated long lists of willful misdemeanors. Transgressions accumulate because the FCC usually treats them leniently as long as the guilty licensee candidly admits error and contritely promises to reform.

Exhibit 11.d

Citizen Involvement: The Landmark WLBT Case

Until the late 1960s, a broadcast station's audience members had no right to take part in regulatory proceedings concerning the station. That situation changed as a result of a court case that began in 1955 when a group of citizens made the first of a series of complaints to the FCC about the conduct of WLBT, a VHF television station in Jackson, Mississippi. The group accused the station of blatant discrimination against African Americans, who formed 45 percent of its audience. The FCC dismissed the citizens' complaints, saying that they had no legal right to participate in a licensing decision. When WLBT's license again came up for renewal in 1964, local groups obtained legal assistance from the Office of Communications of the United Church of Christ (UCC) in New York.

The UCC petitioned the FCC on behalf of the local groups for permission to intervene in the WLBT renewal proceeding, but the FCC again rejected the petition, saying that citizens had no **legal standing** to intervene. At that time, the Commission recognized only signal interference or economic injury (to another broadcaster) as reasons to give parties the right to participate in renewal hearings. Thus, only other broadcasters had standing to challenge existing licensees.

The UCC went to the court of appeals, claiming that the FCC had no right to bar representatives of the viewing public from intervening in renewals or to award a renewal without a hearing in the face of substantial public opposition. The court agreed, directing the FCC to hold hearings on WLBT's renewal and to give standing to representatives of the public (F, 1966). The FCC held a hearing and grudgingly permitted the UCC to participate as ordered. However, it once again renewed WLBT's license.

The UCC returned to court, and in 1969 an appeals court reconsidered the case—14 years after the first complaints had been recorded. The court rebuked the FCC for "scandalous delay" and ordered the FCC to cancel WLBT's license and to appoint an interim operator pending selection of a new licensee (F, 1969). But 10 more years passed before the FCC finally selected a new permanent licensee. Altogether, the case dragged on for more than a quarter of a century.

As the FCC had feared, the WLBT case triggered many petitions to deny the renewal of other licenses. This "reign of terror," as a trade magazine put it, actually resulted in few actual hearings and still fewer denials. An exacting standard of evidence established by the FCC and approved by the court ensures this high rate of petition failure. Only after an opponent presents overwhelming evidence will the FCC schedule a license hearing (F, 1972).

Eventually, another violation or lack of candor causes the FCC to lose patience, and some specific misdeed results in nonrenewal or revocation.

Lesser Penalties

Not all offenses, of course, warrant the capital punishment of license loss. For lesser offenses, the FCC inflicts milder sanctions:

- **Short-term renewal** (usually a year or two instead of the full renewal term) puts a licensee on a kind of probation pending correction of deficiencies evident during its preceding license period.
- **Conditional renewal** is granted pending correction of some specific fault.
- **Forfeitures,** or **fines,** ranging from the base fine of $7,000 up to a maximum of $325,000 per incident may be assessed for broadcaster infractions of FCC rules. Fines against common carriers can be as high as $1 million. Until relatively recently, most forfeitures came from technical violations. Lately, however, more forfeitures have been assessed for violations of the Commission's indecency and children's television rules (covered in the next chapter). Most fines are for much less than the maximum amount. Because cable systems have no license that

the FCC can threaten, fines are the agency's chief means of enforcing cable rules.
- Relatively minor infractions may result in a letter being placed in the station's file for consideration when it applies for license renewal.

11.8 Cable

Cable "licensing," or **franchising,** follows a pattern totally different from broadcast licensing. Local (and, increasingly, state) rather than federal authorities issue franchises because cable systems use streets and other public property that is subject to municipal jurisdiction, rather than federally controlled airways. Federal cable laws contain provisions covering subscriber fees, ownership, equal employment opportunities, programming, customer service, and technical standards. These laws, passed in 1984, 1992, and 1996, amended the 1934 Communications Act. Exhibit 11.e illustrates the somewhat serpentine history of cable regulation.

Cable Acts: General Provisions

The Cable Communications Policy Act of 1984 created a new Title VI of the Communications Act that established

Exhibit 11.e

Changing Cable Regulation

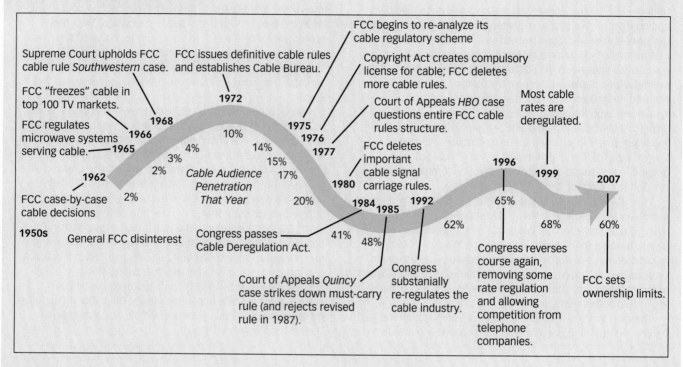

For more than five decades the FCC's regulation of cable television has undergone substantial changes in direction. From virtually no regulation in the cable's earliest years to substantial and detailed FCC regulation of the medium in 1972, cable was steadily more controlled. For the next two decades, cable was progressively deregulated, especially with the 1984 cable act, which removed most remaining local franchise limitations. In 1992, Congress reversed course and passed a strongly re-regulatory cable act, only to change course again four years later. In the mid-2000s, former FCC Chairman Kevin Martin initiated several attempts to impose additional regulations on cable television operators.

a loose federal deregulatory framework for cable television. Key parts of that act were reversed in the strongly re-regulatory Cable Television Consumer Protection and Competition Act of 1992, which amended Title VI. This 1992 legislation grew out of public and congressional anger over sharp increases in cable subscription rates—in some cases three times the rate of inflation—in the five years before it became law. The 1996 act modified a few provisions and authorized a new provider for the delivery of cable services–the telephone companies. The combined result of the three acts includes the following key provisions:

▶ The 1984 act defined cable television as a one-way video programming service; neither it nor the 1992 and 1996 revisions regulate two-way (interactive) services.

▶ The 1992 act transforms the relationship between broadcasters and cable systems. Under this act, each full-power commercial television station has the right every three years either (1) to require cable

systems within its coverage area to offer some valuable consideration for use of its signal (termed **retransmission consent**) or, (2) simply to re-quire that cable systems carry its signal (the **must-carry rule**). If a station and cable system cannot reach agreement on terms, that station will not be carried on that system for at least three years. Stations that fail to choose between must-carry and retransmission consent will, by default, come under the must-carry option. Must carry applies only to a television station's primary program channel; it does not cover a station's digital multicast channels. Local noncommercial stations may claim must-carry rights, but do not have the option of seeking retransmission consent. MMDS and satellite master antenna television (SMATV) systems are also subject to retransmission consent rules.

Cable systems with 12 or fewer channels must devote at least three to local broadcast signals. Systems with more than 12 channels may be required to devote up to a third of their capacity to such signals. None of this applies to the relatively few systems with fewer than 300 subscribers.

- A TV station may also demand carriage on the same channel number on cable that it uses over the air.
- Reversing a key aspect of the 1984 law, the 1992 act required local authorities or the FCC to regulate subscriber rates for basic tiers of cable service. Congress retreated a bit in 1996 by ending all rate regulation of upper-tier basic services. No rate regulation of pay-cable channels such as HBO and Showtime is allowed. Cable systems are exempt from all rate regulation if they serve fewer than 30 percent of the households in their area or are subject to "effective competition" from some other multichannel competitor (MMDS, SMATV, DBS, or telephone companies) that is available to at least 50 percent—and actually subscribed to by at least 15 percent—of an area's households.
- Cable program providers (e.g., ESPN or HBO) that are owned even in part by cable system operators must make their services available to multichannel cable competitors (such as SMATV, MMDS, and DBS) at the same prices offered to cable systems. This provision, which expires in 2012, is designed to give competing delivery systems a chance to get an audience foothold.

Cable Acts: Franchising

Whereas the 1984 act severely limited regulatory powers of state and local authorities, the 1992 law reinstated many of those same powers and added new FCC oversight of many aspects of cable franchising.

- Local franchising authorities may require public, educational, and government (PEG) access channels over which the cable operator has little editorial control.
- The 1984 act called for cable systems with more than 36 channels to set aside 10 to 15 percent of those channels for leased access to outside parties. The cable owner sets rates for leasing access channels but has no editorial control over their content—other than enforcement of obscenity limitations (as discussed in Chapter 12). The 1992 act requires the FCC to set maximum rates for use of such channels.
- Reinforcing existing practices and FCC guidelines, Congress allowed franchise authorities to charge annual franchise fees of up to 5 percent of cable system gross revenues.
- The FCC may require that specific customer service levels and technical standards be included in new and renewal franchise agreements.

Franchise Process

Most areas of the country have had cable television service for many years. State statutes or local ordinances, drafted in many cases with the advice of outside experts, describe the conditions under which cable systems are allowed to operate. Ordinances typically stipulate the following:

- the term of the franchise (usually 10 to 15 years, but sometimes longer)
- the quality of service to be provided
- technical standards, such as the minimum number of channels to be provided, time limits on construction, and interconnection with other systems
- the franchise fee (usually 5 percent of gross revenues)
- PEG channel requirements, if any

Throughout most of the history of cable, franchising authorities usually granted only one franchise in an area, thus making the cable system a local monopoly. In an attempt to stimulate local competition, the 1992 act states that local authorities may not unreasonably refuse the grant of a competing franchise. This requirement became important relatively recently as telephone companies began to seek permission from franchising authorities to provide cable-like services via their fiber optic systems.

Finding that some franchising authorities were making unreasonable demands on the telephone companies or taking too much time to grant new franchises, in 2007 the FCC adopted new franchising rules to speed up the process (FCCR, 2007). According to the new regulations, franchising authorities:

- must make their decisions within 90 days of the phone company's application for a competitive franchise
- cannot mandate that new entrants serve all parts of the franchise area
- cannot force new applicants to provide PEG access in excess of that required for incumbent systems

Several state governments, acting on requests from telephone companies in their states, have granted statewide franchises to existing telcos. In those states, local governments no longer have as much control over the provision of cable services.

Renewals

A franchising authority need not find that renewal will serve the public interest or meet any other standard, but rather may simply renew a franchise without ceremony. If, however, the local authority wants to deny renewal, the Communications Act requires that it hold a hearing, in effect raising public-interest issues by deciding whether the incumbent operator has (1) complied with the law; (2) provided a quality of service that is "reasonable in light of the community needs"; (3) maintained the financial, legal, and technical ability to operate; and (4) prepared a renewal proposal that is "reasonable to meet the future cable-related community needs and interests" (Sec. 626).

11.9 Other Electronic Media

While broadcasting and cable television certainly are the largest electronic mass media in terms of the number of people served, other electronic media are also regulated by the FCC. Based on the characteristics of those media, FCC regulation may vary.

Direct Broadcast Satellite and Satellite Radio

The FCC licensed the first direct broadcast satellite (DBS) systems in the early 1980s much the same as they granted broadcast licenses. More recently, the Commission has granted new licenses through the spectrum auction process. To date, DBS systems operate on a subscription basis and deliver much the same programming as cable systems.

Congress enacted legislation in 1999 that regulates the carriage of local broadcast stations by DBS operators. DBS providers are not required to carry the broadcast stations of any particular local market, but they must carry all local TV signals in the markets they choose to serve. TV broadcasters, led by the NAB, argue that DBS operators should be required to carry all local signals in all markets, but so far the FCC has not adopted such a requirement. The law also permits DBS operators to provide selected TV broadcast signals to households located in so-called white areas—locations where over-the-air broadcast signals are unavailable. Thus, subscribers living in those areas can receive broadcast network affiliates as part of their DBS service, usually for a small extra fee. In addition, DBS service providers must set aside 4 percent of their channel capacity for public-interest programming. FCC equal employment opportunity (EEO) rules apply to DBS licensees.

In 1997, the FCC authorized a new satellite service to deliver multichannel, CD-quality audio service directly to homes, automobiles, and portable radios nationwide. Two satellite radio licenses were auctioned later in 1997, with the stipulation that the two licensees could not merge operations. This rule was intended to guarantee that there would always be competition in the provision of satellite radio service. The FCC was asked to waive this requirement when the two satellite radio providers, XM and Sirius, proposed to merge in 2007. The FCC approved the merger in July 2008 with several conditions, including a three-year cap on subscription prices.

Satellite Master Antenna Television Systems

Satellite master antenna television (SMATV) systems are functionally similar to cable television systems except that they serve multiunit dwelling complexes without crossing public streets or rights of way. As such, they are sometimes termed "private" cable systems, and they are not subject to state or local regulation. Thus, SMATV systems do not need franchises to operate, nor are they subject to local access channel and equipment requirements. The FCC does, however, require SMATV systems to follow broadcast television must-carry rules.

"Wireless" Cable

Wireless cable—sometimes referred to as multichannel television—is a subscription service much like cable television, except that it uses over-the-air microwave frequencies to deliver its signals rather than coaxial cable and fiber. Currently, wireless cable utilizes multichannel multipoint distribution service (MMDS) to distribute up to 30 channels of programming to subscribers. Equal employment opportunity regulations and broadcast signal carriage rules apply to MMDS systems. Because these systems use over-the-air frequencies, state and local governments have no jurisdiction over MMDS services.

Telephone Companies

From the mid-1960s to 1996 the FCC did not allow telephone companies to provide cable TV services in the same area in which they provided telephone service. The Commission enacted this cross ownership restriction so that the powerful telephone companies would not dominate the nascent cable TV business. Congress followed the FCC's lead and codified the cross ownership ban in the 1984 amendments to the Communications Act.

Following several successful court challenges of the cable/telco cross-ownership restrictions in the mid-1990s, Congress removed the ban in the Telecommunications Act of 1996 as part of its effort to stimulate local competition in the multichannel video market. According to the 1996 legislation, telephone companies may now offer video services in their local telephone service areas under four different regulatory regimes: as over-the-air providers, such as MMDS operators, subject to Title III regulation; as common carriers subject to Title II regulation; as cable television operators subject to Title VI regulation; or as a newly created hybrid service called an **open video system (OVS)**.

Operation as an OVS allows the telephone company to deliver programming of its own choosing while giving other programmers access to the company's distribution system. Essentially, the telephone company acts as a cable system operator and common carrier at the same time. The Act requires that if there is more demand for system capacity than exists, then the telephone company may control no more than one-third of the system's capacity; the other two-thirds of the system capacity must be apportioned among other users. Although OVS operators must satisfy some of the requirements imposed on cable operators—signal carriage and EEO, for example—they are exempt from some aspects of cable regulation. OVS systems are certified by the FCC and are not franchised locally. Also, most rate regulation does not apply to OVS operations. Local authorities are permitted to exact a share of the OVS system revenues, much like the franchise fee levied against cable operators.

A couple dozen small telephone companies currently offer video services as OVS operators. The majority of telephone companies offering cable-like services opt for cable regulation under Title VI.

11.10 Media Ownership Regulations

First Amendment theory (more on this in Chapter 12) stresses the value of many diverse and antagonistic sources of information and opinion. Unregulated competition can lead to monopoly control of media outlets, thus limiting the number of speakers in the market. Accordingly, to promote "a marketplace of ideas" and prevent the monopolization of the electronic media, the government limits the number and kinds of media outlets that any one entity can own. This **diversification** of ownership and control has long been a major FCC goal.

Antitrust Law

The Sherman Act of 1890 and the Clayton Act of 1914 together aim to prevent excessive concentration of control by one or a few companies over a particular segment of the economy. They provide the basis for such government actions as the one that led to the 1984 breakup of the giant telephone monopoly AT&T.

Courts have long held that despite the First Amendment, business law—including antitrust statutes—may be applied to media. Section 313 of the Communications Act requires the FCC to consider revoking licenses held by companies found guilty of violating antitrust laws. However, the deregulatory atmosphere of the 1980s and the early 2000s led to a decline in antitrust enforcement. During those periods, the Justice Department rarely questioned huge media mergers and takeovers.

Multiple Ownership

In general, the FCC defines ownership as any active or participating equity interest in the station of 5 percent or more. Complex **attribution rules** pinpoint exactly what other kinds of interests may be deemed ownership under the FCC's rules (47 CFR Sec. 73.3555).

Prior to 1996, the FCC limited the total number of broadcast stations anyone could control. By 1994, those limits generally confined a single owner to no more than 20 AM, 20 FM, and 12 full-power TV stations nationwide. For television there was an additional limit of reaching markets totaling no more than 25 percent of the TV homes in the country (UHF TV stations counted only one-half the homes they actually reached).

The Telecommunications Act of 1996 changed the national ownership rules substantially. Now there are no limits on the number of radio stations that one entity may own. As discussed elsewhere, this led to an unprecedented number of radio station sales, with some owners controlling hundreds of radio stations across the country. Congress also removed the limits on the number of TV stations that can be controlled by one owner. Congress maintained the national audience cap for TV owners, though it raised that limit to 39 percent of TV homes in the country. None of these regulations applies to ownership of noncommercial broadcast stations. Note also that while Congress removed these national ownership limits, local ownership restrictions on both radio and television are still in effect.

Duopoly

On the individual market level, a **duopoly** rule the FCC issued in 1940 and enforced for half a century held that no single owner could have more than one station of the same type (e.g., more than one AM station) in the same market.

In 1992, while changing its radio ownership rules, the FCC struck down the duopoly limitation, allowing ownership of up to four stations in the largest radio markets. In 1996, as part of the Communications Act revisions, Congress went even further and codified new local ownership standards for radio depending on the size of the market (see Exhibit 11.f).

In 1999, the FCC amended the television duopoly rule to allow one entity to own two stations in a market under specific conditions. For one entity to own two TV stations in one market, one of the stations cannot be among the top four stations in the market in terms of audience share. Also, the market must have at least eight other full-power TV stations. The new rules also permit an existing owner to buy a second TV station in the market if the station purchased is a "failed station"— one that is either off the air or is involved in involuntary bankruptcy proceedings (47 CFR Sec. 73.3555). At the time this text went to press, the television duopoly rules were being challenged in court.

Exhibit 11.f

Media Ownership Regulations

Multiple Ownership

	Market Size	Limitation
Radio	45 or more commercial stations	8, no more than 5 in one service (AM or FM)
	30–44 commercial stations	7, no more than 4 in one service
	15–29 commercial stations	6, no more than 4 in one service
	14 or *fewer* commercial stations	5, no more than 3 in one service No more than 50 percent of stations in market
Television		May own 2 stations per market if one station is not among the top 4 stations in market *and* there are at least 8 other full-power stations in market Nationally, group-owned stations may cover no more than 39 percent of U.S. TV households
Cable Television		MSOs may not serve more than 30 percent of U.S. video subscribers
MMDS		Can control only one of two sets of frequencies available per market

Cross Ownership

Newspaper-Broadcast	Except in the top 20 TV markets, cannot own a newspaper and a broadcast station in the same market; existing combinations grandfathered
TV-Radio	May own up to 2 television and 6 radio stations in markets with 20 additional independent media "voices" (full-power TV stations, radio stations, daily newspapers, cable systems) May own up to 2 TV stations and 4 radio stations in markets with 10 additional voices May own a television and a radio station not withstanding the number of independent voices in the market

Note that several of these restrictions are being challenged in court. Students should track these proceedings and be aware that these regulations could change.

Cable Systems

Whereas the 1984 cable act *allowed* the FCC to establish cable ownership rules if it chose (it did not), the 1992 cable act *mandated* the Commission to do so. In 1993, the FCC issued rules limiting ownership to systems that pass no more than 30 percent of all U.S. cable subscribers. The FCC revised this rule in 1999. Multiple system operators (MSOs) are now permitted to serve up to 30 percent of all multichannel video subscribers (which includes not only cable subscribers, but also DBS and MMDS subscribers) (47 CFR Sec. 76.503). Comcast, the largest cable MSO in the United States, has challenged this regulation in court.

The Commission also has limited **vertical integration** by ruling that a cable system can devote no more than 40 percent of its channels to program services in which the system operator has an ownership interest. The limit applies to only the first 75 channels.

Cross-Media Ties

Every instance of media **cross ownership**, such as common control of newspapers and broadcast stations in the same market, reduces potential alternative information sources (sometimes called media **voices**, as opposed to actual **outlets**, such as stations or systems). This may be especially undesirable in small communities, in which the only newspaper might own the only broadcast station or cable system.

The FCC issued rules banning new daily newspaper-broadcasting cross ownership in 1975, but allowed all but a very few existing combinations to continue (a process called **grandfathering**). In 2003, citing many changes and increased competition in local media markets, the Commission rescinded the rule, but that action was reversed on appeal (F, 2005). In December 2007, the Commission took a more modest approach and voted to allow newspaper-broadcast cross ownership in the nation's largest 20 TV markets. This decision has also been challenged in court, by public interest groups who oppose further ownership concentration and by media interests who want the rule change extended to smaller television markets.

In 1970, the Commission prohibited broadcast TV network ownership of cable systems, as well as cross ownership of telephone companies or TV stations and cable systems in the same market (except in rural areas of fewer than 5,000 people). Congress eliminated both the network-cable and the cable-telco cross ownership restrictions in the Telecommunications Act of 1996 (broadcast networks have always been allowed to own cable networks).

Common ownership of a television and a radio station in the same market had been prohibited since the mid-1970s (with existing combinations grandfathered). In 1999, as part of its ruling allowing television duopolies, the FCC amended its television-radio cross-ownership rules to permit common station ownership in the same market. In the largest markets, licensees may own up to two television and six radio stations. Even in the smallest markets, one owner can now control a television and a radio station (47 CFR Sec. 73.3555).

Minority Ownership

For years the FCC ignored minority status of owners as an aspect of diversifying media control. A series of court reversals in the 1960s and early 1970s forced it to reexamine its position, and it slowly began to give an advantage to minority applicants.

Over the years the Commission has taken several steps to enhance opportunities for members of ethnic and racial minority groups (African Americans, Hispanics, Asians, and Native Americans) to become licensees.

► **Tax certificates.** These have encouraged the sale of stations and cable systems to minorities by allowing sellers to avoid or at least defer paying capital gains taxes on their profits.
► **Distress sales.** Normally, the Commission will not permit an owner whose license is in serious danger of nonrenewal to sell anything other than the station's physical assets. But to encourage sales to minority applicants, the FCC permits endangered licensees to recover some, though not all, of the market value of "intangible assets" (effectively, the station license and the operation's public image).
► **Controlling interests.** In 1982, the Commission sought to further encourage minority ownership by allowing members of a racial minority holding as little as 20 percent of the equity in a licensee to take advantage of both tax certificates and distress sale rules—provided that the minority owner had voting control. At the same time, the FCC made cable system sales eligible for tax certificate consideration.

► **Minority enhancements.** When the FCC held hearings to decide which of several applicants would receive a broadcast license, the Commission gave preference to minority owners who pledged to work at the station.
► **Lotteries.** Used in choosing LPTV and MMDS licensees, lotteries gave preference to minority ownership.
► **Bidding credits.** These are awarded to companies owned by minorities or women participating in the FCC's frequency auctions.

Minority preferences came under attack in the 1990s. Congress—angered by reports that Viacom might avoid some $600 million in taxes by selling its cable systems to an African American-owned company backed by TCI, the nation's largest cable operator at the time—abolished the tax certificate program as part of its overall review of equal employment opportunity programs. At about the same time, a Supreme Court decision striking down minority preferences for federal contracting cast doubt on the continuing constitutionality of the FCC's race-based policies (US, 1995).

In response to these actions, the FCC initiated a series of proceedings relating to minority and female ownership of electronic media. The first was a broad-based inquiry seeking insights into its existing minority policies and efforts to extend them (FCCR, 1995). The second sought comments on identifying and eliminating market-entry barriers for small businesses, especially small businesses owned by minorities and females (FCCR, 1996). This proceeding led to the policy allowing bidding credits for small businesses seeking new licenses by way of the Commission's spectrum auctions. Responding to concerns about the declining number of minority and female broadcast owners (e.g., Turner, 2007), the FCC initiated yet another inquiry into minority ownership policies in 2007 (FCCR, 2007).

Foreign Control

Section 310(a) of the Communications Act forbids control of a U.S. broadcast or common-carrier radio station by a foreign entity. Specifically, no more than 25 percent of the station's stock or other means of control can be in the hands of foreign investors. Not all electronic media are restricted in this way: Canadian and other foreign interests, for example, may own U.S. cable systems.

11.11 Deregulation

Many motives underlie efforts to deregulate—in communication and several other economic sectors. Least controversial is the recognized need to discard outdated rules, to simplify unnecessarily complex rules, to ensure that those rules that remain can actually achieve their objectives, to lighten administrative agency loads, and to encourage rapid development of new technologies. Deregulation based on these motives began in the 1970s with wide political support.

A more controversial drive to deregulate stems from ideological motives growing out of a specific vision of a limited governmental role in national life. This view opposes government intervention, advocating instead reliance on the marketplace as a nongovernmental source of control over private economic behavior. This approach first emerged as a force on the national agenda in the late 1970s under President Jimmy Carter, escalated when Ronald Reagan came to the White House in 1981, and continued during subsequent administrations. With respect to the regulation of media content, however, many of the FCC's policies have been distinctly re-regulatory. These efforts to increase government oversight of programming content are addressed in the next chapter.

Theoretical Basis

Deregulatory theory holds that marketplace economic forces can stimulate production of better, more varied, and cheaper consumer goods and services without official guidance. When government regulation is proposed, it should be tested by a cost-benefit formula to make sure that the costs of such regulation do not outweigh its gains.

The FCC did not go so far as to advocate abandoning all regulation. It divided rules into behavioral and structural categories. **Behavioral regulation** controls what licensees may or may not do in conducting their businesses; **structural regulation** controls the overall shape of the marketplace and terms on which would-be licensees can enter. Rules requiring a licensee to limit advertising in children's programs are one example of behavioral regulation; rules preventing a licensee from owning more than a specified number of stations are an example of structural regulation.

Media deregulation, however, tilts toward the structural regulation approach, which enhances competition by making marketplace entry easier, preserves competition by preventing monopolies, and stays away from program-based decisions. Critics argue that deregulation serves mainly to enrich a few companies and individuals, often at the expense of broader public concerns.

Even theorists favoring deregulation admit that **market failure** can occur. Sometimes competition fails to produce expected favorable results. Indeed, uncontrolled competition may produce corporate giants that suppress competition (major airline control of most departure gates at "hub" airports is one example). And some public "goods," as economists call desirable services, may fall outside the realm of marketplace economics and therefore fail to materialize. If, for example, public television is thought desirable, but costs too much to produce with limited private support, marketplace economics may have to be supplemented by giving such broadcasters government aid.

Deregulation in Practice

Although many industry leaders praise deregulation in theory, they sometimes argue against it in practice because regulation often protects them from increased competition. For example, existing broadcasters generally opposed the deregulation of some technical rules necessary for the creation of the new Low Power FM Service. As originally proposed, this service could have added thousands of new radio stations. Likewise, leaders in the cable television business argue for deregulation when it is in their best interests—regarding subscriber rates or signal carriage rules, for example. But the industry strongly opposed the deregulation of the cable-telco cross ownership rules, not wanting the increased competition from the telephone companies.

Technical Standards

In the past, the FCC assumed responsibility for setting technical standards for a new technology when it was made commercially available. Universally mandated standards protect the public—at least to a point—from investing in new products that might later prove incompatible with existing products or of less than optimum quality. The deregulatory approach, however, tends to reject official standard setting, leaving choices to the marketplace. This often works in the consumer electronics market (consider the early competition, for example, between high definition DVD formats, Sony's Blu-ray and Toshiba's HD DVD), but has been less successful when applied to broadcast standards.

The issue was defined when the Commission declined to select a specific standard while approving AM stereo in 1982, a precedent for a decade of refusals to impose standards. Similar "nondecisions" followed regarding DBS, teletext, and other standards, indicating that economists had superseded engineers in Commission policy making, even in largely technical matters.

The "marketplace" in each case actually consisted not of consumers buying receivers but of station owners, operators, and manufacturers choosing equipment. Broadcasters would have to decide for themselves which transmission standard to use, hoping that set makers would eventually gear up to supply receivers that consumers would buy.

In AM stereo's case, that did not happen. A decade later few stations were broadcasting in stereo and few consumers had stereo-equipped AM receivers. Both the industry and the Commission recognized that deregulation had failed to achieve its goals. Finally, acting on a congressional mandate, the FCC in 1993 selected Motorola's CQuam system, although the decade-late decision made little difference for beleaguered AM licensees.

Industry debate over the FCC's approach to technical standards rose to a fever pitch over **advanced television (ATV)** standards. At issue were the same questions: Should government help industry select specific standards, and would selection of a standard stifle technical development? But ATV's financial stakes were far higher—the eventual replacement of all the country's broadcast and consumer TV equipment, and concerns about further imbalance of international trade if ATV devices were largely imported. Perhaps having learned a valuable lesson from its AM stereo debacle, the Commission in the 1990s began the arduous but vital process of setting standards for this new technology, with billions of dollars riding on the outcome. Finally, after years of testing and compromise, the FCC adopted an industry-developed transmission standard for advanced TV services in 1996. For most full-power TV stations in the United States, the transition to the new digital standard concluded in February of 2009. But even in the case of advanced TV services, including high-definition television (HDTV), the FCC left image shape, image resolution, and the method of scanning up to the marketplace.

The Commission simplified the transition to digital radio broadcasting by adopting a digital radio standard in 2002. Unlike the TV transition, which was mandatory, the radio transition is entirely voluntary; individual stations will decide whether and when to offer digital radio services.

Deregulation Critique

Deregulation has had many positive effects. It greatly speeded FCC actions, eliminated outdated rules, encouraged the development of new technology, and gave audiences more program choice.

But deregulation can have negative results as well. The following policy decisions illustrate the sometimes unintended consequences of deregulation.

▶ Abandonment by the FCC of many recordkeeping requirements as a money-saving tactic in the early 1980s left blanks in knowledge about the electronic media. For example, discontinuation of annual broadcasting and cable financial reports limited the FCC's own understanding of the changing financial health of broadcasters and cable systems amid substantial transition.

▶ Deregulation—no matter what the source—tends to put business interests ahead of those of the public. With its 1984 cable act, for example, Congress curbed the right of cities to control cable subscription fees, allowing systems to raise rates freely, given their monopoly status in most markets. Subsequent cable price increases and poor service pushed Congress to reinstate FCC cable oversight eight years later.

▶ The deregulation of media ownership in the Telecommunications Act of 1996 triggered considerable industry concentration both on the national and local levels. As companies consolidated their staffs, many employees found themselves jobless.

▶ The deregulatory vision of all human activity reduced to simplistic economic terms (the marketplace) treated programs as the equivalent of manufactured goods with little concern for diversity, quality, or cultural content—what former chairman Mark Fowler called "a toaster with pictures."

▶ The Telecommunications Act of 1996 was expected to open the way for new competition in media markets. As noted elsewhere, the act instead has led to increased consolidation of media ownership, which some would argue has actually decreased media competition.

▶ Citing the increased competition from cable television systems providing telephone services, several states deregulated the telephone companies. Many phone companies responded by significantly raising their rates for services.

11.12 Other Regulations

Many other federal laws, as well as state and municipal statutes, affect the electronic media. The following sections briefly survey some of the most relevant.

Treaties

The tendency of radio signals to ignore political boundaries necessitates international treaties to prevent interference. The United States and its neighbors have entered into separate regional treaties governing AM, FM, and TV broadcasting. AM agreements cover the widest territory, because long-distance sky-wave propagation affects the scattered islands of the Caribbean as well as the two common-border nations, Canada and Mexico; agreements on simpler FM and TV allocations have also long been in place with both countries.

On American international telecommunications policy, the FCC works closely with the U.S. State Department and the National Telecommunications and Information Administration (NTIA)—an agency of the Department of Commerce that acts as the president's chief adviser on telecommunications questions. The FCC provides technical expertise and helps coordinate private-sector participation.

Press Law

The electronic media share with the print media a body of laws, precedents, and privileges known as the law of the press. Typical areas include defamation, obscenity, trial coverage, freedom of access to information, right of privacy, labor laws, and copyright (many of which are discussed in Chapter 12).

One other area, **reporter's privilege**, concerns the asserted right of news personnel to withhold the identity of news sources and to refuse to surrender personal notes, including any audio and video "outtakes." This and many other aspects of press law fall under state jurisdiction, with results varying widely from state to state.

Regulation of Advertising

The FCC itself has no authority to punish licensees directly for unfair advertising. All it can do is cite fraudulent advertising as evidence that an applicant or licensee lacks the requisite character qualification to be a licensee and refer cases of deceptive advertising to a sister agency, the Federal Trade Commission (FTC).

The FTC settles most cases of alleged advertising deception by **stipulation**, an informal (and hence timesaving) way of getting advertisers to drop objectionable practices voluntarily. If a formal complaint becomes necessary, the FTC can seek a **consent order**, another nonpunitive measure under which the advertiser agrees to stop the offending practice without admitting guilt. Actual guilt has to be proved before the FTC can obtain a **cease and desist order** forcing compliance with the law. Such orders can be appealed in the courts. The appeal process can mean long delays in bringing the objectionable advertising to an end if the advertiser chooses to use it.

The only legal product officially banned from broadcast and cable advertising is cigarettes and related tobacco products. A federal statute adopted in 1971 imposed the ban. Many broadcasters claim that they were unfairly singled out because cigarette ads continue to appear—even increase—in other media.

The FCC does have jurisdiction over commercialization levels for children's television. A 1990 act of Congress limited the time that could be devoted to advertising in children's programs (defined as programming intended for children 12 and younger) to 10.5 minutes per hour on weekends and 12 minutes per hour on weekdays. This regulation applies to both broadcast stations and cable networks. The FCC is in charge of enforcing these rules, and the Commission

has assessed thousands of dollars in fines for violating these limits.

State and Local Laws

Under the Constitution, federal laws prevail over state laws in subject areas designated as being of federal concern. This means that a state law cannot override the Communications Act. Nevertheless, state laws govern many electronic media activities that are not covered by federal statutes. Scores of state laws affect the print and electronic media, especially those concerned with these areas:

▶ individual rights (regarding defamation and privacy, as discussed in Section 12.4)
▶ advertising of specific products and services
▶ noncommercial broadcasting (many states have commissions to coordinate statewide public radio and television activities)
▶ standard business operations (e.g., state taxes)
▶ aspects of cable television—including franchising or cable right-of-way disputes, theft of service, and the attachment of cable lines to utility poles (municipalities, too, have enacted many local regulations on cable franchising)
▶ zoning controls over the placement of antenna towers

Informal Controls

Sometimes just the suggestion of regulation by the FCC can influence industry behavior. A well-timed speech by the Chair of the Commission on the need for more local programs, for example, may prod station managers to provide more programming of local interest. This unofficial cajoling, or regulation "by raised eyebrow" as some pundits have called it, has long been a tool in the Commission's arsenal of tactics to help licensees take the preferred path. Members of Congress wield similar power and often exert it during Committee hearings where they sometimes blast industry representatives for perceived wrongdoing.

Since the 1920s, the White House has found ways to influence electronic media policy. The Clinton administration, for example, took an activist approach to telecommunications policy making. Several times President Clinton invited electronic media leaders to the White House for policy discussions on the topics of violence and children's television requirements. Vice President Al Gore was a leading administration spokesperson for telecommunication reform. By contrast, the George W. Bush administration took a more hands-off approach, relying on the president's appointees at the FCC to carry out administration priorities. The overall effect of White House pressure varies with each administration and its interest in communications matters.

Self-Regulation

Many professions and industries adopt voluntary codes of conduct to cultivate favorable public relations and forestall abuses that might otherwise bring on government regulation. But codes that restrict the freedom to compete often run afoul of antitrust laws.

The National Association of Broadcasters (NAB) began developing a code for radio programming and advertising practices in the late 1920s and extended them to television in 1952. These codes used broad generalizations and many "shoulds" and "should nots," but left most decisions to the discretion of station management. Nonetheless, the codes reinforced generally observed standards, especially as to the amount of time broadcasters should devote to advertising.

Despite NAB precautions to avoid any hint of coercion, the Department of Justice brought suit against the Television Code in 1979. The suit alleged that code time standards "artificially curtailed" advertising, repressing price competition and "depriving advertisers of the benefits of free and open competition." In 1982, a federal district court approved a consent decree by which the NAB disbanded its code-making activities.

Much self-regulation results from media worries about externally imposed controls. Consequently, networks and many stations continued to follow their own internal standards—some even tougher than the former NAB codes.

Consumer Action

The highlight event that crystallized interest in broadcast reform came in the consumerism heyday of the 1960s. The WLBT case (see Exhibit 11.d) gave a station's audience the legal right to file complaints against the station and participate in license renewal proceedings. Hundreds did, though with relatively little lasting impact.

In recent years, consumer action has increasingly taken the form of single-issue groups with specific complaints. The threat of a **boycott** was a popular tactic in the 1980s and 1990s to try to influence electronic media behavior. For example, in 1999 the NAACP threatened to boycott the major broadcast networks to protest the lack of minorities in network programs. Boycotts involve not watching or listening to targeted stations and refusing to buy advertised products. In a pluralistic society, boycotters have difficulty achieving sufficient consensus and discipline to do substantial economic damage.

Beginning around the turn of the century, concerned citizens and special-interest groups began taking their complaints directly to the government through the use of e-mail. Both Congress and the FCC have been flooded with complaints about sex and violence in the electronic media, prompting additional regulation (as discussed in Chapter 12) and industry self-regulation. For example, in response to criticism that many cable TV program tiers contain channels that some subscribers find objectionable, several cable operators began offering "family friendly tiers" that do not include those channels.

Even noncommercial broadcasting, supposedly freer to present more points of view because it does not cater to advertisers, has succumbed to group pressure. Programs on gay lifestyles, avant-garde art, and Third World political movements have all been criticized—and sometimes temporarily removed from the air.

Press Criticism

Coverage of the electronic media in both the trade and popular press often affects policy. Congress, the White House, the FCC, and other agencies closely follow reporting about the media, seeking reports of their actions.

Reviewers in major newspapers and magazines seem to have more impact on news and public-affairs programs than on entertainment shows. Further, they influence producers of such programs more than they do the general audience.

Constitutional Issues and Content Regulation

chapter

he First Amendment to the U.S. Constitution, together with the Fourteenth Amendment (see Exhibit 12.a), prohibits government regulation of speech and press, yet the Communications Act imposes federal licensing and other limitations on those who own electronic media. This paradox isn't unique, as society often demands a balance between the ideal of *absolute* individual freedom and the practical need to limit speech that might harm others (e.g., one may be punished for yelling "fire" in a crowded theater if there is none). The essence of the constitutional controversies discussed here is how to compromise between these opposing goals.

12.1 First Amendment

The freedoms of speech and press guaranteed by the First Amendment were intended from the start—and the courts have construed them since—to encourage a wide-open **marketplace of ideas**. First Amendment theory holds that ideas and opinions from different sources should compete in such a marketplace. As the Supreme Court noted in a landmark electronic media decision, "It is the purpose of the First Amendment to preserve an uninhibited marketplace of ideas in which truth will ultimately prevail, rather than to countenance monopolization of the market" (US, 1969: 390).

Although freedom of expression is only part of one of the 10 amendments that make up the Bill of Rights, that freedom has played a pivotal role in the American political system and is seen as essential to a well-functioning democracy. In the words of Supreme Court Justice William Brennan, the First Amendment "was fashioned to assure unfettered interchange of ideas for the bringing about of political and social changes desired by the people" (US 1957: 484).

"No Such Thing as a False Idea"

"Under the First Amendment," said the Supreme Court, "there is no such thing as a false idea. However pernicious an opinion may seem, we depend for its correction not on the conscience of judges and juries, but on the competition of other ideas" (US, 1974: 339)—again, the marketplace metaphor.

The First Amendment *encourages* disagreement. "A function of free speech under our system of government is to invite dispute," wrote Justice William O. Douglas. "It may indeed best serve its highest purpose when it induces a condition of unrest, creates dissatisfaction with conditions as they are, or even stirs people to anger" (US, 1949: 4).

Anger certainly arose after a talk show host on a Boston radio station urged violence against Muslims. According to complaints filed at the FCC, the host allegedly stated, "I believe that Muslims in this country are a fifth column . . . You believe that we should befriend them. I think we should kill them." The complaints also alleged that the host advocated dropping bombs in the Middle East to kill Muslims. Citing a long line of precedent, the FCC declined to take action against the station, saying:

> It is the judgment of the Commission, as it has been the judgment of those who drafted our Constitution and of the overwhelming majority of our legislators and judges over the years, that the public interest is best served by permitting the expression of any views that do not involve "a clear and present danger of serious substantive evil that rises far above public inconvenience, annoyance, or unrest." . . . [T]his principle insures that the most diverse and opposing opinions will be expressed, many of which may be even highly offensive to those officials who thus protect the rights of others to free speech. If there is to be free speech, it must be free for speech that we abhor and hate as well as for speech that we find tolerable or congenial. (FCCR, 2004c)

Because there was no finding that the broadcast incited a "clear and present danger of serious substantive evil," the complaint was dismissed.

Government Censorship

Many assume that the First Amendment also provides protection from private parties. But, in fact, the amendment aims at protecting people only from government (censorship), not from one another (broadcaster or cable editorial decisions). When controversial radio host Don Imus made insensitive remarks about a women's basketball team, it was his employer, CBS, that took him off the air, not the government. Moreover, station, system, and network officials who edit, cut, bleep, delete, revise, and otherwise mangle programs may be guilty of bad judgment, excessive timidity, and other faults, but editorial control is not censorship, and it does not violate the First Amendment.

Such control becomes a violation only when it results from the kind of government intrusion known as **state action.** In promoting the "family viewing" concept in the 1970s, for example, the FCC attempted to reduce TV violence not by rule but by "jawboning"—pressuring the television industry to regulate itself. When the National Association of Broadcasters (NAB) responded to this pressure by amending its Television Code, a court construed this private action as state action in violation of the First Amendment (F, 1979: 355).

Prior Restraint

The principal evil that First Amendment authors intended to address is **prior restraint;** that is, preventing

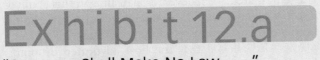

Exhibit 12.a

"Congress Shall Make No Law . . ."

The First Amendment protects four fundamental rights of citizens that governments throughout history have had the most reason to fear and the greatest inclination to violate—freedom to *believe*, to *speak*, to *gather together*, and to ask rulers to *correct injustices*. The amendment conveys all this in only 45 words, of which just 14 guarantee freedom of expression:

> Congress shall make no law respecting an establishment of religion, or prohibiting the free exercise thereof, or abridging the freedom of speech, or of the press; or the right of the people peaceably to assemble, and to petition the Government for a redress of grievances.

These words limit not only Congress, but also state and local governments, thanks to the Fourteenth Amendment, passed in 1868, which says, "No state shall make or enforce any law which shall abridge the privileges or immunities of citizens of the United States." Sec. 326 of the Communications Act of 1934 explicitly extends the First Amendment's protection to broadcasting:

> Nothing in this Act shall be understood or construed to give the Commission the power of censorship over the radio communications or signals transmitted by any radio station, and no regulation or condition shall be promulgated or fixed by the Commission which shall interfere with the right of free speech by means of radio communication.

Source: Photo from Stock Connection.

someone in advance from saying, showing, or otherwise publishing something. Only in the most extreme and exceedingly rare case will a court issue an **injunction** barring, for example, a TV program from broadcasting a story that may be an invasion of privacy (see Section 12.4). When such invasions occur, the remedy is punishment after the fact, not censorship before.

Religious Freedom

Another First Amendment clause guarantees religious freedom. The increasing propensity of preachers of all stripes to exhort their flocks to support specific parties or candidates disturbs many people who are sensitive to First Amendment concerns about the establishment of any specific religion. Yet, the same amendment protects the pastors' right to have their say.

Doubly protected by the freedoms of speech and religion, stations owned by religious groups have often claimed near-immunity from FCC requirements because they regard their right of religious freedom (from any government action) as absolute. Though the FCC holds religious licensees to the same standards as any other broadcaster, it has resisted close monitoring of any licensees. On the other hand, cable operator arguments that rules requiring them to carry religious TV stations violate the systems owners' First Amendment rights to religious freedom have proved unsuccessful.

12.2 Broadcasting's Limited Rights

Just what do the First Amendment words **speech** and **press** mean in today's context? Speech encompasses not only that amplified by public-address systems, but also film, broadcasting, videos, cable, DBS, and the Internet. The press includes pornographic magazines. Can *all* ways of expressing oneself and *all* forms of the press claim equal First Amendment rights?

Broadcasting vs. Print

More specifically, should all regulated electronic media have First Amendment *parity* (equality) with unregulated media, especially the printed press? The answer has generally been no—the First Amendment protects some media more than others. Broadcasting, it is argued, has unique attributes that justify imposing certain regulations that would violate the First Amendment if imposed on newspapers. The three main arguments favoring this assumption follow.

Channel Scarcity

Not everyone who wants to own a station can do so, because intolerable interference would otherwise result. Because of this channel scarcity, the government (the FCC) has to choose among applicants. Where mutually exclusive applications seek facilities whose activation would cause interference, only one license can be granted; thereby abridging the freedom of other applicants. By contrast, anyone who can afford it can publish a newspaper or magazine without limit or license.

The development of new and improved services *has* decreased scarcity as a justification for regulating broadcasting. The huge increase in the number of stations since Congress wrote the 1927 Radio Act—from about 600 to more than 15,000, plus more than 5,000 cable systems—makes scarcity a relative factor at best. And although demand for channels in major markets continues, cable, DBS, and the Internet provide a multitude of additional channels—converting scarcity into abundance.

By contrast, others point to the many applicants for desirable stations that become available, and the huge prices often paid for them, to suggest that scarcity continues. In any event, cable, DBS, and access to the Internet differ sharply from "free" broadcasting by requiring subscription fees over and above receiver expenses.

Others argue that even if spectrum scarcity does exist, that fact does not justify treating broadcasting differently from the printed press in terms of the First Amendment. Judge Robert Bork, in a case before the U.S. Court of Appeals, addressed the issue this way:

> The line drawn between the print media and the broadcast media, resting as it does on the physical scarcity of the latter, is a distinction without a difference.
> It is certainly true that broadcast frequencies are scarce but it is unclear why that fact justifies content regulation of broadcasting in a way that would be intolerable if applied to the editorial process of the print media. All economic goods are scarce, not the least the newsprint, ink, delivery trucks, computers, and other resources that go into the production and dissemination of print journalism. Not everyone who wishes to publish a newspaper, or even a pamphlet, may do so. Since scarcity is a universal fact, it can hardly explain regulation in one context and not another. (F, 1986: 508)

According to this argument, economic scarcity, not physical scarcity, is what drives media ownership. Anybody can speak via a broadcast station—as long as he or she has enough money to buy one.

Conflict in Licensing

When writing the Communications Act, Congress explicitly confirmed "the right of free speech by means of radio communication." Yet, the Act also requires the FCC to grant or renew licenses only if they serve the public interest. It also requires the FCC to ensure that candidates for public office have equal opportunities to use broadcast stations.

Any such requirements by definition place limits on licensees' freedom of speech. That fundamental contradiction came before the Supreme Court in the 1943 *NBC* case, where broadcasters argued that the FCC had the right to regulate only *technical* factors, and that any

further regulation violated the First Amendment. But the Court emphatically rejected this argument, saying:

> We are asked to regard the Commission as a kind of traffic officer, policing the wave lengths to prevent stations from interfering with one another. But the Act does not restrict the Commission merely to supervision of the traffic. It puts upon the Commission the burden of determining the composition of that traffic. (US, 1943: 215)

Intrusiveness

Radio and television enter directly into virtually every U.S. household, readily available to people of all ages and types. Because of the intrusive nature of the medium, people never know exactly what they will see or hear when they first turn on their sets, and that initial exposure might be upsetting. The medium also is easily accessible to children; it requires no special training to turn on a television or radio and flip through the channels or stations. Children who are not yet old enough to read can use a broadcast receiver even when their parents are not around. Because of broadcasting's intrusiveness and easy accessibility to children, Congress, the courts, and the FCC have often imposed content regulation on broadcasters that would not be allowed in the print media. Some content acceptable in other media (e.g., indecency), may be regarded as intolerable in broadcasting, at least when children form a substantial portion of the audience.

First Amendment purists respond that where such distinctions need to be made, the marketplace can make them better than government. If people object to a program, they can, and do, complain to station and system operators, networks, or advertisers, or they can simply hit the "off" button. Regarding protection of children, opponents of content regulation argue that parents, not the government, should be responsible for the viewing and listening behavior of children.

12.3 First Amendment Status of Other Electronic Media

Because of the factors noted in the previous section, broadcasting enjoys substantially less First Amendment protection than the printed press. Generally speaking, as new electronic media emerge, they are not regulated (and thus match the print model) until and unless government takes some specific action (e.g., congressional attempts to control indecency on the Internet). Government must then discern how those media should be treated in terms of the free speech and free press guarantees. The Supreme Court has repeatedly stated that, for First Amendment purposes, each new medium must be judged based on its own unique characteristics. When judging new media, the government tends to analyze them in terms of what is already familiar. Often the analysis comes down to the question, "Is the new service more like print or more like broadcasting?"

On a scale of First Amendment protection, cable TV systems fall somewhere between the print and broadcast media. Courts consistently find that cable is much different than a broadcast station in terms of its physical characteristics. Cable systems do not use the electromagnetic spectrum in the same way broadcasters do, so spectrum scarcity typically is not an issue. Because cable is a subscription service, cable is not considered as intrusive as broadcasting; subscribers choose to bring the service into their homes every month as they pay their cable bills. For similar reasons, cable is not considered as accessible to children. Plus, cable systems have long provided special lock boxes that can block out channels that parents may find unsuitable for children.

For these reasons, certain programming restrictions that have been upheld for broadcasters (e.g., indecency regulations), have been judged invalid when applied to cable TV systems. Critics consider this rather curious. Most consumers do not think much about how their TV signals are delivered so long as they get a good picture with good service. But under the First Amendment rulings, TV content is regulated differently based on how it is delivered to the home. On the other hand, courts have approved content-related regulations for cable systems—the must-carry rules offer a good example—that would never be approved if applied to newspapers or magazines.

Other electronic media whose First Amendment status has been considered by the courts have been treated similarly. Speech and press protections for telephone systems, DBS, and the Internet so far seem to fall somewhere between the protections afforded newspapers and broadcasters. In all cases, the courts must balance the interests of those seeking the broadest protection of speech and those arguing for protection from certain types of content.

12.4 Things You Can't Say

Despite that seemingly strict First Amendment command, "Congress shall make no law . . .," government does in fact make laws that punish *unprotected* speech. This includes defamation (libel and slander), invasion of privacy, and obscenity.

Libel: Protecting Reputations

Libel is **defamation** by published untrue words that may expose their subject to public hatred, shame, or disgrace. Spoken defamation is called **slander**, but because

electronic media spread spoken words far and wide, and because the words are often preserved, broadcast or cable defamation is treated as libel.

Libel laws constitute another example of conflicting social interests. Although libel should be punishable because society has an interest in protecting its citizens, society also needs to expose official corruption and incompetence. Harassing libel suits can serve as a screen to protect dishonest politicians. In the United States all public figures, not just politicians, must be prepared to face harsh, sometimes even unfair and ill-founded, criticism from the media, because it is extremely difficult to prove the **actual malice** standard necessary for their libel suit to succeed (see Exhibit 12.b).

In fact, most libel suits are resolved long before they reach trial: They are dropped, settled, or dismissed by a judge during pretrial proceedings. Even when the media win, however, they spend a lot of money defending themselves. More important, such suits have a **chilling effect** on investigative reporting.

Preserving Privacy

Privacy as an individual right, though not spelled out in the Constitution, is implied in the Fourth Amendment: "The right of the people to be secure in their persons, houses, papers, and effects . . . shall not be violated." The law of privacy is not as well developed as libel law, but several individual privacy rights have been identified:

▶ the right to physical solitude
▶ protection from intrusion on private property or publication of the private details of one's personal life
▶ protection from being presented in a "false light" (e.g., being photographed walking on campus and then being included in a visual accompanying a TV feature about drug use in college)
▶ protection from unauthorized use of one's name or image for commercial gain

Although the courts have held that public officials, performers, and people involved in news events have a lesser right to privacy because of legitimate public interest in those persons or events, privacy laws still limit the media by generally supporting individual rights.

Privacy advocates are concerned increasingly about loss of privacy on the Internet. The computer programs that allow web browsing and on-line purchasing also enable marketers to track an individual's web use. Opinions differ on whether such tracking is benign or pernicious, but many people do not like the fact that their web use can be monitored. Also, computer databases that contain private financial or medical records can easily be copied and transferred without an individual's knowledge or consent. Many groups concerned about privacy rights have lobbied Congress to enact

Exhibit 12.b

Times v. Sullivan Libel Landmark

The leading case establishing the relative protection of media from libel suits filed by public figures occurred during the civil rights protests of the 1960s. By chance it involved an instance of "editorial advertising," not investigative reporting. Supporters of the Montgomery, Alabama bus boycott protesting segregation bought a large display advertisement in the *New York Times* that criticized Montgomery officials. Some of the statements in the advertisement were false, although they apparently were not *deliberate* lies. Sullivan, one of the officials, sued for libel in an Alabama court (all libel suits have to be brought at the state level). The court awarded Sullivan a half-million dollars in damages, and the Alabama Supreme Court affirmed the decision.

On appeal to the U.S. Supreme Court, the *Times* won a reversal. Criticism of public officials, said the Court, had broad First Amendment protection. Even though some of the allegations against the unnamed officials were untrue, they did not constitute libel. Argument over public officials, the Court continued, should be "uninhibited, robust, and wide-open." It may include "vehement, caustic, and sometimes unpleasantly sharp attacks on government and public officials." Such free-wheeling debate would be discouraged if, in the heat of controversy, the critic must pause to weigh every unfavorable word:

> The constitutional guarantees require, we think, a federal rule that prohibits a public official from recovering damages for a defamatory falsehood relating to his *official* conduct unless he proves that the statement was made with "actual malice"—that is, with knowledge that it was false or with reckless disregard of whether it was false or not. (US, 1964: 279)

Subsequent libel cases broadened the term *public officials* to include anyone who, because of notoriety, could be classed as a *public figure*. People so classified have little chance of bringing a successful libel suit against the media. Even when stories about public figures are false, plaintiffs find it exceedingly difficult to prove actual malice.

Restricting Court Coverage

The due process clause of the Fifth Amendment ensures fair play to persons accused of crimes. The Sixth Amendment also spells out some of the elements of due process, among them the right to a fair and public trial in criminal cases. Ordinarily, news media freely cover trials, but that coverage can subject participants to such extensive publicity that a fair trial becomes impossible. In this **free press vs. fair trial** confrontation, the constitutional rights of the media sometimes have to give way to the constitutional rights of criminal defendants.

For decades there was virtually no live or recorded radio or television coverage of trials. After messy coverage of the Lindbergh kidnapping trial (see Exhibit 12.c), the American Bar Association (ABA) recommended in 1935 that judges discourage radio and photo coverage because it tended "to detract from the essential dignity of the proceedings, degrade the court, and create misconceptions with respect thereto in the mind of the public."

By the 1970s, less intrusive equipment and seemingly more mature broadcast journalism judgment persuaded the ABA to recommend that judges be given wider latitude in allowing photo and video coverage of trials. In 1981, the Supreme Court—although it bans cameras and microphones in its own proceedings—noted the improved technology, holding that "the risk of juror prejudice . . . does not warrant an absolute constitutional ban on all broadcast coverage" (US, 1981: 560). Today, all but a handful of states either allow cameras in their courtrooms or have conducted experiments to that end.

Federal courts have remained off-limits to such coverage, despite repeated media attempts to breach that barrier. Late in 1994, after a multiyear experiment with TV coverage of civil cases in six federal district and two appeals courts, the Judicial Conference of the United States voted to restore its flat ban on cameras in federal courtrooms. Exceptions occasionally occur (e.g., the Second Circuit allowed C-SPAN to televise oral arguments in the 2007 case involving Fox television's challenge of an indecency fine), but, in general, cameras and recording equipment are not allowed in federal courtrooms.

Broadcast Hoaxes

While the broadcasting of "news" that isn't really news dates back at least to the 1938 Orson Welles' broadcast of *War of the Worlds*, there have been relatively few cases of intentional news hoax broadcasts. However, a rash of cases in the early 1990s convinced the FCC that it needed stronger rules and a means of fining stations for hoaxes rather than just sending letters of concern. Several stations broadcast stories of false murders, one station said a nearby trash dump was about to explode because of methane gas buildup, another used the Emergency Alert System and said a nuclear attack was

legislation to prohibit the unauthorized use of private information on the Internet, but, other than requiring companies to notify consumers of their privacy policies, Congress seems unwilling to act, preferring that companies engage in self-regulation.

Special privacy rules apply to children. For example, in 1998, Congress adopted the Children's On-line Privacy Protection Act to regulate the collection of personal data from children by web site operators. Pursuant to the act, the Federal Trade Commission adopted rules requiring web sites that cater to children to post their privacy policies. The rules also restrict companies from collecting personal information from children without a parent's permission.

Exhibit 12.c

Covering Courts—Changing Pictures

(A)

(B)

Broadcast coverage of court trials began with the 1925 Scopes case and reached the height of overkill with **(A)** the 1935 trial of Bruno Hauptmann for the kidnap and murder of Charles Lindbergh's son. Reaction to that intrusive coverage by radio and film led to the ABA's "Canon 35," which banned trial coverage for decades. **(B)** An experiment in television coverage in the 1960s, Billie Sol Estes's trial for fraud, led to a Supreme Court reversal because of television intrusiveness. **(C)** Court coverage reached historic proportions in 1994 and 1995 when live cameras, hour after hour, watched every move by the prosecution and defense in the bizarre case of sports and media personality O. J. Simpson, charged with murdering his former wife and her friend.

(C)

Sources: Photo (A) from AP/Wide World Photos; photo (B) © Bettmann/Corbis; photo (C) from AP Photo/Reed Saxon.

under way, and still another reported that a volcano had erupted in a suburban Connecticut town. All were presented as real events, and emergency forces responded accordingly.

In 1992, the Commission adopted a rule against "harmful" hoaxes—those that might divert police, fire, or other safety forces from real events. The FCC made clear that it had the First Amendment in mind as the rule was developed and hence limited its actions to cases where "broadcast of such information will cause substantial public harm, and broadcast of the information does in fact directly cause such harm." Such broadcasts can result in significant fines.

Lotteries

The advertising of illegal lotteries can subject a licensee to a fine and imprisonment for each day's offense, according to a provision of the U.S. Criminal Code (18 USC 1304). This statute concerns broadcasters because they frequently use contests in advertising and promotional campaigns. They must take care not to let an innocent promotional gimmick turn into an illegal lottery—defined as a *chance* to win a *prize* for a *price*.

A contest becomes a lottery if it requires participants to pay any kind of fee or go out of their way (*price* or *consideration*), chooses the winner by lot (*chance*), and awards the winner something of value (*prize*). Contests involving these elements can get a station into serious trouble. The advertising of legal city and state lotteries is exempted from the anti-lottery statute. Restrictions on broadcast advertising for casino gambling were declared unconstitutional by the Supreme Court in 1999 (US, 1999).

12.5 Obscenity and Indecency

One of the most controversial topics regarding electronic media concerns sexually explicit content. Although the terms "obscene" and "indecent" might be considered synonyms in polite conversation, in law they have different and specific meanings, though they both refer to sexually explicit material. If something is found to be "obscene," it has no First Amendment protection whatsoever. According to the Supreme Court,

> All ideas having even the slightest redeeming social importance—unorthodox ideas, controversial ideas, even ideas hateful to the prevailing climate of opinion—have the full protection of the [First Amendment] guarantees. . . . But implicit in the history of the First Amendment is the rejection of obscenity as utterly without redeeming social importance. . . . We hold that obscenity is not within the area of constitutionally protected speech or press. (US, 1957: 484)

"Indecent" speech, on the other hand, is protected expression under the First Amendment, but it can be regulated under certain conditions to protect children from being exposed to it. The major problem with this area of the law, for both students and the media, is defining and understanding the terms "obscene" and "indecent."

What Is Obscene?

The current definition of obscenity dates to the 1973 *Miller* case in which the Supreme Court upheld a California obscenity law. The decision reaffirmed the basic notion that obscene material does not receive protection under the First Amendment. The Court then emphasized that **community standards** vary from place to place: "It is neither realistic nor constitutionally sound to read the First Amendment as requiring that the people of Maine or Mississippi accept public depiction of conduct found tolerable in Las Vegas or New York City."

Nevertheless, the Court warned, state laws must carefully confine what they classify as **obscene** to "works which, taken as a whole, *appeal to the prurient interest in sex, which portray sexual conduct in a patently offensive way, and which, taken as a whole, do not have serious literary, artistic, political, or scientific value*" (US, 1973b: 24; emphasis added).

The *Miller* case, along with later decisions that added minor modifications, restricted obscenity censorship to "hard-core" pornography. Courts now interpret the First Amendment as preventing censors from taking such arbitrary actions as these:

▶ condemning an entire work because of a few isolated vulgar words
▶ using outdated standards no longer common to the local community
▶ applying as a standard the opinions of hypersensitive persons not typical of the general public
▶ ignoring serious artistic, scientific, literary, or political purpose in judging a work

Generally speaking, courts must consider the "average person" when applying contemporary community standards to potentially obscene material. Historically, those standards have been stricter for material available to children.

Limiting Indecency in Broadcasting

Section 1464 of the U.S. Criminal Code reads:

> Whosoever utters any *obscene, indecent,* or *profane* language by means of radio communication shall be fined not more than $10,000 or imprisoned for not more than two years, or both. (18 USC 1464; emphasis added)

Note the use of *indecent* and *profane* in the statute. As with *obscene,* definitions and degrees of control have varied for these terms over the years. For most of its history, the Commission ignored the profanity provision, focusing exclusively on dealing with indecency. In a 1992 policy statement, the Commission defined **indecency** as "language or material that, in context, depicts or describes, in terms patently offensive as measured by *contemporary community standards for the broadcast medium,* sexual or excretory activities or organs" (FCCR, 1992b: 6464, note 4, emphasis added).

The Commission long remained in doubt as to its power to enforce the Criminal Code provision. Because of ready availability of electronic media to children, material acceptable in other media might be regarded as unacceptable by many in the audience. Furthermore, because broadcast and cable network services have national reach, they confront a great variety of local standards.

Broadcasting's traditional conservatism delayed its response to the tolerant social climate of the 1960s, but the liberalization of standards in other media had its effect. In the 1970s, a "topless radio" fad found receptive audiences in some markets. The format invited women to call in and talk on the air about intimate details of their sex lives. Although such talk shows are commonplace today, on television as well as radio, one Illinois radio broadcast in 1973 triggered a flood of complaints. The FCC imposed what was then a fairly steep $2,000 fine on the offending FM station (FCCR, 1973: 919). The Commission had actually hoped that the station would contest the fine, thus precipitating a test case, but the station dutifully mailed in a check instead (for an amount equal to only a few minutes' worth of advertising revenue in a major market).

Pacifica Decision

That same year, the FCC finally got its test case. A noncommercial station, WBAI-FM in New York, included in a discussion of social attitudes about language a recording of a nightclub act by comedian George Carlin (see Exhibit 12.d). Called "Filthy Words," the monologue satirized society's hang-ups about seven sexually oriented words not likely to be heard on the air. This time, though, they were heard—no fewer than 106 times in 12 minutes. The single complaint came from a man who, as it later turned out, was associated with a group called Morality in Media. He heard the early-afternoon broadcast with his teenage son—a crucial element in the case.

On the basis of that lone complaint, the FCC advised station management that the broadcast appeared to violate the indecency statute. The licensee, Pacifica, challenged the ruling as a matter of First Amendment principles. The FCC received an initial setback in the appeals court, but won Supreme Court approval of its reasoning. Focusing its argument on the Carlin monologue as *indecent* rather than obscene (as the Supreme Court had defined obscenity), the FCC stressed that the broadcast came when children would normally be in the audience.

The FCC argued that children need protection from indecency. Instead of meeting the First Amendment directly by flatly banning such material as the Carlin monologue, the FCC said it should be **channeled** to a part of the day when children are least likely to be in the audience.

The channeling concept has precedence in nuisance law, which recognizes that something acceptable in one setting could be an illegal nuisance in others. The Supreme Court agreed with this rationale when, recalling that a judge had once said that a nuisance "may be merely a right thing in a wrong place—like a pig in the parlor instead of the barnyard," the Court added that if the FCC "finds a pig has entered the parlor, the exercise of regulatory power does not depend on proof that the pig is obscene." In other words, explicit language that would not be considered obscene could still be regulated. The Court also accepted the FCC's narrowing of community standards in adding the words *for broadcasting*, saying, "We have long recognized that each medium of expression presents special First Amendment problems. . . . And of all forms of communication, it is broadcasting that has received the most limited First Amendment protection" (US, 1978: 748).

Enforcement

Because indecent speech has some First Amendment protection, the FCC and the courts have held that it cannot be banned on broadcasting 24 hours per day. Accordingly, the Commission has carved out a **safe harbor** during which indecent programming can be aired. The safe harbor consists of the hours between 10:00 P.M. and 6:00 A.M. Airing indecent material outside the safe harbor can lead to fines of up to $325,000 per violation. Group owners of stations carrying network or syndicated programs that have contained indecent material have been assessed fines in the millions of dollars. The possibility of such large fines led several popular shock jocks—Howard Stern, for one—to leave broadcasting for satellite radio, a pay service that is not regulated with respect to indecency. It is important to remember that the stations airing the material are liable for the fines, not the networks or syndicators that producd the programming.

Regulating Profanity

Before 2004, the Commission generally did not fine stations that aired an occasional offensive word when that word was used as an adjective or interjection. The FCC stated that use of these "fleeting expletives," often heard during a live broadcast, were not "depictions of sexual or excretory activities or organs" and thus did not fit into the definition of indecency.

That all changed after Bono, accepting a Golden Globe award on a live broadcast aired by the NBC network in prime time, expressed his joy by saying, "This is really, really [expletive] brilliant." Besieged with complaints, the Commission initially ruled that the use of the expletive was not indecent, thus following the agency's precedent. At that point all heck broke loose and the Commission was roundly criticized by angry parents, religious groups, and many members of Congress. Bowing to pressure, the Commission reversed itself and ruled that such language would henceforth be actionable, suggesting that such language was certainly profane, if not indecent. The Commission defined profanity as "language so grossly offensive to members of the public who actually hear it as to amount to a nuisance" (FCCR, 2004b). According to the new policy, in order to protect children from hearing such language, profanity would not be tolerated outside the safe harbor.

Since changing its policy on indecency, the Commission has issued a confusing series of opinions with respect to when such words can be used and when they would lead to fines. Use of the words was considered appropriate on the prime-time broadcast of *Saving Private Ryan*, but not when used in an award-winning documentary on the blues. Stations were fined when the offensive words were used in live awards shows, but not when uttered during live newscasts.

This lack of predictability led Fox Television Stations to challenge the FCC's profanity policy in court, and in 2007 the U.S. Court of Appeals ruled that the FCC had not adequately explained its change in policy. According to the Court, if the FCC were really concerned about protecting minors from hearing explicit language, the agency would not have made exceptions for certain movies or newscasts. Consequently, the Court declared the new rules invalid and ordered the Commission to better explain its position (F, 2007). In turn, the FCC petitioned the Supreme Court to hear the case, and the Court granted certiorari in March 2008. At press time of this text, the Supreme Court had not yet made a decision.

Exhibit 12.d

Entertainers and Indecency

(A)

(B)

(C)

(D)

The Supreme Court case that upheld the FCC's authority to regulate broadcast indecency spawned from New York radio station WBAI's airing of George Carlin's **(A)** monologue about the seven words you could never say on the radio. Due to the broadcasts of shock jocks such as Howard Stern **(B)**, the FCC extended indecency enforcement beyond the seven dirty words in the late 1980s, subjecting radio stations to millions of dollars in fines. Janet Jackson's **(C)** "costume malfunction" during the 2004 Super Bowl prompted Congress to increase the fine for

individual indecency violations from $32,500 to $325,000 per incident. Bono's **(D)** acceptance speech at the 2003 Golden Globe Awards—"this is really, really [expletive] brilliant"—led the FCC to expand its enforcement once again, this time to include "fleeting expletives" that could be considered profane.

Sources: Photo (A) from AP Photo/The Ames Tribune/Jon Britton; photo (B) from AP Photo/Richard Drew; photo (C) from Frank Micelotta/Getty Images; photo (D) from KMazur/WireImages/Getty Images.

Regulating Indecency on Cable

The cable act of 1984 provided for fines or imprisonment for anyone who "transmits over any cable system any matter which is obscene or otherwise unprotected by the Constitution" (47 USC 639). Although the Supreme Court has held that cable television does have First Amendment protection, it has also said that such protection must be balanced against what it has called "competing social interests," without specifying what those interests may be or how that might be done (US, 1986: 488).

States had previously tried to go even further by applying the Supreme Court's *Pacifica* decision to questionable cable content. Four federal court decisions in the mid-1980s concluded that state and local laws banning cable indecency violated the First Amendment because they were too broad in scope. The courts reasoned that cable is not as "uniquely intrusive" as broadcasting, nor as available to children, because subscribers pay for the service, therefore *Pacifica* does not apply to cable.

Congress also has attempted to regulate indecency on cable systems, with mixed results. The 1992 cable act for the first time gave system operators the authority to prohibit indecent programming on public and leased access channels and empowered system operators to enforce written policy on such programming. Additionally, the 1992 act required cable operators who did allow indecent programming on these channels to put all such programming on one channel and to provide that channel only to subscribers who wanted it (47 USC 612, 638). In 1996, the Supreme Court upheld the provision allowing cable operators to prohibit indecency on leased-access channels, but declared the other requirements of the law unconstitutional infringements on cable programmers' and subscribers' First Amendment rights (US, 1996).

In 1996, Congress passed legislation requiring cable operators to block fully the audio and video of channels primarily dedicated to sexually oriented programming. The intent of this provision was to prevent nonsubscribers from receiving any part of the channel. The law further required that until the full channel blocking is accomplished, the cable operator must protect the child audience by carrying the channel only at times of the day when children are not likely to be watching (47 USC 561). Several adult-oriented programmers, including the Playboy Channel, challenged the law in court. In May 2000, the U.S. Supreme Court declared the law unconstitutional, finding that there were less restrictive ways (e.g., the use of a channel lock-out device) to protect children from indecent programming on cable (US, 2000).

In 1991, the FCC and the Justice Department agreed to divide their overlapping concerns about obscenity and indecency. The Justice Department would take primary responsibility for any actions against cable or pay-cable services, whereas the FCC would concentrate on broadcast cases (Ferris et al., 1983–1992: 8–38/9).

Indecency and Other Electronic Media

Although no precedent exists with respect to indecency standards for other multichannel technologies, such as DBS and satellite radio, so far they have been treated similarly to cable television because they are primarily subscription services. The courts have spoken about the transmission of sexually explicit material on two other electronic media: the telephone system and the Internet.

Since the early 1980s, the FCC had been trying to control the transmission of sexually explicit messages via the telephone, commonly known as "dial-a-porn," but several of its attempts at regulation were struck down by a court of appeals as being too restrictive. Finally, Congress acted in 1988 with legislation that sought to prohibit dial-a-porn by making it a crime to transmit obscene or indecent commercial telephone messages. The Supreme Court unanimously held the statute to be unconstitutional as applied to the transmission of indecent messages. The Court noted that indecent speech was constitutionally protected for adults, and that as long as other techniques were available to block such messages from children, a total ban on telephone indecency violated the First Amendment (US, 1989). Consequently, so long as sexually explicit message providers take steps to make sure that children cannot access their services (e.g., through credit card sales, scrambling techniques, or verifiable passwords), their transmissions of indecent material are protected.

The other great pornography battleground is the Internet. Spurred by press reports of easily accessible sexual material on the Internet, plus anecdotal evidence of children's harmful exposure to this type of content, Congress, as part of its revision of the Communications Act in 1996, passed the Communications Decency Act (CDA). The CDA made it a crime to make, create, solicit, initiate the transmission of, or display obscene or indecent material over the Internet to any person under the age of 18. Almost immediately after the CDA's passage, a coalition of free speech advocates, Internet users, and computer and telecommunications industry groups went to court, arguing that the CDA was unconstitutional with respect to its limitations on indecency.

In June of 1996, a special three-judge panel of the U.S. District Court in Pennsylvania agreed with the plaintiffs in the case. As a first step, the court noted that access to the Internet is much more complicated than access to broadcasting, implying that a different First Amendment standard should be applied. According to the U.S. District Court:

> Internet communication, while unique, is more akin to telephone communication, at issue in *Sable*, than to broadcasting, at issue in *Pacifica*, because, as with the telephone, an Internet user must act affirmatively and deliberately to retrieve specific information online. Even if a broad search will, on occasion, retrieve unwanted materials, the user virtually always receives some warning of its content, significantly reducing the element of surprise or "assault" involved in broadcasting. (FS, 1996: 851–852)

The judges noted that while the CDA criminalized only transmissions to minors, there was no way to know the age of an Internet user. Thus, content providers might stifle their messages not knowing who might receive them. Since indecent speech is fully protected when targeted to adults, the court concluded that this "chilling effect" on such content violated the First Amendment rights of the speakers. The decision was appealed directly to the Supreme Court. In June 1997, the Court, using similar arguments, upheld the lower court's decision, thus making the CDA unenforceable with respect to indecency (US, 1997).

In response to the Court's decision, Congress in 1998 again attempted to regulate sexually explicit programming on the Internet by passing the Child On-line Protection Act (COPA). The act prohibits commercial Internet sites from making available to children material that is deemed "harmful to minors." Immediately after COPA's passage, several groups filed suit, arguing that the law, like the CDA before it, violates the First Amendment rights of adults. Subsequently, a federal judge enjoined the government from enforcing the act while the lawsuit is being considered. Since the lawsuit was filed, the case has bounced around the court system like a ping pong ball, producing five court decisions by the end of 2008. At the time this text went to press, no final decision on the constitutionality of the act had been rendered.

Seeking a Balance

Obscenity/indecency law as applied to the electronic media will evolve as society's standards evolve. After decades of increased liberalization, during which many taboos fell and audiences grew more tolerant of explicit language and scenes, the pendulum swung to a more conservative standard—restrictions aimed at preserving "family values."

By contrast, no indication of a disappearing market for programs that pushed the limits has been evident in recent years. The popularity of titillating new network programs suggests that the search for what was acceptable (i.e., how far one could go) is ongoing.

The trend toward a more permissive interpretation of laws dealing with sexuality for cable as compared to broadcast programming also has continued into the new century. This difference arises largely because cable lacks the universal reach of broadcasting and comes into the home only after a conscious decision to subscribe—a decision reviewed monthly when the bill arrives.

America's appetite for hard-core material appears to be growing. Although an all-out invasion of X-rated cable programs has not yet occurred, cable programmers such as Playboy regularly offer only minimally sanitized pornographic videos. Moreover, commercial Internet pornography sites experienced phenomenal growth over the past decade and now generate more than $3 billion per year in revenue in the United States alone.

12.6 Political Access

The Communications Act regulates programs most explicitly when they involve candidates for public office. Congress correctly foresaw in 1927 that broadcasting would one day exert a major influence on voters. If the party in power could monopolize the electronic media, opposing candidates would stand little chance of winning elections.

Equal Opportunities

The commonly but imprecisely used term **equal time** does not appear in the Communications Act. Indeed, the correct term, **equal opportunities,** requires more than equal time. A literal interpretation of equal time would, for example, permit a broadcaster to run a 30-second commercial for a favored candidate during prime time and run another for the opponent at 4:00 A.M.—a ploy not permitted under the equal opportunities rule.

Section 315 of the Act requires that:

> if any licensee shall permit any person who is a legally qualified candidate for any public office to use a broadcasting station, he shall afford equal opportunities to all other such candidates for that office in the use of such broadcasting station; *Provided*, That such licensee shall have no power of censorship over the material broadcast under the provisions of this section. No obligation is imposed under this subsection upon any licensee to allow the use of its station by any such candidate. (47 USC 315[a])

The Commission has interpreted "equal opportunities" to require not only equal amounts of time, but also access to equivalent audiences and equal financial arrangements. Thus, if a broadcaster gives free airtime to his brother-in-law who is running for mayor, the licensee is obligated under Section 315 to provide a similar amount of free airtime, in a time slot calculated to reach a similar audience, to his relative's opponents as well. Nothing in Section 315, however, requires a broadcaster to sell time to a politician in the first place.

A 1971 amendment to the Act mandates allowing time for *federal* candidates by adding a new basis for license revocation: the "willful or repeated failure to allow reasonable access to" federal candidates (47 USC 312[a][7]). The equal opportunities and reasonable access provisions of the Act apply only to broadcast stations and cable channels on which a cable operator originates programming. Cable networks such as CNN and MTV are not covered by these laws.

Candidates in the News

What about the presence of candidates in news stories? Do such "uses" also trigger Section 315's equal opportunities obligation? At first the FCC said no; later it said yes. Congress thereupon amended Section 315 to exempt news coverage of all candidates:

Appearance by a legally qualified candidate on any

1. bona fide newscast,
2. bona fide news interview,
3. bona fide news documentary (if the appearance of the candidate is incidental to the presentation of the subject or subjects covered by the news documentary), or
4. on-the-spot news coverage of bona fide news events (including but not limited to political conventions and activities incidental thereto), *shall not be deemed to be use of a broadcasting station* within the meaning of this subsection.
   (47 USC 315 [a]; emphasis added)

Although the amendment liberated news coverage from political equal opportunity claims, it also left the FCC with many knotty problems of interpretation. Questions regarding political candidates' rights are among those most frequently asked by licensees seeking interpretation of FCC rules. Some examples of the issues confronting stations are detailed in Exhibit 12.e. In addition to providing paid-for access, the broadcast media have a responsibility to inform the electorate about political issues in a nonpartisan way. This tricky combination of enforced cooperation, profit making, and the obligations of journalistic objectivity continues to create problems for station managers.

Buying Political Time

One of the trickiest problems in political broadcasting is defining what constitutes a station's "lowest unit charge." This phrase in Sec. 315(b) of the Communications Act defines the maximum rate that

Exhibit 12.e

What Does "Equal Opportunities" Mean?

▶ *Who gets equal opportunities?* Candidates for nomination in primary elections and nominees in general elections get equal opportunities. But equal opportunities can be claimed only by candidates for the same specific office; purchase of time by a candidate for Congress, for example, entitles all other candidates for that post in that district to equal opportunities, but not candidates for other districts or other offices.

▶ *Do presidential news conferences count as bona fide news programs?* Yes—they are exempt from equal opportunity claims.

▶ *Do presidential candidate debates count as news?* Though the rules have changed many times, the answer is yes. However, third-party candidates are less likely to be heard (networks or other sponsors exclude them as being of little interest)—a news exception that flies in the face of Sec. 315's intent to let voters hear all the candidates.

▶ *Are regularly scheduled interview and talk programs exempt from equal opportunity requests?* Yes— including "infotainment" programs such as *Oprah*.

▶ *How much time constitutes "reasonable access"?* The FCC refuses to provide any set amount, but stations are prohibited from limiting candidates for federal office to set numbers of spots or amounts of program time, even when their schedules do not easily allow extended political speeches.

▶ *May live news appearances be recorded for later playback and still be exempt?* Yes.

▶ *Is a candidate entitled to whatever time of day he or she wants?* No. Candidates cannot decree when they appear. Stations may keep political spots out of particular periods— such as the times scheduled for news programs.

▶ *May broadcasters require political ads to conform to standard advertising spot or program lengths?* No. Stations cannot ban campaign ads lasting for five minutes or other "nonstandard" lengths of time.

▶ *Must a station broadcast a candidate's use of obscene material?* No. When *Hustler* publisher Larry Flynt threatened to use arguably obscene material in a possible campaign for the presidency in 1984, licensees asked the FCC for policy guidance. The Commission held that the ban on obscenity overrode the "no censorship" provision of Section 315.

▶ *Are photos of aborted fetuses in political ads indecent and therefore not allowed?* No. During recent elections, several candidates ran on anti-abortion platforms, and some used graphic pictures of aborted fetuses in their advertising. Yielding to both viewer and licensee concerns, the Commission held that such depictions, although well within the rights of candidates' uncensored access, might be indecent and thus could be restricted to the "safe harbor" hours of 10:00 P.M. to 6:00 A.M. A federal appeals court disagreed and ruled that broadcasters could not restrict such ads only to the safe harbor hours. The court argued that this would deprive many voters of hearing the candidates' message (F, 1996). Stations can run a disclaimer that federal law required the ad to be carried.

▶ *Must a station carry potentially libelous material by a candidate?* Yes. *Is the station legally liable?* No.

▶ *Are cable systems held to the same regulations?* Regulations apply only to channels on which the cable operator *originates* programming. Cable systems are not responsible for the political content of stations or services whose programs they carry but over which they have no content control.

▶ *May a licensee evade political broadcasting problems by banning all political advertising?* No, at least not for federal candidates (who must receive "reasonable access").

▶ *Is any appearance of a candidate a "use" of broadcast facilities?* Unless it qualifies as a news exemption, yes. Any time a candidate appears on the air—even in an entertainment or other nonpolitical situation—that time constitutes a use subject to equal opportunities.

licensees may charge candidates who buy time for political purposes.

In effect, stations may charge a political candidate no more for a given commercial than would be charged to the lowest-paying advertiser for the same spot. For example, a commercial advertiser might have to buy several hundred spots to qualify for the maximum quantity discount, but a political candidate benefits from that discount even when buying only a single spot.

Even with the lowest unit rate, candidates spend hundreds of millions of dollars on broadcast advertising during political campaigns. This inevitably leads to calls for campaign reform. Over the years, would-be reformers have proposed that broadcasters provide highly discounted or even free time for candidates. Many politicians suggest that this would be a small price to pay for the broadcasters' use of the spectrum. Broadcasters for the most part oppose these plans, arguing that they should not be required to foot the bill for campaign finance reform.

12.7 Public Access

Not everyone with an idea to express can own a station or cable system, nor can everyone expect access to stations or systems owned by others. The FCC long struggled with this problem by trying to provide access to broadcasting for *ideas* rather than for specific *people*. But even access for ideas has to be qualified. It would be impractical to force stations to give time for literally every idea that might be put forward. The FCC mandated access only for ideas about **controversial issues of public importance**.

Rise of the Fairness Doctrine

The FCC slowly elaborated its access ideas into a formalized set of procedures called the **fairness doctrine**. This doctrine obligated stations (a) to schedule time for programs on controversial issues of public importance, and (b) to ensure expression of opposing views on those issues. Both stations and the FCC largely ignored (a), focusing their attention on (b). In practice, therefore, most fairness doctrine complaints came as reactions to ideas that had already been discussed on the air, rather than as complaints about the failure to initiate discussion of issues. Licensees had great latitude in deciding whether a subject qualified as both a controversial issue and one of public importance, how much time should be devoted to replies, when replies should be scheduled, and who should speak for opposing viewpoints.

In 1969, the Supreme Court upheld the FCC's fairness doctrine, as well as its related personal attack and political editorializing rules, in its landmark *Red Lion* decision (see Exhibit 12.f). By unanimously supporting the FCC in this case, the Court strongly affirmed the fairness doctrine concept in an opinion that emphasized four key principles relevant to broadcasting's First Amendment status (US, 1969: 367).

- ▶ **On the uniqueness of broadcasting:** "It is idle to posit an unabridgeable First Amendment right to broadcast comparable to the right of every individual to speak, write, or publish."
- ▶ **On the fiduciary principle:** "There is nothing in the First Amendment which prevents the Government from requiring a licensee to share his frequency with others and to conduct himself as a proxy or fiduciary."
- ▶ **On the public interest:** "It is the right of the viewers and listeners, not the right of the broadcasters, which is paramount."
- ▶ **On the scarcity factor:** "Nothing in this record, or in our own researches, convinces us that the [spectrum] resource is no longer one for which there are more immediate and potential uses than can be accommodated, and for which wise planning is essential."

Although the fairness doctrine is no longer in effect, these underlying constitutional principles remain intact.

End of the Doctrine

By 1985, the FCC, by then largely made up of appointees dedicated to deregulation, had joined a mounting chorus of opposition to the fairness doctrine. After a lengthy proceeding, the Commission concluded:

> [Based on] our experience in administering the doctrine and our general expertise in broadcast regulation, we no longer believe that the fairness doctrine, as a matter *of policy*, serves the public interest. . . . Furthermore, we find that the fairness doctrine, in operation, actually inhibits the presentation of controversial issues of public importance to the detriment of the public and in degradation of the editorial prerogatives of broadcast journalists. (FCCR, 1985b: 143)

Acting on a court remand requiring the FCC to reconsider an earlier fairness decision, the Commission instead abolished the doctrine entirely (FCCR, 1987b: 5043).

Since the FCC rescinded the fairness doctrine, many in Congress have called for its reinstatement. Bills codifying the doctrine were introduced and passed twice but were vetoed both times by President Reagan. President Clinton stated early in 1993 that he would sign a fairness doctrine reinstatement bill if it reached his desk, but Congress never acted. Separate bills were introduced in later Congresses that would have reinstated the fairness doctrine (favored by Democrats) or ban the

Exhibit 12.f

A Place and a Case Called *Red Lion*

An unlikely small-town station formed the setting for one of the leading Supreme Court decisions on electronic media. During the 1960s, right-wing preachers inundated radio with paid syndicated political commentary, backed by ultraconservative supporters such as Texas multimillionaire, H. L. Hunt, through tax-exempt foundations. Purchased time for these religious/political programs provided much-needed radio income in small markets.

The landmark case got its name from WGCB, a southeastern Pennsylvania AM/FM outlet licensed to John M. Norris, a conservative minister, under the name Red Lion Broadcasting. In 1964, one of the Reverend Billy James Hargis's syndicated broadcasts carried by the station attacked author Fred Cook, who had criticized defeated Republican presidential candidate, Barry Goldwater, and had written an article on what he termed the "hate clubs of the air," referring to the Hargis series *Christian Crusade*, among others. Hargis attacked Cook on the air, charging him with communist affiliations and with criticizing the FBI and the CIA—the standard litany of accusations Hargis routinely made against liberals.

Cook then accused the station of violating FCC rules by failing to inform him of a personal attack. When he wrote asking for time to reply, the station responded with a rate card, inviting him to buy time like anyone else. Cook appealed to the FCC, which agreed that he had a right to free airtime for a reply. It ordered WGCB to comply.

It would have been easy for Norris to grant Cook a few minutes of time on the Red Lion station, but he refused on First Amendment grounds, appealing the Commission decision. The court of appeals upheld the FCC, but Norris took the case to the Supreme Court, which, in 1969, also upheld the FCC, issuing an opinion strongly defensive of the FCC's right to demand program fairness.

Several years later, Fred Friendly, the former head of CBS News, but by then a Columbia University journalism professor, began looking into the background of this well-known case for a book about the fairness doctrine (Friendly, 1976). He discovered that Cook had been a subsidized writer for the Democratic National Committee and that his fairness complaint had been linked to a systematic campaign mounted by the Democrats to discredit right-wing extremists such as Hargis.

According to Friendly, the Democrats set out to exploit the fairness doctrine as a means of harassing stations that sold time for the airing of ultraconservative political programs. Cook and the Democratic National Committee claimed that Friendly had misinterpreted their activities, maintaining that Cook had acted as a private individual, not as an agent of the Democratic Party.

doctrine's reinstatement (favored by Republicans). Neither passed.

A *Right* of Reply?

Although the fairness doctrine concerned balanced coverage of controversial issues, two corollaries of the doctrine required a personal right of reply.

The **personal attack rule** required stations to inform individuals or groups of personal attacks on their "honesty, character, integrity or like personal qualities" that occurred in the course of discussions of controversial public issues. Those attacked were then given air time to respond. Indeed, the *Red Lion* case discussed in Exhibit 12.f grew out of a personal attack dispute.

The **political editorializing rule** required that all candidates or their representatives be given a chance to respond if a licensee endorsed any of their opponents. If a station editorially opposed a candidate, that candidate had to be given an opportunity to respond.

The Radio-Television News Directors Association (RTNDA) had long urged the Commission to abolish the rules. RTNDA finally sued and obtained a court order forcing the Commission to consider RTNDA's petition. Consequently, the FCC repealed both the personal attack and the political editorializing rules in 2000 (FCCR, 2000).

Rights for Advertisers

To date, the only legal products or services that cannot be advertised on radio or television are tobacco products. Aside from that, access by advertisers to broadcasting has been governed more by considerations of taste and public acceptance (and income potential) than by government regulation. In deciding whether to accept advertisements, broadcasters have great discretion.

With respect to **editorial advertising**, or "advertorials," however, broadcasters' discretion has not gone unchallenged. Traditionally, the electronic media have declined to let advertisers use commercials as vehicles for comment on controversial issues, arguing that:

► serious issues cannot be adequately discussed in short announcements
► selling larger blocks of time for editorializing by outsiders involves surrender of editorial responsibility
► not everyone can afford to buy time, so selling to those with funds is inherently unfair

The Supreme Court upheld the principle of licensee **journalistic discretion** in a case dealing with a fairness doctrine demand for access to editorial advertising:

> Since it is physically impossible to provide time for all viewpoints . . . the right to exercise editorial judgment was granted to the broadcaster. The broadcaster, therefore, is allowed significant journalistic discretion in deciding how best to fulfill the Fairness Doctrine obligations, although that discretion is bounded by rules designed to assure that the public interest in fairness is furthered. (US, 1973a: 111)

Despite rescission of the fairness doctrine, the question of editorial advertising continually reappears. Controversies arise periodically between advertisers and broadcasters. In several cases, ads that were turned down by broadcasters have appeared on cable or in print—with pointed commentary about the refusal of broadcasters to sell time for such advertising. The controversy over advertising of condoms is one example: Few broadcasters accepted condom advertising or editorial statements calling for their use to prevent AIDS, for fear that substantial parts of their audiences would be offended by such messages. Moreover, the refusal of many broadcasters to air the messages of antiabortion advocates led abortion foes to run for Congress. As detailed in Exhibit 12.e, broadcasters cannot censor the ads of political candidates; this gives anti-abortion candidates an opportunity to put their views on the air.

Editorial Discretion

By their nature, news and public-affairs programs necessarily involve controversial issues, often leading partisans to bring charges of unfairness. It becomes difficult for broadcasting and cable journalists to deal with serious issues if their corporate bosses prefer to avoid controversy. Yet, electronic media cannot win full public respect and First Amendment status without taking risks similar to those the printed press has always faced.

The FCC and courts generally assume that reporters and editors use editorial discretion, which calls for fair and considered news treatment of events, people, and controversies. No one believes that journalists always use the best judgment or that they totally lack bias or prejudice. First Amendment philosophy holds, however, that it is better to tolerate journalists' mistakes—and even their prejudice and incompetence—than to set up a government agency as an arbiter of truth. According to the Supreme Court:

> For better or worse, editing is what editors are for, and editing is selection and choice of material. That editors—newspapers or broadcast—can and do abuse this power is beyond doubt, but that is not reason to deny the discretion Congress provided. Calculated risks of abuse are taken in order to preserve higher values. (US, 1973a: 124)

Localism

The public needs access to diverse voices, but they also need voices of their own. The notion of a broad right of public access has two aspects: access to the ideas of others and to the means of expressing those ideas. The widespread availability of stations and cable systems can facilitate such two-way access, especially within local-market communities.

From its inception until well into the 1960s, the FCC encouraged **localism**—reflection of the local community's needs and interests—by distributing as many local outlets to as many localities as possible and by issuing guidelines that encouraged airing of programs reflecting community needs and interests. The Communications Act gives the Commission its own localism guidelines when it acts on applications for new stations:

> The Commission shall make such distribution of licenses, frequencies, hours of operation, and of power among the several States and *communities as to provide a fair, efficient, and equitable distribution of radio service to each of the same.* (47 USC 307[b]; emphasis added)

This policy of localizing stations has provided listeners in major markets 40 or more radio stations from which to choose, whereas people in rural areas have far fewer or, in some cases, none at all. As cable expanded, it equalized and increased television channel choices in most urban and suburban areas; but it, too, underserves rural areas.

Yet, cable does take pressure off commercial broadcasters, inasmuch as coverage of meetings and local events has largely transferred to local cable government access channels. Most cable systems have public, educational, and government (PEG) channels as encouraged by federal law and often required by local franchise. Though budget problems facing many local governments and school systems have restricted their use, the potential of cable's growing number of channels to serve a variety of local concerns has increased.

Still, when threatened by changing technology (e.g., direct broadcast satellites or telephone industry takeover), broadcasters immediately cite their unique public interest in providing locally relevant programs. They argued long and hard to the FCC and Congress, though to no avail, that cable and DBS are almost entirely national services, whereas broadcasters still hold to the ideal of station-based localism. However, as any discerning listener can attest, while broadcasting and cable do have local *outlets*, the *voices* they carry are increasingly the same nationwide. Evidence of this trend away from local programming abounds. Many radio stations eschew local news and public affairs programming altogether, preferring to program their stations with 24-hour-per-day syndicated music formats delivered via satellite. Some television stations are canceling local newscasts in favor of more profitable syndicated programs.

Concerned over these trends, in 2007 the FCC adopted a Notice of Proposed Rule Making, seeking comment on proposals to stimulate the production of more local programming (FCCR, 2007a). Broadcasters contradicted the Commission's assumptions and vowed to fight any new regulations. At the time this text went to press, no final action had been taken.

12.8 Serving Children

Reacting to constant pressure from Action for Children's Television and others, Congress passed legislation in 1990 regulating the amount of advertising in children's programs as well as establishing a general obligation to serve child audiences. Its major provisions include the following:

▶ Advertising per hour of children's programs is limited to no more than 10 and one-half minutes on weekends and 12 minutes on weekdays. This "limitation" applies to broadcast licensees and cable systems for all programming produced and broadcast primarily for children aged 12 and under.

▶ At license renewal, the FCC must consider whether stations have served the "educational and information needs of children" through their overall programming, which must include "some" (otherwise undefined) programming specifically designed to meet children's needs.

Licensee Duties

The Act directed the FCC to put more specific regulations in place. After considerable input from the broadcast and cable industries and others, including direct intervention from President Clinton at one point, the Commission arrived at the following decisions:

▶ All TV broadcasters should air at least three hours of educational or informational children's programming per week. For purposes of this *programming* regulation, "children" are defined as those 16 and younger (the congressional limitation on *commercials* affects programs aimed at children 12 and under).

▶ Educational programs must be at least 30 minutes in length and must be regularly scheduled at times of the day (7:00 A.M. to 10:00 P.M.) when children are likely to be in the audience.

▶ Broadcasters must file quarterly reports of the programs aired to fulfill these mandates. These quarterly reports must also be placed in the stations' public file.

▶ Program-length commercials for children are forbidden. A program built around a fantasy hero may no longer include advertising for products related to that hero—they must run in another, unrelated children's program. (Since 1974 the FCC had policies against "host selling" and the close intermixing of program and advertising elements.)

The Commission further refined the children's TV rules in anticipation of the transition to digital broadcasting. These new rules require the same three hours of educational programming per week on the broadcasters' primary digital stream. For broadcasters that multicast, an additional three hours of programming is required for every full-time free program stream. Program streams broadcast less than full time are required to provide children's programming on a pro rata basis. The commercial limits on programming for children 12 and under also apply to all digital signals.

The Commission also added rules to deal with special considerations relating to children's web sites. Programs that target children 12 and younger may not list web sites that lead children to commercial sites that include e-commerce or advertising. Only sites that contain primarily program related and other noncommercial content may be listed in children's programs (FCCR, 2004a).

Television Violence

As detailed in Chapter 10, TV violence and its effects on children have elicited more concern and study than any other entertainment program issue. The first congressional hearings on TV violence were held in the 1950s, and there have been many more since then. Until relatively recently, however, the government has declined to regulate violent programming based primarily on First Amendment grounds. Throughout the controversy broadcasters have resisted regulation, arguing that parents and not the government should control children's television viewing. Not satisfied with broadcasters' efforts at self-regulation, Congress finally acted on this issue in 1996.

As part of the Telecommunications Act of 1996, Congress set in motion a process to help parents control the programming their children watch. The legislation required the establishment of a TV program ratings system. The ratings are listed in TV programming guides and displayed at the beginning of rated programs. The legislation also required that new TV sets be equipped with a device known as a V-chip (V for violence), which allows parents to program their televisions to block out all programs of a particular rating. Each program carries its rating in the signal so that the V-chip can identify which programs could be shown and which should be blocked.

Ten years after ratings and V-chip requirements went into effect it was clear that they were generally not effective in shielding children from violent content. Studies showed that most consumers did not even know that their TV sets were equipped with the V-chip, and those that knew either could not figure out how to program the chip (perhaps they should ask their children!) or they just did not care.

Prodded by members of Congress, the FCC began a study on TV violence with a view to recommending whether further regulation would be useful. The Commission's report, issued in 2007, cited many studies suggesting that exposure to media violence can lead to aggressive behavior in children. Noting that the V-chip was mostly ineffective, the Commission recommended that Congress pass a new law requiring that violent programming be channeled to periods of the day when children are not likely to be watching, much the same as how indecent programming is regulated

(FCCR 2007d). As of mid-2008, Congress had not acted on the agency's recommendation.

12.9 Copyright

The Constitution recognizes the fundamental importance of encouraging national creativity. Article I, Sec. 8, calls on Congress to "promote the progress of science and the useful arts, by securing for limited times to authors and inventors the exclusive right to their respective writings and discoveries."

When broadcasting began, authors and composers had to rely on the copyright law of 1909, which dealt primarily with printed works and live performances. Despite amendments, the old act never caught up with the times. After long study and debate, Congress finally passed a new copyright law in 1976, effective for works published in 1978 and later. The act has been updated several times since then, mostly as a response to changing technology.

Basics

Key provisions of the Copyright Act, administered by the Copyright Office (part of the Library of Congress), include the following:

▶ **Purpose.** Copyright holders license others to use their works in exchange for the payment of **royalties**. "Use" consists of making public by publishing, performing, displaying, or broadcasting.

▶ **Copyrightable works.** In addition to traditionally copyrightable works—books, musical compositions, motion pictures, and broadcast programs—works such as sculptures, choreographic notations, and computer programs can be copyrighted. Things *not* copyrightable include ideas, slogans, brand names, news events, and titles. (However, brand names, logos, and slogans can be protected under trademark regulations.)

▶ **Length of copyright.** In general, a copyright lasts for the life of the work's creator plus 70 years. Copyrights initially granted to corporations last 95 years from the first publication of the work or 120 years from the date the work was created, whichever comes first. After that, a work enters the **public domain** and can be used without securing permission or paying royalties.

▶ **Fair use.** The act codifies the traditional copyright concept of fair use, which permits limited use of copyrighted works without payment or permission for certain educational and critical or creative purposes (such as reviews of books and musical works).

▶ **Infringement.** Those who violate the exclusive rights of copyright owners (e.g., the right to make and distribute copies or publicly perform a copy-

righted work), are guilty of infringement. Copyright owners may sue infringers for monetary damages. In some cases, infringement also carries criminal penalties.

Music Licensing

Broadcast and cable programmers obtain rights to use music by reaching agreements with the copyright licensing organizations ASCAP, BMI, and SESAC. Most stations hold **blanket licenses** from these agencies, which allow unlimited air play of any music in their catalogs in return for payment of an annual percentage of the station's gross income. Some radio stations, especially those with news and talk formats, pay on a per-use basis. These licenses, whether blanket or per use, permit the *broadcast* of the music by the stations. They do not cover other uses of the music, such as adding the music to a local commercial or public service announcement. Such uses require additional permission from the copyright owner.

Cable and Copyright

The Copyright Act grants cable TV systems a **compulsory license** to retransmit the copyrighted material of TV stations that they lawfully receive and deliver to their subscribers. The grant of a compulsory license does not require the permission of the copyright owner. Cable systems, in turn, must pay a preset small proportion of their revenue for these rights. Similar regulations apply to DBS operators and telephone systems that carry broadcast stations. The Copyright Office in the Library of Congress establishes the rates that cable systems pay for the compulsory licenses, collects the resulting revenue, and divides the pooled money among copyright holders.

Signal piracy has long been a problem for the cable TV industry. Until the mid-1980s, signal piracy chiefly involved illicit hookups to cable TV feeder lines, enabling cable reception without payment of monthly subscriber fees. As pay cable developed, illegal "black boxes" (decoders) made possible the reception of even scrambled signals. Pirated cable (and satellite) reception violates Sec. 705 of the Communications Act, which defines penalties for the unauthorized reception of communications intended only for paying subscribers. Additionally, more than half the states have passed antipiracy laws prohibiting the manufacture, sale, or use of unauthorized decoders or antennas.

Culture of Copying

In 1976, a number of program producers brought suit against Sony, the pioneering manufacturer of home video recorders, for "indirect" copyright infringement ("indirect" because Sony provided the *means* of infringement—the machines that made recording possible—but did not itself do the copying). A district court found in favor of Sony, concluding that home recordings of broadcast programs not sold for a profit fall within the fair use provision of the new copyright law. The Supreme Court affirmed the decision by a 5-to-4 vote (US, 1984a: 417). The Court cited audience research showing that people record broadcast signals primarily for time-shifting purposes, which it regarded as a fair use.

The decision left unresolved the legality of recording cable or pay programming; the *Sony* case covered only recording of over-the-air, or "free," broadcast material. That distinction was lost on most consumers, however, and many VCR owners taped all nature of programming for both time shifting and to build personal video libraries. About the same time dual deck audio tape players appeared on the market and audio lovers thought nothing of taping and sharing copyrighted materials with friends and family. As a result of the *Sony* case and the ease of making audio copies, a culture of copying developed.

In an analog world, consumer copying of copyrighted material did not draw dramatic attention from copyright owners. Video analog copies had to be made in real time and the quality of analog copies deteriorated with each subsequent transfer. Copyright owners were more concerned with large-scale pirates who made thousands of copies and sold them on the black market or in foreign countries.

All that changed when media began being produced in a digital format. Digital copies are perfect and computers can make hundreds of copies simultaneously. Suddenly, individual consumers became a threat to the creative industries, and copyright interests began pressing Congress for increased protection against infringing digital copying and distribution.

Since 1992, Congress has passed several laws addressing various copying issues.

► The price of digital audio tape (DAT) machines includes a 2 percent royalty fee that is distributed to copyright owners. Similarly, blank digital tapes include a 3 percent fee on their wholesale price.
► Copyright owners may impose technical standards for **serial copy management systems** that prevent second-generation digital copies from being made. In other words, an owner can make a copy, but not a copy of a copy.
► It is illegal to break through any encryption codes that producers use to protect copyrighted material from unauthorized copying.

► The manufacture or distribution of devices or programs that circumvent encryption technology is likewise illegal.

Protecting Digital Broadcast Content

Now that TV broadcasters are delivering high-definition digital signals and HD radio is transmitting CD quality music, the creators of digital programming are concerned about consumers' ability to record and distribute perfect copies of their copyrighted work. Digital video recorders (DVRs) and HD radios can record and store perfect digital copies of programs. This could have a considerable impact on the sale of DVDs or MP3 music files.

To combat wholesale digital copying of television and radio signals, copyright interests have proposed the adoption of a serial copy management system dubbed the **broadcast flag**. Using this system, certain programs could be flagged by the broadcaster. Such flagged programming could be received and copied by the homeowner, but those copies could neither be copied nor distributed. This would require all television and radio sets to come equipped with the copy management technology.

The FCC mandated the implementation of a television broadcast flag system in 2003, but the regulations were struck down in federal court. The court ruled that the FCC did not have the power to mandate such a system (F, 2005a). Since then, both video producers and record companies have pressured Congress to pass broadcast flag legislation. The proposals are very controversial. As of the date this text went to press, Congress had not acted.

Copyright and the Internet

The ease and speed with which information travels on the Internet poses unique and thorny copyright problems. Anyone with a computer can easily put perfect duplicates of copyrighted material into the hands of thousands of Internet users in a matter of seconds. Technically, anytime a copyrighted work is transmitted from one computer to another and copied in the receiving computer's memory, a violation of copyright law has occurred. Thus, sharing music files, games, movies, and TV programs via the Internet without the owners' permission constitutes a violation of copyright law.

Internet user groups argue that the copyright laws should be interpreted as allowing the freest exchange of information possible. They contend that restrictive copyright enforcement will stifle the free-wheeling and robust interchange of ideas that occurs on the Internet. Commercial interests and the government, on the other hand, counter that copyright enforcement on the Internet should be increased in order to protect the economic interests of copyright owners.

Copyright interests have pressed their case against the widespread distribution of protected material via the Internet in three ways: seek legislation that mandates technological solutions; challenge hardware, software, and service providers that facilitate infringements; and sue consumers who engage in widespread file sharing.

Legislation discussed earlier that imposes serial copy management systems and criminalizes the distribution of programs that circumvent encryption systems are examples of technological solutions. The proposed broadcast flag is another example.

Challenges against those who help facilitate infringements have led to mixed results. The *Sony* decision protected home copying of broadcast programs for personal use, and a 1999 court case settled at least one music recording issue: The use of hand-held MP3 players, such as the popular iPod, does not violate copyright law. The court ruled that the players are consistent with the intent of copyright law to ensure the right of consumers to make recordings of copyrighted music for their private noncommercial use (F, 1999).

Other cases have supported the position of the copyright owners. The first popular on-line music sharing service, Napster, was shut down following a series of adverse legal decisions. The service was found guilty of contributing to widespread copyright infringements (F, 2002). The Supreme Court issued a similar decision in 2005 when it found that the next generation of file-sharing programs, like Grokster, could be found liable for inducing infringements (US, 2005).

Questions concerning the liability of Internet carriers and service providers for distributing and posting infringing material was settled by Congress in 1998. The On-line Copyright Infringement Liability Limitation Act shields telephone companies and ISPs from liability when subscribers illegally transmit or post infringing material using their facilities. The legislation protects telcos and ISPs only when they are unaware of the infringing activity (17 USC 512). When informed of the presence of infringing materials by copyright owners, ISPs must remove the offending materials from their sites.

Perhaps the most controversial actions taken by rights holders involve bringing infringement lawsuits against individuals—often college students who use their university's broadband connections to distribute massive audio and video files. In many cases, these lawsuits are settled before going to trial, usually with the defendants agreeing to pay thousands of dollars in reparations. This has led many universities to monitor the use of student Internet accounts and warn them about activity that might draw the attention of copyright interests (see Exhibit 12.g).

Technological innovation has created what some observers consider a crisis in copyright law. Where the balance lies between the legitimate protection of copyrighted material and the use of that material by consumers is a difficult and complex issue. At some point, rather than relying on litigation and stop-gap legislative fixes, Congress may need to step up to the plate and consider comprehensive copyright reform.

12.10 Changing Perspectives

Numerous media compete for attention and consumer dollars, but more can too often become less in a marketplace dominated by giant corporations. These well-financed communicators blanket the nation, reducing the diversity of competing voices.

Two totally different approaches to this problem are actively debated. Here stands the **deregulator**, confident that the marketplace will regulate itself, given maximum competition and unconstrained consumer choice. There stands the **regulator**, demanding that government intervene once more to oppose monopolistic media tendencies and protect the public interest from the effects of unrestrained competition.

Many practical examples of this fundamental clash of views exist:

▶ Should indecency in electronic media have the same First Amendment protections it has on newsstands and in movie theaters? If so, how best can children be protected from such content?

▶ Should electronic media have special responsibilities with regard to airing local programs or controversial issues of social importance? If so, why, and to what degree, should they be treated differently than print media that bear no such responsibilities?

▶ Does violence in the electronic media have such potentially damaging social effects as to justify regulation?

▶ What controls should, and realistically can, be imposed (and by whom) on the unlimited-channel universe of cyberspace, with media that for some are mass and for others personal?

Exhibit 12.g

File Sharers, Beware!

College students beware: If you use popular programs such as Limewire or BitTorrent to send and receive large audio and video files using your campus Internet account, you just might receive something like the following in your mailbox.

Dear Sally Student:

All of us at Great Midwestern State University are happy to welcome you to another year of learning together. It is in this spirit that we are writing to alert you to a significant risk having to do with how you may use the Internet. It is VERY important that you read the contents of this letter.

Briefly, for some time now, music companies have been suing college students for thousands of dollars, because they claim those students have used "peer to peer" software to share songs, television programs, and movies with other people on the Internet without the permission of the people who own them. Lawsuits were filed against 19 GMSU students last year, and we just received notice of another round of "early settlement" letters, which typically have preceded lawsuits which may be filed if students don't settle the claims before the case goes to trial. The music companies are demanding between $3,000 and $4,000 to settle their claims; several GMSU students have paid $4,000 in settlement. If the lawsuits go to trial and the companies can prove their claim of copyright infringement, students could face substantially higher penalties under the law, not to mention significant legal fees. The settlement amounts that GMSU students have paid this past summer have been financially devastating for some families, requiring at least one student to withdraw from school, and others to consider filing bankruptcy.

Many do not realize that it is generally illegal to share copyrighted music, videos, games, and software files over the Internet without the permission of the people who own those works. In some cases there can be criminal penalties, even if students are not exchanging money as part of their file sharing. It is critical that you understand the following:

- If you share copyrighted music, movies, and software files over the Internet using peer-to-peer file sharing programs, you are most likely breaking the law, and, based on recent cases, that's true even if you do not know you are sharing files;

- It is relatively simple for the copyright owners or their agents to identify computers on the Internet from which sharing is taking place, and then use a subpoena to compel GMSU to identify the owner of that computer;

- They may then file a lawsuit against you, seeking thousands of dollars;

- Illegal sharing using Internet access provided by GMSU also violates GMSU policy; and

- If GMSU receives a valid notice that you have used the GMSU network to engage in unlawful file sharing, the University will impose appropriate disciplinary sanctions.

We hope that you understand that it is out of concern for GMSU students and families that we are taking the very unusual step of writing to you.

Sincerely,

Shirley S. Quire
University Counsel

Source: Adapted from letters sent to Indiana University students, November 2007.

Perhaps most fundamentally, with the abundance of media choices that are available today, does it still make sense to treat different media differently under the First Amendment?

As the second decade of the 21st century begins, the debate on how these issues should be addressed continues. Deregulation advocates argue that economic forces, competition, and technological advancements will resolve any problems. Proponents of government intervention counter that the public's interest in receiving diverse and relevant information are not likely to be advanced by commercial profit motives, but are better guaranteed by well-crafted regulations. In fact, the electronic media will continue to be guided by a combination of both approaches, which, it is hoped, will further the First Amendment goals of guaranteeing free speech for all and promoting a free-flowing marketplace of diverse viewpoints.

A Global View

chapter

Few Americans realize that most other countries operate electronic media quite differently than we do. Yet, because radio waves ignore national boundaries (especially when sent from satellites), and telephone and computer networks reach almost the entire world, electronic media are truly international. Countless organizations here and abroad participate in global exchanges of equipment, programs, and training. Fully understanding electronic media in America requires at least a sense of how they operate elsewhere. In recent years, the dynamics of business globalization and new media technologies are shaping a new international media environment. National boundaries are almost impossible to maintain in terms of restricting inhabitants from interacting with other cultures. Many nation states struggle to maintain control over cross-border communications, but the task is daunting in an era of transnational business ventures and new media distribution.

Although countries have the same theoretical potential for using electronic media, each adopts a system uniquely suited to serve its own conditions, economic abilities, and needs. Conventional over-the-air broadcasting invites **government regulation** because it requires the use of the electromagnetic spectrum, which all governments view as public property. In addition, although cable and the Internet do not suffer from any type of spectrum scarcity, some governments still desire to control media content, regardless of the technology used. Each government defines its responsibility to control electronic media in the context of its own history, geography, economics, culture, and, most important, political philosophy. Because it would be impossible to examine the economic and regulatory systems of every country in one brief chapter, we have decided to emphasize concepts over countries. That is, this chapter highlights common approaches and issues experienced by many nations and then offers specific examples to help clarify the topic and provide some real-world relevance. This global view encompasses not only the inner workings of a nation's media system, but also external operations intended to reach the outside world.

13.1 Controlling Philosophies

Controls that a nation imposes on electronic media reflect the government's attitudes toward its own people. Scholars have found several ways to categorize these philosophies. Some have used a three-category approach of permissivism, paternalism, and authoritarianism. In recent years, international media scholars have adopted a more complex approach that supposedly captures more important factors and recognizes that these categories typically combine to varying degrees within a country's media system. One common approach is to introduce six philosophies: authoritarian, libertarian, communist, social responsibility, developmental, and democratic-participant. These approaches influence the types of media ownership, regulation, financing, and program content. No one country operates exclusively under one philosophy. Instead, governments select several and mix them into a kind of "recipe" that makes sense to those who govern.

Authoritarian

Traditionally, dictatorships of whatever political flavor take an authoritarian approach to electronic media. **Authoritarian philosophy** essentially holds that the leader of the country is an all-knowing ruler who deserves total obedience. To this end, authoritarian countries often hold traditional culture as sacred and worry about the negative influences of other rival cultures. From a media perspective, the expectation is that the media exist to serve the state. Media can be either privately or publicly owned, but in either case are controlled by the state either through direct censorship or self-censorship in which the media organizations work in concert with government goals. The media are perceived primarily as a tool for civic education and political propaganda. Some media scholars attribute authoritarianism not to a ruling government, but to the dominance of a small controlling group of media corporations that have cultural and political agendas.

Libertarian

Libertarian philosophy emphasizes the individual in a society and is generally suspicious of government. In particular, the libertarian view favors private ownership and free-market economics as the best means of satisfying the needs of citizens. This includes utilizing the marketplace of ideas as well as the marketplace of commodities in which the best ideas, as well as the best products, will emerge from free competition. Under these circumstances, most media are privately owned, profit-motivated businesses. The function of any government regulation is only to maintain fair competition. The notions of **permissiveness** and **laissez-faire** can be readily applied to the libertarian worldview. These common terms reflect the attitude that government interference in the internal workings of a free-market economy should be discouraged. Essentially, the market should be "let alone."

Communist

Communist philosophy holds that the purpose of the state is to be the caretaker for the well-being of all citizens. As a result, the state becomes a highly centralized distributor of what a society needs to survive and prosper.

The role of the individual is to respect the state's efforts in achieving its goals for the larger society. This means a suppression of individual goals in favor of a larger cause. Contrary to a more libertarian view, which admires capitalism, communist philosophy has its roots in fighting the exploitation of labor by business owners. From a media perspective, communist countries typically advocate state ownership of most property, which in turn places emphasis on teaching communist doctrine. Using the media for this purpose is considered necessary to guard against the temptations of materialism. As with authoritarian philosophy, government censorship is common.

Social Responsibility

Social responsibility philosophy takes a middle ground in that government regulation is encouraged to provide fair and balanced information to the society. Similar to the libertarian viewpoint, vigorous debate in the marketplace of ideas is a primary goal, however, government is seen as a tool to make this happen rather than a threat. From a media perspective, social responsibility philosophy does not object to a government creating regulations that are designed to assure certain standards of quality. These "standards," however, can be troublesome to define precisely and can result in undesirable censorship by overzealous government agencies. Government agencies are intended to assure that public service is not pushed aside by free enterprise.

Developmental

Developmental philosophy holds that media are responsible for specifically improving the social conditions of developing nations. The ultimate goal is not to maintain the status quo, but to bring about dramatic social change. The means to these ends, however, can be quite different from those used by stable, wealthy countries that also seek progress. By definition, developing countries are economically poor and politically unstable. Therefore, the government, not private enterprise, must invest in most of the costly technology, content creation, and distribution systems necessary to help a struggling nation reach true autonomy. On the other hand, developmental philosophy advocates the legal establishment of media freedom. That is, government should provide the necessary media tools, such as equipment and employees, but avoid censorship of what is presented to audiences. Accomplishing this task is not easy and often outside international assistance and pressure may be necessary to keep developing governments from exploiting their power. Many emerging nations make use of government resources to help uplift struggling free-market-based media systems.

Democratic-Participant

Democratic-participant philosophy argues that a citizen's voice is essential to the management of any worthwhile government and, consequently, from a media perspective, citizens are encouraged to be involved in all phases of producing media content. The underlying motivation for this approach has been concern over the dominance of large media corporations and their affiliations with powerful governments. The assumption is that minority groups, defined by such factors as race, ethnicity, nationality, or gender have been denied access to the media-making process. The notion of "citizen-initiated media content" is at the core of this philosophy and has become popular in recent decades with the introduction of new media technologies, such as the Internet, that permit individuals and groups to bypass conventional media roadblocks and reach audiences directly.

13.2 Pluralistic Trend

Today, none of these six controlling philosophies exist anywhere in pure form. Instead, most countries today support a combination of approaches. Compromise leads to combinations of features to create a hybrid approach often referred to as **pluralism.** Pluralism means more than simple competition among rival services. Given that similar motives drive all services, media would merely imitate one another in the absence of pluralistic competition. Pluralism means putting a variety of motives to work, each with approximately equal status—usually a mix of commercial and public-service motives. Advocates of pluralism assert that healthy competition between differently motivated broadcasting organizations can stimulate creativity, encourage innovation, and ensure variety. The result is usually a wider range of genuine program choices than any single-motive system could produce.

Looking at our prior chapter addressing public broadcasting in the United States, we can see an example of pluralism in which a highly competitive, advertising-based media system also supports a tax-supported Corporation for Public Broadcasting to assist thousands of noncommercial radio and TV stations in providing program content not typically found on the pure commercial services. Financing is acquired from several sources, including local, state, and federal governments; corporate underwriters; private grants; and individual citizen memberships. No other country has such an approach to offering an alternative to a well-established free-market system.

One way to appreciate the nature and extent of pluralism is to create a rough continuum, in which at one extreme we would have countries that are relatively isolated from interacting with the rest of the world, exercising considerable government control over the ownership of facilities and the creation and distribution of program content. Often, these nations are just beginning to experiment with free-market economics and media advertising. At the opposite extreme, we have countries that are truly international in their thinking and encourage private ownership of almost all media and advocate deregulation of commerce and content. These nations, however, still maintain enforceable standards of quality and some government-supported, noncommercial media.

Three Examples of Pluralism: People's Republic of China, Mexico, and the United Kingdom

A detailed examination of the dozen or so possible combinations of controlling philosophies is not within the scope of this single chapter, however, a close look at three unique media systems hopefully will give the reader an appreciation of the myriad ways a country can deal with its electronic media. In particular, these three examples demonstrate how government participation and free-market commercialism can coexist. For the sake of keeping this chapter a reasonable length, we will focus primarily on broadcasting to demonstrate this point, knowing that other media, such as cable, satellite, and the Internet, could be analyzed in the same manner. The People's Republic of China, Mexico, and the United Kingdom offer some interesting contrasts and similarities to our American system.

People's Republic of China. The People's Republic of China (PRC) controls its media through a government agency, the State Administration of Radio, Film, and Television (SARFT), which in turn is controlled by the Central Committee of the Communist Party. This agency supervises China National Radio, China Central Television, and China Radio International. Each of these services offers several unique networks or channels. Based on this political structure, it should be no surprise that the government takes a close look at all content and yet there are signs of a more tolerant attitude than in years past. As the country reaches out to the rest of the world for business opportunities, its once strong authoritarian oversight of all media is giving way to notions of a free-market economy. The current government gradually has reduced many of the hard-handed isolationist tactics of the past. In particular, China's broadcasting system, once totally supported by government funding, has accepted commercial advertising since the late 1980s, and the trend has continued with even more advertisers from around the world, including major American advertisers, such

as Proctor & Gable, showing up on Chinese radio, television, and cable. Today, the country supports approximately 700 conventional TV stations, as well as about 3,000 cable channels and 1,000 radio stations. Coinciding with the introduction of an advertising-based business model has been a change in program content. The steady diet of political propaganda has given way to a much broader choice of programming, including imported programs like *American Idol* from the United States. Of course, the government is always close by and has the authority to shut down any media enterprise.

Much of the surprising diversity in the media in China is attributable to the fact that most state media outlets no longer receive large government subsidies and are expected to largely pay for themselves through commercial advertising. Consequently, the media can no longer serve solely as a propaganda tool for the government, but must also attract sizable audiences so that money can be generated through advertising. Although a form of communism remains the official doctrine of the PRC, its waning influence has bolstered the media to be critical of government policies. Increased contact with the West has fostered a desire for more civil liberties, especially freedom of speech. Although far from a pure libertarian approach, the PRC continues to embrace the positive aspects of a free-market media environment while still maintaining a highly visible government presence.

Mexico. A primarily commercial marketplace with strong government regulation is a defining feature of the media system in Mexico. The national government is directly involved in the regulation of broadcast media, though some observers believe that this has diminished somewhat through the country's transition to a more open democracy. Radio and TV stations are privately owned, but licensed and regulated by the government agencies, the Ministry of Transportation and Communication, and the Ministry of the Interior. The privately owned stations are allowed to carry advertising. Noncommercial broadcasting exists and is not funded by the national government, but rather by regional state governments. The Mexican national government, however, does partially fund a 26 station commercial radio network called IMER. In addition, the national government owns the country's main news agency, Notimex, which provides stories to Mexican media outlets. Although stations are provided a fair amount of creative freedom for entertainment programming, news programs receive much scrutiny. Furthermore, the government requires that each station broadcasts free of charge a certain amount of government-produced programs each week. For example, for one hour on Sundays, all radio broadcasters must turn over their airtime to the *National Hour*, a series of progress reports on government activities. A second obligation is *State Time*, a daily series of 30 second government-produced radio and television announcements distributed throughout the broadcast day. Compared to the People's Republic of China, the Mexican government's involvement with the free market has progressed much farther in recent decades, but critics maintain that the private media appear disturbingly close to the government and seldom demonstrate any true autonomy from the powers that license and regulate.

United Kingdom. The British have a long history of nurturing civil liberties and democratic government, but the overseeing of electronic media for many years included a ban on free-market commercialism. Instead, the British advocated a much-admired public broadcasting system composed of two noncommercial authorities: the **British Broadcasting Corporation (BBC)** and the **Independent Broadcasting Authority (IBA)**. The BBC enjoyed a monopoly status until 1954 when Parliament created a competitive, commercially sponsored TV system. Later in the 1970s, further competition was added when local privately owned radio stations were authorized.

Today, the BBC offers five national and several regional TV networks. In addition, it provides a 24-hour cable news channel and web site. The BBC is a quasi-autonomous public corporation that has a mandate to provide high-quality educational and cultural media content distributed through a variety of noncommercial outlets. Similar to the function of the Corporation for Public Broadcasting in the United States, the BBC is run by the BBC Trust and is intended to be free from both political and commercial influence. As part of its charter, the Corporation cannot show commercial advertising on any services—television, radio, or the Internet. The BBC's domestic programming and broadcasts primarily are funded by levying annual TV license fees. Such a license is required to operate a broadcast TV receiver within the United Kingdom. Outside the United Kingdom, the BBC broadcasts commercially funded channels such as *BBC America*, *BBC Canada*, and *BBC World News*.

Independent Television (ITV) is a public service network of British commercial television broadcasters, set up under the Independent Television Authority (ITA) to provide an alternative to the BBC. ITV is the oldest and largest commercial television network in the United Kingdom. Since 1990, its legal name has been **Channel 3**. Fifteen companies provide regional Channel 3 services in various areas of the United Kingdom. Programs from ITV are provided by ITV's in-house production unit and by the independent sector. As well as network programming, each of the ITV licenses provides regional programming to cater to the interests of people living in each area of the United Kingdom.

In 2003, the British government consolidated the responsibilities of five media regulatory bodies into **The Office of Communications** or, as it is more often known, Ofcom. Resembling many of the duties given the FCC in the United States, Ofcom is responsible for the management, regulation, assignment, and licensing of the electromagnetic spectrum in the United Kingdom, and licenses portions of it for use in TV and radio broadcasts, mobile phone transmissions, and private communications networks.

In the United Kingdom, all broadcasters, including commercial broadcasters, are considered to be public service media that have obligations in terms of quality and quantity of certain types of programming. In this case, a social responsibility philosophy is the dominant approach to regulation, but although technically the government could exert considerable pressure on its media, it has rarely done so. Historically, the press has had wide-ranging freedoms and has encouraged criticism of all levels of government.

13.3 Deregulation and Privatization

Along with the explosive growth of new types of media technology, there have been equally important changes in media regulation and ownership. Worldwide, we have come a long way from the monopolistic, nationally controlled media of the past. Starting around 1980, U.S.-inspired deregulatory practices swept the telecommunications world, although American influence alone did not create this trend. Deregulation appealed overseas as it did here for another reason—no regulator could keep up with the fast-changing technology.

Competition

The United States has negotiated aggressively in international discussions to further the deregulatory trend, seeking to stimulate global competition, avoid anticompetitive conduct, and open international markets to foreign participation. Several international trade agreements now make it easier for companies from one country to participate in the telecommunications markets of other countries. These agreements are all subject to ratification by the individual nations involved, and not all countries agree with these goals. Similar agreements have been reached among the members of the European Union (EU), which will be discussed later in this chapter.

With deregulation, traditional public-service operators faced new competition from cable, satellite, and the Internet. Some critics argue that excessive competition may force public-service broadcasters to lower program standards as they struggle to maintain viable audience shares. Others argue that even public-service programming should be "competitive."

Coinciding with the international trend toward deregulation has been an equally powerful trend toward privatization of media. Converting state-owned facilities to private ownership (or creating new private outlets), has rapidly taken hold in Europe, Australia, Canada, Japan, New Zealand, and many Latin American nations. Of course, privatization automatically assumes the fostering of private enterprise in the form of commercial advertising and subscription business models.

An example of one of the most dramatic changes in international media control and ownership occurred in Russia and its Eastern European client states. The fall of the former Soviet Union and the move to democratization brought dramatic change over the past three decades. Nothing in history matches the startling suddenness with which four decades of rigid communist control crumbled almost overnight in country after country. The culmination was the total collapse of the Soviet Union itself in late 1991.

Private broadcasting and cable have made much headway in several formerly communist nations, but history has a way of repeating itself and many of the changes in regulation and private ownership have been reversed. As this text was being revised, Russia has abruptly halted its hands-off policies with the media and has reintroduced government censorship of newscasts and taken back control of most broadcast facilities. In Moscow and elsewhere, journalists have been harassed or physically abused. Reporters investigating the affairs of the political and corporate elite are said to be particularly at risk. The media rights organization, Reporters without Borders, has expressed concern at "the absence of pluralism in news and information, an intensifying crackdown against journalists." In addition, several nearby countries, including Hungary and Slovakia, have placed strong controls on media content, including limits on antigovernment news or statements. Despite periodic setbacks, in general, the world for the past 20 years has continued to move toward less government regulation and less direct government ownership of electronic media.

PTT Deregulation

Deregulation has also had a widespread impact on common-carrier services, loosening control by highly centralized national post, telephone, and telegraph (PTT) monopolies, and spurring competition among new telecommunications service providers. In addition to their telephone operations, some PTTs have long held exclusive rights to install and operate broadcast transmitters and relays, as well as cable facilities. However, in many countries, transmission and programming have been regulated by separate government authorities. For cable television, marketing and promotion play key roles: Consumers need to be convinced that this new service will benefit them. Lack of experience in facing competition generally means that monopolistic PTTs have little marketing expertise. Overall, liberalization and new competition have been boons to consumers throughout most of the world.

13.4 International Cooperation

In addition to important changes in regulation and privatization occurring inside many countries, there have been significant developments in the ways countries deal with countries outside their borders. The growth of electronic media technologies has stimulated efforts in international cooperation and the formation of standing organizations. One such organization is the **International Telecommunication Union (ITU)**. Today, most nations belong to the ITU, a United Nations' affiliate headquartered in Geneva, Switzerland. As sovereign nations, members cannot be forced to obey ITU regulations, though they usually find it in their best interests to accept ITU recommendations and to adopt ITU standardized terms and procedures.

The ITU is also dedicated to helping developing nations improve their telecommunication facilities. In the early 1990s, the ITU underwent its most dramatic reorganization in a half-century—evidence that its dozens of developing members were having more impact on ITU decisions. The ITU attempts to spread equitable, sustainable, and affordable access to information and communication technologies (ICT) as a means of stimulating broader social and economic development. Held every four years, the World Telecommunication Development Conference (WTDC) establishes concrete priorities to help achieve these goals.

Another example of international cooperation has been the **European Broadcasting Union (EBU)**; a confederation of 75 broadcasting organizations, most of which are government-owned public service broadcasters or privately owned stations with public missions. Associate members from the United States include ABC, CBS, NBC, the Corporation for Public Broadcasting, and Time Warner. The EBU claims to be the largest association of national broadcasters in the world, with the overarching goal of promoting cooperation among media organizations and facilitating the exchange of audiovisual content. For example, Eurovision and Euroradio networks, operated by the EBU, carry daily exchanges of programs, music, sports events, and news among members and other media players. Much of the foreign news featured on national news bulletins has passed through the control center in Geneva.

Competing Technical Standards

Thanks to ITU's uniform spectrum allocations and standards, taking a portable radio to listen to abroad works in most places. But don't try traveling internationally with a regular TV set. Although television has similar channel allocations throughout the world, its technical standards are not uniform. No fewer than 14 monochrome and 3 principal color technical standards require converters to exchange programs (as in Olympic or World Cup sports coverage) or to use one country's TV equipment elsewhere.

Today's three basic analog color television systems—NTSC, PAL, and SECAM—reflect American, German, and French government promotion in the 1960s. Each country sought to persuade other governments to adopt its standard. Adoption meant not only national prestige, but also huge revenues from international sales by manufacturers of equipment using the favored system. Today, PAL is primarily used in Western Europe and South America; the American NTSC system is found in Japan; and France, Russia, and most other Eastern European countries have adopted SECAM.

Most developed nations are in the process of making the transition from analog to digital television. As was the case with analog television, the world will not have a singular standard for high-definition television. Current HDTV broadcast standards include ATSC (Advanced Television Systems Committee) for North America and parts of South America and South Korea; DVB (digital video broadcasting) for Europe, Australia, parts of Asia, and Africa; and ISDB-T (integrated services digital broadcasting-terrestrial) for Japan and Brazil.

13.5 Access

Because all electronic media can inform, persuade, and cultivate values, this makes access to them a jealously guarded prerogative. Traditionally, most countries have limited access to professional broadcasters, experts on topics of public interest, people currently in the news, entertainers, and politicians.

Politicians

Democracy requires fairness in the political use of the electronic media—without at the same time crippling the media's role as a means of informing voters. In America, weak parties and candidates have the same theoretical access rights as major parties, provided they can afford to buy advertising time. Although the United States has a reputation for granting politicians considerable access to the media, many countries require by law even more free access in an effort to halt the excessive commercialization of elections. A good example is the United Kingdom, in which national campaigns last only 30 days, and voters are spared the endless merchandising of candidates. Nor do candidates have to beg for donations and accept money from lobbyists to pay for expensive broadcast advertising. The United Kingdom is also one of the few countries that allow live televising of Parliament's debates—similar to C-SPAN's coverage of Congress here. Such a ready means of watching can bring the governing process closer to voters.

Citizens

During the 1960s, people in many countries sought airway access. They argued that if the electromagnetic spectrum is really a shared natural resource, then everybody should get a chance to use it. This access movement paralleled a widespread rise in ethnic and regional awareness. Access seekers petitioned authorities to create regional and community stations. Many did. France, for example, legitimized more than a thousand small, privately owned FM radio stations following passage of a new broadcasting law in 1982. Many had started as pirate stations, which the French government had suppressed rigorously. In Scandinavia, governments finance low-power FM **ndr radio** (neighborhood stations), inviting local groups to help program them, free of virtually all regulation.

Groups

Another way of dealing with access demands is to shift the emphasis from individuals to the groups to which those individuals belong. The uniquely structured access system of the Netherlands has gone farthest in assuring different social groups their own programs on national broadcast facilities. Most program time on government-run networks is turned over to citizen broadcasting associations.

Access can also work in a negative fashion. The once White-controlled *apartheid* government of South Africa for years limited Black access to outside sources of news. Radio news directed at tribal groups in their own languages was channeled onto FM radio. As FM and shortwave tuning were not ordinarily available on the same receiver, the use of FM for controlled domestic news limited Black listeners' access to external news sources.

The Internet has had a profound impact on the ability of ordinary citizens and special interest groups to gain access to audiences by essentially bypassing conventional media organizations and government agencies. The popularity of the Internet and the ability of net users to communicate effortlessly across national boundaries make the medium at once a very liberating or a dangerous technology, depending on one's point of view. On one hand, ordinary people feel liberated in that they can now communicate with the outside word. On the other hand, some governments feel threatened because they can no longer censor communication.

13.6 Economics and Geography

Economics is second only to politics in shaping a country's electronic media. National systems vary widely in audience size, facilities, revenue sources, and the ability to produce home-grown programs. Economic constraints account for these differences, though geography also plays an important role.

Audience Size

More than 200 countries and dependencies have their own radio broadcasting systems. Fewer than 40 countries (mostly small islands) lack TV stations. TV set penetration per household varies from nearly 100 percent in countries like the United States, the United Kingdom, and Switzerland, to less than 10 percent in parts of Asia and Africa. High penetration levels depend only partly on economics; important as well are programs popular enough to motivate TV set purchase and a policy of licensing local stations. But TV set penetration does not tell the whole story of viewing and listening in other countries. Cultural differences can influence the use of electronic media even when TV set penetration levels are comparable. Television viewing time per household in Asia, for example, is much less than in the United States.

Lack of communications infrastructure—electric power, telephones, and relay facilities for networks—further impedes electronic media development. However, a few of the oil-rich Middle East states have achieved relatively high radio set penetration. One clever solution to the lack of electrical power has been the distribution of thousands of hand-crank/solar-powered Lifeline radios to rural Africa so that people in the most remote areas of the continent can have access to news, information, education, and even a little music.

Revenue Sources

Electronic media financial support comes from four main sources: government appropriations, receiver license fees, advertising, and user fees. Most countries' electronic media still depend at least partially on government funds. In industrialized democracies, substantial support depends on user license fees—an annual payment per household or receiver. This somewhat insulates broadcasting organizations from inevitable biases caused by dependence on either direct government funding or advertising. But the protection is only partial, because governments create fee payment rules and set fee levels. As operational costs rise faster than audience fees increase, many formerly fee-supported systems turn to advertising, though theoretically advertising contributes too small a part to give advertisers any real influence over programs. User fees have become more common as countries move to digital technologies. For many years, the most common user fee has been the **subscription,** wherein a user pays a flat monthly or annual fee. This has been a long-standing business model of cable television. Another type of user fee gaining in popularity due to the growth of broadband capabilities is the **per-use fee,** wherein the user pays for each instance of media access, such as video-on-demand. Sometimes the user pays a simple one-time download fee, such as a piece of music to an iPod, that can be played back any number of times. All of these more recent revenue sources are dependent on audiences having the necessary technology and wealth to purchase the items.

Program Economics

Television consumes expensive programs at such a rate that even developed nations with strong economies cannot afford to program several different TV networks exclusively with home-grown productions. As a result, they acquire programming via syndication or other means from other countries. As will be presented in more detail later in this chapter, many nations find this dependence undesirable and consequently place legal restrictions or quotas on the amount of program content that can be imported.

Most imported programs come from the United States, though many come from Britain. A few developing countries, especially Brazil, Mexico, and India, are active in supplying international program markets. In the past decade, the enormous popularity of unscripted, or so-called reality programming, has enabled countries to produce dozens of episodes quickly and inexpensively. Of course, critics can argue over the quality of such programming, but nonetheless, it does make economic sense for nations wishing greater participation in international programming.

Gestures in cooperation have also helped. International syndication and various forms of cost and talent sharing have helped to increase the amount of programming available. Co-production is increasingly used to cover high program costs. Producers from two or more countries combine financial and other resources to co-produce television series or movies. They divide the capital expenses and profits from the distribution of programming in participating countries.

Coverage Problems

Cost-effective media coverage of a country depends on both its shape and size. Alaska and Hawaii, for example, had to await satellite transmission to enjoy same-time coverage with the U.S. mainland. Indonesia's 6,000 or so widely scattered islands with diverse populations speaking many different languages present even more formidable coverage problems. And Russian territory extends so far east and west that national broadcast schedules have to be adapted to serve 10 different time zones (contrasted with only 4 in the continental United States). The same dilemma is true for the People's Republic of China. Program distribution needs prompted these countries to become early users of domestic satellites. As with just about any other aspect of electronic communication, the Internet and, in particular, the adoption of high-speed broadband capabilities has erased many coverage problems. Assuming a consumer can get access to these sophisticated services, any type of long-form programming, from a symphony to a movie, can be streamed to anyplace on the globe.

✗ Signal Spillover

If, in fact, geographical coverage has become less of a problem, the opposite is now true for some countries because geographical borders cannot stop electronic "spillover" from neighboring states. A familiar example for our readers is the 3,000 mile shared border with a northern neighbor. Spillover from the United States has strongly influenced not only broadcasting, but also satellite and cable development in neighboring Canada. Most Canadians live within 100 miles of the American border and can easily receive American broadcast signals off-air and/or by cable and DBS (and vice versa, of course). As a result, Canada became the first heavily cabled country in the world.

Any place on the globe, where a country's borders are not adjacent to an ocean, electronic signals can penetrate easily the arbitrary boundaries set up by governments. Of course, until recently this signal spillover issue has involved more traditional media, but the enormous growth of the Internet and broadband has taken it to a new level.

The term **spillover** implies that these broadcast signals cross borders by coincidence, but in some cases this phenomenon is far more deliberate. As will be discussed in more detail within the section addressing transborder communications (Section 13.9), several European nations bordering large countries have long operated stations that have every intention of reaching audiences and advertisers living and working far beyond its own borders. Commercial motives account for these transborder broadcasters (sometimes referred to as **peripherals**) that beam commercial radio services in appropriate languages to neighboring countries. A good example is the tiny country of The Grand Duchy of Luxembourg, ideally located for peripheral transmitters at the intersection of Belgium, France, and Germany. This country receives much of its national income from international commercial television as well as radio broadcasting. Peripherals in general tend to be rather noncontroversial in their program offerings and are tolerated by their target countries, some of which even invest in them.

13.7 Programs

The previously mentioned sharing of programming across borders simply reflects the fact that similar program formats exist throughout the world. News, commentary, public affairs, music, drama, variety, studio games, sports events—such program types appeal everywhere. National differences are evident only in the ways these genres are treated.

News and Public Affairs

Prime-time daily newscasts are universally popular, but their content and style differ among countries. Parochialism, chauvinism, and ideology affect the choice, treatment, and timing of news stories. Each country emphasizes its own national events, few of which hold interest elsewhere.

As presented at the beginning of this chapter, the underlying controlling philosophy influences the type of program content that is endorsed by a government. This is especially true when looking at news and public affairs content. In predominantly authoritarian countries, such as Iran, Cuba, and North Korea, news focuses heavily on the national leader to the virtual exclusion of all else. Some broadcasting systems devote their news-gathering facilities entirely to reporting on the head of state's every public move and developing a cult of personality. On the other hand, many countries that accept more of a libertarian or social responsibility philosophy of governance are far more tolerant of public criticism and encourage investigative journalism and vigorous debate within the "marketplace of ideas."

Program Balance

Of course, audiences everywhere prefer entertaining comedy and drama to more serious informational content. Accordingly, where audience appeal controls programs—as through audience ratings—entertainment dominates. But even entertainment program content can be manipulated by some governments that are highly concerned with preserving their unique culture.

Censorship can be applied to dramas and comedies as well as newscasts.

Most industrialized democracies (including the United States, thanks to public broadcasting and news/culture-oriented cable channels) try to strike a balance among light entertainment, news, information, culture, and educational programs. Those members of a society who buy most of the consumer products and services and enjoy access to political and social groups see and hear themselves through the electronic media far more than do the poor and powerless. Accordingly, the electronic media depict a largely urban, fairly well-educated, affluent people, whether fictional or real.

Developing nations can afford few local productions with popular appeal, therefore, they import foreign entertainment that attracts audiences for a fraction of what it would cost to produce programs locally. But imports throw schedules out of balance (as discussed in the next section) by overemphasizing entertainment and playing up foreign cultures that are often quite different from the viewer's surroundings.

Schedules

Though common in America, broadcast days of 18 to 24 hours were rare even in other developed countries until quite recently. Traditionally, most foreign radio services would broadcast a short morning segment, take a break before a midday segment, then another break before evening programs, closing down for the night relatively early. Television in much of the world still begins only late in the afternoon, signing off by about 11:00 P.M. Of course, time shifting has become hugely popular in the United States with the introduction of various digital recording devices (DVRs), such as TiVo, that enable individuals to acquire and play back programming at anytime. Again, for less affluent and developing countries, the issue isn't technology as much as economics. That is, the hardware and software exist, but many countries cannot afford to install these services, nor can ordinary people afford to pay for them.

International Syndication

Repeated sales of TV programs, both within the United States and throughout the world, has long been central to the profitability of the television industry. As was discussed in detail in prior chapters addressing programming, **reruns** often are what make a program profitable. This audience acceptance of repeat airings of television content can be found among all countries. In addition, many countries have found it far more economical to purchase the syndicated rights to American television programs than to produce their own first-run product, opening a vast market for American program content. With added demand from new satellite-distributed cable networks, direct broadcast satellite channels, and DVDs, program services vacuum up content from whatever sources they can find. Their enhanced demand has intensified old fears of American cultural domination.

Although the price tag (i.e., syndication fee) for U.S. television programming in the international marketplace is generally based on free-market supply and demand, the prices paid for programs in Europe typically are far higher than those paid in Africa or Latin America. No matter how small the syndication fee, however, the sales of programming produce additional income for their original production companies. Exhibit 13.a provides an overview of the average prices paid by different countries for U.S. syndicated material.

Increasingly, the worldwide TV syndication marketplace has featured productions not always part of the U.S. industry. For example, Brazilian, Venezuelan, and Mexican telenovelas are programmed throughout the Spanish-speaking world. As in the American business context, the profits generated by syndication can be used to produce other material on a speculative basis and to bolster the production of first-run programming.

The stage on which the international players appear are the marketing festivals held several times a year in Europe, the United States, and more recently, Asia. The most important is MIP-TV (International Film and Programme Market for Television) held in Cannes, France. MIP-TV brings international executives together to consider co-producing, buying, selling, financing, and distributing entertainment content across all media platforms. MIPCOM (International Market for Television, Video, Cable and Satellite Films and Programs) also held in Cannes, has become the second biggest event after MIP-TV. Furthermore, the annual National Association of Television Programming Executives (NATPE) convention, held in the United States each year, is another important venue for international syndication.

Cultural differences often impact programming. One major difference between American and foreign television (especially in Europe) is the tolerance of nudity in programs and advertising. Full frontal nudes are not uncommon on some European TV channels. What is acceptable in one country often is not in another, creating problems for program exchange or syndication. American programs, for example, are often criticized abroad for being excessively violent.

13.8 Global Media

The global commercial system is a very recent development. Until the 1980s, media systems were generally national in scope. While there have been imports of books, films, music, and TV shows for decades, the basic broadcasting systems and newspaper industries

Exhibit 13.a

The Global Market for U.S. Syndicated Programming

This exhibit provides an overview of the average prices paid by different countries for U.S. syndicated programming. The figures are the average prices paid by broadcast stations in key territories for selected genres of U.S. programming. Drama prices are by the hour; sitcoms and docs/kids/arts are by the half-hour. Sums paid for feature films fluctuate dramatically according to their theatrical gross in the United States and/or in the territory in question.

Global TV Price Guide

Germany
Feature films: $2.5 million
TV movies: $200,000
Dramas: $150,000
Sitcoms: $80,000
Reality: $50,000
Docs/kids/arts: $25,000

Scandinavia
Feature films: $250,000
TV movies: $75,000
Dramas: $60,000
Sitcoms: $40,000
Reality: $25,000
Docs/kids/arts: $20,000

Hungary
Feature films: $60,000
TV movies: $35,000
Dramas: $45,000
Sitcoms: $30,000
Reality: $20,000
Docs/kids/arts: $7,500

United Kingdom
Feature films: $2.5 million
TV movies: $150,000
Dramas: $300,000
Sitcoms: $200,000
Reality: $150,000
Docs/kids/arts: $50,000

Belgium
Feature films: $200,000
TV movies: $75,000
Dramas: $50,000
Sitcoms: $40,000
Reality: $20,000
Docs/kids/arts: $15,000

Canada
Feature films: $400,000
TV movies: $200,000
Dramas: $100,000
Sitcoms: $60,000
Reality: $50,000
Docs/kids/arts: $25,000

France
Feature films: $1.5 million
TV movies: $125,000
Dramas: $100,000
Sitcoms: $75,000
Reality: $40,000
Docs/kids/arts: $25,000

Austria
Feature films: $100,000
TV movies: $60,000
Dramas: $50,000
Sitcoms: $30,000
Reality: $20,000
Docs/kids/arts: $15,000

Japan
Feature films: $1.5 million
TV movies: $80,000
Dramas: $50,000
Sitcoms: $30,000
Reality: $25,000
Docs/kids/arts: $20,000

Italy
Feature films: $1 million
TV movies: $150,000
Dramas: $80,000
Sitcoms: $40,000
Reality: $40,000
Docs/kids/arts: $20,000

Russia
Feature films: $150,000
TV movies: $100,000
Dramas: $75,000
Sitcoms: $50,000
Reality: $40,000
Docs/kids/arts: $25,000

Australia
Feature films: $200,000
TV movies: $75,000
Dramas: $60,000
Sitcoms: $35,000
Reality: $25,000
Docs/kids/arts: $20,000

Spain
Feature films: $1 million
TV movies: $125,000
Dramas: $80,000
Sitcoms: $40,000
Reality: $30,000
Docs/kids/arts: $20,000

Poland
Feature films: $90,000
TV movies: $60,000
Dramas: $50,000
Sitcoms: $35,000
Reality: $25,000
Docs/kids/arts: $15,000

Mexico
Feature films: $100,000
TV movies: $75,000
Dramas: $30,000
Sitcoms: $20,000
Reality: $20,000
Docs/kids/arts: $10,000

Netherlands
Feature films: $250,000
TV movies: $100,000
Dramas: $75,000
Sitcoms: $50,000
Reality: $25,000
Docs/kids/arts: $15,000

Czech Republic
Feature films: $60,000
TV movies: $35,000
Dramas: $40,000
Sitcoms: $20,000
Reality: $15,000
Docs/kids/arts: $5,000

Brazil
Feature films: $75,000
TV movies: $50,000
Dramas: $40,000
Sitcoms: $25,000
Reality: $20,000
Docs/kids/arts: $10,000

Source: Elizabeth Guider, "Global TV Price Guide," *Variety*, April 12, 2007.

were domestically owned and regulated. The 1980s and 1990s saw the rise of transnational media giants. The deregulation of media ownership, the privatization of many media services, and new media technologies have made it possible for large media companies to establish powerful distribution and production networks within and among nations. Some media observers are concerned about a global commercial media system dominated by a small number of powerful, mostly U.S. corporations. They maintain that a mere 50 or so firms control most of the world's film production, TV show production, cable channel ownership, cable and satellite system ownership, book publishing, magazine publishing, and music production. Among these 50, an elite dozen control most of the business transactions. Media companies such as Time Warner, General Electric (NBC / Universal), Disney, Viacom, Sony, and News Corporation are some of the major players.

One example of a huge transborder success that may be appreciated by students is MTV International, owned by Viacom, that operates several regional and country-specific services: MTV Europe, MTV Asia, MTV Latin America, MTV India, MTV Brazil, MTV Mandarin, MTV Australia, and MTV Japan. These channels, produced in Singapore, Taipei, and London, feature national talent and playlists designed to appeal to each channel's target market.

Cultural Imperialism

American dominance of international syndication has long fed concern about what some media critics call cultural imperialism, or the "Americanization," of other cultures. They argue that images and values shown in imported TV programs undermine local cultures. For example, American shows are criticized for encouraging excessive consumption, materialism, and disregard for other traditions. Further, every imported program denies an opportunity for locals to showcase their own talents. Cheaper imported programs can thus perpetuate dependence on foreigners. This is a special problem with developing countries, but even developed nations with extensive production of their own limit the amount of entertainment their national systems may import.

One prominent example of halting the growth of imported media content is the "Television Without Frontiers" Directive (TWFD) sponsored by the European Union (EU), a group of European countries that participate in the world economy as one economic unit and operate under one official currency, the euro. The EU's goal is to create a barrier-free trade zone and to enhance economic wealth by creating more efficiency within its marketplace. The Directive rests on two basic principles: the free movement of European TV programs within the internal market and the requirement for TV channels to reserve, whenever possible, more than half of their transmission time for European works ("broadcasting quotas"), exclud-

ing the time allocated to news, sports events, games, and advertising. In addition, the policy ensures that European audiovisual programs are given a conspicuous position in TV program schedules. Broadcasters must also reserve at least 10 percent of their transmission time or 10 percent of their programming budget for European works from independent producers. Similar associations exist in Asia, the Middle East, and the Caribbean, although they are not as active as the EU in handling program exchanges.

To avoid being overwhelmed by American programs, and to ensure work for its own creative community, Canada imposes quotas limiting the amount of syndicated programming that the electronic media may import. To help fill the gap, Canada's government subsidizes Canadian production, leading to a vibrant Canadian popular music industry, for example. In addition, some American films and TV programs have been co-produced in Canada to lower their cost to get around import quotas.

American producers understandably strongly resist attempts by other countries to limit program imports. At the newspaper and broadcast industries' request, U.S. diplomats successfully advocated for a *free flow* international communication policy when the United Nations was created in 1945. But many countries that have since joined the United Nations ask what value free flow has for them when it runs almost entirely in one direction—*from* the United States and other industrialized countries *to* developing nations. Instead, they call for **balanced flow**— defined as news and entertainment that treats developing countries fairly and in proportion to their population significance. The debate between these polar positions continues in many international organizations today.

UNESCO's Role

Much of this debate over global media, and in particular the development of international journalism, came to a head in the 1970s and 1980s at the Paris-based UN Educational, Scientific, and Cultural Organization (UNESCO), which led in defining and calling for the establishment of a New World Information and Communication Order (NWICO). The organization called for, among other things, balanced media flow, training (and perhaps licensing) of journalists to operate in other cultures and languages, and support from rich nations to assist the development of poor nations' media infrastructure. American media leaders saw this development as an attack on journalistic independence and free-enterprise advertising. Claiming that UNESCO wasted money (a quarter of its budget came from the United States) and had become hopelessly politicized, the U.S. government withdrew as a member in 1984, leaving an agency that it had helped establish four decades earlier. In 2003, after much of the agency's political and budget turmoil had been resolved, the United States rejoined the organization.

13.9 Transborder Communication

In addition to providing programming to be consumed within the borders of a country, many governments for decades have operated external services intended to reach audiences outside their borders. For the purposes of this text, **transborder communication** is defined as communications that are deliberately aimed at a foreign, rather than a domestic, audience. This content usually is transmitted by means of conventional radio, in recent years content also has been transmitted using direct broadcast satellite (DBS) and the Internet. Historically, the primary purpose for most of these transmissions has been propaganda, particularly during wartime. But even during the Cold War and relative peace, state-operated stations have continued to provide information and news that typically has an ideological slant.

Since the 1920s, the ability to use radio to penetrate political boundaries added a potent element to diplomatic relations. Never before had nations been able to talk directly to masses of foreigners, crossing even the most heavily defended national borders. Today, more than 80 countries operate official external services—programs aimed at foreign countries.

For some countries that have maintained faraway colonies or other types of affiliated territories, transborder communication has served as a means of keeping in touch with expatriates. Probably the most notable example has been the BBC Empire Service created in 1932, with transmissions aimed toward Australia and New Zealand. As the winds of war approached Europe in the mid-1930s, Nazi Germany began a concerted effort to propagandize much of the world with daily programs. When war broke out in full force in the 1940s, Russian, German, British, and Italian international broadcasting services expanded dramatically. In 1942, the United States initiated the *Voice of America* international service, which still operates to this day.

The Cold War led to increased international broadcasting, as Communist and non-Communist states attempted to influence each other's domestic population. Some of the most prominent Western broadcasters were the *Voice of America*, the *BBC World Service*, and the CIA-backed *Radio Free Europe/Radio Liberty*. The Soviet Union's most recognized global service was Radio Moscow (now the *Voice of Russia*). Meanwhile, China used *Radio Peking* (then *Radio Beijing*, now *China Radio International*) to improve its image overseas.

In addition to the superpower states, international broadcast services grew in Europe and the Middle East. For example, under the presidency of Gamal Nasser, Egyptian transmitters covered the Arab world; Israel's service, Kol Yisrael, presented the Israeli point of view to the world. *Radio RSA*, as part of the South African Broadcasting Corporation, was established in 1966 to promote the image of South Africa and reduce criticism of apartheid. With the ending of the Cold War, many international broadcasters cut back on hours and foreign language broadcasts, or reemphasized other language services. However, with the war in Iraq and related turmoil in the Middle East, international services have emerged again. One of the most controversial has been the *Aljazeera* news service, which claims no ideological bias, but often is accused of providing anti-American interpretations of news events.

Governments often do not want their citizens listening to international broadcasters. In some cases, listening to such broadcasts has been considered a crime punishable by jail. The most common method of preventing reception is **jamming**, or broadcasting a signal on the same frequencies as the international broadcaster. Germany jammed the BBC European service during World War II. Russian and Eastern European jammers were aimed against Radio Free Europe, other Western broadcasters, and against Chinese broadcasters during the nadir of Sino-Soviet relations. The Cuban government frequently jams the Voice of America's Radio Marti programs. North Korea restricts most people to a single fixed radio frequency. Another method of preventing reception involves moving a domestic station to the frequency used by the international broadcaster. Jamming can be defeated by using very powerful transmitting antennas, carefully choosing the transmitted frequency, changing transmitted frequency often, and properly aiming the receiving antenna.

Because this textbook is aimed primarily at the American electronic media, we will now take a closer look at several transborder activities sponsored by the U.S. government. Under the supervision of the Broadcasting Board of Governors (BBG), the International Broadcasting Bureau (IBB) provides the administrative and engineering support for U.S. government-funded non-military international broadcast services. Broadcast elements include the Voice of America (VOA), Radio Free Europe and Radio Liberty, Radio Marti, and Radio Free Asia.

Voice of America

The Voice of America (VOA), which first went on the air in 1942, is a multimedia international broadcasting service funded by the U.S. government through the Broadcasting Board of Governors. VOA broadcasts more than 1,000 hours of news, information, educational, and cultural programming every week to an estimated worldwide audience of more than 115 million people. The U.S government created WorldNet as a daily TV service distributed abroad by satellite. Service costs, as well as research showing very small audiences, led to congressional budget cuts. In 2003, WorldNet was merged into the multiplatform system of the VOA. Today, audiences can receive free VOA programming via radio, satellite, web casts, iPods or other MP3 players, as well as mobile phone or Internet-enabled handheld devices.

VOA news and public-affairs programs reflect official American policies. News commentaries are explicitly labeled as coming from the U.S. government. For the sake of credibility, VOA tries to observe the spirit of its original 1942 policy: "Daily at this time we shall speak to you about America. The news may be good or bad. We shall tell you the truth." Truth telling continues to be VOA policy, despite occasional lapses when partisan officials bend facts to suit momentary political objectives.

Radio Free Europe and Radio Liberty

The stated mission for Radio Free Europe and Radio Liberty (RFE/RL) is to provide uncensored news and information to countries where a free press is either banned by the government or not fully established. RFE/RL journalists provide discussion and open debate of local and international news, politics, history, culture, religion, arts, and literature.

Beginning in the early 1950s, Radio Liberty (RL) targeted the Soviet Union, while Radio Free Europe (RFE) aimed its programming at Eastern European states then under Soviet control. CIA support of these services was revealed in the early 1970s, leading to their re-organization under the Board for International Broadcasting. Broadcasting by radio, entirely in the languages of the target countries, RFE and RL provided domestic and foreign news from the listeners' perspective, often with strong messages encouraging resistance to communist thinking and governments. As might be expected, the USSR attempted to jam these broadcasts.

The 1989–1991 collapse of communism in the USSR and Eastern Europe led to major adjustments in RFE and RL. Both stepped up their activity once listening to them was no longer illegal, and they soon added transmitters and news bureaus right in their target countries— something undreamed of in Cold War days. Driven by budget concerns, Congress decided to merge RFE/RL into a new broadcasting bureau (including VOA) within the United States Information Agency (USIA). From its new offices in Prague, RFE/RL broadcasts 800 hours of programming per week in 26 languages to a regular audience of more than 35 million listeners.

RFE/RL programs can be heard on shortwave frequencies by listeners across the entire region. In addition, RFE/RL has also built a network of more than 260 affiliate partner organizations that rebroadcast radio and television programming on over 650 transmitters across 11 time zones. More than 5 million people visit the RFE/RL web site every month to read news reports and hear programming.

Radio/TV Marti

Radio Marti and TV Marti are Spanish language radio and television broadcast services directed at undermining the Cuban government. Supervised by the Office of Cuba Broadcasting (OCB) within the USIA, the program content is aimed at giving Cuba news and information free of Castro-regime bias. Supporters claim that Radio Marti has had a powerful effect, heightening dissatisfaction with the Castro regime by revealing facts it conceals from its own people. The expatriate Cuban community in south Florida, with solid political ties to Washington, strongly supports the operation. Critics suggest that some Cuban expatriates exert too much control over the station, thus damaging its credibility as a news source. There is much debate about the effectiveness of these broadcasts. As with Radio Free Europe during the Cold War, there is no way to judge the station's true audience through the usual listener surveys.

Today, Radio Marti transmits over shortwave transmitters in Delano, California and Greenville, North Carolina and a medium-wave transmitter in Florida. Cuba jams both the medium-wave and shortwave signals, but the shortwave program is heard in Canada and throughout Central and South America.

An hour of Radio Marti's news programs is carried each night, midnight to 1:00 A.M., by Miami's most popular Spanish language station, Radio Mambi (WAQI-710 AM), which blankets the island of Cuba with its 50,000 watt AM signal, although it is jammed in Havana. A low-power Miami TV channel, WPMF-TV, Channel 38, carries TV Marti's half-hour early and late evening newscasts, and the channel is also carried on DIRECTV, which is pirated by many Cuban civilians. Radio and TV Marti pay fees to these stations through the U.S. government's Office of Cuba Broadcasting. The two distributor stations can receive additional revenue through the sale of commercial spots.

Radio Free Asia

The idea of bringing news reports to places otherwise unlikely to hear them also took hold on the other side of the world. In 1993, Congress authorized a Radio Free Asia (RFA) service aimed at potential audiences in the People's Republic of China and other Asian countries.

Today, Radio Free Asia's stated mission is to provide accurate and timely news and information to Asian countries whose governments prohibit access to a free press. Guided by the core principles of freedom of expression and opinion, RFA claims to serve its listeners with information critical for informed decision making. RFA is mandated to broadcast to China, Tibet, North Korea, Vietnam, Cambodia, Laos, and Burma. RFA's programming primarily comprises domestic news and information of unique and specific interest to its listeners. All broadcasts are solely in local languages and dialects. Each RFA language service is distinctive, reflecting the particular culture, language, and preferences of its listeners. Several countries, most notably China and Vietnam, have strongly criticized RFA operations in recent years.

Pirates

The strict definition of a **pirate radio station** is a station that operates from sovereign territory without a broadcasting license, or just beyond the territorial waters of a sovereign nation from on board a ship or other marine structure with the intention of broadcasting to that nation without obtaining a broadcasting license from that nation. Pirate radio culture grows from anarchist culture. It avoids hierarchies, demands total freedom of expression, and holds little respect for authority. These broadcasters don't like asking anyone for permission to broadcast. The first offshore pirate stations began broadcasting from ships anchored between Denmark and Sweden in 1958. Lacking authorization from their target countries, they were often financed by American interests and copied American pop-music formats, advertising techniques, and promotional gimmicks. They quickly captured large and devoted youthful audiences—their very illegality adding spice to their attractiveness. During this same era, several pirate stations operated successfully in Latin America, although the program content was far more political and revolutionary than that found among European pirates.

Some pirates made a lot of money, but at considerable risk. They suffered from storms, raids by rival pirates, and stringent laws that penalized land-based firms for supplying or doing other business with them. The appetite for pop music whetted by pirate stations forced national systems to take notice of formerly ignored musical tastes. The most publicized radio pirates have operated off the shores of Great Britain and had a measurable impact. The BBC, for example, reorganized its national radio network offerings, adding a pop-music network (Radio 1) imitative of the pirates. Some offshore DJs eventually worked for the BBC and other established broadcasters.

From the earliest days of the history of broadcasting, a number of radio stations in Mexico became known to the general public as "border-blasters" due to their excessive use of power to reach their intended audience in American cities far north of the border. The traditional border-blasters were AM radio stations—though there were numerous FM radio and even TV stations along the border that broadcast to the United States from Mexico. Although American broadcasters hated the "pirate" competition and the FCC was not pleased with signal interference, these stations for the most part were officially licensed by the Mexican government.

The most recent example of a true nonlicensed pirate radio station in Mexico has been the short-lived La Tremenda 106.5 in Nuevo Laredo, Tamaulipas, Mexico, which broadcast Spanish and English international contemporary music and news. Beginning operations in 2006, using the fictitious American call sign "KLPR" on its logo, the station was shut down in 2008 by the Mexican federal police.

As national systems become more pluralistic in program appeal, and as more "virtual stations" stream on the Internet, the rationale for pirate stations has declined today, but there are exceptions. For example, a number of offshore radio stations have reportedly been operating from the South China Sea, mainly for political purposes. These include *Voice of the People's Liberation Army*, *Radio Flash*, and *Popular of Peking*. In addition, a study by the United Kingdom media regulator Ofcom published in 2007 estimated that as many as 200 pirate radio stations currently operate in Great Britain; half of them are based in London.

13.10 International Distribution Technology

Today, commercial services increasingly cross borders by using a variety of technological platforms from satellites and cable to DVDs and broadband. Because Chapters 4 and 5 provide detailed descriptions of all kinds of communication hardware, this chapter does not go into such depth, however, it does attempt to provide an overview of the kinds of technologies used in global communications.

International Telecommunications Satellite Organization

The creation of the International Telecommunications Satellite Organization (ITSO), previously known by the acronym INTELSAT, resulted from the efforts of a group of nations to join the United States in 1964 to establish a global communications satellite system. The ITSO is an intergovernmental organization that incorporates the principle set forth by the General Assembly of the United Nations, which establishes that communication by means of satellites should be available to the nations of the world. In 2000, the Assembly of Parties, the highest decision-making body of the Organization, approved the legal instruments and framework necessary to create a commercial and pro-competitive company named "Intelsat, Ltd.," to operate the satellite system. For this purpose, ITSO transferred its global satellite system, including the geostationary-orbital locations, and the brand-name of "Intelsat," to *Intelsat, Ltd*. Since this transfer, Intelsat has invested almost three billion dollars to provide high-quality and reliable capacity for public telecommunications services, including telephony, data, video, and Internet connectivity, to more than 200 countries and territories, no matter their location, size, or level of development. The Assembly of Parties is the governing body of the Organization, currently comprised of the 148 member countries, and meets every two years.

Satellite Launching

The U.S. National Aeronautics and Space Administration (NASA) long monopolized Western capacity to launch communication satellites. In 1984, a consortium of European countries began to challenge NASA's monopoly with its own launch facility, Arianespace (named for *Ariane*, the rocket used). Ariane rockets operate from a site in French Guiana on the northern coast of South America, near the equator. That location gives Arianespace better conditions for attaining equatorial orbit than does NASA's more northerly location at Cape Canaveral, Florida.

Although dozens of countries can build communication satellites, only a small handful have the rocketry necessary to launch this technology into space. Not even counting the cost of a satellite itself, most space launchings now cost $30 million to $100 million. As a result, these countries purchase space on rockets developed by the more capable nations. As of 2008, only seven countries, the United States, Russia, Japan, China, India, and Israel, and one regional organization (the European Space Agency, which includes the United Kingdom and France), have independently launched satellites on their own developed rockets ("launch vehicles"). Several other countries, including South Korea, Iran, Brazil, Pakistan, and Australia are at various stages of development of their own small-scale launch capabilities.

Direct Broadcast Satellite Service

Direct broadcast satellite (DBS) is a term used to refer to satellite TV broadcasts intended for home reception, also referred to more broadly as direct-to-home signals. DBS services have shown promise in countries that do not have high cable penetration. Japan led the world with the first full-time DBS service in 1987. The following year a Luxembourg corporation launched *ASTRA*, Europe's first privately owned satellite suitable for DBS service. In Britain, Rupert Murdoch's *Sky Television* began in 1989 and eventually merged with a competitor to form *BSkyB*. In 1991, *StarTV* began satellite delivery of television programming to all of Asia. *Arab Digital Distribution (ADD)* is a provider of pay television, and interactive and digital services across the Middle East, North Africa, and Europe. *MultiChoice* is a South African company which operates the primary satellite TV service in Sub-Saharan Africa. *AUSTAR* is an Australian telecommunications company providing satellite pay TV, Internet access, and mobile phones.

Premiere is a German pay-TV company offering several channels of digital content via satellite and cable. *Digital+* is a Spanish satellite service offering a variety of national and international channels. *SKY Latin America* refers to two closely related pay-TV providers, one based in Mexico, the other in Brazil. DIRECTV, a direct broadcast satellite service based in the United States, transmits digital satellite television and audio to households in not only the states, but also the Caribbean and Latin America. Its primary competitor is *Dish Network*.

The previously mentioned companies are just a sampling of the growing activity in global satellite communications aimed at individual consumers. Although all these companies derive most of their revenue and profits from providing traditional long-form TV programming, many are looking at secondary services, such as Internet access and telephony.

Radio by Satellite

Americans tend to think of DBS services exclusively in TV terms, but in recent years, radio has come on-board. Offering a meaningful alternative to ground-based radio services in some countries, most notably the United States, **satellite radio** is a digital radio signal transmitted by a communications satellite, which covers a much wider geographical range than terrestrial radio signals. Today, over 60 services are available around the world. Most audiences receive satellite radio services directly by means of home satellite dish or indirectly via cable systems and FM radio stations. Mobile services, such as *Sirius*, *XM* (which have agreed to merge), and *Worldspace*, allow listeners to roam across an entire continent, listening to the same audio programming anywhere they go.

Although *Sirius* and *XM* focus primarily on the U.S. market, other companies, such as *WorldSpace*, based in Washington, DC, covers most of Asia and Europe, plus all of Africa by satellite. Satellite radio services usually are provided by commercial ventures and are subscription-based. The program content is scrambled, requiring the purchase of specialized hardware for decoding and playback. As we found with other new media, developing countries typically lack a sufficient number of affluent customers to sustain a subscription-based radio service, especially when conventional over-the-air radio can be listened to for free.

Cable

Many developed countries had primitive community antenna television (CATV) for years before modern cable emerged. These early systems merely extended domestic broadcast station coverage, sometimes adding a few channels for the purpose of carrying neighboring foreign broadcast networks. Most operated noncommercially, often owned by municipalities. They offered few channels, no local origination, and no pay TV.

Cable television provides TV programming to consumer televisions through fixed optical fibers or coaxial cables, as opposed to the over-the-air method used in traditional TV broadcasting. Today, cable can also provide radio programming, high-speed Internet, telephony, and other nontelevision services. Cable is most commonplace in North America, Europe, Australia, and East Asia, though it is present in many other countries. The biggest obstacle to cable development has been its high installation costs. Because it is not cost-effective to lay cables in sparsely populated areas, in certain regions of the world satellite television is far more popular than cable. Of course, neither technology attracts large audiences because the typical business model for private cable and satellite companies includes subscription fees, which often are cost prohibitive for poor, developing countries.

Over the past few years, many U.S. networks have started to develop cable content for international consumption, such as CNN, MTV, Cartoon Network, Disney Channel, Nickelodeon, ESPN, and others.

Recording Devices

Both as an alternative and as a supplement to cable and DBS, videocassette recorders (VCRs) and now digital video discs (DVDs) have proved a boon to viewers in countries where broadcast services fail to satisfy demand. They offer a relatively inexpensive shortcut to programs banned from, or otherwise not available on, national broadcast or cable channels. Few individuals in developing countries can afford to buy a machine outright, but rentals, club purchases, and group viewings in bars,

Exhibit 13.b

Protection or Exploitation? The DVD Copy Control Association (DVD CCA)

Region Codes and Countries

Region Code	Area
0	Informal term meaning "worldwide." Region 0 is not an official setting; discs that bear the region 0 symbol either have no flag set or have region 1–6 flags set.
1	Canada; United States; U.S. territories; Bermuda
2	Europe; Western Asia; Kingdom of the Netherlands; Egypt; Japan; Lesotho, South Africa; Swaziland; British overseas territories; French overseas territories; Greenland
3	Southeast Asia; South Korea; Non-mainland China (Hong Kong, Taiwan)
4	Oceania; Central and South America; Caribbean; Mexico
5	Africa; Central and South Asia; Belarus; Mongolia; North Korea; Russia; Ukraine
6	Mainland China
7	Reserved for future use (found in use on protected screener copies of MPAA-related DVDs and "media copies" of pre-releases in Asia)
8	International venues such as aircraft, cruise ships, etc.
ALL	Region ALL discs have all 8 flags set, allowing the disc to be played in any locale on any player.

The DVD Copy Control Association (DVD CCA) is a not-for-profit organization for licensing a content scramble system (CSS) to manufacturers of DVD hardware, program content discs, and related products. In particular, CSS prevents movies from being illegally duplicated, protecting the intellectual property of the manufacturers, producers, and writers from theft. The association defends this practice because without sufficient protections, movie studios would not offer their copyrighted films to consumers in this high-quality

digital format, fearing that multiple "pirate" copies could be made from one master disk.

A far more controversial practice is regional coding, a way of imposing geographical limitations on physical media traveling across borders. The system essentially regulates where in the world a DVD can be played. That is, a DVD purchased in one region may not play back in another region. There are many purposes that regional coding can achieve, but a primary one is price *discrimination*, an economic principle of demanding a coffeehouses, and even on buses resolve cost problems. In some cases, heavy censorship encourages purchases—as in Saudi Arabia, where conservative Islamic standards severely limit broadcast television. A worldwide underground market in VCRs, DVDs, and tapes defeats most government attempts to limit sales and rentals. It also undermines the profitability of video sales.

VCR recording has become an obsolete technology, giving way to DVD-video as the dominant form of home video distribution worldwide. In the United States, by 2003, for the first time, weekly DVD-video rentals outnumbered weekly VHS cassette rentals, reflecting the rapid adoption rate of the technology in the U.S. marketplace, and the rest of the world has embraced this recording and playback technology with equal enthusiasm.

DVD-video discs may be encoded with a region code restricting the area of the world in which they can be played. Discs without region coding are called **all region** or **region 0 discs**. The DVD Copy Control Association (DVD CCA) is an organization primarily responsible for the copy prevention of DVDs. The content scramble system (CSS) was devised for this purpose to make copyright infringement difficult. The association is also responsible for the much criticized regional playback control (RPC), the region encoding scheme which gives movie studios geographic control over DVD release dates to maximize their profits. Exhibit 13.b provides a more detailed explanation of this controversial organization.

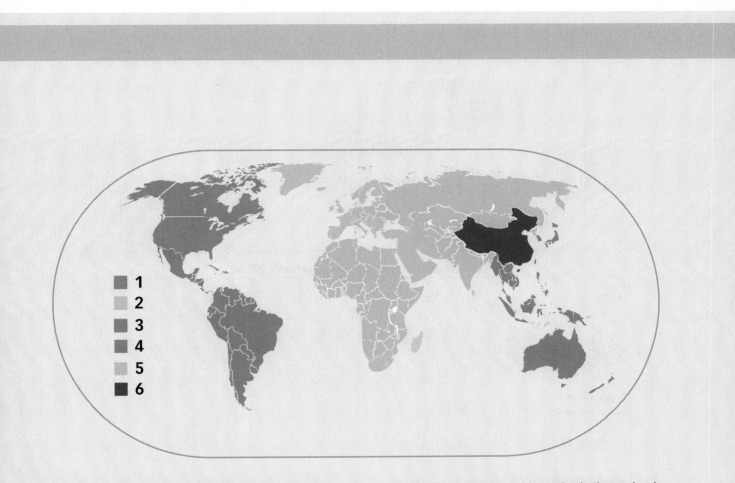

higher price from buyers who are willing to pay more. One can find a great disparity among the regions of the world in how much a DVD will cost. Critics of regional coding argue that the ethical notions of protection have evolved into more sinister notions of exploitation.

A number of international organizations, such as the European Union, and individual countries have objected to the enforcement of regional coding, claiming it is anticompetitive and a violation of certain free-trade agreements. Rather than protecting copyrights, critics maintain that regional coding is solely an attempt to enforce price differentials. As of 2008, many "multi-region" DVD players now reject regional lockouts, allowing the user to manually select a particular region. In fact, some manufacturers of DVD players now freely supply information on how to disable regional lockout.

Teletext and Videotex

Teletext has proved far more successful overseas than in the United States. Though not a runaway success, it has nevertheless found greater acceptance in Europe than in this country, where too many alternative media choices exist. Teletext information is broadcast in the vertical blanking interval between image frames in a broadcast television signal. It is closely linked to the PAL broadcast system, and most PAL televisions include teletext decoders. Other teletext systems have been developed to work with the SECAM and NTSC

systems, but teletext failed to gain widespread acceptance in North America and other areas where NTSC is used. In contrast, teletext has been very popular across Europe, as well as some other regions, with most major broadcasters providing teletext services such as TV schedules, news and sports, plus subtitling for deaf people or in different languages.

Videotex is a computer-based system that some people confuse with the Internet. Although early videotex providers in the 1970s encountered many issues similar to those faced by Internet service providers 20 years later, it is important to emphasize that the two

Exhibit 13.c

Global Internet Usage Statistics

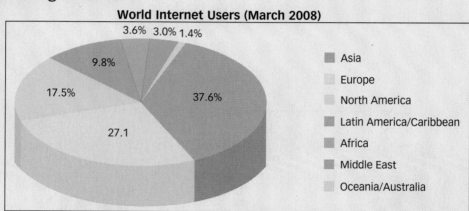

World Internet Users (March 2008)

- 3.6%
- 3.0%
- 1.4%
- 9.8%
- 17.5%
- 27.1
- 37.6%

Legend:
- Asia
- Europe
- North America
- Latin America/Caribbean
- Africa
- Middle East
- Oceania/Australia

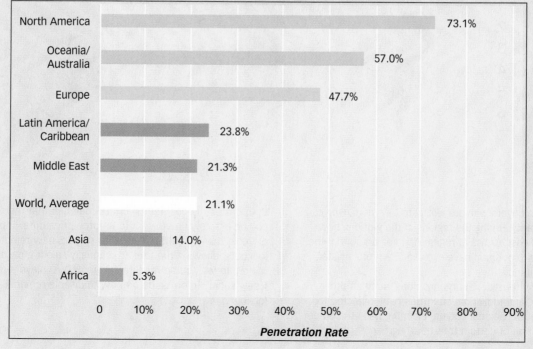

World Internet Penetration Rates (March 2008)

Region	Penetration Rate
North America	73.1%
Oceania/Australia	57.0%
Europe	47.7%
Latin America/Caribbean	23.8%
Middle East	21.3%
World, Average	21.1%
Asia	14.0%
Africa	5.3%

Penetration Rate

technologies evolved separately and reflect fundamentally different ways to computerize communications. Both teletext and videotex provide practical information to consumers in an interactive text format. France leads the world in videotex development with its *Minitel* system. As of 2008, despite the widespread use of high-speed Internet service, about one million terminals remain in service and 4,000 services are available. With few exceptions, such as the French system, most media experts believe that teletext and videotex will soon become obsolete technologies, surpassed by the Internet.

The Internet

Growing access to the Internet worldwide provides a communications link for many people with no hope of access to traditional media. Although Internet usage in most countries is very low (see Exhibit 13.c), people with a will often find a way. Users in Haiti often must use solar power, batteries, and generators to power their computers because there is no electricity most of the time.

Broadband is often called high-speed Internet, because it has a high rate of data transmission and enables end users to take advantage of video on demand

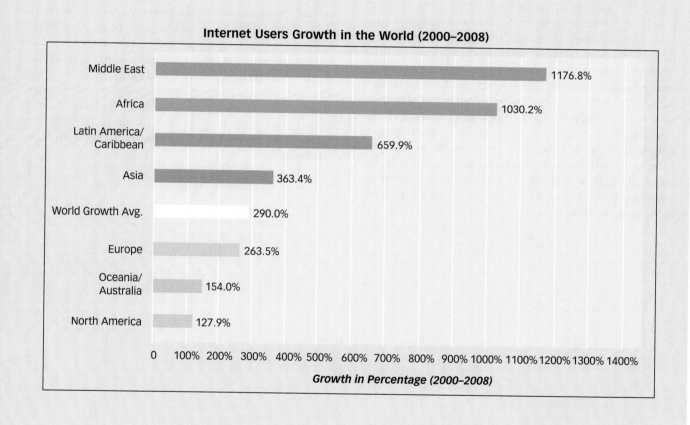

Internet Users Growth in the World (2000–2008)

Region	Growth
Middle East	1176.8%
Africa	1030.2%
Latin America/Caribbean	659.9%
Asia	363.4%
World Growth Avg.	290.0%
Europe	263.5%
Oceania/Australia	154.0%
North America	127.9%

Growth in Percentage (2000–2008)

Growing access to the Internet worldwide provides a communications link for many people with no hope of access to traditional media. Unfortunately, in many regions of the world

Internet penetration is tiny compared to the United States and Europe.

services streamed over the Internet. Many existing radio and TV broadcasters provide Internet feeds of their live audio and video streams. They may also allow time-shift viewing or listening. As discussed in prior chapters, these providers have been joined by a range of pure Internet "broadcasters" who never had on-air licenses. This means that an Internet-connected device, such as a computer or cell phone, can access on-line media in much the same way as was previously possible only with a television or radio receiver.

One of the greatest beneficiaries of high-speed Internet has been YouTube, sometimes described as an Internet phenomenon because of its vast amount of users. Founded in 2005, it is now the leading web site for free streaming video, experiencing an average of 825,000 new video uploads every day.

In many countries, residents seeking access to the Internet must deal not only with a lack of technical infrastructure, but also with a national government hostile to the kind of open communications the Internet provides. Some governments, such as those of Cuba, Iran, North Korea, Myanmar, the People's Republic of China, and Saudi Arabia, restrict what people in their countries can access on the Internet, especially political and religious content. This is accomplished through software that filters domains and content so that they may not be easily accessed or obtained without elaborate circumvention. Even less repressive governments have initiated such screenings. For example, in Norway, Denmark, Finland, and Sweden, major Internet service providers have voluntarily agreed to restrict access to sites listed by police. Typically, these sites deal with child pornography.

Conclusion: Converging Communications and Converging Cultures

Recognizing that the world is changing all the time and communication technologies continue to evolve at an astonishing pace, the future is almost impossible to predict, at least in terms of specifics. However, after reading this text, and especially this final chapter on global communication, it seems safe to say that one basic trend will continue for years to come, and that is the simultaneous convergence of communication and culture. Indeed, one could argue that one actually causes the other to occur, although that assumption could lead to an endless "chicken-or-the egg" debate. What is important is the fact that we as inhabitants of this planet are coming together.

As was brought up in the beginning of this chapter, territorial boundaries are becoming ever more artificial and pointless. Governments can no longer easily isolate their populations from the rest of the world—for good or bad. As electronic media converge, so do the people that create, distribute, and receive program content. Government agencies and media corporations are no longer essential for an individual or a group to express words and pictures to a worldwide audience. From Internet blogs and social networking to video downloads and e-commerce, we are forming global, interactive, virtual communities that in many respects may become more important to us than our designated nationality.

Bibliography

Abramson, Albert. 1995. *Zworykin: Pioneer of Television.* U. of Illinois Press, Urbana.

Albarran, Alan B. 2005. *Management of Electronic Media*, 3rd ed. Wadsworth Publishing, New York.

Albarran, Alan B., Chan-Olmsted, Sylvia M., and Wirth, Michael O. 2005. *Handbook of Media Management and Economics.* Lawrence Erlbaum Associates (Lea's Media Management and Economics Series), Mahwah, New Jersey.

Albarran, Alan B., and Reca, Angel A. 2003. *Time and Media Markets* Lawrence Erlbaum (Lea's Communication Series), Mahwah, New Jersey.

Alten, Stanley R. 1994. *Audio in Media*, 4th ed. Wadsworth, Belmont, CA.

American Academy of Pediatrics. 1999. "Policy Statement, Media Education." *Pediatrics*, 104 (August): 341.

Anderson, Chris. 2006. The Long Tail. "Why the Future of Business is the Selling Less of More." Hyperion Publishing, New York.

Anokwa, Kwadwo; Lin, Carolyn A.; and Salwen, Michael B. 2003. *International Communication: Concepts and Cases*, Wadsworth Publishing, New York.

APA. 1992. "APA Task Force Explores Television's Positive and Negative Influences on Society." News Release. American Psychological Association, Washington, DC.

Arbitron Internet Information Services. 2000. Info-stream Headlines. http://internet.arbitron.com.

ATSC. 2003. *Recommended Practice: Guide to the Use of the ATSC Digital Television Standard, Including Corrigendum No. 1.* Advanced Television Systems Committee, Washington, D.C.

ATSC. 2007. *ATSC Digital Television Standard Part – 1 Digital Television System (A/53, Part 1:2007).* Advanced Television Systems Committee, Washington, D.C.

Auletta, Ken. 1991. *Three Blind Mice: How the TV Networks Lost Their Way.* Random House, New York.

Avery, Robert K., and Pepper, Robert. 1979. *The Politics of Interconnection: A History of Public Television at the National Level.* National Association of Educational Broadcasters, Washington, DC.

Baker, W. J. 1970. *A History of the Marconi Company.* Methuen, London.

Baldwin, Thomas F., and Lewis, Colby. 1972. "Violence in Television: The Industry Looks at Itself," in Comstock and Rubenstein, 290–365.

_____, McVoy, D. Stevens, and Steinfield, Charles. 1996. *Convergence Integrating Media, Information & Communication.* Sage, Thousand Oaks, CA.

Banning, William P. 1946. *Commercial Broadcasting Pioneer: The WEAF Experiment, 1922–1926.* Harvard U. Press, Cambridge, MA.

Baran, Stanley J., and Davis, Dennis K. 2008. *Mass Communication Theory: Foundations, Ferment, and Future.* Wadsworth Publishing, New York.

Barnouw, Erik. 1978. *The Sponsor: Notes on a Modern Potentate.* Oxford U. Press, New York.

Baudino, Joseph E., and Kittross, John M. 1977. "Broadcasting's Oldest Station: An Examination of Four Claimants," *Journal of Broadcasting*, 21 (Winter): 61.

BIB (Board for International Broadcasting). Annual. *Annual Report.* GPO, Washington, DC.

Bilby, Kenneth. 1986. *The General: David Sarnoff and the Rise of the Communications Industry.* Harper and Row, New York.

Block, Alex Ben. 1990. *Outfoxed: Marvin Davis, Barry Diller, Rupert Murdoch, Joan Rivers, and the Inside Story of America's Fourth Television Network.* St. Martin's, New York.

Blumenthal, Howard J., and Goodenough, Oliver R. 2006. *This Business of Television.* Billboard Books, New York.

Boorstin, Daniel J. 1964. *The Image: A Guide to Pseudo-Events in America.* Harper and Row, New York.

_____. 1978. "The Significance of Broadcasting in Human History," in Hoso-Bunka Foundation, *Symposium on the Cultural Role of Broadcasting*, The Foundation, Tokyo.

Bower, Robert T. 1973. *Television and the Public.* Holt, Rinehart and Winston, New York.

_____. 1985. *The Changing Television Audience in America.* Columbia U. Press, New York.

Broadcast Engineering. Monthly. Intertec, Overland Park, KS.

Brooks, John. 1976. *Telephone: The First Hundred Years.* Harper and Row, New York.

Brooks, Tim, and Marsh, Earle. 2003. *The Complete Directory to Prime Time Network TV Shows: 1946-Present*, 8th ed. Ballantine, New York.

Brotman, Stuart N. 1990. *Telephone Company and Cable Television Competition: Key Technical, Economic, Legal and Policy Issues.* Artech, Norwood, MA.

Brown, Les. 1971. *Television: The Business Behind the Box.* Harcourt Brace Jovanovich, New York.

Buchman, Warner, C. 2007. *Media Selling: Broadcast, Cable, Print, and Interactive.* Iowa State Press. Ames, Iowa.

Buckley, Tom. 1978. "Popularity of '60 Minutes' Based on Wide-Ranging Reports," *New York Times* (December 17): 99.

Bucy, Erik P., and Newhagan, John E. 2003. *Media Access: Social and Psychological Dimensions of New Technology.* Lawrence Erlbaum (Lea's Communication Series), Mahwah, New Jersey.

Butler, Jeremy. 2007. *Television: Critical Methods and Applications.* Lawrence Erlbaum Associates, Mahwah, New Jersey.

Buxton, Frank, and Owen, Bill. 1972. *The Big Broadcast: 1920–1950.* Viking, New York.

Cal. (California Reporter). 1981. *Olivia N. v. National Broadcasting Co.*, 178 Cal. Rptr. 888 (California Court of Appeal, First District).

Cantril, Hadley. 1940. *The Invasion from Mars: A Study of the Psychology of Panic.* Princeton U. Press, Princeton, NJ.

Carothers, Diane Foxhill. 1991. *Radio Broadcasting from 1920 to 1990: An Annotated Bibliography.* Garland, New York.

Carter, T. Barton, et al. 1991. *The First Amendment and the Fourth Estate: The Law of Mass Media*, 5th ed. Foundation, Westbury, NY.

_____. 1996. *The First Amendment and the Fifth Estate: Regulation of Electronic Mass Media*, 4th ed. Foundation, Westbury, NY.

Caslon Analytics. 2007. Blog Statistics and Demographics. www.caslon.com.au/weblogprofile1.htm.

CCET (Carnegie Commission on Educational Television). 1967. *Public Television: A Program for Action.* Harper and Row, New York.

CCFPB (Carnegie Commission on the Future of Public Broadcasting). 1979. *A Public Trust.* Bantam, New York.

CFR (Code of Federal Regulations). Annual. *Title 47: Telecommunications*, 5 vols. GPO, Washington, DC.

Chan-Olmsted, S. M. 2006. *Competitive Strategy for Media Firms: Strategic and Brand Management in Changing Media Markets.* Lawrence Erlbaum, Mahwah, NJ.

Christians, Clifford G; Fackler, Mark; Brittain, Kathy McKee; Kreshel, Peggy J; and Woods, Robert H. 2007. *Media Ethics: Cases and Moral Reasoning*, 8th ed. Allyn & Bacon, New York

Churchill, G. A. 2004. *Marketing Research: Methodological Foundations*, 9th ed. Dryden Press, Fort Worth, TX.

Clifford, Martin. 1992. *Modern Audio Technology: A Handbook for Technicians and Engineers.* Prentice Hall, Englewood Cliffs, NJ.

Comstock, George, et al. 1978. *Television and Human Behavior.* Columbia U. Press, New York.

_____, and Rubenstein, F., eds. 1972. *Television and Social Behavior: Media Content and Control I.* GPO, Washington, DC.

Consumer Electronics Manufacturers Association. 1999.

www.cemacity.org/gazette/files3/dtvsales.htm

Coolidge, Calvin. 1926. "Message to Congress," 68 *Congressional Record 32.*

Cooper, Eunice, and Jahoda, Marie. 1947. "The Evasion of Propaganda: How Prejudicial People Respond to Anti-Prejudice Propaganda." *Journal of Psychology* (January 23): 15.

CPB (Corporation for Public Broadcasting, Washington, DC). Annual. *Annual Report.*

Dimmick, J. W. 2003. *Media Competition and Coexistence: The Theory of the Niche.* Lawrence Erlbaum, Mahwah, NJ.

Dominick Joseph R; Sherman, Barry L; and Messere, Fritz J. 2007. *Broadcasting, Cable, the Internet, and Beyond: An Introduction to Modern Electronic Media.* McGraw-Hill, New York.

Donald, Ralph, and Spann, Thomas. 2007. *Fundamentals of Television Production.* Allyn & Bacon, New York.

Dorsey, Tom. 1998. "Cable Was the Worst," *Louisville Courier Journal* (August 19): 2C.

Doyle, Marc. 1992. *The Future of Television: A Global Overview of Programming, Advertising, Technology, and Growth.* NTC Business Books, Lincolnwood, IL.

Drake-Chenault Enterprises, Inc. 1978. "History of Rock and Roll," Drake-Chenault, Canoga Park, CA.

Duncan, James. Five times a year. *American Radio.* Duncan Media, Indianapolis, IN.

Eastman, Susan Tyler, and Ferguson, Douglas A. 2008. *Media Programming: Strategies and Practices.* Wadsworth Publishing, New York.

Eastman, S. T.; Ferguson, D. A.; and Klein, R. A. 2006. *Promotion and Marketing for Broadcasting, Cable, and the Web*, 5th ed. Focal Press, Boston.

Edgerton, Gary. 2007. *The Columbia History of American Television* (Columbia Histories of Modern American Life). Columbia U. Press, New York.

EIA (Electronic Industries Association). Annual. *The U.S. Consumer Electronics Industry in Review* (title varies). ETA, Washington, DC (after 1994: Arlington, VA).

Ellerbee, Linda. 1986. *"And So It Goes": Adventures in Television.* Putnam, New York.

Ennes, Harold E. 1953. *Principles and Practices of Telecasting Operations.* Sams, Indianapolis.

F *(Federal Reporter, 2d and 3d Series).* West, St. Paul, MN. 1926. *U.S. v. Zenith Radio Corp.*, 12 F2d 614.

_____. 1969. *Office of Communication v. FCC*, 425 F2d 543. 1972. *Brandywine-Main Line Radio v. FCC*, 473 F2d 16. 1975. *Natl. Assn. of Independent TV Distributors v. FCC*, 516 F2d 526.

_____. 1977. *Home Box Office v. FCC*, 567 F2d 9.

_____. 1979. *Writers Guild v. ABC*, 609 F2d 355.

_____. 1986. *Telecommunications Research and Action Center v. FCC*, 801 F2d 501, *rehearing denied*, 806 F2d 1115 (D.C. Cir. 1986).

_____. 1987. *Century Communications Corp. v. FCC*, 835 F2d 292.

_____. 1988. *Action for Children's Television et al. v. FCC*, 852 F2d 1332.

_____. 1991. *Action for Children's Television v. FCC*, 932 F2d 1504.

_____. 1995. *Action for Children's Television v. FCC*, 58 F3d 654.

_____. 1996. *Becker v. FCC*, 95 F3d 75, 4 CR 882.

_____. 1998a. *Bechtel v. FCC*, 10 F.3d 875 (D.C. Cir.).

_____. 1998b. *Lutheran Church—Missouri Synod v. FCC*, 141 F3d 344.

_____. 1999. *Recording Industry Association of America v. Diamond Multimedia Systems, Inc.*, 180 F3d 1072 (9th Cir).

_____. 2000. *Time Warner Entertainment Co. v. United States*, 211 F.3d 1313 (D.C. Cir.)..

_____. 2002. *A&M Records v. Napster*, 284 F3d 1091 (9th Cir).

_____. 2005a. *American Library Association v. FCC*, 406 F3d 689 (D.C. Cir).

_____. 2005b. *Promethius Radio Project v. FCC*, 373 F3d 372 (3rd Cir).

_____. 2007. Fox TV Stations v. FCC, 489 F3d 444 (2nd Cir).

FCC (Federal Communications Commission). GPO, Washington, DC. *Annual Report.* Annual.

_____. 1980a. (Network Inquiry Special Staff). *New Television Networks: Entry, Jurisdiction, Ownership, and Regulation.* Final Report, Vol. *1. Background Reports*, Vol. 2.

_____. 1980b. *Staff Report and Recommendations in the Low-Power Television Inquiry.* FCC, Washington, DC.

47 C.F.R. Section 73.3555

47. C.F.R. Section 76.503

47. C.F.R. Section 73.3555

_____. 1999. *Digital Audio Broadcasting Systems and Their Impact on the Terrestrial Radio Broadcast Service.* (Notice of Proposed Rulemaking.) MM Docket No. 99-325. Washington, DC.

_____. 2000. *Report on International Telecommunications Markets for 1999.*

_____. 2002. *Digital Audio Broadcasting Systems and Their Impact on the Terrestrial Radio Broadcast Service.* (First Report and Order.) MM Docket No. 99-325. Washington, DC.

_____. 2007a. *Advanced Television Systems and their Impact Upon the Existing Television Broadcast Service.* (Seventh Report and Order and Eighth Further Notice of Proposed Rulemaking.) MB Docket No. 87-268. Washington, DC.

_____. 2007b. *Annual Assessment of the Status of Competition in the Market for the Delivery of Video Programming.* MB Docket No. 03-172. Washington, DC.

_____. 2007c. *Carriage of Digital Television Broadcast Signals: Amendment to Part 76 of the Commission's Rules.* (Second Further Notice of Proposed Rulemaking.) CS Docket No. 98-120. Washington, D.C.

_____. 2007d. *Creation of a Low Power Radio Service.* (Third Report and Order and Second Further Notice of Proposed Rulemaking.) MM Docket No. 99-25. Washington, DC.

_____. 2007e. *Digital Audio Broadcasting Systems and Their Impact on the Terrestrial Radio Broadcast Service.* (Further Notice of Proposed Rulemaking and Notice of Inquiry.) MM Docket No. 99-325. Washington, D.C.

_____. 2007f. *Digital Audio Broadcasting Systems and Their Impact on the Terrestrial Radio Broadcast Service.* (Second Report and Order, First Order on Reconsideration, and Second Further Notice of Proposed Rulemaking.) MM Docket No. 99-325. Washington, DC.

_____. 2007g. *Third Periodic Review of the Commission's Rules and Policies Affecting the Conversion to Digital Television.* (Notice of Proposed Rulemaking.) MB Docket No. 07-91. Washington, DC.

_____. 2008. *Inquiry Concerning the Deployment of Advanced Telecommunications Capability to All Americans in a Reasonable and Timely Fashion, and Possible Steps to Accelerate Such Deployment Pursuant to Section 706 of the Telecommunications Act of 1996.* (Fifth Report). GN Docket No. 07-45. Washington, DC.

FCCR (*FCC Reports*, 1st and 2d Series; and *FCC Record*). GPO, Washington, DC.

_____. 1952. *Amendment of Sec. 3.606* [adopting new television rules] . . . Sixth Report and Order. 41 FCC 148.

_____. 1965. *Comparative Broadcast Hearings.* Policy Statement. 1 FCC2d 393.

_____. 1973. *Apparent Liability of Stations WGLD-FM* [Sonderling Broadcasting]. News Release. 41 FCC2d 919.

_____. 1985a. *Cattle Country Broadcasting [KTTL-FM].* Hearing Designation Order and Notice of Apparent Liability. 58 RR 1109.

_____. 1985b. *Inquiry into . . . the General Fairness Doctrine Obligations of Broadcast Licensees.* Report. 102 FCC2d 143.

_____. 1987a. *New Indecency Enforcement Standards to Be Applied to All Broadcast and Amateur Radio Licenses.* Public Notice. 2 FCC Rcd 2726.

_____. 1987b. *Complaint of Syracuse Peace Council Against Television Station WTVH.* Memorandum Opinion and Order. 2 FCC Rcd 5043.

_____. 1992a. *Telephone Company-Cable Television Cross-Ownership Rules.* Second Report and Order, Recommendation to Congress and Second Further Notice of Proposed Rulemaking. 7 FCC Rcd 5781. ("Video Dial Tone")

_____. 1992b. *Enforcement of Prohibitions Against Broadcast Indecency in 18 USC 1464.* 7 FCC Rcd 6464.

_____. 1995. *Minority and Female Ownership,* 10 FCC Rcd 2788.

_____. 1996. *Section 257 Proceeding to Identify and Eliminate Market Entry Barriers for Small Businesses,* 11 FCC Rcd 6280.

_____. 2000a. *Repeal or Modification of the Personal Attack and Political Editorializing Rules,* 15 FCC Rcd. 20697.

_____. 2000b. *Review of Commission's Rules and Policies Affecting the Conversion to Digital Television,* 15 FCC Rcd 5257.

_____. 2004a. *Children's Television Obligations of Digital Television Broadcasters,* 19 FCC Rcd. 22943.

_____. 2004b. *Complaints Against Various Broadcast Licensees Regarding Their Airing of the "Golden Globe Awards,"* 19 FCC Rcd 4975.

_____. 2004c. *Greater Boston Radio, Inc.,* 19 FCC Rcd. 13064.

_____. 2007a. *Broadcast Localism,* 23 FCC Rcd. 1324.

_____. 2007b. *Implementation of Section 621(a)(1) of the Cable Communications Policy Act of 1984 as amended by the Cable Television Consumer Protection and Competition Act of 1992,* 22 FCC Rcd 5101.

_____. 2007c. *Quadrennial Review of the Commission's Broadcast Ownership Rules,* Second Notice of Proposed Rule Making, 22 FCC Rcd 14215.

_____. 2007d. *Violent Television Programming and its Impact on Children,* 22 FCC Rcd. 7929.

Federal Trade Commission. 1999. "FTC to Conduct Study on Marketing Practices of Entertainment Industry." Press Release, June 1.

Ferris, Charles, et al. 1983–present. *Cable Television Law: A Video Communications Guide,* 3 vols. Matthew Bender, New York.

Fisch, Shalom M. 2004. *Children's Learning from Educational Television: Sesame Street and Beyond.* Lawrence Erlbaum Associates, Mahwah, New Jersey.

Fowles, Jib. 2000. *The Case for Television Violence.* Sage Publications, New York.

The Freedom Forum, May 1994: 4

Friedman, Wayne. 2008. "Nielsen Reveals First Out-of-Home TV Ratings." *Media Daily News* (September 3): www.mediapost.com/publications/?fa=Articles.showArticleHomePage&art_aid=89738

Friendly, Fred. 1976. *The Good Guys, the Bad Guys, and the First Amendment: Free Speech vs. Fairness in Broad-casting.* Random House, New York.

FS (*Federal Supplement*). West, St. Paul, MN.

_____. 1996. *American Civil Liberties Union v. Reno,* 929 F. Supp. 824.

_____. 2000. *Twentieth Century Fox Film Corp. v. ICRAVETV.* 2000 U.S. Dist. LEXIS 1013 (WD. Pa.).

Gallup News Service. 2007. "Local TV is No. 1 News Source for Americans." www.gallup.com/poll/26053/Local-No-Source-News-Americans.aspx.

Goldenson, Leonard H., with Wolf, Marvin J. 1991. *Beating the Odds: The Untold Story Behind the Rise of ABC—The Stars, Struggles, and Egos That Transformed Network Television.* Scribner's, New York.

The Graphic, Visualization and Usability Center. 1998. Georgia Tech Research Corporation, Atlanta, GA. www.gvu.gatech.edu/gvu/user_surveys/survey-1998-10/.

Greenfield, Jeff. 1977. *Television: The First Fifty Years.* Abrams, New York.

Ha, Louisa S., and Ganahl, Richard J. 2006. *Webcasting Worldwide: Business Models of an Emerging Global Medium.* Lawrence Erlbaum, Mahwah, NJ.

Halberstam, David. 1979. *The Powers That Be.* Knopf, New York.

Harris Interactive Surveys. www.harrisinteractive.com/news/index.asp?NewsID=55 &HLelection =other.

Harris, Richard Jackson. 2004. *A Cognitive Psychology of Mass Communication.* Lawrence Erlbaum (Lea's Communication Series), Mahwah, NJ.

Head, Sydney W. 1985. *World Broadcasting Systems: A Comparative Analysis.* Wadsworth, Belmont, CA.

Henry J. Kaiser Family Foundation. 1999. *Kids & Media @ the New Millenium.* Menlo Park, CA.

Hoskins, Colin; McFadyen, Stuart M; and Finn, Adam. 2004. *Media Economics: Applying Economics to New and Traditional Media.* Sage Publications, New York.

Hurly, Paul, et al. 1985. *The Videotex and Teletext Hand-book.* Harper & Row, New York, NY.

Intellectual Property and the National Information Infra-structure: The Report of the Working Group on Intellectual Property Rights. 1996. GPO, Washington, DC.

Isailovic, Jordan. 1985. *Videodisc and Optical Memory Systems.* Prentice Hall, Englewood Cliffs, NJ.

Jennings, Bryant R. 2008. *Media Effects: Advances in Theory and Research,* 3rd ed. Lawrence Erlbaum Associates (Lea's Communication Series), Mahwah, NJ.

Jessel, Harry A. 2008. *Broadcasting and Cable Yearbook.* RR Bowker Publishing, New Providence, NJ.

Johnson, Bobbie. 2007. "Cerf Predicts the End of TV as We Know It," *The Guardian,* Technology 1 (August 27).

Johnson, Leland L. 1992. *Telephone Company Entry into Cable Television: Competition, Regulation, and Public Policy.* Rand, Santa Monica, CA.

Jowett, Garth. 1976. *Film: The Democratic Art.* Little, Brown, Boston.

Kaltenborn, H. V. 1938. *I Broadcast the Crisis.* Random House, New York.

Katz, Elihu, and Lazarsfeld, Paul E. 1955. *Personal Influence: The Part Played by People in the Flow of Mass Communications.* Free Press, Glencoe, IL.

Katz, Helen. 2006. *The Media Handbook: A Complete Guide to Advertising Media Selection, Planning, Research, and Buying.* Lawrence Erlbaum, Mahwah, NJ.

Kean, John. 2004. National Public Radio. *Host Compatibility Measurements for the Extended Hybrid Mode of IBOC Digital Audio Broadcasting.* Washington, DC.

Keith, M. C. 2004. *The Radio Station* 6th ed. B Focal Press, Boston.

Killebrew, Kenneth C. 2004. *Managing Media Convergence: Pathways to Journalistic Cooperation,* Wiley-Blackwell (Media and Technology Series), New York.

Klapper, Joseph T. 1960. *The Effects of Mass Communication.* Free Press, Glencoe, IL.

Klein, Paul. 1971. "The Men Who Run TV Aren't That Stupid . . . They Know Us Better Than You Think," *New York* (January 25): 20.

Koch, R. 1998. *The 80/20 Principle—Currency.* Doubleday Publishing, New York.

Koch, Tom. 1991. *Journalism for the 21st Century: Online Information, Electronic Databases, and the News.* Praeger, New York.

Labaton, Stephen. 2007. "FCC Set to End Sole Cable Deals for Apartments," (October 29): www.nytimes.com/2007/10/29/business/media/29cable.html.

Leichtman Research Group. 2007. "DVRs Now in Over One of Every Five U.S. Households," (August 21): www.leichtmanresearch.com/press/082107release.html.

Lichter, S. Robert; Lichter, Linda S.; and Amundson, Dan. 1999. *Merchandising Mayhem: Violence and Popular Culture.* Center for Media and Public Affairs, Washington, DC.

McCauley, Michael. 2005. *NPR: The Trials and Triumphs of National Public Radio.* Columbia U. Press, New York.

McCauley, Michael P.; Peterson, Eric E.; Artz, B. Lee; and Halleck, DeeDee. 2003. *Public Broadcasting and the Public Interest: Media, Communication, and Culture in America.* M.E. Sharpe Publishing, Armonk, NY.

McDowell, W. S. 2006. *Broadcast Television: A Complete Guide to the Industry.* Peter Lang, New York.

_____, and Batten, A. 2005. *Branding TV: Principles and Practices,* 2nd ed. National Association of Broadcasters and Focal Press, Boston.

_____. 2008. *Understanding Broadcast and Cable Finance: A Primer for the Non-Financial Manager.* Broadcast and Financial Management Association (BCFM). Focal Press, Boston.

McChesney, Robert W. 2007. *Communication Revolution: Critical Junctures and the Future of Media.* The New Press, New York.

McClellan, Steve. 1999. "This News Hound Still Hunts." *Broadcasting & Cable* (August 8): 18.

Mallinson, John C. 1993. *The Foundations of Magnetic Recording.* Academic, San Diego, CA.

Markey, Edward J. 1988. "Statement Accompanying Congressional Research Service Letter to House Subcommittee on Telecommunications and Finance. Cases Involving the Federal Communications Commission That Were Reversed . . ." (March 21). Library of Congress, Washington, DC.

Mayo, John S. 1992. "The Promise of Networked Multi-media Communications." Speech delivered at Bear Sterns Sixth Annual Media & Communications Conference, Coronado, CA (October 28).

Media International. February 1999.

Media Week, April 14, 1997. No. 15, Vol 1, p.78.

Metz, Robert. 1975. *CBS: Reflections in a Bloodshot Eye.* Playboy Press, Chicago.

_____. 1977. *The Today Show: An Inside Look . . .* Playboy Press, Chicago.

Meyersohn, Rolf B. 1957. "Social Research in Television," in Rosenberg and White, 345–357.

Miami Herald, 2 April 1994: A2.

_____. 9 May 1994: A2.

Minow, Newton N. 1964. *Equal Time: The Private Broadcaster and the Public Interest.* Atheneum, New York.

_____. 1991. "How Vast the Wasteland Now?" Gannett Foundation Media Center, Columbia University, New York (May 9).

Montgomery, Kathryn C. 1989. *Target: Prime Time: Advocacy Groups and the Struggle Over Entertainment Television.* Oxford U. Press, New York.

Mothersole, Peter L., and White, Norman W. 1990. *Broadcast Data Systems: Teletext and RDS.* Butterworth & Co. Ltd., London.

Mullen, Megan. 2008. *Television in the Multichannel Age: A Brief History of Cable Television.* Wiley-Blackwell, New York.

NAB (National Association of Broadcasters). Washington, DC. Annual. *Radio Financial Report* (to 1992). Annual. *Television Financial Report.* Semiannual. *Broadcast Regulation* (title varies). 1978. *The Television Code.* www.nab.org/PressRel/ Dtvstations.asp.

_____. 1999. www.nab.org/Newsroom/Issues/digitalty/ DTVstationsasp

Napoli, Philip M. 2000. *Market Conditions and Public Affairs Programming: Implications for Digital Television Policy.* Benton Foundation: Washington, DC.

National Cable Television Association. Quarterly. *Cable Television Developments.* Washington, DC.

National Telecommunications and Information Administration (a division of the U.S. Department of Commerce). 8 July 1999. *Falling Through the Net: Defining the Digital Divide.* http://ntia.doc.gov/ntiahome/ fttn99/execsummary.html

NCTA (National Cable & Telecommunications Association). 2008. *2008 Industry Overview.* http://i.ncta.com/ncta_com/PDFs/NCTA_ Annual_Report_05.16.08.pdf.

New Century Net. 1997. www.newcentury.net.

Newcomb, Horace. 2004. *Encyclopedia of Television.* Taylor and Francis, Oxford, UK.

NewMedia. Monthly. HyperMedia, San Mateo, CA.

Newseum. 1997. www.newseum.org.

Newspage. 1997. www.newspage.com.

The New York Times. 30 September 1992: 1, B8.

_____. 20 January 1995: C3.

The New Yorker. 6 January 1997: 76.

Ohio State University. School of Journalism. Annual. *Journalism and Mass Communications Graduate Survey: Summary Report.* Ohio State University, Columbus, OH.

O'Keefe, Daniel J. 2002. *Persuasion: Theory and Research (Current Communication: An Advanced Text).* Sage Publications, New York.

Paley, William S. 1979. *As It Happened: A Memoir.* Doubleday, New York.

Parents Television Council. 1999. *Unintended Consequences: With Ratings in Place, TV More Offensive Than Ever.* Alexandria, VA.

Paul Kagan Associates. Annual. *The Cable TV Financial Databook.* Carmel, CA. www.kagan.com/screen/ kmarket/press1l.html.

_____. 1999. www.ncta.com/yearend98_3.html#std.

Persico, Joseph E. 1988. *Edward R. Murrow, An American Original.* McGraw-Hill, New York.

Pew Internet and American Life Project. 2005. "Internet: The Mainstreaming of Online Life Trends 2005," www/ pewinternet.org/pdfs/Internet_Status_2005.pdf.

_____. 2007. "Social Networking Sites and Teens," www.pewinternet.org/PPF/r/198/report_display.asp.

_____. 2008. "Home Broadband Adoption 2008," www.pewinternet.org/pdfs/PIP_Broadband_2008.pdf.

Picard, R. G. 2002. *The Economics of Financing of Media Companies.* Fordham U. Press, New York.

Pichaske, David. 1979. *A Generation in Motion: Popular Music and Culture of the Sixties.* Schirmer Books, New York.

Pike and Fischer. *Radio Regulation* (after 1995 *Communications Regulation*). Bethesda, MD.

Pringle, P.; Starr, M. F.; and McCavitt, W. 2008. *Electronic Media Management,* 6th ed. Allyn & Bacon, Boston.

Ray III, Thomas R. 2008. *HD Radio Implementation: The Field Guide for Facility Conversion.* Focal Press, Burlington, MA.

Richtel, Matt. 2007. "Small New Steps Toward Fulfilling the Promise of PC-TV Links" (September 13): www.nytimes.com/2007/09/13/ technology/circuits/13basics.html.

Richter, William A. 2006. *Radio: A Complete Guide to the Industry,* (Media Industries Series). Peter Lang Publishing, New York.

Rosenberg, Bernard, and White, David Manning, eds. 1957. *Mass Culture: The Popular Arts in America.* Free Press, Glencoe, IL.

Rubin, Bernard. 1967. *Political Television.* Wadsworth, Belmont, CA.

Salwen, Michael B.; Garrison, Bruce; and Driscoll, Paul D. 2005. *Online News and the Public.* Lawrence Erlbaum Associates, Mahwah, NJ.

Schmitt, Kelly L. 1999. *The Three-Hour Rule: Is It Living Up to Expectations?* Annenberg Public Policy Center, University of Pennsylvania, Philadelphia, PA.

Senate CC (U.S. Congress, Senate Committee on Commerce). 1972. *Surgeon General's Report by Scientific Advisory Committee on Television and Social Behavior.* Hearings. 92nd Cong., 2d Sess. GPO, Washington, DC.

Settel, Irving. 1967. *A Pictorial History of Radio,* 2nd ed. Grosset and Dunlap, New York.

_____. 1983. *A Pictorial History of Television,* 2nd ed. Ungar, New York.

Setzer, Florence, and Levy, Jonathan. 1991. *Broadcast Television in a Multichannel Marketplace.* FCC Office of Plans and Policy (Staff Study No. 26, June).

Shannon, Claude, and Weaver, Warren. 1949. *The Mathematical Theory of Communication.* U. of Illinois Press, Urbana.

Shannon and Weaver. 1949. *The Mathematical Theory of Communication.*

Shawcross, William. 1992. *Murdoch.* Simon and Schuster, New York.

Sieber, Robert. 1988. "Industry Views on the People Meter: Cable Networks," *Gannett Center Journal 2* (Summer): 70.

Singleton, Loy A., and Copeland, Gary A. 1997. "FCC Broadcast Indecency Enforcement Actions: Changing Patterns Since *Pacifica*," Law and Policy Division, BEA Annual Conference.

Smith, Bruce Lannes, et al. 1946. *Propaganda, Communication, and Public Opinion.* Princeton U. Press, Princeton, NJ.

Smith, Richard A. 1985. "TV: The Light That Failed," *Fortune* (December): 78.

Smith, Sally Bedell. 1990. *In All His Glory: The Life of William S. Paley—The Legendary Tycoon and His Brilliant Circle.* Simon and Schuster, New York.

Sperber, A. M. 1986. *Murrow: His Life and Times.* Freundlich Books, New York.

Spring, Tom. 2008. *Get Ready for a Crackdown on Broadband Use.* (February 15). PC World: www.pcworld.com/article/142476/get_ready_for_a_crackdown_ on_broadband_use.html.

Steiner, Gary A. 1963. *The People Look at Television: A Study of Audience Attitudes*. Knopf, New York.

Stelter, Brian. 2008. "Charging by the Byte to Curb Internet Traffic (June 15): www.nytimes.com/2008/06/15/technology/15cable.html?

_____. 2008. "Measuring Ratings on the Run," *New York Times* (April 9): http://tvdecoder.blogs. nytimes.com/2008/04/09/measuring-ratings-on-the-run/.

Stephenson, William. 1967. *The Play Theory of Mass Communication*. U. of Chicago Press, Chicago.

Sterling, Christopher H. 1984. *Electronic Media: A Guide to Trends in Broadcasting and Newer Technologies, 1920–1983*. Praeger, New York.

_____, and Kittross, John M. 1990. *Stay Tuned: A Concise History of American Broadcasting*, 2nd ed. Wadsworth, Belmont, CA.

Stone, Brad. 2008. "Netflix Partners with LG to Bring Movies Straight to TV," *New York Times* (January 3): www.nytimes.com/2008/01/03/technology/03netflix.html.

Strong, William S. 1993. *The Copyright Book: A Practical Guide*, 4th ed. MIT Press, Cambridge, MA.

Swartz , Brecken. C. 2007. *Strategies in International Broadcasting: Communication Values Across Cultures*. VDM Verlag Dr. Mueller E.K., New York

Talwani, Sanjay. 2008. "Verizon Makes Its Move." *TV Technology*, (July 9): 1.

TCAF (Temporary Commission on Alternative Financing for Public Telecommunications). 1982–1983. *Alternative Financing Options for Public Broadcasting* (Vol. 1); *Final Report* (Vol. 2). FCC, Washington, DC.

Television Broadcast. Monthly. Miller Freeman, New York.

Television Digest. 28 September 1992: 10.

Thussu, Daya K. 2006. *International Communication: Continuity and Change*, 2nd ed. Hodder Arnold Publication, New York.

Toffler, Alvin. 1970. *Future Shock*. Random House, New York.

_____. 1980. *The Third Wave*. Morrow, New York.

Troudt, Paul. 2005. *Media, Audiences, Effects: An Introduction to the Study of Media Content and Audience Analysis*. Allyn & Bacon, Boston.

Turner, S. Derek. 2007. *Off the Dial: Female and Minority Radio Stations Ownership in the United States*. Free Press: www.stop bigmedia.com/files/off_the_dial.pdf.

TV Technology. Semi-monthly. IMAS, Falls Church, VA. U.S. (United States Reports).GPO, Washington, DC.

U.S. 1919. *Schenk v. U.S.*, 249 U.S. 47.

_____. 1942. *Marconi Wireless Telegraph Co. of America v. U.S.*, 320 U.S. 1.

_____. 1943. *NBC v. U.S.*, 319 U.S. 190.

_____. 1949. *Terminiello v. Chicago*, 337 U.S. 1.

_____. 1951. *Dennis v. U.S.*, 341 U.S. 494.

_____. 1957. *Roth v. United States*, 354 U.S. 476.

_____. 1964. *New York Times v. Sullivan*, 376 U.S. 254.

_____.1968. *U.S. v. Southwestern Cable*, 392 U.S. 157.

_____. 1969. *Red Lion v. FCC*, 395 U.S. 367.

_____. 1973. *Miller v. California*, 413 U.S. 15.

_____. 1974. *Miami Herald v. Tornillo*, 418 U.S. 241.

_____. 1978. *FCC v. Pacifica Foundation*, 438 U.S. 726.

_____. 1981. *Chandler v. Florida*, 449 U.S. 560.

_____. 1984. *Universal Studios v. Sony*, 464 U.S. 417.

_____. 1986. *City of Los Angeles and Department of Water and Power v. Preferred Communications, Inc.*, 476 U.S. 488.

_____.1989. *Sable Communications of California, Inc. v. FCC*, 492 U.S. 115.

_____. 1990. *Metro Broadcasting v. FCC*, 497 U.S. 547.

_____. 1995. *Adarand Constructors, Inc. v. Pena*, 515 U.S. 200, 115 S. Ct. 2097.

_____. 1996. *Denver Area Educational Telecommunications Consortium v. FCC*, 116 S. Ct. 2374.

_____. 1997. *Reno v. American Civil Liberties Union*, 521 U.S. 844.

_____. 1999. *Greater New Orleans Broadcasting Association, Inc. v. United States*, 527 U.S. 173.

_____.2000. *United States v. Playboy Entertainment Group, Inc.*, 529 U.S. 803.

_____. 2005. *Metro Goldwyn Mayer Studios v. Grokster*, 545 U.S. 913.

U.S.C. (United States Code). Regularly revised. GPO, Washington, DC., 47 U.S.C. 315.

_____. 1998. *Children's Online Privacy Protection Act*. 47 U.S.C. 6501 et seq.

_____. 1998. *Children's Online Protection Act*. 47 U.S.C. 201.

_____. 1998. *Digital Millennium Copyright Act*. 17 U.S.C. 1201 et seq.

_____. 1998. *Online Copyright Infringement Liability Limitation Act*. 17 U.S.C. 512.

U.S. Commission on Civil Rights. 1977, 1979. *Window Dressing on the Set: Women and Minorities in Television*, 2 vols. GPO, Washington, DC.

U.S. Education Department's National Center for Education Statistics (NCES). 1998. http://cyberatlas/internet.com/big_picture/demographics/education/article/0,1323,5951_308911,00.html

Valkenburg, Patti M. 2004. *Children's Responses to the Screen: A Media Psychological Approach*. Lawrence Erlbaum (Lea's Communication Series), Mahwah, NJ.

Variety. Weekly. Variety, New York.

The Veronis, Suhler and Associates Communications Industry Forecast: Historical and Projected Expenditures for 9 Industry Segments. Annual. Veronis, Suhler, New York.

Wall Street Journal, 11 July 1994: Al.

Webster, James; Phalen, Patricia F.; and Lichty, Lawrence W. 2005. *Ratings Analysis: The Theory and Practice Of Audience Research*, 3rd ed. Lawrence Erlbaum, Mahwah, NJ.

Wiener, Norbert. 1950. *The Human Use of Human Beings*.Houghton Mifflin Company, Boston.

Williams, Brian K. and Sawyer, Stacey C. 2007. *Using Information Technology: A Practical*

Introduction to Computers & Communications, 7th ed. McGraw-Hill, Boston.

Williams, Christian. 1981. *Lead, Follow, or Get Out of the Way: The Story of Ted Turner*. Times Books, New York.

Williams, Margorie. 1989. "MTV as Pathfinder for Entertainment" *The Washington Post* (December 13): Al.

Wimmer, Roger D. and Dominick, Joseph R. 2005. *Mass Media Research: An Introduction* 8th ed. Wadsworth Publishing, New York.

Zettl, Herbert. 2008. *Television Production Handbook*, 10th ed. Wadsworth, Belmont, CA.

Glossary

Access Time: The prime-time hour preceding network programming. It often delivers the most revenue for network affiliates.

Actual Malice Standard: The Actual Malice Standard was established from the landmark *New York Times Co. v. Sullivan* 376 U.S. 254 (1964) court case which ruled that public officials needed to prove actual malice in order to recover damages for libel. It is defined as "knowledge that the information was false" or, was published "with reckless disregard of whether it was false or not." Reckless disregard does not encompass mere neglect in following professional standards of fact checking. The publisher must entertain actual doubt as to the statement's truth.

Addressability: The ability to receive program orders and address individual pay-per-view decoders.

Addressable Converter Box: A device through which cable or satellite subscribers can order services (usually by remote control, phone, or on-line) and the service operator sends a special signal allowing a subscriber's set top box to provide the service.

Adjacencies: Local commercials that are placed by affiliates that are scheduled next to national spots during network programming.

Adjacent-Channel Interference: Interference between two or more stations operating on frequencies next to each other.

Administrative Law Judges (ALJs): Senior staff attorneys in the Federal Communication Commission (FCC) who preside over initial FCC hearings.

Adult Contemporary: A radio music program format consisting of an array of popular music and older hit songs.

Advanced Television (ATV) Standards: Advanced Television (ATV), also known as Digital Television (DTV), incorporates technologies known as High-Definition Television (HDTV) and Standard Digital Television (SDTV) and marks a complete redesign of North America's television service.

Agenda-Setting Theory: A mass media theory that concentrates primarily on the power of the news media to determine what issues people think are important to their community and personal wellbeing. In short, although media may not tell us what to think, they do tell us what to think about.

All Region /Region 0 Discs: DVD-video discs are encoded with a region code restricting the area of the world in which they can be played. Discs without region coding are called "all region" or "region 0 discs."

All-News Format: A radio format that typically includes both local and network news, costs a lot to produce and often earns low ratings (but high cumes) compared with successful music formats.

Alternative / Progressive Format: A music format featuring avant-garde music not played by conventional commercial outlets. This music format became popular in the 1990s.

Amplitude Modulation (AM): A technique used for transmitting information via a radio carrier wave. AM works by varying the strength of the transmitted signal in relation to the information being sent.

Antenna Gain: The increase in signal strength by the concentration of radio waves by means of directional propagation.

Antennas: Metallic structures used for transmitting or receiving electromagnetic waves.

Apartheid: A system of legal racial segregation enforced by the National Party government of South Africa between 1948 and 1990.

Appointment Television: An idea that successful programs may be scheduled anywhere because serious-minded fans will follow wherever they go.

Asymmetric Digital Subscriber Line (ADSL): A form of Digital Subscriber Line (DSL) service which provides much greater downstream than upstream capacity.

Attenuation: A process through which radio waves lose their energy as they radiate outward.

Audience Flow: The movement of viewers or listeners from one program to another.

Audience Segmentation: A term used to represent the dividing or slicing of an audience into different categories based on factors such as geographic locations, demographic attributes and lifestyle attributes.

Audio Frequency (AF): Periodic vibrations whose frequency is audible to the average human.

Audion: An amplifier device invented by Lee de Forest in 1906. It was the precursor of what is commonly known today as a triode.

Authoritarian Philosophy: A philosophy that gives precedence to the State over its subjects. From a media perspective, the expectation is that the media exist to serve the state.

Avails: Specific units of time within programs that are sold to advertisers. Avails can vary in duration from as short as 10 seconds to as long as two minutes.

Barter Avails: A specific number of commercial avails within a syndicated program that are intended to be sold exclusively by a program syndicator, rather than the local station that owns the rights to the program. (See *Syndicated Programs.*)

Barter Syndication Advertising: Commercials placed by national advertisers inside various syndicated programs airing on local TV stations around the country.

Basic Tier: The cable TV service package that consists of TV channels which at minimum must include the local broadcast television stations and the Public, Educational, and Governmental (PEG) access channels that the operator may be required to offer in accordance with an agreement with the local government. After complying with these minimum requirements, a cable operator may offer additional programming as part of their basic service tier.

Beam Tilt: Television antennas can improve coverage by using beam tilt, which concentrates the radiated energy downwards so that little of it skims over the line-of-sight horizon to be lost uselessly in space.

Behavioral Sampling: A sampling method where behavioral responses of audiences such as turning on a receiver, selection of stations, selection of programs, and turning off the set, are all recorded.

Behaviorism: A theoretical concept developed as part of Social Learning Theory, which postulates that one's environment has significant influence over one's behavior.

Bidding Credits: Credit awarded to qualified small companies participating in the Federal Communication Commission's frequency auctions.

Billings: The amount advertisers are charged by the media outlets.

Binary Digit: Numbers expressed in binary digits consist of only two digits. They are conventionally expressed as "zero" and "one" but can also be regarded as equivalent to "on" and "off."

Bit Speed: The number of bits per second that one channel can handle.

Blanket Licensing: A form of music licensing that most radio stations hold from licensing agencies. It allows the stations unlimited rights to air any music in the agencies' catalogs in return for payment of an annual percentage of the station's gross income.

Blending: A process wherein an HD radio receiver will initially acquire the station's analog signal first in mono and then in stereo, and finally the station's primary digital signal. This process allows the receiver to automatically revert back to an analog-only signal if the digital signal is lost, avoiding any disruption in listening.

Block Programming: Programming strategy that tries to maintain audience flow-through by scheduling programs with similar appeal next to each other; for example, by filling an entire evening with family-comedy programs.

Blogcast: The combination of a blog and podcast into a single website. A blog is a weblog, or journal, that is available on the Internet. A podcast is an audio file that is shared with visitors or subscribers to a site. A blogcast enables participants to freely add text, photos, and music.

Blogs (Web Logs): Publicly available web pages usually maintained by an individual with regular entries of commentary, descriptions of events, or other audio visual materials such as graphics or video.

Border Blasters: A term used to refer to some Mexican radio stations that used excessive power to reach their intended audience in American cities far north of the border.

Border Gateway Protocol (BGP): A set of technical rules for routing data across different networks.

Bottom Line Mentality: A preoccupation with profit-and-loss statements to the exclusion of all else.

Brand Differentiation: A process through which a particular brand differentiates itself from other competing brands in the same product category.

Branding: A marketing strategy wherein a product or a program's reputation is systematically built over time through various promotional strategies.

Breaks/Pods: Avails that are clustered into program interruptions in a specific program.

Bridging: A strategy to weaken the drawing power of a competing show by scheduling a one-hour (or longer) program that overlaps the start time of the competing show.

British Broadcasting Corporation (BBC): One of the two independent non-profit organizations that oversees broadcasting operations in Britain.

Broadband over Powerline (BPL): A technology that allows the use of ordinary power lines to carry high-speed broadband services into the consumer's home.

Broadcast Flag: A system developed for preventing large scale piracy. Using this system, digital bits (flags) inserted into a digital program stream place restrictions on copying and/or re-copying program content.

Cable System Interconnects: Refers to both the physical interconnection or the placement of advertisements on multiple cable systems in a region.

Cable Television: A system of providing television to consumers via radio frequency signals transmitted to televisions through fixed coaxial or fiber optic cables as opposed to the traditional over-the-air method of broadcasting.

CableCARD (CC): A credit card size device that can be inserted into digital TV receivers and other host equipment, such as digital video recorders (DVRs). This device allows customers to view and record digital cable television channels on digital video recorders, personal computers and televisions without the use of other equipment such as a set-top box (STB).

Carrier-Current Stations: Low-power AM signals can be fed into building power lines or steam pipes, which serve as distribution grids. The signals radiate for a short distance into the space surrounding these conductors, usually enough to cover the interior of the building. Services using this propagation are called carrier-current stations.

Carrier Wave: The basic emission of a broadcasting station; an unmodulated wave that conveys information superimposed on it. It is analogous to a road that carries traffic.

Cash Barter Deals: A program purchase transaction in which a broadcast station provides payment to a syndicator in the form of both cash and a specific number of commercials avails that will be sold to national advertisers. (See *Barter Avails.*)

Cathode Ray Tube (CRT): A vacuum tube containing an electron gun and a fluorescent screen. The electron gun scans images on the fluorescent screen. CRT screens are widely used in television and other monitors.

Cease and Desist Order: A formal punitive disciplinary process used by the Federal Trade Commission that forces compliance with the law.

Chain/Network: In early years of broadcasting it was a common practice to call interconnected radio and television stations carrying the same program a chain. Such interconnected stations are now referred to as networks.

Channel: A range of frequencies allotted by the government to each AM, FM, and TV station in which to operate.

Channel Repertoire: A term used to describe the limited array of channels an audience member uses regularly as compared to all channels available to the individual. (Also see *Tuning Inertia.*)

Charge Coupled Device (CCD): A image sensor chip used in video and still cameras that contains hundreds of thousands of tiny light-sensitive elements (pixels). Light is converted (transduced) into electrical charges corresponding to the intensity of the light striking the pixel. The electrical charges making up the image are then transferred (read out) from the chip.

Checkbook Journalism: The practice of paying interviewees for televised interviews.

Checkerboard: A program scheduling strategy in which, over the course of a week, a different program is scheduled in the same time period. For example, a broadcast network will schedule a different program each night at 8:00 PM in prime time.

Chilling Effect: A situation where the conduct of free speech is suppressed because of the fear of penalization self-censorship.

Circuit Court of Appeal: One of the US Courts of Appeal which serves a specific region of the country.

Classic Rock: A radio music program format consisting of familiar songs from popular albums of the 1960s, 1970s, and 1980s.

Clearance: An affiliate's contractual agreement to keep clear in its program schedule the times a network needs to run its programs.

Click Through: An event during which when the viewer clicks on the banner, he or she is directed to the web site advertised in the banner.

Cliff Effect: A term used to describe the all or nothing quality of digital TV reception. The picture is either excellent (with sufficient signal strength) or not available at all.

Clipping: A fraudulent advertising practice where affiliates cut away from network or barter-syndication programs prematurely, usually to insert commercials of their own.

Clusters: Cable systems that are geographically proximate to each other and often owned by one multiple-system operator.

Coaxial Cable: The name coaxial cable is derived from its two conductors with a common axis: a solid central conductor and a braided copper shield conductor. Radio energy travels within the protected environment between the two conductors through the white plastic (or foam) insulator. Cable television relies on this type of conductor, as do many terrestrial relay links that convey TV signals, telephone calls, data and other types of information.

Co-Channel Interference: Interference between any two or more stations operating on the same frequency.

Common Carrier: A business that transports people, goods, or services and offers its services to the general public under license or authority provided by a regulatory body. A common carrier holds itself out to provide service to the general public without discrimination.

Communist Philosophy: A philosophy that advocates state-owned media. Communist countries typically advocate state ownership of most property, which in turn places emphasis on teaching communist doctrine. Using the media for this purpose is considered necessary to guard against the temptations of materialism.

Community Antenna Television (CATV): In 1948 when television broadcasting first started, in areas where over-the-air reception was limited by mountainous terrain, communities often erected large community antennas and ran cables from these antennas to individual homes. These Community Antenna Television systems allowed communities to receive television signals despite territorial constraints.

Compact Disc (CD): A small, portable, high-density, optical, media storage device for electronically recording, storing, and playing back audio, video, text, and other information in a digital format.

Compression: A process for reducing the amount of data that must be stored or transmitted. Compression is accomplished by encoding (and later decoding) a digital data stream. Compression can be "lossy" where some data is permanently lost, or "lossless" where all information can be restored.

Confounding Variables: Variables or factors that sometimes interfere with the results of an experiment or field study.

Consent Order: A formal non-punitive disciplinary process used by Federal Trade Commission to censure advertisers under which the advertiser agrees to stop the offending practice without admitting guilt.

Construction Permits (CPs): A Construction Permit gives its holder a limited time (usually 24 months for television and 18 for radio) to construct and test the station. The CP holder then files a

record of technical testing to apply for a regular license with the FCC.

Content Analysis: Research strategy which involves the estimation of characteristics of media content. The classification of programs into various categories constitutes one form of content analysis. On a more sophisticated level, content analysis categorizes, counts, and interprets message content.

Cookie: The cookie takes space on the user's computer to store information that web services can retrieve and use later. Cookies have been used by web advertisers to track individual users and their activities.

Cooperative Advertising/Co-op: An advertising strategy where local retailers or small businesses share advertising costs with product manufacturers.

Cost per Point: A measurement that estimates advertising returns by dividing the cost of the commercial by the number of ratings points that the program earned. These points can be based on total households or narrower demographic ratings.

Cost per Thousand (CPM): A measurement that estimates advertising costs among competing media. CPM is the cost of reaching 1,000 (represented by the Roman numeral M) households or other defined targets. CPM is calculated by dividing the cost of a commercial by the number of homes (in thousands) that it reached.

Counterprogramming: A programming strategy that seeks to attract the audience to one's own station or network by offering programs different from those of the competition. For example, an independent station might schedule situation comedies against evening news.

Coverage Contour: The geographical area in which a broadcast station's signal could be received.

Cross-Promotion: A program promotional strategy wherein many broadcast networks enter into an agreement with their "sister" cable networks owned by the same parent corporation, through which the networks air promos for each other.

Cultivation Theory: A theory, first proposed by Dr. George Gerbner and his colleagues in the 1960s, examines the power of television to influence people's perceptions, attitudes, and values about the world in which they live. The term "cultivation" was derived from the notion that the long-term repetition of television's mass produced messages and images subtly "cultivate" viewers' perceptions of social reality.

Cumes: Short for cumulative, a cume rating gives a percentage estimate of the number of unduplicated (different) persons a station reaches over a period of time. Cumes may also be expressed as raw numbers rather than a percentage.

Cyber-Squatters: Individuals or institutions who register a domain name (or close variation) of an existing business whose identity is protected by trademarks, service marks, or other intellectual property laws, in hope of selling it for a profit.

Cycle: The complete process where a wave of energy reaches a maximum positive peak, back down through the zero point, then to a maximum negative peak and back to zero.

Dayparts: Blocks of time in which several programs may be scheduled or one consistent type of program content may be offered.

Deficit Financing: When considering the adoption of a new program to its schedule, a major broadcast network will ask the program producer to share in the financial risk, at least for the first season. The "deficit" in deficit financing means that the network does not pay the total cost of creating a pilot program or the cost of creating a few episodes of a new program.

Delayed Broadcast: An agreement reached between a network and its affiliate/s which stipulates that the affiliate may carry the network's programming at a time later than originally scheduled.

Democratic Participant Philosophy: A philosophy which argues that a citizen's voice is essential to the management of any worthwhile government and, consequently, from a media perspective, citizens are encouraged to be involved in all phases of producing media content.

Demographic Breakouts: Also referred to as demographics, a form of measurement where the overall ratings are divided into such subgroups as those for men, women, and teens. Adult audience age group categories typically consist of decade units for radio (such as men 35–44) for radio and larger units for television (e.g., women 18–34 or 25–49).

Designated Market Area (DMA): One or more counties in which TV stations located in a central town or city are the most viewed. DMAs usually extend over smaller areas in the East, where cities are closer together, than in the West. Nielsen assigns each of the more than 3,000 counties in the United States to a single DMA, updating the assignments annually.

Developmental Philosophy: A philosophy which holds that media are responsible for specifically improving the social conditions of developing nations. The ultimate goal is not to maintain the status quo, but to bring about dramatic social change.

Digital Cable Ready (DCR): A digital television set that the consumer can connect directly to their cable service. Usually, these sets contain a CableCARD (CC) slot to receive digital cable signals with full image quality without the need for a traditional cable set-top box.

Digital Light Processing (DLP): Developed by Texas Instruments, DLP sets contain an optical semiconductor chip that contains up to two million, hinge-mounted, tiny aluminum mirrors that reflect light to make a picture. Each mirror is one-fifth the width of a human hair, and represents one pixel. The number of mirrors used determines the resolution of the picture.

Digital Subscriber Line (DSL): Internet service provided through a subscriber's "twisted pair" copper telephone lines.

Digital Television (DTV): A technology for sending and receiving moving images and sound by using digital signals.

Digital Tier: A cable program package which includes several digital channels. Often customers pay extra subscription fees to receive these channels.

Digital Video Discs (DVDs): A popular optical disc storage medium used for audio, video and data storage. DVDs have the same dimensions as compact discs (CDs) but store more than six times as much data.

Digital Video Recorders (DVRs): A device that records video in a digital format to a hard disk drive or other memory medium within a media device.

Digitization: Representing an object, image, document or a signal (usually an analog signal) by a discrete set of its points or samples.

Diode: A two-terminal device that has two active electrodes between which the signal of interest may flow. Most are used for their unidirectional electric current property.

Direct Broadcast Satellite (DBS): A system for the distribution of video and audio streams directly to subscribers over satellite systems.

Direct Waves: Waves that travel in a line-of-sight manner from transmitter antenna to receiver antenna.

Directional Propagation: A process of beaming reinforced signals in a desired direction. Directional propagation has value both for increasing signal strength in a desired direction and for preventing interference between stations.

Dolby Digital/AC-3: A format standard for digital audio.

Domain Name System (DNS): An Internet service that translates domain names into the Internet Protocol addresses used by networking equipment to deliver information.

Domestic Satellites (Domsats): Communications satellite system that allows for the transmission of TV and radio programming throughout the United States.

Down-Converter: A device that translates the high frequencies used by satellites into the lower frequency ranges that TV receivers use. Many systems use a low-noise block converter (LNB), which combines the functions of amplification and frequency conversion in a single device.

Downlinking: A process of establishing a communications link used for the transmission of signals from a satellite or an airborne platform to an Earth terminal.

Downloadable Conditional Access System (DCAS): A system consisting of hardware components and software needed to provide consumers selective access or denial of specific content services in their cable operator's network.

Duopoly: Ownership of two radio or television stations within the same market.

Duopoly: Rule: A rule first issued by the FCC in 1940 and enforced for half a century that stipulated no single owner could have more than one station of the same type (e.g., more than one AM station) in the same market.

Economy of Scale: An economic principle that asserts that as business becomes larger, the costs of production per unit of its product become smaller. Therefore, large businesses often have an inherent advantage over smaller businesses attempting to compete with the identical product.

Editorial Advertising / Advertorials: Advertisements that promote a particular opinion or viewpoint rather than a product or service.

Effective Radiated Power (ERP): A standardized theoretical measurement of Radio Frequency (RF) energy, also referred to as equivalent radiated power (ERP).

80/20 Principal: For businesses, the principle means typically that roughly 20 percent of the products sold yield 80 percent of profit.

8-Vestigial Sideband Modulation (8-VSB): Vestigial sideband modulation with eight discrete amplitude levels.

Elaboration Likelihood Model (ELM): A communication processing model intended to describe the circumstances in which audiences invest a lot of critical thinking (i.e., elaboration) or not about a received message.

Electromagnetism: A field which exerts a force on particles that possess the property of electric charge, and is in turn affected by the presence and motion of those particles. There are three basic common properties to all forms of electromagnetic energy. First, they radiate outward from a source without benefit of any discernible physical vehicle; second, they travel at the same high velocity; and third, they have the properties of waves.

Enhanced Underwriting: A form of corporate sponsorship in public broadcasting. When a station offers enhanced underwriting, it may air announcements up to 30 seconds long and mention specific consumer products.

Equivalent Substitutes: A scenario where a customer finds two or more brands equally satisfying and therefore easily substituted.

Ethnographic Studies: A research strategy where the researcher becomes part of the (usually small) group being studied, and this participant observation over extended time periods allows a realistic "window" to the group that is being studied.

European Broadcasting Union (EBU): A confederation of 75 broadcasting organizations, most of which are government-owned public service broadcasters or privately owned stations with public missions. The EBU claims to be the largest association of national broadcasters in the world, with the overarching goal of promoting cooperation among media organizations and facilitating the exchange of audiovisual content.

Expanded Basic Tier: A cable program package which often includes local channels, Public, Education, and Government (PEG) channels, and the most popular ad-supported cable networks.

Extended Viewing Period: Many television programs now invite viewers to visit their associated websites to learn more about the topic, interact with the program's performers or production staff, comment on the show, enter a contest, or explore the topic in greater detail through links to other web pages. This allows the program sponsors to engage the audiences with the program for an extended period of time.

Fairness Doctrine: A policy of the FCC that required the holders of broadcast licenses to present all sides of controversial issues of public importance in a balanced manner.

Fiber to the Home (FTTH): Networks that send signals over fiber-optic lines from the company's headend to an optical network terminal located in the customer's home.

Fiber to the Node (FTTN): Networks that send signals over fiber-optic lines from the company's headend to an optical node located in the customer's neighborhood.

Fiber-Optic Cable: Hair-thin strands of extremely pure glass (or plastic for shorter distances) that convey modulated light beams with a bandwidth over 1,000 Megabytes per second (MBps).

Field Studies: A research strategy where behavior is recorded in "the real world" without unduly intruding on or otherwise influencing participants.

Financial Interest and Syndication (Fin/Syn) Rules: A body of rules established by the FCC in 1970. These rules prevented the Big Three television networks from owning or acting as the syndicator of any of the programming that they aired in prime time. The rules were progressively relaxed over time and were finally abolished in 1993.

First-Run: A form of syndicated programming that typically has never been on a network.

Flowthrough: The movement of audience viewers or listeners on the same stations or channels.

Format: The organization of an entire service. Most radio stations have adopted distinctive formats, such as country, classical music, or all news.

Format Fragmentation: A term used to refer to the fine distinctions among types of radio programming.

Frequency Division Multiplexing: Modulating two or more separate carriers in the same channel.

Frequency Modulation (FM): A technique used for transmitting information via a radio carrier wave. FM works by varying the frequency of the electromagnetic waves while keeping amplitude constant.

Gatekeepers: A person in an organization or an organization within a larger social context which controls the flow of knowledge and information.

Generic Promotions: Announcements that promote an entire television series.

Genre: (Pronounced "zhahn'-ruh") A denotation of a category of content. Familiar entertainment genres include the situation comedy, the game show, the drama, and the soap opera.

Geostationary or Geosynchronous Orbit: An orbital position directly above the equator at a height of about 22,300 miles. At that height, objects revolve around the Earth at the same rate that the Earth turns on its axis resulting in a constant coverage pattern (footprint).

Global System for Mobile Communications (GSM): A popular standard developed by the International Telecommunication Union for mobile phone and data transmission.

Grandfathering: Allowing existing conditions to continue when new contradictory regulations are adopted.

Graphical User Interface: A type of user interface which allows users to interact with electronic devices like computers by manipulating graphical icons as opposed to text-based interfaces and typed commands.

Gross Rating Points (GRPs): Typically a media–buying term referring to the number of commercials placed with various programs by an advertiser multiplied by the number of ratings points delivered by each program. The data summed from each program produces "gross" figure for the entire week or month.

Ground Waves: Waves that are propagated along and through the surface of the Earth. Ground waves are used in AM radio broadcasting.

Hammock: A programming strategy that tries to establish an audience for a new program, or to recover the audience for a show slipping in popularity, by scheduling the program in question between two strong programs.

Hard or True Interconnections: Several cable systems in a large market interconnect so that commercials (or programs) can be seen on all of them, rather than only one, providing combined advertising coverage equivalent in reach to that of the area's TV stations. System interconnection that involves physical linking of the systems by cable, microwave, or satellite are called hard or true interconnections.

Harmonics: Weaker signals at multiples of the carrier frequency. Harmonic energy can interfere with services on higher frequencies if it is not suppressed before it reaches the antenna.

Headend: The nerve center of a cable system where the operator aggregates TV programming from various sources and delivers it via cable to subscriber homes.

High-Definition Television (HDTV): A digital television system providing a larger screen, vastly improved picture resolution, and multichannel sound.

Hot Switching: Programming strategy that fine-tunes the lead-in strategy through the use of "seamless," commercial free transitions from one show to another.

Households Using Television (HUT): A measure used to calculate audience share. A HUT rating of 55 indicates that at a given time an estimated 55 percent of all TV households are actually tuned in to *some* channel receivable in that market; the remaining 45 percent are not at home, busy with something else, or otherwise not using television. HUT may also be expressed in raw numbers rather than a percentage.

Hybrid Fiber-Coaxial (HFC): Cable network architecture that sends signals from the headend over fiber-optic cable to an optical node located in the subscriber's neighborhood. Traditional coaxial cable is then used for the connection between the node and the subscriber's home.

Hybrid Services: A service that combines more than one regulatory classification. For example, an open video system (OVS) is part common carrier and part cable system.

Hyper Text Markup Language (HTML): The predominant mark up language for creating web pages. It provides a means to describe the structure of text-based information in a document by representing certain text as links, headings, paragraphs, lists, and so on. It also supplements that text with interactive forms, embedded images, and other objects.

Hyper Text Transfer Protocol (HTTP): A communications protocol used for retrieving inter-linked text documents (hypertext). It led to the establishment of the World Wide Web.

Hyping: Deliberate attempts by stations or networks to influence ratings by scheduling special programs and promotional efforts during ratings sweeps.

Iconoscope: The name given to the early television camera tube.

Image Dissector: A device for taking pictures apart electronically for bit-by-bit transmission.

Impression: A single appearance of an advertisement on a web page. Each time an advertisement loads onto a users screen may be counted as one impression.

In-Band, On-Channel (IBOC): The addition of digital carriers to the frequencies assigned to existing terrestrial radio stations allowing them to offer a digital audio broadcast service while simultaneously maintaining their analog service.

Indecency: The FCC defines indecency as "language or material that, in context, depicts or describes, in terms patently offensive as measured by contemporary community standards for the broadcast medium, sexual or excretory activities or organs."

Independent Broadcasting Authority (IBA): One of the two independent non-profit organizations that oversees broadcasting operations in Britain.

Independent Regulatory Agencies: Agencies that Congress authorizes to oversee such often complex areas as power, transportation, labor, finance, and communication.

Independent Television (ITV) Britain: A public service network of British commercial television broadcasters set up under the Independent Television Authority (ITA). It provides an alternative to the British Broadcasting Corporation.

Independents: Radio and television stations that do not have full-service network affiliation. In some instances they may have a partial affiliation with a major network or a regional network.

Inflow: Movement of audience viewers or listeners from competing programs.

Infomercials: Long format commercials that often resemble talk shows, also mix information (or sales pitches masquerading as information) and entertainment.

Injunction: A court order that stipulates a party to resort to some act or refrain from doing a certain act.

In-Tab Sample: The sample actually used in tabulating results and producing a ratings report.

Integrated Circuit (IC): A miniaturized electronic circuit consisting of semiconductor devices as well as passive components that havd been embedded into the surface of a thin substrate of semiconductor material.

Interference Zone: Interference zones form the basis for the FCC's spacing requirements keeping stations operating on the same frequencies geographically apart to avoid interference.

Interlaced Scanning: One of two common methods for "painting" a video image on an electronic display screen by scanning or displaying each line or row of pixels. This technique uses two fields to create a frame. One field contains all the odd lines in the image and the other contains all the even lines of the image. The two sets of fields work together to create a full frame.

Intermixture: Assignment of both VHF and UHF TV channels in the same market.

International Telecommunication Union (ITU): A non-profit organization affiliated with the United Nations and headquartered in Geneva, Switzerland. ITU fosters international cooperation and standard setting in the area of telecommunications among its member countries.

Internet: A global system of inter-connected computer networks that exchange data by a method referred to as packet switching. The Internet uses a standardized set of rules called the Internet Protocol Suite (TCP/IP). The Internet can be referred to as a "network of networks" that consists of billions of private and public, academic, business, and government networks of local to global scope that are linked by copper wires, fiber-optic cables, wireless connections, and other networking technologies.

Internet Exchange Points (IXPs): Physical hubs containing switches and routers used by large Internet service provider networks to forward each other's data traffic without charge.

Internet Protocol Multicast (IP Multicast): A one-to-many routing system that uses Internet protocols to send a single program stream to many devices—usually computers, TVs, and cell phones—that have requested the content.

Internet Protocol TV (IPTV): IPTV uses Internet technology such as Transmission Control Protocol and Internet Protocol (TCP/IP) originally developed for use in computer networks to deliver video content. Similar to using the Internet, a customer makes a request for specific video content which is then delivered to the home.

Intervening Variables: A variable which explains the relationship between an independent and a dependent variable, where there is no clear logical causal explanation to relate directly the two variables.

Inventory: The total number of avails per program that can be sold to advertisers.

Journalistic Discretion: In relation to the fairness doctrine the Supreme Court ruled that because broadcasters cannot possibly provide time for all viewpoints, broadcasters should be allowed significant journalistic discretion in deciding how best to fulfill the fairness doctrine obligations.

Jump: To move back and forth between pairs of channels.

Kinescope: The name given to the early version of the television picture tube invented by Vladimir K. Zworykin. Also, film of television programs photographed as they were displayed on the face of a picture tube.

Laboratory Experiments: A research strategy where some variables are precisely controlled while excluding others. By controlling independent variables (e.g., the items being tested that could lead to a change in attitude) and measuring dependent variables (the attitude being studied), researchers can get closer to determining causation and genuine "effects."

LASER: Light Amplification by Stimulated Emission of Radiation.

Lead-In: A program that is scheduled immediately prior to another program.

Lead-Out: A program that is scheduled immediately after another program.

Least Objectionable Program (LOP): An assumption that no matter what TV programming is offered, audiences are most likely to watch the least objectionable program.

Libel: Defamation by published untrue words that may expose their subject to public hatred, shame, or disgrace, particularly in group viewing situations.

Libertarian Philosophy: A view that favors private ownership and free-market economics as the best means of satisfying the needs of citizens. Under this philosophy media are mostly privately owned, profit-motivated businesses. The function of any government regulation is only to maintain fair competition.

Life Line Service: A cable program package offering a basic set of channels. Such packages often include some local channels and Public, Education, and Government (PEG) channels.

Liquid Crystal Display (LCD): A TV display technology that employs a liquid crystal fluid sandwiched between two plates of glass. An electrical voltage applied to each pixel causes the crystals to twist, allowing light to pass.

Liquid Crystal on Silicon (LCoS): A micro-projection device that uses highly reflective liquid crystals rather than mirrors to form the image.

Local Advertising: Commercials placed by businesses or advertising agencies located in the same market as the radio, TV station or cable franchise. For example, a local car dealer in Boston will purchase commercial time on a TV station licensed to the Boston TV market or Boston cable franchise area.

Local Exchange Carrier (LEC): A term for a public telephone company in the United States that provides local telephone and other related services.

Local into Local: A term used to describe a satellite television operator's strategy of beaming local TV signals back into the local TV market, allowing DBS subscribers to watch local TV stations without disconnecting from their satellite feed.

Local-Origination (LO): Channels controlled and programmed by the cable operators themselves.

Long Tail Principal: A theory that argues products that are in low demand or have low sales volume can collectively make up a market share that rivals or exceeds the relatively few current bestsellers and blockbusters, if the store or distribution channel is large enough.

Lossless Compression: A compression technique in which all original data can be reconstructed after decompression.

Lossy Compression: A compression technique in which only an approximation of the original data can be reconstructed after decompression.

Lotteries: A method once used by Federal Communication Commission in choosing LPTV and MMDS licensees.

Low Power FM (LPFM): FM stations designated to operate with very low effective radiated power (ERP). LPFM stations are not protected from interference that may be received from other classes of FM stations.

Low-Noise Amplifier (LNA): Devices that amplify the incoming signal strength at an antenna by as much as a million times.

Made-for-Cable: A genre of low budget movies that are exclusively made for cable TV.

Magazine Format: A format of television programming consisting of a medley of short features bound together by a personable host or group of hosts.

Make-Goods: For networks and large-market stations and cable systems, the media essentially promise a certain minimum audience delivery reflected in Nielsen and Arbitron ratings. If, in fact, the program or day part does not deliver what was promised, the media often are obliged to compensate for this shortfall—make good on the original promise— by offering additional free commercials.

Market Exclusivity: An agreement which stipulates a particular radio or television station as an exclusive local affiliate of a particular network, or an exclusive provider of syndicated programming in the market.

Marketplace of Ideas: An analogy based on the economic concept of a free market that is used to justify freedom of expression based on the First Amendment. The belief holds that the truth or the best policy arises out of the competition of various ideas in free, transparent public discourse.

Mass Media: Technology-based means of communication that reach large numbers of people delivering news and entertainment that most people find interesting and at a price they can afford.

Media Mix: A term which refers to a strategy of mixing different types of media in an advertising campaign.

Miniseries: A television program that typically runs for three to eight episodes.

Minority Enhancements: Privileges given by the FCC to minority owners that have applied to receive a broadcast license.

Mobile Banner: A form of banner advertising most commonly used in mobile phones and displayed at the top of the phone page.

Mobile Poster: A form of banner advertising most commonly used in mobile phones and displayed at the bottom of the phone page, opened in a mobile phone browser.

Modulation: Ways of imposing meaningful variations on a transmitter's carrier wave to enable it to carry information.

Morning Drive/Midday/Afternoon Drive/Night/Overnight Segments: Dayparts used to report radio station ratings figures.

MPEG-2 Standard: (The Motion Picture Experts Group-2) One of the most popular compression standards used for digital audio and video transmission.

Multicasting: The ability to deliver more than one program on a single transmission channel.

Multichannel Multipoint Distribution Service (MMDS): A system that uses microwave radio signals in the ultra-high-frequency (UHF) portion of the radio spectrum between 2.1 and 2.7 Ghz to distribute cable programming to subscribers.

Multichannel Video Program Distributor (MVPD): Any business entity including but not limited to, a cable operator, a Multiple System Operator, a Direct Broadcast Satellite service, a multiple channel distribution service or a receive only satellite program distributor that makes available for purchase for consumers multiple channels of video programming.

Multiple System Operators (MSOs): Cable companies that own more than one individual cable system.

Multiplexing: A process of simultaneously sending multiple signals through a communication transmission medium.

Multistage Area Probability Sampling: A sampling strategy involving the step-by-step narrowing down of selection areas.

Must-Carry Rules: Rules that mandate that cable companies carry various local television stations within a cable provider's service area.

National Access Points (NAPs): Defined under the U.S. National Information Infrastructure (NII) document as transitional data communications facilities at which Network Service Providers (NSPs) would exchange traffic, in replacement of the publicly financed NSFNet Internet backbone.

National Programming Service (NPS): A PBS service that provides documentaries, arts, children's, and news and public-affairs programming. In prime time, NPS presents signature series like *Frontline*, *American Experience*, *NOVA*, *Nature*, and *American Masters*, as well as a wide range of high-profile miniseries and specials.

National Public Radio (NPR): A producer and distributor of noncommercial radio programming.

National Rep Firm: An agency that acts as an intermediary or broker between an advertising agency and the station. National spot advertising enables advertisers to capitalize on audience interest in local programs, something the network advertiser cannot do.

National Spot Advertising: An alternative to network advertising in which a business wishes not to reach the entire country but prefers to advertise in only selected geographical areas of the country. For example, a company that sells snow blowers would be interested in reaching people living in New England, but certainly not in Florida. National spot advertisers bypass the networks and purchase commercial time from local stations or cable systems.

NATPE: National Association of Television Program Executives. A trade association for television programmers.

Network Advertising: Commercials placed by major advertisers on the broadcast and cable networks intended to reach a nationwide audience. Although the commercials are seen on hundreds of stations (i.e., network affiliates) in local markets, the stations themselves do not share in any of the commercial revenue.

Network Compensation: Cash compensation provided to an affiliate by a network for the right to use their stations to reach their audiences.

Niche Content: Content that focuses more on specialized target audiences or topics rather than a singular, homogeneous mass audience.

Non Sampling Error: Errors not caused by the act of sampling. These errors may be intentional or inadvertent and cause bias or other inaccuracy in research results.

Noncommercial Broadcasting: Broadcasting services that are motivated by public-service goals rather than by profit. The FCC has reserved certain radio and TV frequencies for only noncommercial service.

Non-response Errors: Errors that arise in statistical calculations because of lack of responses from respondents.

Notice of Inquiry (NOI): A document issued by government agencies to gather information on an industry specific issue that needs preliminary comment and research.

Notice of Proposed Rule Making (NPRM): A document issued by a government agency when it wishes to add, remove, or change a rule (or regulation) as part of the rulemaking process.

NTSC: (National Television System Committee) Standards committee established by the FCC in 1940 that set the technical specifications for the analog television system used in the United States, Canada, Japan, Mexico, the Philippines, South Korea, Taiwan and some other countries.

Obscene/Obscenity: The legal definition of obscenity was derived from the *Miller vs. California* 413 U.S. 15 (1973) court case decision. The courts defined obscenity as "works which, taken as a whole, appeal to the prurient interest in sex, which portray sexual conduct in a patently offensive way, and which, taken as a whole, do not have serious literary, artistic, political, or scientific value."

Off-Network: Syndicated program that began on one of the major broadcast or cable networks before being made available in reruns to stations.

Office of Communications Britain: The regulatory body that oversees broadcast operations in Britain. It plays a role that is similar to Federal Communication Commission (FCC) in the United States.

Oldies: A radio music program format consisting of familiar hits from the 1950s through the 1970s.

Open Video System (OVS): A system that allows the telephone company to deliver programming of its own choosing while giving other programmers access to the company's distribution system. Essentially the telephone company acts as a cable system operator and common carrier at the same time.

Opinion Leaders: A term that was born out of the two-step flow of communication propounded by Paul Lazarsfeld and Elihu Katz. Opinion leaders are those who are active media users who interpret the meaning of media messages or content for others. Typically the opinion leader is held in high esteem by those who accept his or her opinions.

Organic Light-Emitting Diodes (OLEDs): Diodes that rely on inks with light-emitting properties that may eventually replace today's LCD displays and eliminate the need for back-lighting while delivering ultra-thin screens.

Outflow: Movement of audience viewers or listeners away from their present viewing or listening selections to either competing programs or turning off their sets.

Owned and Operated (O&O): Radio and television stations that are owned and operated by the broadcast networks.

Pacing Reports: A measure of performance for sales departments that is estimated by using various daily, weekly, and monthly reports and comparing the current pricing and inventory sellout with historical benchmarks.

Package: The practice wherein syndicators typically bundle several dozen titles into a single deal called packages.

PAL: (Phase Alternating Line) A color-encoding system used in broadcast television systems in large parts of the world.

Participating Sponsorship: A financial arrangement where several different advertisers share the costs of a program.

Pay or Premium Cable: Commercial-free premium television services available for subscription through cable and satellite television systems for fees higher than traditional, packaged cable television services.

Pay-Per-View (PPV) Networks: Networks that provide programming through cable systems or DBS that subscribers can access by paying a separate fee for each program they access and watch.

Pay Per View System (PPV): A system that allows viewers to order individual programs from the cable company or DBS operator for a one-time fee.

Payola: The illegal practice of undisclosed payment or other incentive handed out by record companies for the broadcast of recordings on music radio, in which a song is presented as being part of the normal day's broadcast.

PBS Plus: A service intended to complement the National Program Service, which provides the national program schedule to PBS member stations. PBS PLUS consists entirely of fully underwritten continuing series, limited series, and specials in a variety of genres.

PBS via Satellite: PBS offers two full-time satellite channels: the PBS National Satellite Service for C-Band, which is transmitted to the backyard TVRO audience; and the PBS National Satellite Service for Direct Broadcast Satellite, which is provided on DIRECTV and DISH Network. All satellite services are made possible by viewer support of local PBS stations.

Per Subscriber Fee: A fee paid by the cable system operator directly to each network that it carries.

Perceptual Coding: Compression techniques wherein some portions of an original audio or video analog wave containing information that humans do not consciously perceive can be deleted without it being missed.

Per-Inquiry (PI): A payment system that commits the advertiser to pay not for advertising time, but for the number of inquiries or the number of items sold in direct response to PI commercials. Many Internet-based companies have adopted this pricing model.

Persistence of Vision: The human eye and brain cannot distinguish individual images flashed in rapid succession. This persistence of vision causes viewers to see a smoothly moving image rather than a series of individual frames of video.

Personal Attack Rule: A former Federal Communication Commission (FCC) regulation which required stations to inform individuals or groups of personal attacks on their "honesty, character, integrity or like personal qualities" that occurred in the course of discussions of controversial public issues. Broadcasters were required to provide free air time for a response.

Personal Digital Assistant (PDA): A handheld device that combines computing, telephone/fax and network capabilities. PDAs are also called as palmtops, hand-held computers and pocket computers.

Personal Video Recorder (PVR) or Digital Video Recorder (DVR): A device that records TV programming on a large computer hard drive.

Per-Use Fee: A revenue model wherein the user pays for each instance of media access.

Pilot Signal: A signal usually in single frequency, transmitted over a communications system for supervisory, control, equalization, continuity, synchronization, or reference purposes.

Pirate Radio Station: A station that operates from sovereign territory without a broadcasting license, or just beyond the territorial waters of a sovereign nation on board a ship or other marine structures with the intention of broadcasting without obtaining a broadcasting license from that nation.

Plasma Display Panel (PDP): A grid comprised of tiny channels (pixels) filled with gas, usually a mixture of neon and xenon. An electrical charge causes the gas to change to a plasma state, generating ultra violet (UV) light, which in turn reacts with red, green, and blue phosphors to produce visible light. PDPs provide bright images that do not wash out under most ambient light conditions.

Platforms: Different types of media distribution outlets such as over-the-air broadcast, satellite, microwave, cable, telephone, fiber optics and the Internet.

Playlists: A list of songs from which a radio show host must select or even play in the order listed.

Plugola: An unethical practice in which a station or one of its employees uses or promotes on the air a product or a service in which the station or employee has an undisclosed financial interest.

Pluralism: A philosophy that encourages more than just simple competition among rival services. Given that similar motives drive all services, from a media point of view the philosophy underlines that media would merely imitate one another in the absence of pluralistic competition. Pluralism means putting a variety of motives to work, each with approximately equal status—usually a mix of commercial and public-service motives.

Podcasting: The method of distributing multimedia files, such as audio programs or music videos, over the Internet for playback on mobile devices and personal computers. The term podcast, like radio, can mean both the content and the method of delivery. The host or author of a podcast is often called a podcaster.

Political Editorializing Rule: A former Federal Communication Commission (FCC) regulation required that all candidates or their representatives be given a chance to respond if a licensee endorsed any of their opponents. If a station editorially opposed a candidate, that candidate had to be given an opportunity to respond.

Pre-Log/Log: A listing of scheduled programs and announcements in a broadcast.

Primary Affiliate: The network affiliate in a market given the first option to carry the network's programming.

Prime Time: The most important time segment in television broadcasting which commands the largest audiences.

Prior Restraint: A legal term referring to a government's actions that prevent materials from being published.

Processing Rules: Rules that stipulate whether a particular issue may be settled by FCC staff members or whether the issue must be decided by the commissioners.

Product Placement/Product Integration: An advertising strategy in which promotional advertisements are placed by marketers using real commercial products and services in media. Here, the presence of a particular brand is the result of an economic exchange. It is also known as product integration, especially when the product becomes integral to the plot in a program.

Progressive Scanning: One of two common methods for "painting" a video image on an electronic display screen by scanning or displaying each line or row of pixels on the screen one after the other, in a numerical sequence.

Projected Ratings: The estimated ratings and audience viewership that radio and television broadcast networks project for a particular program.

Promos: On-air announcements, similar to commercials in structure and scheduling, but intended to promote a station's or network's programming.

Proof of Performance: The documenting procedure where radio and television networks provide the proof of airing commercials and other announcements. Broadcast stations log the time, length, and source of each commercial and when the commercial was broadcast.

Propagation: The process through which waves travel outward from the antenna.

Public Access: Channels programmed by private citizens and non-profit institutions such as schools and municipal governments.

Public Interest, Convenience, or Necessity (PICON): The "Public Interest, Convenience and Necessity" provision was incorporated into the Radio Act of 1927 to become the operational standard for broadcast licensees. PICON contained a regulatory clause which ensured that broadcasters operated within their assigned frequencies, and at the appropriate time periods. The PICON principal stipulates the obligation to serve the public interest and is integral to the "trusteeship" model of broadcasting—the philosophical foundation upon which broadcasters are expected to operate.

Public Utility Commissions (PUCs): State administrative bodies that regulate intrastate telephone services and other public utilities.

Pulse-Code Modulation (PCM): A high speed sampling process involving the cutting up of an original analog signal and leaving out some pieces of the same. Each sample derived consists of a short pulse of energy, proportional in strength to the original signal's amplitude at that point.

Q-Scores: A form of audience measurement that estimates image (familiarity and likability— not necessarily the same thing) ratings of major performers, artists and the popularity of specific programs among various demographic groups.

Quantitative Ratings: Audience measurements that focus on the number of viewers and listeners rather than qualitative measures such as enjoyment or understanding.

Quantized: The process of labeling each energy pulse with a number representing the level of momentary amplitude from the analog wave. The quantized number is then put into binary form.

Radio Broadcast Data System (RBDS): A system that allows data to be transmitted on an analog FM station's subcarrier for receivers equipped with a special microchip. Stations provide promotional information (such as song title, call letters, or location) in a visual format on special receivers through this system.

Radio Frequency (RF): Frequencies or rate of oscillation within the range of about 3 Hz to 300 GHz.

Radio Networks: A system which distributes programming to multiple stations simultaneously, for the purpose of extending total coverage beyond the limits of a single broadcast signal. Radio networks often pay compensation to major-market affiliates, but radio syndicators usually charge for their programs. Stations can choose from dozens of specialized networks catering to every conceivable audience interest.

Radio's All-Dimension Audience Research (RADAR): Arbitron's report which provides the only ratings service for national network radio listening. RADAR issues reports four times a year, each covering an average week based on the last 12-month period, reflecting the surveys of 250,000 respondents.

Random Sampling: A sampling technique where data are collected from a randomly selected small sample of a large population which will be representative (within a predictable degree of accuracy) of the entire population. Random selection means that, ideally, every member of the entire population to be surveyed has an equal chance of being selected.

Rating Periods: Points in time when researchers gather audience viewing or listening data for calculating ratings.

Ratings: An estimate of the number of households (or persons, in the case of radio) tuned to a specific channel (station, network, or program), expressed as a percentage of available households (or persons). "Available" refers to the entire potential audience, even those who may not have their receivers turned on.

Ratings Thresholds Syndication Contracts: Provisions in which the rights fees can be altered either up or down, depending on audience delivery reflected in Nielsen ratings.

Reality Programming: A genre of television programs depicting the dramatization of "real" events and occupations. These programs consist of "tabloid" television, newsmagazine shows, video-vérité, re-created crime or rescue programs, and family amateur video shows, among others.

Receiving Antenna: A metal apparatus designed for capturing electromagnetic waves over a range of different frequencies.

Reciprocal Determinism: A theoretical concept developed as part of Social Learning Theory which postulates that the world and a person's behavior cause each other.

Redelivery Services: Services that are used for enlarging their audiences by extending signals to unserved areas, beefing up fringe reception, and overcoming local interference.

Refraction: A type of reflection or bending back of AM and short-wave signals when bombarded by high energy radiation from the sun.

Regulation of Advertising by Stipulation: A formal nonpunitive process used by Federal Trade Commission to settle most cases of alleged advertising deception. This procedure allows advertisers to drop objectionable practices voluntarily.

Repeat: A re-airing of an episode of a radio or television broadcast (also known as a rerun).

Repeater Transmitters: A device that receives a signal, amplifies it and then retransmits it.

Repetition: A programming strategy which makes it convenient for viewers to catch a program, such as a movie, because repeat showings are scattered throughout the schedule.

Reporter's Privilege: Part of the press law, concerning the asserted right of news personnel to withhold the identity of news sources and to refuse to surrender personal notes, including any audio and video "out-takes." This and many other aspects of press law fall under state jurisdiction, with results varying widely from state to state.

Repurposing: The reuse of network programming on other media, such as cable networks.

Request for Avails: A written statement submitted by an advertiser or media buyer informing the network or station of the desired target audience, size of budget, and air dates of a campaign. In addition, buyers may stipulate desired audience ratings, plus data on the expected demographic reach and frequency of audience exposure to the commercial.

Reruns: A re-airing of an episode of a radio or television broadcast (also known as a repeat).

Reserved Channels: FM and TV channels that may be used (i.e. they are reserved) only by non-commercial broadcasters.

Resolution: The number of lines making up the image helps determine the resolution. The clarity of an image on a screen depends on the number of lines. The more lines, the greater is the resolution.

Restless Viewers/Grazers: Audiences that use a remote control to switch rapidly among several channels.

Retransmission Consent: A stipulation which allows a full-power US television station to negotiate with a cable system operator for carriage of its broadcast programming. A station may propose that the cable operator pay cash to carry the station or ask for any other form of consideration.

Revenue Potential: An estimate of how much the station plausibly can earn from owning the rights for a particular program.

RSS (Really Simple Syndication): A software program that searches the web for the latest audio feeds to which a user has subscribed and automatically transfers the files to the consumer's player when the player is connected again to the user's computer.

Runs per Title: An agreement clause in a contract between a station and a syndicator which stipulates the number of times a program episode can be run.

Safe Harbor: A time frame created by FCC during which indecent programming can be aired. The safe harbor consists of the hours between 10:00 PM and 6:00 AM.

Sales Promotion: Incentives aimed at helping the sales department attract advertisers.

Sample Surveys: A survey research strategy that involves the estimation of characteristics of an entire population through the use of a very small, but highly representative, sample of an entire population.

Sampling Error: The margin of error in a statistical measurement that arises out of sampling techniques. Using the laws of probability, statistical calculations can determine the sampling error of the results provided from a random sample or a comparison of several random samples.

Sampling Frames: Lists comprised of either telephone numbers, address listings, or maps of housing unit locations from which samples are selected.

Satellite Digital Audio Radio Services (SDARS): Subscription based services that offer customers an alternative to traditional radio broadcasting with an average of 150 channels of audio programming. It is especially popular in areas severely underserved by regular radio stations. Radio signals are relayed via satellites. Strong digital satellite signals eliminate the need for a dish, and programming is delivered directly to mobile- and home-based receivers. Ground-based repeaters are used to fill-in coverage gaps caused by large buildings and other obstructions.

Satellite Radio: A digital radio signal broadcast by a communications satellite which covers a wider geographical range than terrestrial radio signals.

ScanAmerica: A three-pronged single-source system developed by Arbitron providing ratings, audience demographic data, and—through the use of a wand that read universal bar codes—a measure of product purchasing. In 1992, lacking sufficient advertiser interest, Arbitron dropped use of both the wand and the name ScanAmerica and soon after ended all of its broadcast TV and cable ratings activities.

SECAM: An analog color television system first used in France. Historically it was considered as the first European standard for color television. (Also written as SÉCAM (Séquentiel couleur à mémoire), a French phrase which when translated to English means "Sequential Color with Memory".)

Secondary Affiliates: Radio or television stations that typically share affiliation with another station in a given market.

Segment Sync Signal: A signal found in any broadcast signal beginning with each data segment which basically tells the receiver where to begin and end each horizontal line of video.

Separation Guidelines: Advertising guidelines for cable and television networks which prevent the airing of competitors' advertisements side-by-side within the same commercial break.

Serial Copy Management System (SCMS): A digital piracy prevention system that sets an encryption bit in all copies, preventing anyone from making further copies of those first copies. It does not, however, limit the number of first-generation copies made from a master tape.

Set Meter: A term used to refer to Nielsen's Audimeter which was first used to gather data in 1950. Set meters are attached to each TV set in a sample household and record when the set is on and to which channel it is tuned. Researchers refer to the Set Meter as passive because no effort is required on the part of the viewer to record its information, and to distinguish it from the newer People Meter.

Set Penetration: A percentage of all homes that have TV receivers.

Set-top Box (STB): A TV device available from cable and direct broadcast satellite services which the consumer uses to switch TV channels. It can also be used to control subscribers access to content and can unscramble pay-cable programming.

Share: An estimate of the number of households (or persons, for radio) tuned to a given channel, expressed as a percentage of all those households (or persons) actually using their receivers at that time. Recall that a rating is based on all those owning receivers, not necessarily using them.

Sideband: A band of frequencies higher or lower than the carrier frequency, containing power as a result of the modulation process. All forms of modulation produce sidebands.

Signal Compression: The process of removing unnecessary data from a transmission which allows for the efficient delivery of content.

Signal Piracy: The illegal reception of television or radio signals without authorization from the service provider.

Single-Sideband (SSB): A refined form of amplitude modulation that more efficiently uses electrical power and bandwidth.

Skip Zone: A silent zone between the furthest points at which the ground wave can be received and the nearest point at which the refracted sky waves can be received.

Sky Waves: Refracted AM and short-wave signals that are refracted when bombarded by high energy radiation from the sun.

Slander: Defamation by spoken word.

Small Thrusters: Equipment used for moving a satellite, orienting it, and holding it in its assigned position, activated on command from ground controllers.

Social Learning Theory: A theory developed by Albert Bandura, which proposes that much learning takes place through observing and modeling the behavior of others. In particular, social learning theory has been applied to the study of the possible effects of TV violence.

Social Networks: A new genre of software services that provide a collection of various ways for users to interact, such as chat, messaging, twitter, e-mail, video, voice chat, file sharing, blogging, and discussion groups. These networks also offer business opportunities in terms of advertising, membership fees and purchase transactions. The two most popular websites in this category are Facebook and MySpace.

Social Responsibility Philosophy: A philosophy that does not object to a government creating regulations that are designed to assure certain standards of quality. These "standards," however, can be troublesome to define precisely and can result in undesirable censorship by overzealous government agencies. Government agencies are intended to assure that public service is not pushed aside by free enterprise.

Soft Interconnections: System interconnection that involves the simple exchange of programming so that commercials (or programs) can be seen on several cable systems, rather than only one.

Soil Conductivity: The degree to which soil resists passage of radio waves which varies according to dampness and soil composition.

Specific /Episodic Promotions: Announcements that promote and highlight one episode in a series.

Spectaculars: Television specials that are usually one-time only programs, presented with great network fanfare and usually combining music, dance, and comedy routines presented in variety show-type formats.

Spillover: A term used to describe how broadcast signals cross geographical borders.

Spiral of Silence Theory: A political science and mass communication theory asserting that a person is less likely to voice an opinion on a topic if one feels that one is in the minority for fear of reprisal or isolation from the majority.

Sponsor Identification Rule: A rule that attempts to prevent deception by requiring the on-air identification of the person or organization that pays for the broadcast of any programming.

Spots: Short-hand term for commercial messages on radio or TV.

Standard-Definition TV (SDTV): A digital TV format that displays 480 active lines, yielding a picture of about the same general quality as that found on an NTSC receiver.

Static: Interference caused by lighting or electrical machinery that has more effect on the amplitude of a radio wave than on its frequency.

Station Program Cooperative (SPC): A system that was developed as a mechanism for the nation's public television stations to select desired programs from a pool of available offerings, thus diminishing central control of national program selection.

Statistical Significance: A mathematical tool employed in statistical analysis to determine whether the occurrence of a particular result is presumed to be greater than chance.

Stringers: Self-employed professionals who sell individual stories to radio and TV stations, and other media outlets.

Strip Programming: A programming strategy wherein different episodes of the same TV program are scheduled at the same time every weekday.

Stunting: A set of programming strategies which seek to keep the opposing networks off balance by using different tactics. The tactics include making abrupt schedule changes, opening a new series with an extra-long episode and interrupting regular programming frequently with heavily promoted specials.

Subscriber Video on Demand (SVOD): A service that allows subscribers unlimited access to video content for a monthly fee.

Sunspots: Blotches on the sun's surface that increase and decrease over an 11-year cycle. They are known to dramatically increase interference on some radio frequencies.

Superstation: A local television station that typically broadcasts to one specific market, which also reaches hundreds of other markets throughout the country by means of satellite distribution to cable systems.

Surf /Graze: To browse rapidly through the available channels.

Sweep Weeks /Sweeps: Four-week-long period when Nielsen collects data in all television markets. Such data is collected four times a year.

Symmetric Digital Subscriber Line (SDSL): A form of DSL service that provides a more balanced upstream and downstream capacity required for applications like two-way video conferencing.

Syndicated Barter Advertising: A financing mechanism for syndicated programming, wherein an advertiser makes advance purchase of all or some part of the advertising opportunities (commercial spots) in a syndicated program.

Syndicated Exclusivity Rule / Syndex Rule: A rule passed in 1988 which requires each cable system, at a local TV station's request, to delete from its schedule any superstation programs that duplicate programs for which the station holds exclusive local rights.

Syndicated Program: Any program sold, licensed, distributed, or offered to radio and television stations in more than one market within the United States for non-interconnected (i.e., no network) broadcast exhibition.

Tables of Organization/Organization Charts: A visual representation of an institution's form of organization and hierarchy.

Target Rating Points (TRPs): A measure for estimating the reach of a program in terms of audience subgroups such as teens or women 18 to 49 years of age.

Technological Convergence: Development of digital technologies have now enabled conventional print and electronic media content to be digitized and offered to consumers through a variety of electronic sources or platforms, including over-the-air broadcast, satellite, microwave, cable, telephone, fiber optics, and the Internet. The trend wherein the development of digital technologies have blurred the once-familiar distinctions among "television" from broadcasting, "television" from cable, "television" from satellite, or "television" from computers.

Technology Determinism: A reductionist theory which states that a society's technology determines its cultural values, social structure, or history.

Telemetering Devices: Equipment used for reporting a satellite's vital signs to and receiving instructions from the ground controllers.

Telenovelas: Spanish language TV programming similar to American soap operas. Popular with Hispanic audiences, Telenovelas have a fixed number of episodes and are primarily viewed for entertainment, but often carry educational messages, typically promoting approved conduct and family values.

Television Receive Only Antennas (TVRO): An antenna apparatus used for picking up programs relayed by a satellite.

Tent-Pole: A programming strategy that places a very popular program at the center of a programming schedule, hoping that audiences will gravitate to either side of "the pole," capitalizing on the notions of lead-in and lead-out.

Third-Person Effect Hypothesis: A theoretical postulate which states that a person exposed to a persuasive communication in the mass media sees it as having a greater effect on others than on themselves. As a result, people will often advocate media censorship, not to protect themselves from the dangers of undesirable media effects, but to protect others (i.e., third persons) who are more vulnerable.

Time Brokerage: The practice of selling time in blocks to brokers, who then resell it at a markup.

Time Sampling: A sampling method wherein a sample taken every few weeks or months from a continuous program stream suffices for most purposes.

Time Shifting: The audience behavior of recording a program off the air and viewing it at a later time. Hence, shifting the time when the program is exposed to an audience. Time shifting today usually is accomplished with digital video recorders.

Toll Broadcasting: A broadcast model that is widely considered as an alternative to today's advertiser supported broadcasting model. In 1922, AT&T announced its plan to finance its broadcast stations by selling airtime directly to program providers, which it called "toll broadcasting."

Top 40: A radio music program format consisting of an array of the most recent hits where the playlist is restricted to about 20 to 40 songs.

Total Survey Area (TSA): The largest local region on which Nielsen and Arbitron report which includes 98 percent of a market's listening audience, thus covering counties outside the DMA and overlapping with adjacent DMAs. Nielsen also uses the term "station total area" to describe these local regions.

Trade Deal/Tradeout: A business deal wherein a station or a cable system exchanges commercial time for an advertiser's goods or services.

Transduction: In engineering, the process of changing one form of energy into another form. Converting sound energy into electrical energy using a microphone is an example of transduction.

Translator: A type of a repeater that transmits on a different channel from the originating station to prevent interference with the originating station's signal.

Transmission Control Protocol (TCP): A set of protocols that allow information-sharing among different computers in a network.

Transponders: Receiving /transmitting units on satellites that pick up radio signals, amplify them and transmit them back to Earth.

Travelers Information Service (TIS): A radio service offered to help motorists navigate in congested areas, such as busy airports or intersections.

Triode: An electronic amplification device that has three active elements: the filament or cathode, the grid, and the plate or anode. The triode vacuum tube is often viewed as the first electrical amplification device.

Tuning Inertia: Whether because of viewer loyalty to a station or network, or simple laziness before widespread use of remote controls, viewers tended to leave sets tuned to the same station. Tuning inertia still strongly affects radio audiences; in large markets with as many as 40 stations from which to choose, listeners tend to confine their tuning to only two or three favorites.

Two-Step Flow Hypothesis: An idea first proposed by Lazarsfeld and Katz that argued mass media information flows in two steps. Media information is channelled to the "masses" through opinion leaders. The people with most access to media and having a more literate understanding of media content explain and diffuse the content to others.

Underground or Free Form/Progressive Radio Format: A radio format which mixes live and recorded music and talk, usually at the whim of the presenter. Community stations often feature, if not progressive music, a classical, jazz, or diversified format. Small, low-salaried staff supplemented by volunteers mean low overhead, enabling such outlets to present formats that would not be commercially viable.

Underwriting: A form of sponsorship in non-commercial broadcasting. Companies may provide general underwriting support for a station or underwrite a specific program or series but may not directly promote their products or services.

Uniform Resource Locator (URL): (In computing) a system of locating online resources which specifies where the identified resource is available and the protocol for retrieving it on Internet.

Upgrading/Downgrading Provisions in Syndication Contracts: Certain business provisions in which the cost per episode will vary according to the time period in which the program is scheduled. For instance, if a program is rescheduled from early afternoon to late night, the broadcast rights fees probably would decrease. Conversely, if a program is highly successful in a lesser time period and the station wants to upgrade it to a more lucrative time of day, the syndicator may demand a higher rights fee.

Uplinking: A process of establishing a communications link used for the transmission of signals from an Earth terminal to a satellite or to an airborne platform.

Urban Contemporary/Urban: A mix of rap, rhythm and blues, and jazz, favoring black artists.

Uses and Gratifications Theory (U&G): A widely accepted mass media theory that argues the need gratifications and media choices are related. It suggests that people's needs influence what media they choose, how they use certain media, and what gratifications the media give them. This approach differs from conventional media effects research in that it regards audiences as active media users as opposed to merely passive receivers of information.

Vacuum Tube: A device used to amplify, switch, otherwise modify, or create an electrical signal by controlling the movement of electrons in a low-pressure space.

Variety: A genre of programs that once played a role both in viewers' habits and in the world of music. Hosted by stars such as Ed Sullivan (who introduced Elvis and the Beatles to America), Judy Garland, Frank Sinatra, Dean Martin, Perry Como, and Sonny and Cher, these programs once brought hours of music into the home, but their popularity faded as production costs increased and as musical tastes changed.

Video Cassette Recorder (VCR): A device capable of recording and playing back audio and video signals on a magnetic tape housed in a plastic cassette.

Video News Releases (VNRs): Video news program items produced by sources such as government agencies and businesses that are often incorporated into local newscasts.

Video on Demand (VOD): Programming content available at any time that can be accessed by the customer of a cable or DBS system.

Viral Marketing: A marketing strategy wherein companies use pre-existing social networks to produce increases in brand awareness or to achieve other marketing objectives (such as product sales) through self-replicating viral processes, analogous to the spread of pathological and computer viruses.

Voice over Internet Protocol (VoIP): A set of protocols that convert voice into digital packets that travel over the Internet.

Used by cable systems, and other businesses, to provide telephone service.

Voice Tracking: A process wherein many radio hosts prerecord their shows.

Voice-Over Promotions: A promotional announcement often appearing during final credits of a program urging viewers to stay tuned to what follows.

Wave Frequency: The number of separate radio waves produced each second.

Wavelength: The distance from the origin of one wave to the origin of the next.

Web Banner Advertising: The most popular form of advertising among serious web advertisers. Banner advertising functions the same way as traditional advertisements in that the goal is to notify consumers of the product or service and present reasons why the consumer should choose the product brand in question. The web banner is displayed when a web page that references the banner is loaded in a web browser.

Web Traffic Analytics: A way of looking at the data that comes from user activity on a given web site. In most cases, web data comes from log files, capturing all the requests that users make to the web site's servers. Software then translates the coded requests into tables, charts, and graphs that give a picture of what users are doing on the site.

Wi-Fi: A wireless local area network that allows computers and other devices equipped with an appropriate network card to connect wirelessly to an access point that itself has a wired connection to the Internet.

Wi-Max: A wireless wide area network that is similar to Wi-Fi, but covers a much greater area, up to 30 miles. Wi-Max towers can connect to one another using line-of-sight microwave links allowing them to function as backhaul feeds that connect ultimately to the wired Internet.

Wireless Cable: Systems that use terrestrial microwave radio signals to distribute cable programming to subscribers.

Wireless Telecommunications Bureau: A division of the Federal Communication Commissions (FCC) that handles most domestic wireless telecommunications programs and policies including cellular services, paging systems and amateur radio services, but excluding satellite communications. The Wireless Bureau is also responsible for implementing competitive bidding for spectrum auctions.

Writ of Certiorari: A writ that a superior appellate court issues in its discretion to an inferior court, ordering it to produce a certified record of a particular case it has tried, in order to determine whether any irregularities or errors occurred that justify review of the case.

Yield Management: The decisions concerning the pricing and inventory control of a product in order to maximize revenue. For electronic media, this would refer typically to managing commercial pricing and avails within programming.

Zapping: A popular term used to refer to audiences' deletion of unwanted commercials while recording a program.

Zero Sum Market: A term which refers to a status wherein despite the number of brand offerings for a product or service, the total number of customers desiring that product or service remains unchanged.

Zipping: A popular term used to refer to audiences' fast-forwarding through commercial announcements when playing back prerecorded TV programming.

INDEX

Abbreviations and Acronyms from ABC to WWW:

8-VSB	Eight-Level Vestigial Sideband
ABC	American Broadcasting Company
AC	Adult Contemporary
AC	Alternating Current
ACATS	Advisory Committee on Advanced Television Service
ACM	Average Commercial Minute
ACT	Action for Children's Television
ADI	Area of Dominant Influence
ADSL	Asymmetric Digital Subscriber Line
AFM	American Federation of Musicians
AFTRA	American Federation of Television and Radio Artists
AGVA	American Guild of Variety Artists
AIM	Accuracy in Media
ALJ	Administrative Law Judge
ALTV	Association of Local Television Stations (formerly INTV)
AM	Amplitude Modulation
AOR	Album-Oriented Rock
AP	Associated Press
APR	American Public Radio
APTS	Association of Public Television Stations
ASCAP	American Society of Composers, Authors, and Publishers
AT&T	American Telephone and Telegraph Company
ATM	Asynchronous Transfer Mode
ATSC	Advanced Television Systems Committee
ATTC	Advanced Television Testing Center
ATV	Advanced Television
AWRT	American Women in Radio and Television
BBC	British Broadcasting Corporation
BBG	Broadcasting Board of Governors
BEA	Broadcast Education Association
BGP	Border Gateway Protocol
BIB	Board for International Broadcasting
BIT	Binary Digit
BMI	Broadcast Music Incorporated
BOC	Bell Operating Company
C&W	Country and Western
CAB	Cable Television Advertising Bureau
CARS	Community Antenna Relay Service
CATV	Community Antenna Television
CBA	Community Broadcasters Association
CBC	Canadian Broadcasting Corporation
CBS	Columbia Broadcasting System
CC	Cable Card
CC	Closed Captioning
CCD	Charge-Coupled Device
CCIR	International Radio Consultative Committee
CD	Compact Disc
CD-E	Compact Disc Erasable
CD-R	Compact Disc Recordable
CD-ROM	Compact Disc Read-Only Memory
CEMA	Consumer Electronics Manufacturers Association
CHR	Contemporary Hit Radio
CODEC	Compression-Decompression
COMSAT	Communications Satellite Corporation
CONUS	Continental United States
CP	Construction Permit
CPB	Corporation for Public Broadcasting
CPM	Cost per Thousand
CPP	Cost per Point
CRT	Cathode Ray Tube
CSS	Content Scramble System
CTAM	Cable Television Administration and Marketing Society
CTW	Children's Television Workshop
DAB	Digital Audio Broadcasting
DARS	Digital Audio Radio Service
DAT	Digital Audio Tape
dB	Decibel
DBS	Direct Broadcast Satellite
DCAS	Downloadable Content Access System
DCC	Digital Compact Cassette
DCR	Digital Cable Ready
DLP	Digital Light Processing
DMA	Designated Market Area
DNS	Domain Name System
DSL	Digital Subscriber Line
DTH	Direct-to-Home Satellite
DTV	Digital Television
DVD	Digital Video (or Versatile) Disk
DVD CCA	DVD Copy Control Association
DVR	Digital Video Recorder (also PVR)
DX	Long Distance
EAS	Emergency Alert System
EBU	European Broadcasting Union
EC	European Community
EEO	Equal Employment Opportunity
EFP	Electronic Field Production
EHF	Extremely High Frequency
EIA	Electronics Industry Association
ELM	Elaboration Likelihood Model
EM	Electromagnetic
ENG	Electronic News Gathering
ERP	Effective Radiated Power
ETV	Educational Television
EBU	European Broadcasting Union
FBC	Fox Broadcasting Company
FCBA	Federal Communications Bar Association
FCC	Federal Communications Commission
FIN/SYN	Financial Interest and Syndication Rules
FM	Frequency Modulation
FRC	Federal Radio Commission
FTC	Federal Trade Commission
FTTH	Fiber to the Home
FTTN	Fiber to the Node (or Neighborhood)
GE	General Electric
GHz	Gigahertz
GRP	Gross Rating Points
GSM	Global System for Mobile Communications
GSO	Geostationary (or Geosynchronous) Orbit
HDTV	High-Definition Television
HF	High Frequency
HFC	Hybrid Fiber-Coax
HTML	Hypertext Markup Language
HTTP	Hypertext Transfer Protocol
HUT	Households Using Television
Hz	Hertz
IAB	Interactive Advertising Bureau
IATSE	International Alliance of Theatrical State Employees
IBA	Independent Broadcasting Authority
IBB	International Broadcasting Bureau
IBEW	International Brotherhood of Electrical Workers
IBOC	In Band, On Channel
ICANN	Internet Corporation for Assigned Names and Numbers
ID	(Station) Identification (Announcement)
IFRB	International Frequency Registration Board
ILR	Independent Local Radio
INTELSAT	International Telecommunications Satellite Organization
IP	Internet Protocol
IPTV	Internet Protocol Television
IRTS	International Radio and Television Society
ISDN	Integrated Services Digital Network
ISP	Internet Service Provider
ITC	Independent Television Commission
ITFS	Instructional Television Fixed Services
ITN	Independent Television News
ITSO	International Telecommunications Satellite Organization
ITU	International Telecommunication Union
ITV	Independent Television
IVDS	Interactive Video and Data Services
IXP	Internet Exchange Point
JCET	Joint Committee on Educational Television
Kbps	Kilobits per second
kHz	Kilohertz
LAN	Local Area Network
LASER	Light Amplification by Stimulated Emission of Radiation
LCD	Liquid Crystal Display
LCoS	Liquid Crystal on Silicon
LED	Light-Emitting Diode
LEO	Low Earth Orbit
LF	Low Frequency
LMA	Local Marketing Agreement
LMDS	Local Multipoint Distribution Service
LNA	Low-Noise Amplifier
LNB	Low-Noise Block Converter
LO	Local Origination